A Chronological Outline of the History of Bristol, and the Stranger's Guide through its streets and neighbourhood.

John Evans

A Chronological Outline of the History of Bristol, and the Stranger's Guide through its streets and neighbourhood.
Evans, John
British Library, Historical Print Editions
British Library
1824
8°.
010358.g.41.

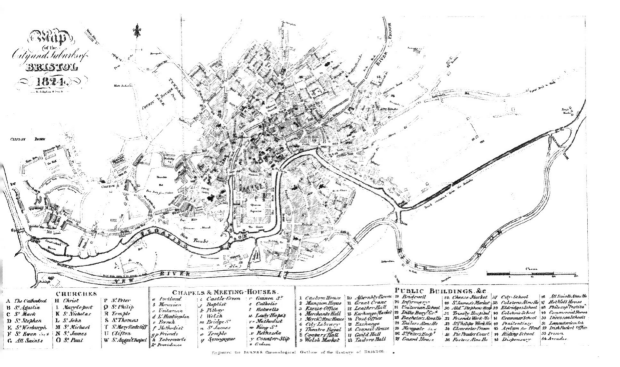

Map of the City and Suburbs of BRISTOL 1824.

CHURCHES		
A	The Cathedral	H Christ	P St. Peter
B	St. Augustin	I Maryleport	Q St. Philip
C	St. Mark	K St. Nicholas	R Temple
D	St. Stephen	L St. John	S St. Thomas
E	St. Werburgh	M St. Michael	T St. Mary Ratcliff
F	St. Ewen &c.	N St. James	U Clifton
G	All Saints	O St. Paul	W St. Augs. Chapel

CHAPELS & MEETING-HOUSES.

a Portland	i Castle Green	v Cannon St.
b Moravian	j Baptist	x Catholic
c Unitarian	k Pithay	t Hotwells
d E. Huntingdon	l Welsh	u Lady Hope's
e French	m Bridge St.	v Methodist
f Methodist	n St. James	w King St.
g p Friends	o Temple	x Bethesda
h Tabernacle	q Synagogue	y Counter-Slip
k Providence		y Gideon

PUBLIC BUILDINGS, &c.

1 Custom House	10 Assembly-Room	19 Bridewell	28 Cheese Market	37 City School	46 All Saints Alms Ho
2 Mansion House	11 Great Crane	20 Infirmary	29 St. James Market	38 Colstons Alms Ho	47 Hot Well House
3 Excise-Office	12 Leather-Hall	21 Unitarian School	30 Ald. Stephens Hosp	39 Eldridges School	48 Philosop. Institu.n
4 Merchants Hall	13 Exchange Market	22 Ditto Bury & c.a	31 Trinity Hospital	40 Colstons School	49 Commercial Rooms
5 Merch. Hall House	14 Post Office	23 Bachelors Almsho	32 Friends Work-Ho	41 Grammar School	50 Tnecation Schools
6 City Library	15 Exchange	24 Taylors Alms Ho	33 St. Philips Work Ho	42 Penitentiary	51 Lancasterian Sch.
7 Theatre Royal	16 Council-House	25 Newgate &c.a	34 Gloucester Prison	43 Asylum for Blind	52 Irish Packet Office.n
8 Coopers Hall	17 Guild Hall	26 St. Peters Hosp.	35 Pie Powder Court	44 Riding School	53 Prison
9 Welsh Market	18 Taylors Hall	27 Guard House	36 Fosters Alms Ho	45 Dispensary	54 Arcades

Engraved for EVANS's Chronological Outline of the History of BRISTOL.

A

CHRONOLOGICAL OUTLINE

OF THE

HISTORY OF BRISTOL,

AND THE

Stranger's Guide

THROUGH ITS

STREETS AND NEIGHBOURHOOD.

By JOHN EVANS, Printer.

Printed at the Office of the late " Bristol Observer," and published by the Author.

SOLD, IN LONDON, BY G. AND W. B. WHITTAKER, PATERNOSTER - ROW;
R. HUNTER, ST. PAUL'S CHURCH-YARD; W. ANDERSON, 184, PICCADILLY;
AND NICHOLS AND SON, PARLIAMENT-STREET.

ALSO BY THE BOOKSELLERS IN BRISTOL.

1824.

NOTE.

The Vignette was reduced from Mr. Smirke's perspective drawing, and pencilled on the wood, by Mr. James Johnson; as was the Shield of the Arms of the City, by Mr. Manning. Both were engraven by Mr. Berriman. The crest, supporters, &c. are described in p. 342.

TO

THE RIGHT WORSHIPFUL

JOHN BARROW, ESQUIRE, MAYOR;

THE RIGHT HONOURABLE

ROBERT, LORD GIFFORD,

MASTER OF THE ROLLS AND RECORDS OF THE COURT OF CHANCERY,

RECORDER;

THE WORSHIPFUL

THE ALDERMEN;

THE SHERIFFS,

AND THE OTHER

MEMBERS OF THE COMMON COUNCIL,

OF THE CITY AND COUNTY OF

Bristol,

THIS

CONTRIBUTION TOWARDS THE STUDY OF ITS HISTORY

IS, WITH PERMISSION,

MOST RESPECTFULLY DEDICATED.

Dear Sir,

  Had not both custom and propriety assigned the Dedication of a work like the present to the Public Guardians and Trustees of our ancient City's peace and security, an accumulation of social feeling and esteem, that has grown with the better portion of our several lives, would not have been satisfied with the second place in an act of duty and gratitude. Whatever may be the consummation of our new-born Chamber of Commerce in regard to " Mayor's dues," and " Town-dues," I am sure that you would have been the last of its members to dispute the precedent which has been set me by the Chamber of Authorship formed by a Hooke, a Barrett, and a Seyer, with respect to the tribute literary, in honour of the municipal store laid up by a long line of predecessors, for magisterial contribution to its integrity.

  At a stage of approach towards manhood when, in your circumstances of paternal fortune, and of which the Annals of Bristol have presented so many proud examples, youth may be scarcely said to commence a scholastic education, fatherly prudence and discrimination consigned you to a station of commercial usefulness which many a learned ignoramus has conceitedly imagined must irredeemably absorb all leisure or relish for enjoyments connected with literature or intellectual taste and refinement. But, to say nothing of the pendulum-habits of a man of business continuing to vibrate in his hours of recreation, if you were thus precluded from the risk of stultifying intoxication at classic reservoirs which too often abstract the student from a comprehensive acquaintance with books as well as with men, you have not shewn yourself the less disposed to drink at every refreshing spring that flows amid thousands of verdant margins, fructifying the present vigorous if not mature age of British science and philosophy.

At the very first approach with which idleness threatened to visit myself for a single day, during more than thirty years after I was raised from school-boy to the exalted rank of apprentice to " a man of letters," you heard me avow my determination to resist her influence at any rate, and, though you did not apprehend the alternative of mischievous industry, recommended me to undertake the task which I have here endeavoured to accomplish, namely, to write a book of moderate bulk, which might be alike interesting to the resident and the stranger. I at first doubted the adequacy of my manuscript-resources; but this doubt was speedily removed when, having carefully read and noted all that had been printed, I communicated my design to such of our fellow-citizens as were most likely to increase my stock of unpublished materials.

Your constitutional indisposition to become an object of popular notice, I trust will yield to the expediency of receiving this address, as the most fitting medium for my acknowledgments to those other gentlemen whose freely proffered and awarded co-operation promoted this attempt—one which has no higher aim than to sharpen the public appetite for a course of reading and inquiry that cannot fail to repay whatever pains and attention it may be possible for probationers in local history and topography to share with other desirable pursuits.

My thanks (which must necessarily bend to alphabetical law) are especially due for the active friendship of
Mr. J. W. Atwood; Mr. Birtill (now at Göttingen); Mr. Arthur Biggs; George Weare Braikenridge, Esq.; Benjamin Heywood Bright, Esq.; Mr. Thomas Blomfield; Mr. Carden; Mr. Cossham; Mr. W. L. Clarke;

Mr. Edward Dalton; Mr. Ewen; W. Farr, Esq.; the Rev. Thomas Dudley Fosbroke, M.A. F.A.S.; Mr. Charles Frost; Mr. T. Gough; Mr. C. Grevile; John Haythorne, Esq. Alderman; Messrs. Hartley & Son; Mr. W. O. Hare; John Scandret Harford, Esq.; Mr. William Haynes; Mr. Howe; Mr. Edward Hodges; Messrs. Hillyard & Morgan; Mr. Isaac James; Mr. Johnson, engraver; James Johnson, Esq. F.R.S.; Mr. H. A. Laurinson (my typographical co-operator and critical "accessary" after very short notices "before the fact"); Mr. J. E. Lunell; Mr. Mallard; Mr. John Mills; Mr. Major; Messrs. Nichols & Son, of London; Mr. Norton; Mr. Page; Mr. Henry Pallin; James Palmer, Esq.; Messrs. Panting & Son; Charles Payne, Esq.; Mr. John Peace; Mr. James Plumley; Mr. Edward Powell; Mr. W. Quick; Mr. Racster; Mr. Rees; J. W. Ricketts, Esq.; Mr. Frederick Ricketts; Mr. Charles Savery; the Rev. Dr. Shaw; Mr. Smith, of Marlborough Hill; Mr. William Smith, the companion of Chatterton; Mr. Richard Smith; Mr. Henry Smith; Mr. Taylor, a proprietor of The Mirror; Mr. Terrell; Mr. Tyson; Sir Richard Vaughan, Alderman; Thomas Weatherall, Esq. of Lincoln's Inn; Mr. S. C. Webb; Joseph Whittuck, Esq.; and Mr. Henry Wood, sculptor.

That you, my dear Sir, with your Father, your Brothers, and all the beloved objects of your and their fire-side solicitude, may long, very long continue to enjoy every blessing which ample means and a judicious appropriation of them can command, will never cease to be the wish of

Your and my Fellow-Citizens' devoted Servant,

No. 9, Somerset-street,
Kingsdown;
September 1, 1824.

Errata.

In p. xxxii., l. 8, for "descending" read ascending. In p. 58, l. 13, for "1289" read 1269. In p. 72, l. 8, for "1305" read 1306. In p. 140, for "1554" read 1544. In p. 143, for "1559" read 1550. In p. 145, last line of text, for "1560" read 1566. In p. 213, for "MSS." read MS. In p. 215, l. 9 from the foot, for "1666" read 1660. In p. 221, l. 11., for "1662" read 1663. In p. 252, l. 3, for "Nov. 20," read 26. In p. 262, the election should be under 1734. In p. 332, l. 27, for "Brickden" read Brigden.

INTRODUCTION.

But words are things, and a small drop of ink,
   Falling like dew, upon a thought, produces
That which makes thousands, perhaps millions, think:
   'Tis strange, the shortest letter which man uses
Instead of speech, may form a lasting link
   Of ages. To what straits Old Time reduces
Frail Man, when paper—even a rag like this,
Survives himself, his tomb, and all that's his!

And when his bones are dust, his grave a blank,
   His station, generation, even his nation,
Become a thing, or nothing, save to rank
   In chronological commemoration,
Some dull MS. oblivion long has sank,
   A grave-stone, found in a barrack's station,
In digging the foundation of a closet,
May turn his name up, as a rare deposit.   LORD BYRON.

HENRY HALLAM, Esq.* in his " View of the State of
Europe during the Middle Ages," remarking upon the
progress of towns in Continental countries, from a condition
bordering upon servitude to wealth and liberty, observes
that " their growth in England, both from general causes
and imitative policy, was very similar and nearly co-incident.
Under the Anglo-Saxon line of sovereigns, we scarcely can
discover in our scanty records the condition of the inhabitants, except retrospectively from the great survey of
Domesday-Book, which displays the state of England
under Edward the Confessor. Some attention to commerce
had been shewn by Alfred and Athelstan, and a merchant
who had made three voyages beyond sea was raised by a

* Son of the Rev. Dr. John Hallam, who was installed Dean of Bristol in 1781.

b

law of the latter monarch to the dignity of a Thane. This privilege was not, perhaps, often claimed; but the burgesses of towns were already a distinct class from the ceorls or rustics, and, though hardly free according to our estimation, seem to have laid the foundation of more extensive immunities. It is probable, at least, that the English towns had made full as great advances towards emancipation as those of France. At the Conquest, we find the burgesses or inhabitants of towns living under the protection of the king, or some other lord, to whom they paid annual rents and determinate dues or customs. Sometimes they belonged to different lords, and sometimes the same burgess paid custom to one master, while he was under the jurisdiction of another. They frequently enjoyed special privileges as to inheritance; and in two or three instances they seem to have possessed common property, belonging to a sort of guild or corporation, but never, as far as appears by any evidence, had they a municipal administration by magistrates of their own choice. Besides the regular payments, which were in general not heavy, they were liable to tallages at the discretion of their lords. This burthen continued for two centuries, with no limitation, except that the barons were latterly forced to ask permission of the king before they set a tallage on their tenants, which was commonly done when he imposed one upon his own. Still the towns became considerably richer: for the profits of their traffic were undiminished by competition; and the consciousness that they could not be individually despoiled of their possessions, like the villeins of the country around, inspired an industry and perseverance, which all the rapacity of Norman kings and barons was unable to daunt or overcome." "In the Saxon period, we find voluntary associations, sometimes religious, sometimes secular; in some cases for mutual défence against injury, in others for mutual relief in poverty. These were called Guilds, from the Saxon verb *gildan*, to pay or contribute, and exhibited the natural if not legal character of corporations."*

---

* " See more of the Anglo-Saxon guilds, in Turner's History, vol. ii. p. 102."—4to.

With the foregoing comprehensive sketch from the hand of a master, as the ground-work of his reflections, the general reader may the better appreciate the particular subject of the succeeding pages, in its multifarious features.

Bristol is situated in lat. 2 deg. 40 min. W. from Greenwich, and long. 51 deg. 30 min. N.; its distance from London being 120 miles, and from Edinburgh 377 miles. It stands upon the confluence of the rivers Avon and Froom, which hence discharge their waters into the Severn, or Bristol Channel, at the sailing-distance of ten miles, but only a crow-flight of seven miles, from Bristol Bridge. Its boundaries (extending to a circumference of about seven miles, without reckoning its aquatic limits, which reach the two islands of Flat and Steep Holm) constitute a distinct city and county, lying between Somersetshire and Gloucestershire, but subordinate to neither, except that for levies of the militia it is included in the county of Gloucester. In all other respects, it is as independent of either as those counties are of each other. The present number of inhabitants of the city and suburbs is nearly 100,000. The criminal jurisdiction, including a court of admiralty, is vested in the Mayor and two Sheriffs for the time being, (annually chosen from among the Common Council,) twelve Aldermen, who are His Majesty's Justices of the Peace, one of whom is the Recorder, presiding as judge of the session of *oyer and terminer*, or general gaol-delivery. The Mayor, Sheriffs, Aldermen, and Common Council, form a body-corporate of forty-three persons, together with the Town-Clerk, Chamberlain, Vice-Chamberlain, Clerk of Arraigns, Steward of the Sheriffs' Court, Sword-Bearer, Mayor's Clerk, Mayor's Chaplain, two Coroners, Registrar of the Court of Conscience, Receiver of Town-Dues, &c.; the Under-Sheriff, Water-Bailiff, Quay-Warden, Governor of His Majesty's Gaol, Keeper of the House of Correction, Inspector of Nuisances on the River, and two Inspectors for the Streets, &c. There are, besides, four Mayor's Serjeants, four Sheriffs' Serjeants, four Sheriffs' Yeomen, two Mayor's Marshals, and a City-Crier. To each of the twelve

Aldermen is assigned a Ward, governed subordinately by a Chief-Constable chosen annually, and a Night-Constable; viz. Trinity, St. James, Castle-Precincts, Temple, St. Thomas, St. Mary Redcliff, St. Nicholas, St. Michael, St. Ewen, All Saints, St. Mary-le-Port, and St. Stephen. To this constitution is appended a Lord High Stewardship in the person of the Right Hon. Baron Grenville. The privileged burgesses, who are so by possession of a freehold, as sons of freemen, by apprenticeship to a freeman, or by marriage of a freeman's daughter, in number 5000 and upward, send two Representatives to Parliament.

Besides those of the Parishes that give name to the twelve Wards (in which the whole are included), the churches are, the Cathedral, St. Mark's or the Mayor's Chapel, St. Augustin-the-Less, St. Augustin's Chapel, Christ-Church, St. Werburgh, St. John, St. Paul, St. Philip and Jacob, St. Peter; in all, nineteen. The suburbian churches and chapels are, those of Bedminster, Clifton, Dowry-Square, and the Orphan-Asylum. Thus far of the Establishment. There are thirty Dissenting Chapels, (exclusive of one of French Protestants, where the Liturgy of the Church of England is adopted,) which are occupied by Friends, Independents, Baptists, Moravians, Wesleyan Methodists, Tent-Methodists, Whitfieldian Methodists, Lady Huntingdon's Society, Swedenbourgians, Seceders from the Establishment, Roman Catholics, "Christians," Jews, Welsh Independents, and Unitarians. There are also two Floating-Chapels for Seamen.

The seventeen parishes within the city-boundaries, and the out-parishes of St. James and St. Philip and James *alias* Jacob, including the closely adjacent parishes of Bedminster and Clifton, contain about seven hundred and twenty streets, lanes, avenues, courts, "places," terraces, "buildings," &c. with ten squares. The buildings and places for transaction of public business amount to about thirty; those occupied as hospitals, schools, and by other charitable institutions, thirty-three, besides nineteen benevolent associations, to whose use no house is exclusively appropriated; Freemasons' Halls, two; in one of which was lately formed a society of literary and philosophical "Inquirers," who are already too numerous for their place of meeting. The places for public amusement are, the Theatre in King-street and the Assembly-Room in Prince's street. A suite of public rooms is nearly completed in Wine-street, to be named the Tyndall-Rooms. To the City-Library, in King-street, has recently been added a sister-institution (the " Bristol Literary and Philosophical") in Park-street; and the increasing disposition of our fellow-citizens to announce themselves " at home" to the whole circle of the sciences, is expected speedily to evince itself in the architectural accession of a projected " Bristol Harmonic Institution," with hospitable accommodations for a Mechanics' Institute and what not? Returning to " such things are," the banking-houses count ten, besides a Savings' Bank; and insurance-offices, not connected with those of London, five. The number of resident barristers-at-law is thirteen; attorneys, one hundred and four; conveyancers, four; law-stationers, three; physicians, twenty-eight; surgeons, apothecaries, and surgeon-dentists, about one hundred. A copy of the last Census for Bristol, &c. may be seen in our Chronicle.

The " Chronological Outline" will be found to contain materials for very voluminous dissertations upon the antiquity and architectural remains of the city and its immediate vicinity. The scheme offered, as the sequel to this introductory essay, for Eight Morning-Walks and as many Evening-Walks or Rides, in a neighbourhood which, for picturesque variety, is without parallel in the same limits, and occasional references to the Topographical Index at the end of the volume, will easily introduce the curious visitor to an acquaintance with the resources of Bristol for either profit or pleasure, without the delay of needlessly retracing the same steps towards whatever point for observation may be selected.

In the arrangement of the Chronological department, the best possible evidence is obtained of the original foundation of the city, in the fourth century antecedent to the Christian era, superadding the advantage of appeal to topographical and geological facts in confirmation of its earliest appellation.

The chain of events is hence, for the first time in a History of Bristol, continued from the Roman occupation of this neighbourhood, in common with the rest of the British islands, through the five very busy centuries of the Saxon Octarchy and Danish Confederacy, till the Norman Conquest,—exciting the unavoidable inference that *Brig-stowe*, or *Caer Brito*, as the frontier-town of Wessex opposed to Mercia, shared in all the transactions that distinguished the reign of Arthur (now no longer of dubious memory), of Cerdic, of Cenrick, of Cealwin, of Ceolric, of Ceolwulph (during which St. Austin and the British bishops congregated), of Cynegils (our first Christian king), of Cenwalch, of his widow Saxburga, of Kentwin, of Ceadwalla, of Ina (whose collection of laws is still extant, and who founded a Saxon School at Rome), of Cuthred, of Sigebyrht, of Cynewulf, of Brightric (the first builder on " Radcleve"), of Egbert, of Ethelwulf, and of Alfred the Great, who succeeded to the throne of Wessex in 871. During the subsequent reigns of Edward the Elder, Edmund, Edred, Edwin, Ethelred, Edmund Ironside, Canute, Harold, Hardicanute, and Edward the Confessor, it will appear that Bristol increased rapidly in military and ecclesiastical importance; and the village of Redland is marked as, in 1063, the place of a brilliant achievement by Harold, then duke of the West-Saxons, upon the palace and ships of Griffin, a theretofore powerful king of South Wales. With William of Normandy come into due notice the family of Harding, the Monastery, and its " tombs of all the Berkeleys"—the Castles or Castle, and fortifications of the City, with the Churches and other religious houses; in remains whereof Bristol is scarcely less rich than any other depositum of architectural eccentricities in the British islands—the wars of the Empress Maud, and Robert, earl of Gloucester, against Stephen; during which the writers on behalf of the latter characterized Bristol as " the volcano whence the kingdom was deluged with fire and sword"— the series of Charters obtained by the Burgesses in return for such of their " things" as each succeeding Cæsar found indispensable to his independence of combinations among baronial Brutuses, and the consequent growing importance l ﾝ

of the Trade and Manufactures, and extension of the civic
boundaries and magisterial jurisdiction—the Great Insurrection and Siege of 1313—the Royal and Parliamentary Sieges
of 1643 and 1645—the previous and subsequent Royal and
gracious visits—the appalling visitation of Judge Jefferys,
in the sequel of his bloody western expedition; and, among
the more tranquil and varied indications of contemporaneous
advancement towards a more diffusive abstract cultivation
of the riches of mind as well as matter, are given a brief
estimate of Chatterton's resources as an historian, and a
short Poem (a reverie on a future state), written by him in
the presence of a gentleman still living, and which has not
before been printed.

By the accession of memoranda after the earlier sheets had
been printed, referring to the periods they embraced, the
Appendix is unavoidably entailed upon the Reader's
patience, for connexion by means of his own pen with the
corresponding dates.

WALKS AND RIDES,

INCLUDING THE POINTS OF MOST COMMON RESORT ON THE WAY.

First Morning. A walk.

LEFT HAND.   RIGHT HAND.

Commencing from either
Corn-street, Broad-street, or Wine-street.
High-street.

LEFT HAND	RIGHT HAND
Chilcott, printer and bookseller, No. 6.	St. Nicholas Market,
Barry & Son, booksellers and librarians, No. 21.	Wedn. and Saturday.
M‘Dowall, printer and bookseller, No. 24.	
	St. Nicholas-street.
Bridge-street.	St. Nicholas Back.
The Bridge and Parade.	
Savings-Bank.	Pitt & Co.'s Bank.
Redcliff-street.	
Red Lion Inn.	[Two or three Printing-offices
Queen's Head Inn.	and Stationery-warehouses
	on either side.
St. Thomas' Church-lane.	Several avenues to
Three-Queen-lane.	Redcliff-Back.
Old Fox Inn.	
Portwall-lane.	

24 DE 61

Redcliff-Pit.

Angel Inn.
Pile-street.
REDCLIFF-CHURCH.
St. John's Lane.

Redcliff-Parade.

Wellington-Place.
Ferry to the Grove.

Guinea-street.

Wesleyan Chapel.

Redcliff-Hill.

The Church and Colston's Parade.
A lane at the east end, to

Pile-street.

The School-house and Chatterton's birth-place.
The Glass-houses.
George Inn.
Saracen's Head Inn.

Site of Temple-Gate.
Pipe-lane.
Rose-street.
Church-lane.
TEMPLE-CHURCH.

Temple-street.

Long Row, lending to
St. Thomas-street.

St. THOMAS' CHURCH.

Bridge-Parade and the Bridge.
St. NICHOLAS' CHURCH and Street.
All-Saints' Row, and Lane.
ALL-SAINTS' CHURCH.

Corn-street, and the Exchange.

———

First Evening. A walk or ride.

High-street and the Bridge.
Bath-street.

Tucker-street.
Mathews's Directory-Office.
Hawkins's Coach-Office.
Bristol Dispensary.
The Talbot Inn, and Coach-Office.

Temple-street.

Countess-Slip, and a
Baptist Chapel.
Beer-lane.
Water-lane.
Church-lane.
Cart-lane.
Pipe-lane.
Old book-shop.
Long-Row.

Mitchel-lane.

Portwall-lane.

Temple-Gate.

George Inn.

Pile-street.
Red-lane.
Saracen's Head Inn.

Bath-Parade.

New Road, Bridge, and Feeder.

Hill's Bridge.

Redcliff-Crescent.   *Left-hand bank of*   New Cut of the Avon.
Coronation-Road to Ashton.

Harford's Bridge.

Redcliff-Hill.

Commercial Road.

New Prison.

Bathurst Basin.

Ride over Prince's Street Bridge, or walk to   The Ferry.

The Grove.

Avenues to Queen-Square.
King-street.

Welsh Market-house.

The Back.

Crow-lane.
Baldwin-street.
St. Nicholas Church-steps.

High-street.

Second Morning. A walk.

Corn-street.

Stamp-Office.   Council-House.
ALL-SAINTS' CHURCH.
Norwich Union Assurance-Office.
All-Saints' Lane and the Rummer Tavern.
Exchange, and Exchange Bank.   Bush-Tavern.
Crown Fire-Office.   Bullion-Bank.
Exchange-Buildings.   St. Nicholas' Market.   Post-Office.
St. Nicholas-street.   St. Nicholas-street.

Blind or Baldwin Steps.

Baldwin-street.   Baldwin-street.

Back-street.

King-street.   King-street.

Charlotte-street.

Cruttwell's waggon-warehouse.
Mayoralty Mansion-House.

Queen-Square.

Custom-House and Excise-Office.

Eastern Avenue.

The Grove.

Mud-Docks. Floating Chapel.

Prince's Street.

Assembly-Room.

Assembly-Room Avenue.

Assembly Coffee-house.

c

Quay.

Thunderbolt-street.

Merchants' Hall.

Broad Quay.

Return to
Draw-Bridge.

Oram, stationer.
Stuckey & Co.'s Bank.

Clare-street.

Pewters, stationer.
Rosemary-lane.
Burnell, engraver.
Howell's music-warehouse.
Marsh-street.
Richardson, bookseller.

Essex & Co. booksellers.
Tyson's old book-shop.
St. STEPHEN's CHURCH.
Hodges's music-warehouse.
Parsons & Browne, stationers.
St. Stephen's Street.

Baldwin-street.

Corn-street.

St. Stephen's Lane.
Old Bank, Elton & Co.

St. Nicholas-street.
Ames & Co.'s Bank.
Bristol Union Fire-Office.
Harford & Co.'s Bank.
Morcom, bookseller.
Norton, bookseller.
Post-Office.

Bulgin, bookseller.
Commercial Rooms.
St. WERBURGH's CHURCH.

Small-street.

Commercial Rooms.

Small-street Court.
Pitching and Paving Office.

Small-street Buildings { Sheriffs' Office.
{ Bristol Fire-Office.
Turpin & Co. bookbinders.

Bristol Mirror-Office, No. 15.
Felix Farley's Journal-Office, No. 20.

Quay-street—St. John's Gate—Broad-street.

———————

Second Evening. A ride.

Corn-street.
Marsh-street.

Merchants' Hall.

King-street.

The Library.

Custom-House Avenue.

The Custom-House.

Queen-Square.
Excise-Office Avenue.
Prince's Street.

Assembly-Rooms.

Prince's Street Bridge.

The Prison.

Bathurst Basin.

Swing-Bridge.
Commercial Road.

Harford's Bridge.
Coronation-Road.

Red Clift: Dowager Lady Smyth's Mansion.
Ashton.

The Avon,
Rownham Ferry,
and the Hotwells.

Return to the Swing-Bridge.
N. bank of the New River.
Circuit round the Prison to the
Old Rope-Walk,
Prince's Street Bridge, &c.

———

Third Morning. A walk.

Broad-street.

The Council-House.
Frost, bookseller.

CHRIST-CHURCH.
White Hart Inn.
White Lion Inn.
New-Market Passage.
Cider-House Passage.
Tailors' Court and
Tailors' Hall.
Dock-Company's Office.

The Guild-Hall.

Bedford, bookseller.
Guildhall-Chambers.

St. John-street.
Prothonotary's Office.
Hall of the Royal York Lodge.
Tower-lane.

Bell-Tavern-lane.

St. John's Gate and Church.

Nelson-street.
Christmas-street.

Quay-street.

Small-street.

St. Giles's or the Stone Bridge.

River Froom.

Under the Bank.

Zed-alley.
Steps leading to

St. Augustin's Place.

Horse-street.
Colston's School.
Lady Huntingdon's Chapel.
Pipe-lane.

St. Augustin's Back.

Draw-Bridge.
Prison in the distance.

Formerly Shiercliff's Library.
Hanover-street.
Denmark-street.
Webber, stationer, &c.
St. Mark's Lane.

Foot of the Green.
CHURCH OF ST. AUGUSTIN-THE-LESS.

Tremlett's Library, &c.

c 2

College-Green.

Trinity-street.
THE CATHEDRAL.   ST. MARK's or the MAYOR's CHAPEL.
Saxon Archway to

Lower College-Green.

Cloisters.
Rope-Walk.   Brandon-street, to

College-street.

College-Place and Reeve's Hotel.

Frog-lane.

Foot of Park-street.   College-Green, to

The Mayor's Chapel, and Red Girls' School.

Return in College-Green to

Unity-street.

Moutrie's Music-warehouse.
The Grammar-School.
Denmark-street.

Orchard-street.

French Protestant Chapel.

Return to

Denmark-street.

Way to Hanover-street.   Red Maids' School,
new entrance.

St. Augustin's Back and Place.

Host-street.

Steep-street.   Zed-Alley.
Queen-street Steps.
City-School (the Bartholomews).
Little Lewin's Mead.

Froom (or the Water) Gate-Way.

St. John's Bridge.

Christmas-street.

St. John's Gate.

Quay-street.

Small-street.

Post-Office.

Third Evening. A Walk.

Small-street.

St. Stephen-street and Quay-Pipe.   River Froom.

Quay.

Tontine-Warehouses and St. Stephen-street.
Bristol Mercury-Office, No. 30.
Clare-street.   Broad Quay.

Draw-Bridge.

St. Augustin's Back.

St. Augustin's Church.

The Butts.

Bridge passing Tombs's Dock.

Sea-Banks.

Trinity-street.

Anchor-smith Lane.

Docks.

Mardyke to Hotwells.
Woodwell's Lane.

Canon's Marsh.
Oil-Gas Co.'s station.
Glass-House.

Brandon-Hill.

Queen's Parade.

Ascend, and descend on the N. W. to

Charlotte-street.

Upper Park-street.

Park-street.

Frog-Lane.

College-Green.

Frog-Lane.

Through the centre.

St. Augustin's Back.

Draw-Bridge.

Clare-street, &c.

Fourth Morning. A walk.

Broad-street—St. John's Gate—Christmas-street—to
Queen-street or Steps.

Steep-street.
Griffin Inn and Lane.

St. Michael's Hill.

Church-Steps.

Church-Lane.

Church-Lane.

St. Michael's Church.

St. Michael's Hill.

King David Inn.

St. Michael's Hill.

Upper Maudlin-Lane.

Pembroke-Court—John Ball's Lane, to
Lewin's Mead.
Moravian Chapel.

Terrill-street.
Alfred-Hill.
Marlborough-street and
The Infirmary.

Lower Maudlin-Lane.

Earl-street.

Blind Asylum.
Eye-Infirmary.
Way to Moravian Chapel.

Whitson-Court.

St. James's Church.

St. James's Church-yard.
Horse-Fair.

Lewin's Mead.
Bridewell-Lane.

St. James's Back.

Broadmead and Haymarket.

Nelson-street.

All-Saints' Street.   Bridewell-Lane.

St. John's Steps.

Tower-Lane.   Tower-Lane.

St. John-street.

Major, stationer, printer, &c.
Hillyard & Morgan, book and
music sellers, &c.
Huntly, bookseller.
Newcomb, bookseller and printer.
Johnson, engraver.

Broad-street, &c.

———————

Fourth Evening.   A walk.

Broad-street—Christmas-street—Queen-street.

Griffin-Lane.

Bristol Steps to
Church-Lane.

Park-Row.

Lodge-street.
The Red Lodge.
Stony Hill. .

Enter the Gate and Shrubbery, to

Tyndall's Park.

Path to the Old Park.
St. Michael's Hill.
The Fort-House.

Brandon-Hill.
Path towards Clifton.

Pass through the Central Shrubbery, north-eastward, to a Lane leading to

St. Michael's Hill.

Road to King's Parade.
Cotham Turnpike.
Base of St. Bewell's Cross, in a field.
Clarence-Place.
Paul-street.   White Bear Inn.
Southwell-street and the
    Montague Tavern.
                                                           Fort-Road.
Robin-Hood Lane.
                                                    Steps to Tinker's, or Tankard's,
                                                        or Tancred's Close.
Colston's Alms-House.   Park-Place.
Horfield-lane.   St. Michael's Church-Yard.
King David Inn.   Church-lane.
Upper Maudlin-lane.
Somerton's Printing-Office.
Compton's Library.   Clark's Hawkers' Tract Depository.

Queen-street Steps—Christmas-street—St. John's Gate,
                    Broad-street.

21

Fifth Morning. A walk.

Wine-street.

pposition Coach-Office.

lume of Feathers Inn.

ing's Head Passage.
age, bookseller.
he Pithay and Tower-lane.

The Castle Bank.
Savery & Co.'s Bank.
Adam and Eve Lane, Tavern, and the
Observer Printing-Office.
Guard-House Passage.
Rees, bookseller and librarian.
The Tyndall Rooms.
The Cheese-Market.
Dolphin-street.
Narrow Wine-street.

Union-street.

ld Town-wall Steps to
Pithay-Gate.

St. James's Market.

Broadmead.

lelson-street.

Hay-Market.

St. James's Back.

ridewell-Lane.

Horse-Fair.

Silver-street.
Lower and Upper Maudlin Lanes.
St. Michael's Hill.
Horfield-Lane.

obin-Hood-Lane.

Terrill-street.
The Prior's or Bird's Garden.
Prospect-House Passage.
Alfred-Hill.

lfred-Place.
olston's Mount, way to Cotham
House, and Redland-Court.
fontague-Tavern.

Montague-Garden.

Montague-Parade.

Marlborough-Hill.

Kingsdown-Parade.

Montague-street.

James's Parade—James's Place.

Spring-Hill.

Dame Pugsley's Well-Field.
Somerset-street.
Spring-Hill.

love-street.

Dove-street.

King-Square.

arolina-Court.
maica-street.

Duke-street.
Dighton-street.

King-Square Avenue.

oke's Croft (Road to Gloucester).
ck Fields and Wilder-street.
ll-Moon Inn.

Charles's Street.
Cherry-lane.

North-street.

Cumberland-street.

Brunswick-Square.

Wilder-street.
Unitarian Burying-Ground.

York-street.
Gloucester-street.

Surrey-street.

Prichard-street.

Cave-street.

Portland-Square.

Dean-street—ST. PAUL'S CHURCH—St. Paul-street.

St. Paul-street.

Norfolk-street.

Wilson-street.
Orange-street.

Newfoundland-street.

Charlotte-street.
Clark-street.

Mills's Place.

Milk-street.

Prichard-street.
Gloucester-street.
York-street.

Callowhill-Steps
Leek-lane.

Square-Avenue.

St. James's Square.

St. James's Terrace.

Wellington-Terrace.

St. James's Barton.

Barrs-street.

White Horse Inn.
Horse Fair.

Milk-street.

Old King-street.

Ebenezer Chapel.
Broadmead.

Baptist Chapel.
Rosemary-street.

Merchant-street.

Black Friars.
Broad Weir.

Merchant-Tailors' Alms-House.
The Castle Mill.

Castle Mill-street.

Castle-Green.

Site of Newgate Prison.

Narrow Wine-street.

Mitchell's Waggon-Warehouse.
Dallimore's Van-Warehouse.
Chequer-lane.
Dolphin-street.

The George Tavern.

Union-street.

Wine-street.

Fifth Evening. A walk.

Broad-street—Christmas-street—St. John's Bridge.

Lewin's Mead Chapel.

Bartholomew or John Ball's Lane.

23

Upper Maudlin-lane.
Terrill-street.
St. Magdalen's Nunnery Garden.   Bedford-Place.
Horfield-lane.
Southwell-street.   Kingsdown.
Alfred-Place.
Paul-street.   Colston's Fort Cottage.
Observatory, formerly a wind-mill.   Portland-House ;
Portland-street.
                                        Portland Chapel.
Road to the Cross-Hands.
Cotham-Lodge and Park.
Castellated Arch on the brow of the Hill.
Park of Redland-Court.

Redland-Court-House (which is built in the style of Strachan, if not under his immediate direction) was originally erected, and the grounds laid out, between the years 1730 and 40, at the expense of Mr. Cousens, a merchant of London; whose taste in the choice of a situation would be better appreciated, were it not, like the light of the Sun, so commonly accessible. The Chapel, for his own private use, was a part of the plan. The House with the Park was given by Mr. Cousens to Mr. Innes, from whom it was inherited by the family of Mr. Baker; on Mr. Baker's decease it was sold to Mr. Seymour, from whom the present occupier, Sir Richard Vaughan, knight, became the purchaser. The field that contains the Arch remains with Mr. Baker's family.

Road eastward to the Cross-Hands.
Lampblack-Hill.
Path to Cutler's Mills, and new cut of the
 Road to Horfield and Gloucester.
Rennison's Baths, Montpelier,
 and Ashley-Court.
Catherine-Place.
Road to Ashley-Place, the Orphan Asylum,
 new Ashley-Court Road to Horfield,
 Baptist Mills and Stapleton.
                          Path to Dame Pugsley's Well Field.

Stoke's Croft.
The Baptist Academy.   Black Horse Inn and site
                                       of Old Theatre, under
                                       Nine-tree Hill.
Back-Fields and Circular   Hillgrove-street.
   Stables.
Lewin's Mead Boys' Free-School
 and Women's Alms-House.
                                      King-Square Avenue.

North-street.
Wilder-street.   Cherry-lane.
Full-Moon Inn.
St. James's Barton.
                             St. James's Sunday School-
                                  House.
Barton-Alley.
                              An old book-shop.

d

St. James's Church-Yard.
Bridewell-Bridge and Lane.

Mrs. Fry's and another old book-shop.   Nelson-street.

St. John's Steps and Street—Broad-street.

———

Sixth Morning. A walk.

Wine-street—Narrow Wine-street—Castle-Mill-street—
Merchant-street.

Merchant-Tailors' Alms-House.   Two ways to the Black Friers.

Rosemary-street.

Coupland's Stables.   The Friends' Meeting-House.
Philadelphia-street.

Water-street.

Callowhill Meeting-House—Old Orchard.

Penn-street.

Whitfield's Tabernacle.

Narrow Weir.

River Froom.

New Ælle-Bridge and Passage.
Ælle-Bridge *alias* Elbroad-street.

Captain Cary's Lane.

Redcross-street.

Baptist Alms-House and
Burying-ground.
St. Philip's Wesleyan Chapel.
Lancasterian Free-Schools.

Tabernacle Burying-ground.

Back-Lane.

Passage to New-street.
West-street.

Old Market-street.

St. PHILIP's CHURCH.

Jacob-street.

Church-Lane, to

Tower-Hill.

Old Market-street.

Castle-Ditch.

Castle-street.

Queen-street to the Ferry.
Golden Boy Court.

Castle-Green.
Cock-and-Bottle-Lane.

St. Peter-street.

St. PETER's CHURCH.
House of Industry.
Bridge-street.

Road to Newgate, &c.
Chequer-Lane.
Dolphin-street.

St. Maryport-street.

Two ways to the CHURCH and
Bridge-street Independent
Chapel.

The Cheese-Market.

Guard-House-Passage.
Adam-and-Eve-Lane.

High-street, &c.

Sixth Evening. A ride.

Wine-street—Dolphin-street—St. Peter-street—Castle-street.
Old Market-street.

Bull-Paunch-lane, and Poyntz-Pool.

West-street.

The Lamb Inn.

Gloucester-lane.

Poyntz-Pool.   Gloucester County Prison and
Wade-street.   Sessions-House.

Stapleton Road.

Armoury.   Baptist-Mills.

Road to the Orphan Asylum, &c.
Ashley-Place and Wellington-Place.

Picton-street.
Road to Redland, Gloucester, &c.

Stoke's Croft—North-street—Barrs-street—Broadmead.
Union-street—Wine-street.

———————

Seventh Morning. A ride.

High-street—the Bridge—St. Thomas-street—Portwall-lane—
Temple-Gate—Bath-Parade.

Hill's Bridge.

Hill's Bridge-Place.

New course of the   Colston-street.
  River Avon.   Somerset-street.
                                                   Langton-street.
                                                   Somerset-Square, &c.
Harford's Bridge.   Redcliff-Hill.

Commercial Road.

New course of   Bathurst-Basin.
  the Avon.   Prince's Street Bridge.
                                                        The Prison.
                                                   View of the Cathedral, &c.

Overfall-Dam.

Cumberland Basin.   Floating-Harbour.

Swing-Bridge.
Cumberland-Place.

Gloucester-House and Steam-Packet Hotel—
  late Barton's, now Warne's.

Dowry-Parade.

Hotwell Chapel.   Dowry-Square.

Green-street.

Albemarle-Row.   Hope-Square and Chapel.

Granby-Place.

Windsor Terrace.   Lower Crescent.
Paragon Buildings.   Royal York Crescent.

d 2

Prince's Buildings. Wellington-Place.

Sion-Hill.

Old Hot-Wells.

New Hot-Wells.

Sion-Place.

Sion-Row.
Gloucester-Row.

Ancient Military Station.

Clifton-Down.

Harley-Place.

Mortimer-House.

Portland-Place.

Rodney-Place. Boyce's Buildings.

The Mall.

Clifton-Hill.

Saville-Place.
CLIFTON CHURCH.
York-Place.

Mr. Goldney's Mansion.
Descent to Jacob's Well.

Clifton Wood.

Belle Vue.

Berkeley-Place.

Clifton Burying-ground.

Road to Jacob's Well.
Upper Berkeley-Place.
Berkeley-Crescent.
Berkeley-Square.

Road to Aust Passage.
Park-Row.

Park-street.

College-Green—St. Augustin's Back—Draw-Bridge—
Clare-street—Corn-street.

Seventh Evening. A ride.

Corn-street, &c. to Park-street.

Aust-Road.

Roads to Clifton.
The White Ladies.

The Park-Gate.
Vittoria-Place.

Turnpike.

Miller's Nurseries.

St. Michael's Hill.

King's Parade.

Black Boy Tavern.

Redland.

Durdham-Down.

Road on the left to Stoke.

Sneed-Park Farm.
On the top of the hill, within
the wall, on the left, the
entire remains of a British
cromlech.
Col. Webb's Mansion.

24 DE 31

Stoke-House, the residence of
Sir Henry Lippincott, bart.

Kingsweston.

Kingsweston Inn.

Lord De Clifford's Park. [See note to p. 269.]

Pen-Pole.
Shirehampton.

Lamplighter's Hall, and Ferry to Pill.

Return the same road, across Durdham-Down, and turn on the left-hand for

Redland.

Redland-Green and the CHAPEL.
Redland-Court.

Road to the Cross-Hands.

Road to Horfield and Gloucester.

Lamp-black Hill—Stoke's Croft—North-street—Barrs-street—Broadmead—Union-street—Wine-street.

————

Eighth Morning.   A ride.

Corn-street, &c. (as in Seventh Evening), across Durdham-Down, to the right.
Westbury.

WESTBURY CHURCH.
Westbury College.

River Trym.   River Trym.

Henbury.

Salutation Inn.

Blaize Castle and the Cottages.

BLAIZE CASTLE.—About the year 1762, Thomas Farr, Esq. a merchant, of Bristol, purchased from Sir Jarrett Smith, bart. an estate at Henbury, including Blaize Wood, so called from the existence anciently, within its precincts, of a Chapel dedicated to St. Blaize, Bishop of Sebastia, in America, who is said to have discovered the art of combing wool. The estate comprises a richly wooded valley interspersed with bold rocks, and commands delicious views of the river Severn, the Welsh hills, and neighbouring country. This had been a favourite scene of Mr. Farr's shooting-excursions when a school-boy; and, to the credit of his decision of character no less than of his fine taste, in being the first to appreciate the beauties of this spot, it should not be forgotten that he thus early determined, whenever he might possess the means and opportunity, to become its purchaser, and make it emulate, as far as its limits would permit, the charms of the far-famed Piercefield Estate, with the owner of which, the lamented Valentine Morris,* Mr. Farr's family were on terms of intimacy. When the propitious era of maturity and competence arrived, Mr. Farr commenced his operations by laying out a walk around the wood, and opening the foliage at places of easy access for the most striking points of view. In 1766, at an expense of about three thousand pounds, he erected on the highest acclivity a castellated building, consisting of a very large circular room, and a few small rooms; which he named Blaize Castle. The structure is elegant; and from its apartments, but especially from the summit of its tower, the eye ranges over an extended prospect, in every direction, rarely equalled for the richness and variety of its features. In digging the foundation of this building, a great number of Roman coins, chiefly of brass, with some few of silver, were found, of the age of Vespasian, Constan-

* For an interesting memoir of this gentleman, see The Devil upon Two Sticks in England, a novel, written by the late Mr. William Combe, the author of Dr. Syntax's popular Tour in Search of the Picturesque, &c.—See also the Gentleman's Magazine, vol. ii. of the year 1823, for some anecdotes of Mr. Combe himself, communicated by the present Chronologist.

tine, Gordianus, &c. a complete catalogue of which has been furnished by the Rev. Samuel Seyer, in the first part of his " Memoirs of Bristol." At the entrance of the wood was a neat rustic building, formed of roots and branches of trees. A gentleman, who was a stranger, having visited the wood, on his return left the following lines upon the table of the root-house, written with a pencil:

> Far I have roam'd, o'er many a foreign soil,
> And view'd the different beauties of this Isle:
> They far excel what many pleasing call;
> But thy improvements, Farr! excel them all.

In 1778, Mr. Farr was induced to part with the estate to —— Skeate, D. C. L. That gentleman within a few years disposed of it, to become the builder of Lambridge House, near Bath; when Blaize Castle was purchased by the late John Scandrett Harford, esq. who considerably improved the whole demesne. In place of the original residence, which was comparatively small and inconvenient, stands a capital mansion, surrounded by pleasure-grounds, in which Art has contributed much to the loveliness that Nature, her fondest, most grateful nurse, had supplied.

The approach to the house is through a gothic lodge on the top of Henbury Hill. After passing through a wood, the road arrives at the side of a hill, whence the house appears across a deep woody glen, which was formerly deemed impassable. However, by cutting away the face of the rock in some places, and building lofty walls in others, to sustain the road, and by taking advantage of the natural projections and recesses to make the necessary curvatures, carriages now pass this tremendous chasm with perfect ease and safety. This masterly improvement was projected by the late Humphry Repton, esq. and executed under his superintendance.

The grounds of Blaize Castle exhibit proofs of the benevolence of Mr. Harford no less striking than of his taste for the picturesque, in the creation of a small hamlet, familiarly known as THE HENBURY COTTAGES. This hamlet was erected in 1810, at Mr. Harford's sole expense, and with the view of providing an asylum for aged persons of deserving character having very small incomes, so as to enable them, by saving the expense of house-rent, to end their days in comfort. The number of cottages is ten; and they are of an architectural character so variously fanciful as to impress the imagination of an untravelled spectator with the belief that they were designed as specimens of the domestic buildings of different countries. The interior of the ground-plan is marked by a ring terrace-walk of irregular curve, and encloses a lawn of naturally undulating surface. Each cottage contains an oven, a boiler, and other conveniences, and stands insulated in front of its own garden. This group of buildings was erected after the designs of John Nash, esq., whose object was to produce the best effect when they should be clothed with the ivy, honey-suckle, jasmin, and other ornamental shrubs, even to the chimney-tops. The whole of this little paradise is covered from the violence of the north-west winds across the Severn by trees of medium growth. The inhabitants are supplied with water from a well sunk upon the edge of the lawn in front of one of the cottages; the pump of which presents a neatly finished column in stone, tastefully relieving and promoting the sylvan aspect of the surrounding structures.

The present proprietor of Blaize Castle, John Scandrett Harford, esq. D. C. L. has decorated the house with a fine collection of paintings, made by himself in Italy, and is pursuing plans of further improvement by planting on an extensive scale. In 1824 he purchased from Edward Hodges Bailey, R. A. who is a native of Bristol, his celebrated statue of Eve, cut from a block of marble that cost the sculptor £400.

Eighth Evening. A short walk.

[Vide the Fifth Morning.]

Dine at the Montague Tavern, with any number of friends, whether few or many, no matter at what price per head, that may suit an honest man's pocket. If cleanliness,

29

attention, pure cates, precise cookery, and excellent wines
or punch-royal, be received as legitimate ingredients towards
' a feast of reason and flow of soul," then let it be remembered that such is the " Bristol fashion" of many another
public table: an every-day ordinary at either of our inns
presents nothing in common with an ordinary dinner.

And if the stranger to Bristol's citizens should choose a
sojourn of length enough to cultivate their confidence, he
cannot fail to associate with Tradesmen who have proved
themselves Nature's nobles, and Merchants worthy to rank
among Princes. But without integrity no less than good
humour and liberal professions, the blandishments of dress
and address must be content to weigh as dust in the balance.
—So far write us down " hogs," but no farther.

Should length of residence in Bristol permit still more
extended excursions than those already described, the following places may be found generally within the distance
of thirteen miles, as marked upon Donne's " Map of the
Country twenty-one miles round the city of Bristol;" which
includes, within its circle between W. and N., Bassaleg,
Newport, Usk, and Trelleg, Monmouthshire;— between
N. and E., Blakeney on the Monmouthshire side of the
Severn, in Gloucestershire; Cambridge Inn, Nympfield
and the seat of Lord Ducie, Kingscote, Beverstone, Tetbury,
Foxbury and Malmsbury Common, Corston, and Chippenham;—between E. and S., Melksham, Trowbridge, Westbury, Frome, Nunney, Wanstrow, Evercreech and Pyle-
street, beyond Shepton-Mallet;— between S. and W.,
Glastonbury, Mark, South-Brent, and East-Brent, and
Brean on the Bristol Channel. This reference will present
a choice of excursions, most of which may be accomplished
within a summer's day, viz.

1. A voyage down the Avon, to Kingroad, may be taken either in a
light boat with sails, which would give time for a deliberate view of its
varied margin of wood and rock, or on the deck of one of the outward-
bound steam-vessels as far as the river's mouth. Opportunities for return
the same day occur most frequently with a flowing afternoon-tide, or
land-conveyance from Lamplighter's Hall.

·2. Leaving Bristol as in the " *Eighth Morning*," and the road to Henbury on the left-hand, with the White Hart Inn on the right, ascend Westbury-Hill, and proceed onward to Crib's Causeway, 5 miles; East Compton, 6; Redwick, 8; Marsh-Common, 9; Aust, 11 miles.

3. From Stoke's Croft pass through Horfield to Filton, $3\frac{1}{2}$ miles; Almondsbury-Hill, 6; Alveston, 10; Thornbury, 11; its *Castle*, $11\frac{1}{2}$ miles. Return by way of Littleton-upon-Severn, Elberton, Olveston, Tockington, and Almondsbury, descending its Hill, to the six-mile stone.

4. By way of Gloucester-lane, go to Stapleton, 2 miles; (*Stoke-House* is on the hill to the left;) Stoke-Gifford; Winterbourn, 6 miles; Frampton-Cotterel; Iron-Acton, 9 miles. Return through Nibley. (Southward of the nine-mile stone is *Says Farm*, the country-residence of Edward Colston.) Cross Coalpit-Heath, to Downend, Stapleton, &c.

5. Turning eastward, about half way between Bristol and Stapleton, pass the Fishponds to Mangotsfield, 5 miles; Pucklechurch, 7 miles; northward to Westerleigh; (the kitchen of the King's Arms there was taken by Bird, R. A. as the scene of his *Country Choristers*;) eastward to Wapley; northward to Sodbury; eastward to Old Sodbury; the Cross-Hands; north-eastward to *Badminton*, one of the seats of His Grace the Duke of Beaufort. Return by Acton-Turville to the Cross-Hands; southward, skirting Dodington-Park on the right, to Hinton-Hill; then south-westward, across Hinton-Common, to Pucklechurch.

6. Progress through Old-Market-street, West-street, over Lawrence-Hill (at an ancient hospital on the left of which, in 1574, Elizabeth stopped to beautify, that she might the more effectively dazzle Bristol's citizens), through St. George's, Kingswood, Warmley, 4 miles; Wick, 7; on the left of which is Abston, with the small river Boyd and its St. Vincent-like rocks; Tughill; Cold Aston, 10; Marshfield, 12 miles. Returning, on Tughill, turn to the left, for *Sir Beville Granville's Monument*, erected on Landsdown in 1643; then through Tracy-Park to Wick, and homeward.

7. The " Upper Road" to Bath is through St. George's: the right-hand road, passing the Church, to Oldland, 4 miles; Bitton, 6; Swineford; Kelston, formerly the seat of the Harington family; and the lower part of Weston, viewing Twerton on the right. Omit not to see *Prior-Park*, the residence of Fielding's *Allworthy*, where his original of *Tom Jones* was found, while the humorist was there a visitor, in one of the beds.* Returning from Bath by the " Lower Road," go through Twerton, by Newton St. Leo; Corston; Saltford; through Keynsham, and over

---

* The prototype of his '*Squire Western*, who lived about 13 miles *west*ward, thus warranted the portrait. A gentleman having remarked that he understood Inigo Jones built the family-mansion: " Its a d—d lie, whoever told you so," replied our 'squire; " for my father built it."——A rich man, by shutting himself up from every society except that in which he may be the sole oracle, is very likely to retrograde in perceptive powers towards a state of nature; *vulgo*, to become *a natural*.

'hat was, till within a few years since, a wild common (now clothed
ith wood and verdure, and crowned by Dr. Edward Long Fox's Asylum
)r the restoration of the precious jewel of the mind to its frail casket the
ody), to Brislington; which of itself, with the Church, site of " St. Anne's
ɪ the Wood," a Summer-house of Langton-Court, now the domicile
f a cotter, in which, to the Pactolean flowings of our Avon, Addison
rote some of his Spectators, and the Castle and Queen-street Gates,
ɪight well invite a *Ninth Morning's Walk.*

8. To Stanton-Drew, from Temple-Gate, leave the Lower Bath-
oad on the left, for Knowle, Whitchurch, Pensford, 6 miles. Beyond
ensford, 1¼ mile to the right, make a right-hand circuit through
tanton-Wick and Stanton-Drew, to the *Druidical Stones.*   Return
omeward through Norton-Malreward† and Whitchurch.

9. Ride over Redcliff-Hill, through Bedminster (the Common of
hich presents a beautiful bird's eye view of the Hotwells, &c.), to
ɪishport; passing Dundry on the right, to Northwick, Chew-Magna,
hew-Stoke, and East-Harptree, 11 miles.

10. Through Bedminster, straight onward to the nine-mile stone;
ɪrning to the right for Wrington, 10½ miles, the birth-place of LOCKE.

11. In Bedminster, turn on the right for Ashton. *Ashton-Court* is
ɪ the right of the road, the *Church* on the left. Go through Long-
shton, to Flax-Bourton, Farleigh, West-Town, Brockley and the
ombe,§ 9 miles. [This may suffice for one day, but intending either
vo days, or a week,]
    Pass onward to Congresbury, 21 miles; Puxton, St. George,
Vorle, and Weston-super-Mare, 12 miles. Here is an Hotel, kept by
ɪe who was butler to the Mayors of Bristol for several successive years,
 Library, Baths, and society enough for ample illustration of what a

* In *The Bristol Mirror* for Oct. 10, 1818, or in the succeeding Bristol Observer,
ay be seen an interesting letter, dated on the 3d from Brislington-House, explana-
ry of a recent article in the *Rouen Gazette*, upon the subject of Dr. Fox's father,
ɪseph Fox of Falmouth, having persevered in his determination to restore his share
' some French prizes, captured by two vessels of which he was part owner, to the
ɪffering proprietors, and in the completion of which liberal purpose the Doctor himself
as instrumental, after his father's decease.——We cannot exactly point out, but doubt-
ss any of his neighbours may, the spot selected by Dr. Fox for his family burying-
ace. A " churlish priest," now gone to his account, once thought he did credit to
ɪristianity by denying interment to one of the Doctor's children in ecclesiastically
ɪnsecrated ground, because of their different religious discipline. The sound of a
ther's sorrowing voice over the grave, and the tears of his surviving family, sanctified
ɪher earth, which its Creator had not rejected; for flowers, we dare say, would grow
ɪere no less quickly than in the church-yard, and smell as sweetly. We honour every
ue Churchman, provided he be no less charitable than sincere; and preachers who
'e not so, need being preached to no less than their flock.
    † Vide Collinson's History of Somersetshire.
  § Vide the " Remains of William Reed," 8vo. by the Rev. John Evans.—We must
fer the *Antiquary* to the Map connected with chap. i. § 66, &c. of the Rev. Samuel
eyer's Memoirs of Bristol.

commercial life in Bristol may produce in the way of good tast: in recreation and general intelligence.

12. Cross the Avon at Rownham-Ferry; ascend the hill to Leigh-Down; pierce the Wood, and view the circumvallations of an *ancient military station*, opposite to that of Clifton Down. [This alone, with a camp tea-equipage, might serve for a *Thirteenth Afternoon*, on foot.] Ride to Failand, Wraxall, Clevedon - Court, and Clevedon. Return through Walton, Weston, Portishead, Portbury, Abbot's Leigh, and Leigh Down, to Rownham. The Lodge on the summit of Leigh Down, with Ionic columns, is the approach to P. J. Miles, Esq.'s mansion,* the successor of Leigh Court, the Royal retreat of 1651.

As on the gates of the city of Seville, we are told, was inscribed, " *He that hath not seen Seville, hath not seen any thing wonderful,*"—so may be read in the countenances of those who shall *tourify* in the courses above described, *He that searches for a greater variety of the pleasures*

> " That grove and valley, hill and field,
> Or woods and steepy mountains yield,"

may have little besides air and exercise for his reward.

Had Bristol and its neighbourhood possessed fewer charms derived from Nature and Art, still, as a brother "Picture"-maker would phrase it, (to whom, notwithstanding he is a namesake, it may be necessary to add, we bear nought but a cosmopolitish affinity,) "unquestionably Bristol has peculiar claims upon the traveller's regard for interesting associations," as the birth-place of a DALLAWAY for *Antiquities and Heraldry*, a LAWRENCE for *Painting*, a SOUTHEY for *Poetry*, and a BAILY for *Sculpture*. Of these, though contemporaries, we may speak, because they are not locally in the tribe of Bristol's worthies; a few of whom we have the happiness to greet with our every-day how-d'ye? and who little suspect the cogitations of the

> " .. chield amang 'em, taking notes,"

and his propensity for "authoring" and "*prenting*" transactions, when they are either dead *or* " gone for good and all."

* We do not quite credit the story, connected with Charles the Second's retreat, of the carter's frock, and the cook-maid, and application of her stick to the King's back. The block, if it ever had an identical existence, should be still in being.

A
CHRONOLOGICAL OUTLINE

OF THE

History of Bristol.

VHENEVER, the Ancients were either unable or, after the
ule of a prophet being without honour in his own country,
nwilling to assign any useful invention to a fellow-mortal,
iey piously and poetically gave it to the gods; and, in the
bsence of written language, so apt were leaders or teachers to
ive, and the million to receive, sensible objects for the enforce-
ient of ideal events, that even the gods themselves were said to
nd birth in any country where their worship was first intro-
uced. Now, as Geoffry of Monmouth, the chief of the most
ncient collectors of British history, did not claim a divine or
iiraculous origin for the towns and cities of Britain, and as
Villiam of Worcester and Robert Ricart, the two elder Bristol
hroniclers, held Geoffry's authorities in some degree of respect,
e are bound to entertain those authorities, until contradicted or
irrected by something of greater weight—matter more tangible,
earing a date, the best of all challenges to farther enquiry and
tter condemnation to the regions of fable and romance. The
eader will, if it pleaseth him, strike out of his estimation all
iatter in the following sheets which is not so warranted; but
ie Writer, or Compiler, or Editor—let whichever appellation
: the most fitting—could do no less than lay before him the
formation of the venerable Geoffry, that about the year of the
orld, before the birth of Christ, 380, Donebante, Dyfnal Moel-
ud, or Dunwallo Molmutius, reigned, the first King of Britain*

---

* For the etymology of Britain, the Reader is referred to "Horæ Britannicæ, or Studies
Ancient British History, containing various Disquisitions on the National and Reli-
ius Antiquities of Great Britain. By John Hughes." 2 vols. 8vo. 1818.—In that work
: claim of Geoffry of Monmouth to consideration and respect is duly estimated. If

so called; who had two sons, named Belin, or Bellinus, and Bren, or Brennus.* Bellinus, having followed the example of his father in constructing roads and highways in Britain, so far contributed to the foundation of Bristol; but William of Worcester, in his Notes on Bristol, asserts that it was founded by Brennus. The Kalendar of Robert Ricart, (compiled about 1479, when he became Town-Clerk of Bristol,) thus states the relative condition of the two brothers.

"Belyne, the eldest sonne, had al the londe a this side Humbre;
"and Brynne had al the londe beyonde Humbre unto Scotlonde. And
"for as moche as Belyne had the more parte and the better parte,
"Brynne wexed wrothe and would have had more. But Belyn would
"not suffre him. So they beganne to werre. But Brynne, the younger
"broder, had no force, nether pouer, against his brother Belyn. So
"Brynne, by counselle of his people, voided into Fraunce, and there
"abode long time, and gotte there grete lordeshippes by marriage; for
"he was Duc of all Burgoynte, by that he wedded the daughter of
"Duc Selvyn, whiche was heire of all that londe. And, whiles Brynne
"bode in Fraunce, King Belyne regned nobly and in peace in this londe
"among his Bretonnes, and made many roiall weies thro al the londe—
"that one from the este unto the west that is called Watteling-strete,
"and that other wey from the south unto the northe that is called
"Ikenelde-strete. And other two waies he made athwert the londe;
"that one is called the Fosse, and that other the Fosse dyke. And [he]
"maynteyned well the lawes that his fadre Donebante had stablished in
"his tyme.
"And in this mean tyme Brynne assembled a grete pouer and a grete
"oste of Burgoinhers and Frenchmen, and came into this lande† to fight
"with his brother Belynne; but they were made accorded bi their modre
"Conuwenn [Conuvena—MILTON] with grete justaunce and labour.
"And then they came togyder, with grete joie, to the citee of New Troie,
"and there dwelled in fere a hole yere. And then they enterprised and
"toke upon them for to go conquere al Fraunce; and so they did, and
"passed then to Rome, Lombardie, and Germaine, and toke homages
"and feantees of earles, baronns, and of al other estates of that land,
"Bi whom Kinge Arthure took his title in al his conquests. And after
"they had this doon, the sade two brethren returned home into this land

the admixture of improbable with probable or possible events, handed down through a long line of ages, is to place the whole out of rational belief, no book whatever may escape proscription. Fables, to find credence within any moderate time of their assumed origin, must necessarily be mingled with generally acknowledged facts, as presenting the only chance of existence in the estimation of posterity. The wisdom of unbelief is of cheap acquisition. Folly need not be long at school, to grow as eloquent and instructive.

* Had the Latin historians of events purely British, forborne thus to transmute proper names, much confusion of identity might have been saved, to later writers in English, unacquainted with British or Welsh.

† The precision of the transcriber might here be doubted; but instances are not wanting of the name of a person being spelt differently on one and the same legal document, in so many as three varieties from the signature.

" of Grete Bretaigne, with their Bretonnes, and dwelled here togyder
" in grete joye. And then Brynne first founded and bilded this worship-
" ful towne of Bristul that now is Bristowe, and set it upon a litell hill;
" that is to say, between Seint Nicholas Yate, Seint Johne's Yate, Seint
" Leonarde's Yate, and the Newe Yate. And no more was bilde, not
" many yeres after. And thenne Brynne repaired home over see into
" his own lordship of Burgoine, and there abode al his lyf,* And King
" Bellyne abode at New Troie, and bilded there a noble gate, fast by
" the water of Tamys, and called it Billingesgate, after his own name,
" and reigned nobly al his lyf, and lieth at New Troie."

Were our task that of compiling an Early History of Britain,
we could give more weight to the preceding extract from the
Kalendar of the Mayors of Bristol than at first sight it may
seem to command, and from sources very recently opened to the
public view; but the insulated fact of the foundation of Bristol
is, in our own opinion, established by the name of the hill or
mount which so closely adjoins and overlooks the whole of the
original town.

Dun, dune, thune, don, ton, being of the Saxon family whence
we derive TOWN,—and as the hill in question must have had a
name before the introduction of any calendar of Saints, whether
provincial or catholic, why may it not have been called by a
name equivalent to *the hill of Brennus' town,* or *Bren town?*
We need only refer to the list of Mayors and Prepositors of
Bristol from A.D. 1216 to 1300, to prove that a place gave name
to persons of inferior rank to that of princes, more frequently
than such persons conferred name on a place. We there find
Robert de Monmouth, Robert de Weston, James de Rowberrowe,
Walter de Ubbley, Hugh de Fairford, John de Broadway, John
de Marsefielde, Nicholas de Portbury, John de Cardiffe, Philip
de Pawlette, William de Leigh, Elias de Axbridge, Richard de
Lemster, Simon de Wedmore, Peter de Cainsham, John de Portes-
head, Robert de Kingwood, Richard de Mangersfield, John de

---

* We find the following in "A Chronological History of France," appended to
Mr. Hervé's "How to enjoy Paris," published in 1816. In his Preliminary Observations, that gentleman says his Chronology was not copied from any table of the kind
that had appeared. Finding a strange variation in the dates affixed by historians to
striking circumstances, and even in their account of the number of years the sovereigns
lived and reigned, he had decided by comparing events, and the different accounts, one
with another.
" 400 years before Christ.—The Gauls under Brennus plundered and burnt Rome,
" but were cut off shortly after by Camillus the Roman general, and in a subsequent
" attack lost 40,000 men.
" 387 B. C.—Brennus, with two other generals, in three divisions, invades Mace-
" donia with an army of 150,000 foot and 60,000 horse, and ravages the country, but
" is defeated in Greece, and puts an end to his life."
Mr. Hervé's remark as to the variation of dates in the French authorities may equally
apply to Geoffry of Monmouth. Perhaps Donebante reigned 480 instead of 380 years
before the Christian æra.

Cheddar, William de Glastonbury, and even Richard de Colepit.
As we shall have to note the existence of two at least of the
Anchorites (one a female) who chose Brandon-Hill as their place
of retirement from the popular world, it is not unreasonable to
conjecture that the first person who selected so conspicuous a
station for solitude was called the Saint of Brandon-Hill, and
that hence was imbibed the notion of a Saint Brandon, to whom
a hermitage on the summit of the mount is said to have been
dedicated.

Bristol, then, we conclude, was founded by Brennus.

British houses were built at some distance from each other,
not in regular streets. These were generally on the banks of a
river, for the convenience of water, or in the woods and forests,
where abundance of forage might be found for the cattle.*
The most convenient of these places was chosen by the prince
for his own residence; and his followers and dependents made
their habitations as near as they could, conveniently, to that
of their sovereign, and also erected stalls for their cattle within
the same limits. A ditch or mound of earth, or ramparts, surrounded the whole. The houses were wooden, circular, (like
windmills,) with high tapering roofs; at the top or centre of
which was an aperture for admitting light and venting smoke.
Such, it is presumed, before the mixture of Roman refinements
and buildings, was the appearance of Bristol.

Between Bellinus and the next sovereign of the Britons whom
it falls within the limits of our plan to name, might be enume-
rated about thirty-three kings, the duration of whose reigns
occupied, the longest thirty-two years, and the shortest seven
months. Considering the vicissitudes to which the written
records of this country have been from time to time exposed, it
must necessarily happen that our own chronicles consist chiefly
of widely disjointed fragments. Among the prose-works of our
native poet, Milton, will be found " A History of Britain, that
part especially now called England, from the first traditional
beginning, continued to the Norman Conquest, collected out of
the ancientest and best authors thereof." A new edition of this
neglected work was published in 1818, with a preface written

* A learned writer, (Carte,) who has sifted all remains of British Antiquity with
great diligence, observes that " the forests were useful for the excellent pannage, or
" mast, they afforded for hogs; whence, as the wealth of the inhabitants consisted in
" droves of those animals, the province itself might have its name from them, and
" from *hukh* (the British name for porkus) be denominated *Huicca*, or, in Latin,
" *Wiccia*, and its people *Wiccii*." Whence may be deduced the probability that the
number of places, of the names of which Wick forms a part, were anciently forests.
The forests in the immediate neighbourhood of Bristol were Kingswood and Horewood,
now Horfield. Of Kingswood Forest, vide note under A.D. 947. Of Horfield, see 1222.

by Baron Maseres. We must content ourselves with simply recommending it to the Reader's notice, which we do with the greater earnestness, because, from the circumstance of Dr. R. Watson, author of the Life of Fletcher, and proprietor of the Stuart archives, having collected also some very valuable documents referring to the history of this country, which had been kept for ages previous to the French Revolution in the Royal Abbey of St. Denis, the time cannot be far distant when annals that have been considered as having originated in the poetical inventions of the cloister, will assume a highly satisfactory degree of credence.

83   Cassivelanus, or Cassibelain, was king of Britain.
70   Diviaticus, king of the Suessones in Germany, a conqueror chiefly in Berkshire and Oxfordshire.*
55   Aug. 26, the Romans, under Julius Cæsar, first invaded Britain.
50   Tenantius, or Theomantius, younger son of Lud, the predecessor of Cassivelanus, king of Britain.
44   March 15, Julius Cæsar killed.
24   Cunobelin or Cymbeline, king of Britain.

. D.   —————

45   Gwydyr or Guidenus or Caractacus, and Togudumus, sons of Cymbeline, kings of the Britons.

     The Emperor Claudius Cæsar sent his general, Aulus Plautius, who subdued great part of the island, including Hampshire, Wiltshire, Somersetshire, and Cornwall, killing Togudumus.

74   Gloucester (Glevum—caer Gloyw) built by Arviragus, in honour of Claudius Cæsar, whose daughter he married.
50   The Emperor Claudius Drusus visited Britain. His general, the successor of Aulus Plautius, was Ostorius Scapula, who hereafter defeated Caractacus, and sent him to Rome.† Leland says that Bristol was now called Caer Oder, or Oser nante Badon, i. e. the city Oder in the valley of Bath. Baxter, in his Glossary, says "the city Caer Brito was, by the Britons, called Caer Oder, i. e. Civitas Limitis, a frontier city;" which agrees with its situation, whether as opposed to the sea, or (in 519) a frontier of the West-Saxon kingdom against the Britons, and (in 582) of the rival kingdom to Mercia. Milton, in his History of Britain, states that "Ostorius disarmed those of the Britons whom he suspected, and, to surround

* See Collinson's "Beauties of British Antiquity," p. 46.
† Vide Horæ Britannicæ.

A. D.

50 them, placed many garrisons upon the rivers Antona and
Sabrina." It is elsewhere supposed that the Britons, in
compliment to Ostorius, for his clemency, and for having
raised fortifications above and below the city, called it Caer
Odera, *i. e.* Castrum Ostorii ; thence Caer Oster, and (by
dropping the s, a common practice to the present day) Caer
Oter, or Otera.* We have, however, a geological memorandum in favour of the *Caer Odor* of the Welsh chronicles,
which places this matter safe beyond the frail foundation of
verbal conjecture. Independently of the various deposits of
alluvial soil recently developed by Mr. Plumley and others
in the level banks of the Avon and the Froom, which immediately border the original town, " *nante* Baddon," (in
the vale of Bath or the Baths,) the fact that, at a very remote
period, the united waters of those rivers† found a passage
between St. Vincent's rocks and Leigh woods, through
some sudden convulsion of nature, receives confirmation
in the following circumstance. Upon excavating the ground
near the mansion of the Dowager Lady Smyth, for the new

* Aust Passage, in Domesday Book, (made by order of William the Conqueror about
1068, deposited in the Tower of London, and which is often brought into Court in
cases of dispute as to manorial demesnes,) is called *Austor* Clive, retaining the name
of Ostorius without the Latin termination. The vestiges of a camp in the parish of
Dinder, near Hereford, still remain, situated on *Oyster* Hill ; which hill, according to
Camden, derived its name from Ostorius.—He died of fatigue during the war, and was
succeeded in his governorship by Aulus Didius Gallus. See a map of the line of
defence fortified by Ostorius, in the Archæologia for 1820.

† The River *Avon* rises near the northern boundary of Wiltshire, passing westward
of Brandon Forest, to the vicinity of Malmsbury, where it receives the junction of
two streams, one of which rises near Tetbury, by which Malmsbury is nearly encircled.
Its course hence, receiving several tributary streams by the way, is to Chippenham,
Bradford (where it passes under a bridge of eight arches), Bath, Keynsham (where the
river Chew falls into it), flowing onward to Temple Mead, where, in 1803, it first took
its present direction on the south side of the city, instead of passing through it, receiving the river Froom through the Trench completed in 1247.

The River *Froom* rises near Dodington in Gloucestershire, passes S. W. of Sodbury,
through Iron Acton, Hambrook, by Frenchay, to Stoke, where it meets a spring from
the Park, and flows through Stapleton to Baptist Mills (so named because, in their
early days, the religious community of that denomination performed the ceremony of
immersion in the Mill-pond), entering the city-bounds at Wade's Bridge. Here it
becomes the pond of the Castle-Mill, the surplus-water discharging itself through a
hatch into a feather that runs in a parallel line under three bridges, crossed by Penn-
street, Philadelphia-street, and Merchant-street, where it is joined by the mill-stream,
and runs under seven other bridges, crossed by Union-street, the site of Aylward's or
the Pithay Gate, Nelson-street, Bridewell-lane, the junction of Lewin's Mead with
Christmas-street (called St. John's Bridge), the site of the Water-Gate, and the way
from Small-street to its north bank, named St. Giles's or the Stone Bridge, where the
Trench above noted began.

The Castle-Mill-Pond is also supplied through the Ditch of the Castle from the Avon,
and has an intermediate relief from its waste-waters through a culvert under Philadelphia-street.

From the Castle-Mill to St. Giles's Bridge (as will be seen hereafter) the Froom
still washes the base of the ancient military wall of the city.

A. D.

50 course of the Avon, in 1804, there were found, at about twelve feet beneath the surface, the trunks of thirty maiden-oak-trees, some of them measuring between sixty and seventy feet, together with a large portion of underwood, chiefly hazel. The oaks lay parallel, with their roots towards Ashton, and their branches pointing to Clifton. Hazel-nuts were found entire, also teeth of the beaver and the wild hog, and a beetle of the brilliant green cantharides species, which are preserved in the museum of James Johnson, Esq. The trees were covered with a bed of washed gravel or small fragments of rock, rounded by attrition in the action of the stream, five or six feet in depth. More trees may be seen remaining in the banks of the new line of river, proving that the body of waters which previously found a way to the Bristol Channel over the moors in Somersetshire, on this side of Bridgewater, at length forced an abrupt passage through a close forest in the town's immediate vicinity. Here, then, is the strongest possible evidence of the " rupture" by which the " chasm" was formed which gave to Bristol one of its earliest appellations, viz. CAER OBOR *nante* BADDON : *the City of the Chasm or rupture in the valley of Bath*. The origin of the present name is said to be Caer Brito, the British town or city, as inhabited by the Britons under the protection of the Romans, and thus distinguished from the Roman stations on the surrounding hills, called Abone, from Avona, the river Avon. The Itinerary of Antoninus notices a camp or station so called (situated between Aquæ Solis and the River Severn) which we think included (with Bristol) Kingsdown, Clifton, Durdham Down, Westbury, Kingsweston, and Henbury.* But, after close consideration of the more than forty modes of spelling Bristol, of which *Brig-stowe* seems to us the genuine root, we have persuaded ourselves that all their fanciful and romantic interpretations must resolve themselves into BRIDGE-TOWN, the *town of the Bridge* that united Wessex to Mercia. Of Clifton, see 1822.

60 The Christian religion first planted in Britain, during the reign of Nero.

* Roman coins have been dug up in the field behind Montague Parade. Sir William Draper, in levelling the ground near the circular specula or outpost on Clifton Hill, (which has parallel vallations on the opposite hill, in Leigh Wood) found a curious Roman urn with two handles, tiles, bricks, and Roman potsherds. Under Kingsweston, near the river, was a common field, called Avon's Town, mentioned in the Rental of Sir Ralph Sadleir, dated 36 Henry VIII. : "One acre in Campo Abone Town."—Coins of Nero, Constantine, Domitian, Trajan, &c. have been found here, and also at Henbury, by J. S. Harford, Esq.

A. D.

61　Boadicea, widow of Prasutagus, king of the Iceni, destroyed 70,000 of the Romans.

62　Suetonius Paullinus, the fifth Roman general, (the fourth, as successor to Aulus Didius Gallus, having been Quintius Verannius,) defeated the Britons, killing 80,000; whereupon Boadicea poisoned herself. It was now that the Romans laid out camps and constructed fortifications; and it was they who first used mortar in building, with which the stones of the Clifton station are cemented.

63　Arviragus, (according to Juvenal, the poet,) king of the Britons. The Roman generals, successors of Suetonius,
69　previous to and about this time, were,—6, Petronius Turpi-
79　lianus; 7, Trebellius Maximus; 8, Vettius Bolanus; 9, Petilius Cerealis; 10, Julius Frontinus; and, 11, Cnæus Julius
84　Agricola, father-in-law of the Roman historian, Tacitus, under whom it appears that the south of Britain enjoyed a state of uninterrupted tranquillity. His warlike operations were directed towards the north, where he defeated
85　the British prince, Calgacus.* It was not until after the Conquest that Britain was discovered to be an island. Agricola now erected a bank and a ditch, with a range of castles at unequal distances, from the German Ocean to the Irish Sea, beginning 5½ miles E. of Newcastle, and ending 12 miles W. of Carlisle, as a barrier against the Picts.

86　Agricola surrendered his command to Salustus Lucullus.

120　Ptolemy says that Bristol was about this time a capital city of the Belgæ. He calls it Venta Belgarum; but, in the Itinerary of Antoninus, this name is given to Winchester.

122　The Emperor Adrian visited Britain, and repaired the works of Agricola, adding some of his own to strengthen them, viz. joining to Agricola's small ditch, which lay towards the north, a large one, making a large rampart, and then finishing, as Agricola began, with a small ditch: all their works running in parallel lines.

125　Marius, king of the Britons.

144　Another boundary-wall, between the frith of Dumbritton and the frith of Edinburgh, erected in the reign of Antoninus Pius. This is now called Graham's dyke.

162　The Emperor Marcus Aurelius reigned.

179　Coilus, son of Marius, king of the Britons.

181　Lucius, king of the Britons, during the reign of the Emperor Commodus.

* Vide N. S. Smith's Translation of Tacitus on the Manners of the Germans, and Life of Agricola. 8vo. 1821.

.D.

200   The Emperor Severus erected a wall of stone, twelve feet
high and eight feet thick, strengthened with eighteen stations or cities, eighty-one castles, and about three hundred
and thirty turrets or watch-towers, at proper distances, and
defended by a ditch and military way, nearly parallel to the
works of Agricola and Adrian, a few paces farther northward, and from the east coast near Tinmouth, to the Sole-
way Firth at Boulness, on the western coast.*

211   Severus died at York. "From hence the Roman empire
declining apace, good historians growing scarce, or lost,
have left us little else but fragments for many years
ensuing."—MILTON.

286   Porphyrius, a philosopher; the first who made mention
of the Scottish nation.

287   Caurasius, a native of Menapia, and of low parentage,
rebelling against Dioclesian, possessed the island. By him
the Saxons became educated in the empire of the ocean.
He granted a charter to Freemasons.

292   Caurasius slain treacherously by his friend Alectus. Constantius Chlorus came into Britain, and defeated Alectus.
He married Helena, daughter of Coilus, Duke of Colchester,
by whom he had Constantine the Great, who was born in
Britain.   Constantius Chlorus died at York, A.D. 306.

305   St. Vincent suffered martyrdom at Valencia. A chapel,
erected to his memory, on the rocks near the Hotwells, was
standing in the time of William of Worcester. It was
twenty-seven feet long and nine feet broad, and stood
twenty fathom (120 feet) from the dry ground—about the
middle of the rock.

306   Constantine the Great, Emperor of Rome.

311   Constantine, eldest son of Constantine the Great, succeeded to the sovereignty of this island, and divided it
into three provinces. "In these days there were great
store of workmen and excellent builders [Freemasons] in
this island, whom, after the alteration of things here, the
Adrians in Burgundy entertained, to build their temples
and public edifices."—MILTON.

340   Constantine slain in civil war with his brother Constans,
who, with his third brother, Constantius, coming into
Britain, seized it as victor. Julian was the next Emperor.

367   Theodosius, father of the first Emperor of that name,
made governor of Britain by the Emperor Valentinian.
London named Augusta.

* See W. Hutton's History of this wall, and its appearance in 1801. 8vo. 2d edit.
13.

A. D.

373   Fraomarius, king of the Almans, appointed successor of Theodosius in England.

382   Maximus, declaring himself Emperor, carried over all the youth of Britain, as well as the Roman forces, into France.

389   Maximus slain by the Emperor Theodosius.

Until now the south of Britain had been exposed to the excursions of Scots from the Irish seas, of Saxons from the German, and of Picts from the north. They were hence successively and successfully opposed under Chrysanthus, son of Marcian, a bishop, made deputy of Britain by Theodosius, and Stilicho, a man of great power, whom Theodosius, dying, left protector of his son Honorius.

395   Theodosius died. In January, his youngest son, Honorius, became Emperor.

408   The Emperor Honorius abandoned Britain, and discharged the Britons from their allegiance.

410   August 24, Rome underwent a third siege and successful assault by Alaric, king of the Visigoths.

423   About this time the Goths finally succeeded in forcing the Romans to leave their conquests, when they took their last farewell of Britain.

449   Three Saxon vessels, bearing Hengist and Horsa, arrived at Ebbo-fleet, in the island of Thanet, near Richborough, as auxiliaries of the Britons against the Picts.

455   The Britons themselves, as well as the Picts, subdued by the Saxons, at Aylesford, in Kent, and again, in 457, at Cranford. The Saxons, in turn, driven from the island, and absent for five years.

461   The honour of Gloucester was held by Eldol, a Briton.

465   Hengist returned, near the spot of his first landing.

477   Ælla arrived in Sussex.

490   Ælla besieged Andredes Ceaster, a city in Sussex.

495   Cerdic arrived with another Saxon colony, in five ships.

501   A band of allies, under Porta, effected a landing, with the companies of two ships, at Portsmouth, and defeated the Britons.

519   The kingdom of West Saxons was the first established, under Cerdic, who, having just arrived in Britain, defeated King Arthur at Chard, in Somersetshire, and thus became chief monarch or king of the English nation. West Saxony, or Wessex, comprised Berkshire, Hampshire, Wiltshire, Somersetshire, Dorsetshire, Devonshire, and that part of Cornwall which was not possessed by the Britons. Bristol (Caer Brito) was now much enlarged, had an external and second wall built about some parts of it, where it had been

A. D.

increased, and became the principal sea-port, mart, fortress, and capital, of Wessex. It formed the frontier-town towards Gloucestershire.* See 582.

530 The battle of Longborth, in which king Arthur commanded the Britons.

534 Cenrick or Kenrick, eldest son of Cerdic, succeeded as second king of the West Saxons, and fourth chief monarch of the Saxon Octarchy.

546 King Arthur perished in a civil feud with Medrawd, his nephew, and was buried at Glastonbury.†

547 Ida arrived, with his Angles, in forty vessels, on the coast of Northumberland.

560 Ella, one of Ida's companions, raised a new kingdom of Angles, on Deira. Cealwin, or Chevline, son of Kenrick, became third king of the West Saxons, and fifth monarch of the octarchy.

568 Ethelbert, fourth successor of Hengist, invaded Wessex, but was defeated by Cealwin, at Wimbledon.

571 The brother of Cealwin defeated the Britons at Bedford.

577 Cealwin and Cuthwin maintained an engagement near Derham, Gloucestershire, in which three British kings fell. Gloucester, Cirencester, and Bath, with the neighbourhood, were the fruits of the victory.

* The following are the various parts of Britain into which, according to Archbishop Usher, the Saxons and their confederates subsequently spread themselves.

The Jutes possessed Kent; the Isle of Wight; and that part of the coast of Hampshire which fronts it.

The SAXONS were distinguished, from their situation, into

South-Saxons, who peopled Sussex.

East-Saxons, who were in Essex, Middlesex, and the South part of Hertfordshire.

West-Saxons, in Surrey, Hampshire, (the coast of the Jutes excepted,) Berks, Wilts, Dorset, Somerset, Devon, and that part of Cornwall which the Britons were unable to retain.

The ANGLES were divided into

East-Angles, in Norfolk, Suffolk, Cambridge, the Isle of Ely, and (it should seem) part of Bedfordshire.

Middle Angles, in Leicestershire, which appertained to Mercia.

The MERCIANS, divided by the Trent, into

South Mercians, in the counties of Lincoln, Northampton, Rutland, Huntingdon, the north parts of Bedfordshire and Hertfordshire, Bucks, Oxfordshire, Gloucestershire, Warwickshire, Worcestershire, Herefordshire, Staffordshire, Shropshire.

North Mercians, in the counties of Chester, Derby, and Nottingham.

The NORTHUMBRIANS, who were,

The Deiri, in Lancaster, York, Westmoreland, Cumberland, Durham.

The Bornicians, in Northumberland, and the South of Scotland, between the Tweed and the Frith of Forth.

Mr. Turner, in his History of the Anglo-Saxons, for sufficient reasons, prefers calling these divisions, collectively, the Saxon Octarchy, rather than Heptarchy.

† Milton, with a truly republican prejudice against "he of Monmouth" and his "cathedral regests," denies the existence of any such British king as Arthur. But the short time that has elapsed, from 1694, has been sufficiently productive of historic discoveries to restore this king to us without fear of a second goose-quill decollation.

A. D.

582 The kingdom of Mercia commenced.

584 On the death of Cissa, the kingdom of Sussex fell into the hands of Cealwin, which he annexed to Wessex.

585 Cridda, first king of Mercia, began to reign. (This kingdom ended in 874.)

591 Cealwin, having abdicated the sovereignty, now died in banishment at Wednesbury, Wilts. His nephew, Ceolric, became fourth king of the West Saxons. Ethelbert, king of Kent, was at this time the fifth monarch of England.

598 Ceolwulph, fifth king of the West Saxons.

603 St. Austin and the British bishops said to have held a conference under an oak which stood on the limits of the Wiccian and West-Saxon kingdom, supposed near Tetbury. Gloucester, about this time, lost its rank as a city, in consequence of its annexation to the province of Wiccia; and Wynchcombe, as a great court of the Mercian kings, took from it the more distinguished rank of the principal town of the county. See 795.

610 Ceolwulph and his forces crossed the Severn into Glamorganshire. Tewdric, father of Mowric, now king of the Cymri, and who had retired for a solitary life among the rocks and woods of Tintern, reassumed the military command, and drove back the invaders over the Severn, but lost his life by a wound in the head, and was buried at Mathern, the abbreviation of Merthyr Teudric. In the sixteenth century his remains were found unconsumed, and the fatal blow on his head was visible.

611 Cynegils, or Quinthelim, sixth king of the West Saxons, and, in 634, their first Christian king; Oswald, king of Mercia, standing sponsor at his baptism.

614 The West Saxons, under Cynegils, obtained a victory at Beamdune (Bampton, Devon) over the Cornish Britons, who lost 2000 men.

628 Penda, king of Mercia, attacked Cirencester, belonging to Wessex. A day's conflict ended in a pacific negociation.

642 Cenwalch, son and successor of Cynegils, expelled by Penda from Wessex, for repudiating his sister. Cenwalch lived three years in exile in Essex, during which time Sussex terminated its subordination to Wessex.

653 According to Bede, iii. 28, at this period Ireland was distinguished for its religious literature; and many of the Anglo-Saxons, both of the higher and lower ranks, retired thither, to pursue their studies or their devotions: while some assumed the monastic life, others, seeking variety of knowledge, went from one master's cell to another. The hos-

A. D.

pitable Irish received them all, supplied them with daily food, and gratuitous instruction.*

658 The Welsh defeated by the West Saxons at Pen, in Somersetshire, being chased with great slaughter to Pedridan, on the river Parret.

661 Cenwalch attacked Wulfhere, Penda's son and successor in Mercia, but lost the Meanware district in Hampshire, which Wulfhere conferred, with the Isle of Wight, on Edilwalch, the new king of Sussex.

672 Saxburga, widow of Cenwalch, became sovereign of West Saxony; but for ten years the nobles shared the government.

674 Æscuin, son of Cenfusus, a prevailing noble, descended from Cerdic, led a powerful force against Wulfhere, and a battle, mutually destructive, ensued, at Bedwin, Wilts.

676 Æscuin dying, Kentwin succeeded in the rule of West Saxony.

681 Cadwaladyr, the last of the Cymri who pretended to the sovereignty of the island, having quitted Wales (which was afflicted by a pestilence and famine) for Bretagne, Alan, king of Bretagne, being on the point of death at Rome, sent his son Ivor, and his nephew Inor, with a powerful fleet, to regain Cadwaladyr's crown. Ivor was at first so successful that he defeated the Saxons and took Cornwall, Devonshire, and Somersetshire. But Kentwin met him with the West-Saxon power, and, chasing him to the sea, again disappointed the hopes of the Cymri.

584 Ceadwalla, descended from Cerdic through Cealwin, and his son Cutha, began to contend for the throne of Wessex. Having been banished by the factious chiefs, he succeeded in drawing the youth of Wessex to his standard. Being assisted by Wilford, bishop of Selsey, with money and horses, he surprised and destroyed the king of Sussex; but being expelled by the royal generals, who had been warring in Kent, he proceeded to secure to himself the crown of Wessex. He hence regained Sussex, and also captured the Isle of Wight.

586 Ceadwalla, and his brother Mollo, for two years plundered Kent; but Mollo, with twelve soldiers, being surprised by the men of Kent in a cottage, perished in its flames. In the

* One of the great blunders of the Reformation was, that in returning the Irish this compliment, England sent among them preachers against the use of an unknown tongue who knew not the tongue of their hearers! (See 1547.) How have we since endeavoured repair this blunder?

A. D.

following year, Ceadwalla made Kent mourn this sacrifice in all its districts.

688   Ceadwalla travelled to Rome, where he was baptized by the Pope, and died in his youth, the following week. He was succeeded in Wessex by Ina, the son of Cenred, who was the nephew of Cinegils, Cenred still living. Ina published a collection of laws, which yet remain. Vide Wilkins's Leges Saxonicæ, p. 14—27.

694   Kent bought its peace from Wessex by thirty thousand marks of gold.

700   According to William of Worcester, whose uncle, Thomas Botoner, was a brother of it, the House of Kalendaries was this year erected in the parish of Christ-Church.* See 1216.

710   Ina waged war successfully with Geraint, the British king of Cornwall.

715   Ina prosecuted a war with Ceolred, king of Mercia. They fought at Wednesbury, but without advantage to either.

718   Inigils, brother to Ina, died. He was the ancestor from whom Egbert and Alfred, and the following Saxon monarchs of England, deduced their descent.—Ina re-erected the Abbey of Glastonbury, which lasted till the Danish ravages.

721   Ina destroyed an insurgent named Cynewulf Atheling. The next year his queen, Ethelburga, besieged Ealdbright in Taunton Castle, which Ina had built, and levelled it with the ground. Ealdbright withdrew into Sussex; whence, in three years afterward, Ina removed him.

725   Ina went to Rome, and formed a Saxon school, for the instruction of those of his countrymen who chose to be educated there, adding a church for their service and the convenience of their burial. To support this, and to provide a subsistence for the English who should dwell at Rome, he imposed the payment of a penny on every family, which was denominated Romescot, and sent to the papal see. Having, at the instance of his queen, from pious motives, resigned his crown, he died at Rome.

728   Æthelheard, a descendant of Cerdic, and successor of Ina, devastated Devonshire, but was vanquished by the Britons, at Heilyn, in Cornwall.

734   Bede, who died this year, says, " Britain was famous in

* We are strongly inclined to believe that this was what has been called the fourth church surrounding the High Cross, as represented in the coloured drawing appended to Ricart's Kalendar. The writer contributed that description of its remains, as they stood in 1816, which forms part of Appendix No. 10, in Corry and Evans's History of Bristol. If there was a tower, it must have stood at the east, and not at the west end of the building, as erroneously suggested in that paper. It has been stated, but we know not on what authority, that it was a church dedicated to St. Andrew.

. D.

ancient times for twenty-eight most noble cities, furnished with gates, and strong bolts, walls, and towers."

741 Æthelheard died, and was succeeded by his relation, Cuthred.

743 In conjunction with Ethelbald, king of Mercia, Cuthred defeated the Britons at Ddefawdan, and returned with much plunder.

748 Cuthred lost his son Cynric in a military sedition.

750 Cuthred suppressed a dangerous rebellion of Edelhun, one of his chieftains.

752 Cuthred at war with his Mercian neighbour, Ethelbald. The rival princes met at Burford, in Oxfordshire; Ethelbald being assisted by the forces of Kent, East Anglia, and Essex. Edelhun, now a willing subject, advancing beyond his line, commenced the battle, by rending the golden dragon,* the splendid banner of Mercia. The king of Mercia, after a terrible conflict, gave to his army the first example of a hasty flight. Wessex was hence rescued from the yoke of Mercia.

753 Cuthred again assailed the Welsh, with success, in their own country.

754 Cuthred died, and was succeeded by Sigebyrht, whose reign was short and tyrannical. When Cumbra, the noblest of his earls, obeyed the solicitations of his people, and intimated their complaints to the king, he was arbitrarily put to death, and the grievances were multiplied. Sigebyrht was deposed unanimously, and Cynewulf, a youth of the royal blood, elected in his place. Deserted by all, the deposed king fled into the woods of Anderida. A swineherd of the murdered Cumbra discovered him in his hiding-place, and immediately slew him.

774 Offa, king of Mercia, cut the great trench from Bristol to Basingwerk, Flintshire, as the boundary of the Britons who harboured in Wales.

777 Offa attacked Cynewulf at Bensington, defeated him, and subjected part of Wessex.

784 Cynewulf assassinated by Cyneheard, brother of the deposed Sigebyrht, while on a visit to a lady at Merton in Surrey. The assassin and his accomplices perished. Brihtric, of the race of Cerdic, who married Eadburga, the daughter of Offa, succeeded to the throne of Wessex.—The Danes now first landed on the English shores. Eadburga, in at-

* A gilt dragon is the form of the vane that decorates the steeple of the present Christ-Church, for the reason that a gilt dragon so distinguished its ancient predecessor. Why may not this have been a token of the triumph and emancipation here recorded, originally erected upon the House of the Kalendaries? See 700.

A. D.

tempting to poison a youth to whom he was attached, also poisoned her husband. She was driven out of Wessex, and at last begged her daily bread at Pavia, where she closed an abandoned life by a deplorable death.

789 Brihtric said to have erected a church and palace called Rud Hall, with the walls of Radcleve.

795 Cenole, now king of the Mercians, built the monastery of Wynchcombe, Gloucestershire. " Saynte Kenelme, marter,'' says the Golden Legend, was king [in 819] of a part of Englond by Walis. His fader was king before him, and was named Kenulphe [or Cenole], and founded the abbaye of Wynchcombe, and sette thereyn monkes. And, when he was deed, he was beryed in the same abbaye. That time Wynchcombe was the beste town of the countre.'' And again,—" Wynchcombe was chief citie of all thise shires,'' i. e. of the shires belonging to the kingdom of Mercia. Wine-street, Bristol, as the chief road leading out of the city towards Wynchcombe, was originally called Wynch-street.

800 Wessex had by this time been again incorporated with Sussex. Egbert, son of Ethelmund, the great grandson of Inigils, the brother of Ina, was now summoned out of the French empire, where he had been educated in the court of Charlemagne, to the throne of Wessex.

813 Egbert penetrated successfully into Devonshire and Cornwall.

820 Ethelmund, or Alemond, the father of Egbert, said to have been buried in Almondsbury church.

824 A monastery at Westbury-upon-Trymme, (anciently Westminster on Trymme,) mentioned in the Acts of the Synod of Clovesho, given by Ethelric, son of Ethelmund, after the death of his mother. See 983.

827 Wiglaf, king of Mercia, consented to be the tributary vassal of Wessex. East Anglia and Northumbria also submitted to Egbert.

828 With a numerous army, Egbert penetrated to Snowdon, and finally reached Denbighland and Anglesey with victory.

832 The Danes ravaged the island of Sheppey, and defeated Egbert at Charmouth in Dorsetshire. The Danes afterward formed an offensive alliance with the Cornish Britons; but Egbert defeated their combined forces with great slaughter.

836 Feb. 4, Egbert died, and was buried at Winchester. He was succeeded by his eldest son, Ethelwulf, then a monk at Winchester, as king of the West Saxons. Alstan, bishop of Sherborne, was his minister.

A. D.

837}
840} The Danes made several descents on the English coasts.

846 Ethulwulf ordained that tithes should be collected, exempting the clergy from regal tributes.

849 After three elder sons, Osberga, Ethelwulf's queen, was delivered of Alfred.

852 In the spring, the Danes entered the Thames with three hundred and fifty ships, plundered Canterbury and London, and defeated Bertulph, king of Mercia, and then entered Surrey. The West Saxons, under Ethelwulf and his son Ethelbald, met them; and at Aclea, the field of oaks, after a long battle, the English triumphed.

This is the date of the monkish story of the Berkeley Witch.

853 Alfred was sent to Rome, with a great train of nobility and others; when the Pope anointed him King; at the request of his father.

855 Ethelwulf went to Rome, accompanied by Alfred; where he continued a year, and rebuilt the Saxon school which Ina had founded.

856 In July, Ethelwulf sued for an alliance with Judith, daughter of Charles, the French king, and was married to her in October. Meanwhile a revolt took place in Wessex, conducted by Bishop Alstan and favoured by the Duke of Somerset, in which Ethelbald was placed at the head of the government. The popular reason was the elevation of Ethelwulf's new wife to the dignity of the crown. The revolt first assumed a serious appearance in Selwood Forest. Ethelwulf, on his return, assented to the plan that Ethelbald should be put in possession of West Saxony, and that he himself should be content with the eastern districts enjoyed by Ethelstan.

858 Ethelwulf died, and Ethelbald married his widow, but put her away on the exhortation of Swithin.

860 Ethelbald died, and was succeeded in Wessex by his brother Ethelbert, who had been already reigning in Kent, Surrey, and Sussex. A large fleet of the Danes being chased from off Winchester, they betook themselves to the Seine, and Charles averted their hostilities by a present of five thousand pounds of silver.

64 The Danes wintered at Thanet.

66 Ethelbert died, and was buried in Shireburn. He was succeeded by his brother Ethelred.—The Danish confederacy began to arrive, under Ingwar and Ubbo, two of the sons of Ragnar Lodbrog, whose reputed Quida, or death-song, has been long celebrated for its antiquity and for its genius. (See Turner's History of the Anglo-Saxons.)

c

A. D.

867 Alfred, now nineteen years old, married Ealswitha, the daughter of a Mercian nobleman.

St. Mathyas's Chapel said to have been built in Redcliff-street. See 1398.

868 Ethelred, with Alfred and the whole force of his dominions, joined the Mercian king, Burrhed, against the Danes, then in possession of Nottingham. It was agreed that the invaders should retreat to York; and the kings of Wessex and Mercia returned home.

869 A famine, and the consequent mortality to men and cattle.

870 The Danes re-commenced hostilities, destroying the monasteries and monks of Bardency, in Lincolnshire, and Croydon, and the nunnery of Ely. They attacked East Anglia, and advanced against Mercia; but, finding the banner of West Saxony waving on its frontiers, they penetrated into Berkshire and took possession of Reading. On the next day, Ethelwulf, earl of Berkshire, defeated them at Inglefield, killing Sidroc the elder, a Danish chief who had much afflicted France. Four days afterward, Ethelred and Alfred joined Ethelwulf and attacked the Northmen at Reading. Ethelwulf was killed, and the West-Saxons retreated. In four days more, the West-Saxons combated the enemy at Æscedun, or the Ash-tree Hill. A long struggle ended in the death of the king Bacseg, of the younger Sidroc, many other earls, and some thousands of the Danes, who fled in general rout. The English chased them all night and the following day over the fields at Ashdown, till they reached their fortress at Reading. Fourteen days afterward, the Danes collected sufficient strength to defeat the kings of Wessex at Basing. The invaders derived an accession of allies by new arrivals from the north. Within two months another battle was fought, at Merton, where Ethelred received a wound, of which he died soon after Easter, and was interred at Wimburn.

871 Alfred succeeded to the throne of Wessex. In this year the West-Saxons maintained eight pitched battles against the Northmen, besides innumerable skirmishes by day and night, by which the nobles and royal officers endeavoured to check their depredations. Many thousands of the invaders fell; but new fleets of adventurers, perpetually shading the German Ocean with their armaments, repaired the havoc caused by the West-Saxon swords. Within a month after Alfred's accession, the Danes attacked his troops at Wilton, in his absence, with a great superiority of force. Wearied with these depopulating conflicts, Alfred made a peace with them, and they quitted his dominions.

874 The Northmen conquered Mercia, and England became
divided into two powers, the West-Saxons and the Northmen, they having subdued all the rest of England.

876 The three Danish kings, Godrun, Oskitul, and Amund,
having wintered at Cambridge, re-commenced hostilities
against Wessex, by stealing into Dorsetshire, surprising the
castle of Wareham, and depopulating the surrounding
country. Money effected a solemn treaty of peace, which
was broken by the Danes in a night, shortly after the solemnity, by rushing clandestinely on Alfred's forces, and
slaying all his horsemen. They used the steeds to mount
a part of their army, which rode immediately to Exeter,
and remained there for the winter.

877 Alfred caused long ships and galleys to be built at the
ports of his kingdom, which he manned with such piratical
foreigners as chose to engage in his service, for the purpose
of intercepting supplies to the invaders. One hundred and
thirty of the Northmen's ships were destroyed at the rock
of Swanwick, on the Hampshire coast. Alfred marched
against the Danes in Exeter; but they had possessed themselves of the castle, and he therefore contented himself
with exacting new hostages, and new oaths that they should
depart from his kingdom.

878 In January the Northmen took possession of Chippenham.
Before Easter, many of the inhabitants emigrated in penury
to other regions. The rest, overawed by the Danish cavalry, submitted to their dominion, and Alfred became a
fugitive. Mr. Turner, in his valuable history of this
period, p. 248—58, furnishes an instructive dissertation upon
the causes of Arthur's flight, and his seclusion, together with
a view of his occupations while it lasted. In this interval,
Ubbo, who had been harassing the Britons in South Wales,
where he wintered, on his return with twenty-three ships to
the English Channel, sailing by the north of Devon, was
attracted by the castle of Kynwith, or Henny Castle, near
Appledore, where many of Alfred's servants had embraced
the protection of the Earl of Devon. Ubbo commenced a
blockade; but Odun, in a vigorous sally during the night,
pierced to his tent, and not only slew him and his attendants,
but made twelve hundred of his host the companions of their
expiring commander. A few reached their vessels and
escaped. Among the immense booty was the Danish magical
standard, the famous Reafan (Raven).

At Whitsuntide, Alfred, from the isle of Etheling or
Athelney, at the conflux of the Perrot and the Thone,

A. D.

878 sent into Wiltshire, Hampshire, and Somersetshire, to re-
unite his followers on the east of Selwood Forest. In the
battle of Eddinton, Alfred became the victorious sovereign
of England. Among the conditions of peace, Godrun
consented to receive Christianity, was baptized in the name
of Ethelstan, and the ceremony was completed at the royal
town of Wædmor. Godrun remained at Cirencester a year,
and then divided East-Anglia among his soldiers for cultivation. The limits of the respective territories were thus
settled by a treaty which still exists: the boundary was
placed in the Thames, the river Lea to its source, and
Watling-street to the Ouse. The spaces thus marked contained Norfolk, Suffolk, Cambridgeshire, Essex, part of
Hertfordshire, part of Bedfordshire, and a little of Huntingdonshire. These regions were subjected to Godrun, and
were filled with Danes. Northumbria was afterwards put
under Guthred, who governed Deira; and Egbert ruled in
Bernicia.

A large fleet of Northmen, under the famous Hastings,
arrived in the Thames, with the object of inducing Godrun
to unite in a new warfare; but, failing in this, after
wintering at Fulham, they sailed for Flanders.

882 Alfred, in a naval conflict, took four ships.

884 A part of the army of Northmen on the Scheld besieged
Rochester, but was forced by Alfred to abandon their horses,
and retreat the same summer to France. He afterwards
captured thirteen Danish war-ships on the coast of East-
Anglia, but suffered a defeat in the mouth of the river,
either by surprise or a larger force. Peace, however, was
soon restored.

893 Hastings again approached England, with three hundred
ships. Mr. Turner's account of the ensuing operations is
highly honourable to the character of the Wessexian
sovereign.

894 The Danish colonists of Northumbria and East-Anglia
assisted the invaders at sea. One hundred ships (a part of
the armament) besieged Exeter, and, reaching the Bristol
Channel, surrounded a fortress in the north part of the
country. Alfred relieved Exeter, and forced the invaders
again to sea, slaying many hundreds, and taking some ships.
Hastings marauded from the Thames to the Severn, but was
pursued to Buttington, on the Severn, and besieged in his
fortress. After great loss, the Northmen made a desperate
burst from their prison, and regained their station in Essex.
Before winter, raising a large army from the East-Anglians

A. D.

and Northumbrians, they reached and fortified Chester on the Wiral. Here they were speedily blockaded by Alfred, and all subsistence from the surrounding country was destroyed.

896 Hastings disbanded his followers.

897. The depredators who remained in England betook themselves to piracy on the coast of Wessex; but Alfred built vessels of superior dimensions, impelled by at least sixty rowers in each, and finally destroyed the pirates. A pestilence of three years followed the waste occasioned by the contest with Hastings. The sovereignty of Alfred hence became established, not only over the Anglo-Saxons, but his power was acknowledged and his alliance sought by the Cymry in Wales.

900 or 901 Oct. 26, Alfred died, aged fifty-two years, of an internal disorder that had afflicted him from the age of twenty.

Edward the Elder, the son of Alfred, chosen as king by the nobles.

905 Guy, afterwards Earl of Warwick, born at Warwick. His father, Gyraldus Cassibelanus, was a native of Northumberland, and of good estate, in the time of the Mercian kings.

912 Edward, and Leoline, prince of Wales, met on the opposite shores of the Severn, the former at Aust, the latter at Beachley. Upon Leoline's refusal to cross the Severn, Edward passed over to him; upon which Leoline threw his royal robes on the ground, advanced into the water, embraced the boat, carried Edward upon his shoulders, made him sit upon his robes, and did him homage.

915 The abbat of Berkeley was chosen bishop of the Wicci. Stowe says that in this year Edward, for the defence of Bristol, built a castle at the mouth of the Avon.

918 Two northern earls, from Armorica, brought a hostile fleet round Cornwall into the Severn, and devastated North Wales. They detached, and plundered in Herefordshire, but were defeated with the loss of one of their chiefs. Endeavouring to escape in two divisions, one was destroyed in Watchet, the other in Porlock Bay, Somersetshire. The miserable remnant sheltered themselves in a neighbouring island, (the Flat Holme,) till famine drove them to South Wales, and finally to Ireland.

The chapel of St. Mary Magdalen, in the Castle, said to have been founded by Ælla, the first warden.

920 Ælla died in Bristol Castle, of wounds received in battle with the Danes. According to Turgot, as quoted by Chatterton, Ælla was succeeded by Coërnicus, after whom Cornstreet was named. Upon the same authority, but without

920 giving a date, the third warden was Harward, "slain near Redcliff, in fighting with the pagans." Smallaricus was the fourth warden. Coernicus, Harward, and Smallaricus, are the only three names for which we depend solely on Chatterton's authority, who (if he invented Coernicus for the purpose above mentioned) failed to notice the probability that from the last of these three was derived Small-street. We have next in succession, from other sources, Vincent, Adelwyn, Egwyn, (in whose time an earthquake threw down many houses,) and Aylward Sneaw, a descendant of Edward, who founded the Castle; of whom see under 930. See also 1130.

Mercia was this year finally incorporated with Wessex, on the death of Ethelfledn, widow of Ethelred, its military commander, and daughter of Alfred.

924 Edward died at Farrington, Berkshire, and was succeeded by Athelstan, his first-born but illegitimate son, who had been a favourite of his grandfather, Alfred.

930 Aylward Sneaw (who was born about 907) flourished at this time. This is the probable date of the second wall of Bristol, that which was washed by the Froom from Newgate* to Froom or Water-gate, at the end of Christmas-street. The Pithay was formerly called Aylward's street, and the gate that stood at the foot of that declivity upon arches under which the Froom passed from Castle Mill, Aylward's gate. See 980.

934 Anlaf, son of Sigtryg, or Sihtric, deceased king of Northumbria, who, upon being expelled thence, obtained a sovereignty in Ireland, being joined by the Welsh and Anglo-Danes of Northumbria and East-Anglia, and fleets from Norway and the Baltic, entered the Humber with six hundred and fifteen ships. The hostilities that ensued were closed by the battle of Brunanburh, supposed to have been in Northumberland, and Athelstan became the first sovereign of all England and nominal lord of Wales and Scotland.—Mr. Turner's estimate of the glory of Athelstan's reign will be found highly interesting.

In the course of this reign, Guy, earl of Warwick, is said to have encountered Colbron or Colbrond, a Danish champion, of large stature, when the king was besieged by the Danish army in Winchester. The contest took place in Hide Mead, near the north gate.

* A gate which stood at Chequer-lane in Narrow Wine-street, and perhaps had been called Ælla's gate, from Ælla, the first warden of the Castle, was hence called Old-gate.

. D.

"In the days of Athelstan," says Roger Hoveden, "it was decreed that there should be, at Canterbury, seven monctaries, viz. four of the king, two of the bishop, one of the abbot; at London, eight, and at Bristowe and other boroughs, one." Though Bristol is seldom named as the place of any particular event in the history of West-Saxony, it is hence impossible to resist the conclusion that she had hitherto borne her proper share in its glories.

941 Edmund, the eldest brother of Athelstan, aged sixteen years, succeeded to the throne.

Anlaf again invaded England, and obtained a pacific agreement that he should possess all that part of England which extended north of Watling-street; but he died the following year.

946 May 26, while the king was celebrating, at Pucklechurch, in Gloucestershire, (where was an Anglo-Saxon palace, the site of which is still to be seen,) the feast of St. Augustine,* he observed among the intoxicated guests one Leolf, whom he had six years before banished for pillage. The king jumped from his seat, seized the man by the hair, and pulled him with himself to the ground. The robber drew his dagger, and in this situation mortally wounded the unhappy monarch in the breast. After having wounded some of the attendants, he was cut to pieces by the others.

Edred, third son of Edward the Elder, was the first who was styled King of Great Britain.

955 Edred died of a wasting disease, and was succeeded by his nephew, Edwin, or Edwy, eldest son of Edmund.

The Benedictine order of monks was about this time introduced to this island. Dunstan, (born in 925, in the neighbourhood of Glastonbury,) a man of genius, far beyond his companions, in cultivation of the mathematical sciences, such as they were then taught, skilled in music, writing, painting, engraving, and working in metals, revenged himself for having been driven from court in his early manhood, as accomplished in demoniac arts, by turning monk. Having become abbot of Glastonbury previous to Edred's coronation, he was chosen by the king as his confidential friend and counsellor, and played such pranks, both with his royal master and his fellow-subjects, as must ever render the abuse of power hateful, whether exercised in the name of God or of man. Mr. Turner gives a circumstantial narrative of the insult offered to the king, in the apartment of his queen,

---

* Kingswood Forest is believed to have been one of the appendages of that nature belonging to the Anglo-Saxon kings resident at Pucklechurch.

955 Elgiva, on the day of his coronation. Dunstan was hereupon banished; but his friend Odo, the primate of England, headed a conspiracy to divorce the king from his wife, on the plea of their kinship. They then seized Elgiva, branded her in the face with a red-hot iron, and banished her to Ireland. On her wounds being healed, she returned to Gloucester in all her beauty, where she was again seized by Odo's fiends, who cut the nerves and muscles of her legs, that she might wander from their vengeance no more. She shortly afterward died.

957 Influenced doubtless by the Benedictine reformation, the Mercians and Northumbrians rebelled against the king, drove him beyond the Thames, and appointed Edgar, his brother, a boy only thirteen years of age, to govern them in his stead. Dunstan was afterwards recalled with honour.

959 Edwin was assassinated before he had reached the full age of manhood. Odo having died before Edwin, Dunstan, not Edgar, was now the monarch of England.

960 Dunstan claimed the faculty of conversing with the spiritual world.

964 Edgar, the strenuous partizan of the Benedictine revolution, boasted that he had made forty-seven monasteries, and declared his intention to increase them to fifty.

965 About this time took place the affair of Athelwold and Elfrida, whom Edgar married, causing her husband to be assassinated. For this, for violating a lady of noble birth, who used a nun's veil as a protection, and other acts of a like nature, Dunstan only imposed trifling penances. This king had not, like Edwin, opposed the monk's thirst for power.

973 Edgar ostentatiously made eight kings, viz. Kenneth of Scotland, Malcolm of Cumbria, Macchus of Anglesey and the Isles, three kings of Wales, and two others, do him homage at Chester, and row him in a boat on the Dee, himself at the helm. — William of Malmsbury says that Edgar fitted out four thousand ships. He stationed three fleets, of twelve hundred ships each, on the east, west, and south coasts of the island. Matthew of Westminster asserts that his shipping amounted to four thousand eight hundred. He exacted of the Welsh three hundred wolves' heads yearly; by which means, in three years, those animals were extirpated.

975 Edgar dying (being buried in the Abbey of Glastonbury), he was succeeded by his eldest son, Edward (the Martyr), by his first wife, Elfleda, now only sixteen years old; in whose reign there were great contests between the regular and

A. D.

975 the secular clergy. The governor of Mercia turned out all the monks; the governor of East-Anglia supported them. These feuds were terminated by the interposition, or rather, imposition of miracles, especially that notable one of a floor giving way under a council of nobles held at Calne, the seat of Dunstan only remaining unmoved.

It is stated in the records of the Abbey of Ely, that its first abbot, Brithonod, had been seen by Elfrida in the New Forest. He went to the royal court on the business of his church, and at his departure took leave also of her. She desired a private conversation with him, on affairs of conscience, and in the interview she acted the wife of Potiphar. The abbot emulated the virtue of Joseph, and the disappointed Elfrida procured his assassination. The power of the queen-dowager compelled his monastery to indulge their suspicions in silence, but in her days of penitence she acknowledged the crime.

978 March 18, Edgar was stabbed, at the instigation of his mother-in-law, whilst drinking at Corfe Castle, in the isle of Purbeck; and thus gave place to her son, Ethelred II. (the Unready) only ten years of age.

980 Aylward Sneaw, governor of Bristol Castle, founded a small monastery in honour of God, St. Mary, and St. Bartholomew, at Cranbourne. This was probably the closing act of his long life. Adelbryhte, Amstuarde, and Algar, elder son of Aylward (see 1010), became successively governors of Bristol Castle, but we can assign no date to either of their appointments. Algar held the manor of Lea, in Gloucestershire, in the preceding reign. See 1030.

Seven Danish ships plundered Southampton and Thanet.

981 Next year, the same sea-king ravaged Cornwall and Devon-
982 shire. In the year following, three ships molested the island of Portland.

983 Ostwald, bishop of Worcester, replaced the monks of Westbury. See 1093.

988 The Danes made an attempt at Wecedport, when the English gained the field of burial.

991 A large force, commanded by Justin and Gorthmund, attacked Ipswich. They were opposed by Brithnoth, governor of Essex, who fell, and the Danes were victorious. Ten thousand pounds were paid them as the price of their retreat. In the raising of this money began direct taxation.

992 Alfric, duke of Mercia, being put in command of a fleet to surprise the Danes, sailed secretly to join them. His vessels were recaptured, but the traitor escaped.

D

A. D.

994 Olave, king of Norway, and Svein, king of Denmark, came into the Thames with ninety-four ships. Eventually, less than ten thousand invaders demanded sixteen thousand pounds as the price of their forbearance. Olave kept his word not to molest England any more; but the army of

998 Svein, after three years respite, navigated along Wessex, and, doubling the Land's End, entered the Severn. Wales, and afterwards Cornwall and Devonshire, were infested.

999 Svein attacked Dorsetshire, Sussex, and Hampshire.

1000 The Danes besieged Rochester.

1001 They exacted twenty-four thousand pounds from the English nation.

1002 Massacre of the Danes on the 13th of November, the feast of St. Brittius, or Hock-tide, though then living at peace with the Anglo-Saxons.

Svein arrived to avenge his murdered countrymen, and proceeded through Wiltshire.

About this time the universities of Oxford and Cambridge were utterly destroyed by the Danes, and all studies ceased for above one hundred years.

Ethelred married Emma, daughter of Richard III. duke of Normandy.

1003 Bedminster Church, in the N. W. abutment of the tower, has been said to have a stone bearing this date: it was a vicarage belonging to the Abbey of Whytland, dedicated to St. John the Baptist, and may have been erected thus early; but the stone alluded to bears no such date. See 1663.

1004 Svein burnt Norwich. Ufketul, duke of East-Anglia, conquered the Danish army. A famine ensued, and the Danes returned to the Baltic.

The old Christ-Church spire was found, in 1765, to have a date of lead let into a stone near the top, 1003 or 4.

1006 The Danes obtained from England thirty-six thousand pounds.

1007 Edric made duke of Mercia.

1008 The king assessed every three hundred and ten hides of land to build and present one vessel, and every eight hides to furnish one helmet and breast-plate, which was calculated to produce seven hundred and eighty-five ships, and arms for thirty-thousand four hundred and fifty men.

1009 The fleet assembled at Sandwich. Brihtric, a brother of Edric, accused Wulfnoth, an officer in Sussex. Wulfnoth, with twenty ships, commenced pirate. Brihtric pursued him with eighty ships, but a tempest wrecked and Wulfnoth burnt them.

A. D.

1010 .The church of St. Leonard, at the foot of Corn-street, built by Algar. See 1297, 1301.

Sixteen counties surrendered to the Danes, and paid forty-eight thousand pounds.

1013 The people gradually seceded from Ethelred, and appointed Svein their king. Ethelred withdrew into Normandy. Svein died at Gainsborough.

1014 Canute, upon the death of Svein, his father, was by the Danish soldiers elected to succeed him; but the English recalled Ethelred, and compelled Canute to retire to Denmark.

1015 Canute returned, and repossessed himself of great part of the kingdom. Wessex submitted to the invaders and gave hostages for its fidelity.

1016 April 22, Ethelred died at London. His body was translated to Hereford by Brictric ("Bristow construxi"), accompanied by Egremund. Ethelred was succeeded by Edmund (Ironside), as king of that part of the island which adhered to his father. He at length agreed with Canute to divide the kingdom between them, Canute to reign in the north and Edmund in the south; but Edmund being assassinated at Oxford, Nov. 30, Canute became king of all England.

1018 Canute married Emma, also called Elgiva, the widow of Ethelred.

1019 Canute went to Denmark.

1020 Upon his return from the Baltic, Canute held a great council in the Easter-festivity at Cirencester, in which he banished the duke Ethelwerd.

1021 Canute exiled the celebrated Turketul.

1025 Canute went again to Denmark, and conquered Norway.

1027 Brictric, son of Algar, born.

1030 St. Nicholas Church founded by Brightrycke, or Brictric, second son of Aylward (see 980), who also held the manor of Lea, in Gloucestershire. (See 1066.) A chapel in this church was held by the fraternity of St. John the Baptist, denominated The Chapel to the Honour of the Holy Cross: The Fraternity of the Holy Ghost was one of the names they assumed.

1031 Canute penetrated Scotland, and subdued Malcolm and two other kings. He then made a voyage to Rome.

1035 Wednesday, Nov. 12, Canute died at Shaftesbury. He had placed Svein, his eldest son, over Norway, and wished that Harold should rule in England and Hardicanute in Denmark.

1039 Duncan, king of Scotland, assassinated by Macbeth.

1040 April 16, Harold died. He was succeeded by Hardicanute.

A. D.

1042   June, Hardicanute died suddenly, at the nuptial feast of a great lord at Lambeth. Edward (the Confessor), only surviving son of king Ethelred, by Emma, his second wife, (afterward the wife of Canute) succeeded to the crown. He married Editha, the daughter of earl Godwin. Godwin was the son of an Anglo-Saxon herdsman, elevated for a personal service to Ulfr, one of Canute's kinsmen, during his invasion, in performing the office of a guide to his fleet, when he had lost his way; and had three sons, named Svein, Harold, and Leofwyne.

1048   Svein, eldest son of earl Godwin, held the honour or lordship of Gloucester.

1049   The king confirmed Leofwyne in the governorship of the Castle of Bristol.

     Thirty-six ships of Irish pirates entered the Severn, and, with the help of Griffith (Milton calls him Griffin), king of South Wales, obtained considerable successes.

1051   Harold and Leofwyne, being proscribed for joining in a solemn league against the king (who had been bred in Normandy), for his attachment to France, introducing its language and laws, they fled to "Brytstowe," and, in a ship provided by their brother Svein, over to Ireland. Their father, with three other of his sons, had already sailed to Flanders. Brictric, son of Algar, succeeded as governor of Bristol Castle. William, duke of Normandy, this year visited England.

1052   Griffith ravaged great part of Herefordshire.

     Harold and his brothers successfully invaded the west of England. They were joined by their father, and, in a great council held at London, the family, excepting Svein, were restored to favour. Svein, having murdered his cousin Beorn, six years afterward set off with naked feet on a walking pilgrimage from Flanders to Jerusalem, and died on his return, in Lycia.

1053   At the king's table, in the Easter-festivity, earl Godwin suddenly lost his speech, and lingered from Monday to Thursday, when he died.

1054   Siward, earl of Northumbria, whose sister had been Duncan's queen, defeated Macbeth, and made Malcolm king of Scotland.

1055   Siward died, and was succeeded by Tostig, brother of Algar, governor of Essex and East-Anglia. Algar was banished without a fault, through the influence of Harold. He fled to Ireland, collected eighteen piratical vessels, and, interesting Griffith in his favour, forced his restoration.

A. D.

1057 Leofric, duke of Mercia, Algar's father, died.

1058 Algar exiled again, and restored by the same means.

1061 "The Welsh made great efforts against the Anglo-Saxons
1062 in this reign. Griffith for some years molested, with good
1063 fortune, *the counties near Wales*, and for some years his
aggressions escaped unchastised. In 1063, Harold resolved
upon his punishment. He marched into Wales with power.
Griffith fled; Harold burnt his palace and ships, and returned."—TURNER's *Hist. Angl. Saxons*, vol. i. (4to.) p. 458.

"The year [1061] passing to an end without other matters
of moment, save the frequent inroads and robberies of
Griffin, whom no bonds of faith could restrain, king Edward sent against him, after Christmas, Harold, now duke
of the West-Saxons [1062], with no great body of horse,
from Gloucester, where he then kept his court; whose
coming, heard of, Griffin, not daring to abide, nor in any
part of his land holding himself secure, escaped hardly by
sea, ere Harold, coming to *Rudeland*, burnt his palace and
1063 ships there, and returned to Gloucester the same day. But,
by the middle of May, 1063, setting out with a fleet from
Bristow, he sailed about the most part of Wales, and, being
met by his brother Tosti, with many troops of horse, as the
king had appointed, began to waste the country; but the
Welsh, giving pledges, yielded themselves, and promised
to become tributary and banish Griffin their prince; who,
lurking somewhere, was the next year [1064] taken and
slain by Griffin, prince of North Wales; his head, with the
head and tackle of his ship, sent to Harold, and by him to the
king, who, of his gentleness, made Blechgen and Rithwallon,
or Rivallon, his two brothers, princes in his stead: they to
Harold, in behalf of the king, swore fealty and tribute;
yet the next year [1065] Harold having built a fair house
at a place called Portascith, in Monmouthshire, and stored
it with provision, that the king might lodge there in time of
hunting, Carradoc, the son of Griffin, slain the year before,
came with a number of men, slew all he found there, and
took away the provision."—MILTON's History, p. 252.

We see no reason to disbelieve that the "*Rudeland*,"
named by Milton but omitted by Mr. Turner, was the
present village of Redland, in the vicinity of Bristol, which,
looking across Durdham Down,* commands a view of the
mouth of the Avon. We have seen that Griffith had twice

---

* *Ham*, in pure Saxon, means eminent dwelling-place, such as a king's palace. The
view of the surrounding country from the roof of Vincent Lodge, erected by Jacob
Willcox Ricketts, Esq. its present occupier, would baffle any attempt at description.

A. D.

1063 succeeded in restoring Algar, opposed to the whole force of England. Mr. Turner acknowledges that he had for some years molested, with good fortune, the counties near Wales, and that his aggressions remained unchastised. What part of Wales (as that gentleman would read Milton) could Harold reach, and with a body of horse, to burn a palace and ships and return to Gloucester the same day? Whence by sea, except from Redland, could Griffin " hardly escape?" — certainly not from Wales, at the approach of " no great body of horse" from Gloucester; for, to invade Wales itself, Harold found it necessary to wait the appointment of a fleet from Bristol, whence he sailed to co-operate with Tosti and his " many troops of horse." This proves, too, that there was no port nearer to Gloucester convenient for a warlike debarkation; for where, higher up the Severn, would a prince of South Wales choose to moor his ships?— Griffith then, we conclude, in the outset of the transactions here recorded, was in sufficient force to keep a court of some sort at Redland, in the rear of his troops encamped on Durdham-Down, with his fleet moored in the Avon, at the foot of its rocks. Harold's approach was perhaps during the neap-tides, when but a small part of Griffin's fleet, thus surprised, could possibly escape.

1065   The Northumbrians revolted against Tostig, and chose Morcar, son of Alcar, for their earl.

1066   Jan. 5, Edward the Confessor died, aged 65. On the evening of his funeral, Harold assumed the crown, in opposition to the will of Edward in favour of William, duke of Normandy, a descendant of Canute, and who, in 1058, had betrothed his daughter to Harold.

WILLIAM THE CONQUEROR.

Sept. 5, William arrived at Pevensey, in Sussex. Oct. 14, he came to an engagement with Harold, and killed him at Battle Abbey. William hence assumed the title of Conqueror.

Brictric, at this time governor of the Castle of Bristol, and who held the manor of Thornbury, (containing Oldbury-upon-Severn, Cowhill, Kingston, Marlewood, Morton, Hope, Buckover, and Palfield,) had been employed in an embassy to *Baldwin*, earl of Flanders, when Matilda, or Maud, the earl's daughter, settled her affections on him, but was rejected. Being now the wife of the Conqueror, with " a woman's hatred and a woman's vengeance," she

A. D.

excited her husband against him, as a Saxon of power and large possessions, and Brictric was arrested at his manor of 1068 Hanley, near Salisbury, and sent a prisoner to Winchester, where he died soon afterward. All his estates, including the Castle of Bristol, were settled by the king on Maud, who was crowned in 1068, and the same year prince Henry (afterward Henry I.) was born.

1069 Early in this year the three sons of Harold, viz. Godwin, Eadmund, and Magnus, landed, with a body of troops from Ireland, at the mouth of the Avon. Bristol was defended by its townsmen, and the assailants retreated to their ships. Thence they went into Somersetshire, but finally retreated to Ireland. They returned from Ireland about midsummer, with four ships, and landed at the mouth of the Taw, near Barnstaple or Bideford. Earl Beorn, earl of Britain, came upon them unexpectedly, with a large army, and slew their bravest men. The few who remained escaped to their ships, and Harold's sons again retreated to Ireland.

Hardinc, or Harding, a second son of one of the kings of Denmark,* had come over with the Conqueror, and was made mayor and governor of Bristol, being rewarded with much wealth, having settled himself as a merchant on the then bank of the Froom, south side of the city;† whence we believe, in compliment to the queen, Harding's mansion and the present street were named after her father. He had also a house at Portbury. His wife's name was Lyvida, by whom he had Robert (Fitz-Harding), with two other sons and daughters. Maud gave Harding the castle, town, and barony of Berkeley. See 1142. " He purchased with money the manor of Billeswick, from Robert, earl of Gloucester—the manor of Bedminster, from the same—the manor of Bray, in Devon, from William de Braiosa—the manor and advowson of Portbury, from Richard de More-ville—the manor and advowson of Were, Somerset, from Julian de Borton, and various others."—SEYER.

A Castle of Bristol is said to have been now erected by Godfrey; but it was not mentioned in Domesday-Book as standing in 1086.

* Mr. Seyer labours this point with his accustomed industry of research, and asserts the conclusion that Harding could not have been a son of the king of Denmark, the Conqueror's rival, but was the son of Ednoth the Stallar, who lost his life in a battle against the sons of Harold, in 1068. He adds that Harding was a lawyer or an advocate.

† The remains of the Great Stone House, often mentioned, but without naming the site, were discovered in 1823, and described in " The Bristol Observer" for Sept. 3, of that year, as standing on the south side of Baldwin-street, where is now the King's tobacco-warehouse and Mr. Pring's leather-warehouse, and the gardens, &c. of which extended backward nearly to Back-street.

A. D.

1070   William had by this time seized upon all the baronies and fiefs of the crown, and distributed them among his Norman followers.

1072   The name of Godfrey, bishop of Constance, or, as it is now pronounced, Coutance, appears affixed to an instrument signed at Windsor, in determination of the cause of the primacy of Canterbury over York.   Godfrey was present at the battle of Hastings, and afterwards commander of the cavalry in other places.

1075   Godfrey in possession of the Abbey of Ely.*

1078   Foundation of the Tower of London laid this year.

1079   Jews first arrived in England.

1080   The survey recorded in "Domesday-Boke" commenced.

1081   Godfrey promoted to be abbot of Malmsbury.

1084   Maud, the Conqueror's wife, died in April, and was buried in a nunnery which she had built at Caen, in Normandy.† William now held the Castle of Bristol in his own hand. Godfrey had the custody of the Castle, by grant either from the king or previous hereto from the queen.   The bishop possessed two hundred and eighty manors, which at his death he left to his nephew, Robert de Molbray or Mowbray. Of these, more than a hundred were in Devonshire, above seventy in Somersetshire, and there were nine in Gloucestershire.   The following were in the neighbourhood of Bristol :—Hutton, Harptree, Clutton, Timsbury, Norton, Farmborough, Weston, Sandford, Easton (St. Georges's), Portishead, Weston (super Mare), Kenn, Backwell, Butcombe, Berrow, Portbury, Wraxall, Twerton, Littleton, Camely, Acton, Hambrook, Wapley, and Alveston.   "His local authority and influence," adds Mr. Seyer, " rendered him therefore the most proper person to command in Bristol."

1086   Domesday-Boke finished.   In this the people of Bristol are styled burgesses : " Bristow, with Barton, an adjoining farm, paid to the king 100 marks of silver [73l. 6s. 8d.] and the burgesses returned that bishop G. [the custos, keeper, or propraetor of the Castle] had [received] 33 marks [28l.] and one of gold."

1087   Sept. 9, the Conqueror died, in his 61st year, and was buried at Caen, in Normandy.‡

* A picture of Godfrey is preserved in the Ely table—a painting hung up in the palace, with the figures of the monks of Ely, and the knights sent to be quartered on them.
† " Nov. 2, 1083."—*Saxon Chronicle.*   " Nov. 3, 1083."—*Mr.* SEYER.
‡ When Castillon took that city in 1562, some of his soldiers opened the tomb in search of treasure, but finding none, they scattered his bones in derision; some of which were afterwards brought to England.

WILLIAM II. *surnamed* RUFUS,

Second surviving son of the Conqueror, succeeded to the crown by appointment of his father. Godfrey and his nephew, Robert de Mowbray, hastened to secure the Castle in favour of the Conqueror's eldest son, Robert Curthose, and plundered as far as Berkeley and Bath, which they sacked and burnt. They were repulsed before Ilchester.

Camden, with other historians, notices that Bristol had a double wall in this reign, said to have been erected by Godfrey.* If Godfrey erected any wall, it must have been that which extended from the Avon, at the commencement of King-street, with a gate, called Back-gate, a second at the end of Back-street, and a third at the end of Marsh-street, round to the Great or Viell's Tower,† opposite the present Drawbridge, and onward to the bank of the Froom; which at this time washed the foot of Small-street (where also was a gate in the original town-wall), and flowed through St. Stephen-street and Baldwin-street. Without St. Giles's Gate a bridge, still standing, continued the wall to Froom-gate, at the end of the narrow part of Christmas-street. Thence the wall was continued along the south bank of the Froom, to Monken-bridge, now Bridewell—to Needless-bridge, erected in 1656, and so called, perhaps in derision, by the populace, who could see no necessity for such an erection—to Pithay or Aylward's Gate—across the centre of Union-street, which passes over a bridge to Old-gate. Returning to the site of St. Giles's Gate, the original town-wall is obviously marked by its counterscarp, Bell-lane, terminating with St. John's Gate—Tower-lane, in which the arch over St. John's Steps was at first called Blind-gate, and supported a tower called successively Dove-tower and Nightingale-tower. A quoin still remains of what was called the Old-gate in Tower-street, descending into the Pithay. The inner wall continued thence to its eastern termination, Old-gate, in Narrow Wine-street, and turned southward at Chequer-lane. Whether a part or the whole of the site of St. Peter's Church was without the wall is matter of doubt, but the wall returned in its western direction with Worship-street, now the north side of Bridge-street, to the gate at the foot of High-street— thence in the direction of St. Nicholas-street to St. Leonard's Gate, at the foot of Corn-street, where St. Leonard's Lane

---

* Godfrey died in Normandy, in 1093.   † More than 30 yards in circumference.

E

A. D.

1087 completes the circle of which we commenced this description at the foot of Small-street.

Sewin, who was præpositor of Bristol in the time of
Edward the Confessor, held from him the manor of Clifton.
At this time it was part of the land of Roger Fitz-Ralph.

1089   The honour and earldom of Gloucester, with the Castle
of Bristol, bestowed by the King on Robert Fitzhaymon,
gentleman of his bedchamber.

1090   Robert de Melhent (Rufus, or the Red Earl) born, a
natural son of Prince Henry, by Nesta, daughter of Rhys,
prince of South Wales.

The Life of Wulfstan, bishop of Worcester, in Anglia Sacra,
contains the following passage, which has been assigned to
this period of the history of Bristol.

" There is a sea-port town, called Bristol, opposite to Ireland,
into which its inhabitants make frequent voyages on account of
trade. Wulfstan cured the people of this town of a most odious
and inveterate custom, which they derived from their ancestors, of
buying men and women in all parts of England, and exporting
them to Ireland for the sake of gain.* The young women they
commonly got with child, and carried them to market in their
pregnancy, that they might bring a better price. You might have
seen, with sorrow, long ranks of young persons of both sexes, and
of the greatest beauty, tied together with ropes, and daily exposed
to sale. Oh! horrid wickedness! to give up their nearest relations,
nay, their own children, to slavery. Wulfstan, knowing the obsti-
nacy of these people, sometimes stayed two months among them,
preaching every Lord's day; by which, in process of time, he
made so great an impression on their minds, that they abandoned
that wicked trade, and set an example to all the rest of England to
do the same."

1093   Westbury Monastery re-edified, to the honour of the
Blessed Virgin : the old lands were recovered, new added,
and the monks restored, by Bishop Wulfstan, who made it a
cell to the Priory of Worcester; but his successor, Bishop
Sampson, in the same reign, revoked the grant, and removed
the monks.

1096   The first holy war undertaken by Christians, at the instigation of the Pope. Robert Curthose was among the
crusaders.

1099   Westminster Hall built.

* Mr. Turner sufficiently proves the prevalence of slavery, in his distinctions of
Anglo-Saxon society. By law, a father, if very poor, was allowed to give his son up
to slavery for seven years, if the child consented to it. It was enjoined by the Synod
held in 816, that at the death of a bishop, his English slaves, who had been reduced
to slavery in his life-time, should be freed.

1100 Aug. 2, the King killed by Walter Tyrrel, a French knight, while hunting in the New Forest, aged 44.*

HENRY I. *surnamed* BEAUCLERK.

Robert Curthose being upon his voyage from the Holy Land, his younger brother, Henry, seized the royal treasure, and was crowned at Westminster, Aug. 5.

1101 The contest between Robert and Henry ended in an agreement that Henry should enjoy the kingdom for life, paying Robert annually three thousand marks, and that the survivor should succeed both to the kingdom of Great Britain and the duchy of Normandy.

1106 The King taking his brother prisoner, all Normandy was reduced to obedience, and Robert was first brought to Bristol, where, upon an attempt to escape, his eyes were put out. He was afterwards removed to Cardiff Castle, upon its erection by Robert, earl of Gloucester. See 1134.

St. Peter's Church, and the tithes of the rents of Brigstou, having been bestowed by Robert Fitzhaymon on the Abbey of Tewksbury, of which he was the founder, the grant was this year confirmed by Henry.

1107 March, Robert Fitzhaymon, earl of Gloucester, died, leaving four daughters, the eldest named Mabile. He was buried in the Chapter-house at Tewksbury—removed into the Church about 1241, and a chapel of stone was erected over him in 1397.

1109 The King's daughter, Matilda, married to the Emperor Henry IV.

1110 Robert Melhent, aged about twenty years, married Mabile, heiress of Robert Fitzhaymon, and was created Earl of Gloucester and Lord of Bristol. The Castle said to have been built, meaning re-built, in the following year. See 1130.

The arts and sciences taught again in the university of Cambridge.

1111 The King planted colonies of Flemings in Pembrokeshire.

1115 Nov. 6, died Hardynge, who was succeeded in his estates by his son Robert, who thence had the surname of Fitz-Harding, and, as will appear hereafter, was founder of the Monastery of St. Augustine, and father of the first Lord Berkeley. Robert's first residence, after Baldwin-street, was in Broad-street.

* The bridle of the horse which he rode is now in the possession of Sir Richard Phillips.

E 2

A. D.

1117   Maurice Fitzharding born.

1118   The order of Knights Templar instituted about this time.

1121   Henry spent his Easter at Berkeley with his queen.

1124   A large body of Northmen, arriving in autumn, spent the winter in Bristol.—*Annals of Margam.*

1126   Robert, duke of Normandy, was taken from the custody of Roger, bishop of Salisbury, and entrusted to the custody of Robert, earl of Gloucester, for confinement in Bristol Castle.

1127   The Emperor Henry IV. died. The nobility swore fealty to Matilda, the emperor's widow and the king's only daughter.

Church-wardens and overseers instituted.

1129   The Priory of St. James, of which the present church, without its tower, was the chapel, dedicated to St. Mary, founded by Robert, earl of Gloucester, for black monks of the Benedictine order. It was consecrated by Simon, bishop of Worcester. The site of this priory extended from the existing Whitson-Court, westward, to the Barton eastward, and consisted, on the east side of the church, of a large mansion-house, with a spacious long hall—a buttery adjoining—a long gallery extending to the church—rooms under and a chamber at the west end of the long gallery—an extensive green court adjoining—a great gate-house, entering by the church-yard into the said green court—a dwelling-house—a great stable in the court—a brew-house and bake-house near to the kitchen-door—a little garden adjoining to the brew-house. Another garden lay between the west end of the church and the said great gate-house; also a little way or lane leading out of the great court to the west part of the gate, entering into the way that parted Shooter's Close and the Montagues—all which was the west part of the said mansion-house. On the east side were galleries and chambers in them, parlours, &c. united with the west part—a little square green court and enclosed ground, with a pigeon-house—a large barton extending from the gate in the Barrs-lane, whereby was the pound, and two great barns, also several buildings lying on both sides the barton.* See 1174.

* The house, latterly occupied by Mr. Tovey, coach-lamp manufacturer, and, while we write, undergoing a division into two tenements, to which others are to be attached, exhibits some of the original masonry of the back part of one of the apartments above described. The garden, with lime-trees, in the title-deeds is called a paddock. The front and back walls of the house of Mr. James, tailor, on the Parade, are of the same ancient erection. In altering the steps of his cellar, a few years since, the workmen discovered a skull, at about two feet and a half under the landing-place in the stone passage.

A. D.

1130 The nobility renewed their oath on the Empress's marriage to Jeffery Plantagenet, earl of Anjou. According to the Historia Minor of Matthew Paris, Stephen, (third son of Stephen, earl of Blois, by Adela, fourth daughter of William I.) who was now twenty-four years old, debauched the empress, on board the ship in which he was conducting her to be married.

Robert, earl of Gloucester, began this year to rebuild Bristol Castle, erecting a palace and other houses, a magnificent tower, donjon or keep (with stone brought out of Normandy), situated in the N. W. part of the castle, and encompassed the whole with strong walls, devoting every tenth stone to the building of the Priory of St. James.* See 1199.

1131 The Abbey of St. Mary of Tintern founded by Walter Fitz-Richard de Clare, for monks of the Cistertian order.

1133 The Empress Maud had a son, afterwards Henry II.

1134 Robert Curthose died at Cardiff Castle, having been a prisoner twenty-six years. Among reasons for disbelieving that he was by his brother Henry's order blinded, a Welsh sonnet is said to have been written by him, in which he mentions the pleasant view from the castle-windows.

1135 Dec. 1, the King died in Normandy, in his 78th year, nominating the Empress Matilda his successor; but she being absent,

STEPHEN

was crowned Dec. 26.

1136 The Welsh made irruptions into England in favour of the empress. After Easter, Robert, earl of Gloucester, returned to England, and did homage to Stephen, but on condition that the King should fully maintain his dignity.

1137 March, Stephen crossed the sea, and on Easter-day following so did the earl. On landing, he was forewarned by persons employed for the capture, that the king intended to make him prisoner. He was with the King in Normandy at the time when Geoffrey, earl of Anjou, invaded that country with a strong force; and he was then suspected, with many others, of an inclination to support his sister's cause. Stephen found Normandy as dangerous as England: Matilda's friends openly shewed themselves in both countries.

* The notion that the Castle was designed for offence to the town would seem contradicted by the adoption of it as a device for the civic seal. See 1361, for the origin of the wall between the town and the Castle.

A. D.

In July, pressed on all sides, Stephen was forced to make a truce with Matilda and her husband.

1138 An insurrection took place in favour of Maud, and (according to Camden) the Castle was scarcely finished before it was besieged by Stephen. Arriving at Gloucester, after the siege of Bedford, "the usurper (says Knighton) laid hold of the Castle of Gloucester and others. This imprudent step, as it proved to be, occasioned Robert, earl of Gloucester, to invite over his sister Maud, the empress, to take the crown." Geoffry Talbot, being driven out of Hereford, about June, took refuge in Bristol, and put himself under the protection of the Earl of Gloucester's son, who had been left in command of it by his father, after furnishing it with a garrison and provisions—Robert returning to Normandy. Stephen now took Bristol by force of arms, and placed in the Castle Sir Bartholomew de Courcill, an ancestor of the great Duke of Marlborough. At midsummer, Robert sent messengers from Normandy to the King (then in London) remanding his homage, because the King had not kept his oath to him nor his sister Matilda. Whereupon the King deprived him of all his possessions in England. The revolt now became general, including Milo, the chief constable of England.

New-gate was built about this time, and held, in two niches on the outside, the statues of Earl Robert and Bishop Godfrey. These are said to be the statues that are still extant at the castellated building, composed of the eastern Castle-gate and other remains of more remote antiquity, erected by Mr. Reeve at Brislington, 1767. They represent very aged men, one holding in his left hand the model of a castle or square tower; the other, in the act of uncovering a chalice.

1139 In September the Empress landed at Arundel, with her brother Robert, and additional forces. The Earl came to Bristol, through the midst of the country occupied by Stephen, accompanied by some soldiers and only ten horse-archers, by way of Wallingford; leaving the Empress and his own wife with Adeliza, the wife of the Earl of Arundel. He afterwards conducted the Empress to this city, where she remained two months; and in October went to Gloucester, to Earl Milo, who held that castle under Robert.

Nov. 7, Robert, at the head of the men of Gloucester, took the city of Worcester, and carried off much plunder and many prisoners. The King, going there with a great army from Oxford, took away the honour of the royal con-

. D.

stableship from Milo, and gave it to William, son of Walter de Beauchamp, sheriff of Worcestershire.—While the King was at Worcester, Geoffry Talbot took Hereford from the king's garrison.

40 Early in this year, the Earl of Worcester destroyed the Earl of Gloucester's magnificent house at Tewksbury.—At Whitsuntide a conference was held between the King and the Empress, near Bath, for the purpose of settling a peace; her brother Robert meeting on the part of the Empress, the Legate and Archbishop on the part of the King; but they came to no agreement.

St. Ewen's Church mentioned in a deed of this date by Robert, earl of Gloucester, who gave it to Thurstan, the priest of Bristol. Thurstan afterward resigned it to God and the parish of St. James, Bristol, and the Abbey of Tewksbury; which was confirmed by William, earl of Gloucester.

Fitzharding began to build the Abbey of St. Augustin, upon the manor of Byleswicke, purchased from the Earl of Gloucester.

141 Feb. 2, the battle of Lincoln, in which Maud defeated Stephen. She was thereupon declared Queen of England in a national synod. Stephen was brought prisoner by Robert to the Empress at Gloucester, who ordered him to Bristol Castle, whither Robert conducted him. Matilda was now acknowledged by the whole kingdom, excepting Kent, which Stephen's queen and William de Ypres, his general, still held, with an army.

On the Friday after Ash-Wednesday, the Empress left Gloucester and proceeded to Cirencester, on her way to Winchester. In the same year, when the Empress fled from the rage of the Londoners, upon her haughty refusal to restore the laws of King Edward, in return for the money she wished to obtain from them, she went to Gloucester, and held a council with Earl Milo,* after which she gave orders to confine Stephen in chains.

July 25, at Oxford, on her way with an army to Winchester, she granted the earldom of Hereford to her friend Milo. Her object was to punish the treachery of the Bishop of Winchester, Stephen's brother, who had theretofore joined her party. Sept. 14, the siege of the Bishop's castle ended in a broken retreat. At Devizes, being almost dead with fatigue, she was tied like a corpse upon a bier, and thus carried by horses to Gloucester. Milo, after having

* Milo had been appointed by Stephen to the governorship of Bristol Castle.

1141 been surrounded, made a wonderful escape, and arrived at
Gloucester almost naked. In his flight, he must have
thrown away his seal, for it was found in a field near An-
dover, in a direct line between Winchester and Ludgershall,
about the beginning of 1795. See Gent.'s Mag. p. 1737.

Robert being taken prisoner in September, at Winchester,
after a battle with the forces raised by Queen Matilda, the
wife of Stephen, he was esteemed an equal ransom for the
King, who on All-Saints' day was released from his cap-
tivity, but left behind him, in the Castle, his Queen, his son,
and two chiefs of his party. On the third day he arrived
at Winchester, and there released the Earl of Gloucester,
who had been brought from Rochester for that purpose;
but the Earl left behind him his son William, as a hostage.
When he arrived at Bristol, he released the Queen and her
party, who in return sent back his son.

Stephen hereupon attempted to retake Bristol, but was
forced to raise the siege, and never again had any authority
here.—The writer of a Latin MS., *Gesta Stephani*, translated by Mr. Seyer, in his " Memoirs," describes the city
at this time as, " by the very situation of the place, the best-
defended of all the cities of England; for (as we read of
Brundusium) a certain part of the province of Gloucester,
being narrowed into the form of a tongue and extended a
long way, forms the city, two rivers washing two of its
sides, and meeting together in a great abundance of waters
on the lower side, where the land itself is defective [meaning
the marsh-ground, which admitted high tides to the city-
wall that extended from the Avon to the Froom, on the N.
side of King-street, &c]. Moreover, a quick and strong
tide, ebbing and flowing abundantly night and day, causes
the rivers on both sides of the city to run back upon themselves into a wide and deep sea; and, forming a port very
fit and safe for a thousand vessels, it binds the circuit of the
city so nearly and so closely, that the whole city seems to
swim on the water and sit on its banks.* But on one side,
where it is esteemed more exposed to a siege, and more
assailable, a castle, raised on a considerable mound, fortified
with a wall and bulwarks, towers, and various machines,
prevents the approach of assailants."

* We beg the reader will, in our allusion to the probable egress of the waters of the
Avon and Froom, in p. 7, for the loose phrase, " over the moors in Somersetshire,"
adopt that of " through the Vale of Ashton, to the sea at Clevedon." We are not
aware of any geological reason why the rise of Ashton-Vale for four or five miles,
according to the barometrical observation of the Rev. W. Conybeare, may not have
been less at the time of the rupture or chasm than now.

A. D.

1141 Stephen about this time reconnoitred Bristol, with his army, and consulted his barons upon the expediency of blocking up the port and inundating the city, but abandoned the design. Philip Gai, a relation of Earl Robert, was at this time in command during the Earl's absence. By the writers on behalf of Stephen, Bristol is characterized as the volcano whence the kingdom was deluged with fire and sword.

1142 About midsummer, Robert crossed the sea, to solicit succours from the Earl of Anjou. The Earl being engaged in hostilities at home, in

November, Robert arrived at Wareham with Prince Henry. The Empress was then at Oxford, closely besieged by Stephen. Robert besieged Wareham, in hope of inducing the King to raise the siege of Oxford, and took it in three weeks. By this time the Empress had escaped, the country being covered with snow, by putting herself and five soldiers in white linen clothes, passing through the middle of the enemy's watch, favoured by only a single soldier of Stephen's army. Thence she went on foot over hedge and ditch, crossed the Thames on the ice, and arrived safely, in the same night, at the Castle of Wallingford, distant twelve miles.

Robert, after visiting his sister, brought his nephew to Bristol, where he was for four years entrusted to the care of one Matthews, to be instructed in letters and bred up in good manners. Matthews lived near the great stone house, the residence of the Hardings; and hence doubtless originated the friendship of Henry with Robert Fitzharding.— "R. F., born in 1085, was now 57 years old, and consequently no companion for a boy of nine years old, nor yet his elder son, Maurice, born in 1117; but it is probable enough that some of his younger sons might have been such. During these same four years, Robert Fitzharding was engaged in building his Monastery of St. Augustin, at the consecration of which Prince Henry was present, and assisted him." See 1148.

1143 July 1, Earl Robert utterly routed Stephen's army at Wilton, taking prisoner William Martel, lord of the Castle of Shirburne, and brought his spoils and prisoners to Bristol. Robert and his sons now succeeded in conquering a very large part of the kingdom, from sea to sea across, subjecting the inhabitants to their laws and ordinances, without any resistance whatever.—Stephen having a garrison at Malmsbury, Robert built three castles near it, and, besides cavalry, brought together an army of infantry, composed of

F

A. D.

Welshmen and Bristowans, and men of other cities in the neighbourhood.—The soldiers of Bristow were next concerned in the taking of Farringdon Castle.

1145 Temple Church founded by the Knights Templar about this time.* See 1460.

1146 The Earl of Anjou requested Robert to send home his son Henry. The Earl accompanied the Prince to Wareham, but returned hastily to Bristol.

1147 After many military exploits, Robert was attacked by a severe fever, and died at Gloucester, the beginning of November. He was buried, by his own direction, in the Chapel of the Priory of St. James—the last day of October, say several authorities—in a stone tomb of green jasper, in the choir.† His son William succeeded him in the governorship of the Castle on the 3d of April following. Perhaps it was in the previous interval of vacancy in this office that "the robbers and freebooters of the Castle, both horse and foot, committed great depredations on the city and country." See 1158.

The Empress Maud, weary of the war, this year left England for Normandy.

1148 This year Robert Fitzharding completed the Church and Monastery of St. Augustine.‡—Six canons of the Monastery

---

* This was ten years previous to the erection by the Knights of their Temple in Fleet-street, London. It has been suggested to us, both by a well-read antiquary and an intelligent parishioner of Temple, upon noticing the crenelled parapet-work or battlement just above the middle of the tower, that there can be no doubt of the base having taken its present inclination when the building had proceeded so far, and that it was carried up to its present height when time had proved that the foundation was completely settled, probably about 1390. (See the notice under that date.) It is evident that, in the latter work, an attempt was made to correct the inclination. The spectator, upon an attentive view of the side presented to Church-lane, must be convinced that, were a miracle to set the base completely erect, the superior division would exhibit a bending posture in the opposite direction. The ground upon which the church and its neighbourhood are built was certainly, at a remote period, the bed of a lake or branch of the Avon; for, on recently digging a well in the yard of Messrs. Ring & Co.'s pottery, which adjoins the church-yard, at the depth of from forty to forty-five feet was found a piece of hewn timber, about twenty inches square. See Rowley's Account of Temple Church, in Chatterton's Works, vol. iii. p. 284. If that account be correct, as to the fact of the consecration not taking place till sixteen years after the erection of the church, when the crenelled battlement and the glazing were completed, 1161 (the year after the date of Henry II.'s charter) may be assigned as the æra of this partial finishing of the tower. The carved shield, over the entrance to the western porch, bears a *lion* and flag.

† In January 1818, Mr. Henry Smith, who enjoys an hereditary love of antiquities, was led to a search for the tomb of its founder in this church; and his discovery of it, concealed by a plastered door and pews, was followed by its restoration, with the effigy, as may now be seen in the south wall on the left hand side of the door nearest the tower. In the stone coffin, immediately under the effigy, were found a thigh and other bones.

‡ The different appearance in the colour of the stones exhibited by the exterior of this and other buildings of the same age in Bristol is accounted for in " Outlines of

A. D.

1148 of Wigmore were inducted on Easter-day, April 11. The ceremony of dedication was performed by Robert, bishop of Worcester; Boniface, bishop of Exeter; George, bishop of St. Asaph; and Nicholas, bishop of Llandaffe. Mr. Barrett, in p. 250 of his History of Bristol, gives particulars of the doles of bread, herrings, pease, and money, on the anniversary of the founder and foundress, to one hundred and fifty poor men, the abbot, prior, sub-prior, almoner, servants, friers, and prisoners in the gaol of Newgate. The first abbot's name was Richard.

Robert Fitzharding resided in Broad-street. Existing appearances warrant the belief that the Cider-House formed part of this residence. He afterwards removed to a great stone house which he built upon the bank of the Froom, part of its offices lying near St. James's. Cecily, his sister, had a house not far off, and Robert, earl of Gloucester, was another neighbour. These mansions were situated in Broad-mead (originally called Newport Meadow), which was laid out by Earl Robert under cover of the city-wall. See 1154.

1149 About the middle of May, Prince Henry, with a large body of horse and foot, returned to England, upon invitation of the Barons of his party. He went to David, king of Scotland, and was knighted with many other young men, at Whitsuntide. He was now about sixteen years old.

1150 In January, Henry crossed again into Normandy.

1151 At Whitsuntide he married Queen Eleanor of Guienne, at Bordeaux.

1152 In January, on the day of Epiphany, the Prince, as Duke of Normandy and Earl of Anjou, again landed in England, with 3000 foot-soldiers and 140 knights, and made Bristol his head-quarters for two years.

1153 Nov. 7, (Stephen's son Eustace having died suddenly,) a general assembly of the principal persons of the kingdom met at Winchester, when the King publicly adopted Henry as his son and successor. In this convention, it was agreed that Stephen should execute the whole office of royalty in the whole kingdom of England, as well in the Duke's part (having Bristol for its capital) as in his own part.

1154 At Easter, Henry crossed over into Normandy.

the Geology of England and Wales," &c. by the Rev. W. D. Conybeare, F.R.S. and W. Phillips, F.L.S. part I. p. 236, 1822; where they treat on the oolitic series of the quarry at Dundry Hill, of which the Abbots of the monastery held a lease. See also p. 233, for a general description of Dundry Hill, geologically considered. Why should we not add that the reader will feel obliged to us for recommending him to study the whole of that work with the closest attention?

1154 Oct. 25, Stephen died of the piles, at Dover, aged 50.
During this reign, eleven hundred and fifteen castles were
built.

HENRY II., *surnamed* COURT-MANTLE,

Arrived in England, Dec. 8, and was crowned at Westminster with his Queen Eleanor, heiress of Guienne and
Poictou, divorced wife of Lewis, king of France, on the
19th of the same month.

Henry knighted his schoolfellow and friend, Robert Fitzharding, now mayor or governor of Bristol after his father.
He had before made him heir of the Berkeley estate of
Roger de Berkeley, lord of Dursley, confiscated for that
nobleman's adherence to Stephen against his mother,
and as a compensation for the elder Harding's supplies of
money in support of the cause. He granted him also the
manor of Bitton. But Roger, lord Dursley, proving a
troublesome neighbour, Robert Fitzharding besought Henry
to take from him again the barony of Berkeley; the Duke,
however, reconciled their difference by promoting a contract
for intermarriage of the two families, which was entered into
in the presence of Stephen, at the great stone house in
Baldwin-street, with these conditions,—Maurice, son and
heir of Robert Fitzharding, was to take to wife Alice,
daughter of Lord Dursley, and with her the town of Slym-
brugge (Slimebridge), and the heir of Roger lord Dursley
to marry Helena, daughter of Robert Fitzharding; and it
was mutually agreed that Alice should have twenty pounds
a year in land of the fee of Berkeley for her dower, and
Helena* was to have the manor of Siston assigned to her in
dower; whereupon all right in the barony of Berkeley was
voluntarily released by Lord Dursley. See 1160.

1155 A few weeks after Henry's accession, Nicholas Break-
spear, an Englishman, was raised to the pontificate, under
the title of Adrian IV. The British monarch sent a formal
embassy to congratulate the new pope on his elevation;
which mark of attention was highly pleasing to Adrian. A
strict friendship arose between them. This encouraged the
King to request a grant of the kingdom of Ireland from the
Pope. Adrian, flattered at a circumstance that acknowledged
in the see of Rome the power of disposing of kingdoms and

---

* Helena died about the 10th of King John.

A. D.

empires, readily granted the request, by a special bull, dated December 1156; but various occurrences prevented Henry from profiting immediately by the noble donation.

1156 Richard Cœur de Lion born.

1157 Henry subdued the Welsh, who did homage and swore allegiance.

1158 "William, earl of Gloucester, and his countess, Hawysia, resided at Cardiff Castle, which he possessed by hereditary right, with the whole province of Gwladvorgan, i. e. *the land of Morgan.* He happened at this time to be at war with Yvor, who was surnamed Modicas, *the little.* He was a man of moderate stature, but of prodigious courage; possessing, after the manner of the Welsh, certain mountainous and woody places, which, however, the Earl was very desirous of wholly taking away from him, or of lessening. On a certain night, therefore, although the Castle of Cardiff, surrounded by very strong walls, was defended by the watch-word of a multitude of guards, by 120 soldiers and by many archers, and although the city abounded with very many hired soldiers, yet, in the midst of so many defences and proofs of security, the aforesaid Yvor secretly got over the walls by means of scaling-ladders, and carried away with him into the woods the Earl and Countess and their little son, the only one whom they had, and did not set them at liberty until he had recovered what had been unjustly taken from him and more."—"Hawis, Haweis, Hawisia, or Avisa, was daughter of Robert, commonly called Bossu, or Hunchback, earl of Leicester. They had three daughters and two sons, Robert and Roger. The latter was a priest and a bishop; but Robert, who was born at Cardiff, died there." See 1163.

1160 A charter was granted about this time, by the King, to his men dwelling in the Marsh,* near the *Bridge* of Bristol. See Barrett's Hist. p. 73 and 663. Robert Fitzharding also granted a charter to his men in the Marsh, &c. recited in Barrett, p. 73. See 1164. The marsh near the Bridge we consider must have been the ground now occupied by the parishes of Temple and St. Mary Redcliff.

1163 William, earl of Gloucester, elected Bishop of Worcester. He was consecrated by Thomas à Becket, Aug. 23, 1164.

1164 The King, at Salisbury, granted a charter (in the Rev. Samuel Seyer's translation, No. 1) to his burgesses of Bristol,

---

* The Robert Fitzharding's or St. Augustin's Marsh included Canon's Marsh and Queen's square.

A. D.

1164 for exemption from toll, passage, and custom, throughout his whole land of England, Normandy, and Wales, wherever they should come, they and their goods. Lord Lyttelton, in his Life of Henry II., quotes William of Malmsbury's authority that Bristol was now full of ships from Ireland, Norway, and every part of Europe, which brought hither great commerce and much foreign wealth. The charter was, doubtless, granted in return for money furnished by the citizens toward the war with France.

It was in this year that Dermot Macmurchad, king of Leinster, carried off, from Ireland, Dearborghil, the wife of O'Ruark, prince of Breffni,* and eventually came to Bristol, with about sixty persons in his suite. Hence he proceeded to Normandy, to implore the protection and assistance of Henry for the recovery of his dominions, promising to hold his kingdom of him, as his sovereign lord, if restored to it by his aid. Henry granted letters patent, empowering his subjects to assist M'Murchad. Relying on this authority, M'Murchad returned to Bristol, where he was entertained by Robert Fitzharding. He shortly afterward formed a treaty with Richard Strongbow, earl of Pembroke, who agreed to reinstate him in his dominions, on condition of obtaining his daughter in marriage, and the reversion of his kingdom after his death.

Keynsham Priory founded by William, earl of Gloucester.

1166 Robert, eldest son of William, earl of Gloucester, died at Cardiff, and was buried at Keynsham Priory, which the Earl now newly repaired and endowed, making it an Abbey of Canons Regular to the memory of his son, " at whose request he founded it." See 1170.

Dec. 24, the King's son John born at Oxford.

1168 " In this year commenced in Bristol the political connexion between England and Ireland."—SEYER.

1170 Feb. 5, Robert Fitzharding died, a canon of St. Augustin's Monastery, aged 75. Eva, his wife, died March 12th following. They were buried between the abbot's and the prior's stall, next the abbot's stall, at the entrance to the

* " The King of Leinster had long conceived a violent affection for Dearborghil, daughter to the King of Meath; and though she had been for some time married to O'Ruark, prince of Breffni, yet could it not restrain his passion. They carried on a private correspondence, and she informed him that O'Ruark intended soon to go on a pilgrimage (an act of piety frequent in those days), and conjured him to embrace that opportunity of conveying her from a husband she detested to a lover she adored. Macmurchad too punctually obeyed the summons, and had the lady conveyed to his capital of Ferns."—O'HALLORAN. The monarch Roderic espoused the cause of O'Ruark, while M'Murchad fled to Bristol, as above stated.

.. D.

170 choir. Robert Fitzharding was succeeded in the barony by his eldest son, Maurice. See 1189. His second son, Robert de Gournay, otherwise de Wer or Warre, was the founder of the Gaunts' Hospital. He had the hundreds of Portbury, Bedminster, and Hareclive, " and also the church of St. Nicholas, by Bristol, and divers land there." He married Hawisia de Gurney. His third son was Nicholas de Tiken- ham, and his fourth son, Thomas, who was archdeacon of Worcester in 1135; his fifth son, Henry, was archdeacon of Exeter, and treasurer to Henry while Duke of Nor- mandy.—After Robert Fitzharding's death, his wife Eva founded the Nunnery of St. Magdalen, of which she became Prioress. The site of this nunnery extended from the King David Inn, on the south, up the hill northward, to a lane called the Montagues, since Upper Maudlin-lane, and now Horfield-lane; thence up the said lane eastwarp, to a lane opposite the Fort-lane, now called Terrill-street, leading down into Magdalen-lane southward, and then up the said lane, westward, to the King David Inn.* See 1229, 1284, 1546. Perhaps it was about this time that William de Clifton gave the Church of Clifton, &c. to the Monastery of St. Au- gustin. See 1822.

St. Maryport Church founded about this time, by William, earl of Gloucester. See 1173.

About this time also commenced Henry's affair with Rosamond.†

171   Dec. 30, Becket killed at Canterbury.

172   The King visited Ireland, landing at Waterford on the 18th of October. At Cashel, Henry produced the bull of Adrian IV., confirmed by his successor Alexander III., which transferred the sovereignty of Ireland from its natural princes to himself. At Dublin, he executed the charter to his men of Bristow (Seyer's No. 2), " giving and granting them his city of Dublin for them to inhabit, with all the liberties and free customs which the men of Bristow had at Bristow and through his whole land."

1173   The Earl of Gloucester was actively employed against the rebel Earl of Leicester, in defence of the King. See 1174.

The King granted a charter of privileges to his burgesses of Dublin; which is almost a literal copy of that granted to Bristol.

* Southmead Manor, now the property of Richard Llewellin, Esq. was parcel of the Priory of St. Mary Magdalen, Bristol.

† Rosamond, according to tradition, was born at Frampton-upon-Severn. For a very interesting description of her person, see Fosbroke's Collections for a History of Gloucestershire.

After a stay of six months, during which time he built a palace in Dublin, Henry returned to England.

1174 William, earl of Gloucester, gave to the Priory of St. James and Monastery of Tewksbury (as per Henry's deed of confirmation, 1181) all his freehold in ecclesia and right to the fair held at Whitsuntide in Bristol—the tenth penny of his mills in Newport, Monmouthshire—Runne, Stapleton, and his burgage-rents out of Newport Meadow (now Broadmead)—a messuage of one Allen, in or near the Shambles of Bristol, and the churches that were his fee, viz. St. John's, Christ-Church, St. Jacobus of the Market, (meaning St. Philip and James, near the Old Market), St. Owen's (St. Ewen's), St. Michael's in Bristol, and of St. Brandon without the vill of Bristol, and the church of Edrieston.—In Whitson Court the Prior of St. James held court for his lands without Lawford's Gate and Redlonde.

1175 About midsummer the Earl of Gloucester surrendered his castle of Bristol to the King, but continued to reside in it.

1176 "The Earl, having no male issue, made the King's youngest son, John, his heir of the earldom of Gloucester, and the King granted that his son John should marry the Earl's daughter, if the Court of Rome should allow it, on account of their consanguinity. If not, the King was to grant in marriage the said Earl's daughter, in some very honourable alliance; and nevertheless the King was to give £100 (equal to £1500 at this time, says Lyttelton) of rents in England to Mabile, the wife of Almar, earl of Evereux, and other £100 of rents to Amice, the wife of Richard, earl of Clare—each being a daughter of the said Earl of Gloucester; and if the Earl should have any legitimate son, then that son, and John, the King's son, should divide the earldom of Gloucester between them. Both parties were under age. The lady's name was Isabella, and she was the Earl's youngest daughter."

1177 "The burgesses rendered an account of eighty marks for Sturmis the usurer, who freed it in the Treasury, and was quit."—"Probably," says Mr. Seyer, "the burgesses had either killed him or plundered his property; and the King, who according to the maxims of that age considered the plunder of the Jews to be his own prerogative, punished the townsmen for infringing it."

1179 The King took the honour of Gloucester into his own hands, and held it for six years, during which time it was farmed to Hugh Bardulf, or Bardolph.

A. D.

1182 The Welsh pirates killed Ranulf Poer, sheriff of the county of Gloucester.

1183 Nov. 23, William, earl of Gloucester, died. " He willed to be buried with his father at the Priory of St. James, but was privily conveyed by night to Keynsham, to which he had given the whole lordship of Marshefel (where there was a nunnery), and impropriated the benefice thereof unto St. James's Priory, and the benefice consequently came to Theokesbyri."

The burgesses of Bristol paid a fine of fifty pounds, to have respite and not be impleaded without the walls of the town, till the King's return to England.

1184 Hugh Bardolph rendered an account to the King, as belonging to the Earl of Gloucester's lands, of £119 7s. 5d. of the rent of Bristow, and of the mills and fairs; and for having a house at Bristow, where the King's rents were received, £3 0s. 10d. (This was afterward " King John's House," which adjoined the gardens of " the great stone house," and was entered from Back-street.)

1185 March 31, the King being desirous of providing a secure and honourable establishment for his youngest son, John, in a council at Oxford, knighted and invested him with the lordship of Ireland, and shortly afterward sent him thither; but the haughty conduct of the Prince, then aged nineteen years, and the insolence of his retinue, disgusted the Irish chieftains. Having therefore squandered away a large sum of money, and lost the best part of his army, the youth returned to England on the 17th of December, leaving the chief direction of affairs to the brave John de Courcy. We cannot doubt that on this occasion the charter, Seyer's No. 3, was granted, which was witnessed at Bristol, among others of John's suite, by Maurice and Robert de Berkeley. John styles himself, in the preamble, simply Earl of Morton, (which he became in 1170) *not* Earl of Gloucester, as he did not become so till 1189, though he might have previously held the honour or lordship. In this charter he " grants and confirms to his burgesses of Bristol, dwelling within the walls and without, as far as the boundary of the town, within Sandbrooke [eastward] and Bewell [northward, a little below Cotham Turnpike], and Brightnee Bridge [westward, meaning Bright Bow, Bedminster], and the spring in the way near Aldbery of Knowle [southward, beyond Totterdown and latterly called Alderburiham], all their liberties and free customs, as well, freely and completely (or more so), as they ever had them in his time, or in the time of his predecessors.

G

A. D.

1185 The burgesses not to be sued out of the town, nor pay fine to the King for murder within its bounds—to be exempt from wager of battle, except for death of a stranger—no person to take an inn or lodging-house without leave of the burgesses—no stranger tradesman to buy leather, corn, or wool, within the town, except of the burgesses—no stranger to have a wine-shop excepting in a ship, nor sell cloth for cutting except at the fair—no stranger to remain for sale of his goods longer than forty days—the burgesses to marry without license of their lords—to grind their corn wherever they choose—may build on the bank of the river, and possess all void places, to be built on at their pleasure."

1186 Philip, second abbot of the Monastery of St. Augustin.

1189 Thursday, July 6, Henry died with grief at the altar, in Normandy, cursing his sons,* and was buried at Fonteverard. His age was 61, of which he had reigned nearly 35 years.

John *sans Terre*, now 23 years old, married Isabella, heiress of the family of Gloucester, and succeeded to the earldom. She was his second wife, the first having been Alice, daughter of the Earl of Morton, or Mortaigne, in Normandy. The marriage took place at Marlborough, contrary to the prohibition of Baldwin, archbishop of Canterbury, because they were cousins in the third degree.

RICHARD I. *surnamed* CŒUR DE LION,

Sept. 3, crowned at Westminster; when the mob, falling upon the Jews, murdered many of them, and plundered their houses.

The body of the famous King Arthur sought for in the Abbey of Glastonbury, by Henry de Soili, the abbot, at the solicitation of the King's mother. See 1276.

1190 Lord Maurice de Berkeley, son and heir of Robert Fitzharding, died. He chose to be buried in the parish-church of Brentford, from some pique to the Abbot of St. Augustin, who had offended him. Robert, his eldest son, (born 1165) was Constable of the Castle of Bristol, and the first founder of the Hospital of St. Catherine, in Bedminster, at Bright Bow, where latterly stood a glass-house, and the site of which is now part of a tan-yard. See 1207.

1192 " Josce, son of Lie, of Bristoll, accounted in the Exchequer for 100s. out of the second thousand marks which

---

* In 1176 he had an amour with Alice of France, the betrothed wife of his son Richard. All of his sons, not excepting John, had rebelled against him.

A. D.

the Jews of England had promised to the King. He delivered it into the Treasury, and was quit."

1193 " The burgesses of Bristow were guilty of some disrespect to the King's Justiciaries, Robert Marmiun and his fellows, in not going out to meet them, as they ought; for which neglect they were fined £100 by those justices."

St. Michael's Church mentioned in a deed of confirmation by the Bishop of Worcester, as part of the endowment of the Abbey of Tewksbury. Richard Cumblain was this year presented to the rectory by the Abbot and members.*

1195 The King, being well-informed of his brother John's seditious practices during his absence, by a solemn judgment of his nobles deprived him of all his honours and seized all his castles and land. It would seem, however, that John's garrison in the Castle of Bristow withstood the King's attempt, " for in 1196 [the year after our present date] one Richard Dorescuilz, &c."—SEYER. Our own authority says, " One Richard Dorescuilz was fined five pounds for having assisted at the siege." Qu. by whom was the fine levied,—by the King, or by John? We should imagine by the latter, for Mr. Seyer goes on to inform us that

" About Whitsuntide, 1195, [the year preceding the fine] the King was in some degree reconciled to his brother by the intercession of their mother Eleanor, and restored to him the earldom of Moreton and the honour of Eye and the earldom of Gloucester, with everything belonging to them except the castles; and, in lieu of his other earldoms and lands, gave him annually 8000 pounds of money of Anjou."

1196 William, bishop of Hereford, Hugh Bardolph, and others the King's justices, taxed the burgesses of Bristol, in common with others of the King's manors and burghs, two hundred marks (£133 6s. 3d.), and for the fairs, ten marks. (£6 13s. 4d.)

John, third abbot of St. Augustin's; his predecessor, Philip, being removed to Bellelande, in Yorkshire.†

1199 April 2, Richard received a wound in France from a cross-bow, shot by a man in revenge for the death of his father and his two brothers, whom the King had killed with his own hand. The King charitably forgave his assailant, and died through neglect of the wound, on the 6th of April, aged 44 years; bequeathing England, on his death-bed, to his brother John, and ordering all his castles to be restored to him.

* It has been asked by one of the most zealous Bristol antiquaries, why all churches dedicated to St. Michael were erected in the most elevated and northern situations?

† Which of these was Bale's Bibert, a Benedictine monk, who wrote a History of his Own Times, also mentioned by Leland?

JOHN,

Fourth son of Henry II. (setting aside Arthur, son of Jeffery Plantagenet, the third son, now thirteen years old), crowned on Ascension-day.

1200   John put away Haweis* and married Isabella, daughter of the Earl of Angoulesme, previously contracted to Hugh, earl of March.   He gave back part of Haweis's fortune, but retained the honour of Gloucester and the lordship of Bristol in his own hands, with the Castle.   Hence it became a royal demesne, and annexed to the crown.

The Church of St. Philip & Jacob. mentioned as parochial before this time.   (See 1174.)   So of St. Thomas.

In deeds of this year, Corn-street, where St. Werburgh's Church is situated, called Old Corn-street.

1201   A treasury in Bristol, and the town paid an aid for the King's passage to Ireland,—Bristol 1000 marks, and the men of Redclive 1000 marks, and the men of the Templars of Redclive 500 marks.

1202   Aug. 4, the Princess Eleanor, with Prince Arthur, John's niece and nephew, were taken prisoners at Mirabel in Normandy; and the Princess was brought to Bristol Castle, where she remained for forty years.

1204   The King confirmed to John de la Warre [see 1220] the grant, made previous to his attaining the crown, of the honour of Gloucester and Castle of Bristol, with (at the request of Queen Isabel) the manor of Bristleton (Brislington), a part of that honour.   He afterwards made Hugo de Hastings constable of the Castle.   See 1386.

1205   St. Bartholomew's Priory and Hospital, without Froom Gate (now the City School), founded by Sir Gawyne de Rokshalle† and Sir Johnne de Toedmage.   This date stands upon Chatterton's authority, and it would be too unchari-

---

* Haweis afterward married Hubert de Burgh, earl of Kent, Justiciary to Henry III., who gave him that earldom in 1227,

† A Sir Galfrid de Wrokeshale was at the perambulation of the bounds of Menedip in 1278.

‡ The more the reader becomes acquainted with the authorities from which the notices in the present work are drawn, the more will he be convinced that Chatterton went through a parallel course of reading. Granting, which we do, most readily, that he took unwarrantable liberties with the MSS. that fell in his way, it is inconceivable that any powers of imagination could help him to names and places the existence of which we have identified from sources that had lain hidden since a much earlier period than his birth, and till long after his death. In his account of St. Mathias's Chapel, afterwards Canynge's Place, vol. iii. p. 337, of the Works, &c. he talks of a Roman front towards

A. D

1205 tably liberal to assign to the youth's inventive faculty all his prose as well as all his poetry.‡ He furnishes also a list of *priors*, commencing, this year, with Richard, brother of Sir Gawin de Rokeshall, and ending with Radulph de Beckington, in 1457; but it appears, from contemporaneous deeds, that there was also a *prioress*. See 1382.

1206 The King granted the town of Bristol in fee-farm to the burgesses, at a yearly rent of £245 (which was paid up to the 9th of Henry III.), the Castle of Bristol excepted; reserving the prisage of beer, as much as the Constable of the Castle and his people there might have need of.

1207 Lord Robert de Berkeley (second of the name) granted to Redcliff Church, at the request of William, the chaplain, his fountain of water from Huge Well, below Lower Knowle; part being conveyed, in a pipe of an inch diameter, to the Hospital of St. John the Baptist, in Redcliff-Pit, for the use of the master and friers there. These hospitallers had a Chapel contiguous to the west end of the Church, dedicated to the Holy Spirit. Their Hospital extended from Redcliff-Pit towards the Avon. There is a lane called St. John's Lane without the site of the gate.

Grants of land also to Redcliff Church bear this date.

Roger de Berkeley (see 1243) gave sixty marks, that it might be enquired into how much his land at Leonard Stanley was worth, which was in pledge to the Jews of Bristol, for a debt he owed them, and that he might have his land again, upon paying the value every year to the Jews.

1208 The Pope's interdict commenced and lasted for six years.

1209 The Pope excommunicated the King.

Lords Mayor of London first appointed annually. London, till now, had no other than wooden bridges.

The King issued a proclamation at Bristol, on his way to Ireland, forbidding the taking of all sorts of feathered game throughout England.

1210 The King compelled the Jews to pay great part of his charge into Ireland. The burgesses of Bristol contributed 1000 marks. A Jew named Abraham, and who is said to have resided without the walls on that part of the Froom called the Broad Weir,* though cruelly tormented, refused to ransom himself. The King ordered that he should every

---

Redcliff-street and a Saxon front towards the river. A Saxon front was first discovered upon digging the foundation of Messrs. Birtill and Co.'s floor-cloth manufactory, as we shall notice under the proper date.

* Quay-street, without St. John's Gate, was formerly called Jewrie-lane.

A. D.

1210 day lose a cheek-tooth till he paid ten thousand marks. He
lost one per day for seven days, and then, having but one
left, paid the money.

John this year coined money in Ireland, equal to the
standard of English money; but it does not appear that he
coined any money in England.

1212 The town was obliged to pay the Constable of the Castle
toll for every vessel of fish that came into the port.
See 1284.

1214 The Pope's interdict ceased.—Geoffrey de Mandeville,
earl of Essex, &c. created Earl of Gloucester.—About this
time Prince Henry was placed at school in Bristol.

1215 The Barons made war upon the King, and obliged him to
confirm their Magna Charta.

June 19, the King procured the Pope to make the Great
Charter void, and to join with him in his wars against all the
Barons, and the Pope interdicted the Barons and their
adherents.

John, or Joseph, fourth abbot of St. Augustin's Monastery, upon the death of his predecessor John, whom Chatterton makes a poet. See the short poem "On the Mynster,"
Works, ii. 115.

Bristol, till now, was governed by a Præpositor, under
the Custos of the Castle.

1216 The Barons invited over the Dauphin of France to their
assistance.

Almerick de Eureux created Earl of Gloucester.

Oct. 18, the King died at Newark, of a fever, in his fifty-
first year. He was buried, his bowels at Croxton Abbey,
and his body at Worcester, under the high altar.

HENRY III.

Oct. 28, was crowned at Gloucester, by Peter, bishop of
Winchester, and Joceline, bishop of Bath; Cardinal Guallo,
or Guala Bicherius, legate of Pope Honorius in England,
assisting. The King was nine years old. Immediately after
his coronation he came to Bristol, when the first Mayor,
Adam le Page, was appointed, with two Præpositors, Stephen
Hankin and Reginald Hazard.

Nov. 11, Guallo held a council in presence of the King,
in which Louis, the French King's son, was excommunicated;
and the Legate recognized the rights of the Kalendaries
(see 700) in the words, *Propter antiquates et bonitates in*

A. D.

1216*ed Gilda repertas.* They were a society of religious and laity, females as well as males, like a college de propagandâ fide, wherein Jews and infidels were converted; and to them were committed the archives of the town, keeping a calendar or monthly register of all the public acts, registering deeds, rolls, &c. See 1318.

Mr. Dallaway observes (p. 47 of Heraldic Enquiries) that the hereditary use of arms was not established till this reign. Before, the son constantly varied from the coats of the father.

1220 St. Mark's Church, originally the Chapel of Gaunt's Hospital, was erected about this time. The boundary of this Hospital is still indicated by a niche in the angle of the corner-house of Pipe-lane, and Frog-lane or Frogmore-street, with, near it, the remains of a winged lion, carved in stone, and part of a similar emblem against the western corner-house of St. Mark's Lane, on St. Augustin's Back. Queen Elizabeth's Hospital was erected upon its site, and Unity-street and Orchard-street are erected upon the orchard of the Gaunt's Hospital. A MS. in the possession of Mr. Alderman Haythorne, (one of the many transcripts from the Mayors' Kalendar which supplied the absence of any printed History of Bristol, and was used as the depository of whatever additional information came within the reach of the possessor,) among other particulars introductory of the list of Mayors, &c. commencing with 1216, states in connexion with the date 1320, which is evidently a mistake for 1220, that " the Gaunts* was founded by Robert de Gurney [otherwise de Ware, or Warre, second son of Robert Fitzharding, first Baron of Berkeley] for the soules [repose] of Mauritius de Gaunte, his uncle (whose heire the said Robert was) for a master, 3 chaplaines, and reliefe of 100 people for ever, to the honour of God, St. Mary and St. Marke. [The endowment was] the manor of Powlet, the mill of Ware, 4 markes rent in Bristol, (viz.) the house of Robert Fitzharding, which David la Ware held, 2 markes; of the the house of Richard Cordonarius, juxta P'isam, one marke; of the house of Peter la Ware, in Bristol, one marke; and his houses in Billeswike. Every of the 100 people aforesaid was to receive bread to the weight of 45lb. with sufficient pottage, made with oatemeale: the bread to be made of equall mixture of flower of beans, barly, and wheate."

* Mr. Seyer, in his " Memoirs, &c." says that " the Hospital and Church of the Gaunts, in the cemetery of the Monastery, were founded by Maurice de Gaunt, son of Robert, second son of Robert Fitzharding; which Maurice took the name of Gaunt from the family-property of his wife, Alice de Gaunt."

A. D.

.1221   May 13, the second Robert Lord Berkeley died, aged 55.
He was buried in the north aisle of the monastery, under
an arch against the high altar, in a monk's cowl, which the
superstition of the time counted sacred and a defence against
evil spirits. This recess is the next but one to the altar of
Sir Maurice. His two wives, Juliana and Lucia, (who survived him, and married Hugh de Gournay,) were buried
near him. Leaving no child, he was succeeded by his brother
Thomas (born 1167), who increased the endowments of St.
Catherine's at Bright Bow. Having offended the King, he,
was obliged to enter himself a Knight Templar. See 1243.

The begging-orders of friers were introduced into England; who, by their superior learning and popularity, considerably injured the monastic reputation.

1222   Huntingford Chase, alias Horewood Chase, was now called
the Chase of Bristol. All the lands of Hugh Gurney were
ordered to be seized, for hunting in a chase of that name
without the King's leave. See 1227.

1223   Before this time, in the out-parish of St. Philip & Jacob.,
on the north side of the road to Bath, was an hospital for
lepers, dedicated to St. Lawrence; whence is derived
Lawrence-Hill. The hospital subsequently belonged to the
College of Westbury.

Ralph of Bristol, educated in the Abbey of Glastonbury,
and heretofore Dean of St. Patrick's, Dublin, this year became Bishop of Kildare. He wrote the life of St. Lawrence,
Archbishop of Dublin. Vide Sir James Ware.

1224   Ralph de Willington, called in the writings of this time
Radulphus de Castello, being made Constable of the Castle,
had also the wardenship of the Chase of Kainsham. See 1323.

1225   The burgesses accounted to the King for £245, the ferm
of this town.

1226   St. Francis patron of the Franciscan friers, came to
Bristol.—This year the Pope demanded an annual sum from
every cathedral-church and monastery in Christendom;
which was refused!

1227   The King declared himself of age, and cancelled the Great
Charter and the Charter of the Forests, which occasioned a
conspiracy against him.

Hubert de Burgh, Lord Chief Justice, (who had married
Haweis, the repudiated wife of John,) created Earl of Kent.

May 1, at Westminster, the King granted Bristol a
charter of *inspeximus*, confirming that of Henry II. (1164),
Seyer's No. 4.

This year, too, a writ passed the Sheriff of Gloucestershire,

1227 ordering that no market should be held in the county, but that all the markets of his bailiwick should follow the King in his expedition to the Vale of Kerry. This was a customary mode of provisioning armies.

"At the general petition of the inhabitants of those parts, and especially of the men of the Forest of Horwood, and for £150 in money, King Henry III., in the 12th and 13th yeares of his reign, did disafforest all the townes, lands, and woods, between Huntingford (where Berkeley hundred and Hugh Gurney's lands parted), and the wood of ffurzes now called Kingswood, within fower miles of Bristoll, and so from Seaverneside to the browe of the hills by Sodbury, excepting only Allestone Parke. And, for more assurance, the Bishop of Bath and Wells, and some other lords, took particular patents of disafforestation of their proper manors."
—MS. SMYTHE, *Family-Historian of the Berkeleys.*

Mr. Fosbroke adds, " A writ passed for disafforestation of King's forest near Bristol, called Huntingford: claus. 12 Hen. III. A fine of twelve thousand marks was paid for the disafforestation of the King's forest of Horewood, on this side Severn: Fin. 12 Hen. III. At the same era the Bishop of Bath and Wells held a charter for disafforestation of his manor of Pucklechurch, within this chase: Cart. 13 Hen. III."

1229 Hugo de Burge, governor of Bristol Castle.

There were grants to Redclift Church under this date.

The Monastery of the Black Friers, near Rosemary-street, founded by Sir Maurice Berkeley de Gaunt, elder brother of Sir Henry Gaunt, buried in St. Mark's, 1268. The site of this Black Friery is marked by Philadelphia-street eastward, the Broad Weir south, Merchant-street west, and Rosemary-street northward. The Bakers' Hall is part of the original building. Passing through the remains of the cloisters, into the court of the Friends' Meeting-house, may be seen the exterior of a large east-window of the Hall, the light of which is now contracted, with a portion of the original stained glass. Looking northward, to the left of the Hall, stands the great Hall of the Monastery, with the Dormitory over it, the south and north walls and the north window-frames of which are still in good preservation, and the florid masonry of the west window retains some of its iron-work.*

---

* With the characteristics of the florid Gothic—

> " Her pendant roof, her window's branchy grace,
> Pillars of clustered reeds, and tracery of lace,"

it will appear that scarcely any place abounds more than Bristol. See Henry VI.— Gothic, or British architecture, first became intermixed with the Grecian orders in the time of Henry VIII. The term Gothic, or barbarous, originated with Sir Christopher

A. D.

1229 Messrs. George and Co.'s sugar-house stands between this and the site of the Chapel of the Monastery. Upon digging the foundation of the sugar-house in 1814, Messrs. Jones and Wilcox found three stone coffins. The following probable history of their contents was copied by William of Worcester from the Register of the Monastery:—"William Courtneys made the great cross in the burying-ground. Matthew de Gourney was one of the founders. *Sir Maurice de Berkeley* of Beverstone [see 1466] and the Lady *Joanna*, his wife, were buried in the choir, on the left-hand side of the altar. *Sir William Daubeny*, Knt: was buried in the choir.* The heart of Robert de Gourney was buried in this church." See 1289.

1230 Maurice Berkeley de Gaunt, founder of the Monastery of Black Friers, was interred in the Chapel of St. Mark. He gave by deed to the King, Beverston, Aylburton, and Weston; whence the bequest is called King's Weston.

William de Putort, sheriff of Gloucestershire, declined to answer for the profits of the county, because the King had granted them for the custody of the Castles of Bristol and Gloucester, and for the maintenance of Eleanor his kinswoman, and the soldiers dwelling in both Castles—including the rent of Berton Regis, 60 marks, and the prisage of beer.

1231 The Patent Roll orders murage for the towns of Bristol, Gloucester, and Carlisle.†

1232 Indulgence granted by John, bishop of Ardfert, dated at Bristol this year, for the repairs of St. Mary Redcliff Church.

1233 William, son of Hugh, and brother of Gilbert, Lord Talbot, had custody of the Castle of Bristol.

1234 Abbot David died, and was buried under a marble slab, with a skull and cross-bones, near the Elder Lady's Chapel. William de Bradstone became the sixth abbot.

1237 Peter Quivell, bishop of Exeter, dating at Radcleve this year, granted an indulgence for the repair of St. Mary Redcliff Church.

1238 "William de Marisco, who by evil practices thought to have slayne the King in his bedchamber at Woodstock (as was said), being apprehended, fled, and fortified the Isle of Lundy, in the Channel of Bristoll, doeing much mischiefe by piracie; but was not long after taken, with 16 of his accom-

---

Wren, in his excessive affection for the Grecian. We know nothing of the *barbarous* except their mixture in one building.

* A massive portion of one of these tombs was used in laying a pier of the wooden bridge crossing the Froom into Ellbroad-street.

† Murage was a toll paid for every loaded beast or carriage entering into a walled town, and was applied to the repairing of the walls.

A. D.

plices, and executed at London, though at his death he denied the plott."

1239 The ground for the Trench, in the Marsh of St. Augustin, (the present course of the Froom from St. Giles's or the Stone Bridge) was purchased or agreed for between Abbot Bradstone and the burgesses, Robert le Bell being Mayor.

Oct. 23, Wells Cathedral dedicated to St. Andrew. It was built by Robert de Lewes and Joceline de Welles.*

1240 The Church of St. Augustine the Less mentioned in Gaunt's deeds—founded by the Abbots of St. Augustin's Monastery, as a chapel for the accommodation of the inhabitants who had erected houses within the precincts of the convent, and whose communication with the town was about to be interrupted by the new trench.

1241 Eleanor, sister of Prince Arthur, died, having been a prisoner in the Castle forty years. She was buried in the Chapel of St. James's Priory, but afterward removed to the Nunnery of Congresbury, Wilts, by a charter of license from Henry III. Shenstone has sung her elegy.

1242 Aug. 20, Abbot Bradstone resigned, and was succeeded by William Long, camerarius de Keynsham. Bradstone lived ten years afterward.

Grey soap sold from Bristol to London, to one John Lamb, who retailed it at a penny per pound, and black soap at a halfpenny.

1243 Nov. 29, Thomas Lord Berkeley died, aged 76 years. He was buried in the south aisle of the Monastery, in the arch next to the chapel that contains the Newtons' monuments, his statue being in the habit and posture of a Knight Templar, opposite to where stood the rood-altar; where also his wife was buried. He was succeeded by his eldest son, the second Maurice (born 1218), who married Isabel de Creoun. He bought a release of all right in the manor of Berkeley, &c., from Henry de Berkeley, lord of Dursley. This Henry was the son of John Berkeley, son of Henry, son of Roger, son of Robert, and of Helena, his wife, daughter of Robert Fitzharding. "This Roger de Berkeley, lord of Dursley, son of Robert Fitzharding's daughter, must be the person who pledged [see 1207] his land in Derelega (Dursley), Stanlega, and Dodington, to the Jews of Bristol and Gloucester, for a debt which he owed to them. He afterward paid to the King a fine of fifty marks, that he might hold possession of the lands, paying the annual value of them to the Jews."

* One of the witnesses to the Bristol Charter, 1247, was " Joceline, bishop of Bath."

A. D.

1244 The King ordained that, as often as the burgesses chose a Mayor, they should bring him before the Constable of the Castle, to be sworn and admitted.

1246 David, archbishop of Cassel, granted an indulgence for the repair of Redcliff Church, as did, the same year, Christianus Episcopus Hymelacensis.

1247 July 28, at Woodstock, is dated Henry's Charter, granting " for us and our burgesses of Redclive, in the suburb of Bristol, that they shall for ever answer, with our burgesses of Bristol, before our justices, as our said burgesses of Bristol answer, and where they answer, and not elsewhere." This, remarks Mr. Seyer, was the first step towards the incorporation of Redcliffe with Bristol, which was before a separate burgh.

Lord Maurice (2) de Berkeley about the same time confirmed to his men of Redeclive the liberties which the second Robert had granted them, in a Charter mentioned by Mr. Barrett, p. 73, 4, and recited literally, p. 663. See 1281.

" A Bridge was now concluded to be built, with consent of Redclive and the Governors of Temple-Fee, at the united expense of the citizens and the inhabitants of Redcliff." Richard Aylward was Mayor this year. Hitherto the river (say some MSS.) had been passed by boat from St. Thomas' Slip to St. Mary-le-Port, then called the Church of our Lady her Assumption, and the port, St. Mary Port. The water from the Froom ran by the Castle into the Avon, while the main stream turned the Castle-Mill, and passed onward, as the ditch of the town, through Baldwin-street, driving a mill (near the foot of St. Nicholas' Steps) called Baldwin's Cross Mill, and discharged itself into the Avon, where now the Back-Hall stands. And when the Trench to the Quay was finished, the water was stopped from flowing at the point near the Red Cliff. And all the while the foundation of the arches of the Bridge was laying, and the masons building, the water of the Avon ran up under the bridges of Redcliff and Temple Gates; and at Tower Harratz the water was bayed, so that it might not pass downward to hinder the building. And, when the Bridge was built, the bays were broken down, and the current ebbed and flowed as before. Then the fresh river, which ran by Baldwin's Cross, was dammed up and made a street. " Thus the two Towns were incorporated into one, both on the Somersetshire side and on the Gloucestershire side; that whereas they had usually on every Monday a great market at the Stallenge Cross*

* Stallar, Stall-master, Stallarius, Stallard's Cross.—SEYER.

1247 [in St. Thomas-street], and in Bristow every Wednesday and
Friday, at the High Cross, and it was much trouble for the
people to pass from one side to the other; the Bridge being
built, the market was kept in High-street, at the High Cross."

That there was previously a bridge in the situation
described there can be no doubt; but being, like those of
London at the same period, constructed of wood, it had for
some time fallen into decay. We need not wonder that a
Bridge is nowhere else mentioned than in the Charters: as a
matter of general notoriety, no one thought it required
to be made the subject of special record.

Previous to the grant of land by the Monastery for the
new course of the Froom, the site of Queen-square was
called Avon-Marsh, and the present Canon's Marsh was
named St. Augustin's Marsh. A part of Avon-Marsh, called
Chanter's Close, probably the nearest to the wall of the city
upon which the north side of New King-street is built, had
been exchanged by the Abbot with the Corporation, for
Treen-Mills, on the south side of the Avon (the pond of
which is now Bathurst-Basin), with reservation of the privilege of hunting the duck there, " for disport of the magistrates," upon paying down a certain sum. The remainder
of Avon-Marsh was at that time subject to overflowings of
the tide.

There seem to be difficulties in all the accounts of the
grant of land for the Trench, which we think may be thus
reconciled. The grant, as has been stated above, was made
or agreed for in 1239, 24 Henry III., in which year Robert
le Bell was the Mayor; whereas the covenant appears to
have been between William de Bradstone on the part of the
Monastery, and " Riccardum Aillard," Mayor, on behalf
of the Corporation. Bradstone continued to be Abbot no
longer than 1242. Aylward was not Mayor till 1247, when
William Long was Abbot, having been so for five years.
How can we account for Aylward, and not Le Bell, being
named on the part of the Corporation, unless it be conceded
that the bargain was first negociated in 1239, and not finally
concluded till 1247, when the Trench was completed?—
One MS. has it, " Anno 1240, 24 Hen. III. as Ricart's
" Kalendar says, some say in 1245, 1246, 1247, the Trench
" or Kay was made from Gybb Tailleur to the Key Con-
" duit,—as well those of Redcliff ward and of Temple fee,
" as of the town of Bristol, *taking their turns* in the labour
" and charge." This " taking of turns" may develope the
mystery of the delay of eight years from the date of the

1247 covenant till its final execution; for, on the 27th of April, in the 24th year of his reign (1240), Henry found it necessary to issue a Mandamus to " all his honest men dwelling in la Redclive," saying, " since our beloved burgesses of Bristol, " for the common profit of the town of Bristol, as well as " of your suburb, *have begun* a certain Trench in the Marsh " of St. Augustine, &c., which trench indeed they cannot " perfect without great charges; we therefore command " you, that since, from the bettering of the said port, no " small advantage will accrue, not only to the said burgesses, " but also to you, who are partakers of the same liberties " which our said burgesses have in the said town, and are " joined with them both in scot and lot, that you lend *the* " *same assistance as they do;* as it will be also very profitable " and useful to you to have the work of the trench happily " completed, according to what shall fall to your share, " together with all our burgesses; and so effectually that " the aforesaid work, which we regard as our own, receive " no delay through any defect in you. Witness myself at " Wyndleshore, 29th of April, 24th year of our reign."

This work cost the commonalty of the City 5000 pounds.

Previous to the market being held at the High Cross, the Gloucestershire market was holden without the Castle, in Old Market-street. The Court of Pied-Poudre continues to be opened there every 29th of September; and the sittings continue for fourteen days. The sort of refreshment taken by the members of the Corporation who officiate, before they proceed to business, namely, toasted cheese and metheglin, marks the remotely British antiquity of this branch of civic jurisdiction.

Before the Froom was turned, the usual places for landing goods were at the Back, where stood the Custom-House, now divided into two tenements, adjoining St. Nicholas burial-ground, and at St. Mary-Port, above the present Bridge. On taking down the Shambles, which continued the line of St. Nicholas-street, to erect the north side of Bridge-street, large Gothic arched cellars, running back almost into St. Mary-Port churchyard, were discovered, used formerly for the reception of merchandize; and an old mooring-post stood in the ground, on entering the north door of the church itself; which post was removed about the year 1750. Before the existence of the Shambles, there were houses close to the river; and the street, from its being a great deposit of wealth under the residence of its owners, was called Worship-street.

1248 Froom Bridge was called Knife-smith-street.

1252 Aug. 17, at Woodstock, the King granted a Charter of confirmation (Seyer's No. 6) of that of John while he was Earl of Morton, with the additional grant, that none of the burgesses should be molested by any justice or bailiff of the forest, for venison found within the walls of the town. Henry was at this time raising money under pretence of an expedition to the Holy Land.

John, Cecily, and Nicholas Aylwarde, granted a penny rent out of a house in Steep-street, a penny out of a house in St. Thomas-street, and a pound of cummin out of a house in Broadmead, towards the endowment of Gaunts' Hospital.

1253 This year began the order of Augustinian Friers, whose house was within Temple-gate, on the western side of the street.

John Att Wood was one of the Præpositors this year. The Attwoods have remained a Bristol family to this day. See 1823.

1255 The King bestowed on his son Edward the town of Bristol, with Stamford, Grantham, Ireland, Gascoigny, and Wales, upon his marriage with the King of Castile's sister.

1256 July 24, at Gloucester, the King granted a Charter (Seyer's No. 7), empowering the burgesses of Bristol to choose a coroner, to attach and present pleas of the crown—burgesses not to forfeit their goods for faults of their servants—goods of intestates not to be confiscated—liberties to be free as in London. Henry was just returned, after having spent seven and twenty hundred thousand pounds, in his various journeyings out of the kingdom. He had previous to this stayed four days in Bristol, at the charge, to his son, of 34l. 9s. 1d. and seven hogsheads of wine.

A famine throughout the kingdom. People often fought for the carcases of dogs and other carrion. Wheat in Bristol sixteen shillings a bushel.

1257 The King came to Bristol, and summoned Lord Percy to attend him here, upon an expedition into Wales.

1258 "A Jew fell into a privy at Tewkesbury on a Saturday, and would not suffer any one to pull him out, for the reverence he had for his sabbath; and the next day, being Sunday, Richard de Clare, earl of Gloucester, would not suffer any one to pull him out, for the reverence he had for his sabbath. On the morrow morning, being Monday, the Jew was found dead."—A very reverential affair!

1259 A dispute between the monks of St. Augustin and the brethren of St. Mark, about the right of burial in College-

A. D.

1259 Green, then the common cemetery of the Monastery. The Bishop of Worcester awarded to the brethren the liberty of burying before their house, but on condition of leaving the ground always level, because of the pleasantness of the place.

1260 Roger de Leeburne, a baron, made Constable of the Castle.

1263 The King being now at war with the Barons, who had suddenly and unexpectedly plundered all foreigners throughout the kingdom, the Prince (Edward) took possession of the Castle, and fined the burgesses one thousand pounds, to oblige them to store it with provisions; but the burgesses resisted, and forced him to retire hastily into the Castle; from which, by a device in which he procured the Bishop of Worcester to assist him, he escaped to Windsor Castle. See 1267.

1264 May, 17, Abbot Long died—buried in the north aisle of the Monastery, to the left of Hugh Dodington. Richard de Malmsbury, eighth abbot.

"Gaurine de Bassingburne and Robert Walerande, keepers of Bristow, made oute sudenly an hoste to Walingford, but they prevailed little."—LELAND. This expedition was designed for the relief of Prince Edward, then a prisoner there, under Simon de Montfort, Earl of Leicester, having been taken with the King at the battle of Lewes, May 19.

Bartholomew de Inovence made Constable of the Castle.

1265 Jan. 23, origin of the House of Commons; the Earl of Leicester having called a Parliament in the King's name, being the first wherein two knights for each county, and two burgesses for each borough, were summoned.

1265 "This year Prince Edward was taken by the Barons, together with the King. His army being discharged, [he] came and abode in Bristol, until the Prince made an escape; and they took arms and went to the battle of Evesham."

Aug. 4, the battle of Evesham, in which the Earl of Leicester was defeated and slain.

1266 December, the King's party gained the ascendancy over the Barons, in the conquest of the Castle of Kenilworth. See 1281.

1267 Edward, Prince of Wales, founded the Priory of the Carmelites in St. Augustin's parish, " on the right ripe of the Froom [the Trench], over against the Key."—LELAND. The Carmelite Friery, and Church on the south-west side of it, were dedicated to God and the Blessed Virgin Mary. Their boundary extended from Steep-street on the eastward, to Pipe-lane westward, and backward including the Red

A. D.

Lodge garden. Leland calls it " the fairest of all the houses of Friers."* This Monastery was supplied with water from the spring rising at the top of Park-street, whence *Pipe-lane;* the same which supplies St. John's Pipe, within the Gate. See 1374 and 1400.

1268 Inscription upon a monument, bearing a statue at full length, in the east aisle of the Mayor's Chapel:—" Henricus de Gaunt, magister primus hujus Domus Sancti Marci de Billeswicke, obiit 1268." Leland says, ": Sir Henry Gaunte was a knight some time dwelling not far from Brandon-Hill, by Bristow." See 1336.

1269 Robert de Gourney, nephew and heir of Sir Maurice Gaunt died. His heart was buried in the Church of the Monastery of Black Friers. See 1229.

1271 " Dominus Johannes Musagres, Constable of the Castle, and William de Stanhurst, Subconstabularius."

1272 Nov. 16, the King died in London, aged 65 years, and was buried at Westminster. The first brass statue was that of Henry III.

EDWARD I., *surnamed* OF WINCHESTER,

was at this time absent, in the Holy Land.

Twelve furnaces at York and twelve at Bristol, for melting silver, in order for hammering and stamping perfect money.

1274 The House of Franciscan or Grey Friers founded in "Lion's mede," on the bank of the Froom, the site of the Unitarian Chapel, Messrs. Stock and Fry's sugar-house, &c.†

Aug. 15, Edward arrived in England with his Queen, Eleanor. At his coronation, five hundred great horses were let loose, for any that would take them.

1276 Sept. 22, the King issued an order concerning the navigation of the Avon between Bath and Bristol.—" King

---

* One MS. calls Edward's foundation " the Fryers near the Ware" (or Weir); and this would encourage the speculation that a small Gothic window, the frame of which still remains in the wall over the water of the Narrow Weir, eastward of the Horse-Pool, was also part of a religious edifice. But this, we believe, was the general style of building all houses of opulent inhabitants at the period in question.

Mr. Seyer conjectures that, before the cutting of the Trench, the principal channel of the Froom was not through Baldwin-street, as stated under 1747, but something nearer its present course. Perhaps its waste-waters found their way over a " Ware" within view of this Priory, and then crossed Back-street, as described in the " Memoirs." See c. xii. § 23, 26, of " a certain *ditch* that bounded the arable land belonging to the Abbey."

† Dr. Burney, in vol. i., p.394, of his History of Music, describes a Musical Tract among the Cotton MSS. in the Bodleian Library, ascribed to Thomas Tewkesbury, a Franciscan of Bristol.

I

A. D.

1276 Edward, with his Queen, and the Arche Bishop of Canterbury, went to Glastonbury, [and] tooke up the bones of King Arthur, to view them.* He altered the coinage of money, causing it to be made round and intire; whereas, before, pence were made on purpose to be broken into halfpence and farthings. Of this new coyne,

> The King's syde was his head and name written,
> The Cross side, wth city it was coined and smitten."
>
> *Mr. Alderman* HAYTHORNE's MS.

Sept. 13, Abbot Richard died, and was succeeded by John de Marina, the ninth abbot.

1277 This year the two Præpositors of Bristol were called Stewards or Seneschals.—The first statute of mortmain enacted.

1278 Four ships of Bristol made prize of a ship, near the island of Scilly, in which was the intended spouse of Llewellin, Prince of Wales, Eleanor, daughter of Simon de Montfort, (the late Earl of Leicester); which was well accepted of the King.†

Robert, bishop of Bath and Wells, this year granted an indulgence for the repair of St. Mary Redcliff Church.

Nov. 9, a visitation by Godfrey, bishop of Worcester.—Barrett (Hist. p. 261) furnishes a curious description of the loose state of discipline in the Monastery. The Bishop found the House of St. Mark in much the same disorder.

1279 Sept. 12, a process was issued, out of the office of the Bishop of Worcester, against Peter de la Mare, Constable of the Castle, and others, his accomplices, for infringing the privileges of the Church, in taking one William de Lay, who fled for refuge to the church-yard of St. Philip & Jacob., for carrying into the Castle and imprisoning him, and, lastly, cutting off his head. Nine or ten being involved in the crime, their sentence was, to go from the Church of the Friers Minor, in Lewin's Mead, to the Church of St. Philip & Jacob., through the streets, naked, except their breeches and shirts, for four market-days for four weeks, each receiving discipline all the way; and it was enjoined

---

* This is elsewhere said to have been done by Henry II., after his visit to Ireland, in consequence of having learnt from the song of a Welsh bard, in his passage through Wales, that Arthur was buried in Glastonbury Abbey. Upon this incident Thomas Warton built his Ode entitled *The Grave of King Arthur.* We have shewn, under 1189, that the search was made after the decease of Henry II., at the instance of his widow.

† Llewellin (or Leolyn) paid a ransom of fifty thousand pounds sterling for his love, and a thousand pounds per annum during his life.

A. D.

1279 Peter de la Mare, that he should build a stone cross, at the expense of one hundred shillings at least,—one hundred poor to be fed around it on a certain day every year, and that he should find a priest to celebrate mass during his life, where the Bishop might appoint. The stone cross is thus mentioned by William of Worcester:—"Altæ crucis prope fossam castro Bristoll." It stood on the south side of the Old Market, near the corner of Tower-Hill.

1280 Abbot John absent through sickness—the Monastery again in disorder.

The Barrs (now Barrs-lane) at this time the residence of common women, who were not suffered to come nearer the town.

1281 April 4, Lord Maurice (2) de Berkeley died, aged 63. He was buried in the N. aisle of the Monastery, next to the altar of Sir Maurice. He was succeeded by his second son, the second Thomas, born 1245, constable and general of a great army serving in France, and one of the plenipotentiaries for negociation of peace with Philip IV. "His elder brother Maurice, had been slain in a tournament at Kenilworth, during his father's life-time." Thomas's wife was Joan, daughter of William de Ferrers, earl of Derby. He spent his pupillage at Berkeley—his next days at Bedminster; which manor was conferred upon him by his father, for support of his youthful expenses and for his initiation in husbandry, having for his guides and instructors the Abbot and Prior of St. Augustin's and the Master of St. Catherine's Hospital. He and his son Maurice had violent disputes with the burgesses of Bristol; of which see Mr. Seyer's Memoirs of Bristol, c. xiii. § 14—22, as carried on in the years 1303 and 4, with great virulence. The contest on the part of the Earl and his son was for the maintenance of manorial rights in Radeclyve and other streets annexed; for resistance of which, by William Randelph, the Mayor, and others, the Earl and his retainers, among other outrages, "assaulted Adam the cheesemonger, first in his house at Bristol, where they beat, wounded, and dragged him from out of his house and cast him into a pit, &c." and afterwards at Dundry fair, where they "brake his legs in such pitiful manner that the marrow came out of his shin-bones." The King eventually assigned John de Bottetort, William Haward ("two good men and of sound understanding"), and Nicholas Fermebrand, constable of the Castle, to hear and determine all the offences complained of; and this lord, his son, and their men, were fined at 3000 marks, but afterwards released

I 2

therefrom upon condition of the service of ten armed horsemen and a captain in the war of Scotland. See 1314.

1282 Another visitation of the Monastery, and to the Houses of St. James and St. Mark. All well, except that the old Abbot was a non-resident, and the convent in debt.

1283 This year was issued out the first regular summons by writ, to the Mayor of Bristol (Peter de Rumeny), &c. requiring that two persons should be sent to serve in the Parliament at Shrewsbury.

Prince Leolyn's head had been set upon the Tower of London, crowned with ivy; and his brother David was drawn at a horse's tail about the city of Shrewsbury, then beheaded, the trunk of his body divided, his heart and bowels burnt, his head sent to accompany that of his brother on the Tower of London, and his four quarters sent to as many cities, viz. Bristol, Northampton, York, and Winchester.

King Edward came from Wales to Bristol, after reducing the Welsh Princes, (furnishing a subject for Gray's "Bard,") and kept his Christmas here (says our authority) with much content, and held a Parliament.*

1284 Giffard, bishop of Worcester, visited the nuns of Magdalen House; where he found nothing to be amended, except that the Vicar of St. Michael's had detained from the nuns, for three years, two shillings and two pounds of pepper and cummin yearly, for rent, to the restitution of which he was condemned by the Bishop, who preached there; his text was, Filiæ tibi sunt, serva corpus illarum, &c. See 1546.

Dec. 30, the King was at Bristol, and restored to the citizens their Charter, which they had forfeited by encroaching on the rights of the Constable of the Castle, in preventing delivery to the garrison of the customary portion of every cargo of fish.

1286 Feb. 26, Abbot John de Marina died. He was buried in the Chapter-house. His successor was

1287 Hugh of Dedyndon, tenth Abbot.

Peter Quivell, Bishop of Exeter, dated at Redclyve this year an indulgence for the repair of St. Mary Redcliff Church.

In November, all the Jews in England were apprehended in one day, their goods and chattels confiscated to the King, and they, to the number of fifteen thousand, banished the

* Mr. Alderman Haythorne's MS. adds—" and the next he kept at Exeter with much mourning, where Alfred Duport, the late Mayor of the said town, and some more, were hanged for the death of Walter Leath Cale, because the south gate was left open that night, and the murtherer escaped." Walter *Lichdale* was first chanter of the Cathe-

A. D.

1287 realm, having only sustenance-money allowed. A writ passed to the Sheriff of Gloucester, commanding him to make proclamation that no one should presume to hurt the Jews, nor take from them those goods the King had allowed them to keep, but, on the contrary, furnish them with a guard, provided they would pay for it, which might secure their passage to London, in order for transportation; provided also that, before their removal, they returned all their pawns or pledges to such as were willing to redeem them.

1288 The burgesses paid £23 9s. 10d. to the Constable of the Castle, in lieu of prise of beer, called tyne; and the Constable accounted for the same to the King, as part of the profits of the Castle.

Bartholomew Badlesmere succeeded Peter de la Mare in the constableship of the Castle; but the precise time does not appear. He was made Constable a second time: we shall find him so in 16 Edward III. Roger Bigod, son of Hugh, nephew and heir to the last Earl, had a grant of the Castles of Bristol and Nottingham for life; which he surrendered again in the 20th Edward I. (1291).

Godfrey Giffard, bishop of Worcester, attempted to make several churches in these parts, of the patronage of the see of Worcester, prebendal to the Monastery of Westbury; which, after great opposition from the Prior and the Convent of Worcester, he effected, and there became a College for a Dean and Canons, in the gift of the Bishop of Worcester, dedicated to the Holy Trinity; which was hereafter augmented by the benefactions of John Carpenter, bishop of Worcester (who sometimes styled himself Bishop of Westbury), Richard, duke of York, and Sir William Canynges, knight, who is said to have rebuilt the College.—*Bishop* TANNER's *Notitia Monastica*, ii. 73.

1289 This year there were twelve furnaces erected in Bristol, for coining hammered money.

Simon de Burton was one of the Stewards this year.

1290 May 3, died Robert de Berkeley, brother of the second Maurice lord Berkeley. The figure of a Knight-Templar in chain-armour, under the N. window of the great cross-aisle of Redcliff Church, is said to have been designed for Robert

dral at Exeter, and met his death as he came from matins, which was usually performed at two in the morning. At Bishop Quivell's request, (adds an Exeter chronicle,) the King, with his Queen Eleanora, came to Exeter for the purpose of furthering the enquiry. See the use Chatterton has made of the royal visit to Bristol, in his poem of "The Tournament," vol. ii. of the Works, &c. p. 57, placing it two years later.

A. D.

de Berkeley, lord of Bedminster and Redcliff,* and is consequently of greater antiquity than the church itself.

1293   Simon de Burton, then Mayor, began to build the Church
of St. Mary Redcliff, and the Alms-House in Long-Row,
St. Thomas-street, for sixteen women; in which he was
buried. See 1721. John Lamyngton was chaplain of St.
Mary Redcliff.

"About the middle of September, 1293, the Earl of
Berre married Elenor, the King's daughter, in the towne of
Bristol," saith Grafton, p. 170.—"Of his [Edward's]
daughters, the eldest, named Eleanor, was first marryed by
proxy to Alphonsus, King of Arragon; but he dying before
the marriage solemnized, she was afterward married at
Bristow to Henry, Earl of Bary in France, by whom she had
issue, sons and daughters."—BAKER's *Chronicle*.

The King's order for payment of his daughter's marriage-
portion of 10,000 marks is still extant, being dated Winterbourn, Oct. 1, in his progress from Bristol towards London.

1294   Simon de Burton, Mayor.

Nov. 26, Abbot Hugh died. He was buried in the north
cross-aisle of the Cathedral, between two other abbots. He
was succeeded by James Barry, the eleventh abbot.

1295   Simon de Burton, Mayor.†

1297   Simon de Burton granted the tenement in which he then
lived, in Corn-street, newly built, within the gate of St.
Leonard, to John Dicto; which afterwards paid 6s. 8d. twice
a year, for the maintenance of a lamp to burn in St. Leonard's
Church. See 1301. St. Leonard's Gate had been called
Baldwin's Gate.

1299   A Chapel at the extremity of the north aisle of Temple
Church, and a piece of ground thereto belonging, was
granted by the King to the Company of Weavers, for ever.
See 1390 and 1460.

Abbot Barry, going to Almondsbury, late in the evening,
many armed men entered, took away what he had there
for his household, and killed his steward.

* This figure was discovered by the late Mr. Goldwyer and Mr. Henry Smith, concealed by boarding and plastering, in its present situation, where it serves as a base for
some of the uprights supporting a gallery erected for the charity-children.

† The following was the mode of assessing the elevenths and sevenths granted to the
King this year, in the County of Gloucester, as preserved by Morant:—" Roger, the
dyer, had, on Michaelmas-day last, in his treasury or cupboard, one silver buckle, price
18d.—one cup, or mazer-maple, pr. 18d.—in his chamber, two gowns, pr. 20s.—
two beds, pr. half a mark,—one napkin and one towel, pr. 2s. In his house, one
ewer with a bason, pr. 14d.—one andiron, pr. 8d. In his kitchen, a brass pot,
pr. 20d.—one brass skillet, pr. 6d.—one brass pipkin, pr. 8d.—one trivet, pr. 4d.
In his brewhouse, one quarter of oats, pr. 2s.—wood-ashes, pr. half a mark—one

A. D.

1300 March 28, at Westminster, King Edward granted the Charter (No. 8 of Mr. Seyer's Collection), confirming that of Earl John, with those of the 11th, 36th, and 40th Henry III., and granting, farther, that the burgesses should be exempt from murage, stallage (a fee paid for setting up a stall in a market or fair), and pannage (money paid to the King or other lord for liberty to feed swine, &c. on acorns and other wild fruits in the woods and forests), throughout the realm. As often as the burgesses chose a Mayor (the time of war alone excepted), they were to present him to the Constable of the Castle for admission, according to custom.

1301 The Chapel of St. Giles united with the Church of St. Leonard. St. Giles's Church stood over the gate at the foot of Small-street. St. Leonard's Church stood over the junction of Corn-street, Marsh-street (previously called Skadpull-street, and then extending to St. Stephen-street, Clare-street not being in existence), Baldwin-street and St. Nicholas-street. St. Leonard's Gate thus had a triangular archway. The tower stood sixty-five feet high from the ground, eighteen feet in front from north to south, and ten feet from east to west. It had four small freestone pinnacles, surrounded with freestone battlements. In the tower were one large and one small bell. Under the bell-loft, within the church, was built, against the east window, a beautiful neat altar, which, at the taking down of the church, in 1770, was sold to the Church-wardens of Backwell, Somerset. The communion-table and rails around it were of mahogany, and part of the floor was laid with black and white marble.

1302 Simon de Burton, Mayor.

1303* Robert le Ware was Patron of the Church of St. Lawrence, adjoining that of St. John, on the west side of the gate.

1304 Simon de Burton, Mayor.

St. Stephen's Church mentioned in deeds of this date. It belonged to the Abbots of Glastonbury (of whom Geoffrey Fromont was living this year), who continued patrons till the dissolution. There was no tower till 1470. The Abbey of Glastonbury possessed five houses in Glastonbury-court, situated on the right hand, with the entrance from Marsh-

---

great fat for dying, pr. 2s. 6d. Item, one cow, pr. 5s.—one calf, pr. 2s.—two pigs, pr. 2s., each 12d,—one sow, pr. 15d.—billet-woods and faggots for firing, pr. one mark. Sum, 71s. 5d. The fifteenth of that, 4s. 9½d." Nor did they spare the meanest person: e. g. " John Fitzelias, weaver, had, the day aforesaid, one old coat, pr. 2s.—one lamb, pr. 6d. Sum, 2s. 6d. The fifteenth of that, 2d."—*History of Colchester*, p. 47.

* See 1281 (p. 67), for civic disputes with the Berkeleys.

street, of Virgin now Maiden Tavern-lane, (see 1445) leading to Baldwin-street. See 1319.

1305 Simon de Burton, Mayor.

Bristol paid a fine of four hundred pounds to be freed from certain payments which the King required of all cities and towns in England. Edward was then at war with Scotland.

William Wallace was executed this year.

1305 The Scots Earl of Marr's son and heir, a child, was this year confined in Bristol Castle, where he remained till 1314.

Nov. 12, died Abbot James Barry. He was buried under a marble slab, on the south side of the rood-altar. Edward de Knowle, or Knowles, the twelfth abbot, much repaired the Monastery, but whether before or after he became abbot does not clearly appear.

The Bishop of Bath and Wells appropriated the rectory of Backwell to the Hospital of St. John, Redcliff-Pit.

1307 July 7, the King died of a flux, on his march towards Scotland, in his 68th year, and was succeeded by his fourth but only surviving son, aged 23 years,

EDWARD II., surnamed CÆRNARVON.

1308 The King accompanied his favourite, Piers Gaveston, to Bristol, on his way to Ireland.

John de Tavernor, Mayor.

1311 This year the Stewards are called Bailiffs.

The rebuilding of St. Augustin's Monastery began about this time, as appears by a grant of the Bishop of Worcester, of the Church of Wotton, to the members of the Monastery, as a remuneration for the expense they had incurred. That an *entire* rebuilding, only one hundred and sixty-three years after its erection, should be necessary, is not probable. The exterior walls have not been changed, though some of the abutments and their pinnacles may have been added about this time; nor is it likely that the mural monuments of the members of the Berkeley family buried previous to this date would have remained: the great tomb, erected about 1368, might have been deemed a sufficient substitute for them. The newly discovered shrine (1822) of the second Maurice Berkeley, who died in 1281, will appear, on inspection at the north and south corners, to have been inserted *after* erection of the stone-work against which it is placed. The elaborate ornaments of the sealing-room, now used as a robing-room, compared with the workmanship within the roof, of the

311 chancel and naves, of acknowledged later date (1463), we think sufficiently prove it to be part of the original building. We may, in print, stand alone in this opinion; but it is not unsupported in the estimation of those who have paid much more attention to this particular subject. It has been remarked to us, also, that the flooring of Anglo-Saxon churches was generally laid a foot or two below the surface without the doors. No building, since the arrival of the Normans, exhibits a similar base to that of the abutments on each side of the principal north door, and at the original termination of the church westward, until 1542. Though it is certain that the excavations for the Trench, about 1247, were laid upon the cemetery, now the College-Green, yet was the surface of the ground not raised so high upon the bases of those abutments as to account for the whole of the present descent into the Cathedral. See 1363.*

312 Mr. Seyer, in his chap. xiv. § 2—25, gives publicity to a series of documents, derived chiefly from the Rolls of Parliament, in detail of what is emphatically called the Great Insurrection; no mention of which appears in any of the numerous copies of the Mayor's Kalendar, nor did Ricart himself give it the slightest notice. The succeeding notices upon this subject will form a brief abstract of Mr. Seyer's regular narrative founded upon those documents.

Fourteen of the principal burgesses, the chief of whom was William Randolph, who had been four times Mayor, had assumed the collection and management of the revenues of the Corporation, in which they were supported by the Constable of the Castle. In this they were strongly opposed by some principal men of the commonalty, as leaders of a large majority of the malcontents. The immediate cause of this tumultuous opposition was the imposing of certain tolls in the market, and a custom called *a cocket*, to be levied on the shipping for the King's use. These tumults induced the King, soon after July 7, the anniversary of his accession, to take the government and revenue of the town into his own hands, and appoint a custos, whose authority was for a time to supersede or to controul the regular administration. Sept. 30, Bartholomew de Baddlesmere, the constable, (a baron of very great power and property, particularly in Kent,) was appointed custos, and the ferm of the town granted him at an annual rent, being authorized to collect all rents, customs, and profits, keep the prison, &c.

---

* See a note of St. Nicholas Church, referring to this date, under 1762.

A. D.

1312 But this the mayor [William Hore], bailiffs [John Beane-flower and Thomas le Spicer], and citizens, violently resisted; so that neither Baddlesmere, nor any person deputed by him, ever entered the town for any of those purposes.

The order of Knights Templar abolished this year, and the manor of Temple-fee granted to the Knights of St. John of Jerusalem.   See 1543.

This was the first year of the Stewards being called Bailiffs.

1313   The King sent a mandate to the Sheriff of Gloucestershire, ordering him no longer to make a return of writs to the Mayor and Bailiffs of Bristol; and various petitions and complaints on both sides having been presented to the King, he appointed Thomas de Berkeley, John de Wylyngton, Richard de Abyngdon, and John de Button [*qu.* Burton], his justices, for the purpose of settling the privileges of the burgesses and commonalty, and of putting an end to the disturbance.   They met in the Guildhall; but the more numerous party objected to the jurisdiction, complaining of foreigners being associated in it, and appealed to the multitude without doors on the danger of utterly losing their liberties and privileges.   Ringing out the common town-bell, they raised a horrible clamour, and put a full stop to the business in hand; then, bursting into the Guildhall, they attacked those of the opposite party with fists and sticks. Nearly twenty men were killed on the spot, and so great was the terror, that many, rich and poor indiscriminately, made their escape out of the Hall through the windows, and, by leaping down into the street from the top of the pentise or leads, broke their legs, and were otherwise grievously wounded.   The Judges were in extreme danger; but at length the Mayor so far restrained the madness of the populace, that they were suffered to depart unhurt. About eighty persons were indicted for this riot before Henry Spigurnel and his fellows, the King's justices, at Gloucester; but, refusing to make their appearance, they were outlawed. Trusting, however, to the strength of the town, and being supported by the rest of the burgesses, who had now the management of the corporation in their own hands, they took measures of defence.   Notwithstanding the King's writ and mandate for their protection, William Randolph and the others of his party, with their wives and children, vassals and tenants, were by fear of violence driven out of the town; and the townsmen seized on wine, salt, and other property belonging to them, to the value of £2000.   Many of the King's bailiffs and officers, who ventured into the

A. D.

1313 town, they imprisoned for several weeks, and then drove them, with others, the King's servants, out of the town. The malcontents were evidently in too much strength to be subdued by the garrison of the Castle; but, to prevent a surprise, they built a wall and forts in the line of the present Dolphin-street, which was long afterwards called Defence-lane, and which probably extended through Wynch-street, on its north side, to the head of the Pithay. From this wall, and from several other streets in the town, they kept up an irregular warfare against the Castle, sometimes shooting into it square heavy arrows, called *quarels*, and other missive weapons. This state of rebellion continued for two years, the King's authority being held totally at nought; every mandate being received with contempt or neglect, as opposed to the civic rights and privileges.

1314 In the spring the Sheriffs of Gloucester, Somerset, and Wilts, collected upwards of 20,000 men, and the Earl of Gloucester took the command, in order to reduce the town to obedience; but John le Tavernor, the mayor, encouraged the townsmen to make a stout resistance, and the King having occasion for all the forces in his war with the Scots, the Earl received private orders not to proceed to extremities, and for the present raised the siege.

The King defeated at Bannock Bourn, where Thomas Lord Berkeley and his son were taken prisoners, in consequence of some Welshmen whom they commanded refusing to fight. See 1321.

The Earl of Marr released from Bristol Castle.

The eight bridges in Bristol at this time, mentioned in Constitutiones Villæ Bristolliæ, were, 1. Bristol Bridge, which passed from High-street; 2. St. Giles's Bridge, at the foot of Small-street; 3. Froom Bridge, under Christmas-street; 4. Monken, now Bridewell Bridge, leading to St. James's Priory; 5. Aylward's Bridge, at the foot of the Pithay; 6. a bridge in Merchant-street, leading northward from the Castle; 7. Ælle Bridge, at the end of the Broad Weir, leading to Ellbroad (Alle-Bridge)-street; 8. Castle Bridge, leading out of the Castle into the Old Market.

1316 After some further proceedings by way of enquiry, and a display of stubbornness by the commonalty, the town was actually besieged. Maurice de Berkeley was employed to cut off all communication by sea, while John de Cheriton, the King's chamberlain, Roger de Mortimer, John de Wyllyngton, and many other barons and knights, with Bartholomew de Baddlesmere, the constable, carried on the siege

1316 by land. Bulwarks were raised against the walls, and battering-engines were brought against them from the Castle. For four days the townsmen made resistance; but, when they found the walls and houses shaken by the engines, they surrendered themselves to the King's mercy. The besiegers entered the town, and the principal burgesses were thrown into prison, and many were sent to the Tower of London.

William de Randolph appointed Mayor.

Maurice, son of Thomas Lord Berkeley, custos of the town and castle, Simon Ward being his deputy.

Dec. The King signified his pleasure in council to grant the commonalty a pardon for all their past enormities, and ordered that for this pardon they should come to a fine. This was submitted to by a deputation of twelve to the King, carrying with them a letter patent under the common seal, dated the 20th, imploring the King's favour, which was granted upon submission to a fine of 4000 marks, half of which was to be paid at certain times then agreed on, and the other half to remain on good behaviour.

Such matters, in 1824, are better ordered by a Chamber of Commerce, and its bloodless war of rags, goose-quills, and lamp-black.

This year was such a dearth and famine, that the living could scarcely suffer to bury the dead. Horses and dogs' flesh was accounted good meat, and prisoners plucked and tore the flesh of such as came newly to prison, and devoured them half alive. Towards the borders of Scotland, men and women were obliged to eat their own children.

A duty was paid the King, for every sack of wool carried out of the port of Bristol, of half a mark; for every three hundred sheep-skins, half a mark; and for every last of hides, one mark. Martin Horncastle was collector and receiver.

1317 Under this date, in Memoirs, c. xv. § 3. b., Mr. Seyer notices a transaction of the 3d Maurice de Berkeley, relative to some houses and lands in the suburbs of Bristol, as "a specimen of the violent and rapacious means whereby the great men of that age laid their hands on the property of their neighbours who were not able to resist their power."

1318 June 8. According to a deed in possession of the Chamber of Bristol, it appears that, by a mandate of this date at Chisebury, from the Bishop of Worcester, an inquisition was held in All Saints' Church, into the rights, charters, and liberties of the fraternity of the Kalendaries, by which it

A. D.

1318 appeared that the beginning exceeded the memory of man; and the place of meeting of the brethren and sisters of the same was Christ-Church,* in the time of Aylward Sneau and Brictric his son, Lords of the said town before the Conquest. Afterward [1216] Robert Harding, by consent of King Henry and Earl Robert, connected it with the Church of All Saints; and, in a general council in Bristol, the King, and Gualo, cardinal of the apostolic see and general legate, approved and confirmed the said gild and fraternity, on account of its antiquity and goodness found therein; which Legate commanded and enjoined William de Bleys, Bishop of Worcester, and his successors, to protect the said gild, to the praise of God and all saints, and amendment of devotion and unity of the clergy and laity of Bristol. See 1333.

1319 The Chapel of St. Giles, which belonged to St. Leonard's Church (see 1301), being ruinous, was pulled down, and the chancel, bells, books, and vestments, destroyed.—William of Worcester mentions the parish of St. Egide in Small-street, which about this time was united with the parish of St. Leonard. It contained a chapel or temple for the use of the Jews, who had been banished from the whole kingdom in 1287. Quay-street, as already noted, was called Jewry-lane. St. John, St. Lawrence, St. Egide, and St. Leonard, stood in the circular wall of the old city. So lately as 1655-6 the Chamberlain's accounts mention St. Giles's Gate, with a tenement over it.

1320 The Bishop of Worcester, at a visitation of the Monastery of St. Augustin, ordered all the hounds kept by the monks to be removed—the almoner, frier Henry de Gloucester, to be displaced, and enquiry to be made concerning frier John de Scheftesbury, accused of incontinence with certain women unknown, and concerning William Barry, for sowing dissension among the brethren—that the sick be better provided for—that the brethren have a sufficiency, but in cash, as hath been accustomed—that the mass of the Blessed Virgin be duly and solemnly celebrated—that the forty pence be distributed in the convent, and not be detained by the prior or sub-prior—that William Barry, under a sentence of excommunication for apostacy, be absolved, and that his penance of drinking water only, which he has done constantly on a Wednesday, be dispensed with, and that he may drink beer and eat pulse, but abstain from eating fish.

* Meaning, as we believe, the *parish* of Christ-Church. See note to A. D. 700.

A. D.

1320   The day before the ides of July was consecrated the
Convent of the Brothers Eremites of St. Augustin, within
Temple-Gate on the north side, founded by Sir Simon and
Sir William Montacute.*   The church was very small.

The King granted to Hugh Despenser the younger the
castle and town of Bristol, he paying therefrom £210.

1321   The King, being early in this year at Bristol, issued orders
for the preservation of the peace of the town to Thomas
de Berkeley, who was probably constable of the Castle.

July 23, Thomas (2), lord Berkeley, died, in his 76th
year, at Berkeley Castle: He was buried with his wife, in
the south aisle of the Monastery, in the arch between the
vestry and the south aisle. He was succeeded by his
son, the third Maurice, who was married at eight years and
father of a child at fourteen years old. His first wife, Eve,
the daughter of Eudo de la Zouche, was buried at Portbury,
in 1314. His second wife, Isabel, daughter of Robert Clare,
earl of Gloucester, died in 1338. " Bedminster was his
first seat, where, and at Nailsea, from his marriage till
he reached about twenty years, he much frequented those
downs in all martial exercises, running with lances,
hastiludes, spear-plays, and the like, suitable to those
active times." Sir Richard Baker says that Lord Maurice
Berkeley was at this time among the Barons opposed
to the King, in consequence of his attachment to the
two Spencers; but, seeing the King's power increasing,
he, with the two Roger Mortimers, Lord Hugh Audley,
and others, yielded to the King's mercy. They were notwithstanding sent to divers prisons. Lord Maurice was sent
to Wallingford Castle. See 1326.

1322   Feb. 17, the King, at Gloucester, confirmed the Charter
of 1300—Seyer's No. 7.

March 16, was fought the battle of Burrowbridge, in
Yorkshire.

March 22, Thomas, earl of Lancaster, was beheaded at
his own castle of Pontefract; and among his partizans, who
were executed in different parts of the kingdom, Sir Henry

---

* A piece of ground, whereon are built the houses, east side of Marlborough Hill (late
Bull Hill), was formerly called The Montagues, probably in right of or compliment to these
brothers or their family.—What reader, who lives either by " good eating," or by eating
what is good, can mount this hill without some of the fondest, most grateful recollections?

     " I do remember a RESTAURATEUR,
     " And hereabout he dwelt."—ROMEO AND JULIET.
     " - - - - - Birnam* - - - - - - ."—MACBETH.

* I would wager the price of this dry volume, dished up as it is to feed all posterity, against the cost of
one of Master Pring's " feasts of reason" or reasonable feasts for a single day, that Shakespeare and
WE here mean his predecessor, honest and honourable JOHN BURNHAM.—PR. DAY.

A. D.

1322 Womyngton and Sir Henry Montfort, bannerets, suffered in Bristol.

Sir Henry Womynton, or Willington, or de Wyllington, was lord of the manor of Culverden, Gloucestershire. In the following year orders were issued to arrest persons who pretended that miracles were done over his body.

Sir Bartholomew Baddlesmere (who had deserted the cause of the King) was taken at Stow Park, in the manor of the Bishop of Lincoln, who was his nephew, and hanged near Canterbury, April 14.

Peace in the Monastery now restored, and the dispute with the brethren of St. Mark's, about the cemetery, settled.

1324 The Queen, Isabel, with her son, Prince Edward, went to France, with the Bishop of Exeter in her suite. Here she favoured the young Roger Mortimer, earl of March, who had recently escaped from the Tower of London; and the Bishop secretly returned to the King with the news.

The old Lord Mortimer, uncle of the above, after five years' imprisonment, died, and was brought to Bristol and buried.

This year Lawford's Gate (in the Saxon called Hlaford's Gate*) was kept by William Corbet, of Chadsley, who held a tenement there for this service. The custody of Kingswood forest was about this time granted to Thomas de Bradestone. The forester of this chase then received from the Constable of Bristol Castle the wages of sevenpence-halfpenny a day.

1325 The Queen and all her adherents declared enemies to the kingdom.

* " I find that our ancestors vsed, for.*Lord*, the name of *Laford*, which (as it should seeme), for some aspiration in the pronouncing, they wrote *Hlaford*, and *Hlafurd*. Afterward it grew to be written *Louerd*, and by receiuing like abridgment, as other our ancient appellations haue done, it is in one syllable become *Lord*.

" To deliuer hereof the true etymologie, the reader shall vnderstand that, albeit wee haue our name of *bread* from *breod*, as our ancestors were wont to call it, yet vsed they also, and that most commonly, to call *bread* by the name of *hlaf*; from whence wee now only retain the name of the forme or fashion wherein *bread* is vsually made, calling it a *loaf*; whereas *loaf*, comming of *hlaf* or laf, is rightly also bread it selfe, and was not of our ancestors taken for the forme only, as now we vse it.

" Now was it vsuall, in long foregoing ages, that such as were endued with great wealth and meanes above others, were chiefly renowmed (especially in these northern regions) for their housekeeping, and good hospitalitie; that is, for being able and vsing to feed and sustaine many men, and therefore were they particularly honoured with the name and title of HLAFORD, which is as much as to say, as, *An afoorder of laf*; that is, *A bread giuer*, intending (as it seemeth) by *bread*, the sustenance of man; that being the substance of our food, the most agreeable to nature, and that which in our daily prayers we especially desire at the hands of God."—*A Restitution of Decayed Intelligence: In antiquities. Concerning the most noble and renowned English Nation. By the studie and trauell of* R[ICHARD]. V[ERSTEGAN]. 4to. pp. 374. 1628.

A. D.

"Donald, earl of Marr, was made guardian of the Castle of Bristol, being a Scot; which he kept until Q. Isabell presented King Edward the 2d before it, to whom he then delivered it, and returned into Scotland."

1326 May 31, Maurice (3), lord Berkeley, aged 46, died a prisoner in Wallingford Castle, where he was interred; but his body was afterward brought to the Monastery, and buried in the south aisle, opposite to the then choir-door, immediately within the wooden screen. He was succeeded in the barony by his son, the third Thomas, now 30 years old, whose wife was Margaret, daughter of Roger Mortimer,* earl of March, whom he had married about St. James's Day, 13 Edward II. He was a prisoner with his father at this time, but was released on the 16th of October, out of Pevensey Castle, by order of Queen Isabella. "In 6 Edw. II. he purchased divers houses and lands in Bristol, of several persons, by divers deeds." See 1348.

The Queen married her son to Philippa, daughter of the Earl of Hainault; and, raising an army of 300 men, Sept. 22, landed in Essex. Marching from Oxford by way of Gloucester, she besieged Bristol, arriving here Oct. 22; and, on promise of being received into the Queen and Prince's protection, the citizens delivered the town and castle to the Earl of Kent.

"Oct. 25, Sir Hugh Spencer, the father, [aged 90,] was drawen, hanged, and behedded at Bristowe, and his body hanged up with two strong cordes; and after four dayes it was cut to pieces, and dogges did ete it; and, because he was Count of Wynchester, his hedde was sent thither."—LELAND.

Previous hereto, upon the approach of the Queen, and not knowing where to look for friends, the King and Hugh the son, (Earl of Warwick,) early in the morning of Oct. 16 entered a little vessel behind the Castle (sailing out at the port which still remains†), with design to get to the Island of Lundy in the Bristol Channel, a place plentiful of provision, abounding with conies, fish and fowl, and the island hard of access, as having but one place in it where it could be entered, and that so narrow that a few might easily keep

---

* She died 5th May 1337, and was buried in the great tomb under the arch between the Elder Lady's Chapel and the north aisle. See 1368.

† A ship sailing out of such a port furnished the device for the present arms of the city. When it superseded the ruder device of a double tower and warder, or watchman, looking out from the battlement, preserved in the front of the Guildhall, we have yet to learn.

326out many. But meeting with contrary winds, having first landed at Chepstow, where they heard of the design to pursue them, after fifteen days they landed on the coast of Glamorgan, where the King kept himself close concealed in the Abbey of Neath. Hugh defended himself in Caerphilly Castle, but was at length obliged to capitulate to the Queen's forces, with a promise of safety as to life and limb. After which he rejoined the King; but, on the 16th of November, with other attendants, (Chancellor Baldock, Simon de Reading, and a few others,) both were retaken. On the 10th, the King had sent the Abbot and others on a message to the Queen, and received a letter of protection and safe conduct; notwithstanding on the 20th, at Monmouth Castle, the great seal was forced from him. Thence they were all brought by Sir Henry Beaumont, to Hereford; whither the Queen had removed from Bristol, after the execution of the elder Spencer. Nov. 24, about a mile from Hereford, Hugh Spencer the younger was drawn, hanged on a gallows fifty feet high, and quartered, his head sent to be set upon London Bridge, and his four quarters bestowed in several cities. Simon of Reading suffered on the same gallows, ten feet lower; but the Chancellor Baldock was committed to Newgate, London, where he shortly afterward died.

Immediately after Christmas the Parliament agreed to depose the King and set up his son.

1327 Jan. 25, at Kenilworth Castle, a formal resignation was extorted from the King, by the Bishops of Winchester, Hereford, and Lincoln, assisted by William Prussell, Speaker of the Parliament.

EDWARD III. *surnamed* WINDSOR.

Aged fourteen years.

Lord Mortimer created Earl of March.

Edward II., after his deposition, was kept a close prisoner in Kenilworth Castle; whence he was removed, in April, to Corfe Castle, and then to Bristol Castle, where he remained closely confined until it was discovered that some of the town had formed a resolution to assist him in making his escape beyond sea. Upon this discovery he was removed by his keepers, Sir John Maltravers and Sir Thomas Gurney, to Berkeley Castle. "These champions," says Stowe, " bring Edward towards Berkeley, being guarded by a rabble of hell-hounds, along by the grange belonging

L

A. D.

1327 to the Castle of Bristowe; where that wicked man Gorney, making a crowne of haye, put it on his head; and the soldiers that were present mocked him, saying, ' Tprut, avaunt, Sir Kinge!' making a kind of noise with their mouths as if they broke wind backwards. They feared to be met of any that should knowe Edward; they bent their journey towards the left hande, riding over the marish-grounds lying by the river Severne; moreover, desiring to disfigure him that he should not be known, they determined to shave his head and beard; wherefore, as they travelled by a little water that ran in a ditch, they commanded him to lyghte from his horse to be shaven with the said cold water by the barber, who said that ' that water must serve for this time.' Edward answered, ' would they, nould they, he would have warm water for his beard,' so shed tears plentifully."—The deposed King arrived at Berkeley Castle on the 5th of April, and Lord Berkeley was ordered to use no familiarity with him, but deliver up the Castle to Maltravers and Gurney; which he did. His Lordship retired to a house in the Park, which was, it is supposed, his *secret house*, or *lodge*,—a place where at certain times of the year the nobility retired, dismissed part of their servants on visits to their friends, put the rest on board-wages, and permitted nobody to speak to themselves. The King was confined in a small room on the right hand of the keep-staircase, where a cast of *K. Charles I.* is still shewn for him; £5 a day was allowed for his board. He was now in the 43d year of his age. On the 22d of September his keepers put their bloody orders into execution, by thrusting a red hot iron through a horn pipe up his fundament; which burnt his bowels; and by this horrible murder the unhappy Prince expired. In order to conceal their execrable deed, the two murderers sent for some of the inhabitants of Bristol and Gloucester to examine the body; and there appearing no marks of violence, they concluded he died a natural death. This examination was carefully attested by witnesses, and immediately dispersed over the whole kingdom.* His heart was now put in a silver vessel, and the Berkeley family attended the carriage which conveyed the Royal corpse to Gloucester, where he was buried, Dec. 20, in the Monastery of St. Peter's, by the

---

* For having been thus surreptitiously made parties to a deed so atrocious, it would appear that the citizens of Bristol thought they could not do enough to mark their veneration for the memory of the unfortunate monarch. There are still (1824) in existence more sculptured memorials of Edward II., scattered throughout the remains of ancient buildings, than of all our other sovereigns united. One may be seen in the

A. D.

1327 Benedictine friers. Lord Berkeley was afterwards (when, in 1330, the young King, becoming convinced of Mortimer's familiarity with his mother, exhibited articles against him in Parliament for the murder) tried for his participation in the crime, and pleaded that he was sick at Bradley, and had lost his memory. Though it is plain he had no concern in the very act, because he was sent from the Castle on account of his compassion, yet Mr. Smythe (the family-historian of Berkeley) says that the plea was untrue, because he did not go to Bradley till Michaelmas, and sent Gurney, the regicide, at the very time, with letters to the Queen and Mortimer, at Nottingham Castle; and, by a second direction from them, kept the King's decease secret till All-Saints' day following. One of this unhappy monarch's faults was, that he was much given to drink. This, superadded to his overweening attachment to favourites, who perhaps encouraged his propensity, may account for the progressive contempt to which he at last fell a victim.

1329 Edmund, earl of Kent, the King's uncle, beheaded, for intending the restoration of Edward II.

1330 Mortimer, found guilty of procuring Edward's death, of familiarity with Queen Isabel, and other crimes, was drawn, and hanged at the Elmes, since called Tyburn, for two days. The Queen-mother herself was confined to a castle, where she remained for thirty years, till her death.

The King this year granted to the Mayor and Burgesses of Bristol a confirmation of all their charters and liberties, including the provision in the Charter of 31 Henry III., "that Radclive-street should answer unto and be within the jurisdiction of the Burgesses of Bristol, and nowhere else." See Mr. Seyer's Memoirs, c. xv. § 3 c.—7, for examples of the revived public spirit of the citizens in opposition to the influence of the Berkeley family. See 1373 for the final determination of these disputes, in the precise definition of the extent of the city and liberties.

Seventy families of cloth-workers, from the Netherlands, settled in England, by the King's invitation. See 1340.

1331 Oct. 16, at Westminster, the King confirmed the Charters of 1247 and 1322, and farther provided for the indemnity of orphans and minors against waste and fraud by their

arched ceiling of St. Nicholas crypt; another, as a corbel, in the kitchen of the Giants' Castle public-house, Temple-street, formerly one of the trading-halls; another, from the house occupied by Mr. Orlidge, in Small-street, was affixed by Mr. E. Hodges over a gothic door-way in the back-court of Dr. Ridley's prebendal-house; and the Chamberlain possesses one, taken from the large room of the late Mulberry-Tree tavern, in Broad-street. The entire catalogue would be long.

A. D.

1331 guardians—also secured to the burgesses the view of frank-pledge in their own courts, meaning the suretyship for each other's loyalty and good behaviour, which was generally held by the sheriff or other officer of the King, or by the lord at the leet.

1332   Abbot Knowles died.   His tomb is in the north wall, before the place of the rood high altar—his figure in pontificals, lying on his back, with a crosier in his hand and a mitre on his breast.   He was succeeded by John Snow, the thirteenth abbot and first president of the Abbey summoned to attend a Parliament.

1333   The Abbot granted the fraternity of the Kalendaries permission to rebuild and enlarge their house towards Corn-street.   See 1340.

1334   The merchants of Gascoyne complained to the King in Parliament of outrages committed against them in many parts of England, particularly in London and Bristowe.   See 1347.

1336   May 17, an inquisition was taken in the Castle, relating to the right of patronage of the House of St. Mark, before Hugh le Hunte, the deputy-constable.   See 1487.

So great was the plenty this year, that wheat was at 3d. a bushel; a fat ox, 6s. 8d.; a fat sheep, 7d.; six pigeons, 1d.; a fat goose, 2d.; a pig, 1d.

1337   In this year it is probable was the great tomb erected in the Monastery, to receive the body of Margaret, wife of the third Thomas, Lord Berkeley.   See 1361.

1338   Richard de Kingheston, Constable of the Castle.

A Charter granted to the fraternity of Tailors.   See 1398.

1340   " This year the King met with the French navy upon the sea, and in the fight slew 30,000 men and took 200 ships. The rest fled."—The King quartered the arms of England with those of France, and took the motto, *Dieu et mon droit.*

The woollen manufacture was first introduced here about this time, principally in Tucker-street and Temple-street. See " Memoirs," c. xv. § 12, 13.

July 10, an inquisition was taken by Wulstan, bishop of Worcester, in Bristol; after which it was ordained that the brethren of the Kalendaries, clergy and laity, were to meet on the first Monday in every month.   See 1434.

1341   July 12, died Abbot Snow.   Ralph Asche was the thirteenth Abbot; who petitioned to be exempt from the necessity of attending Parliaments, because it was productive of intolerable burthens to the revenues of the house over which he presided.

Thomas Blanket was one of the Bailiffs this year.

A. D.

1342 Temple Church was made a vicarage, by Ralph, bishop of Bath and Wells. See 1390.

1345 William de Coleford, recorder of Bristol, drew up in writing the laws and liberties of the town. No leprous man to stay within the precincts, nor any common woman. If such were found, the doors and windows to be unhung and carried by the Mayor's sergeants to the house of the constable of the ward, and there to be kept till the woman was removed. No w——e to appear in the streets, nor even to appear within the *bars* in St. James's, without her head being covered, &c.

"Esquire" first appended to the names of persons of fortune not attendant on knights.

1346 Cannon (invented 1330) first used by the English, at the siege of Calais.

The battle of Cressy fought, Aug. 26.

1347 Agnes de Gloucester, prioress of St. Mary Magdalen, Bristol —brother John, rector, and the Bishop of Worcester, patron.

Great troubles ensued to Lord Berkeley in delivering the gaols in the County of Gloucester, " wherein none proved more troublesome than the appearinge and punishinge of a very great assembly of most riotous and rebellious persons of the countyes of Gloucester, Somerset, and Bristol, who had (as the record speaks) taken upon them regall powers, and chosen a captaine, in the nature of a kinge, to govern them, and, after proclamation by them made, had entered upon divers ships, laden with corne and other provisions, ready to goe, by the King's command, into Gascoigne, and by violence had taken the same away, and had beaten and wounded divers of the mariners."

April 24, at Reading, witness Lionel, the King's third but second surviving son (not nine years old), guardian of the realm during the King's absence at the siege of Calais, a Charter was granted (Seyer's No. 11), giving leave to erect a place of confinement for very many evil-doers and disturbers of the peace, wandering and running about, by day and night, in the town of Bristol, doing harms, mischiefs and excesses, in various ways; and, for the better keeping the assize of bread, the Mayor, &c. were empowered to draw bakers who offended upon sledges through the streets, and otherwise punish them, as practised in like manner with regard to such bakers in London.—The cage for the bakers, thus placed as between two grindstones, (the rage of a populace dreading starvation, and a lively market,) was in the meal-market, now the Guard-house, Wine-street.

A. D.

1347 August. Calais surrendered. " This was [part of] the roll of Edward's fleet at the siege:*

Weymouth, 20 ships, 204 men	Bristol, 23 ships, 608 men
Lyme 4 —— 62 ——	London 25 —— 662 ——
Poole 4 —— 94 ——	Seaton 2 —— 25 ——"
Wareham 3 —— 59 ——	

1348 Famine's sister, the Plague, " passed into Devonshire, Somersetshire, and Bristol, and raged so that the Gloucestershire men would not suffer the Bristol men to have access unto them, or into their country, by any means; but at length it came to Gloucester, then to Oxford, and finally spread over all England; and (says Stowe) so wasted and spoyled the people, that scarce the tenth person of all sorts was left alive."

The grass grew several inches high in High-street and Broad-street. See " Memoirs," c. xv. § 19—23.

April 25, Thomas (3) Lord Berkeley founded a perpetual chantry in the abbacy of St. Augustin. See 1361.

1349 Edward Blanket one of the Bailiffs. See " Memoirs," c. xv. § 12.

1350 Stephen Snowgale gave to All Saints' Parish a tenement in All Saints' Lane, which was made convenient for an almshouse, to receive eight old women. See 1739.

1351 Lucy de New Chirche repeatedly offered to the Bishop of Worcester, and desired leave, to be shut up in the hermitage of St. Brendan, of Bristol, and to quit the world; which, after due enquiry into her conduct and purity of life, and necessary virtues for it, was granted her on the 7th of May. She held a piece of ground and a croft near the ground of St. Brendan. (A local saintship, probably ascribed to the first hermit.) See 1403.

---

* Mr. Page possesses a parchment-roll, measuring 18 feet 15 inches by 8¾ inches, thus headed:—" Hereafter followeth the names and Armes of the principal Capitains as well of Noblemen as of Knights that were with the victorious Prince King Edward at the asciege of Callis ye ivth yere of his reigne." The arms, fully emblazoned, comprise 117 shields, beginning with those of the King and Princes Edward and Henry, and ending with that of Sir Peter Despayne, and are accompanied by an enumeration of the number of armed men of different classes under each commander. The reverse contains " The rates of wages of peace and warre expencis necessarye of officers and other charges concerning the howshold of the Prynce, during the expedition;" a list of " The south Flete," enumerating fifty-one ports, that supplied 448 ships and 4630 men, and the " North Flete," of thirty-three ports, (the chief of which was Yarmouth, 43 ships and 1415 men), supplying together 217 ships, 4521 men. Grand total of the English fleet, 665 ships, 9151 men. " Estrangers," from " Bayon, Spayne, Ireland, Flaunders, and Gelderland," 38 ships, 805 men. Sum of all the army, 37,346. These occupy the entire length of the roll.

A. D.

1353 March 1, died Abbot Ralph Asche, who was buried in the middle of the choir. William Coke, or Cooke, the fifteenth Abbot.—Mr. Barrett, in p. 259 of his History, gives the translation of a Latin deed, dated March 7, which describes the form observed in electing the Abbot, under license of the patron, Queen Philippa.

1353 and 1354. Richard Spicer, Mayor; who founded the Chapel of St. George, adjoining the Guildhall.*

1356 Sept. 19, the battle of Poictiers. See 1361.

1357 Walter le Frampton, Mayor, who was the founder of the present St. John's Church. See 1174. He is styled, by William of Worcester, *mercator nobilis.*

1360 A chapel across the centre of Bristol Bridge, dedicated to the Virgin, was completed—said to have been founded by Edward and Philippa; but the expense of erecting and supporting it was defrayed by the citizens. Its dimensions were twenty-five yards by seven yards; and it contained four great windows on each side, a high window over the altar, and a small chapel with an altar on each side. Under it was an arched room of the same extent, for the use of the aldermen of the town. The chapel was dedicated Feb. 4, 1361. See 1644.

Queen Philippa granted to Edmund Flambard the constableship of the Castle, which he resigned; and she then gave the appointment to Robert de Foulehurst, which the King confirmed.

1361 Richard Brandon, Mayor; William Canynges one of the Bailiffs. See 1369. William Younge, M.P. Of his son, see 1411.

Oct. 27, Thomas (3), lord Berkeley, died, aged 68. He was buried in Berkeley Church. His eldest son, the fourth Maurice and ninth Baron, married in August, 12 Edward III., Elizabeth, daughter of Hugh Lord Spencer.. It is recorded

* Stephen le Spicer was Mayor in 1338, 1343, 1344—John le Spicer, in 1348, 1351 —Richard Spicer in 1353, 1354, and 1371. See 1377.

Under 1313 (p. 74) is the earliest mention of the Guildhall. Unless accident has thrown any record of it in the way of Mr. Seyer, the date of erection is entirely lost. The front taken down in 1813 was built preparatory to Queen Elizabeth's visit in 1574, when the present corbel-heads, twenty in number, affixed to the wooden arches of the ceiling, were purchased (probably from the ruins of the religious houses then recently demolished) for forty shillings. The rudeness of construction in the beams and arches is evidence of very remote antiquity.

The ancient arms of the city placed in the centre of the front of the Guildhall, alluded to in the note at p. 80, should have been described, more properly, as the front-gate of a castle, with its moat, but without a drawbridge. On one side of the gate, within the walls, is a large square tower or donjon; on the other, a smaller tower, with the figure, on its top, of a page or warder, in the act of sounding a trumpet. See the "Charges of the Enterteignement of the Queenes Majestie, &c." under 1574.

A. D.

1361 of this lady, that in the year of her husband's sickness she made a new gown for herself, of cloth, furred throughout with cony-skins out of the kitchen. He was wounded by a sword that passed through both his thighs, at the battle of Poictiers, 19th Sept. 1356. He remained a year at the house, in Picardy, of the 'squire who wounded him, before he was well enough to return, and then paid 6000 nobles for his ransom. See 1368.

    Sir Thomas de Berkeley died this year, and was buried in St. Mark's Chapel. The statues of Sir Thomas and his lady (daughter of John Lord Bottetourt) were restored from the obscurity of white and yellow washing by the taste of John Haythorne, Esq., Mayor, in 1819.

1362 The staple of wool established here by the King. The Mayor had the addition of " Mayor of the Staple of Bristol," and held a court called the Staple Court.*

    Edward Blanket was M. P. for Bristol this year.†

1363 Abbot Cook resigned, in October.

    The Monastery completed; Lord Maurice (4) of Berkeley liberally assisted. See 1368.

1364 April 8, Abbot Cook died. He was buried before the door of the Lady's Chapel; a cross and skull cover his grave. Henry Shallynford, alias Bleburne, became the sixteenth abbot.

1366 Sir John de Gourney, lord of Knowle, granted the ground for an aqueduct from Pile - Hill to Temple - Gate, near the friery of the Brothers Eremite of St. Augustin, from a fountain called Raveneswell, at a place called Hales.

1368 June 8, Maurice (4), lord Berkeley, aged 37 years, died at Berkeley, of his wounds at the battle of Poictiers, and lies with his mother (who died May 5, 1337) in the great tomb under the arch between the old Chapel of Our Lady and the north aisle. He was succeeded by his eldest son, the fourth Thomas, born Jan. 5, 1352; who married Margaret, daughter of Warren de Lisle. See 1417.

    Aug. 20, Hugh Segrave appointed Constable of the Castle.

   * See Fuller's History of the Revival by Edward III. of the Trade of Clothing throughout the kingdom, as quoted by the Rev. Dudley Fosbroke, in his Abstracts of Records and MSS. respecting the County of Gloucester, &c. i. 33; also his notice of the origin of the family-name of Webb.

   † At the Dissolution, St. Stephen's Church contained four chantries,—two founded by Richard White, one by Edward Blanket, and the other by Thomas Belcher. There were three of the Blanket family: Edward, Edmund, and Thomas. They were the first who manufactured that comfortable appendage to a bed, the BLANKET. Cervantes makes his Sancho Panza laud " the man who first invented *sleep*." That redoubted 'squire would not have forgotten to praise the men who contributed so important a preservative of sleep—the veritable mantle of Somnus.

A. D.

1369 Aug. 15, Queen Philippa died. Her Majesty's person would seem to have been regarded in Bristol with much esteem. Sculptured likenesses of her head, in stone, still remain (1824) in St. Philip's Church, and in the crypt of St. Nicholas. One other head of a female, in St. Philip's, was probably designed for Joanna of Navarre. See 1401. Queen Philippa's head, with that of the King, still support the arch of the west entrance, under the tower, of St. Michael's Church, and held a correspondent station under the tower of the late Clifton Church.

William Canynges one of the Bailiffs this year. He was the original founder of the present Redcliff Church, which was finished by his grandson, the Dean of Westbury, in the reign of Edward IV. See 1375.

1371 Richard Spicer, Mayor.

The King demised the town to Walter de Derby and Henry Derneford, for one year,—the garden below the Castle and the garden towards the Barton only excepted,—for 100l. "The garden below the Castle" we conjecture to have been that afterwards called William of Worcester's garden, to the southward of Old Market-street; and "the garden towards the Barton," the ground now occupied by the east-side of Old King-street, &c. See "Memoirs," c. xv. § 27.

The King sent a letter to the Bishop of Worcester, ordering him to visit the Monastery of St. Augustin; as Abbot Henry had wasted the rents, by excessive charges and other mismanagement, whereby divine service was almost at an end, all almsgiving ceased, and the canons nearly dispersed, for want of support.

1372 Walter Derby and John Stoke, the last burgesses of Bristol returned to Parliament by the Sheriffs of Gloucestershire.

1373 Aug. 8, at Woodstock, the King granted a Charter (Seyer's No. 12), at the petition of the Mayor and Commonalty, in consideration of the inconvenient distance of the towns of Gloucester and Ilchester, of the good behaviour of the burgesses, and the services in times past of their shipping and other things, and of the sum of 600 marks (£400),—

That the town of Bristol be for ever separated from the counties of Gloucester and Somerset, and that it be a county of itself, called the *County of Bristol;* and that the Burgesses enjoy, within certain metes and bounds, the following liberties and acquittances, viz. The Mayor to be escheator, with one Sheriff, to account at the Exchequer, holding a county-court from month to month on Monday—the Mayor to hold a court for collection of accustomed

M

1373profits—to account by their attorney, and not go out of the town
for that purpose—the Mayor to be sworn before his predecessor in
the Guildhall, without being presented to the Constable of the
Castle—the Sheriff to make oath by writ of *dedimus potestatem* before
the Mayor—the Mayor and Sheriff to hear and determine causes
concerning all manner of misdemeanours, trespasses, disturbances
against the peace, champerties,* conspiracies, confederacies, am-
bidextries,† extortions, oppressions, counterfeitings, and other
misprisions, whatever, and concerning victuallers, workmen, labourers and artificers, and to punish transgressors by fines, amerce-
ment, and imprisonment, and make due executions—estreats of
fines to the Crown to be delivered at the Exchequer on the morrow
of St. Michael—the Mayor and Sheriff also to hear and determine
felonies, make arrests and commitments, deliver the gaol, and
have power to replevy—the Burgesses to have the keeping of the
gaol—to have infangthiefe and outfangthiefe‡—the Sheriff and
Coroner to have power to receive appeals of death and all other
felonies, and arrest the offenders for trial—the Mayor and Sheriff to
have cognizance of all pleas, &c. with respect to lands, tenements,
rents and tenures, and of all trespasses; but pleas in the Tolzey
Court still to be held before the King's Steward, &c.—no other
justices or officers to interfere except in cases of errors and of sub-
sidies—the Mayor to have power to recognize deeds for record,
with power to levy fines—the Mayor and Sheriff permitted to
receive probates of wills and put them in execution—writs to be
directed to the Officers of Bristol—the town not to send more than
two men to Parliament, who shall answer both as knights of the
county and as burgesses of the town and borough of Bristol—
" and that, if in any usages or customs or rules had and practised
arising anew in the said town of Bristol, its suburbs and precincts,
there shall be any difficulties or defects in which no remedy is yet
applied, the same Mayor and Sheriff, and their successors, with the
assent of the Commonalty of the town and its suburbs and precincts,
shall be empowered to elect successively, from time to time, forty
men of the better and more honest men of the same town, suburbs,
and precincts; which Mayor, Sheriff, and forty men, for the time
being, by their common consent, shall have power of ordaining and
establishing a competent remedy in the cases aforesaid, such as shall
be reasonable and useful to the commonalty aforesaid, and to others
who resort to the town of Bristol"—the Mayor, &c. to have power
to levy rates and taxes—two Treasurers to be appointed, who shall
be accountable before the Mayor for the time being; and others to

---

* A species of *maintenance*, whereby a person agrees to assist another in the recovery of land, &c. by law, on condition of receiving a part of the land, &c.—See
BENTHAM *on Usury*, Letter 12.

† The taking from both parties for giving a verdict.

‡ Privilege to the lord of a manor, of judging a thief taken within his fee, and of
reclaiming a thief taken out of his jurisdiction, and judging him in his own court—an-
tiquated, and long since gone.

A.D.

1373 be deputed for the purpose by the commonalty of the town. And if any of the town, or of the forty men, be disobedient to the ordinances of the said Mayor, Sheriff, and forty men, or " procurers, abettors, or maintainers, for the purpose of drawing the men of that company to make debates and hindrances, from whence discord may arise between the commonalty and the Mayor and Sheriff and other officers, or for the purpose of making rebates and discord about the election of Mayor, Sheriff, or other officer," they shall be punished in due manner by the Mayor and Sheriff, according to the law and custom of the kingdom.

Sept. 1, letters patent were issued from Westminster, appointing that commissioners should make a perambulation, for the purpose of placing certain marks, metes and divisions, which may be known for ever, between the precincts of the County of Bristol [see 1186] and the Counties of Gloucester and Somerset, and certify the same in Chancery.

Sept. 30. The Perambulation of the Bounds now returned to Chancery states that, the King's letters patent and writs being directed to his Reverend Fathers in Christ, John, bishop of Bath and Wells, and William, bishop of Worcester, and his beloved in Christ, Walter, abbot of Glastonbury, and Nicholas, abbot of Cirencester, and his faithful Edmund Cliveden, Richard de Acton, Theobald Gorges, Henry Percehay, Walter Clopton, and John Sergaunt,—each of the Sheriffs of Gloucestershire and Somersetshire, and the Mayor of Bristol, came to Temple Gate, in the confines of the three counties, on Friday the morrow of St. Michael, and returned a pannel of twenty-four as well good knights as other good and lawful men, for this purpose; and proclamation being made, &c. the justices and twelve men of each county proceeded to make the perambulation,* on the metes and divisions of the outside of the precincts of the County of Bristol. Beginning at Tower Harratz, the following are the names of places that occur in the course of the perambulation (for the more minute particulars of which, but with change of many of the names and numbers of the stones, we cannot do better than refer to Barrett's History), viz.

The ditch of Hales Croft (see 1366), on the road from Temple Gate towards Bath ; Pill or Pile-Hill Bridge ; a spring near it ; Aldeburiham, in the road to Pensford ; a meadow called Ware-mead ;

* The Jurors of Bristol were Robert Chedre, mayor in 1362 ; Walter Frampton, mayor in 1365 and 1374 ; Walter Derby, mayor in 1363 and 1367 ; Elias Spiller, mayor in 1369 ; Richard Brandon, mayor in 1361 ; William Combe, bailiff in 1350 ; John Jackson the Elder ; William Woodford, bailiff in 1363 ; William Somerwell, mayor in 1360 and 1361 ; John Vyell, bailiff in 1368, sole sheriff under William Canynges in 1372, 1373, and mayor in 1388 ; Henry Vyell, and John Somerwell.

A. D.

1373 a croft that belonged to the fraternity of Satinors (of whom we
believe there is no other mention); Red Lane; Ergle Croft; path
from Knolle to Redcliff-Church; east corner of the church-yard;
Langcroft, belonging to the Hospital of St. John the Baptist;
Langmead; a gutter and trench along Lokeing Croft (the same
with Bedminster Brook); the middle of Brightnee (or Bright Bow)
Bridge; Katharine Mead; Cardiff's Croft; Trenelly-Mill; Bishop's
Worth Brook; the pool of Trene Mill; the margin of the water of
the Avon, to Crockerne Pill; the margin of the water of the Severn,
to Portishead-Ford; a rock called Clevedon's Hoe; north corner of
the island called Steep Holme, "which island is the division between
Somersetshire on the southern part, Bristol on the eastern part, and
Gloucestershire on the northern part;" northward to the south
corner of the Flat Holme; eastward to the south corner of the little
island called the Duny; eastward to Avon road, on the north side
of the water of Avon; eastward on the river-side to a stone east
of a rivulet called Woodwill's Lake (running from Jacob's Well);
northward along its course to a conduit of the Abbot of St. Austin's
(Jacob's Well); northward along Woodwill's Lane; Langcroft
Wall; Bartholomew's Close (now Berkeley Crescent, &c.); Fokeing
(alias Pucking) Grove; Cantoke's Close (now part of Tyndall's
Park); a croft belonging to the houses of the religious of Magdalen
and Bartholomew of Bristol; the highway from Bristol to Henbury;
Bewell's Cross (the stone in the late Gallows Field); Bewell's Well
(the pump in Cotham); Brompton's Close (the site of Clarence Place,
Paul-street, &c.) the Mill Lane (Cottle-street); Prior's Croft (the
north-west side of Southwell-street); Maudlin-lane (now Horfield
Road, continued over Colston's Mount, back of the Montague
Tavern); Prior's Croft (top of Bull or Marlborough Hill); Prior's
Orchard (since called the Montagues); Doucer Croft (within Hill-
grove-street); high road from Bristol to Thornbury (now Stoke's
Croft); path called Apsherd (the way to Nine-tree Hill); Mere
Furlong, and a ditch afterward called Shuter's Ditch; a close called
Beane-flower Croft; a croft called Longesden's Land; Cock's Croft;
Piked Croft; the road from Bristol to Stoke; Wrington's Croft;
road from Bristol to Lekenbridge (since called Wilder-street, after
Peter Wilder, a land-holder); road to the Key-Pipe Conduit (still in
existence, between the Orphan-Asylum and Baptist Mills); a spring
called Begger-Well; the ditch of a garden called Ditche's Orchard
(now Newfoundland-lane); thence (through East-street, across the
feather-stream or back-ditch) to the river Froom, and along its north
bank (the Rope-walk), crossing the river within Quaker's Bridge and
New-street to Lawford's Gate; thence eastward, to a corner of a
stone in a ditch; thence westward, to the south side of St. Philip's
Church-yard; corner of the King's Orchard; St. Philip's Lane;
ditch of the Castle of Bristol; nether-gate (end of Castle-street);
north side of the ditch to New Gate; the moat-ditch (crossing
between St. Peter-street and Castle-street) into the Avon; eastward,
to the end of the common wall of the town, extending westward to

. D.

73Tower Harratz, where the perambulation began. The subscribing witnesses were Robert Chedre and Walter Frampton, of Bristol; Ralph Wales and John Crooke, of Gloucestershire; and John Beckett and Walter Lawrence, of Somersetshire.

Oct. 30, the Perambulation was exemplified; and Dec. 20 was granted the Charter of Confirmation, by consent of Parliament. (Mr. Seyer's Nos. 13, 14, 15, 16.)*

See Mr. Barrett's History, p. 143, for a copy of the first Writ (discovered in the White Tower) for return of Members to Parliament by the Sheriff of Bristol. Walter Derby and Thomas Beaupine were the representatives so returned.

William Canynges was the Mayor, and John Vyell the Sheriff, this year. There were no Bailiffs.

74 The city increasing towards St. James's Priory, the inhabitants petitioned Thomas Chesterton, abbot of Tewkesbury, and the Prior, for permission to hear mass, &c.; to which the Prior agreed, upon having a moiety of the profits of fixing the pales, &c. in the Church-yard, at the Fair; the parish to build the belfry at their own expense, but the Prior to find the stone and earth for the mortar. The bells to be at the joint expense of both parties.

Aug. 27, the Prior of the Church of Worcester (the see being then vacant, through the death of Bishop William de Lynne, Nov. 18, 1373, whilst mounting his horse to go to Parliament), issued a decree for the regulation of the Monastery of St. Augustin, then in great disputes and disorders.

75 William Canynges, Mayor; Harry Vyell, Sheriff. No Bailiffs.

The King presented Wickliffe with the prebend of Aust, in the collegiate church of Westbury-on-Trym. John Purney, one of the most active of the Lollard preachers, was his curate or assistant, and often preached in Bristol. See "Memoirs," c. xvi. § 11—15.

76 June 8, Edward the Black Prince died of consumption; buried at Canterbury.

Redcliff Church finished this year. The tower and spire two hundred and fifty feet high. Ricart's Kalendar of the Mayors says, "This yeare William Canynges builded the body of Redcliff Church, from the cross-iles downwarde; and so the church was finished as it is nowe"—meaning the 18th of Edward IV.

We have been thus diffuse in our notice of these interesting documents, because, ing been professionally initiated in the fact of only 380 copies being printed, we can ert that few of our readers are likely to have the pleasure of any other than the sent reference to their contents.

A. D.

1376 " This year was appointed that the Mayor, the Sheriffs, and two Bayliffs, should be chosen by the Common Council of the Town, upon Holy-Rood day, before Michaelmas-day; and upon St. Michael's day they should take their oath, solemn, in the Guildhall, prepared for that purpose, before the Commons of the town ; and afterwards, in the afternoon, all the whole Council should go to accompany the Mayor to St. Michael's, and there reverently offer to the Saint called St. Michael."

Oct. 1, Walter Derby being Mayor, an agreement was made with Hugh White, plumber, at his own cost during life, to bring the water to the Key Pipe, All Saints' Pipe, and St. John's Pipe, at the yearly sum of £10. See 1534.

1377 Wickliffe wrote in opposition to the Pope's supremacy. Both monks and friers now began to decline rapidly in general estimation.

June 21, Sunday, the King died, in his sixty-fourth year, at Richmond, and was succeeded by his grandson,

RICHARD II.,

son of Edward the Black Prince, in the eleventh year of his age.

The Mayor and Commonalty of Bristol *lent* the King five hundred marks; which was the first instance of a lay-community lending to the Crown, excepting that in London.

Richard Spicer (mayor in 1353, 1354, and 1371) gave seventeen tenements to the city, the site of Spicer's Hall, now the Back-Hall, in Baldwin-street.

1378 Feb. 8, the King, at Westminster, confirmed the Charters of Dec. 20, 1373, and 1347.—Seyer, No. 17.

Feb. 28, the King confirmed the Charter of 1331.—Seyer, No. 18.

Plays were first performed in England.

This year took place the rebellion of Wat Tyler, in which, provoked by an act of injustice, the mob assumed a power that they soon abused; which must ever be the case when power is lodged in the hands of *ignorance*, let the depositories of it be of what rank they may ; and there can be no other first approach than *knowledge*, in the broadest application of the term. towards " emancipation" of any kind. " Know thyself" is inscribed on the first step. " Knowledge is power."

1379 The Mayor, &c. lent the King one hundred marks.

A. D.

1380   John Canynges was one of the Bailiffs.

Several wills, dated about this time, gave money for the fabric, and towards repairing the Church of St. Mary Redcliff; and, among others, that of John Muleward mentions a gift in money, ad opus Beatæ Mariæ de Radcleve: "To the work of the Blessed Mary of Redcliffe."

Before this time there was a trading-guild or fraternity called the Fraternity of Canynges. See 1398.

1381   William Canynges was Mayor.

1382   Robert Cheddre left a legacy to the *sisters* of St. Bartholomew's Hospital. See 1386.

1383   Lamyngton's Lady-Chapel (afterwards called St. Sprite's Chapel), in Redcliff church-yard, was granted to the Society of the Holy Ghost, by the Principal of the Hospital of St. John, in Redcliff-Pit. Johannes Lamyngton was chaplain in 1393. When the chapel was taken down in 1766, in the wall under the west window of the church was found a stone coffin, with a figure carved on the lid, bearing his name; which is now to be seen in the Church.

1384   Walter Derby, Mayor; who died in 1385, and gave forty pounds, by will, towards rebuilding St. Werburgh's Church. By indenture, dated April 11, 1385, John Warwyke, the rector of St. Werburgh's, assigned to the parish a house in Corn-street, for the purpose of erecting a tower to the church, for which he had a house in the church-yard. (See 1761.) Walter Derby also gave to the Mayor and Commonalty seventeen tenements, to be sold, and the money arising from them to be applied to good and charitable uses.

1385   William Canynges, Mayor.

1386   The citizens lent the King two hundred pounds, to provide against the threatened French invasion, with 1287 ships; which was as much as York, and more than any other place, excepting London.

In a deed of this year, Lord de la Warre is named as the patron of St. Bartholomew's Hospital. See 1523.

1388   April 2, Henry Wakefield, bishop of Worcester, by deed in the White Book at Worcester, annexed the then rectory of St. Philip to the Monastery of Tewkesbury. This church has been mentioned under 1174, 1200, and 1279. It must have been previous to the latter date that what is now the chancel formed the whole of the church.

Dec. 2, Abbot Henry, of St. Augustin's, died. He was buried in the nether-tomb of the presbytery, which he had caused to be made, beside the high altar. John Cerney became the seventeenth abbot.

A. D.

1389   William Canynges was Mayor of Bristol for the sixth time.
       12 Richard II., Bristol was excused from pursuing the
       statute of 47 Edward III., relating to the aulnage of drabs.
1390   Bernard Obelly, and, in 1397, Reginald Taylor (see
       1403), by will, bequeathed money towards the building of
       Temple Tower. See 1460.*
1392   John Canynges, Mayor, father of the Dean of Westbury.
1393   Oct. 5, Abbot John died—buried in the over-tomb of the
       presbytery. John Daubeny, the eighteenth abbot.
       A deed of this year, and another of 1471, mention an
       hospital opposite the house of the Augustinean Brethren
       in Temple-street. In the latter it is called Domus Elemo-
       synaria Johannes Spycer, juxta portam Temple. The site
       of this hospital is now marked by the Swan public-house, &c.
1395   September, the King was in Bristol, on his way to Wa-
       terford; when probably the townsmen suffered annoyances
       from the King's officers, which were corrected by the Char-
       ter of 1396.
       Simon Oliver, Recorder of Bristol.
       Thomas Canynges born, who was Lord Mayor of London
       in 1456.
       John Barstable, Mayor.—William of Worcester says,
       Lawford's Gate was built anew by Walter Barstable, in the
       time of Edward III. or Richard II. John Barstable was
       Mayor also in 1401 and 1405, and founded Trinity Hos-
       pital, commonly called the Dial Alms-house, on the south
       side of the Old Market, within the Gate, for ten widowers
       and ten widows, a bed-maker, and a washerwoman. He
       died in 1411. Isabella, his wife, who died in 1404, is said
       to have founded the Hospital on the north side, within the
       Gate, for twenty-four women. They were both buried
       near the communion-table, in the chapel of the Dial Alms-
       house. These hospitals were licensed by letters patent,
       Feb. 15, 4th Henry V. See 1617.
1396   April 1, at York, the King granted the Charter, Seyer's
       No. 19. By this it was granted that the steward and clerk,
       marshal or clerk of the market of the King's household,
       should not sit within the liberties of Bristol. One of
       the witnesses hereto, Richard Metford, canon of Windsor,

* This must refer to the completion of the tower, from the point where it was
partially finished, in 1161, nearly two hundred and thirty years having passed in
testimony of the solidity of the foundation. Whether Chatterton's " Gremondei, a
Lumbard," was the original architect or not, cannot be readily disputed; but we may
reasonably doubt the survival of his contemporary, " John à Brixter," for that portion
of the work of which we think 1460 is the true period.

A. D.

1396 at this time bishop of Salisbury, had been long imprisoned in the Castle of Bristol. John, duke of Aquitaine, the famous John of Gaunt, was another of the witnesses; so was his son, afterwards Henry IV.

Nov. 1, the King married, at Calais, the daughter of the King of France, Isabella, aged only eight years, who was crowned at Westminster in January following. Her portion scarcely paid the charges of his journey to fetch her, which cost him three hundred thousand marks.

1398 By will, dated the 25th of May, John Vyell (Mayor in 1388) gave " Fraternitati de Canynges" 40s., adding " fraternitati quæ sum." (See 1460). He also bequeathed " to the Church of St. Stephen, one ring, in which was set a stone, part of the very pillar to which Christ was bound at the scourging; to be kept among the relics for ever."

Oct. 15, John Thorp and John Sherp, burgesses, obtained a Charter from the King, for a guild of the Wardens and Society of Master-Tailors, consisting of brethren and sisters; to whom belonged, in the south aisle that joined the nave of St. Ewen's Church, a chapel dedicated to St. John the Baptist. This guild always kept the chapel in repair, till its dissolution, in 1552; and they had additional privileges from Queen Elizabeth. See 1615.

1399 May. The King was in Bristol, on his way to Waterford; meanwhile Henry, duke of Lancaster, landed at Ravenspur, in Yorkshire.

In July, four of Richard's advisers, viz. William Scroop, earl of Wiltshire; Sir John Bushy, or Bussey, knight, who had been Speaker of the House of Commons; Sir Henry Green, and Sir James Bagot, knights, in escape from the Duke of Lancaster, came to the Castle of Bristol, with the design of making a stout resistance. They were soon followed by the Duke; when the gates of the town were opened to his forces, and he commanded the Castle to be stormed; which in four days surrendered at discretion. Scroop, Bushy, and Green, were brought bound before the Duke, and the day afterward arraigned before the Constable and Marshal, found guilty of treason for misgoverning the King and the realm, and presently beheaded at the High Cross. Bagot escaped to Ireland.

Sept. 21, Richard was taken prisoner and sent to the Tower.

Sept. 29, he resigned his crown.

Thomas Norton, Esq., M. P. for Bristol this year, lived in St. Peter's Church-yard. See 1422.

N

HENRY IV., *surnamed* BOLINGBROKE.

1400   Feb. 13, Richard was murthered in Pomfret Castle.

Thomas Lord Spencer, earl of Gloucester (grandson of the Sir Hugh Spencer executed in 1326), beheaded by the Commons, without judgment, at the High Cross, Bristol, for joining in a conspiracy against the new king; and his head was sent to London. He had just escaped, with the Duke of Exeter, from Cirencester, where their fellow-conspirators, Thomas Holland, duke of Surrey, and John de Montacute, earl of Salisbury, were beheaded by order of the Mayor of that town. "The King granted by writ to William Flaxman a certain gown of motley velvet of damaske, furred, which lately belonged to Thomas lord le Despencer, in which gown the said Thomas was taken prisoner outside the house of the Mayor of Bristol."

The Grand Prior and Proctor of the Priory of St. James granted the parish of All-Saints a little conduit of water (that which is situated in Maudlin-lane, at the N. E. corner of the Moravian Chapel court), to which the spring rising in the Prior's orchard (the garden above) was conveyed, and thence, through leaden pipes, to Corn-street. See 1601.

1403   Aug. 14, forty days of indulgence granted by William of Wickham, bishop of Winchester, to all benefactors of the Chapel of St. Brendan, and to Reginald Taillor, the poor hermit there, by his letters for one year only to continue.

1404   Thomas Knapp gave twenty pounds to St. Nicholas Church, and one hundred and thirty-three pounds to the Chamber, to be applied to good and charitable uses,

Philip Baunt, merchant, gave by will to John Canterbury, chaplain in St. Mary Redcliff, "quendam libram meum de Evangelis Anglice, qui est in custodiâ Joannis Stourton."

1405   John Canynges died, and was buried in St. Thomas Church. His son William was at this time six years old.

1409   In this year died Sir James, brother of Thomas (4) lord Berkeley. He married the daughter of Sir John Bluett, by whom he had James, the next baron (1417), and was Governor of Tretwr Castle. He was buried in St. Augustin's Monastery, supposed in the great tomb.

In Parliament, the commons of Somerset, Bristol, and Wilts, petitioned for power to remove all obstructions in the Avon, between Bristol and Bath; for, before Richard the Second, the river was navigable from hence to Bath, and wine, wax, salt, wool, skins, and cloth, used to be conveyed

A. D.

1409 in vessels between both cities. A writ was directed to the Mayor of Bristol, and Richard Tikehull, Sheriff of Somerset, for that purpose.

Oct. 28, the King issued writs for summoning a Parliament in Bristol, Jan. 27 following. Mr. Seyer's Memoirs, c. xvii. § 6, contains a proclamation, dated Nov. 12, addressed to John Greyndore, knight, Sheriff of Gloucestershire, John Joyce, and Henry Moton, empowering them to arrest persons of the Forest of Dean, who should continue, as they had done, to hinder persons who wished to carry corn, flesh, fish, or other victuals, to Bristol, where the Parliament was ordered to be holden.

1411 Thomas Young, a great merchant, was Mayor this year, and M. P. in 1414. He married Joanna, widow of John Canynges, and mother of William. His will was dated March 14, 1426, in which he ordered his body to be buried before the altar of St. Nicholas, in the Church of St. Thomas, and left legacies to the Friers Mendicant of Bristol; and to his wife, his mansion in Temple-street, and other messuages there and in the suburbs of the city.

1412 The King, by Charter, exempted the Mayor and Commonalty of Bristol from the jurisdiction of the Admiralty of England.—BARRETT's *Hist.* p. 175.

Hugh Lutterel appointed Constable of the Castle.

1413 March 20, the King died of apoplexy, in his 47th year.

HENRY V., *surnamed* MONMOUTH,

Crowned April 9.

1415 Oct. 24, the battle of Agincourt. Bristol lent the King on this occasion eight ships, laden with Spanish wines as ballast.

William of Worcester supposed to have been born this year. His parents were whitawers, skinners, and glovers, living on St. James's Back. His maternal name was Botoner. He studied at Oxford, and was patronized by Sir John Fastolf, whose biographical memoir he drew up. See 1410.

1416 According to the will of Belinus Nansmoen, dated March 20, there were many poor scholars choristers, and several chaplains, attached to the Church of St. Mary Redcliff.

1417 July 13, The fourth Thomas Lord Berkeley died, and was buried at Wotton-under-Edge.* He was succeeded by his

* Over the kitchen-chimney in the manor-house of Wotton-under-Edge, formerly a leasure-residence of the Abbot of the Monastery of Kingswood, Wilts, were carved a

A. D.

1417nephew James, son of Sir James Berkeley, younger son of the
     fourth Maurice.   Sir James died in 1409.   The chief part of
     Thomas's possessions, including his houses in Bristol, went
     to his daughter Elizabeth, married to Richard Beauchamp,
     son of the Earl of Warwick; the remainder went to his heir-
     male.   James married Isabella, daughter of the Duke of
     Norfolk, who died at Gloucester, in 1442, and was buried
     in the chancel of the church of the Friars Minor (the Grey
     Friars) at Gloucester, now [1822] Mr. Goodyear's breakfast-
     parlour.   See 1463.

1421   Feb. 4, Queen Katherine crowned at Westminster, but
     all the feast was fish, in observation of the Lent season.
     After this (adds Sir Richard Baker) the King took his
     progress through the land, hearing the complaints of his
     poor subjects, and taking order for administering of justice
     to both high and low.   But it does not appear that he visited
     Bristol.

1422   Aug. 30, the King died in France, in his 34th year, of a
     fever and flux, while engaged in war.

          HENRY VI., *surnamed* WINDSOR,

     Nine months old.
          A mint for coining established in Bristol, in the mansion
     late Norton's,§ St. Peter's Church-yard.

1424   Freemasons forbidden in England.   See 1429.
          In the church-books of St. Leonard this year was charged,
     " 2d. for a quart of wine—2d. for two sacks of coals—
     2d. for two pounds of candles—8d. for washing the
     sepulchre."†

1426   Thomas Young's will is dated March 14, this year.   (See
     1411.)   His eldest son, also named Thomas, was an eminent
     lawyer.   He was returned M. P. for Bristol, in the 15th,
     20th, 25th, 27th, 28th, 29th, and 33d of this reign.   In
     1453 he moved, in the House of Commons, that, as King
     Henry had no issue, the Duke of York be declared heir-
     apparent of the Crown; but he was committed to the Tower
     for the motion.

1428   Jan. 26, died Abbot John Daubeny.   He was succeeded
     by Walter Newbury, the nineteenth abbot, who was unjustly

Tiger, Hart, Ostrich, Mermaid, Ass, and Swan; the initials of which make Thomas
(Berkeley), a benefactor.

† By the sepulchre was probably meant the crypt or crowd.   See 1770.

§ *Qu.* the connexion between the Nortons severally mentioned under 1399 and 1446.

expelled for five years, and one Thomas Sutton intruded, who was himself thrust out for dilapidations and neglect.

1429 The cities of Bristol, Gloucester, and Worcester, complained that the Welsh of the marches and other privileged places, where the King's writ did not run, seized their dregs and floats, in order to compel the hiring of the Welsh trows, to carry their goods, and the giving the Welshmen what they were pleased to ask.

Freemasons tolerated by Act of Parliament. William Horwood, who about this time contracted for rebuilding the collegiate church at Fotheringay, is styled a Freemason. See 1445.

1430 The Parliament-rolls of this year complain of divers galleys lying in wait on the Severn, in order to seize the boats of the people of Gloucester and Worcester.

The Mayor and Commonalty of Bristol lent the King £333 6s. 8d. for the defence of the kingdom, in part of £50,000, of which London contributed £6666 12s. 6½d.; Salisbury £72, York £162, and Gloucester 50 marks.

In this year was Joan of Arc taken prisoner and burnt.

1431 Sir John de Welles, this year Lord Mayor of London, gave the rich sword embroidered with pearls, to the town of Bristol; on the hilt of which is written,

"John Wellis, of London, grocer, Maior,
Gave to Bristol this Sword feire."

William of Worcester sent to Hart's Hall, Oxford.

Dec. 7, the King was crowned at Paris.

1432 William Canynges was one of the Bailiffs this year.

1434 June 17, died Sir Thomas Marshall, a kalendary, who built a house near All-Saints' Church, for the perpetual residence of its vicars.

1438 William Canynges, Sheriff; Thomas Mede, one of the Bailiffs.

1439 March 24, died Sir John Inyn, knight, Recorder of Bristol, and one of the Chief Justices of the Common Pleas. His remains are in Redcliff Church. He had a country-seat at Bishopsworth, near Filwood, now or lately a farm-house. His second son, Christopher, had a daughter who was married to Lord Paulet, of Hinton St. George.

John Shipward, who built, at his own expense, the present St. Stephen's tower, was one of the Bailiffs this year.

1440 William Grocyne was born about this time. See 1520.

John Gyllard, Prior of the Kalendaries.

1441 William Canynges, Mayor; John Shipward, Sheriff.

A. D.

1442 Jan. 16, Sir John St. Loe made Constable and Porter of the Castle of Bristol; which he held till his decease, in 1447.

A naval force being necessary, to send Lord Talbot with three thousand men over into Normandy, the Commons pointed out where eight large ships were to be had. "At Bristol, the Nicholas of the Tower, and Katherine of Burton." The Nicholas was the ship that captured the Duke of Suffolk, whose head was immediately struck off on the gunwale of the boat. The Katherine belonged to William Canynges.

"In the year 1442 was John Atherley [or Aderley], the son of John Atherley, of Bristol, Lord Mayor of London."

1443 All-Saints' steeple repaired. See 1713.

"A post of brass, yet standing [in 1669] on the Key of Bristoll, neere to the conduit, was set up in the time of this Mayor, John Stanley's yeere, as appears by the names yet there to be read."

1444 The King granted the manor and hundred of Bristol, with other things, to Henry de Beauchamp, son of the late Earl of Warwick, in reversion from the death of Humphry, duke of Gloucester; but the grantee died June 1445.

John Shipward, Mayor of Bristol.

Dec. 13, died Sir Richard Newton Cradock, of Barr's Court, one of His Majesty's Justices of the Common Pleas.

1445 March 6, the King, by letters patent, granted to Nicholas Hill, Mayor, the town, with the gates, ditches, and walls, also the lands, tenements, rents, and services, with the flesh-shambles, which Joanna, the late Queen, (second wife of Henry IV.) held for her life; also the Precincts, the Castle excepted; but notwithstanding granted the watercourse running down in the ditch toward the mill under the Castle, with the banks, for four feet in breadth toward the Castle, for a term of twenty years. The tithes of the town were then £14 10s., payable to the Abbot of Tewkesbury. Newgate Mill paid 60s. to the Prior of St. James. The porter and watchman of the Castle, and the forester of Kingswood, received £39 4s. 6d.—The sum of £102 13s. 4d. was settled on Queen Margaret of Anjou (whom the King married April 22 this year), for her life.

"A religious guild was instituted, 24th Henry VI., that, for the soul's health and good of the King, the Mayor and Commonalty, and for the prosperity of the Mariners, who were exposed to manifold dangers and distresses, there should be a fraternity erected to the worship of God, Our Lady, St. Clement, St. George, and all the Saints in Heaven,

1445 to be founded in such place in Bristol as the Mayor should direct, for a priest and twelve poor mariners, to pray daily as above; to the support of which the master of every ship, barge, &c., after his voyage performed, at his arrival in the port, should pay four pence per ton of goods imported, in two days, to two Wardens chosen for the craft of mariners, and admitted by the Mayor, and all sworn by the articles and orders of the fraternity; on pain of 6s. 8d. if a master; if a seaman, 3s. 4d.; if a servant, 1s. 8d., &c. &c."
—Vide Barrett's History, p. 180. The Chapel originally erected, in conformity with the ordinance of the pious Henry, adjoined the old Merchants' Hall, in Virgin or Maiden-lane. Entering the lane from Marsh-street, the Hall stood on the left hand side (N.) about half-way through the lane; the door-way of which still remains. Millard's four-sheet map, published in 1673, contains a drawing of the building, which fell down, from decay, in 1812 or 1813. The arms of the Society of Merchant-Venturers stood over the fire-place, carved in freestone. The whole of the ground-floor was occupied as the kitchen, excepting that taken up by the stair-case. The Chapel adjoined the Hall, and is now a smithy. The Virgin (after the Reformation called Maiden) Tavern, stood on the right hand side of the lane, going into Baldwin-street.

The wages of a Freemason, or a master-carpenter, was now four pence a day; without meat or drink, five pence halfpenny.

1446 The King came to Bristol. " This yeare K. Henry came first to Bristol, and made his residence neere Redcliff Churche; which house, as some say, he bestowed on Knights Hospitallers, being that on which lately [1669] stood a crucifix, and neere to Redcliff Gate."

In a storm, the steeple of Redcliff Church was blown down. William Canynges and others repaired the church, by new covering and glazing it, at their own expense.

The right of election of Members in Parliament for Bristol was at this time vested in freeholders of forty shillings per annum, in free tenement. Thomas Young and John Sharpe, jun.* were returned; who had two shillings for their expenses, and no more.

This year Humphrey, duke of Gloucester, fourth son of Henry IV., was arrested by the Lord High Constable, Beauchamp, upon his attendance on the King and Parliament at Bury, and strangled in prison.

---

* John Sharpe was Mayor in 1439.

A. D.

1446 Thomas Norton, the Bristol alchemist, died.

1448 " This year the King came again to Bristowe."

1449 William Canynges, Mayor. The King this year addressed
two letters in his favour,—one to the Master-General of
Prussia, the other to the Magistrates of Dantzic, styling
him, " his beloved eminent merchant of Bristol."

The Mayor and Common-Council ordered that the Mayor
and Sheriff, one at St. John's night, the other at St. Peter's,
should dispense wine, to be disposed of to the Crafts at
their Halls, viz.

Gallons.		Gallons.		Gallons.
Weavers 10	Skinners 4	Masons 3
Tuckers 10	Smiths..........4	Tylers 3
Tailors 10	Farriers 4	Carpenters 3
Cornesers 8	Cutellers 4	Hoopers 3
Butchers 6	Lockyers 4	Wiredrawers 3
Dyers 5	Barbers 4	Cardmakers......3
Bakers........5	Waxmakers.... ..4	Bowers 3
Brewers 5	Tanners 4	Fletchers........2
Shermen......5	Whitawers.......4	

" This yeare was much money laide out for the repairing
of the Back; and slips, both of timber and stone, before
decayed, were now again made fit to unlade and discharge
goods."

1450 The rebellion of Jack Cade.

1451 Sir John Gyllarde, prior of the Kalendaries, died. He
erected a curious wainscot-ceiling over the N. aisle of All-
Saints' Church, and expended two hundred and seventeen
pounds upon the public library over the same aisle, under
the government of the Prior and the Mayor. John Hem-
mynge, alias Davy, was the new prior.

1452 Thomas Mede was Sheriff this year. He never (as Mr.
Britton would have it) served the office of Mayor.

1453 Of Sir Thomas Young's motion in the House of Commons,
see under 1426.

1454 The Duke of York, as protector of the realm, finding it
necessary to send out a fleet for the protection of trade,
raised money by way of loan on the sea-port towns, London
contributing £300; Bristow, £150; York and Hull, £100;
New Castell upon Tyne, £20, &c.

1455 John Shipward, Mayor.

" There was some trouble, this year, between the citizens
and some Irishmen, that for some occasion were admitted
burgesses; but Henry May, and some others, abusing their
freedome, were disfranchised, and a payment laid on them,

A. D.

untill they redeemed their freedom which the said mulct laid on them."

1456 William Canynges, Mayor. His brother, Thomas, a knight, was Lord Mayor of London at the same time.

Queen Margaret was this year in Bristol, with a great train of nobility, and was honourably received and entertained. The King was about the same time under the protection of the Duke of York.

1458 Philip Mede, Mayor. " In this year was a tumult made by one Thomas Talbot, esq., who abused and beat the King's Searcher, one John Welsh. The esquire resisted the mayor, and got away out of town at Temple-Gate, otherwise he had been imprisoned."

1459 Philip Mede was this year member in two Parliaments, at Coventry and Westminster.

A ship belonging to Robert Sturmey (mayor in 1453) having been plundered in the Mediterranean by the Genoese, the King arrested the Genoese merchants in London, seized their goods, and imprisoned them until they gave security to make good the loss; so that they were charged with six thousand pounds due to Mr. Sturmey.

1460 William Canynges, Mayor. St. Mathyas's Chapel, being in ruins, was this year erected by him into a Freemasons' Hall.* Deeds in the City-Chamber mention a house called Canynges' Lodge. This was subsequently converted into a Chapel, the east front of which extended to the common frontage of the houses in Redcliff-street. The late Mr. Birtill, sen. about 1803, shortening the Hall, erected a new eastern wall, to give room for a shop, &c. leaving the western wall, which is of massive thickness, as it stood originally. His surviving heir, Mr. John Birtill, recently discovered, under the boarded flooring of a parlour adjoining the Chapel or Hall, a pavement formed of die-moulded and glazed bricks or tiles, which have been inspected by Sir George Nayler, who copied several of the coats of arms and Latin inscriptions upon the larger devices. The wainscoting of that room is in the style of the time of the Stuarts. The fact of a Chapel having existed previous to the erection at this period of our Chronicle, is corroborated by a circumstance of which Chatterton, in like manner with ourselves, could be acquainted only from real documents; viz. On digging

* " There is a celebrated chesnut-tree in the parish of Tortworth, Gloucestershire, oeval with King John. This timber was much valued by our ancestors, for the roofs f great halls."—FOSBROKE. We believe the roof of Canynges' Hall to be of chesnut. t is not blackened by age or chemical action of the atmosphere, as is the case with oak.

o

A. D.

1460 the foundation for a floor-cloth manufactory, in 1803 or 4, Mr. Birtill found an arched subterranean passage leading from the Hall, and a row of Anglo-Saxon columns, forming the base of the exterior western front of the premises, facing the river, upon Redcliff-back. We feel more and more reason to regret that poor Chatterton thought it necessary to piece out his real fragments, by inventing matter to give a plausible degree of roundness to his narratives; but he wanted not precedents of high and grave authority for such an expedient.

" Temple Tower rebuilt," or, rather, completed. See *ante*, 1390, and 1576.

The cost of a breakfast, &c. on Corpus Christi day is thus entered in a book of St. Ewen's Church:—" Item, for a calve's head and hinge, 3*d.* Item, for two rounds of beef, 6*d.* Item, for bread and ale, 8*d.* Item, for Master Parson [Sir Thomas Seward], for his dinner, 4*d.* Item, for the Clerk, 2*d.* Item, for bearing the cross, 2*d.*"

1461 March 4, the Duke of York proclaimed King in London; and this is considered the last day of the reign of Henry the Sixth. (He lived ten years afterward, but was killed in the Tower, June 20, 1471.) Thus ended the line of Lancaster.

EDWARD IV.,

Descendant of the *third* son of Edward III.—the late King being a descendant of the *fourth* son.

March 24, Palm-Sunday, was fought the battle of Towton, Yorkshire; whereupon Henry and Margaret retired to Scotland.

Sir Baldwin Fulford had, in 1460, given bond to Henry VI., that he would either take away the life of the Earl of Warwick, who was then plotting to dethrone the reigning sovereign, or lose his own head. Stowe says, " After he had spent the King 1000 marks, he returned again." Edward seized and imprisoned him and his two accomplices, —— Bright and —— Hessant, esqrs. in Bristol Castle; and in September the King came to Bristol, and witnessed their passing by to their fate, from the great window of St. Ewen's Church, in Broad-street, about the beginning or middle of that month.* The family of Fulford was of great note and antiquity in the

---

* " Item, for washynge the church payren against K. Edward 4th is comynge to Brystow, iiijd. ob."—*St. Ewen's Church-Warden's Book.*

D.

1461 county of Devon. The following further particulars of this transaction are stated in the Act that passed in 7 Edw. IV. for the restitution in blood and estate of Thomas Fulford, knight, eldest son of Baldewyn Fulford, late of Fulford, in the county of Devon, knight. The preamble of this act, after stating the attainder by the act of Edward IV., goes on thus: " And also the said Baldewyn, the said first yere of your noble reign, at Bristowe, in the shire of Bristowe, before Henry Erle of Essex, William Hastyngs, of Hastyngs, knt., Richard Chock, William Canyng, the Maire of the said towne of Bristowe, and Thomas Yong, by force of your letters patentes to them and other directe, to here and determine all treesons, &c. doon withyn the said towne of Bristowe before the vth day of September the first yere of your said reign, was atteynt of dyvers tresons by him doon agenst your Highness, &c."—The Mayor was Philip Mede.*

Oct. 22, at Westminster, was granted a Charter (Seyer's No. 21), exempting Bristol from the Court of Admiralty (in confirmation of the Charter of 1412), and granting a commission for trying Admiralty causes.

Dec. 14, at Westminster, the King confirmed the Charter of 1396—Seyer's No. 20.

1462 Feb. 12, the King resumed the Letters Patent of 24 Hen. VI. (1445), but made the same grant of the town, &c. to be holden for ever, with all fines, forfeitures, &c. including fines before the Justices of the Forest, for stealing wood and venison.

1463 John Shipward, Mayor; Thomas Young (noticed under 1453), Recorder. See 1476.

April, the Battle of Hexham, in which Henry's forces were defeated.

Sept. 3, died Abbot Walter. He was succeeded by William Hunt, the twentieth abbot; " who rebuilt the roof of the Church and aisles, and caused the lead to be recast, all from the tower eastward." The tower itself is in the style of this period. The new and old workmanship may be discriminated by noticing that the slender pillars against the north and south walls are completely insulated, while the corresponding pillars opposed to them in those aisles are not insulated, but laid close to the main shaft, and not so neatly finished. The rebuilding " from the tower eastward" was contrary to the custom, in entirely new erections, of beginning in the north-east, and finishing a part

* Upon this execution, Chatterton founded his affecting poem, the " Bristowe Tragedie, or the Dethe of Syr Charles Bawdin."—Works, &c. ii. 83.

A. D.

1463 sufficient for the performance of religious worship; and
accordingly we find the ceiling of the new work, excepting
that upon which the tower was raised or re-erected, less
ornamented than that of the sealing-house, now a clothing-
room, leading to the vestry.

Nov. 3, James, lord Berkeley, died, and was buried in
Berkeley Church. He was succeeded by his son William
(born 1426), who was created Viscount Berkeley, 21st April
21 Edw. IV., and 5th March 23 Edw. IV. (1483) made one of
the Privy Council. Under his command was fought the famous
battle of Nibley-Green. (See 1470.) He wasted the greater
part of his property. He had three wives, but no issue.
See 1489.

1464 Henry taken in disguise in Lincolnshire, and conveyed
to the Tower with his legs tied under his horse's belly.

In a deed of ordinance made by the Bishop of Worcester,
mention is made of the Library of the Kalendaries recently
erected at the Bishop's expense,—also, a weekly lecture by
the Prior—three inventories of the books, one to remain
with the Dean, one with the Mayor,* and the third with
the Prior; and other regulations for the better security of
the books. See 1466.

1465 John Cogan, the Sheriff, paid £102 15s. 6d., charged on
the Mayor and Commonalty, for the fee-farm to the Queen
(Elizabeth Grey), settled on her for her life.

From a deed in Latin by William Canynges, dated 6
Edw. IV., it appears that he now formed the chantry of
St. Catherine in Redcliff-Church.

Henry Abingdon was Master of St. Catherine's Hospital,
Bright Bow, this year; which is thus mentioned by William
of Worcester: " Hospitalis domus in ecclesiæ Sanctæ
Catherinæ, ubi magister Henricus Abyngdon, musicus de
capella regis et magister."

1466 William Canynges, Mayor; Thomas Rowley, one of the
Bailiffs.†

" This Mayor, having buried his wife, whom he dearly
loved, was moved by the King to marry another wife, whom
he ordained [see note to 1474]; but Mr. Canynges, as soon
as he had discharged his year, to prevent it, took on him
the order of priesthood, and sung his first mass on Whit-
Sunday, in the Lady's Chapel, at Redcliff; and was afterwards Dean of Westbury; which College, by Richard,

* We hope it will appear that the Mayor's copy of the Catalogue is still in existence.
† It is reasonable to suppose that, if Chatterton had seen a list of the Mayors and
Bailiffs, he would not have made Thomas Rowley a priest.

1466 duke of York, and Edmund, duke of Rutland, was founded, and a Dean and Canons placed. King Edward gave them the Hospital of St. Lawrence, in the hundred of Barton Regis, near Bristol. To this College Mr. Canynges became a great benefactor, and was Dean, as also to Redcliff Church, &c." It appears, from the register of the Bishop of Worcester, that Mr. Canynge was ordained Acolythe by Bishop Carpenter, Sept. 19, 1467, and received the higher orders of Sub-Deacon, Deacon, and Priest, March 12th and April 2d and 16th following.

See Barrett's History, p. 179, for the Ordinances of the Society of Merchants.

May 5, died Maurice de Berkeley, of Beverstone. He was buried in the Monastery of Black Friers.

The Library of the Kalendaries destroyed by fire, through the carelessness of a drunken point-maker.

John Chanceller, of Keynsham, gave one hundred marks towards the re-building of the House of the Kalendaries. (See 1479.) On the site of the House of the Kalendaries was built the London Coffee-House, and the Pipe of All Saints, since removed back into the lane; but this must have been long subsequent to the date under which we are writing. Of Coffee and Coffee-Houses, see 1650.

" In this year was [John] the son of Thomas Younge (a Bristol-man and a grocer in London) Lord Mayor, and knighted in the field;"—the King and the Earl of Warwick being then in arms against each other.

1467 Sheep from England first permitted to be sent to Spain. Of this the citizens of Bristol complained, also on account of removing the staple from Bayonne, where was a great sale of Bristol drapery.—Columbus noticed the Bristol trade to Thule, in Iceland. See Life, by his son, c. iv.

1468 Philip Mede, Mayor; Michael Harvey, Recorder.

1469 The King taken prisoner, in his bed, by the Earl of Warwick, at Woolney, four miles from Berwick, and committed to the care of the Archbishop of York, at Middleham Castle; whence he soon escaped. The Earl had in the mean time dismissed his army.

Robert Ricart's Kalendar says, " one of Lord Herbert his brothern was slayne at Bristowe, at Seynt James his tyde."

" The battle of Bamberry, where much Welshe people were distressed. And there were beheded the Lord Herbert, the Lord Ryvers and his son, and many others; and Sir Richard Herbert, a gentil knight and a manly, was there slayne. And one of the Lord Herbert's brethren was

slayne at Bristowe the same yere, at St. James's tyde."—*MS.*
See 1527, when it would seem that this death of a Herbert
was revenged.

"King Edward, advertised of these mischances, wrote to
the Sheriffs of Somersetshire and Devonshire, to apprehend
the Lord Stafford of Southwick (who had treacherously
forsaken the Earl of Pembrook), and if they could take him,
to put him to death; who being soon after found in a village
within Brentmarsh, was brought to Bridgewater, and there
beheaded."—BAKER's *Chronicle.*

John Shipward, Mayor; who about this time erected the
present St. Stephen's Tower—not as it just now appears,
but in its pristine fullness and beauty of a few months
since (1821), to which we hoped it would soon be restored.
A small part only of what an individual could accomplish
altogether, in 1469, we imagined would not now be too much
for the means or architectural taste of a whole parish or city.
See 1472.

1470 Warwick, having obtained reinforcements in France,
drove Edward out of the kingdom.

March 20, was fought the battle of Nibley-Green ("the
very counter-part of Chevy Chase," says Mr. Seyer), between
William lord Berkeley and the Lord Viscount Lisle, each
attended by a strong body of men. Many of the inhabitants
of Bristol were concerned in the fray. On the death of
Thomas lord Berkeley, in 1417, a quarrel and law-suit
arose between the three daughters of his daughter Elizabeth,
and their husbands, on the one side, and his nephew and
heir, James, on the other side. The present Lord William,
afterward viscount and marquess, inherited this quarrel from
his father, and carried it on with Lord Viscount Lisle, a
young man of 22, who possessed the manor of Wotton-
under-Edge. The discovery of a plot by the latter produced
a challenge from him to Lord Berkeley in the afternoon of
March 19, to meet at Nibley-Green early the next morning.
Lord Berkeley, and his brothers Maurice and Thomas,
came to the field with one thousand men, raised during the
night, in the Forest of Dean and the neighbourhoods of
Berkeley, Thornbury, and Bristol. The Bristol men were
raised by Philip Meade and John Shipward. Lord Lisle's
men were not so numerous. The Berkeley party lay close
in the outskirts of Michaelwood Chase, out of which his
lordship sallied when he first beheld Lord Lisle and his
followers descending the hill from Nibley Church. They
came to a stand at Fowleshard, where the onset was given

A. D.

1470 by a shower of arrows from the Berkeley men; when one of them, called Black Will, a Dean forester, pierced Lord Lisle's left temple, his beaver being up, with an arrow, and a dagger was afterward thrust into his left side. A few beside being slain, Lisle's men fled, and Lord Berkeley led on his men to Wotton, where he rifled the manor-house of all the written evidences and documents which, as he supposed, belonged to that estate, together with a piece of arras, wherein the arms of the Viscount and the Lady Joan, his mother, daughter and coheir of Sir Thomas Cheddre, were wrought, and then returned to Berkeley. See " Memoirs," c. xx. § 6—10.

May 2; at the suit of the Viscountess Lisle and her friends, the Mayor of Bristol [John Shipward himself!] examined twenty persons on oath, as to the suspicion of Philip Meade and John Shipward having sent armed men from Bristol; who all " acquitted them of that scandal and imputation." The historian of the Berkeley family nevertheless believed the allegations to be well founded.

Smythe concludes his narrative of this transaction in these words: " And thus did all the sonnes ioyne in revenge of the innocent bloud of that vertuous and princely lady, Isable, their mother, malitiously spilt at Gloucester seventeen yeares before, by Margaret, this viscount's grandmother, and whose heire and ward he was. And this wounde stroke the deeper, for that the blowe thereof swept away all her issue male from the earth, and in the same quarrell wherein the bloud of the said Lady Berkeley was shed."

Nov. 4, Queen Elizabeth was delivered of Edward V. in the Abbey of Westminster; where she had taken sanctuary, upon leaving the Tower at Warwick's approach.

A Parliament called, by which Henry VI. was reinstated in the government, and Edward attainted as a traitor and usurper.

1471 March 12, Edward, being assisted by the Duke of Burgundy, landed in Yorkshire, and the Duke of Clarence came over to him. April 11, he took London, and re-imprisoned Henry. April 14 (Easter-Sunday) he obtained the victory of Barnet, in which Warwick was killed. The same day, Margaret, Henry's queen, with her son Edward, landed at Weymouth, and raised forces against K. Edward. The Prince and the Duke of Somerset came to Bristol, on their way to Tewkesbury. May 4, King Edward routed Margaret's army at Tewkesbury, and took Prince Edward

1471 prisoner, whom, May 21, he suffered to be killed in his
own presence. June 20, Henry VI. was murdered in the
Tower, in his 50th year. Margaret also was taken prisoner,
but ransomed by her father, the Duke of Anjou.

John Gaywode, in his will, mentions several hospitals to
which he was a benefactor. Vide Barrett's Hist. p. 60.

Philip Mede's will, dated Jan. 11, this year, directed his
body to be buried at the altar of St. Stephen, in Redcliff-
Church.

Caxton brought Printing into England. The first book
printed in the English language bears this date.

1472 John Jay, who was Sheriff this year, married Joanna,
sister of William of Worcester. He died May 15, 1480,
and was buried in Redcliff-Church.

John, earl of Oxford, who surrendered to the King at
Barnet, was confined in Newgate, Bristol, previous to his
being " sent over sea to the Castle of Hammes, where, for
the space of twelve years, he was shut up in a strong prison
and narrowly looked to; whose lady [the sister of the great
Earl of Warwick] all that time was not suffered to come
unto him, nor had any thing to live upon, but what people
of their charities gave her, or what she could get by needle
or other work."—Sir R. Baker.

William of Worcester, having translated Cicero on Old
Age, this year presented it to Wainfleet, bishop of Winchester.

Dec. 14, John Shipward, sen. died. He was buried in
St. Stephen's Church. He left large estates to the poor,
especially to the fraternity of St. Clement, and gave to St.
Stephen's Church two curious missals, a large gilt chalice,
rich vestments for the high altar, the Guillows [Guilders?]
Inn, in High-street, with other tenements; six gardens, for
two chaplains to celebrate his obiit: the rector, with nineteen chaplains, and the Mayor, Sheriff, and their officers,
to attend, who were to choose the chaplains, and dismiss
them if incorrigible.

1474 The King was in Bristol, and lodged in the Abbey of
St. Augustin. In June, he invaded France. As there was
no money raised by Charter on this occasion, it is probable
that, preparatory to his departure, the King obtained from
William Canynges the " 3000 marks for his peace, to be
had in 2470 tons of shipping," as described on his tomb in
Redcliff-Church. Indeed the MS. belonging to Mr. Alderman Haythorne, under this date says, " The King came to
Bristoll and lay at St. Augustine in the Abbey, and got

A. D.

1474 much money, by way of *benevolence*, of the townsmen and dwellers neere to it, to helpe him in his warrs which he had in hand."—This was the first time of resorting to such a mode of obtaining money.*

Robert Strange, Mayor; *William* Rowley, one of the Bailiffs.

Nov. 7, William Canynges died. He was buried at the altar of St. Catherine,† in Redcliff-Church. A MS. in the Bodleian Library says he gave five hundred pounds to the parishioners of St. Mary Redcliff, towards repairing the Church, and for the maintenance of two chaplains, and two clerks in St. Mary's Chapel there, and of two chantry-priests.‡ An almshouse, on the west-side of Redcliff-Hill, in the road from the Church towards Bedminster, was founded by William Canynges, for fourteen persons. On cutting a new course for the Avon through its site, in 1805, the house was re-erected with a southern aspect, facing the river. See 1493.

1475   *Thomas* Rowley, Sheriff.

1476   Bristol, as well as London, exempted from sealing their cloths, kerseys, &c. with a head, according to a statute, 4th of this reign, by which all other places were bound.

Thomas Younge, recorder of Bristol, buried in Christ-Church, London. He died seized of the manor of North-Wraxal, Wilts, with the advowson of the church, and the manor of Easton in Gordano, Somerset.—William Canynges, in his deeds, calls this Thomas Younge his brother. Sir George Younge, of Devonshire, is lineally descended from this Bristol family.

---

* " King Edward, amongst others, having called before him an old rich widow, merrily asked what she would willingly give him towards his great charges? By my troth (quoth she) for thy lovely countenance, thou shalt have even twenty pounds. The King, looking scarce for half that sum, thanked her, and lovingly kist her; which so wrought with the old widow, that she presently swore he should have twenty pounds more, and paid it willingly."—*Sir* RD. BAKER. The same writer adds, " he could make advantages of disadvantages, for he got the love of the Londoners by owing them money, and the good-will of the citizens by lying with their wives." This characteristic, we think, sufficiently accounts for William Canynges' unwillingness to take a wife by Royal command. He had doubtless heard of Shore's wife, and did not choose so far to prove his loyalty.

† Besides the altars of St. Stephen and St. Catherine, in Redcliff-Church, there were altars dedicated to St. Blaze, St. Nicholas, and St. George.

‡ From the looseness of the narrative upon the painted board affixed to his tomb, contrasted with the general precision of monumental inscriptions, and the character of the writing, we are disposed to believe that it was placed there, partly upon traditional authority, at a comparatively late period, probably since the ravages committed upon the entire edifice during the puritanic furor of the interregnum. A divine right to do wrong has been often assumed by a people with no less arrogance than by kings, and with much more irremediable injury.

P

A. D.

1477 Sebastian Cabot born.

1478 March 11, the Duke of Clarence, having been previously
      attainted by Parliament, was murthered in the Tower, by being
      drowned in a butt of malmsey. He was buried at Tewkes-
      bury, by the body of his Duchess, who, great with child,
      had died of poison a little before. It was returned (Esch.
      17 Edw. IV., No. 47) that George, late duke of Clarence,
      and Isabel his wife, held in right of the same Isabel a
      certain great court of the honour [honorary possession] of
      Gloucester, in Bristol, called the Erle's court, in his demesn,
      as of fee; which court had been used to be held, time out of
      mind, within the precincts of the Priory of St. James the
      Apostle, or in the church-yard of the parish-church there
      [under a large tree], from month to month; at which court
      all the tenants of the above Duke and Isabel his wife [de-
      scended from the Beauchamps] holding of their moiety of the
      honour of Gloucester, in that county and Somersetshire,
      owed suit and service from month to month; which honour
      and court was held *in cap.* of the King by knight's service,
      and was worth per annum 100s. By the attainder of the
      Duke of Clarence, this court came to the Crown; but the
      Staffords' moiety escaped; the office of the bailiwick of the
      liberty of the honour of Gloucester, in the same county, late
      Henry, duke of Buckingham's, being granted to Catherine,
      duchess of Bedford, Buckingham's widow, till her son by
      the last duke came of age. (Rot. Parl. 1 H. V.) The
      attainder of the son brought that bailiwick also to the Crown.

1478 " This year Thomas Norton, esq., dwelling in St. Peter's
      church-yard, accused Mr. Mayor [William Spencer] of high
      treason, which was done for ill will; for, as soon as the
      King understood the reasand of the truth, he set the Mayor
      free, who had of his good will yielded himself into prison, soe
      soone as he was apprehended, where he remained prisoner
      thirteen days, until he had the King's letter, which was sent
      him honourably with great love and favour, being highly
      commended of the King for his wisedome; and the said
      Norton was severely check'd of the King."

1479 Robert Ricart, a Kalendary, and one of the five chaplains
      or chantry-priests, was elected Town-Clerk of Bristol. He
      commenced the Mayors' Kalendar or Register. The two
      red books, and the book of wills, orphans, &c., contain
      curious notices by him. See 1503.
          " This year one Symbarbe caused Robert Marks, a towns-
      man, to accuse Robert Strange, who had been Mayor, [and,
      says William of Worcester, had twelve ships at one time]

A. D.

1479 for coining of money, and for sending of gold over the sea unto the Earl of Richmond; wherefore the King sent for him [Strange], and committed him to the Tower, where he remained seven or eight weeks; but, when the truth was known, his accuser, Robert Marks, was had to Bristol, and was hanged, drawn, and quartered, for his false accusation."

William Rowley, of Bristol, buried in Flanders.

1480 The Church of St. Augustin-the-Less re-erected; to which Abbots Newland and Elliott seem to have contributed materially.

Sept. 26, William of Worcester visited the Chapel of the Hermitage of St. Vincent, which he describes, in his Notes on Bristol (edited by Nasmyth), as twenty fathom (120 feet) from the low ground in height, about the middle of the rock. He also notices the Hotwell-spring.

The same writer gives the following account of the Castle at this time:

P. 208.—" The road from the gate of the entrance to the Castle of Bristol" [meaning the gate of the deep ditch across the bridge to the doors of the entrance—p. 217] " is near the E. part of the church of St. Peter; and you go on marching by the *wall of the ditch* of the walls of the Castle, through New Gate and along the street called the Weer, and over Weer-bridge, leaving the watering-place on the left hand, and making a circuit by the wall of the Castle-ditch towards the south, near the Cross in the Old Market; thus continuing to a great stone about a yard high, of freestone, erected at the extremity of the bounds of the city of Bristol; so proceeding on to the gate of the first or eastern entrance of the Castle, at the west part of St. Philip's Church, which is at the end of a lane behind the Old Market. This contains, in a circuit of one part of the tower and walls of the Castle, four hundred and twenty steps."

At p. 217 he says, " the whole circuit contains two thousand one hundred steps." His steps vary, but are about twenty-one inches.

In another place (p. 259) he mentions it in English, thus:*

" The quantite of the Dongeon of the Castell of Bristol, after the informatione of . . . . porter of the Castell. The tour called the Dongeon ys in thykness, at fote, 25 pedes, and at the ledying-place, under the leede

* We follow the original closely, except as to punctuation; our object being to present to the reader, with the least possible trouble to himself, a perspicuous view of this important feature of the " olden time" in Bristol.

1480cuvering, 9 feet and dimid; and yn length, este and west, 60 pedes, and, north and south, 45 pedes; with fowre toures standyng uppon the fowre corners; and the hyghest toure, called the mayn, i. e. myghtyest toure above all the fowre toures, ys 5 fethym hygh abofe all the fowre toures; and the wallys be in thykness there 6 fote. Item, the length of the Castelle, wythynne the wallys, este and weste, ys 180 virgæ. Item, the brede of the Castelle, from the north to the south, wyth the grete Gardyn, that is, from the Water-gate to the mayng rounde of the Castelle, to the wall north-ward, toward the Blak Frerys, 100 yerdes. Item, a bastyle, lyeth southward beyond the Water-gate, conteynyth yn length 60 virgæ. Item, the length from the bullwork at the utter gate, by Seynt Phelippes chyrch-yerd, conteyneth 60 yerdes large. Item, the yerdys called sparres of the Halle Royalle conteynyth in length about 45 fete of hole pece. Item, the brede of every sparre at fore conteynyth 12 onch and 8 onches."

At p. 269 he again describes in Latin: " The Porch or entrance into the Hall is ten yards long, with an arched vault over, at the entrance of the Great Hall. The inner entry into the porch of the Hall is 140 steps,—meaning the space and length betwixt the gate of the Castle-walls, and the walls of the area of the utter-ward. The length of the Hall is 36 yards, or 52 or 54 steps; the breadth of the Hall is 18 yards, or 26 steps. The height of the walls outside the Hall is 14 feet, as I measured them. The Hall, formerly very magnificent in length, breadth, and height, is all tending to ruin. The windows in the Hall double, the height (de 11 days) contains 14 feet. The length of the rafters of the Hall is 32 feet. The Prince's Chamber, on the left side of the King's Hall, is 17 yards, in breadth 9 yards, and has two pillars made with great beams, but very old. The length of the front before the Hall with . . . . is 18 yards. The length of the marble stone table is 15 feet, situated in another part of the Hall, for the King's table there sitting. The length of the Tower, in the east part of it, is 36 yards; its breadth at the western and south part is 30 yards. The length of the utter ward of the Castle, from the middle gate, and lately separated from the inner ward of the Chapel, the principal chamber of the Hall, is 160 steps. The length of the first entrance to the Castle, by the gate, is 40 steps; that is, from the street of the Castle, by entering at the first gate of the Castle into the utter ward. The Chapel in the utter ward, or first ward, is

., D.

480dedicated in honour of St. Martin; but, in devotion to
St. John the Baptist, a monk of St. James ought to celebrate
the office every day, but does it but Sunday, Wednesday,
and Friday.—There is another very magnificent Chapel, for
the King and his Lords and Ladies, situate in the principal
ward, on the north side of the Hall, where beautiful chambers were built, but are now naked and uncovered, void of
planchers or roofing.—The dwelling of the officers of the
kitchen belong to the inner ward near the Hall, on the left
side, that is, on the south part of the Hall. The dwelling
of the Constable or Keeper is situated in the first or utter
ward, on the south part of the magnificent tower, but is all
pulled down and ruinous, which is great pity."

Guided by the foregoing description, the Rev. Samuel
Seyer and Mr. Henry Smith have severally drawn a survey
of the Castle. That of Mr. Seyer is published in his
" Memoirs of Bristol." From Mr. Smith's we here attempt
to localize the prominent features in William of Worcester's
description.

The entrance-gate from the town stood at the termination
of St. Peter-street, but nearest to the left-hand line of houses
in Castle-street. A dry ditch, walled in front, extended
from New-Gate, north, to the Avon, southward.

The great tower, called the dongeon, donjon, or keep,
was situated just within this gate, between Castle-street
and Castle-green, taking the Bear-and-Ragged-Staff public-
house as built upon the site of its north tower, and the
house occupied by Mr. Hunt, cutler, as projecting westward of its south tower. The base of the whole tower
extended about two-thirds of the distance from the point
noted towards Roach's Lane, now called after the Cock-and-
Bottle public-house at its north-west corner.

South of the dongeon, standing between the yard of the
George Inn, now a wool-warehouse, and Golden Boy Lane,
but nearer to the former, stood the Governor's House or
Constable's Hall; westward of which, at the termination
of the George-Yard, and close to the water's edge, stood a
round tower, forming the extreme point of the Castle-walls
on that side.*

St. Martin's Church stood north of the dongeon, at the
entrance of Castle-Green, and adjoining the Tower connected with New-Gate.

Mr. Garrard, the Chamberlain, was lately in possession of a handsome stone
del of a castellated tower, which formerly served as a sign in front of the George
. It is now the property of Mr. Baker, of Blagdon, Somerset.

A. D.

1480   There was a double wall on the north side of the Castle;
the inner wall stood on the summit of the bank marked by
the frontage of the houses on that side of Castle-green.
Parts of the outer wall still remain.

Where the large house in a garden or court adjoining
Messrs. Ambrose Oxley & Co.'s warehouse is situated, stood
a square tower on the inner wall, and a larger tower on the
outer wall or terrace.   From these two towers the wall that
separated the " outer ward," ballium, or court, from the
inner yard, cutting diagonally the lower part of Cock-and-
Bottle lane towards Castle-street, crossed the latter, to a
small tower on the bank of the Avon, which tower stood
mid-way between the extreme western round tower, above
noticed, and a square tower next to the Water-gate, where
the ditch is entered from the river, the place of the unfortunate second Edward's debarkation, in his attempt to seek
an asylum at the Island of Lundy.

The sally-port was in Queen-street, at the Brewery-
warehouse, in an inner wall on the bank of the ditch;
that inner wall being continued from the Water-gate round
to the eastern or Nether-gate, at the end of Castle-street.
From the Water-gate the outer wall followed the curve of
the Avon, close to the water's edge, to a round tower,
between which and the western round tower, near the Mint,
the Water-gate formed a point nearly central.   The outer
wall, proceeding hence north-eastward, towards St. Philip's
Church, continued up the present Tower-street to the
eastern gate, at the end of Castle-street.

The space enclosed by the inner and outer wall on this
side, into the middle of which Queen-street descends, was
called the King's Orchard, or Castle-Mead, and comprised
two acres.

The site of the houses without the Castle walls, between
Tower-street and Church-lane, south of the Old Market,
was William of Worcester's garden.   The Cross erected by
Philip le Mare, in 1279, stood near the house, with a figure
of Time (which has so often, to the great annoyance of our
boyhood, stood still), just without the nether gate.

From this gate the wall continued, on the bank of the
ditch, to a square tower behind the back of Mr. Hartland's
house and the Cold Bath; and the ditch washed the foot of
a square tower which commanded Ælle or Weir bridge,
whence the outer wall continued onward to Newgate.—We
have thus traced the circuit, though reversing the progress,

A. D.

480 which William of Worcester describes as containing two thousand one hundred steps.

Within the Castle-wall, on the eastward, the ground, now occupied by houses in the angle formed by the north side of Castle-street and the east angle of Castle-green (which division of it was formerly called Tower-street), comprised, next to Castle-street, the servants' apartments. In Castle-green are still to be seen the walls and arched ceiling of the entrance-porches to the Great Hall and the Chapel; adjoining whereto, northward, and facing the longer division of Castle-green, westward, were the Royal apartments. At the back of Mr. Hartland's house, situated behind the Gas-Company's late offices, still stands a castellated look-out, indicating the back of those apartments.

That part of the inner ballium or ward which lay next the Avon was called the Great Garden. See 1534.

481 John Newland, alias Nail-heart, the twenty-first Abbot. He was frequently employed, during the succeeding reign, in foreign embassies. He wrote a History of the Monastery, including Memoirs of the Berkeleys. See 1515.

John Foster, Mayor; who, with John Easterfield, founded the almshouse in Steep-street, formerly Stripes-street. See 1504.

482 Robert Strange, Mayor.

Gold angels, 79 grains — groats, and two-pennies, coined in Bristol.*

Dundry Church built.

The first book printed on paper made in England: "Bartholomæus de Proprietatibus Rerum." Translated into English, and printed by Wynkin de Worde. Folio. The English version was by John Trevisa, vicar of Berkeley.†

483 April 9, the King died at Westminster, of ague, in his 42d year. He was buried at Windsor; where, March 11, 1789, his corpse was found undecayed.

---

* For Tables shewing the relative value of the coins of this country, in silver and gold, from the Conquest to 1816, see "Essays on Money, Exchanges, and Political Economy, &c. by Henry James." 8vo. 1820.

† According to a Lecture on English Literature, delivered by the Rev. T. F. Dibdin, at the Royal Institution, on the 7th of February, 1807, very little of John Trevisa is known with accuracy. His translation of [Higden's Polychronicon was said to be first printed by Caxton, in the year of our text. The question of his having *translated the Bible* was particularly discussed. From the private information of a friend, Mr. D. observed that there was recently preserved in the Vatican, at Rome, a work translated by Trevisa, given by some of Lord Berkeley's ancestors to Charles I., when Prince of Wales, and resident at the papal court. It was supposed to be a translation of the Bible into English.

EDWARD V.,

Aged eleven years, proclaimed April 9.

John Twynho, Recorder of Bristol.

June 18, the young King deposed by his uncle and protector, Richard, duke of York, who had taken off the heads of Lord Hastings, Earl Rivers, the Queen's brother, and her son, Lord Grey, and now declared his brother, Edward IV., and the Duke of Clarence, as well as Edward's issue, bastards. Richard was now in his 30th year.

RICHARD III.,

July 6, crowned at Westminster, with Anne, his queen, youngest daughter of the great Warwick, and relict of Prince Edward, son of Henry VI.

1484 Oct. 15, there was a great flood in Bristol, in which more than two hundred men, women, and children, were drowned, and the merchants' cellars suffered much damage. Several ships were lost in Kingroad. The Moon was eclipsed between two and three hours.*

John Spine, a native of Bristol, was a Carmelite and D.D. in Oxford, where he died this year, leaving some books of his writing.

William of Worcester also died this year.†

1485 Aug. 7, the Duke of Richmond landed at Milford-Haven.

Aug. 22, Richard was killed at the battle of Bosworth, near Leicester.

HENRY VII.,

Aged 29 years. He was born in Pembroke Castle. His father, Edmund, earl of Richmond, was the eldest son of Owen Tudor and Queen Katherine, relict of Henry V. His mother was Margaret, sole daughter of John, duke of Somerset, who was son of John, earl of Somerset, son of John

* This was the flood that interrupted the progress of the Duke of Buckingham at Gloucester, in his way to join Hugh Courtney and his brother Peter, bishop of Exeter, arrayed against Richard in Devonshire and Cornwall—cooling the courage of his Welsh forces, and leaving him to Richard's tender mercy.

† His "Common-place Pocket-book" was published by Mr. Nasmith, with Simeon Siméonis, in 1778.

of Gaunt, duke of Lancaster, by his third wife, Katherine Swinford.

1486 Jan. 18, the King married the Princess Elizabeth, eldest daughter of Edward IV.

Jan. 30, died John Milverton, a Carmelite frier of Bristol, and provincial of the order; who, when he had been just elected to the bishoprick of St. David's, preached against the office in favour of the orders of monks and friers, and was imprisoned three years in the Castle of St. Angelo, at Rome. Bale, Cen. Oct., p. 619, gives a catalogue of his productions.

The King came to Bristol on the se'nnight after Whit-Monday, and lodged at St. Augustin's Monastery. His Majesty had dined at Acton with Sir Robert Poyntz, Sheriff of Gloucestershire, and was met, three miles out of Bristol, by the Mayor, the Sheriffs, the Bailiffs, with their brethren, and a great number of other burgesses, including the Recorder, named Treymayle, who in their names "right cunningly welcomed him." On a causeway within Lawford's Gate, the King was received by a procession of friers, and at the end of the causeway the procession of the parish-churches received him; "and in the entry of the town-gate (New-gate) there was ordained a pageant, with great melody and singing; after which, there was a King [Brennus], who had a speech of thirty-five verses—"miserable rhymes," as Mr. Seyer justly calls them, and certainly not coined at the mint of Rowley and Co. (See Memoirs, c. xxii. § 4.)—Chatterton never saw the MS. in the Cotton Library, printed in Leland's collection, from which Mr. Seyer makes his extract, or he would have contrived to make his Bristol bards of the fifteenth century write nearer to this humble standard.— " At the High Cross there was a pageant, full of maiden children richly beseen," and Prudentia had a speech complimentary. Thence " the King proceeded *ad portam sancti Johannis*, where was another pageant of many maiden children, richly beseen with girdles, beads, and *onches*," where Justitia held forth with

"Welcome, most excellent, high and victorious!
Welcome, delicate rose of this our Briton; &c. &c."

On the way towards the Abbey, a baker's wife cast out of a window a great quantity of wheat, crying "Welcome!" and " good luck!" Then there were " the Shipwrights' pageaunt, with pretty conceits playing in the same, without any speech," " another pageant of an olifaunt, with a castle on his back, curiously wrought. The resurrection of our

A D.

1486 Lord in the highest tower of the same [castle], with certain imagery smiting bells, and all went by weights marvellously well done. Within St. Austein's Church, the Abbot and his Convent received the King with procession, as accustomed. And on the morn [morrow], when the King had dined, he rode on pilgrimage to St. Anne's in the wood [Brislington]. And on Thursday next following, which was Corpus Christi day, the King went in procession about the great Green, there called the Sanctuary; whither came all the processions of the town also; and the Bishop of Worcester preached in the pulpit in the middle of the aforesaid Green, in a great audience of the Meyre and the substance of all the burgesses of the town and their wives, with much other people of the country. After evensong, the King sent for the Meyre and Sheriff, and part of the best burgesses of the town, and demanded of them the cause of their poverty [complained of in the ditty of King Brennus]; and they shewed his grace that it was by reason of the great loss of ships and goods which they had suffered within five years. The King comforted them that they should set on and make new ships, and exercise their marchandize, as they were wont to do; and his grace would so help them by divers means [negatively, perhaps, in not asking them for money] like as he shewed them: so that the Mayre of the town told me, they had not heard these hundred years from any King so good a comfort; therefore they thanked Almighty God, that had sent them so good and gracious a sovereign lord. And on the morn [morrow] the King departed to Londonward." See 1490!

From Sept. 21, throughout October, a sickness prevailed in all the kingdom, called the sweating-evil. The remedy was, for those who were attacked in the day-time to lay down in their clothes for twenty-four hours; and for those who were seized in the night, to remain in bed for the same space of time.

1487 Nov. 3, the masonry of the Tower of St. Mark's Chapel was finished, as recorded on a slate let into a stone at the top, now (1822) in possession of Mr. Garrard, the Vice-Chamberlain. See 1667.

John Easterfield, Mayor. (See 1500.) "The Mayor, Sheriff, and Bailiffs, were summoned before the King; which they accomplished, and accused certaine Ireish of Waterford with counterfeite coine."

1488 Feb. 5, at Westminster, the King confirmed the two Charters of 1461, also that of 1462.

A. D.

1489 Jan. 4, William (2), viscount Berkeley, created Marquess
of Berkeley, Earl of Nottingham, and Earl Marshal of England. He had from Edward IV. one hundred marks per
annum out of the customs of Bristol. He excepted against
his brother, the fifth Maurice, as a successor, because he had
married an inferior, Isabella, daughter of Philip Mede,
(see 1458, 1459,) then alderman of Bristol, and gave all his
lands from him. See 1491.

1490 This year the High Cross was painted and gilded.—" The
towne of Bristoll this yeere bestowed twenty pounds in
pitching the streets beyond Avon, and Broade-streete and
others."—" This year divers streetes in Bristowe were
new paved, y^t is to say, Hors-stret, Knightsmith-strete,
Brode-strete, High-strete, Redclif-strete, Thomas-strete,
Temple-strete, Towker-strete, the Bak, Baft-street, Seynt
Mary-strete, Lewin's Mede. And the High Cross was
peynted and gilt, which cost £20."—RICART's *Calendar.*

"This yere the King was at Bristowe, where he had a
benevolence of eighteen hundred pounds."—*Ibid.*

Another MS. says, " The King and the Lord Chancellor
came to Bristol, and lodged at St. Augustine's; and the
commons were made to pay twenty shillings for every one
that was worth twenty pounds, because their wives went so
sumptuously apparelled. The town gave the King five
hundred pounds as a benevolence."—(A third MS. places
this *visitation*, &c. under 1492.)

The stone bridge on the Weir was made.*

1491 Robert Strange died. "This Maior built St. John's Almeshouse, and lyeth in St. John's Church-yard with his wife,
in a monument of freestone, nere the said Almeshouse."
See 1640.

Feb. 14, William, lord Berkeley, died. He was buried at
the St. Augustin's Priory, London, which he had repaired
or newly built, but was burnt in 1666. He was succeeded
in the barony by his brother, the fifth Maurice, third son of
James and Lady Isabel, born 1435. He thus, at 56, became
heir of his father's barony, but without any of its land.
" He was married in his 30th year, and lived with his wife
at Thornbury, where he had lands, until the fifth year afterward, when he assisted his elder and younger brother in the
encounter at Nibley-Green, where the Lord Lisle was by
them slain; for which felonious act he was outlawed, and
inforced, for some time, to withdraw himself and leave

* *Qu.* at Merchant-street or the Narrow Weir?

Q 2

A. D.

1491 Thornbury, whither afterward he returned and for many
years remained. The wife of this Lord Maurice was Isabel,
daughter of Philip Mead, Esq. and of Isabel his wife—son
of Thomas, son of Thomas Mead, descended of the ancient
family of Meads, of Mead-Place, in Feyland, in the parish
of Wraxall, near Portbury, in the county of Somerset; she
was at the time of this marriage a widow, and mother of
three children, who all died very young; and at the same
time her father was an alderman of Bristol, &c. Her dowry,
besides personal estate, consisted of lands in Somersetshire,
and others in Thornbury, where this lord also had lands of
his own purchase and of the gift of his elder-brother, and a
lease of Mead's Place for 21 years. Lady Isabel's brother
dying, she became heir to property in the county of Gloucester, also in Bedminster, Felonde, Ashton, Wraxall, and
Middle Tickenham, Somersetshire. She died in Coventry,
8 Hen. VIII., aged seventy, having outlived her husband nine
years. Her issue were, Maurice, Thomas, James, and Anne.
James married Susan, daughter of Henry Viell, and widow
of William Vele, Esq. See 1506.

Columbus discovered America for the Spaniards. ·

Maud Easterfield gave a ring to the image of Our Lady, in
the north porch of St. Mary Redcliff.*

1492 Beer first introduced into England. It had been used in
Scotland, in 1482†.

1493 The Alms-house in Lewin's Mead, founded by William
Spencer, executor of William Canynges, out of his residuary
goods and estates, for thirteen persons. This is the same
that is now called Spencer's Alms-house. See 1604.

1495 " William Regent, mayor, with two thousand townsmen,
clad in black, met the dead corps of Jasper, duke of Bedford, and accompanied him to Keynsham, where he was
buried. He died at Thornbury. The King and Queen came
shortly afterward to Bristol, and gave the Mayor greate
thanks." The King and Queen lodged at St. Augustin's
Monastery.‡

The High Cross gilded and painted.

" The Sanctuary of St. Mary of St. Augustine's Green was
broken."§

* This lady was probably the wife of John Easterfield, mayor in 1487, and mother of
Harry Easterfield, mayor in 1494.
† Malt-liquor was used in Egypt, 450 B.C.
‡ Perkin Warbeck was at this time in Ireland.
§ In his seventh year the King had obtained from Pope Alexander, his holiness's
authority that no place should be a sanctuary for treason, all traitors being pronounced
enemies to the Christian faith. By the above extract from a MS. it would appear that

A. D.

1495 March 5, Letters-Patent were granted to John Cabot, and his sons, Lewis, Sanctius, and Sebastian, to make discoveries. The King gave license to John Cabot, to take six ships in any haven or harbour of England, of two hundred tons or under, with all necessary outfit, and such masters and men as were willing to go with him. See 1497.

Perkin Warbeck having been entertained by the King of Scots, who invaded England in support of the pretender's claim, the King obtained the consent of Parliament for a subsidy of six score thousand pounds, to enable him to revenge this indignity. Against payment of the subsidy, the people of Cornwall arose in arms, headed by Thomas Flammock, a lawyer, and Michael Joseph, a smith. One of the Bristol MSS. says, " The Cornish rebels, under Flammock and others, being at Wells, sent to the Maior [Phillip Kingston] to billet two thousand men; which he not only denyed, but forbade him on his perill to approach the town. This message was soe ill taken, that the rebells intended revenge; but such provision was made to entertain them, that they desisted. The gates were fortifyed, and such shipps as were of force brought upp to the Marsh. The whole strength of the town were in readyness; for which they received greate comendation of the King." At Wells the rebels were headed by James Touchet, lord Audley, who conducted them to Salisbury, Winchester, and Blackheath. Here they were defeated by the King's forces under Lord Daubeny, the Earl of Kent, and other noblemen, with the loss of 2000 killed, and a great number taken prisoners, many of whom the King pardoned; but Lord Audley was on the 24th of June beheaded at Tower-Hill, and Flammock and Joseph hanged, drawn and quartered.

1497 June 24, St. John's day, John Sebastian Cabot discovered Newfoundland. On his return from this voyage, finding himself neglected, (the nation being still engaged in the war with Scotland,) he went to Spain, where he was furnished with ships, and discovered the coast of Brazil and the river Plate. He was afterward constituted Pilot-Major to Spain. See 1502. There is a portrait of Sebastian in the possession of the Chamber.

1498 " This year there was no Court kept, nor Bayliffs, nor Constable of Temple Fee, for the space of ten weeks. Many were apprehended for heresy in Bristol; for which some were burnt; and some abjured and bore faggots."

the Elder Lady's Chapel had been heretofore the place of sanctuary for the town, and that the privilege was now done away altogether. The handicraftsmen, who then took refuge in the precincts of the Monastery, occupied the College-Green as a rope-walk.

A. D.

1499 Dec. 17, at Knolle (the archiepiscopal palace, near Seven-Oaks, Kent,) the King granted the Charter, No. 24 in Mr. Seyer's Collection. It is a recital chiefly of that of Edw. III. in 1373. The new matter is, the addition to the Mayor and Commonalty, of six Aldermen, including the Recorder for the time being: the other five to be chosen by the Common-Council, and to have the same power as the Aldermen of London. The Mayor and Aldermen to be Justices of the Peace, for proceedings on all indictments whatever at the suit of the King or any other person; the Mayor and Commonalty to have all fines, without giving account to the Exchequer, and appoint a Chamberlain at pleasure, with a seal, and authority the same as in London; the two Bailiffs of the Town, elected by the Mayor, &c., to be also Sheriffs of the County, and hold County-courts, rendering their accounts yearly at the Exchequer. Letters Patent of Sept. 24, 1485, appointing Thomas Hoskins, Water-bailiff, confirmed—providing that upon his death the office shall be vested in the Mayor and Commonalty, to appoint a deputy.

The King presented his own sword to the Mayor, to be borne before him on all occasions of state.

1500 John Greville, Recorder of Bristol.

At the east end of the S. aisle of St. Peter's Church was a Chapel dedicated to the honour of the Blessed Mary of Bellhouse;* to the fraternity of which, now newly established, William Spicer gave a garden and a house in Marshall [now Merchant]-street; as did others. John Easterfield (mayor in 1487), who died Feb. 18, 1507, had a yearly obiit solemnized in the same chapel.

1502 Prince Henry (afterward Henry VIII.), now about twelve years old, contracted to the Infanta Katharine, his late brother Arthur's virgin-wife.

A patent granted to James Elliott and Thomas Ashurst, natives of Bristol, and to John Gonsalez and Francis Fernandez, natives of Portugal, to go with English colours in quest of unknown lands.

1503 The Princess Margaret, King Henry's eldest daughter, married to James IV. king of Scots. (These were the

* In one of the Stage-Moralities written during the succeeding reign, called *Hycke-Scorner*, the principal character, whose name is the title of the piece, gives the following list of a fleet which he describes as having been lost in the Irish Channel.
" Herken, and I wyll shewe you theyr names eche one:
Fyrst was the Regent, with the Mygbell of Brykylse,
The George, with the Gabryell, and the Anne of Foye,
The Starre of Salte-Ashe with the Ibesus of Plumoth;
Also the Hermytage, with the Barbara of Dartmouth,
The *Nycolas*, and the *Mary Bellouse* of *Brystowe*,
With the Elyn of London and James also."

1503 parents of the unfortunate Mary, so fatally the object of Elizabeth's jealousy.) To portion the Princess, the Parliament granted £30,000; towards which London was rated at £618 3s. 5d., Bristol £185 8s. 1¼d., Gloucester £98 10s. 1d., and Bath at £13 6s. 8d.

Robert Ricart ceased to be Town-Clerk of Bristol.

[We learn from the labours of this venerated kalendary, that it was usual, at Michaelmas, for all the chantry-priests, whose compositions, i. e. the copies of Charters and customs of the City, and Rules for the regulation of the different Crafts, were kept among the City-Records, to be sworn before the Mayor, faithfully to record such compositions. It was the custom, too, on Allhallows-day, for the Corporation, and other citizens who chose to assemble with them, after dinner, to go into Allhallows Church, there to offer; and then proceed to the Mayor's, to an entertainment. It was also usual, on St. Katherine's eve, for the Corporation to go to St. Katherine's Chapel, within Temple Church, there to hear their even-song, and then to walk to St. Katherine's Hall, there to be received by the Wardens and Brethren; and in the Hall they were entertained with drinkings, with spices, cakebread, and divers sorts of wine, the cups being sent merrily round (the *humming* stuff thus holily emulating the patron-saint's own wheel), and good fires burning. And after departing home, *St. Katherine's Players* (see 1532) performed before the houses of the Corporation, who gave them drink, and rewarded them for their performance. (These were, doubtless, the journeymen-weavers.) The morrow after St. Katherine's day, the Corporation assembled at Temple Church, and thence walked in procession about the town, and returned again to the church, to hear mass and make their offerings.

On St. Nicholas' eve the Corporation went to St. Nicholas' Church, to hear even-song, and on St. Nicholas' day to hear mass and offer, and hear the Bishop's sermon and receive his blessing. The Corporation, after dinner, assembled at " the Counter" (afterwards called the Tholsel or Tolzey), and while they waited the coming of the Bishop, they amused themselves by playing at dice. It was the business of the Town-Clerk to find them dice, and he received for every raffle one penny. (We can imagine the bronze-tables of the Exchange *now* so occupied, and Mr. Town-Clerk looking out for his pence with one eye, and for the approach of the Reverend Father with the other!) And on the arrival of the Bishop, his choir sang there, and the Bishop gave his blessing. And he and the whole of his Chapel were entertained with bread and wine; and afterward the Corporation went again to St. Nicholas, to hear the Bishop's even-song.

It was usual for the Mayor and Sheriff to be at the Counter every day at eight o'clock, and sit till eleven, and (Saturdays excepted) from two till five in the afternoon, to hear complaints between parties.

A. D.

1503 Proclamation was made just before Christmas and other feasts, for the observance of good order during the holidays. No person whatever was permitted, after the ringing of the *bombell* at St. Nicholas, to carry any kind of light through the streets, nor to be armed with any weapons, on pain of fine and imprisonment. Perhaps the *humming stuff* of those days was apt to make folks quarrelsome and mischievous. It now too often leaves them harmlessly stupid, food for Apoplexy.]

St. Nicholas Church partly rebuilt.

1504 John Foster (mayor in 1481) founded the Chapel of the Three Kings of Cologne, and the Alms-house, Steep-street. After his death, the charity was augmented by his executor, John Easterfield (mayor in 1488 and 1495), and further increased by Dr. George Owen, physician to Henry VIII. (See 1558.) The magistrates are the patrons. The funds are blended with those of the Grammar-school in Orchard-street. See 1702.

1506 September, Maurice (5) lord Berkeley died, leaving great estates, recovered for the most part out of his brother's grants, by law-suits with the possessors. He was buried in St. Augustin's Friery, London, and was succeeded by his nephew, the sixth Maurice, who built the chapel in the Monastery, with a rainbow-arch, in which the Newtons are buried. His wife was Katherine, daughter of Sir William Berkeley, of Stoke Gifford. She died in 1526, and was buried at Yeate. See 1516.

1509 April 22, the King died of consumption, at Richmond, in his 53d year.

HENRY VIII.,

Aged eighteen years. June 3, he married Katherine.

1510 May 10, at Westminster, the King confirmed the Charters of 1488 and 1499—Seyer, No. 25.

1512 John Elliott, Mayor; Thomas Brook, one of the Sheriffs.

1514 Robert Thorne, Mayor. " This Thorne was Knt. civill [a Knight of Seville]. He gave five hundred pounds to the use of cloth-making; and did also give the greatest almes that ever were given in Bristol before this time." He never was sheriff. He was previously hereto a merchant-taylor of London.

1515 Abbot Newland or Nailheart died. He was buried under a stately monument on the south side of the Choir. Sept. 27, was elected Robert Elliott, the twenty-second abbot; whose initials appear in bricks on the floor, and carved in

A. D.

the wood-work, and his statue is one of those on the south side of the Monastery gate. His escutcheon, bearing a heart pierced with nails and bleeding, appears over the arched entrance to the Bishop's Palace from College-square, and in many other parts of the monastic remains.

1516 Peter Martyr, of Angleria, wrote his 3d decade, chap. 6, describing Sebastian Cabot's voyage to the North Seas.

"Whereas there was a custom in this town of Bristol, for the relief of the prisoners in Newgate, that every country-person that brought any thing to be sold in the Market should pay to the jailor, for pitching every pot or sack, one halfpenny; but, because the jailors convey'd it to their own profit, Mr. Richard Hobbington [sheriff in 1515], with the consent of the Mayor, Mr. John Jay, to reform the disorder'd custom and abuse, and to ease the country-people, did put down this disorder'd use; and the said Mr. Hobbington, at his own cost, purchas'd a perpetual stipend, to find them victuals, wood, and straw."

Miles Salley, abbot of the Monastery de Einsham, and episcopus Landaff, buried in St. Mark's Chapel.

Maurice (6) lord Berkeley, High Sheriff of Gloucestershire. See 1522.

1517 Sir John Seymore obtained a grant of the constablewick of the Castle, for his own life and that of his son Edward.

1518 "This yeare William Dale, sheriff, [apothecary,] with divers other young merchants, fell at great strife with the Mayor and others of the Councell, and with John Fitzjames, the Recorder, for certain duties to be paid the Mayor and Recorder yearely by the Sheriffe, of ancient custom."

This year it continued to rain from Whit-Sunday till Michaelmas.

1520 Oct. 4, by an Act of Common-Council, the Burgesses serving in Parliament were ordered to have twenty shillings paid them every session. The following also were fixed as yearly wages: Keeper of the Key, 28s. 8d.—of the Back, 26s. 8d.—Porter of New-Gate, 30s.—of Redcliff-Gate, 20s. —of Temple-Gate, 26s. 8d.—of Froom-Gate, 13s. 4d.—of Pithay-Gate, 13s. 4d.

George Lilly, who lived some time at Rome, with Cardinal Pole, this year published the first exact map of this island. He was the son of William Lilly, the famous grammarian, who was born at Odiham, Hants, and first master of St. Paul's School.*

* Maps and sea-charts were first brought into England by Bartholomew Columbus, in 1490. The mariner's compass was invented in 1302.

R

A. D.

1520 William Grocyne, a native of Bristol, died, in his 80th year.
He was bred at Winchester School, where, in his youth, he
was said to be an excellent poet. The following tetrastick
is attributed to him, as made extempore, on his mistress pelt-
ing him with a snow-ball.

> Me nive candenti petiit mea Julia; rebar
> Igne carere nivem, nix tamen ignis erat
> Sola potes nostres extinguere Julia flammas
> Nou nive, non glacie, at tu potes igne pari.

He afterwards went to Italy, where he studied under Deme-
trius Chalcondilus and Politian. Returning to England, he
was the first public professor of the Greek tongue in Oxford.
Erasmus owns him, in his Epistles, " pro patrono suo et
præceptore."*

William Crop, Prior of the Kalendaries.

1521 " This yeare the duke of Buckenham came to Bristoll.
Shortly after, he was beheaded, May 17th, 1521." — Sir
Richard Baker says, " The chief witness suborned against
him by Wolsey, in revenge for a supposed indignity, was one
Charles Knevet, who had been his surveyor; who confessed
to the Cardinal that the Duke had once fully determined to
make away the King; being brought into a hope to be king
himself, by a vain prophecy, which one Nicholas Hopkins, a
monk of an house of the Charter order, besides Bristow,
called Henton, sometimes his confessor, had opened to him."

" This year John Mathews, of the parish of St. Ewen,
gave all his land, save one tenement in Marsh-street, to the
alms-house at Lawford's Gate; and that one tenement he
gave to the parish of St. Ewen."

1522 Feb. 2, the King received a Bull from the Pope (Adrian
VI.), giving him and his successors the title of Defender of
the Faith, for writing a work against Luther.

Maurice (6) lord Berkeley made Governor of Calais, and
Baron.

1523 " Every man was sworn as to what he was worth."

Sept. 12, Maurice, lord Berkeley, died at Calais, without
legitimate issue, and was buried there in Trinity Chapel,
St. Nicholas' Church. He was succeeded by his brother,
the fifth Thomas, who was only Constable of Berkeley Castle,
the property being then vested in the Crown, by virtue of

---

* " We are told that learning, by which I believe is only meant the scholastic
ontology, had begun to decline at Oxford from the time of Edward III. And the fifteenth
century, from whatever cause, is particularly barren of writers in the Latin language.
The study of Greek was only introduced by Grocyn and Linacer under Henry VII.; and
met with violent opposition in the University of Oxford, where the unlearned party
styled themselves Trojans, as a pretext for abusing and insulting the scholars."—
HALLAM's *Middle Ages*, iii. 595.

A. D.

1523 the will of William, marquess of Berkeley, who died in 1491. See 1532.

St. Bartholomew's Priory, in Christmas-street, purchased of Sir Thomas West, knt. and Lord de la Warre, patrons and founders, by the executors of Robert Thorne. Leland describes this as one of the hospitals in ruins at the time of his visit.

"This year crosses were throwne and pulled downe."

1524 Sept. 1, an Ambassador from the Pope (Clement VII.) brought the King a present of a tree forged of fine gold, with branches, leaves, and flowers resembling roses.

1525 Cardinal Wolsey obtained license of the King to erect a College at Oxford and another at Ipswich; and towards the charge got leave to suppress forty small monasteries, that he might employ their goods and lands for maintenance of the Colleges; for which he also obtained the Pope's confirmation.

"This yere Master Maire, as well with hys own costs as with the costiz of the Commons of this worshipful towne, causid to be taken downe Stalenge Crosse, beyng right old, corrupt, and feble, and causid the Crosse there nowe to be made of the new; not only that cross, but also he commanded that the heddes of the Crosses at the Gallowes [Bewell's] and Market-place [the High Cross] shulde be made of the newe, as they nowe be."—*Mayors' Kalendar.*

This year the reverend martyr, Dr. Barnes, wore a faggot at his back in Bristol.

1526 John Somerset, the twenty-third Abbot.

Roger Eggeworth, Prior of the Kalendaries.

Previous to this date, the Bristol merchants traded with the Canaries, by means of vessels from St. Lucar, in Spain, principally in cloth and soap.

1527 "This yeare, upon midsomer-night, there was made by the Welshmen a great fray in the King's watch; and at St. James tide next following, as the Mayor [Thomas Brooke*] and his brethren came from wrasling, a *Welshman* killed Richard Vaughan,† mercer, on the Bridge; and they escaped cleare away in a boate with the tide, without any hurt done to them for it." Another MS. (that of Mr. Alderman Haythorne) thus relates the same circumstance: "This yeere one Mr. William Vaughan, a mercer, on the Bridge, was killed on St. James's day, by William Herbert, after Earl of Pembroke (saith the Catalogue). Mr. Vaughan

* See note to 1534, of Richard Brooke, &c.

† Harry Vaughan was mayor in 1492; Richard Vaughan in 1500 and 1506; and John Vaughan in 1507 and 1520.

R 2

1527 had been Sheriffe before, in 1516. Mr. Herbert, with much adoe, escaped by a boate that was prepared for him, the water being then ebbing. It seems the murther was committed for want of some respect in complement.'' See 1469.—Aubrey (Lives, p. 447) gives the following version of the same event: " One time, being at Bristowe, he [William Herbert, first earl of Pembroke, by fresh creation] was arrested, and killed one of the Sheriffes of the city. He made his escape through Back-street, through the *then* great gate, into the Marsh, and gott into France. *Mem.* Upon the action of killing the Sheriff, the city ordered the gate to be walled up, and only a little posterne gate or door, with a turnstile for a foot-passenger; which continued so till Bristowe was a garrison for the King, and the great gate was then opened, in 1644 or 1645. When I was a boy there, living with my father's mother, who was married to Alderman John Whitson [mayor in 1603], (who was my godfather,) the story was as fresh as but of yesterday.'' See 1561.

Robert Thorne advised Dr. Ley, ambassador to the Emperor Charles V., of an adventure of fourteen hundred ducats in a fleet from Seville, the outfit of two Englishmen going with Sebastian Cabot to the Moluccas.

By will, dated the 4th of May, John Hawkys (mayor in 1471) gave a third part of his estate, valued at nine hundred pounds, to the rectors and proctors of the Church of St. Leonard, adjoining St. John's.

1528 Nicholas and John Thorne, Sheriffs. Robert and Nicholas Thorne* founded the Grammar-School, on the site of St. Bartholomew's Hospital, without Froom-Gate. See 1532.

The King's scruples first appeared this year, against the lawfulness of his marriage with his brother's widow.

1529 William Warham, archbishop of Canterbury, and Nicholas West, bishop of Ely, doctors of law; with John Fisher, bishop of Rochester,† and Henry Standish, bishop of St. Asaph, doctors of divinity, and others, allowed as Counsel for the Queen; who protested against the hearing, and appealed to the Pope. Cardinal Wolsey, being aware of the King's affection for Anne Boleyn, daughter of Viscount Rochford, and wishing him to marry the Duchess of Alanson, the French King's sister, sent privily, not to prevent, but

* Robert Thorne was bred a merchant-tailor in London, and died a bachelor, aged 40 years, in 1532. He was buried in St. Christopher's, London. Nicholas died Aug. 19, 1546, aged 50, and was buried in St. Werbugh's church, Bristol. Their portraits are preserved in the Grammar-School, Orchard-street.

† Richard Hall, D. D., who died at St. Omer's, in 1604, wrote the Life of this John Fisher, bishop of Rochester.

A. D.

1529 to influence the Pope against giving sentence in favour of the divorce for a time. Upon discovery of this correspondence, Oct. 18, the great seal was transferred from Wolsey to Sir Thomas More, Speaker of the Parliament, (the first layman that had borne the office of Lord Chancellor), and the Cardinal was afterward adjudged to have incurred a præmunire for procuring bulls from Rome to execute his legantine powers, and disgraced and deprived accordingly.

A High Court of Parliament called, in which the Commons complained sharply of their grievances against the Clergy, and passed three bills, one of mortuaries, another of the probate of testaments, and the third for non-residence, pluralities, and the taking of farms by spiritual men.

John Hilsey, a black frier of Bristol, made Bishop of Rochester.

Thomas White, of Coventry, Mayor of Bristol. See 1541.

"This yeare was a faire appointed at Candlemas-day, at St. Mary Redcliffe."

1530 The New-Testament in English, by Tyndale, Joy, and others, forbidden to be read, and copies of it burnt in St. Paul's Church-yard. See 1536.

An Act passed that the Bishops should pay no more money for bulls to the Pope; and another, against appeals out of the realm to the Court of Rome.

Cardinal Wolsey, who still held the bishopricks of York and Winchester, arrested at Cawood, near York, on a charge of high treason. Nov. 18, at Leicester-Abbey, on his way to the Tower, he died of a flux.

The whole clergy of England charged by the King's Counsel to be in a præmunire, for supporting and maintaining the Cardinal's legantine power. The process was stayed by an offer, in convocation, of one hundred thousand pounds for their pardon in Parliament; and in their submission the clergy called the King, Supreme Head of the Church.

Queen Katherine confined.

1532 Jan. 22, Thomas (5) lord Berkeley died. He was at first buried in Mangotsfield Church, but removed, as he had requested, in eight months, and re-interred in the same tomb with his wife Eleanor, under the arch between the north aisle and the Elder Lady's Chapel. This Thomas was the last of the family who was buried in the Monastery.

Now, and in several succeeding years, actors, under the protection of noblemen, were hired by the magistrates to exhibit in the Guildhall.*

* In the Retrospective Review, 8vo. vol. i., for 1820, will be found a curious account of the representation of a Morality before the Corporation of Gloucester about this

A. D.

1532   The King's marriage with Queen Katherine dissolved by the Parliament.

May 16, Sir Thomas More delivered up the great seal.

Sept. 1, the King created Anne Boleyn Marchioness of Pembroke, giving her £1000 a year in land; and on the 10th of October took her with him to Calais, where he met the King of France.

Nov. 14, the King was privately married to Anne Boleyn.

"Thomas [Cranmer], archbishop of Canterbury, came and tarried here nineteen days, and reformed many things amiss, and preached at St. Austin's and other places."

1533   June 1, Whit-Sunday, Anne Boleyn crowned Queen.

Sept. 7, the Princess Elizabeth born.

1534   Jan. The statute of Hen. VI. against heretics repealed.

William Burton became the twenty-fourth Abbot. This is the same whose initials appear so frequently about the present altar of the Cathedral, on each side the device of a tun, with a tree springing from the bung-hole.

Sept. 9, Abbot Burton, with seventeen others of the Monastery, subscribed to the King's supremacy.

Sept. 11, the Hospital of the Gaunts was resigned to the King. The " church, houses, and buildings appoynted to remaine undefaced," were, " the church there, appointed for the parish-church, as heretofore hath been used. The lodgings, called the Master's lodging, with the hall, bottery, pantry and kitchen, (committed to the care of Edward Carne, doctor of law), deemed to be superfluous,* divided into honest tenantries, with convenient rents reserved to the use of the King. Bells remaining in the steeple there, vj., whereof iij assigned to the parish, and remain to the use of the King's majestie, iij—poiz by est. mmlb. weight."*

time, and the effect it produced upon the author, who was then very young, extracted from a book entitled " Mount Tabor, or private exercises of a penitential sinner," by R. W., published in 1639, when the author was 75 years of age.

* In February, 1824, in the house occupied by Mr. Franklyn, perfumer, which is attached to the western wall of the Chapel, a closet, in a dressing-room on the first floor (the window of which overlooks the Grammar-School garden), proved to have been used as a private oratory. It is a recess formed in the wall of the Chapel, from which the upper part is separated only by a thin partition of stone. In the wall on the left-hand side of the closet is a picinæ or niche for a vessel of holy water, cut in the tomb of a painting of the Resurrection. On each side of the Saviour a crowned and a mitred figure kneel in adoration; and between them the words Jesu, Maria, &c. are repeated, in the text-character of the time when the chapel was founded. In the corner on the same hand is a double-sighted aperture, through which a part of the altar in the chapel may be seen and the service heard. Facing the entrance of the closet, the stone partition is painted with two more subjects, in compartments of about twenty-two inches square, one representing the Stable at Bethlehem, with the Virgin, the Child, Joseph, and Magi; the other, Christ in the garden near Bethany, resting his right hand on a spade, with Mary at his left side, the sister of Lazarus in a supplicating attitude before him.

1534 This year there was a controversy between the Lord Prior
of St. John of Jerusalem in England and the Mayor and
Commonalty of Bristol, relating to the privilege of sanctuary
in Temple-street, and of having a law-day, to hold court
with the usual privilege, and returning a brevium and
execution of the same in the same street; claiming also that
his tenants and inhabitants within the said street, not being
burgesses, might vend their merchandizes there in open
shops. All which articles were denied by the Mayor; and
the matter was referred to Sir J. Fitz-James, Ch. J., and
Richard Brooke, Ch. Baron;* who ordered that the liberty
of sanctuary should be void, and that processes should be
served in the said street by the city-officers without disturbance of the Lord Prior. The other matters in dispute
were referred to another time; but Henry contrived to settle
them after his own supremely radical fashion.

The King and Queen being at Thornbury, the Mayor sent
ten fat oxen and forty sheep to the King, and a silver cup
and cover, with a hundred marks of gold, to the Queen.

Great disputes about laymen preaching, who were
favoured by the Mayor. Priests sent to Newgate.

Hugh Latimer, whose benefice was at West Kington, in
Wiltshire, preached on the second Sunday in Lent two
sermons, one in St. Nicholas-Church and the other in the
Black Friers. He also preached on the Monday following.
See Memoirs, c. xxiii. § 9—18, and our notice under 1539.

John Leland visited Bristol Castle about this time, and
thus describes it:—" In the Castle be two courtes. In the
utter courte, as in the north-west part of it, is a great dun-
geon-tower, made as it is said of stone browghte out of Cane
in Normandy, by the redde Erle of Gloucester. A praty
churche and much loggyng in the area: on the southe syde
of it a great gate, a stone bridge, and three bullewarks, in
læva ripa ad ostium frai. There be manie towres yet
standynge in both the courtes; but alle tendith to ruine.
The Castle and most part of the Towne by northe standith
upon a grownde metely eminent, betwyxt the ryvers Avon
and Fraw, alias Froom."—*Itin.* vii. 84, 2d edit.

The same writer gives the following description of the
Bristol Conduits:—" *Conducts ci pontem*—St. John's, harde

* John Brooke, who lies buried in Redcliff-Church, at foot of the high-altar steps,
was Sergeant-at-law to the King, one of the Judges of Assize on the Western Circuit,
and Chief Steward of the Abbey of Glastonbury. His son David was Chief-Baron of
the Exchequer, 1 Mary, and married Catherine, daughter of John, Lord Chandois.
See 1541.

A. D.

1534 by St. John's Gate. The Key-Pipe, with a very fair castellette, All-Hallow Pipe, hard by the Kalendaries, without a castelle. St. Nicholas Pipe, with a castle. [See 1764.] *Ultra pontem*—Redcliffe-Pipe, with a castellet, hard by Redcliffe-Churche; witheowte the Gate.   Another Pipe without Redcliffe-Gate, haveing no castelle.   Another by Port-Waulle, without the waulle."

1535   Jan. 18, the King assumed the title of Head of the Church of England, in the presence of his whole Court.

1536   Jan. 8, died the Dowager-Queen Katherine, at Kimbolton. She was buried at Peterborough.

Oct.   The King sent Dr. Lee and others to visit the abbeys, priories, and nunneries; who set at liberty all that were disposed to forsake their habits, and all that were under the age of twenty-four years.

Dec.   A survey was taken of all chantries, and the names of such as had the gift of them.

"This year William Tyndale was burnt at a town in Flanders, between Brussels and Mechlyn, called Villefort, for translating into English, the New Testament and divers parts of the Old; who, having been long imprisoned, was, upon the Lord Cromwell's writing for his deliverance, in all haste brought to the fire, and burnt."   In 1520, he resided with Sir John Welsh, at Little Sodbury, as tutor to his children, and frequently preached on Sundays in Bristol. He had often debates with the abbots and clergy, who frequented the house of his patron, and with his approbation, but not entirely to the satisfaction of the lady his wife. From the family of this martyr, we believe, is descended that which gives name to one of the most pleasant resources of the citizens of Bristol for air and exercise, Tyndale's Park.

Morgan Guilliam ap Guilliam,* the last abbot of St. Augustin's Monastery.

1537   Feb. 4, in Parliament, an Act was made, giving the King all religious houses, with all their lands and goods, that were of the value of three hundred marks a year and under. The value of the lands so sequestrated was £32,000 per annum—of the moveables, £100,000; and the number of persons put out of those houses was more than 10,000.

---

* Nothing could be more unlikely than that an Abbot elected at such a period could be found so void of circumspection as to be detected in keeping "a snug scraglio of six lewd women," as charged upon Guilliam's memory by Fuller and Speed. Upon the principle of " new brooms, &c." his remains would hardly have been suffered to be deposited within the walls of a church in a state of purgation, though the Royal chastity that held the besom was not itself immaculate.

A. D.

1537 May 19, the Queen beheaded, on a scaffold upon the Green within the Tower.

May 20, the King married Lady Jane Seymour, who at Whitsuntide was openly shewed as Queen.

William Chester, point-maker, Mayor of Bristol. He founded the alms-house on St. James's Back, called the Gift-House. See 1549 and 1602.

Sept. Lord Cromwell, now Vicar-General under the King, set forth injunctions that the Lord's Prayer, the Ave, the Creed, the ten Commandments, and all Articles of the Christian Faith, should be translated into English, and so taught by all parsons and curates to their parishioners. Several insurrections hereupon took place in different parts of the north of England; which were suppressed by force of arms and individual executions under martial law.

Oct. 12, Queen Jane delivered of a son (Edward VI.); and Oct. 24 she died.

1538 Divers roods were taken down by command of the King; and all the notable images, objects of special pilgrimages and offerings, also taken down and burnt. All the orders of friers and nuns, with their cloisters and houses, were suppressed.

1539 "This yeare, the 15th day of May, a Scott named Geo. Wysard [Wischarde] set forth [in] his lecture at S. Nicholas Church of Bristowe, the mooste blasphemous heresy that ever was herd, openly declaring that Christ nother hathe or coulde merit for him, ne yet for vs; which heresie brought many of the commons of this towne into a grete error, and dyvers of theym were persuaded by that hereticall lecture to heresy; whereupon the said stiff-necked Scott was accused by Mr. John Kearne, deane of this diocise; and sone aft he was sende to the most reverend Father in God the Archebishopp of Cantrebury, before whom and others, that is to signifie, the Bishopps of Bathe, Northwiche, and Chichestre, and others; and he before theym was examyned, convicted and condemned in and upon the detestable heresy abovementioned. Whereupon he was enjoyned to bere a faggot in St. Nicholas Churche forsaid and the parishe of the same, the 13 day of July, and in Christe-Churche and parishe thereof the 20 day of July abovesaid; which injunction was duely executed in form forsaid."—*Mayors' Kalendar.*

John Knox, in his "Historie of the Reformation of Religion within the Realme of Scotland," (printed at Edinburgh in 1644), bestows 23 of his close quarto pages upon the progress, in that kingdom, of "that blessed Martyr of

A. D.

1539 God, Master George Wischarde," who entered Scotland in company of the English army and commissioners in May 1544, and, after various adventures consequent upon his bold preachings and prophesyings, was arraigned for heresy before Cardinal Beaton at the Abbey-Church of St. Andrew, and burnt on the 2d of March 1546. This burning lighted the flame of revenge that produced the assassination of the Cardinal, in the Castle, on the 29th of May following; and the sturdy reformer himself shortly afterward first assumed the vocation of a public preacher.

William Rowley one of the Sheriffs.

Nov. 14, Richard Whiting, abbot of Glastonbury, executed at the Tor, with Roger James, and John Thorn, two of the monks—he for hesitating to surrender the Monastery, and they for giving him ill advice.

Dec. 9, Abbot Guilliam surrendered the Monastery of St. Augustin into the King's hands. He obtained for himself a pension of eighty pounds per annum, and an annual allowance of between seven and eight pounds for the monks who chose to continue in observance of their monastic vows. Guilliam lived till 1552, and was buried in the Cathedral. In 1554, the junior ex-monk was made a prebendary of the bishoprick.

The site of the Black Friers' Monastery, near Rosemary-street, was granted to William Chester, esq. See 1549.

1540 Jan. 6, the King married Lady Anne, sister to the Duke of Cleve, a protestant prince—not because he had any affection for her protestantism, but because she was offered to him without the condition of a license from the Pope.

Jan. 9, Robert Circester, prior of St. James, surrendered the priory, and was allowed a pension of £13 6s. 8d. for life.

In April, Lord Cromwell, who had made the match between the King and Anne of Cleve, was made Earl of Essex.

July 9, Lord Cromwell was arrested in the Council-Chamber for heresy and treason, and, on the 28th, beheaded on Tower-Hill.

July 10, the King was divorced from Ann of Cleve; but she lived sixteen years afterward.

Aug. 8, the King was married to Lady Katherine Howard, niece to the Duke of Norfolk, and daughter of Lord Edward Howard.

The office of Lord High Steward of Bristol this year commenced in the person of Edward Seymour, duke of Somerset. See 1551.

The church-plate was forwarded from Bristol to London.

A. D.

540 The Knights of St. John of Jerusalem suppressed by Act of Parliament.

The House of St. Magdalen, St. Michael's Hill, sold to Henry Brayne, a merchant-tailor of London, and John Marsh. The lands were sold in 1546.

541 Jan. 14, by deed, Thomas White gave the manor of Dirham to the Corporation of Bristol, to exempt the Severn vessels from customs in the port of Bristol, and for other charitable purposes. See 1555.

David Brook, serjeant-at-law, Recorder of Bristol.

542 Feb. 12, Queen Katherine Howard and Lady Rochford were beheaded on the Green within the Tower.

Thomas Sylke became Prior of the Kalendaries.

The King having determined to establish six bishopricks, viz. Westminster, Oxford, Peterborough, Bristol, Chester, and Gloucester, on the 4th of June Paul Bush, an Augustinian frier of Oxford, canon of Salisbury, and one of the King's chaplains, was appointed Bishop of Bristol; the Abbey to be hereafter called Trinity College of the City of Bristol. The town was accordingly proclaimed a City and Bishoprick. The endowment of the bishoprick and chapter is dated Nov. 18—the establishment to consist of a bishop, a dean, six prebends, six minor canons, a deacon, a sub-deacon, a præcentor, six choristers, and an organist. It was doubtless in the interval of three years now elapsed since the suppression of the Monastery, that the church westward of the tower underwent the dilapidation so evident upon a view of the exterior on that side. We believe, too, that the choir heretofore commenced at the entrance of the nave between the first pair of shafts supporting the tower, and that the present organ-screen was the rood-loft. On its west side, to the left of the arch, are the arms of the King, with his initials, H. R.; and on the right, the Prince's plume, with the initials, E. R. See 1645.

The College Grammar-School was founded at the same time.

Out of the lands with which the King endowed the College, he ordered that twenty pounds per annum should be bestowed in repairing the highways about Bristol. See 1613.

543 July 2, the day of the Visitation of Our Lady, the Litany was first sung in English, in a general procession from Christ-Church to the Church of St. Mary Redcliff.

July 12, the King married his sixth and last wife, Lady Katherine Parr, widow of Lord Latimer, and a protestant.

A. D.

She was not without her chance of the axe, a warrant having been issued for her apprehension as a heretic; but the Royal caprice, though labouring under a sore leg, was for this time diverted.

1554   June 30, the Corporation purchased of the King the patronage of Temple-Church, and part of the lands. See a copy of the deed in Barrett's Hist. p. 545, signed Edward Beynton and Gyles Dodyngton.

In July, twelve ships sailed out of Bristol, to assist at the siege of Bulloigne, under the command of Matthew, earl of Lenox. "When Henry came on board Bristowe's fleet (fitted out to assist him against the French), he asked the names of their ships; and they answered, the barque Thorne, of 600 tons—Pratt, 600 tons—Gourney, 400 tons—Younge, 400 tons—Winter,* 300 tons—Shipman,† 250 tons—Elephant, 120 tons—Dragon, 120 tons." The King rejoined, "he wished he had more such Pratts and Gourneys in his land."

Nicholas Thorne, Mayor, kept his Admiralty-Court at Clevedon.

"The stews were put down, and Aston was burnt."

A great plague in Bristol, which continued a whole year.

1545   June 26, it was proclaimed at the High Cross that the five gates (Newgate, Redcliff, Temple, Froom, and Pithay) should be free for all strangers or goods going out or coming into the city, and the Quaý and Back to be free for all merchandize except salt-fish. This was in return for the contributions made by the vestries and private persons towards the purchase, by the Corporation from the King, of St. Mark's endowments and other property of the suppressed monasteries, &c.

This year also there was set up in the Castle a mint for coining‡ the confiscated monastic plate, and a press for printing church-homilies, &c. in English.

July 17, a thunder-storm lasted from eight o'clock at night till four the next morning.

1546   Edward, earl of Hertford, Lord High Steward of Bristol.

Tobias Matthews was this year born, on Bristol Bridge. He was the son of a linen-draper.

Sept. Thomas, duke of Norfolk, and Henry, earl of Surrey, his son and heir, were committed to the Tower.

1547   Jan. 13 (the King then lying at the point of death—the ruling passion on him still) the Earl of Surrey was arraigned

---

* After Sir William Winter.   † Mayor in 1521, 1529, and 1533.

‡ Testons, groats, half-groats, and pence, in silver, with "Civitas Bristolliæ" on the reverse.   The Master of the Mint was William Sherrington.   See 1549.

A. D.

1547 in the Guildhall, before the Lord Mayor, the Lord Chancellor, and other Lords then in commission, for bearing certain arms that were said to belong to the King and to the Prince; which the Earl justified, as belonging to divers of his ancestors, and in which he had the opinion of Heralds. A common jury found him guilty, and on the 19th he was beheaded on Tower Hill. (The Duke, his father, remained under attainder till the first year of Queen Mary.)

Jan. 28, the King died of an ulcerated leg and fever, in the 56th year of his age. This man's profession of the Catholic faith must have been alone sufficient to induce his subjects to seek for examples of better practice in the newly found *ism* of Protestants. He was buried at Windsor. One of the very few good works that follow him is an Anthem, to be found in Boyce's Collection of Cathedral Music.

EDWARD VI.

Succeeded, by his father's last will, in the tenth year of his age.—Edward Seymour, earl of Hertford, the King's uncle, afterward Duke of Somerset, chosen Lord Protector.

July 12, at Westminster, was granted the Charter of Confirmation of that of 1510—Seyer's No. 26.

Injunctions set forth against praying to saints or for the dead,—the use of beads, ashes, and processions,—masses, dirges, and praying in any unknown tongue. For want of preachers, homilies were appointed to be read in the churches. An Act was passed, giving the King all the chantries which the late king had not seized.

1548 An order of Council for removing images out of the churches.

April. England continuing at war with Scotland, Mary, the young Queen of Scots, now six years old, was conveyed into France and married to the Dauphin Francis.

At Bedminster Church, this year, there were three hundred and twenty communicants—supposed to have been rendered so numerous by the custom of wake-days of the church that prevailed, admitting sports by the young people in the afternoon, as now in France and other Roman Catholic countries.

A man named Bond was hung in chains at the hither end of Durdham-Down, for murthering his master in the very same place.

The Protector's brother, Lord Sudely, Admiral of England, beheaded.

A. D.

1549 Robert Kelway, High Steward of Bristol.

Upon the alterations of religion in the past and present year, much tumult took place, particularly in Cornwall, Devonshire, Norwich, and at Bristol. The Castle and city-walls were repaired and mounted with cannon; most of the city-gates were made anew, and guards of soldiers were established by day and night. Sir William Herbert was Constable of the Castle. One MS. says, "In the month of May there was a great insurrection in the city of Bristoll, and many young men pluck'd up hedges and thrust down ditches with [*filled up the ditches of*] inclosed grounds near this city; and afterwards they rebelled against the Mayor [William Pikes], so that he and all his brethren with him were forced to go into the Marsh with weapons; and there the matter was closed up, and within four days after all the rebells were taken, one after another, and put in ward; but not one suffered for the insurrection." We elsewhere learn that the malcontents were appeased by the prudence of Mr. William Chester (mayor in 1537, and point-maker), in procuring a general pardon for them. After which the soldiers of the garrison, who were under the command of Lord Grey of Wilton, marched to Honiton, and defeated the rebels there. The public records referring to other places sufficiently prove that plunder was more the object, than piety the motive, of these commotions.

May 25, by deed, Bishop Paul Bush surrendered to the King the manor of Abbot's Leigh; and Sept. 23d following the King granted the reversion of it, after the death of the Bishop, to Sir George Norton and his heirs for ever. (From the Nortons it went to the Trenchards.) See 1651.

The King allowed to Sebastian Cabot an annuity of £166 13s. 4d., and appointed him Grand Pilot of England. He was also made Governor for life of the Russia-Company.

Aug. 14, the plate of All Saints' Church weighed 423½ ounces. Some of it was now taken for the use of the King's mint here, and nearly all the rest for the same purpose in 1552.

1549 Sir William Sherrington, Master of the Mint, a creature of Admiral Seymour, (brother of the Protector Somerset, who resided at Longleat,) put the Mint of Bristol into the hands of the Admiral, who was to take thence £10,000 per month for his rebellious purposes. Yet Sherrington was pardoned and restored.—WALPOLE's *Anecdotes of Painting.*

1550 May 24, the King granted the Charter for the September Fair; the profits to go to the poor of the parish, excepting twenty shillings to the Corporation.

A. D.

1559 " This yere the newe Tolset was bylte; and in this same yere the Stipe-strete, going up to St. Michaels, was brought lower and in good fashion, also Redcliff-strete and Thomas-strete new pight."

1551 Mr. Hippisley, Lord High Steward of Bristol.

" July 12, the 12d. was cryed down to 9d., and the 4d. to 2d. In August, the 12d. was cryed down from 9d. to 6d., and the 4d. to 2d. and the 2d. to a penny, and the penny to a halfpenny, to the great loss of the King and his subjects."

" Altars were pulled down, and tables made for to receive the Communion."

" Sweet wine was sold for 12d. and Gascoine wine for 8d. the gallon."

" The sweating-sickness reigned in the whole realm."
" The pestilence reigned in the City of Bristol very sore for the time it lasted; for it swept away many hundreds every week; the which endured from Easter until Michaelmas."

" Wheat sold at 4s. 8d. per bushel, and the poor could scarce get bread for money; but the Mayor [David Harris, apothecary] prepared wisely for them, for he caused every baker to bake bread for the commons at a price which the mayor and the bakers agreed upon."

Bridewell erected.

Dec. 14, by letters patent the King incorporated the Society of Merchant - Venturers, with four consuls and twenty - four assistants. Sebastian Cabot was the first Governor.

Edward Seymour, duke of Somerset, Lord Protector (who built the palace called Somerset-House), beheaded.

1552 Sebastian Cabot promoted a voyage to the North Seas, which procured the trade to Archangel.

The old Chapel of the fraternity of St. John, south side of St. Ewen's Church, having been granted in 1551 by the parson and parishioners to the Corporation, they this year built a Council-House upon its site, with a piazza, supported by five stone pillars, under which were placed three tables similar to those now in front of the Exchange. This building was erected, as was also its successor of 1704, without taking down the west wall of the Chapel, in which was the frame of a large window of the pointed style. See 1824.

John Walshe, esq. Lord High Steward of Bristol.

Wheat sold at sevenpence a bushel.

The inhabitants of Edgeware, Middlesex, were this year presented for not having a Ducking-Stool. Bristol was not without such a machine for the correction of scolding women.

A. D.

1552 A post was set up in the water of the Froom, at the mouth of the ditch, under the awful frown of the Castle-walls. Across this post was placed a transverse beam, turning on a swivel, with a chair at one end of it; in which when the culprit was properly placed, that end was turned to the stream, and let down into it, once, twice or thrice, according to the tender mercy, gallantry, or auricular sensibility of the operators. The writer last beheld the venerable remains of this silence-imposing post about the year 1785. See 1718, for an account of the latest example of its virtues.

Taverns restrained, by Act of Parliament, to forty in London, eight in York, four in Norwich, three in Westminster, six in Bristol, three in Lincoln, four in Hull, three in Shrewsbury, four in Exeter, three in Salisbury, four in Gloucester, four in Chester, three in Hereford, three in Worcester, three in Southampton, four in Canterbury, three in Ipswich, three in Winchester, three in Oxford, four in Cambridge, three in Colchester, four in Newcastle-upon-Tyne. One MS. says, " This year was six taverns *more* erected in Bristol."

" One William Gardiner, born in Bristol, servant unto one Mr. Pagett, a merchant of the same city, and by him employed in Portugal, at a marriage there, seeing the superstitious adoration of the sacrament, did openly tread their host under foot, and overthrow the chalice; whereupon he was at present wounded and shortly after burned, and a spark of the fire fired one of the King's ships near the place."

1553 July 6, the King died of consumption, at Greenwich, in the sixteenth year of his age. He provided by will, at the instance of the Duke of Northumberland, that his cousin Lady Jane Grey, who had married Lord Guilford Dudley, the Duke's fourth son, should be his successor; and so the Council proclaimed; but, on the 19th, Mary (only daughter of Henry by his first wife, Katherine,) also was proclaimed.

" Sept. 17, the Earl of Surrey, the Duke of Norfolk's son and heir-apparent, came to Bristowe, and was received by the Mayor and Aldermen upon the Bridge of Bristowe, and there was a banquet given him," in the arched room under the Chapel. See 1360.

MARY.

Aug. 23, the Duke of Northumberland was beheaded on Tower-Hill.

1553   John Holyman, a monk of Reading, second Bishop of
        Bristol; Paul Bush being deprived because he had married,
        being a priest. He retired upon the rectory of Winterbourne.
        The stalls of the altar and the episcopal throne were erected
        by Bishop Bush.

        The mass, with the Latin services, &c. restored.

1554   Feb. 12, Lady Jane Grey, aged 17, and her husband, Lord
        Dudley, beheaded within the Tower.

        Feb. 17, Thomas lord Grey, the Duke of Suffolk's brother,
        and Feb. 23, the Duke of Suffolk, Lady Jane's father, be-
        headed.

        "There was great joy in this city that Queen Mary was
        married to Philip, Prince of Spain; and Friday, 4th of
        August, he was proclaimed King at the High Cross, under
        the title of Philip and Mary, by the grace of God King and
        Queen of England, France, Jerusalem, and Ireland, Defenders
        of the Faith, Princes of Spain, and Civil Archduke of Austria,
        Duke of Milan, Burgundia and Brabant, Countess of Har-
        purge, Flanders, Triale."

        Wheat sold at 6s. 8d. a bushel.

1555   April 4, four men, (John Walters, Robert Haddy, Gilbert
        Sheats, and John White), were drawn, hanged, and quartered,
        and their quarters set on the gates, for coining money.

        The Rose-penny fell to be nought. Wheat at 5s. a bushel.

        William Young, Mayor; Thomas Shipman and John
        Griffith,* Sheriffs.

        Oct. 7, William Shapton, weaver, was burnt for religion.

        Sir Thomas White, alderman and merchant-tailor, of
        London, founded St. John's College, Oxford, and allowed
        two fellowships in it to Bristol, worth thirty pounds a year
        each, for two qualified boys from the Grammar-School.
        See 1560.

---

* Mr. Alderman Haythorne's MS. says, " The Sheriff, Mr. John Griffith, was a very
forward man in apprehending the martyrs, and, with David Harris [mayor in 1550]
and Dalby, the Chancellor, deserve to be enrolled. Three suffered in Bristol [referring
probably to those noticed under 1557]; and more had done, had not Queen Elizabeth's
coming to the crown hindered; which brought back again from banishment Mr. Pacy
and Mr. Huntingdon, two preachers of this city. The said Mr. Huntingdon, after his
return, preaching at the Cross in College-Green, charged those men, there present, with
ill using both those that suffered and those that escaped, in these or like words. ' Oh !
' cruelty without mercy, that a man should act, so laboriously, that which, without
' hasty repentance, shall hasten his damnation. Know you not who made the strict
' search for Mr. Pacy, whom, if God had not hid, as Jeremiah, you had burned, stump
' and all,—he being lame ? Yet you had no pity; and you know who went to Redland,
' to buy green wood, for the execution of those blessed saints that suffered, when near
' home, at the Back or Key, he might have had dry. Take heed ! a little sorrow will
' not serve. God may call you into unquenchable fire, worse than the soultering of
' green wood.' "

T

A. D.

1556   Wheat sold at 8s. per bushel, and, at the fall of the year, at 22s. a bushel.

1557   May 7, " Richard Sharp, a weaver, and Thomas Hales, a cobbler, were burnt at St. Michael's Hill, for religion. Aug. 13, Thomas Benion, a shearman, for denying the sacrament of the altar to be the very body and blood of Christ, really and substantially." Another MS. adds that a young man (a carpenter) and Edward Sharp, a Wiltshireman, aged three score, were also burnt. Bishop Holyman refusing to officiate, the burnings were superintended by W. Dalby, chancellor of the diocese. The same executions are thus narrated in Mr. Alderman Haythorne's MS.: " Three men suffered as martyrs: 1st, Richard Sharp, a weaver, of Temple-parish; who, being examined by Dalby, the Chancellor, March 9th, 1556 [6-7], and by him persuaded to recant, he did so; of which he sorely and openly repented, and shortly after was brought to the flames. 2d, Thomas Hale, who shook hands with the said Richard Sharp at the fire, May 7, 1557. He was a shoemaker. He was, by David Harris, alderman, and John Stone, one of the common-council [mayor in 1562 and 1568], caused to arise out of his bed, and committed to the watch, and by them charged to convey him to Newgate; and shortly after [ward] he suffered. 3d, Thomas Benion, who was burned Aug. 27, 1557. More were questioned, but escaped."

Wheat 7s. a bushel.

1558   Oct. 11, Bishop Paul Bush died, at Winterbourne.

Oct. 19, died George Owen, physician to Henry VIII., Queen Katherine, and Edward VI. (See 1504.) He attended Cardinal Wolsey in his last illness, by express order of the King. He was a fellow of Merton-College, Oxon, and lived at Godstou, in Oxfordshire, in close friendship with John Smyth, mayor of Bristol, in 1547, ancestor of the Ashton-Court family.

The hire of a horse per day was at this time sixpence.

Nov. 17, the Queen died of dropsy, in her 43d year. She was buried in a chapel in the minster of St. Peter's Church, Westminster, without any monument or other remembrance.

ELIZABETH.

1559   March 1, at Westminster, the Queen confirmed the Bristol Charter of 1547—Seyer's No. 27.

A. D.

1560 "The Queen restored to her subjects fine and pure sterling money—gold and silver, for their base coin."*

This year Hugh Draper, of Bristol, merchant; Leonard Bilson, of Winchester, clerk; Robert Man, of London, ironmonger; Ralph Poyntz, of Feckenham in Worcestershire, miller; Francis Cocks, of London, yeoman; John Cocks, of Winchester, clerk; Fabian Withers, of Clerkenwell in Middlesex, salter; and John Bright, of Winchester, goldsmith; were taken up for conjuration and sorcery, and, being committed to the Fleet, were tried at Westminster, and confessed their wicked actions; and in open court bound themselves by a solemn oath to abstain from the like acts for the future. After which they were led through Westminster-Hall, and, by the special command of the Queen and her Council, were set in the pillory before the Queen's palace, below the same Hall. See the Lord Chief-Justice Coke's Entries, p. 1.

1561 John Pikes, Mayor. "This year the citizens of Bristol, by the industry and cost of this mayor, were exempted for ever from the marches of Wales, which before did them much harm."†

"All outlandish money was forbidden to be taken."

Temple-Conduit built in the centre of Temple-street, a little southward of its present situation. There is a tradition in the parish, that the cast in lead, of the figure of Neptune, was the gift of a plumber. His name has not been preserved. (See 1824.) The fountain-head is on the high bank of the Avon, near the turn of the Bath road from Totter-down.‡

---

* At the Conquest, a pound troy-weight, containing 11 oz. 2 dwts. of fine silver, was coined into twenty shillings. The same standard of fineness was, in the succeeding reigns, gradually split into forty-five shillings. In 1543, Henry VIII. debased the pound troy to 10 oz. fine, and made forty-eight shillings of it. In 1546, he had brought the pound troy to 4 oz. fine for the same amount. In 1549, his son Edward's councillors made seventy-two shillings out of 6 oz. fine in the pound, and in 1551, the same sum out of 3 oz. fine; but in the same year the fineness was increased to 11 oz. in the pound troy, and the number of shillings coined out of it was reduced to sixty. Elizabeth, at the point of time above noted, added 2 dwts. to the fineness, but did not lessen the number of shillings coined out of the pound. In 1600 she made sixty-two shillings out of the pound, and the same standard of fineness continued till 1816, when George III. coined it into sixty-six shillings.—Perhaps Elizabeth called in all the inferior coinage previously issued. The value of the gold coin was regulated by that of the silver.

† The anecdote of William Herbert, earl of Pembroke, related under 1526, has been supposed to have some connexion with this exemption; as, among other offices, the Earl held that of Lord President of the Council in the Marches of Wales.

‡ The Church-wardens and Vestrymen, with becoming gallantry and devotion, were till lately accustomed to pay an annual visit to the Nymph of the Spring; blending a portion of her purer "radical moisture" with the "radical heat" extracted from the

A. D.

1562 The Queen sent an army of 6000, under the Earl of
      Warwick, to assist the French Protestants under the Prince
      of Condé.

1564 In October commenced "a hot plague, which continued
      a whole year, and of which died in this city two thousand
      five hundred at least."

      At Christmas the river was frozen over, so that at King-
      road people went over on foot, to the St. George's side.

1565 "This year [at the end of St. James's fair] there came
      seven hundred soldiers to Bristol, with their furniture, to go
      to Ireland against the arch-traitor, one Ald; and whilst they
      abode here [six weeks], looking for a wind, three or four ruf-
      fians of them began a comotion at the High Cross, against the
      citizens, about nine of the clock at night; and though many
      blows were given on both sides, yet no man was wounded,
      by reason the magistrates and captains came quickly thi-
      ther, and appeased the matter." ["The fray was ended by
      the coming of Capt. Gilbert, one of their own captains,.
      who, being lodged at the New Inn, behind All Saints'
      Church, came with his sword and target, requiring peace."]
      "But the next day Capt. Randall, their commanding-officer,
      [who lodged at the Castle,] being advised thereof, sent the
      offenders into prison who begun the fray. And, two days
      after, he would have executed martial-law upon them, and
      commanded a gibbet to be set up in the midst of the High-
      street [before the end of St. Maryport-street, against the
      Mayor's door], and also commanded that all the soldiers
      should come thither without their weapons, to see them
      executed; but, when the time of execution was come, after
      long intreaty and much suite by the Worshipful Mayor
      [John Northall, pewterer] and others of this city, with the
      captains and other gentlemen, the Generall, against his
      purpose, was constrained to pardon them; but presently he
      discharged them, and put them from the band." Their
      names were Lawes, Herring, Carvell, and Grant. The
      troops departed the 8th of October.

      A windmill erected on Brandon-Hill, by Mr. Read, the
      town-clerk, where before stood a chapel called the Chapel
      of St. Brandon. See 1625.

      Sebastian Cabot died about this time.

      June 19, Mary, Queen of Scots, delivered of a son, after-
      wards our James I.

juice of the grape and of the sugar-cane, and contriving to dissipate the atmospherical
stillness of her cave, so friendly to gout and rheumatism, by exhalations of the cogi-
tabundous Indian weed.

A. D.

1566 Feb. 13. From March 25 in the preceding year till this
time, 188 persons died of the plague.

Sir Thomas White bequeathed to the Corporation of
Bristol, and St. John's College, Oxford, two thousand
pounds, in trust also for twenty-two other cities.

1568 Mary's friends having been defeated by Murray, she fled
to England for Elizabeth's protection.

"Thomas, duke of Norfolke, came from Bath to Bristol
upon Trinity-Sunday, accompanied with the Earle of Worcester, Lord Berkeley, Lord Richard, and others; but he
was sent for by the Queen from hence with all speed."
Mr. Ald. Haythorne's MS. adds that "the Duke went to
Redcliff, May the 24th, to sermon, and after to Temple,
where he had the bells rung, to try the truth of the report
of the tower's shaking at such times,"—a proof of the close
adhesion of its several parts.

1569 Thomas Chester, merchant, Mayor; who purchased the
manor of Almondsbury, and was High Sheriff of Gloucestershire in 1557. He died Sept. 24, 1583, and was buried
in St. James's Church.

"This yeare, John Willis, chamberlaine of this city,
died; who caused to be made all the causewayes, seven
miles every waye, about this city, and built the Bell Taverne
in Broad-streete [on the site of which now stands a wool-
warehouse], and obtained the Back-Hall for a gift to the
city, wherein himself died."

The Earl of Bedford, with his son, came to Bristol, and
was entertained at Mr. Wiggins's, in Small-street.

1570 Robert, earl of Leicester, Lord High Steward of Bristol;
Lord Chandos, commander of the garrison.

A plan of the city printed in a book called " Civitates
Orbis Terrarem," Hoëfnagel, sc.

"This year there was great variance about choosing the
Burgesses of the city, so that the Sheriffs were at great
debate a long time after."

Dec. 11, William Tucker, draper, Mayor, at his own
charge, obtained Letters Patent for a market to be kept in
St. Thomas-street every Thursday. Michael Sondley, with
the rest of the vestry of St. Thomas, built the market-place
along the breadth of the church and church-yard, for the
purpose of the said market, in the sale of wool, yarn,
cattle, &c. It commenced on the Thursday after the following Lady-day. In return for this privilege, the feoffees
of St. Thomas granted the Mayor, &c. two houses and land,
on which the Meal-market was kept in Wine-street, now
the Guard-House.

A. D.

1571 John Popham, esq. High Steward of Bristol.

"The Mayor kept a watch at midsummer-night and St. Peter's night." "At midsomer were the watches by the companies as delightfull shews."—This mayor was John Hone, brewer, who died June 24, 1575, and lies buried in Temple-Church, with his four wives.

1572 "This year the Mayor (John Browne, merchant) turned the watch into a general muster upon midsummer and St. Peter's days; and the burgesses did then muster with all kinds of warlike furniture and weapons; and every craft and company had their proper ensigns."—A MS. brought down to 1669 says, "The shooting on midsummer, St. Peter, and St. Bartholomew's day, began this year, and the butt of artillery made in the Marsh for that purpose, which hath still continue "—The same mayor increased the size of the barrels and kilderkins.

Jan. 7, the Duke of Norfolk beheaded on Tower-Hill.

1573 Thomas Kelke, Mayor; who afterward resided in Small-street, where are now Mr. Visger's offices and Messrs. Over-bury and Son's warehouses.

1574 "Aug. 13, the Pelican [now the Talbot Inn], in St. Thomas-street, was blown up, and ten men burnt therewith."

Aug. 14, the Queen came to Bristol, in her progress to Wales, and remained till the 20th. She kept her court at the residence of Sir John Young (knighted to receive this visit), on St. Augustin's Back.

"She first alighted at St. Lawrence Hospital, changed some apparel, was met at Lawford's Gate by the Mayor (Mr. Kelk) and Council, riding in scarlet with their foot-clothes and pages. At the gate she was received with an oration made by John Popham, esq." "While she remained here, many pleasant shews and fights upon land and water were by the citizens made to her, which much delighted Her Majesty."

"*Churchyardes Chippes*," one of the scarce pamphlets reprinted in "The Progresses and Public Processions of Queen Elizabeth," by John Nichols, F. S. A. Lond. Edinb. and Perth, contains "The whole order howe our Soveraigne "Ladye Queen Elizabeth was receyved into this citie of "Bristow, and the speaches spoken before her presens at "her entry; with the residue of versis and matter that "might not be spoken (for distance of the place), but sent "in a book over the waetter." By this legitimate specimen of the most fashionable if not the best clerkship of the day, it appears that Her Majesty was first addressed by *Faem*, in twenty-four of Mr. Churchyard's choicest verses, at the High

, **D.**

574Cross. At St. John's Gate, and (proceeding through Christmas-street and Host-street) near her Highness's lodging, a
boy representing *Salutacion* spouted eighteen, and another,
called *Gratulacion*, twenty verses; *Obedient Good Will*, a
third boy, was ready with eight more, but could not speak
them, " time was so far spent." Then three hundred soldiers, by whom the Queen had been conducted, " shot of
thear peeces in passing good order; at which warnyng the
great artillery went of, a hundred and xxx cast peecis; and
so the watche charged, and a hundreth shot apoynted for her
gard."

On the Sunday the Queen went to the College, " to hear
a sarmond, whear thear was a speetch to be sayd and an
imme to be songe. The speech was left out by an occasion
unlooked for; but the imme was songe by a very fine boye."

[The reader is elsewhere told that " some of the speeches,"
and among the rest, perhaps, that designed for the College,
" could not be spoken, by means of a scholemaister, who
envied that any stranger should set forth these shoes."
" Thomas Churchyard, gentilman," had been engaged by
the Corporation to produce this pageant, to the great annoyance of the resident Apollo, whose name we should have been
glad to immortalize.* Now for the " imme," which Master
Churchyard here calls]

" THE SONGE.†

" O happy ower of blis, O colledg thou dost se,
The shado gon, the substance com, nay Sun doth shien on thee:
Away you bosum snacks that sowes dissenshon heer,
To make your neasts whear serpents breed; this soyll and coest is clear.
Enchant no man with charms; ye shall receyve check maet,
If that you play with paltring pawns before so great a staet.
She hateth Hidras heads, and lovs the harmles mind,
A foe to vice, a friend to grace, and bent thereto by kind.
Which grace and grashos God now gied her whear she goes,
With treble grace throw troblous time to tread on all her foes."

A large fort had been erected on the Bedminster side of
the river, in Trene-Mill-Meade, over against Gib-Taylor
[now Prince's Street Bridge], and a large scaffold of timber
in the Marsh, for the Queen to witness a contest promoted
by *Dissension* between *Warrs* and *Peace*, in which, on the
first day,

" A littel fort, standing upon the hill beyond, [Redcliffe,] called

---

* We think " we have found it!"—Master Robert Recorde, that voluminous writer
of quaint arithmetical books, about this time held an office in the Mint at Bristol. See
Introduction to Part I. of " The Bristol Charities," 12mo. 1822. p. xv.
If Rowley and Chatterton were not identically the same in person, then the sixteenth
century had sadly retrograded from the poetical taste of the fifteenth.

† What would not an Amateur, and an Antiquary too, give for the tune?

'A. D.

1574 Feble Pollecie, was wan with great fury, and so rased, and over-
thrown down to the earth." " The mayn fort in the mean while
did send sutch sucker as they might; but prevayling not, they wear
in like sort driven back, and their fort besieged, and mutch ado about
the saem; which drove out that day, and then by tortch light the
prince from her skaffold went to her lodgyng, and in the mean
season som fier works wear seen; and so the watch was charged."

" The second day was thear maed a new aproetch to the mayn
fort, for a better order of warre, and to the ayde of the fort cam
divers gentilmen of good callynge from the court, which maed the
shoe very gallant, and set out the matter mutch.

" Now sarved the tied, and up the water from Kyngroad cam
three brave galleys, chasing a ship that cam with vittayls to the fort.
The fort seyng that their extremitie within was great, sent a gentilman to the prince for aid, who brought her a book covered with
green velvet, which uttred the whoell substance of this device. The
gentilman had a speech of his own makyng, as follows. After he
had swam over the water in some danger, cloes and all, he speak his
part to the prince.

" Mr. JOHN ROBARTS,* of the Temple.

" Eskaept from waltryng waves, from sword and fier, and enmies sleight,
From storms and sturdy flaws, from roeryng shot and fearful fight,
I com to quiet land, whear noble prince doth pastims vew,
And bryng a book in hand of all the shows and matter trew
That must by practies pas before your highnes as it fauls;
And suerly sent I was, by those that keeps your warlike wauls,
To crave your curteys ayd, in their defence that peace desiers,
Whoes staet is maed afrayd by fals Dissenbons kindled fiers.
As your poer people have throw peace possest great gayn and good;
So still sutch peace they crave as may avoyd the losse of blood.
As heer I cam a mayn, so have I promesd, if I may,
For to return agayn throw salt sea from [foam] the saem self way."

" So he departed, and all this while the businesse was great about
the fort (which hazarded the gentilman's lief), and in a wonders
bravery the broyll continued, with a shoe of fight on land and sea,
till the very night approtched; at which time the prince partted, and
stoed [shoed] marvelously well contented with that she had seen."
[The Mayors' Kalendar says—" which marcial experiment being
verie costly and chargable (especially in gun-powder), the Queen
and Nobility liked verie well of; and gave Mr. Mayor and his bre-
theren greate thankes for therie doeings."]

" Now yon must conceyve that Warres (with blodsheds, mizeries,
and other horly borlees) waxt a weery; and that neither the fort,
nor the wickednes of the world (which warres represented) was
desirous of further trobuls, but rather glad to have the matter taken
up in any resonable condicions; for the which purpose was devised
that Perswasion should go and tell his taell, and unfold what follies
and conflicts rises in civill broyle, and what quietness coms by a
mutuall love and agreement."

* Probably a son of the Sheriff of that name in 1563-4, and Mayor in 1578—9.

1574   Then we have " Perswasion to the Citie, called the Main Fort," thirty-four verses; and " The Cities answer to Perswasion," thirty-eight more, containing the following boast:

> " Wee make the sivill lawes to shien, and, by example mield,
> Reform the rued, rebuek the bold, and tame the countrey wyeld.
> We venter goods and lives, ye knoe, and travill seas and land,
> To bring by trafick heaps of wealth and treasuer to your land.
> We are a stay and stoerhouse boeth to kingdoms farr and neer,
> A cawse of plentie throw foersyght whan things wax scarce and deer.
> And thoughe our joy be most in peace, and peace we do maintain,
> Whearon to prince and realm throwout doth ries great welth and gain,
> Yet we have soldyars, as you see, that stoers but when we pleas,
> And sarvs our torns in howshold things, and sits in shop at eas."

And ending,—

> " . . . . O England, joy with us,
> And kis the steps whear she doth tread, that keeps her country thus
> In peace and rest, and perfait stay; whearfore the God of peace,
> In peace by peace our peace presarve, and her long lief encrease."

"This was to be don and put in exersies befoer the Queen cam to the knitting up of the matter; but, Perswasion beyng dismist, the battry was planted befoer the Fort, and they within so straitly enclosed, that they must needs abied the mercy of the sword and cannon.

574   " At which instant, in the afternoon that present day, the prince was in her skaffold to beholde the successe of these offers of Warre; and so went the battry of, and the assaut was given in as mutch order as might be: the enemie was three times repolsed, and beholdyng nue suckors commyng from the courte to the forts great comfort, the enemye agreed on a parley, whearin was rehersyd that the cortain was beaten down, and the fort made sawtable; and yet the enemye, to save the lives of good citizens and soldiors thereof, would give them leave to depart with bag and bagaeg, as orders of warres required. To the which the fort maed answer, that the cortayns nor bulwarks was not their defence, but the corrage of good peple, and the force of a mighty prince (who saet and beheld all these doyngs) was the thyng they trusted to; on which answer the enemie retired, and so condicions of peace were drawn and agreed of; at which peace both the sides shot of their artillery, in sien of a triumphe, and so crying ' God save the Queen,' these triumphes and warlik pastimes finished. The prince, liking the handlyng of these causes verie well, sent ij hundreth crowns to make the souldiors a banket. Now heer is to be considered that the prince went into the gallees, and so down to Kyngroed, aer these things wear brought to an end.

"At her highnes departuer a gentilman in the confiens of the towns liberties spaek" a ' Dolfull a Due' of twenty verses, in which the citizens are made to say,

> " Our deuties are not half discharged, no, thoghe we kist the gronud
> And prostraet fall full flat on face whear her footsteps are found,
> The Persian daer not cast up eies, nor look upon thear king;
> Shall Christians then presuem to preace on sutch a sacred thyng,

And sho no part of duties bownds? O God forbid I say;
But that the Lord's anointed should be honor'd every way."

Having been indulged with a perusal of the original record of " *The charge of the Queenes Maties enterteignem^t to the citie of Bristol*," we made the following extracts:

	£	s	d
Gilding and painting the High Cross, and making new beams	66	13	8
Newly rafting and plastering of Laford's Gate, on both sides; Newgate, and both the Froome Gates, on both sides; and for setting up of scaffolds and taking down the same	16	6	1
Painting and gilding the said gates	26	13	4
Pitching the streets [sanding, various several charges]	13	18	10
Setting up a scaffold at the High Cross, for the oration	0	8	3
Setting up the Queen's arms and the Town's arms, in freestone, in the Guildhall wall [the same now standing]	10	14	0
The purse of gold, silver, and silk, wherein the 200 angeletts was presented	1	12	0
Setting up a gallery in the Marsh, for the Queen's Majesty to see the triumphs	19	4	3
Mending the way in Magdalen-lane, where the Earl of Lincoln lay	0	6	8
Fees and charge to the Queen's Clerk of the Market, and to the Yeoman of the Bottles	5	0	0
Making the Queen's way through Temple-Mead, at her going away	0	14	3
Mr. Domynyck Chester, for charge of the two forts, with other business, as by his accompt	81	8	4
John Field, for his pains in dressing the Marsh	1	0	0
Captain Shute, for his travaile, who was captain of all the army	16	13	4
Mr. Churchyard, for his travaile both in the forts and concerning orations	6	13	4
To eighty-six Pioneers who wrought at the forts	4	5	0

The whole of the items count fifty-eight, and the sum total is £1053 14s. 11d. The charges included herein for gunpowder amount to £210 7s. 8d. The price seems to have been from 1s. 1d. to 1s. 2d. per lb.

Lord Burghley and the Earl of Oxford joined the Queen while she was in Bristol.

" Aug. 21, the accord at Bristol, between the commissioners, David Lewis and William Aubry, for the Queen's Majesty, and the King of Spain, for restitution of the goods arrested 1568."—*Lord* Burghley's *Diary*, printed at the end of vol. ii. of his State-papers. " Some articles of agreement between the English and the Dutch agreed upon in Bristol,

A. D.

1574 by the King of Spain's consent, for the Low-Country traffique."—*Mr. Ald.* HAYTHORNE's *MS.*

This year a proclamation was issued for putting the sumptuary laws against excess of apparel into execution.

"By the Queen's authority, halfpence of copper were made at Bristol for the use of that opulent city, having on one side a ship, and on the other C. B., signifying *Civitas Bristol;* and these went current for small things at Bristol and ten miles round; and for want of some such money the latter end of her reign, every chandler, tapster, victualler, and others, made tokens of lead and brass for halfpence."— *Historical Account of English Money*, by STEPHEN MARTIN LEAKE, *Esq. Clarencieux King at Arms.* 8vo. 1745.

1575 "This year the plague was very hot in Bristol, whereof died nineteen hundred and upwards; and Mr. Northbrook, preacher both in word and deed, did very much good in teaching publicly and privately, from house to house. And in this plague died John Northall, pewterer, John Stone, brewer, [and] John Cutt and William Carr, merchants, all which have been Mayors of Bristol." From July 3 to Jan. 20, 1576, one hundred and thirty-seven died in St. James's parish.

"A new order was taken for orphans and their goods."

July 9, the Queen was at Kenilworth Castle.

"A ship richly laden was lost in Kingroad, the goods of Thomas Williams, merchant."

1577 Sept. 25, three out of four mariners who had, at the preceding St. James's fair, stolen an Irish barque out of Crogan's Pill, for the purpose of robbing the barques that came from the fair, which they carried to Wales, were tried at the sessions, and hung upon a gibbet set up in Canons' Marsh, over against Gibb-Taylor, at the point, near to the river, that the tide might come over them.

Bridewell, of old called Monkenbridge, or Munkbridge, once a tower and fortification, newly built. Meg Lowrey, who feigned herself mad, was the first ill person there corrected.

"This year, Captain Martin Frobisher, in the Queen's ship called the Ayde, alias Anne, of the burthen of two hundred tonns, came into Kingroad, from his voyage attempting to find the north-west passage to the East-Indies, China, and Catayo. He brought with him much supposed gold ore; which, being tried in the Castle, proved not so. He brought also with him a man of Cathay, called Cally Chough, with his wife, called Ignorth, and child, who gave suck, casting

A. D.

1577 her breasts over her shoulders. They were clothed in stags'
skins, having neither linen nor woollen. And the 9th of
October the man rowed up and down the river at the Back,
it being full sea, in a boat made of beasts' skins, in forme
like unto a longe barge or trowe, but sharp at both ends,
about fourteen feet long, having but one round place for him
to sett in; and, as he rowed up and down the river, he killed
a couple of ducks with his dart. And at the Marsh he brought
the boat out of the water, upon his back. They could eat
nothing but raw flesh; and within one month after they all
three died."

Three houses at the Tower of the Key were burnt to the
ground. The fire commenced in the house of one Wolfe, a
joiner, in the night.

Thomas Colston, merchant, was Mayor this year. See
1597.

1578 Mr. Antony Parkhurst, who had been four years at Newfoundland, wrote Mr. Hackluyt, from Bristol, with a natural
history of the island, &c.

A ship, the Golden Lion, of 540 tons, laden with 200 tons
of salt and 60 tuns of sack, not being well moored, drove
upon the rocks in Hungroad, and, upon the tide leaving her,
she fell over. Much pains and cost were employed to get her
up, but she was finally broken in pieces.

1579 Thomas Younge, soap-maker, Mayor.

This year died, at Namur, John Fowler, printer, of Bristol;
a good poet and orator. He abridged Thomas Aquinas, and
translated Osorius into English; but, not liking the Reformation, he went to Antwerp.

1580 The Church of St. Lawrence (which had been sold, with
much other ecclesiastical property, to Henry Brayne, merchant-tailor, of London) going to decay, and having but a
small parish, was united and incorporated with St. John's.
William of Worcester describes it as twenty-eight yards long
and nine yards wide. The walls and arched frame-work
of the roof still (1824) remain, the wood being in remarkable preservation.

An earthquake was felt in Bristol on Easter-Tuesday.

An army of soldiers, commanded by General Lord Grey,
came in their way to Ireland.

1581 July 24, a ship called the Dominick, laden with spices and
oils, was wrecked about Portishead Point, and twenty-seven
men cast away in her.

July 28, at Westminster, the Queen granted the Charter,
No. 28 in Mr. Seyer's translation, which recites the Charter

A. D.

1581of 1499, &c. and increases the number of Aldermen to twelve
—the Mayor and other Aldermen allowed to remove any of
the Aldermen, except the Recorder, and choose others.

"The Earl of Pembroke came to Bristol and was royally
entertained, being met by sixty horsemen of honest burgesses; and the Mayor, Aldermen, and Common-Council
received him in Wyne-street. Which love of the city caused
him much to respect it. Mr. Temple (a preacher) made
him an oration in Latin at the Tolzey."

Manufactories for pins and stockings established in Bristol.

1582 Thomas Aldworth, merchant, Mayor; who advised Sir
Francis Walsingham of the merchants' intention to furnish
1000 marks and two ships, of 60 and 40 tons, for discoveries
on the coast of America.

Now commenced the adaptation of our Kalendar to the
Julian year, by the use of a double date: thus, 158⅔ is to be
received as indicating the year that commenced with March
25, 1582, and ended March 25, 1583. This mode of dating
continued till 1752.

1583 A subsidy of 16d. a pound was laid on the city by the
Mayor and Council, for repair of the Key.

September. Three aldermen, viz. Thomas Chester,
Thomas Kelke, and William Tucker, died and were buried
in one week.—Mr. Halton, the chamberlain, died. Nicholas
Thorne was chosen to succeed him.

Mr. John Haydon, sheriff of London, gave one hundred
pounds to this city.

The Earl of Ormond brought from Ireland the Earl of
Desmond's head, taken off at Mane Castle; which was shewn
to the Mayor (Walter Pikes) and his brethren at the Tolzey,
" pickled in a pipkin. The man who struck it off, the
Queen's 'well-beloved subject and soldier, Daniel Kelly,'
was rewarded with a pension of twenty pounds yearly, which
he enjoyed for many years, but was ultimately hanged at
Tyburn."—CROKER's *Researches in the South of Ireland.*

" Nov. 3, Walter Glesson was committed to Newgate by
Mr. Mayor, for non-payment of a fine of twenty pounds, for
that he was not able to be sheriff, and there remained prisoner
eight days; and then, upon sureties for the payment of £20,
he was released. And Nov. 22, the said Walter Glesson
gave in a supplication, by the hands of Mr. Webb, sheriff,
and thereupon it was agreed by the whole house that the
said Walter Glesson should stand discharged for ever."

1585 Thomas Harman, esq. Lord High Steward.

The Earl of Pembroke was made Lord Lieutenant of the

A. D.

1585 trained soldiers in Bristol, Somerset, and Wilts. March 7, the Earl came from Wells, to take a general muster; and, while here, he presumed to take the upperhand of the Mayor, Richard Cole, mercer. The Queen, being informed of this, sent for the Earl, chid him severely, and committed him to the Tower till he paid a fine for the offence.

"Wheat sold at 17s. per bushell, and all other graine very dear; and, for reliefe, the commons begun to make an insurrection; but the Mayor wisely pacified them, and caused the Pensford bakers to come into the city with bread every day in the week. And the Mayor also having notice that a barque, being in Hungroad, had taken in kinterkins of butter for France, he himself went down by water aboard the barque, and seized the butter; and notwithstanding the sailors resisted him what they durst, and misused him in reproachful words, yet the butter was unladed into a barge and brought up to the Key; and the Mayor caused it to be sold for 2½d. per pound." The sailors who resisted the Mayor were committed by him to ward, " where they lay in irons until they had paid the price set upon them for their disobedience." The Mayor also procured corn from Dantzick, and a great quantity of rice was imported, and sold at 4s. a bushel.

1586 April 10, John Carr, by will, gave his manor of Congresbury towards founding a hospital for maintaining and educating poor orphans and other children, after the manner of Christ-Church Hospital, London. See 1589.

Ralph Dole gave his son Richard a house in the Shambles, upon condition of paying twenty shillings per annum toward the repairing of St. Peter's pump for ever. This payment is now made out of the chop-house in Bridge-street, at the corner of the steps leading into St. Maryport-Church-yard.

1587 Feb. 8, at Fotheringay Castle, Mary, Queen of Scots, was beheaded. She was attended at the block by Richard Fletcher, fifth bishop of Bristol, father of the celebrated dramatist. He impoverished the see by leasing out the estates to courtiers. In 1593 he was translated to Worcester, when the bishoprick of Bristol lay vacant ten years. He married a second wife, Lady Baker, a handsome widow—became the object of the Queen's displeasure, and (tobacco being now a new means of solace for dolour) smoked himself to death as Bishop of London, June 15, 1596.

April 15, the Earls of Leicester and Warwick came from Bath, and lay at Mr. Robert Kitchen's, in Small-street. And " upon Easter-day, after dinner, the Earl of Leicester,

A. D.

1587 with the Mayor and Councell, gathered together in the Councill-House, about some secret matters; and the next day they departed."

July. Mr. Seyer, in his c. xxvi. § 35, relates an affair of force of arms employed in Kingroad, by Mr. Thomas James (afterward M. P. for Bristol) and twelve others, to prevent the shipping, by Edward Whitson, tanner, of Newland, of a parcel of calf-skins on board a French ship, the Esperanso, for which he had not compounded with certain Bristol merchants who possessed the Queen's letters patent for exclusive transportation of that description of merchandize. A musket and half-pikes were the chief weapons of the searcher's pinnace. The crew of the wood-bush boat of Brockwere had well fitted themselves with bows and arrows, pikes, targets, and privy-coats. Some men were hurt on both sides, and John Gethen, master and owner of the boat, killed. The two Sheriffs interfered, and Mr. James was indicted and arraigned at the Marshalsea, as having shot off the musket; but, no evidence appearing against him, he was acquitted.

1588 April 20, four of Her Majesty's men-of-war, viz. the Great Unicorne, the Minion, the Handmaide, and the Ayde, sailed from Bristol, well furnished with men and ammunition, to meet the rest of the fleet at Plymouth. All the canvas brought to St. James's fair, and deposited in the Back-Hall for sale was bought, to make tents for the camp at Tilbury.

July 28 was printed, by order of the Queen, the first newspaper published in England, entitled *The English Mercury*. A copy of it is in the British Museum.

Nov. 24, a general thanksgiving was celebrated in Bristol, for the defeat of the Spanish Armada. The Mayor, Robert Kitchen, and incorporated companies, attended the Cathedral, to hear a sermon; when the Magistrates received the Holy Communion; and, upon their return home, they, with other well-disposed people, gave money to the poor.

1589 William Bird, draper, Mayor; who gave the Corporation a silver cup and cover, double gilt, weight thirty ounces.

The Hospital founded by John Carr in 1586 was opened in the mansion-house of the late Hospital of St. Mark, including the site of the cloisters in Orchard-street. The original number of boys was twenty-eight, The names of the benefactors, &c. appear in the Chapel. It was called Queen Elizabeth's Hospital. " Mr. Bird, the Mayor, freely gave in his life-time five hundred pounds, and also disbursed

A. D.

1589 money to buy the house and orchard for the poor children's lodging; and in this his mayoralty he obtained of the merchants and others, for eight years, to pay, for every ton of lead that came to Redcliff-Hill, 4*d*., and for every ton of iron that came to the Key, 4*d*., and for every piece of raisons, 2*d*.; and so every thing was rated accordingly."* See 1769.

" Richard Ferris, a wherryman, of London, having liberty given him for twelve months to saile from London to Bristol, and that upon a great wager laid down by him, gave the adventure, and departed from London in his wherry upon midsummer-day, being the 24th of June; and upon the 3d of August he came safely to Bristol, at halfe-ebb, up against the tide, with his wherry under saile, and landed at the lower slipp of the Back; and presently his wherry was brought upon men's shoulders up to the Tolzey, and so put in storehouse under the Guildhall for a monument."

1590   William Hopkins, fishmonger, Mayor.

1592   Sir George Snigge, Recorder, (upon the death of Thomas Hammond) from this time till 1604.

Thomas Aldworth, Mayor.

1594   The Mayor and Aldermen of Bristol authorized by the Privy Council to strike farthing-tokens.

Sept. 5, died Robert Kitchen, who was Mayor in 1588. He was buried in St. Stephen's Church. He left four hundred pounds, in trust, for loans to young tradesmen. On a beam over the entrance of the New Market in Broad-street, (so called from containing butchers' shambles) is the following carved inscription : " This Building is at the charge of Robart Kitchen, late Alderman of Bristoll, for the Reliefe of the Poor." " R. K. 1598." John Rocque's four-sheet Plan of the City, published in 1743, marks a building on each side within the entrance of this passage.

" This year [1597-8] the new shambles in Broad-street was built by the executors of Mr. Robert Kitchen, deceased. Their names were, Mr. John Barker, Mr. Matthew Haviland, Mr. Abel Kitchen, and Mr. John Rowborough."—*Mr.* PAGE's *MS.*

* In 1590, March 21, the Queen granted a Charter, and in 1597 an Act of Parliament was passed, for the same purpose. Mr. Bird died Oct. 8, 1590, and was buried in the Chapel. We have been favoured with an inspection of the Charter, which is curious from the beauty of the pictorial embellishments of the head and margin. The miniature-portrait of the Queen (which would seem to have been copied from a three-quarter length in oil, possessed by Mr. Henry Ricketts) presents more of intellectual character than any other of the numerous likenesses of Elizabeth that have come under our notice: we cease to wonder at the extent of her personal influence with her ministers and other immediate dependents.

A. D.

1594 One of the bronze tables now [1824] standing in front of the Exchange bears the following inscription on the ring of its surface: " This post is the gift of Master Robert Kitchin, merchant, some time maior and alderman of this city; who dec. 1 Septemb. 1594." On the garter beneath,—" His executors were fower of his servants, John Barker, Matthew Haviland, Abell Kitchin, aldermen of this city, and John Roborow, sherif. 1630." See 1625.

" Paid, 26th March, for 104lb. butter received out of Gloucestershire, whereof 16lb. at 3½d. and the rest at 3d. the lb., 1l. 6s. 8d. Salt for the said butter, 6d. Carriage of the said butter from Bristol to London, 4s. 6d."—*An old Household Account.* 4lb. soap in the same account is charged ten pence.

1595 The Queen committed to Robert Webbe the farms of the subsidy and ulnage of saleable cloths for thirty-one years, at the annual rent of £72 6s. 8d., in the cities of Gloucester and Bristol.

Alderman John Browne (mayor in 1572) bequeathed £30 6s. per annum to the poor of St. Nicholas parish, inclusive of the inhabitants of an alms-house. See 1656.

1596 An Act of Parliament passed relative to the moneys, &c. given to charitable uses within the city.

A famine throughout the realm. Wheat 20s. per bushel; malt and rye, 10s. But for corn from other parts, and Dantzic rye, both rich and poor had been in a very miserable condition; " wherefore it was concluded upon by the Mayor and Aldermen of this city, that every alderman, with the rest of the Worshipful Burgesses, should keep and find, every day at their own houses, so many poor, during the dearth; and they did so, every man according to his ability, because there might be no insurrection, and that they might not perish." One MS. says, " Eggs two a penny, and other wares excessive deare." See an anecdote of Mr. John Whitson, connected with this subject, in Memoirs, c. xxvi. § 4.

William Yate was Mayor this year. The carved device of *a gate*, with the initials W. and C. B., on the brackets of the bow-window over the arch of the Guard-House passage, in Wine-street, mark the residence of this magistrate. See 1631.

1597 Nov. 6, died Thomas Colston. He was buried in All-Saints' Church.

1598 The Red Lodge, and Sir John Younge's lower house, (now Colston's School) sold to Nicholas Strangeways, of Bradley, in the county of Gloucester. Sir John Young's

A. D.

1598 monument is in the south wall of the Cathedral-choir, in the place of the confessionary. His wife, Joan, died June 14, 1602, aged 70 years.

Feb. 28, died Thomas Aldworth, mayor in 1582 and 1592.

March 7, died Sir Charles Somerset, fifth son of Henry, earl of Worcester, aged 64 years. He was buried in St. James's Church, where his monument informs us that he was standard-bearer to Her Majesty's band of gentlemen pensioners, and his wife the daughter and co-heir of Henry Brayne, esq.

1599   Sir Henry Newton, of Barrs-Court, died this year. One of the same family lies in St. Peter's Church.

1600   John Hopkins, Mayor; who " sett forth a shipp, and in person went captaine to Cales action; at whose returne he was with much joy mett by the citizens on Durdam Downe." This refers to the successful expedition against Cadiz, in 1595, under Robert, earl of Essex, and Charles Howard, admiral of England, in which one thousand of the nobility and gentry served as volunteers.

1601   The Quay-Conduit and All-Saints' Cistern rebuilt.

Religious buildings, &c. did not cease to be plundered till this the 44th year of Elizabeth, a criminal process being now threatened by proclamation against the offenders.

The Witchcraft-Act passed. See 1736.

1602   The inhabitants of Bristol taxed to defray the expenses of the Queen's entertainment.

Sir John Stafford, knt., as a reward for his valour, had been made Constable of Bristol Castle. March 6, this year, the Mayor and Commonalty presented a petition to the Privy Council, representing the loose manner in which Sir John held his office, being a non-resident, and leaving a mean and unworthy deputy, who suffered forty-nine families, consisting of about two hundred and forty persons, to inhabit the Castle, who subsisted chiefly by begging and stealing; and praying that Sir John might take order for removing them into such places where they last dwelt, and that none should be admitted to inhabit but only such as he would undertake for their sufficiency and good behaviour, " to the end that the city be not further charged or molested by them, nor Her Majesty's Castle pestered with any such base cottagers or scandalous inmates." Sir John Stafford died Sept. 28, 1605, and was buried at Thornbury, where his monument bears a long inscription.

1603   March 24, the Queen died at Richmond, in the 70th year of her age, having appointed James VI. of Scotland, son of her unfortunate rival, to be her successor.

JAMES I.

Aged 36 years, the first " King of Great Britain." His Queen was Anne, Princess of Denmark, whom he married Aug. 10, 1589.

March 28, the King was proclaimed in Bristol by the Recorder, Sir George Snigge, and the two Sheriffs, at the High Cross; his picture being placed on the Cross, over their heads. The Mayor (Ralph Hunt, grocer) and Corporation heard divine service on the occasion, at St. Nicholas Church.

July 18, a pestilence began in Pepper-Alley, Marsh-street, and lasted all the year. From Aug. 20 till March 22, 1604, 390 persons died in St. James's parish. In the whole city, from July 28, there died of the plague, 2600—of other diseases, 356. One MS. says, "From July 25, 1603, to Oct. 27, 1604, died nearly 2700; and in St. Philip's parish only, 491. It continued nearly a year and a quarter." No person was allowed to come from London to St. James's fair, to sell goods, without a certificate from the Lord Mayor, that the house from which such person came was not infected with sickness, nor within six weeks before.

The inhabitants taxed by two shillings in the pound for the expenses occasioned by the plague.

John Whitson, Mayor; " who, with Mr. Robert Aldworth and others, set forth a ship for a discovery of the North-West Passage, under the command of Martin Prinne, being then but twenty-three years of age; who afterward proved a very good seaman in the East-India voyages. He is buried in St. Stephen's, on the north side of the chancel." The north side of the chancel is not now a part of the church.

1604 January. The present received translation of the Bible ordered.

July 7, the King prorogued his first Parliament in displeasure. Sir George Snigge, recorder, and Thomas James, alderman, were the representatives for Bristol. The new Recorder was Sir Lawrence Hyde.

July 12, at Westminster, the King confirmed the Bristol Charters of 1559 and 1581—Seyer's No. 29.

An additional tax of sixpence in the pound, on account of the plague.

Alice Cole left four pounds per annum, to be divided between the inhabitants of the Gift-House, St. James's Back, and of the Poor-House, adjoining it, under the care of the church-wardens. She also bequeathed four pounds

A. D.

1604 to twelve of the persons in Spencer's (Canynges') Alms-House, in Lewin's Mead. (See 1493.) Also four pounds a year to the Tailors' Hospital, in Marsh-street, and four pounds a year to the poor in Strange's Alms-House.

1605 Thomas James, Mayor. "This year was the gunpowder-treason. This Mayor, being a very judicious man, was chosen a Burgess of Parliament, and a Commissioner, amongst divers others, concerning the Union of England and Scotland."

1606 John Barber, merchant, Mayor, and the rest of the Council, "took a lease of the Dean and Chapter, for to have so much room in the Cathedral as to build a fair gallery, for the Magistrates to sit in and hear sermon; the which was built this year, at the cost of the Mayor and Council. It stood upon pillars, right against the pulpit; all the fore-part being of joiners' work, curiously wrought; wherein three seats, placed by the middle pillar, were reserved for the Mayor, Dean, and Council of this city, and, if occasion were, for the King, or any Nobleman that should come into the city. And upon the top of the seat was the King's arms guilded and painted. Under which gallery there were seats placed in like order, for the magistrates' wives."

London barrels and kilderkins allowed to be made in Bristol.

The brewers sold their double beer for 7s. per barrel, and their single beer for 3s. 4d. per barrel—best sort of ale, for 3½d. per gallon, and the second sort for 2d. per gallon. This regulation was set by the magistrates.

"Lecture began at St. Walburge, and Mr. Yeamons, of St. Philip's, first lecturer, which he held twenty-seven years."

1607 Tuesday, Jan. 20, at high water, there arose so great a flood that the sea broke over the banks and deluged all the marsh-ground in Wales and on the English coast, drowning the cattle and carrying away the corn and hay. The water rose so high and came so fast upon them, that the people, to save their lives, climbed upon the tops of the houses and into the trees. When the flood began to abate, it carried away many houses and trees, and many people were drowned. In the marsh-country, about Aust, the water remained so deep that the people in the trees could not come down. Having abode there two or three days, and the Mayor (Mr. Barber) hearing of this their distress, he ordered cock-boats to be hauled thither, to fetch them, that they might not perish with cold and hunger. In this city, at the Back, the water was four feet and a half above the streets.

A. D.

1607 In St. Stephen, St. Thomas, and Temple Churches, it was half way up the seats. The merchants and others suffered great loss in their store-houses and cellars, in sugar, woad, and salt. The Bridge was stopped, so that the water was bayed up higher towards Temple and Redcliff sides than in other parts, rising five feet at Treen-Mills. At the return, it brought down great trees, but did no harm to the houses on the Bridge.

April 10, "a strange fish" was caught in Kingroad, and brought to the Back in a Cardiff boat. This scaly stranger however soon found a name, being called "a Fryer." It was five feet long and three feet broad, "having two hands and two feet, and a very gristly wide mouth. The which was hauled upon a dray to Mr. Mayor's house."

Sept. 13, the Mayor died. He was buried in St. Werburgh's Church, where his monument bears a carved figure.

"This year was a view taken in this city, to know how many people were in it; and there were found of all sorts, 10,549 in the whole. It was done because they would know how much corn would serve the whole by the week."

William Child, Doctor of Music, born in Bristol. He lived 90 years. See Burney's History, and Boyce's Cathedral-Music.

Nov. 20 commenced a severe frost, which lasted till the 8th of February, 1608. The Severn and the Wye were so hardly frozen, that people went from one side to the other, and played, and made fires to roast victuals upon the ice. No long trows nor wood-bushes could come to Bristol. When the ice broke, it came down with the tide, doing much damage to the shipping in Kingroad. The frost made great havock with the birds, and did much injury to the corn in the ground.

A smith was *whipped in the pillory,* at the High Cross, for putting out horses' eyes.

1608 John Boucher, draper, Mayor.*

The house of Henry Hobson, innkeeper, in High-street, was shut up for a fortnight, and no one allowed to frequent it, on account of the plague which raged there. It was guarded by watchmen.

The Society of Merchant-Venturers purchased the manor of Clifton. See 1822.

"This year there was a great dearth throughout the realm, and many people had perished with want, if the Lord, in

* The widow of this gentleman, Mrs. Kitchen Searchfield, gave the Corporation a covered cup and a skinker, silver double gilt, weight sixty ounces, and a basin and ewer of silver, double gilt, weight eighty-six ounces and a half.

1608 mercy, had not supplied our scarcity, by sending in store of corn from foreign markets into this land. Into this city came great store of corn from Dantzick and other places. The ships that came into the port of Bristol, from the 23d of July 1608, to the 24th of July, 1609, were in number sixty, and brought, as appears by the Custom-House books,

					£	s.	d.
Of Wheat,	34629	bushels,	at 5s. per bushel,		08657	05	00
Of Rye,	73770	ditto	4s. per bushel,		14754	00	00
Of Barley,	04040	ditto	3s. per bushel,		00606	00	00
Quantity,	112439				24017	05	00

Wheat was sold at first for 6s. 8d. and 6s. a bushel, and rye, 5s. and 5s. 4d., until the latter end of the year; but it pleased God to send such a plentiful harvest, that the best wheat sold in the market for 4s. a bushel before the end of August."

This year Virginia was planted by the English.

1609   Mr. John Guy and his son, a little before he was sheriff (in 1605), went to Newfoundland, to begin a plantation there, and now returned, having left his son there to continue it. See 1611.

Feb. 8, the Bishop, Dr. Thornborough, who had been absent from the city two years, sent men to pull down the gallery in the College, which Mr. Barker, in his mayoralty, with the Council, by consent of the Dean and Chapter, had built; and the reason was, because they had not his consent, neither had built a place for him. Whereupon Mr. Abel Kitchen [sheriff in 1598] and Mr. John Guy were sent to London, to the Lord High Steward of Bristol; who made the case known to the King; and commissioners were appointed to ascertain whether the gallery did ' make the church like a playhouse,' as the Bishop and others of the College had alleged, who had set their hands and seals to the grant of the lease for the building thereof. And a report being returned by the Commissioners to His Majesty of the contrary, the King caused the Bishop to set the gallery in its former place, at his own cost; but he rebuilt it only two or three feet above the ground, and set the pulpit on the lower pillar, next the clock-house. The King, when the Bishop went to London, checked him for this ungracious perversion of His Majesty's commands; so that he abode at Dorchester, and " would not come to Bristol for shame and disgrace." The Bishop " would have forced the Mayor and all the Worshipful Aldermen to come to sermon to the

A. D.

1609 College, as they were used to do on every Sabbath and festival-day, and therefore would not suffer any bell to ring in the city;" but the Mayor sent to the Lord Archbishop of Canterbury, who gave authority to the Corporation to have as many sermons in the city as they would, and where the Mayor might appoint. Accordingly the Corporation did not go to the Cathedral for several years together, but on festival-days went to Redcliff-Church. (We have heard an expression of high authority, for the belief that the law and the bishop went hand in hand.)

John Fownes gave the Corporation sixty-six pounds thirteen shillings and fourpence, to pay annually four pounds to rake and clean the walks in the Marsh, now Queen-Square.

Monday, April 10, the King's uncle, Lodowick Stewart, duke of Lenox, came to Bristol, and was honourably entertained by the Mayor. He slept at Sir John Younge's house, on St. Augustin's Back, where the Bishop then dwelt. The next day he went down to Hungroad by water; and on Wednesday departed for London, being sent for by the King.

Robert Aldworth, Mayor; Thomas Aldworth, one of the Sheriffs. See 1634.

Goods brought by Irishmen from London, and other places infected with the plague, were deposited without the city, till they could be shipped.

1610 Thomas White, D.D. founded the alms-house in Temple-street, entered under the Tuckers' Hall. It was completed in 1613, for six men and six women. He was the son of John White, and born in Temple-street—a student in Magdalen College, Oxon, 1566—rector of St. Dunstan's in the West—became D.D. in 1584, and a prebendary of St. Paul's—canon of Christ-Church, Oxon, 1591, and canon of St. George's Chapel, Windsor, 1593. He died March 1, 1623. In the Chamber of Bristol is his portrait, with some verses ending

" Quique ALBOS cœli portamque invenit apertam."

The new work over against All Saints' Church, at the Tolzey, was built.

The Magistrates lent money to set up the Colchester bays manufacture at the Smiths' Hall. All beggars and poor people were set to work at spinning and stocking-making, under inspection of the parish-officers.

May 9, the Duke of Brunswick came to Bristol, and was honourably entertained by the Mayor (Robert Aldworth) and his brethren. He was saluted on his arrival with the

A. D.

1610 discharge of twenty-five pieces of ordnance in the Marsh. He slept at the White Lion, Broad-street. At supper-time " many volleys of small shot were given him, by 300 of the trained bands of the city; and the next morning the Mayor with some of the Magistrates gave His Grace a walk about the Marsh, to shew him some pleasure; and in the mean time the ordnance was twice discharged. And after being accompanied by the Mayor and Magistrates to his lodging, they took·their farewell of each other; and so His Grace departed the same day, being Easter-evening, for London."

July 12, by a decree of the Court of Chancery, the Mayors, for the time being, were made special Governors of the Grammar-School, St. Bartholomew's Hospital. See 1783.

Dec. 27, at ten o'clock at night, John Snigge, eldest son of Baron Sir George Snigge, attempting to cross the river at Rownham, in his way to Sir Hugh Smyth's, on horseback, was drowned. The body was not found until the 10th of June following, when it was taken up at the graving-place without either hands or legs. His remains were buried in St. John's crowd. The same year, Richard George was drowned at the same place, in attempting to ride across the river.

1611   William Cary, Mayor.   " This mayor was afterward Keeper of the Back Hall; in which time his wife, an ancient woman, died; and, fourscore years old or more, he married his servant, by whom he had a son, having then sons living that were nearly threescore years old."—Mr. Ald. HAY-THORNE's MS.

A very dry summer: not one day of rain in four months; so that butter was sold for sixpence a pound, cheese, 33s. 4d. per cwt., and hay for three pounds a load.

Sept. 20, the new work was set up at the Tolzey before Richard Bossell's window.

Dr. White's Alms-house in Temple-street erected.

This year were the posts and rails set in at Gibb-Taylor by the merchants and others.

1613   " In April, the Lord President of Wales, the Lord de la Ware, the Lord Clifton, with divers other knights and gentlemen, with their ladies, came to this city."

" Friday, June 4, the Queen [Anne of Denmark] came from Bath to Bristol; the Earl of Worcester being in the coach with Her Grace, and the Mayor [Abel Kitchen], with all the Magistrates and Councilmen, in their scarlet robes, and Mr. Hyde, the Recorder, rode two by two in their foot-cloaths, on horseback, accompanied by the chiefest Master of all the Companies, in their hoods, to Lawford's Gate; where the Recorder made a very learned oration to

. D.

313Her Majesty, after which the Mayor presented her with a richly embroidered purse of gold.—And the Mayor with all the Magistrates took horse again, the last of the Common-Council riding foremost, the Mayor, bareheaded, with a chain of gold about his neck, riding next to the Royal coach. And when they came through Wine-street, all the train-soldiers of the city were arrayed on each side. After the Mayor, &c. had conducted the Queen to her lodgings, at Sir John Young's house, then occupied by the Lady Marques, and upon their return, the soldiers drew towards the Quay, and every one loading his musquet, and at a private notice from the Earl of Gloucester (who, being at a house on the Quay, held a handkerchief out of a casement), they all fired; and at the same instant were discharged, at the Great Tower on the Quay, forty-two pieces of ordnance. And after they had marched to the Green, and given another volley before the Queen's Court, they all departed, leaving a guard of honour at Her Majesty's residence.

" On Sunday, the 6th of June, the Mayor, with the Council, in their scarlet robes, but without the sword, came on foot to bring Her Majesty to College to hear a sermon. The trained soldiers formed a line of passage into the Cathedral; and, when the Queen descended from her coach, the Earl of Worcester, on her right hand, and the Bishop of Bath and Wells on her left, conducted her to the Chancel. The sermon was preached by Dr. Robson, the Dean; and after it Her Grace was re-conducted home in the same manner.

" To shew Her Grace some recreation that might delight her, the next day there was a fight made upon the water, at the Gibb, and there was built a place in Canons' Marsh, finely decked with ivy-leaves and flowers, for Her Grace to sit and see the fight. And when the time came, the Mayor and Aldermen, in their black gowns, brought Her Grace thither, they riding before her, in their foot-cloaths; and so, having placed Her Grace, up came an English ship under sail, and cast anchor, who, striking top-masts, and lowering ancients and flags, made obeisance to the Queen. Having hoisted flags, &c. again, up came two galleys of Turks, who set upon the ship; where was much fighting and shooting on both sides— the Turks boarding the ship and putting off again with loss of men. Some of the Turks, running up the shrowds to the main-top, to pull down the flag, were cast overboard into the river, and the ship's side ran over with blood. At last the Turks were taken and presented to Her Majesty, who, laughing, said they looked like Turks indeed, not only by their apparel, but by their countenances. This fight was excellently performed, and so delighted Her Majesty, that she said she never saw any thing so neatly and artificially performed in her life. And then she was re-conducted to her lodging by the Mayor and Aldermen, with a band of soldiers. 'In the evening the Lady Drunman, belonging to Her Majesty's suite, presented the Maire with a faire ring of gould, set with diamonds, as a favour from the Queene.'*

* By his will, executed in 1639, Mr. Alderman Abel Kitchen devised that this ring (said in most of the MSS. to have been worth £60) should not go out of the family, but

Y

1613 " On Tuesday, about two o'clock, the Mayor and Council attended Her Majesty to Lawford's Gate, where the Mayor on his knees took leave of Her Majesty, who thanked him and the whole city for their love, saying that she never knew she was a Queen till she came to Bristol."

Her Majesty, on leaving the city, went to Syston-House, Gloucestershire, then the residence of Sir Henry Billingsly.

This Royal visit was versified by " one Robert Naile, a prentice in Bristoll, who dedicated his booke to the Maior and Aldermen here." For this Poem at large, see " The Bristol Memorialist," p. 229. It comprises about 460 verses. The " Bristoll bands" who received the Queen at Lawford's Gate are thus described:

> " 3 bands there were whose worthy praise my muse cannot rehearse:
> The first in white & violet clad, the second blacke & white,
> The third with white & scarlot was in martial order dight."

The Recorder's address occupies 52 verses. Of the array in Wine-street we learn that

> " First stood a rank of hardy pikes, much like a thorny wood,
> next after them the nimble shot in order ready stood.
> Here waves the ensignes in the winde, there stands the fife & drum,
> attending when her maiestie would through their squadrons com.
> All to their captaines collours were with scarfes & feathers bright
> adorn'd, not wanting ought was fit to please her princely sight."

The Queen's coach was drawn to the Cathedral by

> " 4 milk-white coursers braue;" and
> " . . . . next her did aproach
> the Ladies on theire trampling steeds, like faire Diana's traine
> hunting in the Arcadian woods (as doo the poets faine).
> The reuerend Senats two and two all marching on a row,
> foremost of all in theire degrees unto the church did goe.
> Lastly on foot before her grace with all her noble traine
> of lords and knights into the church the worthy maior came.
> The queene then set in chaire of state with all the residue,
> in their degrees, the maior and sherifes and the nobillity.
> Where learned doctor Robson did a godly sermon frame,
> in setting forth God's mighty works and lauding of his name."

The sham sea-fight is described with accordant spirit. In a marginal note we are told that the sanguinary feature of the fray was produced by " 6 bladders of bloud poured out of the scubber-holes."

The end of the Poem is crowned by the following epilogue

> " *Concerning the Author, Ro: Naile.*
> It is good to keep alive what would be dead,
> Therefore hee hits the naile not on the head.
> But yet he hath done the office of a naile,
> To fix that fast, which otherwise would faile.
> As now proues true, his name matching his fate,
> In nailing fame on eaternities firme gate."

be handed down to posterity. Two or three of his descendants are at this time (1824) pensioners of the Chamber, but the ring has not been heard of since his decease.

A. D.

1613 June 9, died the Chamberlain of Bristol, and Mr. Thomas White succeeded; but the same year he broke for debt, and Mr. Nicholas Meredith was put in his place.

There was a Parliament kept this year. Thomas James and John Whitson, aldermen, were chosen Burgesses.

No stage-players were allowed to play in Bristol this St. James's tide, in consequence of the danger that was apprehended from the plague being in many places in Wales.

The corn (wheat, rye, and barley) imported into Bristol, from Sept. 1613 to June 1614, in one hundred and four vessels, was 25,105 quarters.

Thomas White, D.D. settled one hundred pounds per annum for repairs of highways about Bristol, particularly ten miles on the road towards Oxford, the whole road to Bath, and five miles in every market-road to Gloucestershire and Somersetshire. Feoffees, the Mayor and Aldermen.

Robert Redwood gave by will a house in King-street, for a library for the public use. See 1615.

1614 Mrs. Elizabeth James, wife of Dr. James, gave the Corporation a silver cup and cover, double gilt, weight thirty ounces.

April 28, several men were killed in a cellar in St. Nicholas-street, by under-digging of a pillar of salt that had been a long time in the cellar.

William Yeamons set up a stone in the Marsh, before the Alms-house. (No name of this family appears in the Corporation annals till 1641.)

1615 " This year was erected and built the Library in the Marsh." See 1636, and also 1772, for some further details of the Library, connected with this period.

This year were elected three new Serjeants, two for the Mayor and one for the Sheriffs.

Aug. 28, the King, by Letters Patent, confirmed the Book of Ordinances of the Master, Wardens, and Society of Merchant-Tailors, containing thirty-five articles, acts, and rules. These were ratified by Charles I., May 15, 1640.

" The walk of All-Saints' finished, being made higher and longer than it was before."

No cart, &c. bound with iron, was allowed to come within the walls of the city, except to St. Peter's Pump and the end of Broadmead. See 1636 and 1651.

" One Phelps, a felloner, pressed to death in Newgate, because he would be tried by God and Somersetshire, and not by his country; which was no plea to his indictment."

This year was the Fish-market in the Shambles built.

A. D.

1616 " The Tolzey was enlighten'd, and the leads made higher, and the walks longer." See 1782.

April 23, died William Shakespeare, aged 53 years.

1617 The Book of Sports published, giving leave for innocent recreations after evening-prayers on Sunday.—Vide Lord Somers's Tracts.

Nov. 11 died, aged 73, Sir George Snigge, knt. serjeant-at-law, and one of the Barons of the Exchequer. He was a native of Bristol, and many years its Recorder. His body lay in state six weeks, at the Tailors' Hall, and was buried in St. Stephen's Church.

This year-date appears in the present door-frame of the Dial Alms-house, Old Market-street.

George Harrington, Mayor, went through the city, trying the weights and measures, and renewed all that were faulty. Moreover, he tried the colliers' sacks, cutting to pieces those that held not their measure. Butter being dear, he brought it out of the ships that were outward-bound, and sold it in the market at a reasonable price.

" The Earl of Arundel [a privy councillor] came to Bristol, and had no entertainment of the city; which he much resented; and he afterward refused the courtesy proffered him." The Earl was a Roman Catholic.

1618 John Guy, merchant, Mayor. " He set up the rayles at the Kay, where shipping is built." These enclosed a yard at the mouth of the Froom, on the east bank.

Oct. 29, Sir Walter Rawleigh was beheaded in Parliament-Yard.

1619 March 1, Queen Anne died, at Hampton-Court.

1620 " This year the new walk was made about Christ-Church, and the frame covered with lead over it."

A motion was intended to be made in Parliament by the Bishop of Bristol, to increase the livings of the Clergy in Bristol. The Corporation determined most strenuously to oppose it.

The Society of St. Stephen's Ringers commenced. They continue to hold an annual festival at the Montague Tavern, on the 17th of November. See *The Bristol Mirror* for Dec. 7, 1822.

1621 Sir William Penn, knt. father of the founder of Pennsylvania, born in Bristol.

The Earl of Pembroke, Lord High Steward of Bristol.

Lord Chancellor Bacon convicted of bribery.

1622 John Guy sent for to London, to consult about the decay of trade and coin.

A. D.

1622 In Whitsun-week, Earl Grey, his brother, and Lord
Clanrickarde, their father-in-law, came from Bath, and
were entertained by the Mayor, Robert Rogers, soap-maker.
They slept at the White Lion, Broad-street, and walked
about the Marsh. " This Maior, as his estate was greate,
soe he possessed the same not without trouble. Leaving it
to his son, a knight, he enjoyed not the same above three
yeares, and then dyed; and his stately house, fitt for a
King's pallace, [was] turned into a tavern."—*Mr. Alderman
Haythorne's MS.*

" This yere Mr. Thomas Cecill, for his misdemeaners, was
put out of the Councell." (See 1628.) He was a wire-
drawer, and sheriff in 1618.

John, lord Digby, baron of Sherborne, was created the
first Earl of Bristol. He received the honour, Sept. 15, and
shortly afterward came to see the city.

Dr. Thomas White enfeoffed to the Corporation the property appropriated to Temple Hospital.

1623 Robert Wright, ninth Bishop of Bristol. He had the
stone pulpit made, and the opposite seats for the Corporation. " He caused the lower window in the College
to be made, whereby the church had much more light
than formerly. He set up also the organs and the pictures
about the church." Of the organ, see 1630; and of a new
west-window, see 1704. The pictures were those of a
representation of the Deluge, and the Prophets and Apostles,
in the organ-screen. The latter were plastered up during
the Commonwealth, and have been restored to view within
the last twenty years.

1624 " The Corn-Market in Wine-street built, and a great
well sunk at the end of it, and the pump set there at the
City's charge." The margin of Millerd's four-sheet map
contains a drawing of the Market-House. The roof of it
rested upon sixteen pillars, divided by four arched entrances;
over which, in the pediments, were placed coats of arms, &c.
The pavement was mosaic.

Seven persons were hanged; viz. two for *witchcraft*, two
for murder, and three for unnatural practices.

1625 " By an Act of the Common-Council, Brandon-Hill was
adjudged to the Mayor and Sheriffs, but the citizens were
allowed to dry clothes there."—The more correct version of
this grant is, that " Brandon-Hill was purchased by the
Corporation from —— ——, esq. of Clifton, to be holden
yearly by the Mayor and the two Sheriffs for the time being, at
the yearly rent of two marks, or £1 6s. 0d., on the following

1625terms, viz. 'They keeping it well prepared, and maintaining the hedges and bushes, and admitting the drying of clothes by townsmen and townswomen, as had anciently been accustomed.'"

CHARLES I.

About the beginning of April, a Turkish Ambassador landed at Plymouth, and coming here, in his way to London, at the same time when the King was proclaimed, he dined with the Mayor, John Barker, merchant. In the evening the merchants gave him a supper at the Guilders Inn, in High-street, and made him a present of a fine gelding and furniture, suffering him not to spend anything in this city. He left Bristol for London the following day. [The Guilders Tavern, in front of the inn, was on the site of the house now occupied by Mr. Taylor, silversmith.]

May 11, the King's marriage with the Princess Henrietta Maria of France, youngest daughter of the great *Henri Quatre*, solemnized at Paris, the Duke of Chevereux acting as the King's proxy. June 13, the Queen landed at Dover, and the marriage was consummated at Canterbury. A plague raged at this time in London, which swept away 35,417 persons; "from which," says one of the MSS. "God miraculously preserved Bristol: it came as near as Lawford's Gate; which merciful preservation was so deeply taken to heart by Mr. Yeamons, the pastor of St. Philip's, that scarcely any exercise passsed him all his life afterward, without commemorating the same."

The inscriptions on one of the bronze tables placed in front of the Exchange (that nearest to All-Saints' Church), though originally moulded in bold relief, is now [1824] become totally illegible, by the constant wearing of bakers' baskets and other porters' burthens, for which only, since mercantile transactions ceased to be in ready money, or dicing the public holiday-amusement of the magistrates, it has served, as a resting-place. The florid ornaments of the supporting pillar also distinguish it as the most ancient of the four.—On the garter below the surface of a second of these tables is this record: "Thomas Hobson of Bristol made me, anno 1625. Nicholas Crisp of London gave me, to this honourable city, in remembrance of God's mercy, in Anno Domini 1625. N. G." In the ring of the surface, "Praise the Lord O my soule, and forget not all his benefits. He saved my life from destruction and . . . . . . to his mercy and

A. D.

loving-kindness. Praise . . . ." The rest is worn out. See 1631.

1626 Aug. 18, at Canterbury, the King confirmed the Charter of 1604—Seyer's No. 30.

The Corporation purchased of Sir Charles Redcliff Gerrard, knt., for four hundred and fifty pounds, the advowsons of St. James, St. Peter, Christ, St. Ewen, St. Michael, and St. Philip's Churches.

Christopher Whitson, Mayor. "This Mayor was never married, nor was he exceeding liberall."

1627 Alderman John Whitson, by will, left an endowment for the Red Maids' Hospital, to educate and maintain forty daughters of free burgesses. Trustees, the Mayor and Aldermen. He also left, for disposal by the Aldermen in their several wards, to twenty-six men and twenty-six women, at Michaelmas and Lady-day, seventy-eight pounds per annum. He bequeathed likewise fifty-two pounds for poor lying-in women, at disposal of the Mayoress, or (if the Mayor be a widower) the wife of the senior Alderman; and two exhibitions from the Grammar-School to St. John's College, Oxford, of ten pounds a year each, at the disposal of the Mayor and Aldermen. See 1634.

The Mayor, John Gunning, merchant, gave ten shillings per week (after the manner of Alderman Kitchen), during his life-time.

Jan. 4, the ship Charles, of 300 tons and thirty guns, launched at Gibb-Taylor.

1628 "The Society of Merchant-Venturers of the City of Bristol, their gift to Capt. Samuel Pitts, for bravely defending his ship Kirtlington Gally, the 7th of June, 1628, against a Spanish Rover, in his passage from Jamaica to Bristol."—Inscription, upon a richly chased silver monteith and collar, weighing 266 oz. 11 dwts., sold at auction by Mr. Harril, Dec. 31, 1821, for £148 16s. Purchased by the Corporation.

In July came into Bristol 1500 soldiers, who were very unruly. When tidings came here that the Duke of Buckingham was stabbed at Portsmouth, by Lieut. Felton (Aug. 23), "those soldiers were like lambs, walking about the streets as if they were apparitions or ghosts, not knowing what to do; and, soon after, they were all sent to Ireland."

Tobias Matthews, archbishop of York, died this year.

Mr. Barrett, in his History, p. 589, says that Redcliff-Church "had been at different times endowed with large estates," not only for support of the fabric and of divine

1628 offices celebrated therein, but " for charity to the poor, the aged, and infirm of this parish." Any such endowment heretofore for the latter purpose, we have ascertained, does not appear; and the malversations in respect of " lands to the full amount of £400 per annum," which he erroneously assigns to the time of the Commonwealth, were in fact redressed by proceedings in Chancery, which were brought to issue in this year, the 4th of Charles I. (See 1622, of Cecil, the delinquent named by Mr. Barrett.) The ensuing rebellion brought no mischiefs of the same description.

1629   April 13, at Westminster, the King granted the Charter. (Seyer's No. 31) which recites that of 1373, relative to the separation of Bristol from the adjoining Counties, excepting the Castle, and states that, because no Justices of the County of Gloucester dwell near the Castle of Bristol, to controul its occupation by thieves, malefactors, or other disorderly livers, including persons proper and fit for service in war, who have fled there when there has been occasion for their services, and at the request of the Queen,—the Castle is separated from the County of Gloucester, and made part of the City of Bristol. The King was at this time upon the look-out for ways and means to avoid the " impertinences of Parliaments."

    Alderman John Whitson died, aged 71 years.

    The Manor-House, &c. formerly the Hospital of St. Lawrence (see 1223), was in the possession of Robert Hooke, of Bristol. It comprised two hundred and five acres.

    Humphry Hooke, merchant, of Kingsweston, Mayor, this year. His wife, Florence, was the daughter of Sir Hugh Smyth, of Long-Ashton. See 1661.

    The sum of thirty pounds had been paid, yearly, by the Chamber, for the purpose of keeping the City clean; but general complaints having been made of the continued foulness of the streets, the salary of the Common-Raker was augmented by the addition of forty pounds, which was apportioned on the several parishes. His salary then amounted to £70 per annum.

    A new organ erected in the Cathedral, together with a new west-window, the horologe, and other ornaments, by means of contributions of individuals obtained by the Bishop. See a copy of the roll of subscriptions, hung up in the Chapter-Room; by which it appears that the old organ was sold to " St. Steevens" for thirty pounds.

    Oct. 26, at Westminster, by Charter (Seyer's No. 33), in consideration of nine hundred and fifty-nine pounds, the

A. D.

629 King granted the Castle to the Mayor, burgesses, &c. with all its rights, members, and appurtenances, including a mansion-house then in the occupation of Francis Brewster, yeoman; a close, lying outside the ditch, called the King's Orchard, two acres; a piece of ground called the Inner Green; a wood-yard, three gardens, and forty-three tenements with appurtenances, held by persons named in the Charter; the whole of which, with the walls, towers, fosses, banks, and ditches, enclosing the Castle, had by Letters Patent, dated Aug. 23, 1626, been leased to Francis Brewster, for the term of eighty years, at the annual rent of one hundred pounds. Advowsons, knights' fees, and mines, were excepted from this purchase, the Corporation paying a rent to the Crown of forty pounds per annum.—In Sept. 1634, the City purchased John Brewster's estate, and one life more to come, for five hundred and twenty pounds.

Sir Charles Vaughan died, and was buried in the Cathedral, south side of the north aisle.

" This year wheat was at 8s. the bushell in the city, and dearer would have been, as it was in other places, but that much came in by shipping."

" Now the old prerogative statute for knighthood comes in place, whereby those who had estates of forty pounds per annum were summoned to appear a little before Christmas, to be knighted; and, upon default, to be fined. By which means, about one hundred thousand pounds were brought into the Exchequer."—BAKER's *Chronicle*, Phillip's Continuation, for the 4th edition.

631 " This year the Armour-house in the Castle was built. Also a Tower in the Church-yard of St. Ewen, which cost £196." What remained of this tower, upon the Church being taken down, was connected with the Council-House, as an office of the Mayor's Clerk. See 1824.

Henry Yate, Mayor; who survived ten sons, and died without issue male.

Under 1625 we have noted two of the bronze tables erected on the Exchange-pavement, in Corn-street. The third in respect of age was referred to under 1594. The fourth, which stands nearest to the Post-Office, presents the following information in the ring of the surface:

" A.D. 1631. This is the guift of Mr. White, of Bristoll, merchant, brother unto Doctor Thomas White, a famous benefactor to this citie." Six lines in verse, and a shield with armorial bearings, engraven in the centre of the table, are obliterated. On the garter round the exterior,—" The

z

A. D.

Churche of the livinge God is the pillar and ground of the trueth. So was the work of the pillars finished." See 1634.

1632   John Locke born, at Wrington, Somersetshire.

Henry Hobson, innkeeper, Mayor.

1633   The High Cross taken down, enlarged, raised higher for the admission of four new statues, and protected with iron palisadoes. It now stood 39 feet 3 inches. The cost, to the Chamber, of these improvements, was two hundred and seven pounds; but whether this sum included the four new statues is not known. The order of their appearance was as follows:

North, facing Broad-street { Charles I. / John } West, facing Corn-street { Elizabeth / Edw. III.

East, —— Wine-street { Henry VI. / Henry III. } South, —— High-street { James I. / Edw. IV.

Dr. Wright being translated to Coventry and Lichfield, he was succeeded in the bishoprick by Dr. George Cook.

Nov. 1, died Mr. William Yeamans.

1634   August. The old Crane on the Back rebuilt, at the cost of more than £100.

St. Peter's Pump built and repaired.

The fathers of the two Sheriffs elected this year, John Langton and Thomas Hooke, served as Sheriffs together in 1614.

Nov. 6, died Robert Aldworth, without issue. He was buried in St. Peter's Church, at the upper end of the south aisle. He bequeathed all his estates to Giles Elbridge, merchant, who married his niece. Near the church-yard of St. Peter was an alms-house, erected by Robert Aldworth, who also built the parsonage-house (now, 1824, occupied by a basket-maker, with the date 1613 on its front) opposite the well of St. Edith. One MS. says, " he builded the faire house in St. Peter's church-yard, with all the sellars and lofts for refineing of suger. Another large building he raised in the Marsh; made two docks there for shipping, which came to nothing."

The Bishops enjoined not to let any more leases on lives, but for years.

" This year men were taxed with ship-money."

The Red Maids' Hospital opened, on the site of the Gaunts' Hospital. See 1655.

George White gave an exhibition to St. John's College, Oxford, of five pounds per annum.

1635   Bristol paid above £25,000l. for customs, and gave £2163 13s. 4d. towards fitting out a fleet against France and Holland. See 1638.

A. D.

1636 No person was allowed to drive a dray through the city, under the penalty of 3s. 4d. This was in consequence of the carelessness of drivers. See 1651.

Nov. 13, Edward Colston born, son of William Colston [sheriff in 1643], by Sarah, daughter of Counsellor Bettins.

Elway Bevin, a scholar of Tallis, organist of Bristol Cathedral, gentleman-extraordinary of the Chapel-Royal, and master of Dr. Child, was dismissed from all his appointments, on discovery of his attachment to the Romish communion.

637 William Jones, grocer, Mayor; and Abraham Edwards, apothecary, one of the Sheriffs.

638 Tyndale's Park appointed as a fit place for examining persons infected with the plague, and for airing of goods; and hovels were built for the infected.

From September to December (the King being determined not to convene a Parliament, and wanting money to force Scotland to receive Episcopacy), this city was never free from commissioners and pursuivants, who examined merchants, on oath, as to what commodities they had shipped, what entries were made at the Custom-Houses, what foreign goods imported, for years past; whereby some were compelled to accuse each other, and were sent for to London. Shopkeepers also underwent this inquest, and suffered great exactions. Soap-makers paid £4 custom per ton for soap,—the brewers forty marks per annum for a license. Four aldermen and some merchants being deputed to complain to the King, His Majesty embraced them most graciously, and was sorry for having acted upon wrong information, but could not recall the commission. He gave them liberty, however, to prepare a bill in the Star-Chamber, and retain counsel. They stayed in London at a great expense, for the hearing, but nothing was determined. His Majesty wished them to follow up their suit, and, when it came to the highest, His Grace would mediate between them.

Corn was scarce this year: wheat sold at 9s. a bushel.

In St. James's week, eleven boys were drowned by the launching of a ship, which was thence called the Drown-boy.

640 Mr. Barrett, in his History, p. 487, states that "a commission was this year held by Dr. Wright, the late Bishop of Bristol, to inquire into the trust for the charity of Mr. Robert Strange (mayor in 1475, 1483, and 1490*), who

* Meaning 1474-5, 1482-3, and 1489-90.

z 2

A. D.

1640 founded an alms-house at the foot of St. John's steps, and endowed it with lands by the Castle-Mill up to Newgate, and the Spur-Inn, in Wine-street; by which it appeared that the revenues had been embezzled, several leaves having been cut out of the parish-books, and the inscription on his tomb in the church-yard entirely defaced."—We suspect that Mr. Barrett's authority for this " commission to inquire" was simply loose tradition, and that by 1640, as may be guessed by the sequel, he meant 1630. A vellum-book in possession of the vestry, commencing its entries so early as 1469 (when Robert Strange might have been a benefactor to the parish, for he was one of the Bailiffs in 1461-2, and Sheriff in 1468-9), mentions, among other church-lands the rent of which was applicable to general purposes, the two tenements, or their site, in Wine-street, now (1824) occupied by Mr. Evans, hatter, and Mr. Green, draper and wine-merchant, and which may possibly have been formerly united as " the Spur Inn;" but the five tenements, which fill the area between Newgate and the Castle-Mill, were first named in the parish-rental for 1553, and as alike applicable for general purposes.* The earliest mention of the alms-house in the parish-books is under 1550. It appears, by an old copy of proceedings in Michaelmas term, 1629, that a suit was instituted in Chancery by Walter Strange, claiming as a descendant of Robert Strange, against James Dyer and others, being the feoffees and vestry-men of the parish of St. John; the object of which appears to have been, to charge the feoffees with a misapplication of the rents and profits of certain premises without Newgate, extending to Castle-Mill, and from the street or highway to the river Froom, charging that the same had been settled by the said Robert Strange for the benefit of the alms-house, also alleged to have been founded and built by him in the said parish of St. John the Baptist. The Answer negatives in express terms, not only such endowment by the said Robert Strange, but declares also a disbelief that such alms-house was ever built by him, as surmised by the Bill. It admits that there was such an alms-house, and that the same was used by the parish for their own poor, put in at the discretion of the vestry. It admits also the possession in the parish of the tenements without Newgate, but shews that they had been church-property for a long period before, and applicable to general purposes for the good of the parish, as they

* The carved wood-work, in front of the house next to Newgate, bears the initials R. A. and date 1543.

A. D.

1640 have always been since treated. The same document bears this memorandum, evidently of coeval date: "Upon this Answer made to Strange his Bill, he surceased his suit, and paid seven nobles costs, in 1630."

March 24, John Glanville, recorder, and Humphry Hooke, merchant, were chosen Burgesses for the Parliament, which was shortly afterward begun and presently afterward dissolved.

May 15, the King ratified the ordinances of the Society of Merchant-Tailors. See 1701.

Edmund Prideaux, Recorder.

Two hundred soldiers were impressed in this city, to go against the Scots.

John Taylor, merchant, Mayor. [This gentleman was killed Sept. 9, 1645, when Sir Thomas Fairfax's men entered and took Prior's Hill Fort and the rest of the suburbs.]

Nov. 3, the Parliament met, with whom begun the Commonwealth; William Lenthall, Speaker. Humphrey Hooke and Luke Hodges were the Burgesses for Bristol; but Mr. Hooke being dismissed, Richard Aldworth was chosen in his place.

1641 Jan. 21, Thomas Westfield, twelfth Bishop of Bristol, on the removal of Bishop Skinner to Oxford.

Feb. 14, a Bill for Triennial Parliaments passed the Royal assent.

" Feb. 21, two hundred men went from Bristol into Ireland, to Duncannon Fort, under Capt. Wildings and Capt. Austen. Three hundred more went to Minehead, to be transported under the Captains Pinchback, Manners, and Roberts."

Feb. 26, Laud, archbishop of Canterbury, impeached of high treason by the Commons.

May 12, the Earl of Strafford beheaded on Tower-Hill, for high treason.

August. An order of the Commons for removal of all scandalous pictures, crosses, and figures, within churches and without.

1642 The expenses of repairing and pitching the streets of Bristol were at this time defrayed by the Chamber.

Jan. 5, the King went to the House of Commons, with a guard of pensioners and courtiers, five hundred in number, and demanded the persons of the members, Pym, Hampden, Hollis, Sir Arthur Haslerig, and Strode.

Jan. 11, the Sheriffs of London and the trained bands, with an armed multitude, carried the obnoxious Members in triumph to their seats at Westminster.

1642   Feb. 23, the Queen and Princess Mary (born Nov. 4, 1630, afterward married to the Prince of Orange) embarked for Holland.

March 2, the King left London for Newmarket.

Denzil Hollis appointed by the Parliament to the command of the militia in Bristol; and he himself subscribed one thousand pounds for its maintenance.

Bishop Westfield deprived by the Parliament. He was a good orator, and wrote his own epitaph.

April 23, the King went from Hull to York, with intent to secure the magazine there; but was denied admittance by Sir John Hotham, who held it for the Parliament.

William Penn was this year made captain.

May 13, Sir Nicholas Kemeys, knt. of Keven Mabley, in the county of Glamorgan, created a baronet.

Aug. 22, the King set up the Royal standard at Nottingham.

Oct. 23, the battle of Edghill, Warwickshire.

By this time the Castle and walls of Bristol were repaired by the Magistrates, also a fort built on Brandon-Hill, with a communication to another on St. Michael's Hill, where previously stood a wind-mill (which was afterward improved as a royal pentagonal fort), and to another, on the site of a garden behind the existing house erected by Mr. William Raester, at Montague Parade, which, after the first siege was called Colston's Mount,* from the circumstance of William Colston (father of the benevolent Edward) having then the command of it, and being also, under the Duke of Beaufort, Deputy-Governor of the City and Castle. The Mayor, Richard Aldworth, refused Lord Paulet, who sent to him Sir Fernando Gorges† and Mr. Smyth of Ashton, to bring troops of horse into the city; he having received express orders from the King to admit no troops of either party, but to keep and defend the city for His Majesty's use.

Dec. 2, Col. Sir Alexander Popham sent 500 horse to Bedminster, with the intention of making up 1000 on behalf of the Parliament; but the Corporation then refused him, and placed guards of the trained bands accordingly. The gates and portcullisses were repaired, and strong rails, with long iron spikes, fixed without every gate, so that no horses

---

* On this mount Mr. Carden, in 1823, built a neat residence, which is called *Colston's Fort* House.

† Sir Fernando Gorges at this time occupied Sir John Young's lower house, now Colston's School. Sir Ralph de Gorges, the first knight of that name, was at the siege of Karlaverock Castle, Scotland, in the reign of Edward I.

A. D.

1642 could pass by or over them. The great Tower of the Castle was well repaired, and ordnance were planted on the top.— In expectation of the arrival of Colonel Thomas Essex, with forces from Berkeley and Thornbury, on behalf of the Parliament, the city-gates had been double warded, for resistance. The third day, Dec. 5, the citizens arrayed themselves, and, Essex being expected at Froom-Gate, two guns were planted there, and two at the High Cross. The Magistrates were in council at the Tolzey, when Mrs. Mayoress, Mrs. Rogers, (widow of the mayor in 1621), Mrs. Vickris (wife of one of the sheriffs in 1636), and many other women, came with petitions that the Parliament's army might be received. An affray took place at Froom-Gate; during which Essex was admitted at Newgate, and he immediately took upon himself the governorship of the City and Castle. The citizens now began to feel the weight of martial law.

1643 Jan. 23, Col. Essex shot one of his soldiers with a pistol, for asking for his pay.

Feb. 16, Col. Nathaniel Fiennes (son of Lord Say), Col. Popham, and Clement Walker,* arrived with five troops of horse, and, Feb. 18, five companies of foot.

Feb. 22, the Queen landed at Burlington-Bay, Yorkshire, bringing with her money, arms, and ammunition, raised in Holland, by pawning the Royal jewels. She was conducted to York by two troops of horse, headed by the Earl of Montrose and Lord Ogleby, where she commenced forming her army.

Feb. 27, Sir Edward Hungerford's forces arrived in Bristol. The same day Col. Essex, being at a feast at Captain Hill's, at Redland (in a house which formed part of that now occupied by Mr. Coathupe), and having only three or four of his servants at hand, was made prisoner by Col. Fiennes, upon pretence that he intended to deliver up the city to the King's forces. Fiennes thereupon took upon himself the governorship.

A tax was laid upon the city, to pay the Parliament's forces, of £55 15s. per week, assessed on lands, goods, money at interest, and stocks in trade; the first payment, March 1; the tax to be continued for three months, or until the King's troops should be disbanded. This was afterwards confirmed by Parliament.

March 6 (Monday), Prince Rupert, his brother Maurice, George Lord Digby, and others, with an army of 10,000

* The same who, with Mr. Pryn, as Members of Parliament, exhibited articles of cowardice against Fiennes, in a court-martial at St. Alban's, Dec. 14, this same year.

horse and foot, arrived from Basingstoke at Chipping Sodbury. The approach to the city on the side of Somersetshire
had been prevented, by the breaking down of Keynsham
Bridge, agreeably to a resolve of Col. Fiennes's council of
war.

Tuesday, March 7, the Royal forces advanced to Horfield
and Westbury, and on Wednesday appeared on Durdham
Down, where they brought hay ⸱ ⸱d provisions, and burnt
fires all night.

It was now discovered in the city, upon the information
of some females, that an association had been formed to admit the King's troops, by surprising the main-guard and the
guard of Froom-Gate, and giving the signal, by ringing the
bells of St. John's and St. Michael's Churches, for a rising
of the King's friends in all parts of the city, who were to be
distinguished by wearing pieces of white ribbon or incle in
their bosoms or hats, and the word " Charles."

Thursday, about one in the morning, intimation was given
to the council of war, then sitting, that a party was met in
consultation at the house of Mr. Robert Yeamans, in Wine-
street, one of the last year's sheriffs and now an alderman,
and another portion of the same party, at the house of Mr.
George Boucher, a wealthy merchant, in Christmas-street, near
Froom-Gate. Accordingly, Capt. Buck was sent, with forty
musketteers, to the house of Mr. Yeamans; and there, after
some show of resistance, he and twenty-four men in arms
surrendered themselves prisoners. Sixty men with muskets
were found at Mr. Boucher's, fifty-one of whom, with himself,
were seized; and the whole were sent, under a strong guard,
to the Castle.

" *A briefe Relation, abstracted out of several letters, of a
most hellish, cruell, and bloudy Plott, against the City of
Bristoll, &c.*" ordered by the House of Commons, March 13,
to be forthwith printed, and from which we have extracted
the preceding particulars, adds, that " the chiefe actors of
" this mischievous designe were the aforesaid *Robert Yeo-*
" *mans*, and *George Butcher*, Mr. *Iohn Taylor*, Mr. *Cole-*
" *stone*, and his brother, Mr. *Fitzherbert*, two *Colsons*, and
" two *Herberts; N. Cole* [sheriff in 1644], *E. Arundle,*
" Mr. *Caple*, and Captain *Cole* of *St. Augustin's*, who with
" at least one hundred more Actors and Accessories are
" already taken and imprisoned in the Castle."—" *Two-*
" *good's* * house was searched, and therein were found many

* See 1646.

A. D.

643 " papers that did discover the whole plot, and between three
" and four thousand pounds in money and plate, and twenty
" muskets charged with bullets, besides divers instruments
" to murther and destroy with cruelty, such as wee never
" saw before."

A writer who signs I. H. [perhaps Capt. Hill, of Redland]
says,—

" This plot being spoiled, and the gates kept close, that none
" should goe out to give Prince Rupert and his forces notice, made
" them expect till morning, when our gunner from the fort let fly
" at them and killed a horse, which was found dead there the next
" day by our scouts; immediately upon this, they all marched away,
" and were heard to curse the seamen that had betray'd them.

" On Thursday Prince *Roberts* trumpeter came to towne, but as
" a spy, his errand was to demand two dead bodies that we killed
" upon the *Downe*, one whereof was one *Stroud*, as he said.   The
" trumpeter enquired for mee and said, my Lord of *Cleveland*
" desired me to send him a pound of tobacco, but I being out of the
" way, Colonell *Fines* sent him one pound, and Colonell *Popham*
" another.   We expected to hear of them again last night, but they
" came not, and since they are marched quite away towards *Cicenster*
" and *Oxford*."

" The Country came in to us very strong, and wee are very
" couragious (God be praised) and when that Sr. *William Whaller*
" comes, wee shall be so strong as to drive them out of these parts.
" He is not above 12 or 14 miles from us, and we expect him on
" Monday at the farthest; but he doth much good service as he
" comes along."

Mr. Yeamans and Mr. Boucher* were kept chained by
their necks and feet, in a dungeon of the Castle, twelve weeks;
when they were brought to trial before a court-martial,
at the house of Mr. Robert Rogers (soap-maker, mayor in
1621), at the Bridge-end.   This was on the site now occupied by Pitt & Co.'s bank: a drawing of its highly ornamented north front is given in the margin of Millerd's
four-sheet map, and copied for chap. vii. of the Memoirs.

Col. Fiennes's name appears under this date, in the
appointment of a new commission to bring up a speedy
account of the weekly assessments of the army in the
County of Gloucester.   In this month he had prisoners, of
the King's friends, Sir Walter Pye, Sir William Crofts,
Col. Coningsby, &c.

May 30, Mr. Yeamans and Mr. Boucher were executed in

---

* Nathaniel Boucher, merchant (sheriff in 1624), died, aged 40 years, March 22,
1627, leaving nine children. He was buried in St. Werburgh's Church. For a predecessor of this name, see 1608.

A a

1643 Wine-street, near the Guard-House, opposite to the Nag's Head Tavern,* now Savery & Co.'s banking-house. It was intended that this tragedy should be performed exactly before Mr. Yeamans's own door, but the Corn-Market then stood in the way. "Langridge and Clifton," one account says, "were the hangmen, under Col. Fiennes and his associate, Robert Baugh, the sheep-skin dresser." Many persons are said elsewhere to have been struck down for praying for them. The assistance of the Rev. Mr. Towgood and the Rev. Mr. Standfast was denied them in their prayers; and three schismatics, named Cradock, Rosewell, and Fowler, were chosen for that purpose; who, instead of comforting them in their last moments, reviled them, charging them with hypocrisy and apostacy, to the last moment they were turned off the ladder.

The King had sent a trumpeter with a letter, from Oxford, to endeavour to save them.

Mr. Yeamans recommended his mother to the care of a guardian, and his wife, who was great with her ninth child, (having eight little ones, the eldest not being able to put on its own clothes,) to Mr. Yeamans, his father-in-law. His body was interred in St. Maryport-Church; where, March 15, 1814, upon sinking into a vault, near the vestry, in the north aisle, under a mural monument of the style of Henry VII., which has been always called the tomb of William Little, the Bristol grammarian, in a lead coffin, Mr. Yeamans's remains were discovered in extraordinary preservation. Mr. Richard Smith, senior surgeon of the Bristol Infirmary, published at the time an interesting account of the state in which the body was found. We have also seen, still in MS., the late Mr. Goldwyer's report of the same subject. Mr. Henry Smith, solicitor, made a coloured drawing of the corpse *in situ*. The heart is deposited in Mr. R. Smith's Anatomical Museum. The Rev. W. Waite preserved a portion of the shirt, which was of fine linen, very elegantly worked. Mr. H. Smith has another piece, also a piece of the blue-and-white handkerchief that bound up the head. Mr. Francis Hill, of Burton-Hill, Malmsbury, who is a relative of the family, possesses a portrait of Mr. Yeamans, in his magisterial robes, as sheriff, on which is marked his age, 37 years. Mr. Norton's illustrated copy of the "Memoirs, &c." contains a coloured drawing after this picture. His estate, which was of great

* Whence the Nag's Head Cake, sold to this day in St. Nicholas-market.

1643 value, was seized, and his widow was obliged to redeem the small remainder, in comparison with the rent, at a loss of five hundred pounds.

Mr. Boucher was buried in St. Werburgh's Church. In the corner of the north aisle was a small square stone-table to his memory, bearing the following verses:

> *" Sanguis Martyrum semen ecclesiæ.*
> " Whoever chanceth this way, pass not by
> These sainted ashes with a careless eye:
> They are undaunted dust, and did outbrave
> While they retain'd a soul, Death and the Grave,
> And still bear witness, in our Martyr's right,
> That they dare murder, who yet ne'er durst fight.
> Ne'er was so bold a lion by such hares
> Worried to death—so merciless their snares;
> Yet he so stout, that whether, none can tell,
> His courage or their cruelty did excel.
> Mirror of Patience! Loyalty! thy fall
> Hath proved yet a successful funeral;
> Since 'twas guilt of thy death, no battery
> That storm'd these forts, that gain'd us victory:
> For though our foes were fenced with wall and roof,
> Yet there's no wall, no fence, is conscience-proof.
> Thus is thy murdering-wreath to us become
> A laureate—to thee a crown of martyrdom.
>   G. B."

About this time Walter Stephens (linen-draper, and one of the sheriffs after the surrender of the city in 1645), a leader among the Parliamentarians, demolished the Virgin Mary's Chapel on the Bridge.

July 5, the King's forces were drawn up by Sir Ralph Hopton and Prince Maurice, upon Toghill, or Tughill, about eight miles from Bristol, on the road to Marshfield. The Parliament-troops, commanded by Sir William Waller, were stationed at Landsdown, where they had a battery; whence Sir William detached a strong party of horse and dragoons, with a regiment of cuirassiers, to attack the King's horse, who had never before turned from an enemy. The attack was so vigorous, that they were broken and routed. A fresh party belonging to the King's, winged by some Cornish musketeers, came up, and, attacking in their turn, drove back the Parliament's forces; and, after a very bloody engagement, they gained the summit of the hill, and took possession of the battery. It was now that Sir Beville Granville, at the third charge, and at the head of a stand of pikes, his horse falling, after other wounds, received a mortal blow from a pole-axe. Upon this, Sir William Waller retired behind some stone walls, where both parties continued in sight of each other during the remainder of the day; and at midnight the Parliament-forces retreated to Bath, leaving lighted torches in the walls, to deceive the King's troops; who, in the morning, found themselves masters of the field of battle. Sir Beville Granville, after he was wounded, was taken to the parsonage of Cold-Ashton, where he died. A handsome monument (etched by Mr. Lysons) was erected to his memory, and may now be seen upon Landsdown.

July 17, Col. Fiennes gave orders to demolish St. Peter and St. Philip's Churches; but on the 22d Prince Rupert and the Marquess of Hertford appeared, with 20,000 men, to attack the city.

July 24, the attack was made in six different parts; which obliged Fiennes to withdraw his forces from the Castle, consisting of 2500 foot and a regiment of dragoons, to defend the walls of the city. The shipping in the port were seized the same day.

July 26, although, in the attack on the Somersetshire side, led on by the Marquess of Hertford and Prince Maurice, some of the assailants mounted the wall, yet, by the vigorous defence from within, they were driven back with great slaughter. But, on the Gloucestershire side, where Prince Rupert commanded, Col. Washington, finding a weak place in the curtain, forced a passage through the hollow way between Brandon-Hill Fort and Windmill Fort, secure from the shot of either, to Froom-Gate; not, however, without the loss of five hundred of the King's forces, killed out of the windows of the houses.

July 27, Col. Fiennes ordered a parley to be beat; and it was agreed that the garrison, with divers of the citizens, should march out of the city.

We gather the further particulars of this siege from the trial of Fiennes (which took place at St. Alban's, on the 14th of December following), before a Council of War, assembled by special order of Parliament to Mr. Pryn and Mr. Clement Walker, " for cowardly surrendering the City and Castle of Bristol."

The charges were,—

1. The removal of Col. Essex, on pretence that he intended to deliver up the City and Castle to the enemy.—2. The execution of some of the chief citizens, by martial law, for only intending to deliver up the City to Prince Rupert, though they did not actually surrender it.—3. The putting the Parliament, City, and County, to great expense, as for a defence of three months, having promised several gentlemen to defend it so long, if it should be besieged.—4.

. D.

643 That when the enemy came before the town, with no extraordinary forces, and before they had taken any outworks or raised the least battery against the City or Castle, he had cowardly and traitorously delivered up the same, without the consent of Parliament.— 5. That without the privity of a council of war he demanded a parley, when several officers and soldiers advised the contrary, and would have repulsed the enemy; and when the council of war had unanimously voted that it was neither safe nor honourable to depart the town, unless they might march away with half their arms and their colours, he told them plainly that they must deliver up all to the enemy, but what was excepted in the articles, and leave their arms and colours behind them;—that he caused the town to be delivered up an hour before the time agreed on, and suffered the enemy to possess themselves of it before the soldiers were marched out; * whereby many of them were pillaged, and the best of the inhabitants plundered.—6. That during the three days siege he gave no encouragement to the soldiers, though they killed nearly 1000 of the enemy, with the loss only of eight persons, by his own account; and when a small party, not 200, of the enemy, had entered the line of communication on the 26th of July, and gave themselves up for lost, not being followed by any more for two hours, he neglected to beat them out again, as advised by Capt. Bagnal, Col. Davison, and others, who would have undertaken the service, but, on the contrary, called off the soldiers from the line and outworks, and sounded a parley, when the enemy were so beaten that they threw down their arms and cried 'quarter,' insomuch that the soldiers and inhabitants cried out, they were betrayed.—7. That he had an intention, before the siege, to deliver the city to the enemy, by refusing to send away the prisoners, formerly taken, out of the Castle, saying he would detain them to make his own conditions; and by commanding Mr. Hassard, the master-gunner, to lay aside thirty barrels of powder, with bullets proportionable, for a reserve in case of extremity, and yet surrendered before he was reduced to this last reserve; and by moving Sir William Waller to depart from Bristol before it was besieged.—8. That he surrendered when he had sixty barrels of powder in the Castle, besides twenty more in the City, and other ammunition and provisions proportionable, sufficient for 1000 men for three or four months.—9. That by printed relations and letters he had presumed to justify this dishonourable action, casting an extraordinary blemish on the Houses of Parliament, and their General, the Earl of Essex, by suggesting that, if he had held out the city to the last, he could not have expected any relief from them in less than six or eight weeks; whereas Gloucester, since besieged by a greater force, was relieved in half that time, having held out a month's siege, as Bristol might have

* Fiennes's precipitate admission of the besiegers is said to have produced the following accident: When Prince Rupert's advanced guard marched down Steep-street, some the garrison, stationed in the Ship public-house, fired upon them. Rupert's party revenged themselves by putting all the assailants to the sword.

done.—10. That Bristol was so cowardly delivered up to the enemy, that they had since published, in print, that " the said Colonel bestowed the same on His Majesty, and it was delivered up beyond their expectation, and they could not have taken it, if it had been defended by the Governor."

Fiennes answered to the first charge, that

With regard to Col. Essex, he had received an express order from the General, to remove him from the city, where he commanded a regiment.—2. That after Essex's departure he discovered a conspiracy between divers citizens and some officers of his (Essex's) regiment, to deliver up the city to Prince Rupert;—he had received the thanks of Parliament for apprehending several of the conspirators, and held the council of war in which Yeamans and Boucher were condemned by order of Parliament and a commission from the General, but forbore to execute them until he received a vote of the Commons and his Excellency's commands, when it was done at noon-day, and in the middle of the town.—3. He denied the sufficiency of the garrison.—4. Defended the goodness of the conditions of surrender, but imputed the breaking of them to the unfaithfulness of the enemy, and the disobedience of some of his soldiers. The enemy being lodged in the suburbs, by Froom-Gate, the Castle could not prevent them from immediately entering the town.—5. He was advised to the parley by far the greater part, if not by the unanimous consent of the council of war;—denied the private agreement, in opposition to the council, to leave their arms and colours, but bid the soldiers, gentlemen of the country, and citizens, severally to make conditions for themselves;—the enemy agreed that the troopers should have their horses and swords, but, while they were debating the other point in the council of war, six or seven of his officers came out of the town [to the council-room in the Great Garden], and told him that they could not get six men a piece of their companies together, they ran over to the enemy so fast;—that he gave orders to his Captain-Lieut. Stokes, to stay with his company in the Castle, till Prince Rupert sent to demand it, and ordered the rest of his officers to draw their men into the Marsh, whither he repaired to them about nine o'clock, and stayed within the town an hour or two afterward; but the enemy, contrary to the articles agreed on, entered the town an hour or two before nine, and fell upon their men, disarming, dismounting, and pillaging of them; by means whereof many citizens and soldiers were plundered.—6. That the enemy were at least 200 when they first entered, and soon afterward dug down the rampart of earth, so that their horse and foot might enter, and then possessed themselves of walls, houses, Essex [afterward the Royal] Fort, and other places of advantage;—that, within less than an hour afterward, 300 foot more, and a regiment of horse, with ordnance, entered, and, after that, horse and foot, as fast as they could;—that he himself made all the haste he could to the breach; but, before he could get thither, his men were

643come off the lines for half a mile together, and his own troop, which he was following, beaten off—that he did not cause a parley to be sounded till his men were beaten back by fresh forces ; and he could not get 200 men together, of 10 or 1200 that were on that side the town ; whereupon, by advice of a council of war, he sent to demand a parley.—7. He denied the charge relating to the prisoners. Sir William Waller left the town of his own will, as intended, should the enemy advance towards Bristol; which would otherwise have been sooner lost.—8. Among other points of reply, he asserted that some citizens, who were upon guard at the Castle, made such haste to get their goods out on the Thursday morning, that they left their posts, and the gates of the Castle were so thronged that there was no getting in nor out—that in the mean time some of the prisoners there got loose and disorderly, and some of the enemy got in before their time ; whereupon he (Col. F.) went thither, and with his sword drawn cleared the passage, drew up the bridge, and got some of his soldiers to their posts again, and had drawn all of them into the Castle, if he had not received news that the enemy had broke into the town contrary to the articles, and were disarming and pillaging his men ; whereupon he ordered his Lieutenant, Stokes, to keep the Castle and deliver it up to Prince Rupert, and was forced to go himself into the Marsh with Captain Terringham, one of the enemy's hostages, for the security of the soldiers both horse and foot, and of his friends in the town.—9. Denied any dishonourable action, and doubted not that he could make it appear that he had a harder task to defend Bristol for four days than Colonel Massey had to defend Gloucester for four weeks.—10. That the testimony of an enemy could not be admitted against him.

In the course of the trial, Mr. Pryn stated that

Fiennes took upon himself the office of Governor long before he had a commission—that he drew up his ordinances to pass the House, to enlarge his power and territories twenty miles round Bristol, and create him absolute Governor there—that he accepted of the commission, and yet never acquainted either the City or the Committee of Parliament with it, doing all things in an imperious manner, without their privity.

It was proved in evidence (by Joan Battin, her husband John, and others) that

Major Langrish had guard of the breach where the enemy entered, who quitted it without charging ; which being seen by Lieutenant Rousewell, he called the Major 'coward,' and with three or four musketteers bravely defended it for a time, till he received the wounds of which he afterwards died, and was forced to retire for want of support,—that the enemy, being generally repulsed with loss, retired in disorder to their quarters, and one whole regiment of horse retired as far as Whitchurch, four miles from Bristol, resolving never to come on again, if the news of demanding a parley and the hopes

1643 of surrender had not brought them back;—that from three in the morning, when the enemy entered, till ten or eleven, they were charged only by Lieut. Rousewell and Capt. Nevill, who charged them down hill with only twenty horse,* and could have beaten them out, if he had been seconded by thirty or forty horse and foot; —that Fiennes commanded the soldiers, on pain of death, to draw off from the lines, leaving the works naked of all defence for two miles together, into the Market-place [Wine-street], where they stood idle, without any orders to sally; and many of them left their colours and went to the ale-house or to bed, so that their companies were not half full;—that the sally was not made till eleven o'clock, and then with but 200 men, drawn from the line, instead of the fresh men from the body of reserve and in the Castle;—that the enemy were so beaten in the sally, that they cried ' quarter,' and the women with their children offered to march up to the cannons' mouths and deaden the bullets, and encouraged the soldiers to fight, working up in the very face of the enemy, and blocking up Froom-Gate, where they were likely to enter, with woolsacks and earth; and the soldiers, generally, offered to fight it out to the last; yet was the defendant's cowardice such, that even then he sent out twice to demand a parley; † which made some of the soldiers say they were betrayed, break their arms, and swear they would never serve the Parliament any more. And he made such haste to quit the town, that he left Capt. Blake and Capt. Husbands in Brandon-

---

* This charge must have been made from Church-lane into Park-row.

† Joan Battin and Mrs. Dorothy Hassard [Hazard] were among the witnesses to this part of the evidence; and Mary Smith was a witness as to the strength of the Castle.— Mrs. Hazard was the wife of Matthew Hazard, who, previous to the surrender, was Rector of St. Ewen's Church, and thence became Vicar of Redcliff till 1660. She was one of five persons only, who, in 1640, commenced the society of Dissenters now meeting in Broadmead under the pastorship of Dr. Ryland. They were among the Parliamentary adherents who quitted the city with Fiennes, but returned upon its surrender by Prince Rupert in 1645. The society's early meetings were holden occasionally in the great room of the Dolphin Tavern (on the site of which now stand the Bush-stables) and a house on St. James's Back, one on the Tholzey, and another in Christmas-street, where the Sacrament of the Lord's Supper was first administered to them by a young man named Nathaniel Ingelo. This gentleman, who was of a genteel figure, gave offence to the rigid notions of his communicants, by his careful attention to dress; and especially by his love for music, his company being much in request among harmonious parties out of the strict line of his flock. To a remonstrance upon this species of indulgence, Mr. Ingelo replied, " Take away music, take my life!" He was selected by Bulstrode Whitelock, Cromwell's Ambassador to Christina of Sweden, in 1653, (who probably became acquainted with him during his recordership of Bristol, and who had himself been a professor of music),* to be one of his two Chaplains and Rector Chori. He was a fellow of Eton College, and became D.D. He was the patron of Benjamin Rogers, for whom, in 1658, he obtained the degree of Bachelor of Music at Cambridge, and whose compositions had been repeatedly performed in the presence of the Queen of Sweden by whom they were very much applauded. In 1660 he published a folio novel, learnedly allegorical, called " Bentivoglio and Urania." A MS. in the possession of Mr. Isaac James (from which some of the foregoing particulars are extracted) adds that, after the Restoration, Dr. Ingelo was Master of the King's Band.

* See Dr. Burney's History of Music, for Whitelock's account of Shirley's masque, " The Triumph of Peace," performed about Allhollandtide, 1633.

D.

543Hill and Prior's Hill* Forts, giving them no notice of the articles, nor any warrant to surrender them to the enemy;—that there were above 140 bombs in the Castle, with a mortar-piece; and when one of the gunners importuned him to let him make a shot at the enemy out of the mortar-piece, the defendant forbade him, on pain of death; though many bombs were shot into the town. It appears that the place where the defendant stood with his troop was more than common proof, being under Alderman Jones's house; when, a bomb accidentally falling among them, without doing any hurt, he removed to a place of still greater security. The hostages had so mean an opinion of his courage, that they swore they would come in by Froom-Gate, the shortest way, and not by New-Gate; but Froom-Gate was so barricadoed that it was impossible. His contradictory commands and pale looks were attested, among others, by Mary Smith. Colonel Charles Gerrard, the King's commissioner, having witnessed the outrages contrary to the articles, by letter to Fiennes " protested against these being imputed to the King, charging them upon his own neglect; and if this did not satisfy him, he was ready to meet him, sword in hand."

Mr. Pryn told Fiennes, in the course of his argument upon the defence, that

Even the women in the streets called him coward, and even his own mother (Lady Say) would not believe that he had so suddenly delivered up a place of so much consequence, where it had been proved he " promised to lay his bones, making the flag of truce his winding-sheet, rather than quit it." The enemy's commanders, upon viewing the works of the Castle, had said, " G— damn them, all the devils in hell could not have taken the Castle, had not the Governor cowardly surrendered it; and that they might thank Fiennes for it."—He had 2500 men in the place, while the besiegers were at first not above 7 or 8000 men, and those mostly horsemen; of whom more than 1400 were killed or wounded during the siege. Mr. Saville had deposed that he was in Bristol two days after the surrender, and there being a general muster of Prince Rupert's foot in the Marsh, they did not amount to above 1400 soldiers; and demanding of the men how they came to have so few men and so many colours (of which there were about forty or fifty) he was answered, that many of their men were killed or wounded in the siege. The Bristol garrison might have held out as that of Gloucester had done, especially being furnished with good store of *Bristol milk* (sherry), strong wines, and water. There was no sickness, no want of provisions or necessaries, and no loss but of eight men. How, then, the city could be surrendered on pretence of an impossibility to keep it longer, it was not easy to conceive, especially when the very women were so brave as

---

* Prior's Hill (belonging to the Priory of St. James) now Kingsdown. This fort, stood in the angle formed by the east end of James's Place and Somerset-street, near the summit of Nine-Tree-Hill, so named from nine trees which formerly grew there.

to offer to march with their children to the mouths of the enemy's cannon, and damp the bullets? There were 1400 weight of match, besides a dray-load in the Castle, when it was surrendered, and a match-maker with materials in the town to make more, besides a great deal in the city; and 90 barrels of powder in the Castle, besides what was in the city. Had the defendant really saved 1500 unarmed men, as he alleged, this was but a poor equivalent for the loss of a place of that consequence, strength, shipping, trade, and command by sea and land, with the hazard of the whole kingdom. The loss of Bristol would probably cost the Parliament 30,000 lives; and it was an excellent piece of good husbandry, to endanger the loss of 30,000 to save 1500!

Fiennes, in the conclusion of his defence, prayed that,

" As he had served his country faithfully, and done many good services for it, so he might by this Honourable Council be justified in his faithfulness, and repaired against the prosecutor in his honour, more dear unto him than his life—that so," added he, " after all my public services, I may not be *cast behind the door like a dish-clout*,* unfit for any further employment."

The trial lasted three days, and on the 29th of December Fiennes was sentenced to be beheaded. He entered an appeal in claim of his privilege as a member of the House of Commons, but, on better advice, withdrew it; and was afterward pardoned by the General, on condition of leaving the kingdom.

Of the King's party in this siege were killed, Col. Herbert Lunsford and the Lord Viscount Grandison; and Mr. Bellasis was wounded by his own sword, which was struck to his head by a musket-shot, when they rushed in upon the works. One thousand of the garrison-soldiers remained in the Castle for the King's service. The quantity of powder left in the city was 1700 barrels, with match and bullets in proportion—60 brass pieces of good ordnance, and all the arms—eighteen good ships in the river, belonging to merchants, and four ships belonging to the Earl of Warwick, which arrived on the eve of surrender, with store of ammunition. The citizens gave £1400 by way of composition, to save themselves from being plundered; upon which His Majesty sent a proclamation that it should be death for any soldier to plunder. There was found in the Castle £100,000. —The day before the surrender, all the family-plate of John Harington, esq. of Kelson, was for security removed into the Castle; among which was a golden font, in which Sir

* Is this figure to be received in honour of the Colonel's rhetorical taste, or of the cleanly economy of housewives in the seventeenth century?—" Pah! it smells so."

A. D.

1643 John Harington was christened—a present from his god-mother, Queen Elizabeth.

Aug. 1, the King, accompanied by Prince Charles and the Duke of York, came from Oxford to Bristol, to compose some differences between Prince Rupert and the Marquess of Hert-ford. His Majesty arriving after the hour when Temple-Gate was closed, and the drawbridge raised for the night, the Royal party took up their residence in a small house on the bank of the moat, still standing in Pile-street (now the property of Messrs. Henry Ricketts & Co. and opposite to the windows of their show-room), which was thence called " the Palace."*

Aug. 2, the King and his sons entered the city, and were entertained at Mr. Colston's house in Small-street. His Majesty lodged at Mr. Alderman Creswicke's, in the same street, and Prince Charles and the Duke of York at Mr. Alderman Holworthy's, directly opposite. On the Sunday they attended divine service at the Cathedral.

Sir Ralph Hopton was made a Baron and Governor of Bristol.

Aug. 8, by an ordinance of this date, made by the Lords and Commons, all monuments of idolatry and superstition, as altars, crucifixes, images, representations of the Trinity, &c. were to be destroyed; but images, pictures, coats of arms in glass or stone, set up for any monument of a king or a nobleman, or person not reputed a saint, to be continued.

Aug. 10, the King summoned and invested Gloucester; the siege of which was raised by the Earl of Essex, on the 5th of September.

Humphrey Hooke, esq. merchant, Mayor; William Colston and Henry Creswicke, merchants, Sheriffs of Bristol.

Dec. 4, Edmond Turner, esq. commissioned by the King, as Treasurer of the garrisons of Bristol, Bath, the town and castle of Berkeley, Nunney Castle, Farley Castle, and Portishead Point. †

1644 Jan. A ship from Bristol, bound for Chester, with arms

* The premises of the Phœnix Glass-Company stand without the city-wall, partly on the moat, and partly on its bank. In sinking the well of their steam-engine, at thirty-three feet below the surface, was found an oak-pollard and a piece of a boat with a nail in it.—The embattled wall, between the two gates, Temple and Redcliff, may be seen extending nearly the whole length of Port-wall-lane.—In excavating for the new cut of the Avon, were found cannon-balls of different weights, which had imbedded themselves in a direction proving that they were discharged from the garrison.

† See " Remarks on the Military History of Bristol, containing the Royal Commission appointing Sir Edmond Turnor, knt. Treasurer, &c. By Edmond Turnor, esq. M.P. F.R.S. F.S.A." 4to. 1803. The Treasurer was not knighted until 1663.

1644 and ammunition for the relief of the King's forces there, was carried by the crew into Liverpool.

Feb. 19, the King granted a pardon to the Mayor, Burgesses, and Commonalty of Bristol. Nathaniel Fiennes, Richard Cole, Walter White, Thomas and Richard Hippisley, Robert Baugh, and Herbert, late provost-marshal at Bristol, were excepted, being actors, or advisers and assistants, in the murder of Messrs. Yeamans and Boucher.

March 26, an Act was passed by the Parliament, and committees were appointed in the several counties, to enquire after the clergy and school-masters not well affected to the Parliamentary government.

May. An ordinance of the same tendency with that of Aug. 8, 1643, was passed by the Lords and Commons, against ecclesiastical ornaments. In the Convocation, all the organs in the kingdom were saved from demolition by a single vote.

October. Prince Rupert removed Sir Francis Hawley from being Governor of Bristol.

1645 Sir John Cadman, knt. was beheaded in the Castle, for killing Miles Callowhill, an officer of the garrison.

April 12, Thomas Howell, who had been nominated by the King in the preceding July, was consecrated Bishop of Bristol (the thirteenth) by Archbishop Usher.

June 14, the King was defeated at Naseby, in Northamptonshire, losing all his foot, artillery, arms, &c. with his cabinet of papers; whence, on the 15th, he retired to Lichfield, thence proceeding to Ragland Castle, the seat of the old Marquess of Worcester, who entertained His Majesty for three weeks there, while he assembled his troops. It must have been in the course of this visit, notwithstanding no light is thrown upon it by the "Iter Carolum," in the second volume of "Collectanea Curiosa," that the circumstance recorded in the following quotation took place, and we think July 24.

" What is now called the New Ferry or Passage over the Severn may dispute antiquity with the Old Passage. The former belonged, time immemorial, to the respectable family of St. Pierre, and was suppressed by Oliver Cromwell, from the following occurrence:— The unfortunate Charles, being pursued by a strong party of the enemy, rode through Shire Newton, and crossed the Severn to Chiswell Pit, on the Gloucestershire side. The boat had scarcely returned, before a corps of about sixty republicans followed him to the Black Rock, and instantly compelled the boatmen, with drawn swords, to ferry them across. The boatmen, who were loyalists, left them on a reef, called the English Stones, which is separated

645from the Gloucestershire side by a lake, fordable at low water; but the tide, which had just turned, flowed in with great rapidity, and they were all drowned in attempting to cross. Cromwell, informed of this unfortunate event, abolished the Ferry, and it was not renewed until the year 1748. The renewal occasioned a lawsuit between the family of St. Pierre and the Duke of Beaufort's guardians. In the course of the suit, depositions taken by a Commission of Chancery, held at Bristol, proved Mr. Lewis's right to the Ferry, and confirmed this interesting anecdote."—FOSBROKE's *Collections, &c.* i. 57.

Whitelocke, in his " Memorials, &c." says, under the date July 31, " The Scots advanced through the Forest of Dean, and had intelligence that the King passed over the Severne, towards Bristol,—that about 80 of his horse, endeavouring to pass over Severne, were taken by one of the Parliament's friggots."

July 16, some Parliament-ships arrived in Kingroad, to blockade Bristol, sent by Vice-Admiral Moulton, then at Milford-Haven.

In July, Bath was given up to the Parliament-forces by Sir Thomas Bridges.

After the reduction of Sherborne by the Parliament-forces, Aug. 17, the council of war resolved to march for Bristol, in preference to pursuing General Lord Goring into the north of Devonshire. In the mean time, Nunney Castle surrendered to Col. Rainsborough. Two thousand horse were sent before, under Commissioner-General Ireton, to preserve the neighbourhood of the city from plunder and firing, and thus secure quarters. Bedminster Church now became a stable.

Here it is necessary to describe the outworks of the city, as established by the King's party.

Commencing from the water of the Avon, west of the Limekiln Glass-house, at late Tombs's Dock, the line of fortification proceeded across Cow-lane, now Limekiln-lane, to a fort erected at the foot of Brandon-Hill, called *Water-Fort*, in which were mounted seven guns, commanded by a master-gunner, whose pay was 17s. 6d. a week, a mate at 14s., and three gunners at 10s. per week. The line continued thence to the summit of the hill, on which stood *Brandon-Hill Fort*, containing six guns, a master, a mate, and two men. Descending the hill, and crossing the southeast angle of Berkeley-Square, above the junction of Park-street and Park-Row, which latter was then the only road (where Washington's breach was effected in 1643), the line ascended to what was now converted from Windmill-Fort to a pentagonal construction called the *Royal Fort*, mounting twenty-two guns, with a master, a mate, six gunners, and a commissary of victuals. Thence the line crossed St. Michael's Hill, northward of Southwell-street, touching the line of the county-bounds at Alfred-Hill, to *Colston's Mount*, the site of which has been already described, on which was a fort or redoubt mounting seven guns, with a master, a mate, and two gunners. The line of fortification continued onward at the back of Montague-Parade and Kingsdown-Parade, and crossed diagonally the ground now dividing the parallel ranges of building called James's Place and James's Parade, to *Prior's Hill Fort*, the form of which is still partly traceable: here there were thirteen guns, a master, a mate, and three gunners. The line then descended on the north-east side of Hillgrove-street, touching the county-bounds at the bottom—crossed Stoke's Croft, the ground now occupied by Wilder-street, the Lewin's Mead Chapel burial-ground, Surrey-street, Pembroke-street, Norfolk-street, and Newfoundland-street, the Meadow, the feather of the river Froom which rejoins the main stream at the Castle-Mill, the Froom itself, and so onward, within the line presented by New-street, to *Lawford's Gate*, which was defended by seven guns, a master, a mate, and six men. The line of outworks continued thence, on the west side of the upper angle of Jacob.-street, direct to Unity-street, where it turned in a south-west direction, and crossed Bread-street, Cheese-lane, and the river Avon, to *Tower Harratz*,—thence, with two intermediate towers, to *Temple-Gate*, which had fourteen guns, a master, a mate, and five men. As indicated by the still remaining "Port-walls," the line was completed by *Redcliffe-Gate*, where there were fifteen guns, a master, a mate, and four gunners,—and the water of the Avon. At the Castle-Gate there were sixteen guns, with a master, a mate, eleven gunners, and a commissary, who was rated at 30s. per week. Froom-Gate and Pithay-Gate had two guns each, with two gunners.

Aug. 21 (Thursday), General Fairfax and Lieut.-General Cromwell reconnoitred the city, appointed guards on the south side of the Avon, and quartered themselves at Keynsham, whither several noblemen sent for passes to go beyond sea,* but were refused.

---

* It was the same species of aristocratic imbecility that left France a prey to the horrors of her Revolution, from which she was rescued by Buonaparte. The English nobility, the legitimate guardians and protectors of the people, must by the time of

.D.

645 Friday, Aug. 22. A general rendezvous of horse; Col. Welden's brigade first shewing themselves to the city, on Pile-Hill, within musket-shot of the walls. Guards were completed on the Somersetshire side, notwithstanding the besieged had succeeded in firing Bedminster, upon hearing that 2000 men were to be quartered in it; and the besiegers plied their small shot all night. The head-quarters of Fairfax were removed to Hanham.

Saturday, Aug. 23. Fairfax and Cromwell were employed the whole day in settling the quarters and guards on the Gloucestershire side. The cannon played from the Royal Fort and Prior's Hill Fort, but hurt only one dragoon, who had his thigh shot off. The Prince caused a traverse, or blind of earth, to be made within the draw-bridge at Temple-Gate; while the besiegers began some breast-works and a battery at Knowle-Hill, with a traverse across the road. A sally was made by the Royal cavalry, who were driven back; when Sir Richard Crane, their commander, was mortally wounded. A battery was raised by the besieged in the Marsh, to secure the river, and scour the fields beyond it. Fairfax's head-quarters were removed to Stapleton, at Stoke-House, the present seat of the Duchess-Dowager of Beaufort.

Sunday, Aug. 24. A sally from the port near Prior's Hill Fort, repulsed by Col. Rainsborough's brigade and horse.

Monday, Aug. 25. Instructions for the delivery of the City to the Parliament, signed "Thomas Fairfax" and "Oliver Cromwell," addressed to the citizens, were intercepted, and measures taken accordingly, by imprisonment of suspected persons and the personal presence of the Prince, to prevent a surprisal of the Royal Fort.

Tuesday, Aug. 26. A third sally, on a post held by Col. Welden, at Bedminster, in which ten of the besiegers were killed and ten wounded. Sir Bernard Ashley and Colonel Daniell riding out of the works to see the Parliament's leaguer, Colonel Daniell was slain, having received seven bullets in his body, and Sir Bernard Ashley was made prisoner, who also died, a few days afterward, of his wounds. The Prince, it seems, this day fully expected that the city would be stormed, and accordingly double-manned the line.

ur text have sadly degenerated, both in the council and in the field. Luxurious refine-
ient, and effeminate indifference to the feelings and habits of the mass of a community,
in do much towards alienating hearts that ought never to be severed. With indolence
f mind is ever connected ignorant self-will and unpatriotic tyranny, in superiors—
ie great sources from which have ever sprung the destructive assumptions of mob-law.

A. D.
1645 Thursday, Aug. 28. Sir Thomas Fairfax having raised
2000 men in Somersetshire, they joined a party of his army
and took the fort on Portishead Point, after four days' siege,
with six pieces of ordnance, a demi-culverin, and 200 arms.
Thirty-six, of the garrison had terms to return to their
houses; the rest had run away before. One of the conditions was an oath never to bear arms against the Parliament.
Thus was opened a communication with the ships in Kingroad. Five Parliament-ships arrived, and forced Captain
Broom, who commanded the Tenth Whelpe, to run up the
Severn for security.

Friday, Aug. 29. A fast was observed by the besiegers,
"to seek God for a blessing upon the designs against Bristol;"
but they nevertheless amused themselves by making a bridge
across the Avon, to conjoin their quarters. Mr. Del and
Mr. Hugh Peters (whom, Sept. 9, we find before the House,
to give an account of the siege) kept the day at the head-
quarters, but were disturbed by a sally about noon upon the
quarters at Lawford's Gate; in which three or four soldiers
were taken prisoners.

Sunday, Aug. 31, Capt. Moulton, from Kingroad, conferred
with General Fairfax, and offered to storm the city with his
seamen.

Monday, Sept. 1. About noon, Prince Rupert, with 1000
horse and 600 foot, made a sixth sally, upon the Parliamentary
horse-guards, with much fierceness, and, before retreating,
killed Capt. Guilliams and took Col. Okey prisoner. Orders
were now given by Fairfax to view the line and works—the
soldiers to make faggots and all fitting preparations to storm
the city.

Tuesday, Sept. 2. In a council of war, the storm was determined upon—the manner referred to a committee of Colonels, who were to report in writing to the General the next
morning. Col. Welden, with his brigade of four regiments,
were to storm in their places on the Somersetshire side, one
of which was Temple-Gate, with its drawbridge. The general brigade, under Col. Montague's command, consisting of
the General's, Col. Montague's, Col. Pickering's, and Sir
Hardress Waller's regiment, to storm on both sides Lawford's
Gate, both towards the river Avon and to the lesser river
Froom; the bridge over the Froom (where now is Wade's or
Traitor's bridge), to be made good against horse with pikes,
or to be broken down. Col. Rainsborough's brigade, consisting of his own, Major-Gen. Skippon's, Col. Hammond's,
Col. Birche's, and Lieut.-Col. Pride's regiment, to storm on

A. D.

1645 the north side of the Froom, beginning at the right hand of the sally-port, up to Prior's Hill Fort, and to storm that fort itself, as the main business. Two hundred of this brigade were to go up in boats, with the seamen, to storm Water-Fort, if it could be attempted. One regiment of horse and a regiment of foot to be moving up and down in the closes before the Royal Fort, and to play hard upon it, to alarm it, with a field-officer to command them. The regiment of dragoons, with two regiments of horse, to carry ladders with them, and to attempt the line of works by Clifton and Washington's Breach.

Thursday, Sept. 4. Sir John Seymour brought 1000 men to the leaguer. The weather, which had been extremely wet, began to change, and the great guns began to play from the new battery erected on Montpelier (a little N. W. of the farm-house still standing) against Prior's Hill Fort. A long summons was sent to Prince Rupert; to which he replied by requesting leave to send a messenger for the King's pleasure therein.

(An article dated " at the Leaguer before Bristol, 8 Sept." in the *Mercurius Britannicus*, one of the one hundred and eleven newspapers published during these civil wars to the Restoration, says " the trumpeter was at first something loath to go, because he had heard that Rupert should swear that if any trumpeter came into him with any message from Sir Thomas Fairfax, he would hang him; but seeing our resolution, that if he should offer any such thing, we should retaliate; Sir Bernard Ashley being with us, and others of note, he passed over these doubts and went with his message into Bristol; and so soon as the Prince received the paper, he looking into it, swore God damn him, it was a summons, and called for a cup of sack, and sat down and read it; and detained the trumpeter in Bristol until Friday.")

[*Mother Pugsley's Well-field*, in the S. E. portion of which stood Prior's Hill Fort, is associated with the most delightful portion of many a Bristolian's existence; but we believe that few are acquainted with the history of the lady from whom it derived the name. That and other surrounding land was, at the time of our text, the property of a young man, recently married, named Pugsley, who held a command under Prince Rupert during this siege. He received his death by a shot fired from the redoubt on Montpelier, and fell in or near a ditch where now stands a wall, the boundary of the gardens on the declivity of Nine-tree-Hill, a continuation of the same field in its descent towards Stoke's Croft. After the surrender of the city, he was buried with military honours, beneath the turf stained with his blood. A monumental tablet in the former

A. D.
1645 wall marked the spot.   His widow, a young and beautiful woman, resisted every importunity to change her forlorn condition;
wearing mourning-habiliments till the day of her death, which was
not until she had passed eighty years of age.   We find the manner
of her funeral thus recorded, in a MS. originally the property of a
contemporary family of the Society of Friends, named Farnham,
who resided in Castle-street :—

    " 1700, August 4th, an old woman of the name of ——— Pugsley
died, and desired to be buried in the following manner: to be
wound up in her wedding-sheet, having on her wedding-shift also,
and be carried on a bier to the field adjoining unto the ground commonly called the Nine Trees (by reason of such a number of elms
there planted), and two maids should go before the corpse with herbs,
and strew them as they went; and that the bells of Saint Nicholas
church should ring as her body was carried under the gate.   And
she further ordered that a fiddler should play before the corpse.   All
which was punctually performed, to the admiration and in the view
of at least ten thousand spectators.   She had no coffin."

    Elsewhere we learn that ' Gammer Pugsley' bequeathed money
for a sixpenny loaf and a ninepenny loaf at Easter, and a twopenny
loaf on Twelfth Day, to each of the sixteen women inhabiting St.
Nicholas' Alms-house.

    About twenty-eight years since, the then proprietor of the field,
Mr. Thomas Edwards Freeman, sold it to some building-speculators,
who dug clay, erected a brick-kiln (now used as a cow-house), and
sunk the foundation of several houses, part of the plan of an immense crescent; but three years of possession failing to produce
also completion of the contract, occupation was resumed, and the
turf restored to its original verdure.

    It is in contemplation to rail in the spring as formerly, enlarge
the basins, and render the water more available for the use of the
inhabitants of Kingsdown in dry seasons.   By crowning the fountain with a rustic dome, which should bear on its brow an inscription

          TO EVER-BLOOMING CONNUBIAL AFFECTION,

Dame Pugsley's troubled Spirit of the Spring might be appeased,
and the verdant scene of thousands of happy hours of childhood
would become still more interesting to the matured spectator.]

    Friday, Sept. 5.   Gen. Fairfax rejoined, with objection to
so much delay, and requested to know whether the Prince
had any more positive answer to give from himself.   By this
time everything was prepared for the storm—the General
in the field, and the soldiers ready with faggots at their
backs.

    Saturday, Sept. 6.   " Sir Thomas Fairfax dined in the
fields, on Somersetshire side towards Redcliff-Church; and
after dinner, having ordered Col. Ireton to keep two regiments of horse in waiting at the bottom of the hill near the
sally-port, to be ready in case the enemy should attempt a

1645 sally, he went about in person to view the enemy's works, sometimes by himself, and sometimes with Col. Birch and eight or ten other officers; but no soldier was to shew any obedience to him as General, lest the enemy, seeing it from their works, should take notice and make shot against him to endanger his person. And when he had viewed all, he came to his own cannon, to see how they were planted and levelled, particularly the great twisted piece, and what was not well he caused to be altered. He now went so near to the enemy's works, that in viewing the Great Fort he was within pistol-shot of their breast-work near the Little Fort, which is by the Royal Fort. The meanwhile, Lieut.-Gen. Cromwell viewed the horse, and gave orders to their quarters."—*Merc. Brit.*

Sunday, Sept. 7. The Prince, after a council of war, having transmitted seventeen propositions, that, during the treaty, he might strengthen the works within and hear from the King, in answer thereto, Sir Thomas Fairfax proposed three commissioners, viz. Colonels Ireton, Fleetwood, and Pickering, to conclude a treaty, provided such treaty could be ended by nine o'clock the same evening. But the Prince requested that any doubts and exceptions to his propositions might be made in writing, to which he would give a speedy answer, dated the same day.

Monday, Sept. 8. The storm had been fixed to take place this morning at two o'clock; but the request of the Prince delayed it, for the production of another letter from Fairfax, dated at Stapleton, containing twenty propositions. In these, however, the Prince finding sundry omissions, and some clauses wholly left out, he returned a letter the same day, stipulating that all the forts and lines, excepting the Castle, should be sleighted and demolished, and he would send commissioners to regulate and settle things between them.—Nunney Castle was this day burnt, to prevent the possibility of its future service to the King.

Tuesday, Sept. 9. Fairfax, by another letter, insisted on his own propositions, protesting against further delay. The trumpet having returned with an unsatisfactory answer, at twelve at night the General was in the field, to give orders about drawing out the men, and managing the storm the coming morning.

Wednesday, Sept. 10. At two o'clock this morning the signal was given, by setting fire to some straw and faggots at the top of Montpelier, and the firing of four great guns against Prior's Hill Fort, from the place at which the

1645 General was to reside all the time of the storm, being an old small farm-house, opposite the Prior's Hill Fort, conveniently lying upon any alarm. (There the remains of the redoubt are still to be seen.) The storm instantly became general around the whole city, and was terrible to the beholders.

Colonels Montague and Pickering, with their regiments, at Lawford's Gate, entered speedily, and recovered 22 guns and took many prisoners in the works; and having laid down bridges for that purpose, Col. Desborough advanced with the horse, having the command of the General's regiment and that of Col. Groves. Then the foot advanced to the city-walls, where they possessed the great Gate against the Castle-street, wherein were put 100 men, who made it good.

Sir Hardresse Waller's regiment, and the General's regiment commanded by Lieut.-Col. Jackson, entered between Lawford's Gate and the River Froom.

Col. Rainsborough's regiment assailed Prior's Hill Fort.

Major-Gen. Skippon and Col. Birch's regiments entered nearer to the Froom; and the regiment commanded by Lieut.-Col. Pride was divided; part, under Col. Hammond, being assigned to the service of Prior's Hill Fort, and the rest to alarm the Royal Fort; and afterwards they took a little garrison of Welshmen, in Water-Fort.

The seamen, who were designed to storm the Water-Fort, the tide failing, assisted in storming the line and works generally. The horse who entered on that side, besides the forlorn hope, led on by Capt. Ireton, were severally commanded by Major Bethel, Major Alford, and Adjutant-General Flemming, being formed of Col. Whaley's, Col. Riche's, and part of Col. Graves's regiment. After the line had been broken down by the pioneers, and a sufficient gap made, the horse entered, and within the line met a party of the Royal horse, whom they forced to retreat, mortally wounding Col. Taylor, formerly a member of the House of Commons, and taking several prisoners. Perceiving the besieger's foot to be master of the line, the Royal horse returned no more to the charge, but retired in a body under the cover of the Royal Fort and Colston's Fort.

Meanwhile, Prior's Hill Fort obstinately held out for nearly three hours, playing fiercely with round and case shot from four pieces of cannon for two hours after the line was entered. The besiegers' men returned the compliment in at the port-holes, until ladders were brought up to the wall; but the works being high, a ladder of thirty rounds

A. D.

1645 scarcely reaching the top, some that ascended were beaten down. They however returned to the assault, creeping in at the port-holes as well as scaling the top of the walls. Lieut.-Col. Bowen and others were two hours at push of pike, standing upon the palisadoes; but nevertheless they could not enter, until Col. Hammond, having forced the line towards the Froom, came up withinside the works, and stormed the fort on that side also; not, however, without receiving a shot with two pistol-bullets, which broke his arm. Capt. Lagoe, of Lieut.-Col. Pride's regiment, was the first to seize the colours; and, in the end, the men of the fort were forced to run below, into the inner rooms, where, from the stubbornness of their opposition and refusal of quarter when it was offered, they received little mercy. The commander, Major Price, a Welshman, with nearly all the officers, soldiers and others in the fort, were put to the sword, except a few, who were spared at the entreaty of the besieging-officers.

Thus the line from Prior's Hill Fort to the Avon was in possession of the assailants.

Had the storm been by day-light, Prior's Hill Fort could not have been attempted,—the approach being so completely under the command of the Castle on one side, and of Colston's and the Royal Fort on the other.

The Royal Fort, which had the reputation of strength, lay open to Brandon-Hill Fort; which, if taken, would have commanded the whole plain; but it does not appear that the success of the besiegers in that part of the line extended to Brandon-Hill Fort. The storm on the Somerset-side was not attended with success equal to that on the side of Gloucestershire. The assailants were often forced to retreat. The works were so high that the ladders could not nearly reach them, and the approach to the line was under great disadvantage.

Lest, during the storm, Prince Rupert should endeavour to escape with his horse, Commissary-General Ireton, Col. Butler, and Col. Fleetwood's regiments of horse (part of whom kept up the alarm in the vicinity of the Royal Fort), were appointed a moving-body on Durdham-Down, as the most likely channel of escape, in case the Prince foresaw the town would be lost.

To cover the foot, Col. Okey's dragoons kept up the alarm against Brandon-Hill Fort and the line towards Clifton.

About four hours after the taking of Prior's Hill Fort, a trumpet was sent by the Prince, to desire a parley; a proposal which Gen. Fairfax embraced, on account of the city

A. D.

1645 being on fire in several places,* and on condition of the fire being extinguished. This was done—the treaty proceeded, and by seven in the evening articles were agreed upon, to the effect that His Highness, and all noblemen, officers, gentlemen, and soldiers, with all other persons whatsoever, should march out of the City, Castle, and Forts, with colours, drums, pikes, bag and baggage—the Prince, gentlemen, and commissioned officers, with their horse and arms—servants with their horse and swords, and common soldiers with their swords. 250 horse besides to be at the Prince's disposal—his life-guard of firelocks with their arms, and each of them a pound of powder and proportion of bullets. The sick or wounded to be protected till their recovery, and then have safe conduct to His Majesty. The persons marching out to have convoy to a Royal garrison at not exceeding fifty miles from Bristol—to have eight days allowed for the march, free quarter by the way, two officers to attend them, and twenty waggons for baggage, if needed. The citizens to be exempted from plunder and violence, secured in their persons and estates, and enjoy all the common rights and privileges of other subjects under protection of the Parliament. The City, Castle, &c. to be delivered up by one in the afternoon of the morrow, Thursday, Sept. 11. Col. Okey and all other prisoners to be set at liberty, &c. &c. Signed, as Commissioners on behalf of the Prince, by John Mynne, W. Tillyer, and W. Vavasour—on the part of Sir Thomas Fairfax, by Ed. Montague, T. Rainsborough, and John Pickering.

While Fairfax and Cromwell were sitting on the top of Prior's Hill Fort, a bullet from the Castle grazed within two hands' breadth of them, but without hurting either. During the storm, several of the Parliament-officers, both horse and foot, were killed, and many wounded. Major Bethel was shot, as he entered the line, and died soon afterward.

Thursday, Sept. 11. Prince Rupert marched out of the Royal Fort, with eight noblemen, many ladies and gentlemen, 500 horse, and 1400 foot-soldiers.

Cromwell sent the Parliament a long account of this affair, calling it "the work of the Lord, which none but an Atheist could deny,"† and stating that 140 cannon were taken, 100

---

* "The town was fired in three places by the enemy [the besieged], which we could not put out; which began to be a great trouble to the General, and all his officers, that so famous a city should be wasted; but whilst they were viewing that sad spectacle, the Prince sent a trumpet to the General, desiring a treaty for the surrender."—*Mercurius Veridicus*, Sept. 17 to 20.

† The Parliamentarians' word, during the storm, was "David," and after the line was entered, "The Lord of Hosts."

A. D.

1645 barrels of powder, &c. with the loss of only about 200 men. Provisions were found in the Royal Fort, sufficient to serve 150 men for 320 days; and the Castle was victualled for about half that time.

Prince Rupert was severely censured by the King; which induced His Highness to draw up a vindication of his conduct. This appeared in the shape of a pamphlet, entitled " A Declaration and Narrative of the State of the Garrison and City of Bristol;" by which we learn further, among other particulars, that

" On the Prince's coming to Bristol, the constitution of the garrison was settled at 3600 men, including Nunney, Portishead Point, &c. but that the presidiary soldiers, who went for 8 or 900 men, were really not more than 5 or 600 effective. The auxiliary and trained bands, by reason of the interruption of trade, poverty, and the pestilence that raged in the City, were reduced to 800, and the mariners betook themselves to other parts, or to the enemy. The Commissioners, entrusted for the contribution and the support of the garrison, abandoned the City upon the enemy's approach; and many considerable persons had leave to quit the City, which disheartened the rest. His Highness had originally mustered 2800 men; but, after the approach of the enemy, he could never bring to the line 1500; and it was impossible to keep them from getting over the works; and many of those were newly levied Welsh and unexperienced men. Having given orders for all the inhabitants to victual themselves for six months, upon a strict survey, of 2500 families then remaining in the City, 1500, through indigence, could not provide for themselves. The line of defence was about four miles in compass, generally three feet thick, and the extreme height five feet. The graff was commonly six feet broad—seven at the widest; the depth in most parts four feet—five feet where deepest. The ditch of the Royal Fort, on the right hand of the gate, before the face of the bulwark, was not four feet deep, and eighteen broad, so that horses did go up and down into it. The highest work of the Fort was not 12 feet high—the curtain but 10 feet. Within 100 feet of the Fort was a deep hollow way, where the enemy might lodge what troops he pleased, and might be in the graff before night; and that part of the Fort was minable.—Brandon-Hill Fort was about 12 feet above the level of the Great Fort. The hedges and ditches without the line were neither cut nor levelled."

The Prince produced the Narrative from which we have made these extracts, in a council of war held at Newark, on the 18th of October following; and the King, at a second hearing, on the 21st, was pleased to say that " his nephew was not guilty of the least want of courage or fidelity to himself in the surrender; but withal believed he might have kept the Castle and Royal Fort a longer time, for the chance of relief."*

* To Prince Rupert the Fine Arts are said to be indebted for the discovery of mez-

Preparatory to the 15th of September, the Mayor (Alexander James) and the Council sent to Sir Thomas Fairfax, to know whom they should choose to be the new Mayor; and he sent them word that they were to follow their ancient custom in this respect. Accordingly they chose Francis Creswicke, merchant; who continued in office only till the 21st of October, when he and twelve more of the council (including Aldermen Hooke and Long), upon the advice of Richard Aldworth, M.P.† were set aside, as of the King's party, and John Gunning was chosen Mayor.

Sept. 15, Farley Castle surrendered to the Parliament's army.

Oct. 1, Col. Fleetwood was made Governor of Bristol.

Nov. 21, Major-Gen. Philip Skippon was appointed the Parliament's Governor of the Castle.

Three thousand persons died of the plague this year; of which number, from April 11, 1645, to Feb. 18, 1646, 403 died in St. James's parish: 180 died in the parish of St. Michael.

Serjeant "Whytlocke," Recorder of Bristol.

The Bishop's Palace was now turned by the army into a malt-house, and a mill erected. The Palace was previously uncovered of its lead, exposing the Bishop's wife, in child-bed, to the wind and rain; she died soon afterward. The Bishop himself was dragged violently out of the Palace, and died within a fortnight, in 1646. He was buried at the entrance of the choir from the south aisle, under a plain stone, with only "Expergiscar."—The see remained vacant until 1660, fourteen years.

We may assign to this period the partial destruction and plastering up of the two altars at the east end of the north and south aisles of the Cathedral, as well as the plastering of the portraits of Prophets and Apostles on the west side of the organ-screen. About this time also Redcliff-Church underwent much over-righteous dilapidation. Many of the ornaments and all the lofty pinnacles around the Church were torn down. Within, brass plates were stolen from the monuments. The organ was broken down, and a bonfire made of the Bibles, prayer-books, and books of homilies, with cushions, cassocks, &c. The streets were paraded with streamers made of surplices, and the organ-pipes used as trumpets.

zotinto engraving, in the accidental effect of scraping a copper-plate with the head of an old nail.

† He was a barrister, and probably son of the Richard Aldworth, mercer, who was sheriff in 1627 and mayor in 1642.

A. D.

1645   Dec. 2.   The sum of £800 per month was assessed on the County of Gloucester, for maintenance of the Castle of Bristol; but a neglect ensuing in the committee appointed to enforce the collection, assessments were made in the following form:

	£	s.	d.
The hundred of Pucklechurch..............	17	6	5 per week.
Langley and Swinshood ..	42	4	0
Grumbald's Ash	49	1	9
Barton Regis	11	1	1
Thornbury	32	1	2
Henbury	42	6	5
Total....£194	194	0	10

1646   Feb. 17, a fire, about one in the morning, in the house of Mr. Edwards, apothecary, on the Bridge, destroyed all the houses on both sides (twenty-four or five), from that called the Chapel towards St. Nicholas' Gate. They were rebuilt with the lead and timber taken from Ragland Castle and Parks, upon the surrender to Fairfax, Aug. 19, in this same year.

Feb. 20, the standing-committee for Bristol sequestered the Rev. Richard Towgood,* vicar of St. Nicholas, and soon afterward the Rev. Richard Standfast, rector of Christ-Church, and committed them to the Castle. One Evans, a tailor, was made preacher of Christ-Church. The Rev. Mr. Pierce, vicar of St. Philip's, was also sequestered; and Edward Hancock, a butler to Sir George Horner, knt., put into his living; who, when removed at the Restoration, kept a public-house at Horfield. The Rev. Mr. Brent, vicar of Temple, was also deprived; and many other orthodox clergymen and others, fifty in number, were confined close prisoners in the Castle.†

Richard Vickris, Mayor; ‡ Walter Sandys and Edward Tyson, Sheriffs.

By the 12th of November, Fairfax had reduced all the King's garrisons.

* We believe the "Twogood" mentioned in "A briefe Relation" under 1643.
† Thanks to Joseph Lancaster and Dr. Bell, the most popular of the dissenting sects now begin to think "human" Learning an essential qualification for their preachers, and do not rob the Creator of his glory by denying that a capacity for it is derived from any source inferior to that of Heaven itself. We hear no more of scholastic knowledge being carnal. The scions of Oxford and Cambridge, we therefore hope, will look about them—not simply contenting themselves with the possession of a good chest of tools, but resolving to use them like workmen. All congregations are becoming more and more critical. To the Dissenters and some of the Churchmen we would hint, that unpremeditated extemporaneous discourses are not likely long to remain in fashion. What they themselves would be ashamed to review on paper cannot be the fruit of inspiration.
‡ He lived at the corner of High-street and the Shambles, within St. Nicholas' Gate.

D d

1646 Dec. 11, the House of Commons voted Skippon to be Governor of Newcastle and Tinmouth, to keep the command of Bristol by deputy, and to command in chief the convoy of £200,000 to the Scots, as the price of their surrender of the King into the hands of the Parliament.

1647 Jan. 30, the King was delivered up accordingly, and brought to Holmby, where he wrote *Eikon Basilike,* or *The Portraiture of the King.*

The use of the Common Prayer-Book prohibited by Act of Parliament, under fine and imprisonment for the first offence. Stage-plays also were prohibited.

June 3, the King was taken from Holmby by Cornet Joyce and 500 horse, conveyed to Childersley, and thence to Newmarket; afterwards to Hampton-Court.

July 19, the House voted that Bristol Castle and the Great Fort of Carnarvon should be continued—the keys of the garrisons to be delivered to the Mayors and Corporations, to be governed as formerly.

Sept. 2, a petition was presented to the House of Commons, in the name of the inhabitants of Bristol,

1. For settlement of peace, and to prevent another war.—2. To answer the grievances of the army, and to vindicate them.—3. To preserve the just rights and liberties of the people from tyranny.—4. To free the people from unlawful powers and endeavours to suppress their petitions.—5. To remove out of the House, and from places of justice, unfit and uncapable persons.—6. That faithful persons may be trusted.—7. For tenderness in imposing the Covenant.—8. That tender consciences might not be grieved.—9. For an act of oblivion.—10. For speedy trial of prisoners.—11. Against long imprisonments.—12. To compassionate widows and maimed soldiers.—13. That accounts might be given.—14. To find out a way that suits of law might be less chargeable and dilatory, and the laws in a less volume and in English.

The petitioners were called in, and told that the House could not approve of some things in the petition, but gave them thanks for their good affection.

Nov. 11, the King escaped to Tichfield, and thence to the Isle of Wight.

Nov. 23, letters were received by the House from Bristol, of a mutiny in the garrison, and that the soldiers had secured an Alderman there, till they should have a month's pay. The House sent a letter to the General, to discharge the Alderman, and to prevent the like abuses by the soldiers for the future.

Wheat was sold in Bristol this year for 12s. a bushel, rye at 10s., barley at 8s., peas at 8s., and oatmeal at 12s.; fresh butter 7d. a pound, and all other provisions exceedingly dear.

A. D.

1648　Sir Harry Vane, jun. knt. Lord High Steward of Bristol.

May 2, a vote of the House for £6000 for Bristol.

May 10, an ordinance for money, for fortifying Bristol in some new places.

June 21, an ordinance for settling the militia, and £1000 for the fortification and victualling of Bristol.

June 30, an ordinance for £10,000 for Bristol.

Dec. 12, petitions from Bristol, complaining of neglect in guarding the coast. Ten merchant-vessels taken by the Irish, last week.

Dec. 23, the King was brought to Windsor.

1649　Jan. 9, a new great seal ordered, with the inscription, "In the first year of Freedom, by God's blessing restored, 1648."

Jan. 15, the King brought from Windsor to St. James's.

Jan. 27, the King sentenced to death.

Jan. 30, the King beheaded, in the 48th year of his age.

THE PARLIAMENT—CHARLES II.

Sir William Cann, Mayor of Bristol, proclaimed that there was no King in England, &c.

March 6, the estates of the Bishopric of Bristol were sold for £8390 7s. 9½d.; the Gate-House included, at £18 13s. 4d.

March 17, an Act was passed for abolishing kingly government, and an Act for abolishing the House of Peers.

April 30, an Act was passed for the sale of Dean's and Chapter's lands. The Bishop's Palace and Park (now College-street, &c.) were sold to Thomas and John Clark, for £240.

May 29, an Act passed, declaring and constituting the People of England a Commonwealth and free state.

June. The bells of St. John's Church were newly cast, and a new frame made for them. — Christ-Church dials newly set up.

July 4, a letter was received by the House, of 1660 barrels of beer, with other provisions proportionable, being ready at Bristol, for the soldiers destined for Ireland.

July 17, Saturday, Lieut.-General Oliver Cromwell came to Bristol, on his passage to Ireland.*

---

* None of the many copies of the Mayors' Kalendar that we have seen contain any particulars of the ceremonials of this progress. The late Mr. Francis Harris, stationer, one morning found, in the garden of his residence in St. James's Square, the carcass of

A. D.

1649   July 21, Col. Leg ordered to be committed in Bristol, for high treason.

Oct. 4, Col. Scroop made Governor of Bristol Castle.

1650   Jan. 5, three soldiers were sentenced to death in Bristol, for killing a citizen.

The walls about the Royal Fort made by order of Parliament, who gave £1000 towards the building.

May 31, Cromwell, returning in triumph from Ireland, took up his lodgings in the Palace at Whitehall.

June 26, an Act passed, constituting Oliver Cromwell, esq. Captain-General.

Sept. 8, Cromwell defeated the Scots at Dunbar.

Miles Jackson, merchant, Mayor of Bristol; William Dale and William Yeamans, merchants, Sheriffs.

Dec. 24, Edinburgh Castle surrendered to Cromwell.

The sect of the Quakers commenced this year.

Jews now first appeared in England since the banishment of that people in 1287.*—The first coffee-house in England opened by a Jew at Oxford.

an exhausted sky-rocket. The writing-character attracting his attention, he unfolded the tube, and found it to be a particular narrative of Cromwell's public entry into this city. A short time previous to Mr. Harris's departure for America (where he died, October 2, 1823) he told the writer that he lent the fragment to a gentleman who said he had lost it. We still hope it will come to a better light than that from which it had so narrow an escape. In the mean time it may suffice to make the following extracts from other sources:

" This evening (July 10), about five of the clock, the Lord Lieutenant of Ireland began his journey by the way of Windsor, and so to Bristol. He went forth in that state and equipage as the like hath hardly been seen, himself in a coach with six gallant Flanders mares, whitish grey, divers coaches accompanying him and very many officers of the army: his life-guard consisting of 80 gallant men, the meanest whereof a commander or esquire, in stately habit, with trumpets sounding, almost to the shaking of Charing-Cross, had it been now standing. Of his life-guard many are colonels; and, believe it, it's such a guard as is hardly to be paralleled in the world."—" The Lord Lieutenant's colours are white."—*Mod. Intel.* July 5 to 12.

" By letters from Bristol we are certified that the Lord Lieutenant came thither on Saturday night last, where he was royally entertained by the soldiers and officers in arms, and others who held offices by order of Parliament. The citizens likewise expressed much joy at his coming, and entertained him with great respect."—*Perfect Diurnal,* July 16 to 23.

" The Lord Lieutenant of Ireland is yet at Bristol; money is sent him, and under God, his lordship will some 7 days hence meet it at the water-side; and about a week after launch for Ireland."—*Perf. Occ.* July 20 to 27.

* So long had ceased the anti-christian policy of tolerating the Jews as leeches, to relieve individual subjects from the abuse of wealth, that they might, sponge-like, be occasionally squeezed, to discharge debts or accomplish works of Royal caprice or extravagance! We suspect that compunctious visitings were never without relief by some such salvos as the paper (of which we think it likely that the forthcoming portion of the " Memoirs" will furnish a transcript and translation) No. vii. in No. 957 of the Harleian MSS. in the British Museum, thus entitled: " *Narratio de filio civis Bristolliæ per quendam Judæum crucifixo temp. Henrici iij.*" The crucifixion is said, by the gentleman to whom we are indebted for this reference, to have taken place in the parish of St. Mary Redcliff.

A. D.

1651 Jan. 1, King Charles II. crowned by the Scots at Scone.

July 7, a letter was received by the Parliament, stating that the house of Alderman Jackson, near Bristol, had been burnt, with his children in it.

Sept. 3, the battle of Worcester was fought; in which the King's forces were defeated.

Oct. 15, after wandering about in disguise for six weeks, the King embarked at Brighton in a small merchant-vessel, with Lord Wilmot, and arrived at Paris on the 30th. Cromwell had forbidden relieving or concealing the King, on pain of death, and offered £1000 reward for his discovery.

His Majesty first stopped at White Ladies, about thirty-five miles from Worcester, committing himself to the care of the Pendrels, five brothers, who were Catholics; then successively in a hut and an oak-tree in a wood near Boscobel, at Madely, again at Boscobel, and Moseley, where he met with Lord Wilmot.

"Here (says Father J. D'Orleans, of the Society of Jesus, who wrote at Paris in 1695, from a MSS. of the King's personal relation) the danger daily increasing, His Majesty resolved to draw as near the sea as he could, to be in readiness to embark upon the first opportunity. Having communicated his design to Whitgrave [his host at Moseley, to whose care he had been consigned by the Pendrels] and one Mr. Lane [Colonel Lane], a neighbour of his, a safe man, the latter readily undertook to convey the King towards Bristol, and in order to it, took him away to his own house at Bentley. Lane had a discreet sister [Mrs. Jane Lane], who being let into the secret, by the King's consent, found the means to go to Bristol, which His Majesty approved of, and succeeded well. She had a kinswoman ready to lie in, at a place called Norton [meaning at Mr. Norton's residence,* Abbott's Leigh], near that city. Under colour of visiting that kinswoman, Mrs. Lane got up a horseback behind the King, who was in another disguise, and passed for her servant. A woman a horseback, behind another man [Col. Lassells and his wife], followed for decency, and Wilmot went with them, carrying a hawk on his fist."—"The King and his company thus looked like a country-family making a neighbourly visit."—"During this journey, which lasted three days, the King met with several adventures, some of which diverted, and others made him uneasy."

The route hence was Bromsgrove, Stratford-upon-Avon, and Cirencester.—Having, the preceding night, slept at Marshfield, at the house of a kinswoman of Mrs. Lane, the King arrived at Bristol, and, entering at New-Gate, he could not resist the inclination to turn aside and view the

* On its site was lately erected Nash-House, the mansion of Philip John Miles, esq.

.1651 Castle, which had been the scene of so many important transactions.

"At Norton" [Mr. Norton's], continues the writer of the History of the Revolutions of the Stuarts, &c. "he was still looked upon as a servant; but, that he might have a good bed, and be better used than the others, Mrs. Lane, who passed for his mistress, pretended he was troubled with an ague, and therefore had him lodged in a little room, where there was a good bed; and she sent him something to eat. That fiction gave the King an opportunity to discover that there was a loyal spirit in that quarter. A physician coming to see him, and perceiving he was not very sick, drank the King's health, and forced him to pledge it. The next day, when he was at breakfast, a man, who said he came from Worcester fight, and had seen the King there, put His Majesty into some uneasiness, for fear he should know him; but it soon appeared that what he said was false, when, being asked about the King's shape and mien, whom he affirmed he had seen twenty times, he answered, very short: 'He is four inches taller than you.'—Whilst the King was recovering himself of the fright that extravagant fellow had put him into, another discreeter person knew him through his disguise. This was one Pope, butler to the gentleman where he was, who, having formerly served under him, when he was Prince of Wales, remembered his features too well to be mistaken. He stayed till they were alone, to discover to him that he knew the secret. Then, casting himself at his feet, he said, ' You are the very same, Sir! It was not long before I ' knew you, and it would be in vain for you to conceal yourself from ' me: you may safely own it. But consider that others may dis- ' cover it too, and make haste out of the way where so many are ' searching after you and seeking your destruction. If I can be ' serviceable to you, I shall think myself happy. Make trial of my ' zeal, and rely upon my loyalty.' His Majesty was surprized and at a stand with this fresh accident. He saw the danger of trusting a man he did not know, and of seeming to distrust one who might make out what he said. In this confusion, the sincerity that appeared in the man made him resolve to deal plainly. The event shewed he had judged right. Pope did His Majesty very considerable service, and was one of those that contributed not the least towards his escape. It was he that advised him to [Col.] Windham's house [at Trent, in Dorsetshire], where that monarch spent nineteen days in much safety, waiting for an opportunity to embark."

The King and Lord Wilmot embarked at Shoreham, as two Isle-of-Wight coal-merchants, on the 15th of October; soon landed at Feschampe, near Havre de Grace, and arrived at Paris on the 30th of October. See 1660.

Sept. 12, Cromwell entered London in triumph from Scotland.

Cromwell, Lord High Steward of Bristol, with a salary

A. D.

1651 of five pounds per annum, and a pipe of canary and half a ton of Gascoyne wine as a bonus.

By order of the Mayor and Corporation, no carts or waggons used in Bristol, but only drays.

Brass farthings or tokens, having on one side " Bristol Token,"; and on the other the arms of the city, issued by the Corporation, for the benefit of the citizens.

In consequence of the great increase of " hot water " houses in the city, being the resort of idle and drunken persons, as common tippling-houses, the Magistrates, in order effectually to put down this nuisance and scandal to the city, directed that every keeper of such house, and every person found tippling therein, should be fined 6s. 8d.

Estimated rent of the Ferry from Queen-street to Temple-Back, forty shillings.

1652 Sir William Penn, Vice-Admiral of England.

1653 April 20, Cromwell dissolved the Parliament.

July 5, Cromwell's Convention met, and chose Rouse for their Speaker; whom, on the 12th, the sergeant-at-arms attended with the mace.

Aug. 16, an Act passed for solemnizing marriages by Justices of the Peace.

Aug. 26, the Shire-stones of the City of Bristol were searched and rectified. A map of the city and liberties was drawn by Philip Stainrcad, mathematician, and deposited in the Council-House.

THE PROTECTORATE—CHARLES II.

Dec. 16, Cromwell was declared Lord Protector of the Commonwealth of England, Scotland, and Ireland, and of all the dominions and territorities thereunto belonging.

1654 " This year the city was much troubled by a sort of people called Quakers, who interrupted the ministers in their pulpits. Therefore the *Apprentices* rose to turn them out of the city." (See 1666.)—The Protector addressed a letter to the Mayor, with a caution against French spies in the garb of Quakers. [We could here, to the extent of many pages, present a lesson of no ordinary interest, to such as conceive the public peace best served by either civil or religious intolerance; but the milder and more liberal spirit of our own times, as exemplified in the forbearance shewn towards Joanna Southcott and her followers, has rendered it unnecessary for us to do more than refer the reader, whose

1654 general respect for the office of the magistrate is not likely to be shaken by particular instances of its abuse, to " *The Sufferings of the Quakers, from* 1650 *to the Act of Parliament* 1689. *By Joseph Besse. Lond.* 1753." 2 vols. folio. Reprinted, 1738, in 3 vols. 8vo. By this work it may be seen that the Quakers arose superior to persecution, alike inflicted under the sanction of all the governments embraced by the above dates.]

No ship of above one hundred tons was allowed to come up to the Quay or Back, under the penalty of ten pounds.

" OLIVER P.　　　 [Copy.]

" These are to authorize you forthwith to demolish the Castle, within the City of Bristol; and for so doing this shall be your warrant.　　　 " Given at Whitehall,

" To the Mayor and Commonalty　　28 day of Dec. 1654.
　 of the City of Bristol."

The constables were sent to warn every householder to assist in the demolition personally, or appoint a substitute. The destruction of the Castle was completed in a fortnight.

One Charles Evans was taken about twenty miles from this city, and brought hither, under suspicion of being the King of Scots. He was kept a prisoner at the Feathers,* in Wine-street.

1655　May. Admiral Penn and General Venables took the island of Jamaica from the Spaniards.

——　A bridge was made from Castle-street to the Old Market.

August. An order came for the demolition of the Royal Fort, and to disband the garrison.

Walter Deyos, Mayor.

This year were six marshals chosen, to be constables, and to attend the Mayor in their long gowns, with the City-arms on their staves.

Every citizen not attending the nightly watch in his turn, or neglecting to find a substitute, was fined, in summer sixpence, in winter eight pence, for every neglect.

The lead was taken off the Cathedral, and deposited in the care of the Chamberlain; but a stop being put to any farther spoil, an order was made, Jan. 8, 1656, that the lead so removed should be sold, and the proceeds laid out in the necessary repairs of the Cathedral.

* In 1629 and in 1656, deeds mention this house as bearing " the Prince's arms." The republican modification of " the Feathers" was soon hereafter changed for " the City of Bristol Arms;" the dining-room having the Ship and Castle carved over the fire-place.

A. D.

1655   The Red Maids' Hospital completed.

A frigate called the Islipp, of 30 guns, was launched here.

Sept. Penn and Venables returned home, and were both laid aside for their ill conduct, and sent to the Tower.

1656   A frigate launched, called the Nantwitch, of 44 guns, built by —— Bailey.

Oct. 31, a Committee of Parliament appointed to examine into the blasphemy of James Naylor, the Quaker, who personated our Saviour at Bristol and other places. Nov. 10, the Protector sent for James Naylor, Dorcas Erbury, and other Quaker-preachers, to London. Dec. 8, the Committee resolved that Naylor was guilty. Dec. 17, the Speaker pronounced judgment,—whipping, the pillory, and boring his tongue with a hot iron. He stood once in Palace-yard, and once at the Old Exchange—was whipped from Westminster to the Old Exchange by the common hangman, where his tongue was bored, and the letter B marked on his forehead —sent to Bristol, and conveyed through the city on a horse, with his face backward—here publicly whipped on a market-day, and then committed close prisoner to Bridewell, London, during the pleasure of Parliament. [Naylor's extravagancies doubtless increased the public prejudice against the Quakers generally. He was discharged Sept. 8, 1659; when he came to Bristol, and made a public recantation in a meeting of his friends, in so affecting a manner, that they were convinced of the sincerity of his repentance, and became reconciled to him. He died on a journey from Rippon to Wakefield, near King's Rippon, Huntingdonshire, aged 44 years.—Vide Sewell's History of the Quakers.]

The bridge over the Froom, between Broadmead and Haulier's Lane, called Needless Bridge, was built.

The way that formerly came in at Lawford's Gate, and to the Weir, along by the Castle-wall, and so in at Newgate, was for the most part left off, by reason of a way made directly from Lawford's Gate, through the Castle, into St. Peter's Street. A new gate was made over the Castle-ditch. Houses likewise began to be built, to continue the street through the Castle, to St. Peter's.

St. Nicholas Alms-house, in King-street, near Back-street, erected, for sixteen elderly females.

1657   July 11, Cromwell proclaimed Lord Protector, in Bristol.

Oct. 5, the Mayor ordained, by virtue of several Acts of Parliament, that £909 should be yearly levied, by assessment on each parish, for support of the Ministers of Religion, viz. St. Michael and St. Augustin, £50—St. James, £50—

A. D.

1657 St. Thomas, £12—Temple, £48—Redcliff, £40—St. Philip and the Castle, £20—St. Stephen, £90—St. Nicholas, £120—St. Werburgh and St. Leonard, £85—All Saints and St. Ewen, £70—Christ-Church and St. John, £120—St. Maryport and St. Peter, £96.

Dec. 8, the Mayor (Arthur Farmer) received a letter from the Protector, dated the 2d, saying, " I do hear on all hands that the cavalier-party are designing to put us into blood;" giving authority to raise the militia, and promising a troop of horse to quarter in or near the city.

1658   Feb. 14, the Corporation contributed £100 towards support of the Ministers.

June. Richard Cromwell, the Protector's son, came to Bristol, and was very honourably entertained by the Mayor and his brethren.

" *Bristol*, July 3.—On Thursday last, the most illustrious Lord, the *Lord Richard*, (having received two or three invitations in the name of this City,) set forward from Bath hither, attended by a numerous train of Gentry, and was met three miles from the town by the Sheriffs [John Willoughby and Henry Appleton, mercers], accompanied with at least 200 horse, whence, after their salutation and compliment in the name of the City, they conducted his Lordship with his Lady, and the Hon. Col. William Cromwell, Mr. Dunche, &c. into Bristol, waited on by near 400 horse; at whose entry the artillery was fired from the Marsh and the ships that lay in the road; and his lordship, riding forward, was encountered by the Lord Mayor and Aldermen, and was by them waited on to a house, provided for his lordship at Colonel Aldworth's in Broad-street, and there received with hearty demonstrations of their affections to their highnesses (whom they said they had formerly the honour to see there), and particularly to his lordship. The next day his lordship rode out, to be witness of the beauty of the place, and was at his return entertained with a noble dinner, at which it is observable that (although there were exceeding plenty of wine, &c.) yet there was so much respect had to their prudent orders and civil decorum, that that great entertainment was void of that rudeness, excess, and noise, into which the liberty of feasts, in these our days, do often betray their guests. The same evening his lordship, passing through another part of the city, round the Town-Marsh, was complimented with the discharge of the great guns upon the place, and in his way forth treated particularly by the Mayor, with a banquet, &c. and returned safe to Bath. Throughout this whole entertainment there appeared as clear a face of duty and affection as ever was seen at any time upon the like occasion; yet it is no more than what is paid to that noble lord in every place, by such as have had the honour to observe his great humanity, joined with so great hopes, and the noblest inclinations of a virtuous mind."—*Merc. Pol.* July 1 to 8.

A. D.

1658 "Aug. 12, the Bristol-men born held a feast at the great house at the Bridge-end, over against the Bear-Tavern. Mr. Arthur Farmer, the mayor, being born in Bristol, was treasurer. They paid for their dinner 5s. a-piece."

Sept. 3, Friday, the Protector died of a fever, at White-hall, in the 60th year of his age.

Sept. 4, Richard Cromwell proclaimed Lord Protector. His age was about 28 years.

Sir Henry Vane, High Steward; John Stephens, Recorder.

The house now the Orphan Asylum, part of "Hooke's Mills," bears this date, in the carved work of one of its fire-places.*

1659 Castle-Gate completed. (See 1766.) Queen's Gate also erected about this time.

May 8, upon the Army's invitation, the remnant of the Long Parliament resumed their sitting, and the new Protector's influence thereupon ceased.

1660 Feb. 2, the Apprentices of Bristol assembled, and cried up for a Free Parliament, keeping the city a week.

Feb. 4, General Monk marched into London from Scotland, and took up his quarters at Whitehall.

Feb. 8, a troop of horse came into the city, to suppress the insurrection of the Apprentices, who went into the Marsh

---

* Besides the mention of this family in preceding pages as filling honourable situations, Humphry Hooke, merchant, was a sheriff in 1614, and mayor in 1629. Thomas Hooke, merchant, was sheriff in 1634. Humphrey Hooke, merchant, was mayor in 1643. (See a Sir Humphrey Hooke, M.P. in our text of 1661.) Abraham Hooke, merchant, was sheriff in 1706. "Andrew Hooke, Esq. Native thereof," was the Author of *Bristollia*, &c. noticed under 1748; and Andrew Hooke, Esq. who was of the commission of the peace for Gloucestershire, (probably the same with the Author of Bristollia, and not the Andrew Hooke, M.D. alluded to by Gough, in his Anecdotes of British Topography, as "having the management of the printing-office in Bristol,") erected the present Ashley-Court, on the summit of Ascliga, part of the endowment by Earl Robert of his Priory of St. James. A house of previous erection still forms its west wing. It is now, with some of the adjoining land, the property of Mr. Samuel Lunell. The house in the valley, seated on the stream supplied by the spring called the Boiling-Well, and known as Lower Ashley-House, is of much more ancient date. It was the country-residence of Sir Michael Foster, recorder of Bristol from 1735 to 1762, and is now [1824], being in a state of great decay, about to be taken down, in conformity with other projected improvements of that part of the estate, by its owner, Mr. John Evans Lunell. The eastern approach to this mansion, across the stream, was by a gothic gateway and bridge of stone.* Here, in the writer's schoolboy-days, the force of example co-operating with the then vulgar error that "it was no sin to steal for the belly," the surrounding elms, if they could speak, might remember him as one of an apple-munching crew, engaged in "*boxing the fox*" about Ashley-Orchard; and when the distinctions of *meum et tuum* began to find more lively consciousness, old IZAAK WALTON himself might have rejoiced to behold a "contemplative" disciple, seeking to make captive the lively thornbacks of the brook, by the mighty means of a hazel-twig, a needleful of thread, and a crooked pin, baited with a caddis, drawn from its crusted tube, that had been found inanimately pacing the side of the stone bank at the head of the adjoining miniature-cascade.

* "The Mansion-Place, or Foster's Place," occurs in deeds descriptive of premises between Temple-street and St. Thomas-street, dated 1566 and 1602. In 1789 the same were occupied by Ann Bloom.

A D.

1660 and laid down their arms; but not before articles were drawn between them and the Mayor (Edmund Tyson) for the sake of quietness, yet he sent three or four of them to prison. [These lively young gentlemen had been invested with political importance by a declaration of the Parliament, in 1642, "That all Apprentices, who will list themselves in "their service for the publike cause, shall be secured from "indemnity of their masters during their service, and their "time included, to go on towards their freedome: and all "their respective masters are to receive them again when "they shall return." By which means an infinite number of apprentices were induced to enlist themselves in the army.]

On the eve of Shrove-Tuesday, the city-bellman, by order of the Mayor, proclaimed that *dogs* were not to be tossed nor *cocks* squailed; for which the bellman had his bell cut from his back. On Shrove-Tuesday the apprentices signified their obedience to the Mayor's order by tossing *bitches* and *cats*, and squailing *geese* and *hens*. A goose was squailed before the Mayor's door in St. Nicholas-street; which brought Timothy Parker, one of the Sheriffs, with the design of dispersing the revellers; but he failed, with a broken head for his labour.

Christ-Church bells new cast, eight in number, and chimes set up, by Richard Grigson, vintner, church-warden, who was appointed one of the Sheriffs this year.

March 15, the Parliament dissolved. Admiral Penn was a candidate to represent Bristol in a new parliament; but the Corporation favoured the Recorder, John Stephens, who was elected with John Knight, sen. merchant.

April 25, both Houses of Parliament met at Westminster-Abbey, and after sermon went to their respective chambers; where the Earl of Manchester was chosen Speaker of the Lords, and Sir Harbottle Grimstone of the Commons.

May 1, the King's letters and declaration read to the two Houses, and the Commons voted £50,000 for His Majesty's present occasions.

THE RESTORATION.

May 8, the King solemnly proclaimed. The proclamation was made in Bristol by Francis Gleed, sheriff, assisted by the Mayor and Aldermen.

May 25, the King landed at Dover.

A. D.

1660   June 1, the King made a speech to both Houses.

Henry Creswicke, merchant, Mayor of Bristol ; Richard Grigson, vintner, and Thomas Langton, merchant, Sheriffs.

Dec. 1, Gilbert Ironside, a native of Hawksbury, near Sodbury, elected fourteenth Bishop of Bristol.

Dec. 17 and 19, the Parliament ordered that Francis Windham, esq. and Mrs. Lane be presented each with £1000, for their service in preserving the King after the battle of Worcester.

Dec. 29, the Convention-Parliament dissolved. One of their acts was the establishment of a Post-Office. See 1662.

The Royal Society first instituted this year.

The St. Patrick, of 52 guns, launched in this port.

1661   Sir Humphrey Hooke and Sir John Knight chosen representatives for Bristol, in the new Parliament that met the 8th of May.

May 15, Hugh Smyth, Esq. of Long Ashton, created a baronet.

Nathaniel Cale, soap-maker, Mayor; Thomas Stevens, grocer, and John Hicks, mercer, Sheriffs.—This mayor new-modelled the Common Council, turning out all whom he supposed to be disaffected to the King and attached to the Rump-Parliament or the Covenant.

One hundred pounds issued from the Chamber, in consideration of the Society of Merchants enlarging the New Key from the Lower Slip to Aldworth's Dock or Key, and making a road for coaches and horses by Rownham and the Hotwells.

1662   April 23, the Infanta Catherine of Portugal married to the King, by proxy of the Earl of Sandwich, at Lisbon.

April 30, the Princess Mary, eldest daughter of the Duke of York, born; who was afterwards married to William of Nassau, Prince of Orange, and our William III.

May 19, the Act of Uniformity passed.

May 21, the Queen landed at Portsmouth. Her age was 24 years.

Aug. 24, St. Bartholomew's day, the Act of Uniformity taking effect, " about 2000 ministers of the Geneva stamp lost their preferments."

Sept. 13, Sir Robert Cann, knt. of Compton Greenfield, created a baronet.

Sir Robert Cann, knt. and bart., Mayor; John Wright and Robert Yeamans, Sheriffs.

Many inconveniencies having happened to the river and haven by the coming up of ships out of Kingroad, the Corporation ordered that no vessel of above sixty tons should come from Kingroad to this city, under the penalty of ten pounds.

1663   Sept. 5 (Saturday), the King and Queen, with James, duke of York, Prince Rupert, and several noblemen, came from Bath, and were received at Lawford's Gate by the Mayor and Aldermen in their formalities, when the Mayor, kneeling, presented his sword of state to the King; which His Majesty returned to him. The streets were sanded all the way through the Old Market, the Castle, Wine-street, and High-street, to the house of Sir Richard Rogers, at the Bridge-end, where the royal and noble visitors dined. One hundred and fifty pieces of cannon were discharged in the Marsh, one volley on the King's arrival at the Bridge-end, one when he had dined, and the third at his departure for Bath. Previous to which, at four in the afternoon, the King knighted the Mayor, Robert Cann, his son William, John Knight, and Robert Atkins, jun. [the historian of Gloucestershire].* The royal party left the city at Lawford's Gate. The following week, Robert Yeamans, the sheriff, attending His Majesty at Bath, likewise received the honour of knighthood.

Sir John Knight, the new Mayor; John Bradway, vintner, and Richard Streamer, merchant, Sheriffs.

In December, the Old Speedwell broke from her moorings at the Limekilns, and was overturned by a gust of wind, drowning two men.

The postage of a letter from London to Bristol was now three pence, as appears by one from Edmund Saunders, a solicitor, with this superscription: " To Mr. John Hellier, at his house in Corn-street, in Bristol Citty. These, &c."

Bedminster Church appears to have been this year restored in some measure to its former state. The stone inserted in the north-west abutment bears the following characters: " T.I. I S. C W—1663." A clumsy and we must add impious attempt has been made to convert the " 66" into 00.

1664   April 22, at Westminster, the Charter (Seyer's No. 23) was granted, confirming the several Charters of 1626, 1629, and 1630.

Sir William Penn appointed Great Captain Commander, under the Duke of York, preparatory to the successful engagement with the Dutch fleet, commanded by Opdam, on the 3d of June, off Harwich.

Aug. 17, James, duke of Ormond, Lord Lieutenant of Ireland, came to Bristol, remained at Sir Henry Creswicke's

* See 1681. Sir John Atkins's residence was Wick-Court, still in good preservation. See 1761, for its celebrity as a hospital of sufferers by witchcraft.

A. D.

1664 house in Small-street, four days, and then departed for Ireland by way of Milford-Haven.

John Willoughby, merchant, Mayor; William Crabb, carpet-weaver, and Richard Crump, soap-maker, Sheriffs.

Saturday, Nov. 1, the new Speedwell was cast away in launching, at the Gibb-Taylor, and four men and boys drowned.

1665   Jan. 12, John Yeamans, esq. of Bristol, created a baronet.

"This year the city of London was most greivously visited with the pestilence; the contagion whereof spread as farr as Bristoll. It began at Bedminster; where it raged much, and soe likewise at Barton Regis. Yea it came within Lawford's Gate. Some houses in Haulier's lane and Redcliff-street were infected, and some other places; as at the Mermaide on the Back; and when it was believed it would overspread the whole city, as it had done London, it pleased God, of his wonderful mercy, to restraine it, soe that it went noe furthur."—*Mr. Ald.* HAYTHORNE's *MS.**

1666   The St. Patrick frigate, of 52 guns, launched at Gibb-Taylor; the Mayor and Corporation being present. This mayor was Sir Thomas Langton, knighted upon going to London shortly after he had been sworn.

The Custom-House on the Back built and finished. The cost was between 3 and £400.

Five or six hundred men impressed in Bristol, for the King's service against the Dutch, French, and Danes. One hundred men were enlisted as foot-soldiers under Lord Herbert, earl of Worcester.

Sept. 3, the great fire in London, consuming in four days 89 churches, including St. Paul's Cathedral, the city-gates, the Guildhall, and many other public structures, hospitals, schools, libraries, a vast number of stately edifices, 13,200 dwelling-houses, 400 streets, which covered 436 acres.

1667   The Duchess of Monmouth came privately to Bristol, and dined at the house of Edward Hurne, vintner (and sheriff in 1669), on St. Michael's Hill; where she was visited by the Mayor (Edward Morgan, upholder) and some of the Council. They went thence to the house of Richard Streamer (sheriff in 1663), where she was visited by Mrs. Mayoress; and where a banquet was prepared for her grace and her retinue. She was conducted, on her departure, as far as the Castle.

* This rich MS., so often quoted, and frequently without acknowledgment, we have learnt, since the preceding sheets were printed, was originally the property of Mr. Abel Deane, surgeon, and transmitted through the family of Mr. Alderman Curtis, of Mardyke-House.

" One Joan Beale had a child by her own father; which child she murthered; for which murther she was condemned and hanged at Mile-Hill."

1667   The father of Colley Cibber now flourished as a sculptor. Consequently the monument of Mrs. Baynton, of Bromham, Wilts, in St. Mark's Chapel, is *not* to be received as a specimen of the art at this period; neither should we so esteem that of Charles II. which at the time we write decorates the front of the Guildhall. A similar figure in front of the Council-House being shewn to Nell Gwyn (see 1674), as a compliment to her royal lover, she replied that " it looked more like a great clumsy porter, placed there to keep the entrance." The lady evinced her own better taste for the fine arts in the present of a new window to the Cathedral. See 1680.

1668   William Penn, now 24 years old, first appeared as a preacher among the Quakers.

July 29, the Edgar frigate, of 72 guns, launched, built by Mr. Bailey, of Bristol. Burthen, 1046 tons; to carry 432 men.

Thomas Stephens, grocer, Mayor.

Jonathan Blackwell, vintner, at his own cost, commenced making new the steps on St. Michael's Hill, called Queen-street—finished 1669.

William Gagg, a baker, in Castle-street, repeatedly dreamed of the virtues of the Hotwell-water in his particular case, and was thereby cured of a diabetes.

1669   Sir Robert Yeamans, Mayor; Charles Powell, apothecary, and Edward Hurne, vintner, Sheriffs.

Capt. Sturmey descended Pen-Park Hole, the immense remains of an ancient lead-mine, as described by him in the Philosophical Transactions. The Cotham-stone, a marl, indurated by iron, is the product of this place. Polished, it is a beautiful English marble.

Sept. 16, Sir William Penn died, aged 49 years, at Wanstead, Essex. His body was brought to Bristol; where it lay in state at the Guildhall till the 3d of October, when it was buried in St. Mary Redcliff-Church. He left £30 to the poor of that parish.

The Quakers' Meeting-house built on the site of part of the Monastery of the Black Friers. The Friends had previously held their meetings on the same spot, and at Brislington.

1670   Sir John Knight, M.P. having informed the King that the Mayor (John Knight, sugar-refiner) and most of the Council

A. D.

1670 were fanatics, Sir Robert Yeamans was sent for by His Majesty, and committed to the Tower. The Mayor was then sent for and examined; when the contrary soon appeared, and the informer was obliged to beg pardon of the King on
1671 his knees. Sir Robert Yeamans returned on the 21st of February, and was honourably conducted into the city by 220 horsemen. The Mayor returned on the 20th of April, and was conducted in like manner by 235 horsemen. Sir John Knight came to Lawford's Gate, and privately crossed the water to his own house in Temple-street.* See 1679.

Aug. 30, the City purchased of the Crown, for £3024 15s.1d. the ground-rents paid for certain lands which belonged to religious houses dissolved at the Reformation, including the forty pounds reserved in the purchase of the Castle in 1630.

John Millerd published, this year, his "Exact Delineation of the Famous Cittie of Bristoll and suburbs thereof, composed by a scale and ichnographically described," in a plate of 9 inches by 10; also, in 1673, his four-sheet map. By the latter it appears that between Queen-street and the King David Inn, St. Michael's Hill, stood a mansion in a court, called the White Lodge, to which the turret of Messrs. Jones & Willcox's counting-house, lately modernized, was an appendage. The Old Park was called the Little Park. At the foot of Queen-street, and opposite to the entrance of St. Bartholomew's Hospital, was a slip, with only one house standing between it and Froom-Gate, called Prior-slip. The Pest-House was at the end of Newfoundland-lane, on the spot where latterly stood a farm-house, once occupied by Mr. Driver, a former keeper of the Gaol. The bridge at the end of Queen-street, Castle-Precincts, was called Castle-Bridge; and Limekiln-lane, Castle-mead, now Bread-street, leading to two limekilns. Cheese-lane, bounding St. Philip's Churchyard, passed a glass-house on the left, and was there named Old Harbour. Some brick-kilns stood in a field enclosed on the right, and the Marsh was called King's Marsh, lying parallel with Temple Meads, on the opposite bank of the Avon. "Tower Harriots" was a larger building than the

---

* The King seems to have felt no difficulty in turning a deaf ear to complaints of this nature. This whole reign, and the next, present little else than a series of endeavours, on the part of the Throne, to tolerate Dissenters, and on the side of the Parliament and the Establishment, to suppress conventicles, from dread of giving encouragement to the Sovereign's Papistical predilections. Had subscription to the Bible instead of the 39 Articles been now the only test of Protestantism, superadded to learning and moral habits, it is highly probable that Dissenters from the Church of England would never have been heard of, and the Papal Church would, long ere this, have witnessed a wider diffusion of the right of private judgment: Romanists and Protestants, Jews and Gentiles, must have become more like what they really are, the children of one common Father.

A. D.

1671 other three towers standing between that and Temple-Gate. Pipe-lane was called Back-Avon Walk. Three-Queen-lane was called Ivie-lane; that opposite to it was Mitchell-lane. A glass-house, now a pottery, stood in the quadrangle formed by Three-Queen-lane, St. Thomas-street, Port-walls, and Redcliff-street. Redcliff-Hospital stood at the distance of six houses beyond the Saracen's Head Inn. Guinea-street was called Trine-Mill-lane, and passed a wind-mill on the right, making a circuit to Trine-Mills, on the left of the passing-slip, where now is the lock of Bathurst Basin. There was a glass-house on Redcliff-Back, *within* the City-wall. On the Quay, between the Dial and the Drawbridge, were two slips: that nearest the Dial was called Lower-slip; the other leading obliquely downward to the stream, was called Tower-slip, indicating the site of the "Great Tower." The court which has now a turner's shop at the entrance was called Rose-lane, and Old Nick's entry was Swan-lane; both led in a parallel direction from Marsh-street, to the river below the Draw-bridge.

1673   The Countess of Castlemain came to Bristol, attended by Sir John Churchill, of Churchill [the Recorder of Bristol named in the Charter of 1684], and Sir Thomas Bridges, of Keynsham, with their ladies. They were entertained at the Three Tuns Tavern, in Wine-street, at Sir John Churchill's expense. The Mayor was Richard Streamer.

St. Thomas' Conduit, which stood in the middle of the street, removed to the end of Church-lane. The sheep-market kept in a court adjoining, over which was built the wool-market.

The Cathedral, Christ-Church and its spire, and St. Stephen's Church with the tower and pinnacles, repaired and embellished.

1674   June. A water-mill, to grind corn, built upon a lighter at Gibb-Taylor, by Thomas Jayne, house-carpenter; which, every ebb-tide, ground two bushels an hour, and turned to profit; but it was pulled to pieces on St. James-tide following.

" This year King Charles the 2d his effigie was removed on the leads nearer the Councill-house, by the perswasion of the Dutches of Cleveland, being then in Bristol; it being before (as she said) as a porter or a watchman."

The John Hellier noticed under 1663 drew a presentment to the Grand Jury, complaining of " sismatical preachers, sectaries, and a conventicle in the Castle, the doors of which were shut against the Bishop and the Mayor's train;" and Sir John Knight, M. P. is called upon " to communicate to

A. D.

1674 Sir Humphrey Hooke, knt. and the others of our Representatives, and the Colonel of the City Militia and the Trained
Bands, for the city, to aid in repressing the evils presented."

The Oxford, of 54 guns and 683 tons, for 274 men,
launched.

1675 Robert Aldworth, Town-Clerk, dying, John Romsey was
chosen his successor, " who made it his utmost endeavour
to set the King against the City." See 1685.

Dec. On St. John's day the weather-cock of St. John's
steeple was blown down. Another was put up on the 3d of
May 1676.

This year was born in Bristol, John Lewis, author of the
Life of Caxton, &c. See Dr. Rees's Cyclopædia.

1676 William Crabb, carpet-weaver, Mayor.

1677 July 11, Queen Catherine came from Bath to Bristol,
guarded by the Earl of Ossory and his troops, and was received by the Mayor and Corporation at Lawford's Gate,
with the usual ceremonies. Her Majesty was entertained at
Sir Henry Creswicke's, in Small-street, at the City's expense;
and after dinner she rode in her coach to the Hotwells, and
drank of the water, returning to her court in Small-street;
whence she went back to Bath the same evening.

1679 April 6, Alderman Stevens, by will, endowed with lands in
the parish of Abstone and Wyke, Gloucestershire, the alms-
house in Temple-street, for twelve widows or daughters of
freemen of Bristol, and an hospital in Old Market-street, for
sixteen freemen's widows or daughters.

At a vestry of St. James's Church, four persons were held
guilty, being convicted of a most heinous crime, and cited
into the Spiritual Court, for purloining the Lord's day, in
travelling to Bath on foot; for which they confessed their
sins, and paid twenty shillings for the use of the parish.

The Northumberland, of 1096 tons, for 70 guns and 446
men, launched.

" The Mayor (Joseph Creswicke) being ex officio one of
the deputy-lieutenants, and by commision one of the captains
of the trained bands of the city of Bristol, had his commission
taken away and his deputation revoaked, for his following
the advice of his father-in-law, Sir John Knight, the old
ratt." See 1681.

1680 Aug. 20, died, in Bristol, Bedloe, the coadjutor of Titus
Oates. He was buried on the 22d, below the steps at the
entrance of St. Mark's Chapel, at the expense of the City
Chamber; his goods being all seized for debts.

1681 The votes of the House of Commons first printed.

A. D.

1681 April 12, at the quarter-session, Sir John Knight was
presented by the Grand Jury, for affronting and assaulting
Mr. Mayor in the execution of his duty; also for stigma-
tizing and branding His Majesty's subjects with the odious
and ignominious names of Papists, &c.—Sir John Knight,
Sir Robert Atkins, and John Lawford, aldermen, were presented for publishing a writing under the title of a Petition,
in which were contained divers reproachful untruths and
falsehoods.—Several persons were presented for preaching at
unlawful conventicles; and the constables of several of the
wards were presented for *not disturbing* unlawful conventicles.

May 28, the King dissolved his last Parliament.

The King granted to William Penn the province named
after him, Pennsylvania. In June 1682 he took shipping for
the voyage, and he, that "Great Penn, who," according to
Father O'Leary, "deserved half the world for teaching
sovereigns how to govern the other," laid down the lesson in
two short years; when he returned to England.

Aug. 27, died Richard Standfast, aged 78 years. He had
been rector of Christ-Church 51 years—14 years sequestered
during the Commonwealth, and had performed the duties of
the church for twenty years after he became blind, assisted by
his son. He published "A Handful of Cordial Comfits;"
which was reprinted in 1767, by his great grandson, Standfast Smith, apothecary; also "A Caveat against Seducers."
He once escaped his malicious accusers by putting on the
habit of a thatcher, and working upon a house at Thornbury.*

October. At the session, Sir Robert Atkins, Knight of
the Bath, Recorder, was presented by the Grand Jury for
withdrawing himself and departing from the gaol-delivery,
also for the denial to swear Sir Richard Hart, an alderman,
being duly elected.—Sir Robert Atkins, Sir John Knight,
John Lawford, esq. and Joseph Creswicke, esq. aldermen,
were presented for assembling and uniting themselves and
calling a Court of aldermen, and electing Mr. Thomas Day
an alderman in court.—Many persons were presented for
not going to church, and many for keeping inmates in their
houses.

* The last representative of this family, that bore the same name, was the man, in
appearance, who within a few years resided on St. James's Parade in the Church-yard,
and constantly annoyed the ears of common sense, not excepting on Sundays, by pro-
fane and indecent ribaldry, chiefly addressed to children. He sometimes, in a rare fit of
cleanliness, attracted notice by dressing in a scarlet coat, with ruffles and a cocked hat.
He at last became pious, or affected piety, and committed suicide while on a visit to
take possession of some newly acquired property in Scotland.

A. D.

1682 January-Session. Many persons were presented for riots in December and this month, and joining in conventicles.—The constables of St. Leonard's presented that there was no popish recusant in their parish, to the best of their knowledge.—The Grand Jury presented that the running races and driving of horses in the Marsh on Sundays was a profanation of the Lord's day.—The constables of Redcliff-parish presented a list of about 200 names of such as were recusant within the parishes of Redcliff and St. Thomas, in not going to church and receiving the sacrament, from the day of October last to the 27th of January, together with their children of nine years and upward, and their servants.—The presentments here alluded·to shew that the Friends were not the only objects of jealousy in these feverish times.

" This year there was a fire in Broad-street, in the house of one Abraham Nichols, a strong-water-man; which could not be extinguished till it had consumed the house to the foundation; two houses of each side being also much damaged. The brandy and other strong waters running into the street, and so to St. John's Gate, along the channel, all on fire, to the great amazement of the spectators."*

" Sir Robert Atkins, Recorder of the City of Bristol, having too much abetted with the fannaticks, did, by order from His Majestie, resigne his place of recordership in December, this year; whereupon Sir John Churchill, of Churchill in the County of Somerset, was, *nemine contradicente,* elected in his place."†

Dec. 2, the dukedom of Beaufort created, in the person of Henry, only son of Edward Somerset, the marquess of Worcester, who stands in Mr. Walpole's list of Royal and Noble Authors for " A Century of the Names and Scantlings of such Inventions, &c." and " Certamen Religiosum, or a Conference between King Charles I. and Henry, late marquess of Worcester, concerning Religion."

* How great would be the " amazement of spectators" in 1824, at seeing waters of any *strength* so *burn!*—Corporal Trim talks of the " radical heat" of burnt brandy, but he does not tell us that the " radical moisture," ditch-water, would burn with it.

† Sir Robert Atkins (the elder) was made a knight of the Bath at the Coronation of Charles II. In 1671 he was appointed one of the King's Serjeants-at-law, and in the following year, one of the Judges of the Court of Common Pleas, which station he resigned in 1679. Having been a promoter of the Revolution, in May 1689, King William made him Lord Chief Baron of the Exchequer. In October following he succeeded Lord Halifax as Speaker of the House of Lords, and so continued till the Great Seal was given to Sir John Somers, in the beginning of 1693. In June 1695, being then in his 74th year, Sir Robert resigned his office of Chief Baron, and retired to his seat at Saperton·Hall, Gloucestershire, where he spent the last fourteen years of his life in ease and tranquillity, dying in 1709. He was the Author of " Parliamentary and Political Tracts," in one vol. 8vo.

A. D.

1682 Dec. 13, an Order of the King's Council against kidnapping and spiriting people away to the Plantations.

1683 Feb. A Writ of Quo Warranto was brought against the old Charter of Bristol, by Sir Robert Sawyer, Attorney-General. The Common Council, for some years previously, had exceeded the number of forty-three persons, and this was the only ostensible reason for seizure of the Charter. (See Seyer's No. 34.) In the course of the proceedings in the Court of King's Bench, in Hilary Term, against the City of London, the Attorney-General stated that " the liberties of the City of Bristol were seized, and the custody of it granted to certain persons, for divers contempts and injuries done by the Mayor and Commonalty, &c."

March 22, the King and the Duke of York escaped the effect of the Rye-House plot. A party to this plot was said to have been formed in Bristol, who held their meeting in a summer-house of a garden in Baldwin-street. On the 30th of April, 1684, James Holloway, a linen-manufacturer and merchant of Bristol, who had been outlawed as one of the conspirators, was hung at Tyburn. See 1685.

Ralph Oliver, vintner, was chosen Mayor, but died the day after he was sworn. The Sheriffs, Nathaniel Driver and John Arundel, merchants, were particularly nominated by the King.

Oct. 80, by His Majesty's special command, William Clutterbuck, grocer, was chosen Mayor; and, about two months after being sworn, he was knighted. See 1685.

Nov. 9, by an instrument of this date, the Common Council surrendered their privileges to the King. See Seyer's No. 35.

Dec. 7, Algernon Sidney beheaded on Tower-Hill, for high treason, particularly in a libel, wherein he asserted " Power to be originally in the People, and delegated by them to the Parliament, to whom the King was subject, and might be called to account."

Richard Towgood, dean of Bristol (who had suffered under the Protectorate), died, aged 89.

George Williamson, B.D. sub-dean, presented the brass eagle to the Cathedral, which, in 1802, was sold for the purpose of making an addition to the sacramental plate, and is now in St. Maryport Church.*

* The perpetrator of this transmutation was (with the consent of his Chapter) Dean Layard. Mr. George Ady, a most determined Cathedral-goer (certainly not merely for " the music there," for that he might have heard with more advantage in the cloisters), and a sore annoyance to irreverent singing-boys of all statures, being much

A. D.

1684 June 2, at Westminster, was given the Charter, in Mr.
Seyer's Collection No. 36, granting that " the citizens and
inhabitants of Bristol, and their successors hereafter for ever,
may and shall be a body corporate and politic, in deed, fact,
and name, by the name of *The Mayor, Burgesses, and
Commonalty of the City of Bristol;*" with a common seal—
naming the existing Mayor and Sheriffs to be in office till the
15th of September, and the Common-Council of forty-three
to be in office during their natural lives; John Romsey
nominated Town-Clerk for life; John Robins, Steward of
the Sheriffs' Court; George Lunell and Rowland Searchfield,
Coroners. Corn brought by land to be sold at the ancient
market-place in Wine-street; that by water at the Key,
from the place called Aldworth's Slip, thence thirty yards
towards the Gib*—as well as at the Back. Three cloth-fairs
to be holden annually in King-street, viz. April 18 and
June 18, each to last two days, and the first Thursday after
the feast of St. Michael; † and five horse-fairs, viz. Jan. 25,
in Temple-street, to continue during the feast of St. Paul—
March 25 and 26, at Redcliff-Hill—May 25, 6, in Broadmead—Sept. 25, 6, 7, in Temple-street ‡—Nov. 25, 6, 7,
on Redcliff-Hill, with the Court of Pie-Powder in the same
places.§

June 20, arrived John Lake, seventeenth Bishop of Bristol,
one of the seven who were committed to the Tower by
James II., in June 1688.

scandalized at this supposed profanation of " Jove's sacred bird," rescued it from the
unhallowed hands of the melter for twenty-seven pounds odd, and, in hope of propi-
tiating a better fate for his bargain, offered it for sale by public auction; but finding no
bidder, he made a present of it as above, there to remain for ever. We well remember
the astounding clamour this affair produced against the poor Dean: where two or three
only were met together *out* of church, he who ventured a word of apology for him
could scarcely reckon upon the safety of his nose from toothsome amputation. Even
Dissenters, who affect to despise such toys, were not the least intolerant of bitter
speech. The Dean himself, upon chiding a merry vagrant, more rogue than fool, for
disturbing the King's peace on the Green, was silenced by the gibe recognitory, " Hah!
who stole the *magpie* out of the church ?—thee hold *thy* tongue!" The Dean died soon
afterward, and common report prevailed to the effect that this bar to his previous
reputation for usefulness, excited by a course of lectures on the Church-Catechism,
hastened his dissolution.

* The market-house erected about this date, on the spot described, is the insulated
building long occupied below by a block and pump-maker, and above by a carpenter, &c.
near the Assembly Coffee-house.

† The wearing-trade had not yet left Bristol.

‡ " This was the first of all the new fairs kept in Bristoll."

§ The writer possesses a MS. copy of all the Charters in Mr. Seyer's Collection,
excepting the above and No. 2, which was the property of Alderman John Bartlett,
mayor in 1741-2, and doubtless transcribed for his personal use. From the circumstance of No. 36 not having a place in that MS., it is fair to presume that the Body
Corporate, after the new Charter of Anne, considered it of no value as a subject of
reference in direction of their duties.

A. D.

1684 July 10, in the Guildhall, the oaths of allegiance, &c. were administered to the Corporation, by Charles, marquess of Worcester, Sir John Smythe, bart., Sir James Herbert, knt. and John Fitzherbert, esq.

1685 Feb. 6, the King died at Whitehall, of a fit of apoplexy, in the 55th year of his age.

JAMES II.

Feb. 7, Sir George Jefferys, knt. and bart., made Lord Chief Justice of the King's Bench, &c. &c.

Feb. 8, the King went publicly to mass at St. James's Chapel.

Feb. 18, the King published two papers, taken out of the late King's strong box, to prove he died a Papist.

May. The election of Members of Parliament observed to be more peaceable and unanimous than had been heretofore known.

May 13, Sir George Jefferys created Baron Jefferys, of Wem, in com. Salop.

The Duke of Argyle landed in Scotland with a body of troops, and raised a rebellion there. Each House resolved to assist the King with their lives and fortunes. The Duke was taken prisoner June 17.

June 1, the Duke of Monmouth landed at Lyme in Dorsetshire—proclaimed King at Taunton, June 10.

June 11, in the evening, the news arrived in Bristol; upon which the militia were ordered to watch, two companies each night; one company in the Guildhall, and the other in St. Thomas-street, by the church.

June 16, the Duke of Beaufort arrived in Bristol, to take the command of the militia, and to keep them in readiness for service. The Duke of Somerset also arrived on the 20th.

June 23, Lord Feversham came to Bristol, with about 250 horse of the King's Guard, and early the next day marched for Bath.

June 24, the Duke of Beaufort caused twenty-one companies of foot to be mustered in Redcliff-mead, and six companies of horse at the Lamb-ground at Lawford's Gate; and there appeared a troop of horse freely, being several citizens and country-gentlemen.

The following is extracted from a narrative of the Duke of Monmouth's expedition, in *"The Life and Death of George*

A. D.

1685 *Lord Jeffreys,*" appended to " *The Western Martyrology, or Bloody Assizes.*" 5th ed. 1705.

" We tarried here [at Taunton] till Sunday morning [June 21], and then marched for Bridgwater. We were now between 4 and 5000 men, and, had we not wanted arms, could have made above 10,000. We were received here as in other places, but did little more than read our Declaration, which we did also in all other towns, the Magistrates standing by in their gowns; and likewise our Proclamation; and so marched forward for Glassenbury. From Glassenbury we designed for Bristol, three days march from that place, designing to attack it."

The Duke's forces, says other authority, passed over Bedminster-Down, and at this time (the 24th, in the evening) the ship Abraham and Mary was on fire at the Quay, which was quenched. About the same instant, the backward stables of the White Lion, in Broad-street, were set on fire; in one of which were two of the Duke of Beaufort's best saddle-horses burnt, " and supposed by the malice and envy of the fanatics, of whom a great many were sent prisoners from Bristol to Gloucester, and there kept till the rebellion was over." A third account states that this latter fire did not take place till the 8th of July, during the rejoicing for Monmouth's defeat.

" Accordingly (continues the Narrative) we arrived at Canshum-Bridge, a little town, three miles English from Bristol, intending to enter next morning; the Duke of Beauford being there with a garrison of about 4000 men. Being here lodged in the town, we were on a sudden alarmed with the noise of the approach of the enemy, being in no small confusion on this unsuspected news. The Duke sent one up the tower [of the church] to see whether he could discover them marching. As soon as he came up, he saw them at the very entrance into the town, fighting with our men. Here we had a small skirmish, our men being in the fields adjoining to the town, refreshing themselves; but it lasted not long; for, before he could bring word, they were fled, being not above 60 horsemen. They did us mischief, killing and wounding above 20 men; whereas we killed none of theirs, only took four prisoners* and their horses, and wounded my Lord Newburg, that it was thought mortal. They came thither, thinking it had been their own forces; and had not our undisciplined fellows been a little too eager, and suffered 'em to come a little farther on, they would have entered the town, and we must have had every man of them. Their infantry was following, but, on their return, came not forward. These forces being so near, and Bristol being so well manned also, the Duke was loth

* " Three Bristol men, Andrew Herbert, Charles Pope, and Edward Taylor, and Capt. Savage, belonging to a troop of horse of Gloucestershire, who were brought back to Bristol, July 6."

G g

A. D.

1685 to pass the bridge for Bristol; though some gentlemen that came over with us, and were proscribed upon the account of the former [the Rye-House] plot,* being Bristol men, and knew the hearts of the townsmen, begged him heartily to proceed towards it, offering themselves to go in the head of them into the town, by some private ways which they knew; assuring him they [the citizens] would make no resistance; but could not persuade him; which had we been possessors of, we could not have wanted money nor arms, the only things needful for us in that juncture. For, had we but had arms, I am persuaded we had by this time had at the least 20,000 men; and it would not then have been difficult for us to have marched to London, with the recruit of Bristol, the King not being able to make 7000 men for the gaining of so many kingdoms. But God saw it not fit for us, and over-ruled our consultations to our own ruin, for this was in the top of our prosperity; and yet all the while not a gentleman, more than went over with us [to Amsterdam], came to our assistance.

" So we marched on to Bath. We lay before it in the afternoon, and sent in our trumpeter to demand the town; but they refused to give us entrance, having a strong garrison, it being a stout people, and a strong place. Having no mind to spend time in laying sieges, we marched on that day to a little town called Phillips-Norton, and there lay that night, being now Sunday, the 26th of June, Old Style."—[The Narrative proceeds to describe a skirmish with the enemy, as the writer's party was about to leave Philip's Norton for Frome. At Frome they received the news of Argyle's defeat, and of the advance of the King's forces from London, with considerable baggage and thirty field-pieces. Hence, after suffering a loss of numbers by desertion, they retrograded toward Bridgwater, and arrived there on the 3d of July. The King's forces reaching Sedgmoor on Saturday afternoon, Monmouth's infantry marched out upon them, with a guide, about eleven o'clock at night, and attacked them in their tents at one in the morning. The result appears below.]

July 2, " This day a small vessel belonging to Berkeley was going down the river, and the watch of Rownham calling to them to stop, to shew their let-pass, the tide carried the vessel a little lower than ordinary; upon which a soldier fired at them, and shot one Barker, an alderman of Berkeley, being a soldier here, but who had got leave to go home. Also we had news that Monmouth and his forces were gone towards Bridgewater, and that he had broken their organs and burned their minister's linen surplice."

July 6, the Duke of Monmouth was defeated by the Earl of Feversham and Lord Churchill, at Sedgmoor, near Bridgewater. The Lord Grey was taken the next day, and the

* See 1683.

A. D.

1685 Duke on the 8th instant. He was beheaded at Tower-Hill, on the 15th following.

Aug. 27, Lord Chief Justice Jefferys proceeded into the West, both as Judge and Lieutenant-General, with command of what troops he wished, to attend his orders from place to place. He began at Winchester, and proceeded to Salisbury, Dorchester, Exeter, Taunton, and Wells. The executions in consequence were,—at Lyme 12, Bath 6, Philip's Norton 12, Frome 12, Bruton 3, Wincanton 6, Shepton Mallet 13, Pensford 12, Wrington 3, Wells 8, Wiveliscomb 3, Chewton Mendip 2, Chard 12, Crewkerne 10, Somerton 7, Yeovil 8, Nether Stowey 3, Dunster 3, Dulverton 3, Bridgewater 12, Redcliff-Hill, Bristol, 6 (see Nov. 6), Ilminster 12, Stoke Courcy 2, Wellington 3, South Petherton 3, Porlock 2, Glastonbury 6, Taunton 19, Langport 3, Axbridge 6, Cutherston 2, Minehead 6, Ilchester 12, Stogumber 3, Castle Cary 3, Milborne Port 2, Keynsham 11 —in all, 251.

Sept. 21, Monday, the Lord Chief Justice came to the Guildhall, Bristol, and delivered the Charge, from which the following are extracts:—

" Gentlemen,—I am, by the mercy of God, come to this great and populous city—a city that boasts both of its riches and trade, and may justly indeed claim the next place to the great and populous Metropolis of this Kingdom. Gentlemen! I find here are a great many auditors, who are very intent, as if they expected some formal or prepared speech; but, assure yourselves, we come not neither to make set speeches nor formal declamations, nor to follow a couple of *puffing Trumpeters*; for, Lord, we have seen those things twenty times before! No, we come to do the King's business—a King who is so gracious as to use all the means possible to discover the disorders of the nation, and to search out those who indeed are the very pest of the kingdom: to this end, and for this purpose, are we come to this city. But I find a Special Commission is an unusual thing here, and relishes very ill: nay, the very women storm at it, for fear we should take the *upper hand* of them too; for, by the by, gentlemen, I hear it is much in fashion in this city for the women to govern and bear sway. But, gentlemen, I will not stay you with such needless stories: I will only mention some few things that fall within my knowledge. For points or matters of Law I shall not trouble you, but only mind you of some things that lately hath happened, and particularly in this city (for I have the Kalender of this city in my pocket); and if I do not express myself in so formal or set a declamation (for, as I told you, I came not to make declamations), or in so smooth language as you may expect, you must attribute it partly to the pain of the stone, under which I labour, and partly to the unevenness of this day's journey.

1685   " Gentlemen, I may say that even some of the youngest amongst
us may remember the late horrid Rebellion, how men, under colour
of Law, and pretext of Justice, after they had divested a most gracious and most merciful Prince of all his royal power, by the power
of the sword—they, I say, under colour of Law, and pretext of Justice,
(which added the more to the crime, that it was done under such
pretended Justice,) brought the most mild and meekest Prince (next
to our ever blessed Saviour, Jesus Christ, if we may but compare him
to a Man) to die a Martyr, the first blessed Martyr (pardon the expression) besides our most blessed Jesu, who suffered for us on the
Cross—I say, besides that blessed Son of God,—this, I say, was the
first Royal Martyr; not suffering him to speak for himself, or make
his defence—a liberty which is given to the vilest traitor; and this
was done (not to descant on the number*) by *forty-one!* The rebels, not resting here, for Rebellion is like the Sin of Witchcraft,
divested the lineal, legal, and rightful Heir of the Crown of all his
power and prerogative, till the Mighty God of Heaven and Earth,
God Almighty, restored him to his just right.   And he, as if begot
in mercy, not only forgave all offences, and pardoned voluntarily
even all that had been in actual arms against him (except those ac-
cursed Regicides), but made it a crime for any one that should but
remember or upbraid any of their past crimes or rebellions.   Good
God! O Jesu! that we should live in such an age, in which such
a Prince cannot be safe from the seditious contrivances of pardoned
rebels!   Had we not the *Rye* conspiracy, wherein they not only
designed to have murthered that most Blessed (for so now we may
conclude him to be with God Almighty) and Gracious King, but
also his ever dear and victorious brother?—Had we not the Bill of Ex-
clusion, which our most Gracious King told us he could not, without
a manifest infringement of the Royal Prerogatives of the Crown,
(which are too sacred for us to touch) consent to?—Had we not the
cursed counsel of *Achitophel?*†—Kings are God's Vice-Regents on
Earth, and are indeed Gods on Earth, and we represent them.   Now,
when God Almighty had of his infinite goodness called this Blessed
Prince unto himself, he sends a Prince, who assures us he will
imitate his royal brother and renowned predecessor in all things,
especially in that of his clemency and mercy, and that, too,
upon the word of a King!—a King, I assure you, that will not be
worse than his word; nay (pardon the expression!) that dare not
be worse than his word.   Which of you all, that had a Father murthered by another, (and that deliberately, too, under colour of Justice, which added to the crime, and your brother, nay, yourselves,
thrust out from your inheritance, and banished from your country,
nay, that sought your blood likewise),—would not, if it was in
your power, revenge such injuries, and ruin such persecutors?—But
here our most Blessed Prince, whom God long preserve! hath not

---

* A shrewd hit at the number of Bristol Common-Councilmen.
† Meaning Anthony Ashley Cooper, the Earl of Shaftesbury.

A. D.

1685only forgiven, but will venture his life for the defence of such his enemies. Has he not ventured his life already as far as any man; for the honour of these Kingdoms? Nay, I challenge this City to shew me any one man of it, that perchance may not be worth a groat, that has ventured his life so far for the safety of these Kingdoms, as this Royal Prince hath done?—Good God! what an age do we live in! Shall not such a Prince be secure from the sedition, rebellion, and plots of men? He is scarce seated on his Royal throne (where God Almighty grant he may long reign!) but on the one hand he is invaded by a condemned rebel and arch-traitor, who hath received the just reward of his rebellion; on the other hand up starts a Poppet Prince, who seduces the mobile into rebellion, into which they are easily bewitched; for I say Rebellion is like the Sin of Witchcraft. This man, who had as little title to the Crown as the least of you, (for I hope all of you are legitimate,) being overtaken by justice, and by the goodness of his Prince brought to the scaffold, he has the confidence (good God! that men should be so impudent) to say that *God Almighty did know with what joyfulness he did die*; (a Traitor!) having for these two years last past lived in all incontinency and rebellion, notwithstanding the goodness of an indulgent Prince so often to pardon him; but it is just like him! Rebellion (as I told you) is like the Sin of Witchcraft. * For there was another, which I shall not name, because I will not trample on the dust of the dead, but you may remember him by these words of his speech: he tells you that *he thanks his God that he falls by the ax, and not by the fiery trial.* He had rather (he had as good have said) die a Traitor than a Blessed Martyr.

"Great God of Heaven and Earth! what reason have men to rebel? But, as I told you, Rebellion is like the Sin of Witchcraft. *Fear God and honour the King* is rejected by people for no other reason, as I can find, but that it is written in St. Peter. Gentlemen! I must tell you, I am afraid, I am afraid that this city hath too many of these people in it; and it is your duty to search them out: for this city added much to the ship's loading. There was your *Tylys*, your *Roes*, and your *Wades*,† men started up like mushrooms, scoundrel fellows, mere sons of dunghills: these men must forsooth set up for Liberty and Property!—A fellow that carries the Sword before Mr. Mayor must be very careful of his Property, and turn Politician, as if he had as much property as the person before whom he bears the sword, though perchance not worth a groat! Gentlemen! I must tell you, you have still here the *Tylys*, the *Roes*, and the *Wades*. I have brought a brush in my pocket, and I shall be sure to rub the dirt wherever it lies, or on

* Whatever the *unread* Reader may think, this was said in sober sadness. It was not until 1736 that discovery was made of more old women in *breeches* having ruled the guiding-stars of the nation, than those who were suspected to have bestrid broomsticks in *petticoats*. The world is still advancing in its state of probation. We have now only to bid God b'w'ye! to those who, like Judge Jefferys, are "no conjurers."

† Whence, perhaps, Wade-street, and Wade's alias Traitor's Bridge. See 1711.

1685 whomsoever it sticks.* Gentlemen! I shall not stand compli-
menting with you: I shall talk with some of you before you and I
part. I tell you, I tell you, I have brought a besom, and I will
sweep every man's door, whether great or small. Must I mention
particulars?—I hope you will save me that trouble; yet I will hint
a few things to you, that perchance I have heard of. This is a
great city, and the Magistrates wonderful Loyal, and very forward
to assist the King with men, money, and provisions, when the
Rebels were just at your gates. I do believe it would have went
very hard with some of you, if the enemy had entered the city,
notwithstanding the endeavours that was used to accomplish it.
Certainly they had and must have great encouragement from a
party within, or else why should their design be on the city?—Nay,
when the enemy was within a mile of you, that a ship should be
set on fire in the midst of you, as a signal to the Rebels, and to
amuse those within; when, if God Almighty had not been more
gracious unto you than you was to yourselves (so that wind and tide
was for you) for what I know, the greatest part of this city had
perished; and yet you are willing to believe it was an accident!
Certainly here is a great many of those men which they call *Trimmers*.
A *Whig* is but a mere fool to these; for a Whig is some sort of a
subject in comparison of these; for a Trimmer is but a cowardly
and base-spirited Whig; for the Whig is but the Journeyman-
Prentice, that is hired and set on in the Rebellion, whilst the Trimmer is afraid to appear in the cause: he stands at a doubt, and says
to himself, I will not assist the King until I see who hath the best
of it, and refuses to entertain the King's friends for fear the Rebels
should get the better of it. These men stink worse than the worst
dirt you have in your city; these men have so little Religion, that
they forget that he that is not for us is against us. Gentlemen! I
tell you I have the *Kalendar of this City* here in my hand. I have
heard of those that have searched into the very sink of a Conventicle,
to find out some sneaking rascal to hide their money by night.
Come, come, Gentlemen! to be plain with you, I find the dirt of
the ditch is in your nostrils. Good God! where am I?—In *Bristol?*
This city, it seems, claims the privilege of hanging and drawing
amongst themselves: I find you have more need of a Commission
once a month at least. The very Magistrates, which should be the
Ministers of Justice, fall out with one another to that degree, they
will scarce dine with each other; whilst it is the business of some
cunning men that lie behind the curtain to raise divisions amongst
them, and set them together by the ears, and knock their logger-
heads together. Yet I find they can agree for their interest, or if
there be but a Kid in the case; for I hear the Trade of Kidnapping
is of much request in this city. They can discharge a Felon, or a
Traitor, provided they will go to Mr. Alderman's Plantation at the

---

* An Alderman, in one of the towns of previous visitation, offering to vindicate and
give bail for his son, was answered by Jefferys, that *" he knew many Aldermen were
villains, and he hoped to beat some fur out of their gowns;"*

685 West-Indies!—Come, come, I find you stink for want of rubbing. Gentlemen! what need *I* remind *you* of these things?—I hope you will search into them, and inform *me*. It seems the Dissenters and Phanaticks fare well among you, by reason of the favour of the Magistrates! For example,—if a Dissenter, who is a notorious and obstinate offender, comes before them to be fined, one Alderman or other stands up, and says, He is a good man (though three parts a Rebel)! Well, then, for the sake of Mr. Alderman, he shall be fined but 5s. Then comes another, and up stands another Goodman Alderman, and says, I know him to be an honest man (though rather worse than the former)! Well, for Mr. Alderman's sake he shall be fined but half-a-crown! So *manus manum fricat:* you play the knave for me now, and I will play the knave for you by and by. I am ashamed of these things! And I must not forget to tell you that I hear of some differences among the Clergy—those that ought to preach peace and unity to others. Gentlemen! these things must be looked into. I shall not now trouble you any further. There are several other things, but I expect to hear further of them from you; and if you do not tell me of some of these things, I shall remind you of them. And I find, by the number of your Constables, this is a very large city, and it is impossible for one or two to search into all the concerns of it; therefore mind the Constables of their duties, and call on them for their presentments; for I expect every Constable to bring in his presentment, or that you present him. So adjourn, &c."

The chronicler of this *radical* charge adds,

" Upon affidavits read, and other evidence, against Sir W[illiam C[lutterbuck] the Mayor, Alderman L[awford], and others, for kidnapping, there being Bills preferred to the Grand Jury by J— R— [John Romsey, the Town-Clerk], and being found, he made the Mayor and Aldermen concerned to go from the Bench to the Bar, to plead to the Information, saying of the Mayor, *See how the Kidnapping Rogue looks!* &c."*

Another writer, disposed to consider Jefferys, "when under no state-influence," as "sometimes inclined to protect the natural and civil rights of mankind," states that

" The Mayor and Aldermen of Bristol had made a practice of transporting convicted criminals to the American Plantations, and selling them by way of trade. This turning to good account, when any pilferers or petty rogues were brought before them, they threatened them with hanging, and then some officers who attended earnestly advised the ignorant intimidated creatures to beg for transportation, as the only way to save them; and in general their advice was followed. Then, without more form, each Alderman took one, and sold him for his own benefit."†

* These proceedings were stayed by the Revolution.

† Granting these Fathers of the City to have presented a bad school for their children and fellow-citizens, yet Edward Colston was now growing into manhood, to outshine this blot in our civic escutcheon.

1685   But it is evident that Mr. Town-Clerk *Romsey*, in ferreting out matter for this information, was actuated more by subserviency to the Court than humanity or a love of Justice for her own sake : the Aldermen might have kidnapped all their fellow-citizens with impunity, had they not been violently suspected of either Whiggism or Trimming. Jefferys had had not so far sated his thirst for blood, in his progress, but that he wished to have another taste in this its termination. This was *not* the best way to keep his Sovereign on the throne.

The death of the Lord Keeper, North, having taken place, Sept. 5th, Jefferys was immediately hereupon made Lord Chancellor.

About 200 of the persons concerned in Monmouth's rebellion were brought to Bristol, in order to be transported beyond sea.

Nov. 6, " This day at Bedminster were executed three persons for being with Monmouth, viz. [Edward] Tippet, a shoemaker of this city ; one [Philip] Cambridge, of Sodbury, a fishmonger ; and one countryman, said to be a grocer. Tippet continued cheerful, not changing his colour to the last moment. He said he only went to see Monmouth's army—that he never had any arms, nor design to wrong any person in life or estate. The other two were very sick and weak. They were drawn, hanged, and quartered. The grocer's quarters were begged and buried."

The list of the condemned given in " *The Life and Death of George Lord Jeffreys*" furnishes this extract :

" **Ratcliffe-Hill** at **Bristol** 6.

Richard Evans	*Edward Tippot*
John Pinckwell	*Philip Cumbridge*
Christopher Clerk	*John Tucker alias Glover*."[*]

Jonathan Trelawney, eighteenth Bishop of Bristol.—A regiment of soldiers under the command of Col. Charles Trelawney, the Bishop's brother, was quartered here, partly in 1685 and partly in 1686.

1686   May 17, all the imprisoned Quakers were set at liberty.

About this time was built a new market-house on the Quay.

Aug. 25, the King came here, accompanied by George, Prince of Denmark, and the Dukes of Beaufort, Somerset, and Grafton, "with many other noble and great persons of this realm." They were received by the Mayor (Abraham Saunders, soap-maker) and Aldermen, at Lawford's Gate,

---

[*] Our copy of " The Western Martyrology, &c." has the autograph, " John Wraxall, May 26th, 1705."

A. D.

1686 with the usual ceremonies, and conducted through the Castle-Gate, Castle-Green, and Wine-street, to Sir William Hayman's* house in Small-street, where they were entertained at Alderman Lane's house, on St. Augustin's Back, at the charge of the city.

On the 26th, " the King rode on horseback into the Marsh, where the soldiers had their tents pitched, which they had brought with them from the camp. From thence they went along the Key, and up St. Michael's Hill, and along to Prior-Hill, and so along Barton-lane, into St. James's parish; from thence up to Newgate, and so to his lodgings again; and then he touched several for the King's evil. After dinner, the King went through the city to Redclift; and from thence to Porset Poynt, attended by several noblemen and others. He returned again in the evening; and that night Mr. William Merritt,† the present Sheriff, was knighted, as also Mr. Charles Winter, of the Forest of Dean, who was also the present High Sheriff for the County of Gloucester." The next morning, early, the King went hence to Sedgmoor, to view the place where his army overthrew the Duke of Monmouth—hereafter called King's Sedgmoor.

1687 April 7, the Declaration was brought hither, for indulging all persons in their religion, of what kind soever, and in building meeting-houses, acquainting the next justice of the peace therewith; for which the Dissenters presented addresses of thanks from all parts of the kingdom.

Sept. 12, the King and Queen, being at Bath, were invited by our Magistrates hither, to a splendid entertainment provided for them and their retinue, at Mr. Richard Lane's great house, on St. Augustin's Back. They remained only two hours, returning to Bath at four o'clock. In their way hither, they were met by many citizens on horseback, including a deputation of Quakers, who presented the King with an address, which was read by Charles Jones, a resident in Castle-Green.

This year Count Dada, the Pope's Nuncio, came to Bristol, and dined at the Three Tuns Tavern, in Corn-street.

In the winter, Col. Kirke's regiment of soldiers was quartered in Bristol.

" This year [1687-8] great changes in the Justices of the Peace and Lords and Deputy Lievetenants of the severall counties, and most cities and Corporations purged, parti-

---

* Mayor in 1684.   † See his monument in St. Philip's Church.

H h

A. D.

1688cularly this City of Bristol, where, on the 4th the Mayor
Feb. [Richard Lane, merchant], both the Sheriffes [John Sandford, mercer, and Samuel Wallis, ironmonger], six Aldermen
[including Sir William Clutterbuck and Alderman Lawford],
John Rumsey, Town-Clerke, and eight or more of the Councill,
were turned out; and in the places of the Mayor and Sheriffes
were put Thomas Day, sope-maker, Mayor; John Hine,
sugar-baker, and Thomas Saunders, haberdasher, Sheriffes.
And Nathaniel Wade,* who was concerned in Monmouth's
rebellion, made Town-Clerke, and diverse others, *of different
opinions*, made Aldermen, and brought into the Councill—
in the whole, twenty-eight. This was done by speciall
commission under the Privy Seale,"—with which Nathaniel
Wade had arrived from London on the 2d instant.

March 25, " Charity Schools" first began in England.

June 12, came to Bristol the news of the Queen being
delivered of a son. " They rang the bells a little while,
but made but very small demonstrations of joy. They had
a small bonfire at Newgate."

June 15, the Seven Bishops, who had refused to publish
the King's declaration for liberty of conscience, gave re-
cognizance to stand a trial the 29th following, by a Middlesex
jury. The " news of which coming to Bristol the Monday
following, all the bells rung, and gave very large expressions
of joy, and at night bonfires were made in many parts of
this city."

June 29, the Seven Bishops acquitted. Rejoicings in the
Camp upon Hounslow-Heath.

Aug. 24, the King proposed to call a new Parliament
on Nov. 27th.

Sept. 26, the displaced Deputy-Lieutenants and Justices
ordered to be restored.

Sept. 28, Proclamation, announcing the meditated invasion
from Holland, and revoking writs for calling a Parliament.
A proclamation for a general pardon.

" On the news of the great preparations in Holland, and
that the Prince of Orange was certainly designed for England,
the determined Councils cooled, and then quite ceased; so
that the Church of England men, whose cause the Prince had
espoused, were restored again to the commissions and trusts
they had lately been deprived of."—*Life of Jefferys.*

Oct. 2, the Charter of London restored. " It was brought
to Guildhall by the Lord Chancellor; though he was not

* See 1711, for " Traitor's Bridge," leading to Wade-street.

A. D.

1688 attended by the shouts and acclamations he expected, nor seemed so florid or frolicksome as heretofore; which some looked upon as a bad omen. And, it is reported, soon after being asked by a Courtier, *What the Heads of the Prince's Declaration were?* he should answer, *He was sure his was one, whatever the rest were.*"—Ibid.

Oct. 17, Proclamation for restoring Charters generally.

Oct. 22, " This day came to Bristoll the Duke of Beaufort, being received by the trained soldiers of the city, all in their arms, and had his lodging at the house of Sir William Poole, our Collector, being the great house in the Marsh.

Oct. 23, William Jackson, merchant, who had been chosen Mayor of Bristol, Sept. 15, was restored; but the Sheriffs, Thomas Lifton and Joseph Jackson, merchants, remained displaced; Thomas Cole, merchant, and George White, draper, being appointed in their room.

Nov. 1, the Prince of Orange set sail. On the 5th he landed at Torbay.

Nov. 17, the King set out for Salisbury, and arrived there on the 19th. Nov. 26, he returned to Whitehall. Nov. 28, he issued writs for a Parliament to assemble at Westminster on Jan. 15th.

Dec. 1, " marched into Bristol a regiment of foot-soldiers of the Prince's, being a new-raised regiment under Sir John Guise, a person of Gloucestershire, who had for some time been in Holland, by reason he had said something of the Duke of Beaufort. With them also came two troops of dragoons, one Dutch, the other English, who stayed but three or four days, and marched for Gloucester. This day, before they came hither, the rabble rose in a great number, and went to Mr. Whitney's, a collar-maker, in Castle-street, being a papist, and quite ruined his household goods and what they could find, burning many books and much of their goods, and some stealing away the rest of it; and they greatly abused his wife, he at the same time being at London. From thence they went into King-street, to two other such houses, and did much harm. And the week following they got thither again, and committed great insolence; upon which Sir John Knight, Sir Richard Crump, Sir Thomas Earl, and some others, drew their swords, which so daunted the rabble that they fled. Seventeen of them were taken and put in prison, and the rest of them escaped."

Dec. 2, the Lord Delamere, with six troops of horse, came into Bristol, and declared for the Prince and the Protestant religion.

1688 Dec. 10, the King took water at Whitehall-stairs, and embarked for France.

Dec. 12, Jefferys taken prisoner at Wapping.

"The brutality Jeffreys commonly shewed on the Bench, where his voice and visage [though handsome] were equally terrible, at length exposed him to a severe mortification. A scrivener of Wapping having a cause before him, one of the opponent's counsel said he was a strange fellow, and sometimes went to church and sometimes to conventicles; and it was thought he was a Trimmer. At this the Chancellor fired: 'A Trimmer!' said he; 'I have heard 'much of that monster, but never saw one. Come forth, Mr. 'Trimmer! and let me see your shape.' He then treated the poor fellow so roughly, that, on his leaving the Hall, he declared he would not undergo the terrors of that man's face again to save his life, and he should certainly retain the frightful impression of it as long as he lived. Soon after, on the arrival of the Prince of Orange, the Lord Chancellor, dreading the public resentment, disguised himself in a seaman's dress, in order to leave the kingdom, and was drinking in a cellar at Wapping, where this scrivener entering, and, seeing again the face which had filled him with such horror, started; upon which Jeffreys, fearing he was known, feigned a cough, and turned to the wall with his pot of beer in his hand. But the scrivener, going out, gave notice that he was there; and the mob, rushing in, seized him, beat him, spit in his face, shewed every mark of detestation, and carried him before the Lord Mayor, who sent him with a strong guard to the Lords of the Council, by whom he was committed to the Tower."—[He died there of disease, about nine in the morning of April 18, 1689.]

Dec. 16, "This day the remainder of dragoons that came hither marched hence, being a convoy to six horses laden with money, which was raised by customs and excise in this city.—Note, Tobacco paid 5*d.* per lb. duty."

Dec. 16, the King, driven back by contrary winds, returned to Whitehall, and the same night published an Order of Council against tumults. "He was received by the multitude with such shouts, acclamations, and expressions of affection, as can scarce be expressed. That was a day of triumph for him: no man remembered he had ever seen the like. Ringing of bells, bonfires, and all things used on the greatest solemnities, to testify joy, was now practised."—*History of the Revolutions under the Stuarts.*

Dec. 17, the King was removed at midnight, under a Dutch guard, to Rochester, which he chose in preference to Hampton-Court.

Dec. 23, he embarked for France, finally.

Bristol was taken possession of, for the Prince of Orange, by the Earl of Shrewsbury and Sir John Guise.

1689 Jan. 11, at the election for representatives of Bristol to the Convention, Sir Richard Hart and Sir John Knight were chosen; Mr. Thomas Day and Mr. Robert Yates being the unsuccessful candidates.

Jan. 12, the new Parliament met.

Feb. 2, both Houses agreed that James II. had abdicated the Government, and that the throne was thereby vacant.

WILLIAM AND MARY.

Feb. 13, proclaimed King and Queen.

March 12, King James landed at Kinsale, with French troops.

March 16, in a speech to Parliament, King William intimated his desire that the Dissenters might be admitted into places of trust and profit, and that new oaths might be framed for their satisfaction; but the Houses rejected the proposal.

April 13, Gilbert Ironside, nineteenth Bishop of Bristol; Jonathan Trelawney having been translated to Exeter.

May 24, the royal assent given to the Toleration-Act.

July 22, an Act for abolishing Episcopacy in Scotland received the royal assent.

Sept. The standings of the fair in St. James's Church-yard produced to the Church-Wardens about £80.

1690 Feb. 24, Monday, commenced an election of Representatives in Parliament for Bristol; candidates, Sir Richard Hart, Sir John Knight (the former representatives), the Recorder of the city, and Mr. Robert Yates, merchant. The polling continued till two o'clock in the afternoon of Friday, when the Sheriffs declared Sir Richard Hart and Sir John Knight, duly elected.

July 1, the battle of the Boyne.

Sept. 5, the King and Prince George of Denmark sailed from Ireland. On the 6th they arrived in Kingroad, and lodged at Sir Robert Southwell's, at Kingsweston, that night. Sir Robert was His Majesty's Principal Secretary of State in Ireland, and companion of his journey. (See 1748.) "The next day, being Sunday, multitudes of people went from Bristol to see him. They came from thence the same day, in the Duke of Beaufort's coaches to Bristol, and, without staying any, rid directly to the Duke of Beaufort's houses." Another MS. says, "The King was received by the Mayor (Arthur Hart, merchant) and Aldermen; who walked in their scarlet gowns, bareheaded, to Lawford's Gate, where

A. D.

1690 they took their leave of him; His Majesty being then going to the Duke of Beaufort's, at Badminton; so that he made no stay in this city, not so much as to alight from his coach." The King and Prince arrived at Kensington on the 10th.

1691   Jan. 11, Sir John Duddlestone, knt. and tobacco-merchant, created a baronet.*

March 4, an earthquake was felt in Bristol.

Newgate re-built, by a tax on the inhabitants of 6d. in the pound. The cost was about £1600.—The Tolzey adjoining the Church in St. Thomas-street finished.

Edward Colston, esq. purchased of the Corporation 2 acres 3 quarters and 37 perches of pasture-ground, on St. Michael's Hill, just above the site of St. Mary Magdalen's Nunnery, called the Turtles, or Jonas Leages, on which he built the Alms-house and Chapel, and three other messuages. The alms-house contains twelve men and twelve women. Trustees, the Society of Merchant-Venturers. The charge of building and finishing this house amounted to about £2500.

John Hall, twentieth Bishop; with whom began the annual feast of the Clergy and Sons of the Clergy.†

Sir John Knight, mayor, raised a wall around the Hotwell-spring, to prevent the tide from mixing with the water.

Richard Lane, sugar-baker, mayor, occupied the great house, St. Augustin's Place. William Opie, tobacconist, one of the sheriffs, made a gift of 26s. a year to St. Peter's parish, for three poor people, in bread, weekly.

1692   The Great Crane on the Quay erected.

1693   "The new Key, from the Lower Crane to the Slip was built, and the Slip made."

"1. Cook, 1693," over the entrance to Cooke's Folly.

---

* When did John Duddlestone previously receive the honour of knighthood?—The recent post-haste go-by to the Magistrates, coupled with this addition to Sir John's dignity, would imply belief in the story, so ridiculously related, of his exclusive hospitality to Prince George. The Prince had visited Bristol, with his father-in-law, James, in 1686, and (as noticed, p. 241) dined at Sir William Hayman's in Small-street. Perhaps his visit incog. was when James became unpopular, and those who envied Sir John's blushing honours trumped up the story alluded to, in which he is said to be a bodice-maker, and his lady the wearer of a blue apron, with a style of phrase not exactly suited to a resident in so principal a situation as that of Mr. Norton's, the bookseller, where they lived. Both lie in All Saints' Church, on the right of the entrance by the north door.—This Corporation did not recover from the Royal slight. The equestrian statue was not erected until 1736. See 1701.

† Bishop Hall left a legacy of £70 per annum, to be distributed in Bibles, at the pleasure of his executors and administrators. That sum is now (1824) paid by Thomas Spilsbury, esq., the Bishop's grand-nephew, to the Bible-Society, and Bibles to the amount are received at the Society's abated prices.

A. D.

1693 Sept. 24, bayonets first used by the French, in a charge under Catinat, against the Confederates, near Turin.

1694 Froom-Gate removed,* with the house over it.

The St. James's Poor-house in Barr's Street built. See 1752.

Nov. An eagle shot in Sir John Smyth's Park at Ashton.

Dec. 28, Queen Mary died of small pox, aged 32. Bristol High Cross was hung with black.

WILLIAM III.

1695 Jan. 5, William Penn married Hannah, daughter of Thomas Callowhill, merchant, of Bristol.†

" This year guineas were advanced from 22s. to 30s. each, occasioned, as is supposed, by the clipt and counterfeit coin now amongst us; sixteen shillings of which have been weighed against one of King Charles's milled crowns, and found lighter."

June 15, a widow Scarlett, shop-keeper, in St. Thomas-street, was applied to by a soldier, for a pennyworth of tobacco, and he gave her a broad shilling for change; but not liking the tobacco, he required his money again, when she gave him a small clipped shilling. Upon complaint and search, instruments for clipping were found in her house, and on trial she was sentenced to be burnt in the street. The general lightness of the coin had produced many more such offenders in different parts of the city; of whom this was the first detection.

Guineas reduced to their legal value, by which many people sustained considerable loss. The base silver called in.

An Act of Parliament gave to a " Bristol Water-works Company" the right, title, and privilege, to serve and supply the inhabitants of Bristol with fresh water for two hundred years, upon payment of £166 13s. 4d. to the Chamber of Bristol every seventh year. A reservoir, still existing (1824) at Lawrence-Hill, was supplied from a place at Hanham called the Engine-Mill. See 1679.

Dec. 12, a mint set up to coin money, in the sugar-house behind St. Peter's Church.

Dec. 31, the Commons resolved to raise a supply of £1,200,000, to make good the deficiency of the clipped money,

* The wood-work doors of Froom-Gate, studded with iron, were transferred to the entrance of Edward Young & Co.'s premises in Lewin's Mead, where they still continue.
† From whom *Penn* (alias Tabernacle) street, and *Callowhill*-street, near what was called the Old Orchard.

A. D.

1695 by a tax on windows of 4*s.* per annum where there were ten, 8*s.* for twenty and more—to continue seven years.

1696   The Corporation of the Poor instituted by Act of Parliament, to commence after the 12th of May.   First meeting, at the Guildhall, May 19.

The Society of Merchants built the western wing of their Alms-house in King-street.

An Act of the 10th of this reign for erecting Hospitals, &c. in Tiverton, Devon, reciting this Bristol Act of the 7th and 8th, enacts additional clauses.   See 1714.

The Hotwell-House erected, with the pump raising the water 30 feet, at the cost of Sir Thomas Day (mayor in 1594), Robert Yate (mayor in 1593), Thomas Callowhill, and other citizens; a lease having been granted for that purpose by the Society of Merchants, as lords of the manor, for ninety years, at £5 per annum.

Oct. 28, a pamphlet, entitled "An Account of the Proceedings of the Commons in relation to the recoining the clipt money, and falling the price of guineas," was ordered to be burnt by the common hangman.

The Land-Bank, that had been established by Act of Parliament last year, and was to have raised two millions and a half, did not produce anything; which reduced the Government to very great straits.   About this time Bank-notes were discounted at 20 per cent. and Government-tallies at 40, 50, and 60 per cent.; which was no small inducement to the Court to listen to proposals of peace.   Nor were the French in a better condition; which made them equally pliable.

1697   Jan. 10, all hammered silver-money ceased to be lawful.

Sept. 20, Peace concluded at Ryswick, in which Matthew Prior was the English Secretary.   Oct. 29, proclaimed at the High Cross, St. Peter's and Temple Cross, St. Thomas and the Quay Pipes.   The conduits were set running with wine.   There was a great display of colours on the shipping, and on the tops of houses of the principal citizens, but very few of the churches had colours on their towers and steeples.

"The new river water brought into the city through elm-pipes from Hanham Mills."—Considering the number of more ancient conduits of water into the heart of the city, that even now (1824) bestow their original plenitude of supply, and the facility with which water is everywhere obtained by piercing to no great depth, it is not surprising that this speculation soon failed.   The freehold and leasehold land near Bristol, and a small piece of leasehold land in the parish of Bitton, belonging to the Company, were sold by auction

A. D.

1697 on the 27th of June 1811. The Bristol Dock Company purchased Hanham Mills, but not the right of supplying water. See the Schedule of the Dock-Act.

The Mint ceased to work, after coining 40,050,000 pounds. There had been brought into Bristol, of hammered money and wrought plate, as much as made, in weight, 146,977 oz. The house was purchased by the Guardians of the Poor, to employ the pauper-youth of the city in spinning cotton.

1698 The High Cross repaired and very richly painted and gilded, so that it was thought very few if any such erections in England surpassed it.

St. James's Church repaired, at an expense of £600.

The bulks of the houses on the Bridge taken down.

" This year a pile of brick building was erected on Broad Key; the first brick building in this city."

The Square in the Marsh commenced building.

1699 The Society of Merchants built the eastern wing of their Alms-house in King-street, rebuilt the old centre, and united both angles.

May 20, Christopher Codrington, esq. fellow of Allsouls, Oxford, made Captain-General and Governor of the Caribbee Islands, in the room of his father, Col. Codrington, deceased.

1700 Aug. 4, died Mrs. Pugsley. Her history and the particulars of her bequest to the inhabitants of St. Nicholas Almshouse, are appended to the narrative of the siege of 1645, p. 201.

Dec. 14, the Commons, enquiring into the forfeited estates in Ireland, found that 49,517 acres had been granted to the Earl of Romney, 108,633 acres to the Earl of Albemarle, 135,820 acres to the Earl of Portland, 26,480 acres to the Earl of Athlone, 36,148 acres to the Earl of Galloway, and 95,649 acres, being the private estate of King James, and worth £25,995 per annum, to the Lady Elizabeth Villars, countess of Orkney, a she-favourite of King William's.

Dec. 15, the House resolved to bring in a Bill of Resumption, to apply all the forfeited estates and interests in Ireland, and all grants thereof, and of the revenues of the Crown there, since the 30th of Feb. 1688, to the use of the public.

1701 Jan. 18, the Commons resolved that the passing of the said grants had been the occasion of contracting great debts upon the nation, and levying heavy taxes on the people.

April 11, the royal assent given to the Resumption-Bill.

Temple Church ceiled and beautified.

The Merchants rebuilt their Hall in King-street.

The Merchant-Tailors also rebuilt their Alms-house in

A. D.

1701 Merchant-street. One account says, " it was erected by
Sir John Duddlestone, bodice-maker, and
doublet-maker." The former Hospital was in Marsh-street.
Sir John Duddlestone was for several years Governor of the
Corporation of the Poor.

1702   Feb. 21, the King thrown from his horse in riding from
Kensington towards Hampton-Court, which broke his right
collar-bone. March 6, he died, in the 52d year of his age.

ANNE,

Daughter of King James and youngest sister of the late
Queen Mary, aged 37 years.

April 23, St. George's day, the Queen was crowned. The
following ceremony took place in this city:

The same day the Mayor (John Hawkins, brewer), Aldermen,
Sheriffs, &c. went to the Cathedral; before whom marched the
Militia—the Hospital and Mint Boys—the Companies with their
colours—twenty-four young maidens, dressed in night-veils and
white hoods, with fans in their hands, being led, as their captain,
by a comely young woman, clad in a close white dress, wearing
on her head a perriwig and hat, carrying in her hand a half-pike—
the Constables of the Wards attended at a convenient distance,
followed by the Mint-Maids with their Overseers; then came the
Red Maids, each of them carrying a sprig of holly or box, gilded
with gold; after whom, preceded by two drums, followed eight
young men in Holland shirts, with a large knot of ribbon on their
shoulders, having the inscription, " God save the Queen," and a
naked sword in their hands, on their heads a coronet of laurel.
Then came twenty-four young damsels in sarsnet hoods, with ribbons in their bosoms, &c. bearing in their hands a gilded bow and
arrow. Then came several of the principal citizen's daughters, the
two last supporting a very splendid crown before Mrs. Mayoress,
followed by the wives of the Aldermen and all the Common-Council,
the City-Musicians playing before them. The churches, houses,
and ships, were all decorated. St. Stephen's Church-porch cost
£30, as did St. John's Gate, in the devices and ornaments that
were about them. There was an incessant firing from the shipping
and the cannon planted in the Grove* for that purpose.—In the
evening appeared a company of young men in Holland shirts, with
a naked sword in one hand, and leading in the other each a young
woman in a white waistcoat and red petticoat, with night head-
dress and a white straw hat. After them came a number of men who
were more robust, bearing the effigy of the Pope, dressed as an

* The Grove facing Redcliff-Back has been despoiled of its trees within the last
three or four years. 1824.

702old man, with a long beard and white locks, on his head a triple crown and in his hand a crosier; a scarlet mantle on his shoulders, trimmed with white ermine, &c. Before him went many with vizors and crosiers in their hands, preceded by an officer with a little bell; and, finally, they flung the Pope into a bonfire.

May 18, the Proclamation of War against France and Spain was read at the High Cross and other usual places, by the Sheriffs, with the Mayor and Aldermen.

Sept. 1, the Queen and Prince George, her husband, were received at Lawford's Gate, by the Mayor (John Hawkins, brewer) and Corporation, and conducted from Temple-street, through the Long-Row, to Sir Thomas Day's house at the Bridge-end, in the following order: A great number of horsemen, including sixty captains of ships—twelve of the Queen's coaches, containing her suite—eighteen of the clergy, bareheaded—the Common Council, the Aldermen—the Mayor, carrying the pearl sword—part of the Queen's guards before and behind her coach—coaches of the nobility and gentry. Her Majesty was dressed in purple, mourning for the late King. The Royal coach and trappings of the horses were black, as were those of the nobility. With the Queen rode the Prince and two ladies of honour. The dinner was at the expense of the City; and between four and five o'clock, after knighting Mr. Mayor,* the Royal and noble visitants returned to Bath. The Square in the Marsh was hence named Queen-Square.

Queen Elizabeth's (formerly Gaunts') Hospital began to be rebuilt in a more commodious manner. The number of the boys increased to 40. See 1783.

Foster's Alms-house, on St. Michael's Hill, rebuilt by the Corporation.

Dec. 14, the Queen ordered *semper eadem* to be used as the motto in her coat of arms.

1703 Edward Colston, esq. proposed to increase Queen Elizabeth's Hospital, by a further endowment from himself, for 100 boys instead of 44, provided the Corporation would erect a fabric equal to their reception; but this was not agreed to. See 1709.

Aug. 20, the Queen and Prince visited Bath, where the Mayor of this city (William Lewis, soap-boiler) and some of the Aldermen, with the Town-Clerk, waited upon them;

* Sir John Hawkins's mansion and brewery, were the premises on the east-side of Temple-street, the original front of which remains, now divided between the Colston's Arms public-house and another tenement, with Mr. Shurmer's waggon-warehouse and stables, extending in depth to Temple-Back.

1703 and the Queen conferred upon the Mayor the honour of knighthood.

Nov. 20, about midnight, the wind at W. S. W., commenced a tremendous storm of thunder, hail and rain, in which the Cathedral suffered much injury.* Three of the pinnacles of St. Stephen's Church fell through the roof, into the body of the church. A boat might have sailed through the whole of Temple-street. The loss to the city was about £100,000. In the Thames, the royal navy, just returned from the Straits, suffered the loss of four third-rates, one second-rate, and four fourth-rates; and many others of less force were cast away upon the coast of England. Fifteen hundred seamen were lost, besides those cast away in merchant-vessels. At the Palace, in Wells, Dr. Kidder, bishop of that see, and his lady, were both killed in their bed, by the fall of a stack of chimneys.

1704 Jan. 17, the Queen published an order for the regulation of the Play-houses, prohibiting them to act anything contrary to religion and good manners. In Bristol the acting of stage-plays was prohibited, and the Theatre in Tucker-street converted into a Meeting-house.

The number of ale-houses limited to 220.

" This year, and the last year, the Councill-house was new-built and faced with freestone."—This re-building was but partial. See 1788.

Mr. Henry Smith, from the collection of Mr. G. G. Catcott, possesses a pen-and-ink drawing, by Henry Blondel, of a remarkable tree, at this time growing in the western part of Redcliff Church-yard, the arms of which were supported by six or seven props. The fence of the church-yard was now a thick-set hedge, and the gate facing Bedminster, a common field-gate.

1705 The first brass made in England, at Baptist-Mills. The workmen were brought from Holland. Copper first made in England by Sir Simon Clark, whose assayists, Messrs. Coster and Wayne, established a copper-manufactory near Bristol, in conjunction with Sir Abraham Elton, bart.

1706 March 6, the Act for ratification of the Articles of Union with Scotland received the royal assent.

The pent-house against St. Nicholas Church-yard, on the Back, was built.

Aug. 10, at the general quarter-session, the Grand Jury presented " Mr. Power and his company for acting of plays

---

* The great west-window and the north-window over the principal entrance bear the date 1704, and the window over the principal north door, 1705.

1706 within the liberties of this city."—This, we believe, was in the building at present occupied as Lady Huntingdon's Chapel. The Theatre at Jacob's Wells now probably became the place of retreat for the drama.

Oct. 28, the Queen's husband, Prince George of Denmark, died of asthma and dropsy, aged 55 years.

1708 The winter of 1708-9 was very severe. Wheat advanced
1709 from 4s. to 8s. and 9s. a bushel.

May 21, a body of about two hundred colliers came into the city from Kingswood, and, being joined by some of the idle poor, it was thought necessary to muster the militia. The mob being promised to have wheat at 6s. per bushel the next market-day, the tumult was appeased.

The bank or island called the Green Bank, on the river Froom, above the Great Tower, was walled in, and the Quay thereby greatly enlarged, and two ships were built thereon.

The College-Green railed in, and the walks laid out with young trees.

Redcliff-Church repaired, &c. by means of a brief for £5000. The Chamber contributed £200.

Edward Colston, esq. purchased of the widow of Alderman Lane, sugar-boiler, the great house on St. Augustin's Back, and established it as a hospital, with a master and two ushers, for 100 boys, to be fed, clothed, and instructed in writing and arithmetic, till they should attain 14 years, with £10 each as fee of apprenticeship.* The expense of erection and endowment, all in his life-time, was £40,000. The estates in lands and ground-rents produced at this time £1318 15s. 6d. The charge of fitting up the school and dwelling-house was about £11,000.

The Custom-House, Queen-Square, commenced building.

Now began the political fever of High Church and Low Church.

Sept. Sir John Elwill, of Bristol, knight, created a baronet.

1710 July 24, at Westminster, the Queen, upon the petition of the Mayor, Burgesses, and Commonalty, granted what is called the Great Charter of Bristol. See the last in Mr. Seyer's Collection.

In this Charter, Her Majesty confirms all the grants of her predecessors, unless contradicted by her own; and, without expressly abrogating, pardons all who may have offended against the Charter of 1684.† The designation of the Body Corporate is, " the Mayor, Burgesses, and Commonalty." The Mayor is nominated on the 15th

* See 1782. † See note, p. 231.

1710 of September, yearly. The Recorder is first Alderman; and, with eleven other Aldermen, to remain so during good behaviour. Forty-two persons, besides the Mayor, form the Common-Council. Out of these are chosen, annually, the two Sheriffs. The Town-Clerk, and the Steward of the Sheriff's Court, and two Coroners, respectively, continue in office so long as they behave well. The Mayor and Common-Council fill up all vacancies, impose penalties upon such persons as refuse to take offices to which they may be elected, and make any such ordinances for the government of the city as are not contrary to the laws of the realm. On the death of an Alderman, the Mayor and Aldermen are to choose a successor from the Common-Council-men. The other officers to be elected by the Common-Council. The Recorder to be a barrister of five years, and the Town-Clerk and Steward of the Sheriff's Court barristers of three years standing. The Mayor, Recorder, and Aldermen, to be Justices of the Peace; the Mayor, Recorder, and any one of the Aldermen, to be Justices of Oyer and Terminer and Gaol-delivery. Not to be accountable to the Sovereign for fines, forfeitures, &c. Three Justices (including the Mayor or Recorder, and two of the five senior Aldermen) to hold four Sessions of the Peace in every year. Oaths of Aldermen and Justices to be taken before the Recorder, or, in his absence, the Mayor. Mayor, Aldermen, &c. no longer removable by the Crown. The Common-Council have power to alter the time and place of the markets, and make by-laws for their regulation, but which are to be put in writing.

Sept. 9, the Moon being nine days in her wane, the tide, or first of the flood, which should have been about eleven o'clock, came in about eight o'clock, flowed one foot at the Gibb, and then ebbed; it came in again, the same morning, at eleven o'clock; so that it flowed and ebbed twice in twelve hours.

Abraham Elton, Mayor; Edward Mountjoy and Abraham Elton, Sheriffs.

Nov. 25, Edward Colston and Joseph Earl, esqrs. returned to Parliament for Bristol.

Cross-rows of lime-trees planted in Queen-square. There were also four rows planted off the Gibb, along the river's side, on the back of the south angle of the Square. A sufficient reason why they were not suffered to remain, it would be difficult to produce.

1711 An Act of Parliament obtained, at the expense of the Duke of Beaufort, to complete the navigation from Bristol to Bath. See 1724.

Edward Colston endowed the Boys' School in Temple-street, of which parish he was a native, for the instruction of forty boys, and new clothing them every year.

The tower of All Saints' Church rebuilt.

A. D.

1711   The Custom-House in Queen-Square completed, which cost £2777 7s. 5d.

A stone bridge built over the river Froom, at Earl's Mead, at the charge of Nathaniel Wade, Abraham Hooke, and some others. This is vulgarly called Traitor's Bridge.

Sept. 3, Dr. Robinson, bishop of Bristol, made Lord Privy Seal, in the room of the Duke of Newcastle, who was killed by a fall from his horse.

Dec. 23, the Bishop was appointed one of the Plenipotentiaries for the Treaty of Utrecht.

1712   July. A very prevailing influenza.

July 12, died Richard Cromwell, in his 90th year.

William Goldwin, A.M. of King's College, Cambridge, master of the Bristol Grammar-School, published his "Poetical Description of Bristol;" folio, pp. 28.

The Dock at Sea-Mills was begun.* See 1750.

1713   May 19, Peace proclaimed, at the usual places, by the two Sheriffs.

May 22, Newspapers first franked.

John Gray founded the Charity-School for Girls, on the western side of Temple-street. The school was originally instituted on Temple-Back; to which Mrs. Mary Gray gave £50, in 1699. See 1740.

A German work, "The Principal Routes in Europe," printed at Hamburg, stated that the principal inns at this time in Bristol were *The Man of War* and *The Prodigal Son*.

Monday, Sept. 7, an election for Parliament commenced, in which Sir William Daines was the favourite of the low party, Mr. Thomas Edwards, jun. of the high party, and Col. Joseph Earl divided both parties. The expenses were £2257 9s. 7d., including "Bonney's note for printing, £27." —The contest lasted till the Tuesday se'nnight, and broke up with broken heads, in every respect a drawn battle.

Nov. 2, Mr. Colston's birth-day, the annual dinner of the Loyal Society. Mr. Colston† being aged, he was not present, but represented by Henry, duke of Beaufort.

* This was about the commencement of that enormous wen upon the face of funding-speculations, the "South-Sea Bubble." In 1718, the King was appointed Governor of the company. In June 1720, the stock rose to 890. In Sept. it fell to 150. In Jan. 1721, the King gave orders to discharge such of the Directors as held offices under the Crown; and in February the Lords resolved that their declaration of dividends was a villanous artifice, to delude and defraud His Majesty's good subjects. The whole history of South-Sea Stock is curious and instructive.

† In the Cathedral, affixed to the canopy of the stall now assigned to the Archdeacon of Dorset, are three small carved shields, bearing this gentleman's armorial ensign, and his initials, E. C. The venerable philanthropist was a daily attendant upon divine service, and just previous to his decease had made a contract to re-pave the whole of the choir with marble, at his own private cost, to the amount of £600.

A. D.

1714   March 8, Dr. Smalridge made Bishop of Bristol and Lord
Almoner.

An Act of Parliament, among other matters, to increase the
number of Guardians of the Poor, by appointment of the
Church-Wardens, repealing the clauses of 10 W. III. " to
render more effectual, &c."

Aug. 1, the Queen died of apoplexy, in the 50th year of
her age, leaving none behind her out of eighteen children.

The European Magazine, vol. 23, (for Jan. 1793,) p. 47,
contains an engraving and description of a remarkable
cobweb, discovered in the summer-house of Mr. Brayne,
cooper, in a garden in Baldwin-street, on the day when the
news of the Queen's death arrived in Bristol: Mr. Henry
Smith possesses the original drawing, by H. Blondel, and
part of the cobweb, as preserved by the Rev. A. S. Catcott.

GEORGE,

Elector of Brunswick Lunenburgh, succeeded to the Crown,
by virtue of several Acts of Parliament for securing the Protestant succession.

Sept. 18, the King and the Prince-Royal landed at Greenwich. Great rejoicings in this city, by ringing of bells, a
discharge of cannon from Brandon-Hill, &c. The shops
were shut, and the city illuminated.

Oct. 15, John lord Harvey, of Ickworth, created Earl of
Bristol.

Oct. 20, the coronation-rejoicings in the city were disgraced by attacks, in the evening, upon the windows of
Dissenters. The house of Mr. Stephens, a baker, in Tucker-
street, was entered, partitions were broken down, boxes and
drawers forced open, and bread, plate, and other goods,
plundered, upon pretence of the provocation given by
Stephens and his son in defending their persons and property. Two people were killed and several wounded. A
Quaker, who stood in the entry, endeavouring to persuade
the mob to desist from their violence, was by one of them
knocked down and trampled upon in such a manner that he
died the next day. One of the mob was shot in the head, as
supposed by young Stephens, and died a few days afterward.
Stephens, jun. ran another through the body, but the wound
did not prove mortal. Thirteen of the depredators were committed to Newgate; but the greatest criminals absconded.
—Upon application of the Magistrates, His Majesty sent a

A. D.

1714 special commission to try the rioters in custody: three of the judges and four counsellors arrived Nov. 25, and the proceedings lasted nearly a week. About ten persons, indicted as rioters, were each fined twenty nobles and imprisoned three months, to give security for nine months more; one, indicted for felony, was ordered to be whipped; the rest were acquitted.

The Draw-Bridge, with two arches of stone, completed, at an expense to the City-Chamber of £1066 6s. 1d. Previously, the only communication between the centre of the city and the Cathedral was through Christmas-street and Host *alias* Horse-street.

1715 Jan. The first newspaper published in Bristol, now appeared; the same which was known, till 1809, as "Sarah Farley's Bristol Journal."

April 22, an eclipse of the Sun. It commenced a little after eight o'clock, and continued for two hours. The total darkness lasted about two minutes; during which the stars became visible, and the birds and other animals seemed to be in great consternation.

Mr. Stephens, at the assize in September, before Judge Powis, sued four of the persons who had been convicted of rioting at his house, and recovered sixty pounds. Mark Goddard also sued James Harris and John Cox, for damages sustained by rioting at the election in 1713, and recovered £187 16s.

On the day of swearing the new Mayor, arrived the Earl of Berkeley, Lord Lieutenant of the counties of Gloucester and Bristol; and, at the same time, Brigadier Stanwix's regiment of foot was quartered here, for the prevention of insurrections.

Sunday, Oct. 2, discovery was made of a design to seize this city for the Pretender; whereupon the militia were mustered, the gates shut, and cannon placed at several of them, and divers of the citizens (including William Hart, esq.*) were apprehended and committed to the Marshalsea, on suspicion of being in the interest of the Pretender, or not well affected towards His Majesty's person and government.

St. James's Square (commenced in 1707) was completed this year.

A severe frost, from the latter end of November till the 8th of February. Much distress among the poor. Relieved by collections in the parishes. The Corporation contributed £100.

* Sir Richard Hart was mayor in 1680. Arthur Hart, at the same time one of the sheriffs, was mayor in 1689.

K k

A. D.

1716 This summer, an alms-house, the gift of Mr. Alderman
George Stevens (mayor in 1706-7) was erected in Temple-
street, for twelve poor persons. (It is intended, upon the rebuilding of Doctor White's Alms-house, to place the figure
of Neptune as guard over the waste-pipe in front of this
building.)

Dec. 26, about three o'clock in the afternoon, a fire commenced in Wine-street, and continued for seven hours. It
began at the house of Mr. Plomer, a mercer, near the High
Cross, and burnt two more houses to the ground. The wind
being WW. by N. with a brisk gale, and several other houses
being on fire, the inhabitants also of High-street and St. Maryport-street were in great alarm.

See " Memoirs of himself, by Mr. John Fox," or an extract in the Monthly Repository, vol. xvi. p. 193. Mr. Fox
was in London this year, and became acquainted with Mr.
Jeremiah Burroughs, a dissenting-preacher at Blackfriars,
who was a musical amateur, and hereafter became Collector
of the Customs in the port of Bristol, having married a niece
of Mr. Knight, cashier to the South-Sea Company.

1717 A dome, &c. added to the tower of All Saints' Church.
This must have been at least five years in progress. Mr.
Goldwin, in his " Poetical Description of Bristol," published
in 1712, after lauding the Council-House, as one of " two
noble structures" " on either side the publick Tolzey," adds,

> " The adverse frame unpolisht greatness shows,
> And, true Church-work, in slow advances grows;
> Not want of zeal, or chearful gifts of gold,
> But jarring schemes the pious work withold:
> When nimbler hands th' imperfect Dome compleat,
> 'Twill shine in beauty, and its rival greet."

The Fish-market removed from High-street to the Quay,
north side of St. Stephen's Church; the ground allotted for
the purpose being considerably raised and railed in; and, to
give room for it, the Conduit was taken down and rebuilt
nearer the river. See 1771.

The Quay-wall lengthened 280 feet, as far as the Gibb, up
the river Avon, and the slip made for the Ferry to Redcliff-
Back; another at the graving-place, opposite Trine-Mill,
and a third at the Gibb.

May 29, " guards were placed at several parts of London,
who sufficiently corrected the insolence of those who dared
to wear oak-boughs in memory of the Restoration."

June 20, died the Mayor of Bristol, John Day. He was
buried in St. Werburgh's Church; the funeral being attended
by fifty - two coaches, and " two hundred and fifty-eight

A. D.

1717 persons, all men of note, besides bearers and officers, and six ministers."

June 26, John Clements elected as Mr. Day's successor, for the remainder of the year. In the account of the ceremony of swearing in at the Guildhall, we find mention of " the Charters both old and new, the four swords, the red book, the pocket and other seals, &c."

Dec. 6, Abraham Elton, sen. of Bristol, esq. created a baronet.

1718 The first insurance-office in Bristol against fire, The Crown, established; capital, £40,000.

An Act of Parliament, repealing the appointment, in 1714, of Junior Church-Wardens, as Guardians of the Poor, and " for the better explaining, &c."

Edmund Mountjoy, Mayor. In this mayoralty the *ducking-stool* on the Weir was used as a cure for scolding, in one particularly inveterate instance; but the husband of the lady whose " evil spirit" was so " laid," when the year of civic supremacy expired, brought his action of battery in behalf of his peaceful rib, before Sir Peter King at the Guildhall, " and the man (says our authority) recovered such damages, that the Ex-Mayor could not endure the mention of *cold-duck* any more." (Qu. Was this species of discipline the origin of the endearing domestic appellation, *my duck?*)— Peace to the remains of that preserver of " a quiet life!" As true-bred antiquaries, we would not have its strength and beauty restored for the world. In the nineteenth century is seldom heard a wish to revive its influence. *We* let the sweet tongues wag without restraint, either wet or dry. The fair interlocutors enjoy their tea the better, and sleep the sounder, for the free exercise of their loyal and dutiful lungs.

May 17, 18, so much rain, that the river Froom overflowed as high as the wall at the ducking-stool.

720 The wife of the Rev. Samuel Bury, named Elizabeth, aged 76, celebrated in an elegy by Dr. Isaac Watts, buried in St. James's Church. Her husband died in 1729.

721 Sir Abraham Elton, bart. and Joseph Earl, esq. chosen representatives in Parliament for Bristol.

The Gaunts' Chapel, St. Mark's, since the sequestration used as a chapel for French Protestant refugees, fitted up for the constant use of the Corporation, with a new peal of bells. A Chapel for the French Protestants built in Orchard-street; completed in 1727. See 1818.

Strange's Alms-house rebuilt, below St. John's steps. See 1630.

A. D.

1721 Simon de Burton's Alms-house, Long-Row, St. Thomas-street, rebuilt.

Bridewell (of old a fortified tower, with *Monken Bridge*) rebuilt by the Corporation, at the expense of £1053 3s.

The Quay-wall at the Back continued upward, from the end of King-street.

An Act of Parliament obtained to build an Exchange.

April 28, William Codrington, esq. of Doddington, Gloucestershire, created a baronet.*

Oct. 11, died Edward Colston, aged 85 years. He gave £100 towards erection of the organ of St. James's Church, and left more than £100,000 among his relatives, notwithstanding his immense public largesses.

1722 A gunpowder-repository built at Tower Harritz by the Corporation; which cost £143 18s. 5d.

Stoke's Croft School and Alms-house founded by Abraham Hooke, merchant (sheriff in 1706), and others of the Lewin's Mead Society of Protestant Dissenters.

Mrs. Elizabeth Blanchard died, who had founded an alms-house at the north-east end of Milk-street, for five poor women, being Baptists of the society meeting in the Pithay, which in 1815 removed to Old King-street.

The head of the Back, on the Avon, from the Conduit to the first Slip (the Henroost-slip, from a public-house opposite), was widened.

The wharf "under the Bank," north side of the Froom, was erected for the landing of timber.

1724 The plan for completing the navigation to Bath (see 1711) began to be put in execution, by dividing the estimated expense into thirty-two shares, for which subscriptions were obtained.

Sept. 7, died Sir William Daines, alderman of Bristol, and several times its representative in Parliament. He was succeeded by James Dunning, esq.

1725 The Conduit on the Back was rebuilt.

1726 An Act of Parliament obtained for Turnpikes around the city. The colliers rioted, because they were not exempted from the toll, and entirely destroyed the gates.

Queen-Square completed. The wharf continued on the Back, south of Queen-square, for 180 feet forward. The cost was £488 12s. 7d.

The street opened, and the Market-house (now the Cheese-market) between Wine-street and St. Maryport-street, com-

* There was a Francis Codrington, sheriff in 1542, and a Richard Codrington, master of the Mercers and Linen-Drapers' Company in 1668.

A. D.

1726menced erecting for the sale of corn; and in the following year the old Market-house, in the centre of Wine-street, was taken down.

1727 June 11, the King died of paralysis, at Osnaburgh, on his progress to Hanover, aged 67. Succeeded by his eldest son,

GEORGE II.

Born Oct. 30, 1683.

Peter Day, Mayor of Bristol; Ezekiel Longman and Henry Combe, Sheriffs.

Dec. 27, the navigation to Bath completed; when the first barge was sent to that city, laden with deals, lead, and meal.

About this time the notion prevailed that title-deeds, &c. were enclosed in Mr. Canynges' cofre, deposited with other chests in the unglazed muniment-room over the north porch of St. Mary Redcliff Church. Such deeds as appeared of value were removed to the vestry-room. The uncle of Chatterton's father was then sexton of the church. The poet's father was master of Pile-street School. See 1739.

Sir Abraham Elton, bart. and Baron Scroop chosen representatives in Parliament for Bristol. " Mr. Hart (says one MS.) sold his election." This gentleman was the leading capitalist in the clothing-trade.

1728 May. The Princess Amelia came from Bath by water, and was received by the Corporation at Countess *alias* Counter Slip. Her Royal Highness was entertained at the Merchants' Hall, " in such a manner as greatly surprized Mr. Nash, the then Master of the Ceremonies at Bath." The Princess returned the same evening.

July 23, Baron Scroop chosen Recorder of Bristol, upon the resignation of Lord Chief Justice Eyre, who had filled the office upward of twenty years.

Eight new bells cast for All Saints' Church.

1729 Sept. 29, while the Corporation was at Church, preparatory to swearing in the new Mayor (Samuel Stoakes), the weavers, who had been riotously disposed on account of wages, assembled without Lawford's Gate, and came to the house of Stephen Feachem, on Castle-Ditch, a very considerable manufacturer, determined to level it with the ground and murther him, unless he would raise their pay from 7s. to 8s. per piece; but, with the assistance of a guard of twenty soldiers, they were repulsed, seven of them being killed

A. D.

1729 and many wounded.   The serjeant who commanded was
killed by an accidental shot from his own party.   The rioters
however persevered, till the whole regiment was drawn out,
with the Sheriffs, &c. at their head; when the proclamation
was read, and several of the rioters still refusing to disperse,
they were seized and committed to Newgate.   But at the
ensuing session they were discharged; no evidence appearing
against them.

1730   Redcliff-Gate rebuilt.

Another Turnpike-Act was passed, in amendment of that
of 1722, and exempting the colliers from the toll; but the
gates were nevertheless soon cut down.

1731   Arthur Taylor, Mayor, who resided in the house now
occupied by Messrs. Franklyn and Co. St. Nicholas Back;
from an unfinished sketch of which, made during the
mayoralty, by " Rt. Harman," a finished drawing has been
executed by Mr. O'Neill, as well as of several parts of the
highly ornamented interior.

1733   The Great Crane near the Gibb erected by Mr. Padmore,
and the Mud-Dock completed, at the expense of the Society
of Merchants.

Sir Abraham Elton, bart. and Thomas Coster, esq. chosen
MM.P.   Baron Scroop had rendered himself unpopular by
voting for the Excise-Bill.

August.   Mr. John Vaughan, silversmith, residing opposite
to the High Cross, in the house now the Castle Bank,*
offered to swear before the magistrates that in every high
wind his house and life were endangered by its shaking and
threatening to fall.   The Cross was therefore taken down,
and the parts deposited in the Guildhall.

1734   Feb. 21, the Prince of Orange, being at Bath for his
health, visited Bristol.   He was met at Brislington Common
by the principal inhabitants, wearing orange-coloured
cockades.   Jacob Elton, esq. was the Mayor.   An -elegant
entertainment was provided for His Highness at the Merchants' Hall, and there was a ball in the evening for the
ladies, which he opened by dancing a minuet with Mr.

* We have learnt, but without the requisite appendage of a date, that the proprietor
of this house, of another situated near to it, and of the house formerly occupied by
Mr. Norton, bookseller, and latterly by Mr. Crisp, shoemaker, being in Holland, "took
a fancy" to as many different styles of front; and brought over the wood-work of all
three in one ship from Amsterdam.   The lovers of the picturesque in street-architecture
deplore the loss of two out of these three ingredients in the charm of variety; but the Castle
Bank is designed to retain, while old father Time shall permit, the stability of its proprietors.   The Chamber receives a ground-rent for about six feet square of the east end of the
banking-shop, towards the street, devised by will of Alderman Whitson.

A. D.

1734 Sheriff Pope's lady. About nine His Highness retired to his lodgings at Mr. Peter Day's, in the Square, and the next morning returned to Bath. March 14, His Highness was married to the Princess Anne, the King's eldest daughter.

S. and N. Buck's two Views of this city, north-west from Brandon-Hill, and south-east from Pile-Hill, bear this date.

Temple-Gate rebuilt.

Thomas Secker, the twenty-sixth Bishop of Bristol.

The Deanery (Dove-House) considerably repaired, by Dean Creswicke.

The sect called Methodists first appeared.

1735 The High Cross re-erected in College Green, and finely beautified.

Aug. 6, Baron Scroop having resigned, Michael Foster, esq. was chosen Recorder of Bristol.

In this month the equestrian statue of King William was erected in Queen-square, after a model presented by Rysbrach. It cost £1800. The operative artist was not Rysbrach himself, but Van Oost, who then resided in Dublin, and taught flower-painting. This we derive from Mr. Gahagan's recognition of the style.

Sept. 10, was tried, before the new Recorder, Capt. James Newth, for the murther of his wife.—See the Gentleman's Magazine of this date, for a description of the treatment of his body by the mob, after it had been buried in a cross-road near the city.

736 March 25, the Act against Witchcraft repealed.

A survey made this year states that Bristol and its suburbs contained 1300 houses and 80,000 inhabitants.

The Bristol Charters published, as translated by the Rev. Charles Godwyn, B.D. at the request of the Corporation. See 1812.

737 The Mayor, Nathaniel Day, caused the table of Loan-money and Benefactions to be put up in the Council-House, for public inspection.

Dec. 13, the Bristol Infirmary opened in Earl-street, on part of the site of the present building. The house was built and finished at the sole expense of John Elbridge, deputy comptroller of. His Majesty's Customs. See 1745.

"That part of the penthouse at the Back-Gate, which much incommoded the passage of carriages, was taken down, and likewise the house that stood between the gate and the river, and the way laid quite open." This gate adjoined the site of the Cross-Keys public-house.

738 The Prince and Princess of Wales visited Bristol. They

A. D.

1738 were received by the Corporation (William Jefferys being Mayor, and Henry Combe and Giles Bayly, Sheriffs,) at Temple-Gate, where a platform was erected, and the Recorder addressed their Royal Highnesses in an elegant speech. The trading-companies* headed the procession up High-street, and onward through Marsh-street, to Mr. Sheriff Combe's house in the Square; where the royal pair received the addresses of the Clergy, the Merchant-Adventurers, &c.; and they were afterwards entertained at the Merchants' Hall. The evening concluded with a display of fire-works by Dr. Desaguliers.

The City-Library finished.

The purchase of lands for the Exchange resolved upon.

1739 The Corporation erected an additional building to Barstaple's Trinity Alms-house, on the north-side of Lawford's Gate.

Snowgate's Alms-house, in All-Saints' Lane, sold for £420; and the south and east parts of the Exchange built on its site. The poor were removed to a new building adjoining St. John's Alms-house. See 1743.

Redcliff and St. Thomas Charity-School, for boys, founded in Pile-street. The house was built by Giles Malpus, pin-maker, in St. Thomas-street.

Sept. 30, died Mr. Coster, M.P. at his house in College-Green. He was succeeded in the representation by Robert Southwell, esq.

John Elbridge, esq. founder of the Infirmary, died. He bequeathed £3000, to endow a school which he had erected at the north entrance of Fort-lane, St. Michael's Hill, for the clothing of twenty-four female-children, once a year, and for teaching them reading, writing, and sewing. In 1748 his executors erected the present house, with two apartments, for the habitation of the master and the mistress.

1740 Jan. 18, Sir John Dinely Goodere, bart. seized by his brother, Captain Samuel Goodere, who procured him to be murthered on board the Ruby man-of-war in Kingroad, the next morning. See Captain Goodere's confession, in the Bristol Memoralist, p. 72. The White Hart public-house, in College-Green, where the gang assembled, is the house now [1824] occupied by Mr. Smith, book-binder.

The foundation of the Bristol Exchange laid by Henry Combe, Mayor. To effect this, the Guilders Inn, in High-

---

* The principal of these were glassmakers, on horseback, in Holland shirts, with swords of glass and other glassical devices—woolcombers in their shirts, with wigs of wool and white wands tipped with wool; then the weavers, &c.

A. D.

street, the houses in Corn-street from All-Saints' Lane to Cock-Lane, and so throughout to St. Nicholas-street, were pulled down.

1741 This year was published by Benjamin Hickey, book-seller, the four-sheet survey of Bristol by John Roque, embracing on the north-west the line formed between the points marked Jacob's Wells and Bewell's Croft—on the south-east, that indicated by Totterdown-Hill and part of Lawrence-Hill—on the south-west, near the centre of the plan, Bright-Bow, and on the north-east, the Conduit in Earl's Meads. Copies of this survey are not very scarce, though the writer believes he purchased the last in the hands of the publisher's representatives, and which Mr. Cossham possesses, coloured, to distinguish the parish-boundaries. Mr. Plumley's survey, upon the same scale, is more exten-sive, including the whole of the vicinity shewn in the Map placed at the head of this volume.

The alms-house, south-west corner of Milk-street, for five old bachelors and five old maids, built by Thomas and Sarah Ridley, brother and sister, of Pucklechurch, Gloucestershire.

John Jayne, of Temple parish, mariner, gave £140, the interest to be applied towards clothing and educating the poor girls of that parish, for ever. See 1713.

1742 Sir Abraham Elton, bart. M.P. father of the Mayor, died, and was succeeded in the representation by Robert Hoblyn, esq.

Robert Fitzharding's monument in the Cathedral repaired.

1743 March 27, the Exchange-Market was opened.

Sept. 27, the Exchange itself was opened with great solemnity. Mr. Wood (author of a Description of Bath, in 2 vols. 8vo.) was the architect. The cost was about £50,000. The following, according to the printed account of this cere-mony, were now the incorporated crafts of Bristol:

1. Masons	7. Turners	13. Tanners	19. Hoopers
2. Tilers	8. Hatters	14. Cordwainers	20. Smiths
3. Porters	9. Saddlers	15. Wire-drawers	21. Surgeons,
4. Hauliers	10. Innholders	16. Joiners	with music before them.
5. Carpenters	11. Bakers	17. Dyers	22. Weavers
6. Tobacco-pipe-makers	12. Butchers	18. Whitetawers	23. Tailors.

The Mercers and Linen-Drapers' Company also was now in being; but the members, perhaps, considered themselves sufficiently represented on this occasion by those of their brethren who were of the Corporation. We have had a perusal of " *The Booke of the Mercers and Linnen-Drapers*

A D.

1743 *Companie*," containing " The Coppy of the Master's Oath when he is sworne before the Mayor"—" The Coppy of the Oath to bee administred to all such as are to bee admitted into this Companie"—and the yearly audits of all the Masters and Wardens, from 1647, when John Young was the Master, and Fabian Hill and William Knight the Wardens, being the commencement of the institution, to 1729, the mastership of Paul Fisher. Between the leaves we found an Excise-Office receipt for 5s. duty on 100 oz. of the Company's plate, from Richard Camplin, dated 27 Oct. 1757. The book contains the well-written autographs of all the members, including the names of many families still flourishing, among which that of " Mark Harford" stands prominent for its peculiar neatness. The " Schedule of the Goods and Ornaments" for 1667, and its " Continuation" in 1677, comprise " Mr. Hart's Picture" and " Mr. Timothy Parker's Picture." (Mr. George Hart was a sheriff in 1650, and Mr. Parker, sheriff in 1659.)—Oct. 4, 1669, Richard Codrington, master, signed an order against revealing matters debated in the Company; and that order will for the present influence our abstract of the " Booke." The number of members fluctuated between twenty-seven and forty. In 1663 (when John Capper opened the book with party-coloured and ornamental entries of the previous Masters and Wardens, only) the list, in Henry Gleson's mastership, amounted to thirty names. The greatest number (forty) was during the respective masterships of Peter Muggleworth in 1709-10, and Austin Goodwin, in 1710-11. In 1729 there were thirty-six members. Their first " Hall" was in St. Thomas-lane, in premises rented of Mr. Gunter at £8 per annum, of which they sub-leased a part (retaining for their own use the Hall, with an inner room) to Mr. Townsend, for £5 10s. per annum. This was quitted, in 1681, for a Hall in St. Nicholas-street, for which they paid " John Batchellor" (sheriff in 1693 and mayor in 1699) £4 per annum. Mr. Alderman Batchelor's name appears in the list of the Company for the last time in 1718, when he served as one of the Wardens; and there is no mention of " our Hall" afterward. The meetings would appear to have been subsequently held at the Three Tuns, the Nag's Head Tavern, the Elephant Coffee-house, the Fountain, and the Bush. " For St. Paul's Fair," in 1718, they met at the Three Cups and Salmon; and " for St. James's," at the Lamb. Their more secret meetings were at the houses of members. In 1729 is a charge " To cash paid Mr. Bartlett's maid, as customary, 5s."

1743 Previous to 1683, the admission-fee for a new member was £2, and £1 10s. This was afterward reduced to 3s. 4d., with a continued quarterage of 1s. 8d., and every member taking an apprentice paid £2. The first item of this class is, in 1702, "To cash received of Alderman Bacheler taking Hen. Combe apprentice." (Henry Combe became sheriff in 1726, and mayor in 1740.)—The Beadle, alias "Beagle," at first had a salary of 10s. per annum. In 1678 he began to sport " a livery," that cost £1 1s. 10d. In 1685, he had a new coat, price £1. In 1703, "paid for a coat and hat, and making the coat, &c. £2 6s. 3d." In 1708, these matters amounted to £2 18s. 7d.; and Roger Grant's salary was increased to £1. In 1709, "paid for the staff that is carried before the Company, 10s." In 1710, the said Roger being neglectful, 7s. 6d. was paid to a substitute, and Roger was mulcted in 5s. out of his 20s. In 1712, his year's " sallory" was advanced to £2. In 1718 we find the following indications of " pomp and circumstance" for the edification of all Londoners keeping open shops in the fairs, and all hawkers and pedlars who were not free of the Company.

" Paid for a Hatt and Lacing for Roger.... £1 3 6
————— a pair of Scarlett Stockings 0 4 6
————— 3 yards and ¼ of drab Cloth at 8s. 1 6 0
————— Trimming to Mr. Cadell as per note 0 10 6
————— Making yᵉ Coate, Back Silk, &c. 0 7 0
————— Painting the Stick and cutting the Armes .... 0 8 6"

In 1727, a new hat cost 9s. and the gold lace 13s. 7d. To the drab cloth was added ¾ yard scarlet cloth, 14s. 3d. The making and trimming, 12s. 6d. The scarlet stockings, 5s.

In 1725, £14 14s. was paid for a present to Mr. James Birch of his " Pickture and Frame," which he acknowledged by a contribution of £21 to the Company's fund; the balance of which was latterly kept sufficiently low by increased expenses of free prosecutions of foul traders in the fair.

[According to a Survey of this part of the city now laid down by Mr. Glascodine, copies of which are in possession of the Chamber and of the Vestry of St. Nicholas the Guilders Tavern, in High-street, stood where (in 1824) is the house of Mr. Taylor, silversmith ; the Inn behind it occupying a large space. Cock-lane lay parallel with the present passage from the Post-Office to St. Nicholas-street, and was entered from Corn-street, opposite to the junction of Mr. Mereweather's house with the Bullion-Bank. John Milton, engraver, resided on the east side of Cock-lane. The entrance to the Coopers' Hall was on the west side. Surgeons' Hall stood in a court south

A. D.

1743 of Coopers' Hall, and was the present West-India Coffee-house. The Star public-house stood on the east side of the lane. The Three Tuns Tavern faced the Bush Tavern, and had an entrance also in All-Saints' lane, facing All-Saints' passage from High-street. All-Saints' lane was not a thoroughfare, but a court to the Rummer Tavern. Next to the Rummer Tavern, forming a western angle to its front, was Snowgale's Alms-house above noticed; and adjoining thereto, northward, was the Elephant Coffee-house. Surely no *alms*-folks could be more snugly accommodated! The Tolzey was continued in front of St. Werburgh's Church. The Shambles, on which the north side of Bridge-street is erected, ran upon the same line with St. Nicholas-street, within the Gate.]

Zinc manufactured by Mr. Champion. A patent was afterwards obtained by Mr. Emerson. The manufactory was at Hanham.

1744 The library in the Bishop's Palace repaired, and partly rebuilt, by Bishop Butler. Whilst these repairs were in progress, a parcel of plate fell through the floor in a corner of one of the rooms, and discovered a room underneath, containing a great many human bones, and instruments of iron, supposed to have been designed for torture. A private passage, too, was found, of a construction coeval with the edifice, an arched way, just large enough for one person, in the thickness of the wall, one end terminating in the dungeon, the other in an apartment of the house which seemed to have been used as a court. Both entrances of this mural passage were so concealed, as to make it appear one solid thick wall.

[The prebendal house held by the Rev. Dr. Ridley had, previous to its improvement by Mr. Edward Hodges in 1821, a strong room on the ground-floor (now divided to form a wine-cellar, &c.) which, from its stone seat, strong hatch-divided door, and strongly barred aperture for light, must have been used as a place of confinement for the refractory. This house is separated from the western original termination of the monastic church, by a wall of six feet in thickness.]

1745 The citizens assembled at the Merchants' Hall, and subscribed £36,450, to raise men against the Pretender's son, who had marched as far as Derby. They gave a bounty of £5 a man, and sent sixty men as a reinforcement of the King's guard in London.

July 12, two London privateers came into this port with the money, &c. taken in two Spanish ships, viz. 1093 chests, weighing 1573 cwt. 29 lb. nett weight, (2,644,922 oz.) besides five chests of wrought plate, several tons of cocoa, a gold church in miniature, and other valuables.

1745 The whole was conveyed hence to London in twenty-two waggons.

Oct. 7, the Trial privateer and her prize, destined for Scotland, with arms and £6000, brought into Kingroad.

The Bristol Infirmary this year admitted 493 in-patients and 823 out-patients. The disbursements for the year amounted to £1005 3s. 8¼d. Yearly subscribers, 281; the receipt from whom was £741 6s. See 1752.

1746 April 17, the battle of Culloden.

The Town-Clerk, William Cann; his deputy, John Mitchel, and their clerk, James Briton, all three insane. Mr. Cann cut his own throat, and the other two were sent to the receptacle at the Fishponds.

For Bristol, in the new parliament, Robert Hoblyn and Edward Southwell,* esqrs. were elected representatives.

1747 An Act passed for the relief and support of maimed and disabled seamen, and the widows and children of such as might be killed, maimed, or drowned, in the merchant-service. Trustees, the Society of Merchant-Venturers. Ground was once laid out for an hospital under Brandon-Hill.

1748 A piazza on the Back for a Corn-market erected.

A new Turnpike-Act having been obtained, for continuing the two former Acts, gates were erected all round the city, but most of them were soon cut down. While these were re-erecting, the commissioners placed chains across the roads, and collected the tolls in person. The Somersetshire country-people, enraged at this disappointment to their love for dust and mud in preference to the comfort of their horses and the preservation of their carts, assembled in a body of several hundred, and marched towards Redcliff-Gate; but that being shut against them, they proceeded through Pile-street to Temple-Gate; which also being fast, they went to Totterdown, and began cutting down the gate there. The Sheriffs with their officers and the constables, several of the commissioners, and a party of sailors armed with cutlasses,

* This name has occurred in connexion with Kingsweston, under 1590. The family is descended from a younger branch of the Viscounts Southwell in Ireland. Edward Southwell, esq. the Member of the House of Commons for Bristol, was born June 16, 1705. The biographer of Mr. Mylne, the architect of Blackfriar's Bridge, relates that "being employed by Mr. Southwell, to alter his splendid mansion at Kingsweston, Mr. Mylne commenced his operations by a plan of the house. Whilst thus occupied, he discovered a small room to which there was no means of access, and, on cutting into it, they found a quantity of old plate, together with the records of a barony granted to the family by Henry III. The apartment had probably been shut up during the rebellion against Charles I." The present baron was born June 23, 1767. His aunt Margaret, countess of Leicester, and baroness de Clifford, dying in 1775, his claim was allowed, April 24, 1776, to the baronies de Clifford, Westmorland, and Vesci, of Alnwick, co. Northumberland. His father, Mr. Southwell, died Nov. 1, 1777.

A. D.

1748 came upon them before they had finished their mud-brained work, and put them to flight, wounding some and taking about thirty prisoners. In their way towards Bristol, they had pulled down a house at Bedminster. The prisoners were confined in Newgate till Salisbury assize; at which they were tried by a special commission. Thus ended this chapter of reformation to people for whom the legal maxim, " he who runs may read," could have been scarcely applicable. Surely there is no greater enemy to mankind than ignorance!

Andrew Hooke published his " Dissertation on the Antiquity of Bristol; wherein Mr. Camden's Opinion of the late rise of that ancient City is shewn to be not only contradictory to general tradition, and the opinion of all the Antiquaries before him, but also inconsistent with his own authorities, as well as other positive and direct testimonies." 8vo. 62 pages. Dedicated, in ten more pages, to Buckler Weekes, esq. Mayor; the Hon. Sir Michael Foster, knight, Recorder, and the Aldermen his brethren, and to Joseph Daltera and Isaac Baugh, esqrs. Sheriffs, and the rest of the Commonalty. This was merely the introduction to "Bristollia, or Memoirs of the City of Bristol, both Civil and Ecclesiastical." Mr. Hooke acknowledges the readiness and unanimity with which the Corporation granted his request of having free recourse to the city archives; but nothing further was published.*

1749 St. Peter's Church repaired.

1750 Bishop Butler recommended to the Corporation of Bristol to build a church at Kingswood, and he himself subscribed £400. The Bishop had expended nearly £5000 in repairs of the Palace. He was this year translated to Durham. Dying at Bath, in 1752, his remains were brought to the Cathedral.

John Conybeare, twenty-ninth Bishop of Bristol. He remained in this see till his death, July 13, 1756. His Sermons, in four volumes, were published after his decease, with an immense list of subscribers, headed by the King.

---

* Mr. Barrett, in the Proposals for his " History," acknowledged that Mr. Hooke was very capable, but added that, " as he possessed few materials for such a work, his undertaking dropt of course." Mr. Barrett himself, who published in 1783, wanted not materials; but it is left for the Rev. Samuel Seyer to complete his design; and the writer of this " Outline" will feel happy in the proof that he has assisted in exciting a thirst for this species of reading, the gratification of which may reward Mr. Seyer for the great labour and expense which he has for years devoted to his " Memoirs, Historical and Topographical," now in course of publication. His Parts I.—III. only had appeared when this page passed the press.

A. D.

1750 Two whales brought to Sea-Mill Dock, and the blubber boiled there.

Aug. 1, the first Bank opened in Bristol, in Broad-street (at the house now [1824] occupied with the offices of Messrs. Osborne & Ward), by Mr. Isaac Elton, Mr. Harford Lloyd, Mr. William Miller,* Mr. Thomas Knox, and Mr.——Hale. Mr. Edye was their principal clerk. There was at this time no other banking-house out of London, except one kept by a Jew at Derby. The instant deposit of gold was very great.

1751 March 8, Sir Nathaniel William Wraxall born in Queen-Square. He was educated in Bristol. See " Biographical Dictionary of the Living Authors, &c." Colburn, 1816. John Wraxall was Master of the Mercers and Linen-Drapers' Company of Bristol, in 1723. (See note to p. 240.) Nathaniel Wraxall was a Sheriff of Bristol in the same year.

March 20, died Frederick, Prince of Wales, father of George III.

In France, the commencement of the year with January began, under Charles IX., in 1564: it had previously commenced with March. The retrograde adaptation of the English kalendar to the Julian year, which we noticed under 1586, prevailed chiefly with regard to ecclesiastical computations—why, it is difficult to imagine, unless for the reason that Pope Gregory, in that very year, set us the example, by reforming the kalendar of the rest of Europe, which England at last now saw fit to adopt.† The present March 24 terminated the last *regular* year of Old Style, thus marked in all parliamentary and legal documents; 175⅟. This year, 1751, terminating with Dec. 31, comprised only 282 days. The first correction of the kalendar, and strict adaptation to the solar or Gregorian year, was made in 1752, by calling the next day after Sept. 2, Sept. 14—that year thus comprising only 355 days. See the Acts 24 Geo. II. cap. 23, and 25 Geo. II. cap. 30.‡

* This gentleman resided at the house in Queen-Square since occupied by Mr. Alderman Evans. David Hume, in his Memoirs by himself, says, " In 1734, I went to Bristol with some recommendations to eminent merchants, but in a few months found that scene totally unsuitable to me." He was clerk to Mr. Miller; but David's taste in English composition being offended by the merchant's letter-book, and venturing to 'reform it altogether,'—" I'll tell you what, Mr. Hume!" exclaimed his employer, " I have made £20,000 by my English, and I won't have it mended." Had our fellow-native liked Mr. Hume's English better, the world might have remained without the History of England.

† Protestant prejudice seemed to feel alarm at the notion of giving even " the Devil his due," if he happened to domicile at Rome.

‡ We are indebted for the notice of these three years of irregular calculation, to Mr. Cossham. Without the possession of tables formed hereupon, for the years 1750, 1751, and 1752, what a confusion of numbers and ideas must occur upon every calculation of interest or other legal reference connected with this point of time!

1751   The Castle-Mill was this year rebuilt.

1752   March 3, David Peloquin, mayor, laid the foundation-stone of St. George's Church, Kingswood. The church and vicarage-house were completed at the cost of £2,853 17s. 7¼d. The Corporation gave £500 towards the erection, and the Society of Merchant-Venturers, £105. The Act of Parliament (24th of the reign) obtained by Bishop Butler, alienated a part of the Out-parish of St. Philip and Jacob. for this purpose, but for the church-rate only: the other taxes to remain in common as before. Thomas Chester, esq. lord of the manor of that part of the late Forest or Chase, granted a piece of ground for the site of the church, church-yard, vicarage-house and gardens. The first vicar was William Cary.

" In St. George's parish (says Mr. Fosbroke) was a ruined chapel of St. Anthony's; and in the highway, near the church, stood a penitential cross, which, from *Domm. Johan.* (Domine Johannes, the name of the benefactor perhaps) has obtained the name of *Don John*'s Cross, and made the place where the body of a *noble Spaniard* rested, in its way to Spain for interment! *from whence it was so named!*"—ii. 66. Describing a Survey of the Forest, in vol. i., p. 119, the same author has "*Dungel*'s Cross," between which and *Don John*'s Cross the corrupt transition is less violent.

June 21, the anniversary of the King's accession to the throne, the Mayor appeared in a new state-coach, for the first time.

Nov. 20, Thomas Chatterton was born. His father died in the preceding August.

St. James's Poor-house, Barrs-street, rebuilt by the parish. It heretofore consisted of nine small tenements, inhabited by both men and women.

The Bristol Infirmary this year received 725 in-patients, including 105 casualties and 1676 out-patients. The disbursements amounted to £1686 5s. 6¾d. The number of subscribers was 389, who contributed £920 17s. See 1783.

1753   Whitfield's Tabernacle, in Penn-street, founded.

May 26, several hundred colliers entered the city at 'change-time, and complained at the Council-House of the dearness of bread, insisting upon having twelve pounds weight for a shilling. The Magistrates reasoned with them, but to no purpose—the Proclamation was read, but not regarded. They immediately went to the Quay, and boarded a vessel laden with corn for exportation, broke open the hatches, and plundered the cargo. The constables now came down and

1753 partly dispersed them, driving several overboard into the mud. Enraged, they returned to the Council-House, and poured a volley of stones in at the windows, wounding several persons. The constables and inhabitants rallied, and drove them out, some through the city and some through the river Avon.

On the Thursday a still greater mob of colliers and other country-people approached Lawford's Gate. The Sheriffs, (Daniel Woodward and Edward Whatley) who were at the Guildhall with the constables, &c. proceeded thither, and a skirmish ensued, in which some of the rabble were wounded, and others taken prisoners. About nine o'clock the same evening, the Mayor (John Clement) being informed that there was a large body of rioters without the Gate, who intended to besiege the city, the drum beat " to arms!" and the posse, headed by the Mayor, went to meet them; but the besiegers had retired. The gates were kept shut, and the guards patrolled the streets all night.

In the morning (Friday) a detachment of the Scots Greys arrived from Gloucester, and just as they got into quarters there was a fresh alarm. Their drum beat, they were drawn up for action, and the city-guard also were under arms. Between twelve and one o'clock, the rioters came round to Bridewell-Gate, with the intent of releasing one of their gang who had been taken prisoner; but, by the time they had forced the Gate, they were surrounded. A few shots threw both " pitmen" and " topmen" into such consternation, having little expected that they should be " vired at wi' baal," that they ran in all directions for an escape, and skirmishes took place in different parts of the city, by which several were killed on the spot and many wounded. Twenty-nine were taken prisoners. The soldiers had been drawn up, to assist the magistrates, and received orders to fire; but the rioters were dispersed without it. A small party of gentlemen continued the pursuit without Lawford's Gate, and a battle ensued, wherein one of the colliers, named Fudge, was killed, but not, as was commonly reported, by Mr. Brickdale, for we happen to know by whom. Three of the gentlemen were wounded and two for some time missing. He who was so unhappily successful, after being exposed to a search by the rioters, with pitchforks, in a hay-talhot to which he had retreated, was at night brought home safely by the late Mr. Howorth, mercer, of High-street, then a warehouseman of Mr. Alderman Bartlett's, in Broad-street.— The ringleader, named Job Phipps, and eight others, were

1753committed to Newgate, for trial by a special commission, which sentenced several of them to two years imprisonment, and to find sureties for their good behaviour.*

Nov. 15, the Exchange was re-opened, after repairs amounting to £1500.

The steps and terrace, west of Redcliff-Church, new laid, with Purbeck stone.

1754   April 5, a general election. Candidates for Bristol,

Richard Beckford, esq. who polled votes 2283 } returned.
Robert Nugent, esq.................. 2622 }
Sir John Philipps, bart. 2217

April 16, the first stone laid of St. Giles's Bridge, at the head of the Quay. The cost of erection was £1825 14s. 4½d.

1755   King-Square and the adjacent streets laid out and commenced.

Henry Dampier, Mayor; Henry Weare and James Hilhouse, Sheriffs.

Nov. 1, the Hotwell-water became red, and the water of a well in a field belonging to Mr. John Harrison, near Clifton Church, black as ink. This was the day of the earthquake that destroyed Lisbon.

The Draw-Bridge rebuilt.

1756   Feb. 28, Mr. Beckford's death having occasioned a vacancy for this city in Parliament, the Hon. John Spencer and Jarrett Smith, esq. were candidates. Mr. Smith was returned by a large majority.

Lord Chancellor Hardwicke, High Steward.

Ann Yearsley, the Bristol milkwoman, born. (See Corry and Evans's History of Bristol, vol. ii, p. 402.) Had Mrs. Yearsley's knowledge of herself, and correspondent command of temper, been equal to her genius, she might have experienced less of the "calamities of authors." Worse lady-poets have been more successful. She died May 8, 1806.

Upon a survey, the city, &c. were found to contain 13,000 houses and 90,000 persons.

---

* Rioting is rarely the effect of *want*, but rather the spirit of *wantonness*, blended with cowardly apprehension of want, as its pretext for violence and destruction of the means of plenty. We have often, on such occasions, wondered how honest men, who loved their families, could *afford*, not only to lose their present time for honest labour, but to risk the esteem of those only who were capable of giving them employment thereafter, the orderly and industrious in *mind* as well as body. Without greater labour of mind than rioters evince, Kingswood might again become a forest, and the inhabitants wild beasts.—We regard *mobbing*-elections as the nursing-days, and those who would prefer them to voting by registry at the vestries as the foster-fathers, of all riots. It is a sad joke to call men "free and independent" burgesses, and then *pay* them for the time employed in giving their votes; unless it be intended, in all humility, that the representative shall approximate his constituents in the slavery of poverty.

A. D.

1756 August. " The privateers of London, Bristol, Liverpool, Guernsey, and Jersey, had great success against the enemy this month." Perhaps to this point of time may be referred the anecdotes of Capt. Patrick, of the Fame letter of marque, of this port, recorded by John Harriott, esq. resident magistrate of the Thames Police, in vol. i. p. 64, of his " Struggles through Life," 12mo. 1815.

Chatterton dismissed, at *five* years old, from Pile-street school, for dulness. The master was perhaps the dullest of the two, and had never learnt how to keep a preparatory school for genius.

Hogarth's three paintings, of Christ and the Woman of Samaria, the Sealing of the Tomb, and the Resurrection, put up in Redcliff-Church, for which he was paid 500 guineas. The whole, with the frames, alterations, &c. cost £761 0s. 1d. Hogarth was assisted by John Simmons; for a memoir of whom (by Mr. Tyson), see The Bristol Memorialist, p. 33.

An Act passed for the due making of Bread, and to punish persons who should adulterate meal, flour, or bread.

Nov. 1, the Belliqueux, of 64 guns and 415 men, having entered the Bristol Channel in mistake, the Antelope, stationed here, proceeded off Ilfracombe and brought her into Kingroad.

Nov. 27, Mary Robinson born, in the Minster-house of the Cathedral.—We shall never pass the grave of Bird the artist, out of the Cloisters into the Cathedral, without imagining the youthful Mary's form and rapt countenance, seated on the steps, listening to the organ's solemn peal. She died Dec. 26, 1800. Her " Memoirs" require to be revised. We have had in our hands a lock of hair with its envelope, the first token of favour from her royal admirer, and have also read a kind letter in reply to an application for pecuniary assistance, written with his own hand, fifteen years after their separation. That separation was occasioned more by her own violence of temper and epistolary virulence than by the fickleness of her patron. We have seen, too, the portrait of herself, that remained in her own possession till her decease; and, beautiful as she was, the artist has not given the most amiable expression to her eyes. Having consented to a compact which she knew could be neither legal nor moral, she had no right to assume an implied individuality of attachment; which she did, with reference to an object of jealousy, in terms that no young man of spirit in common life could treat other than with total silence.

M m 2

A.D.

1759   In the mayoralty of Jeremiah Ames (33d of the King) an Act of Parliament was obtained, to value the houses on the old Bridge and build a new one. Carriages and horses laden with coal, or with grains as back-carriage, were to be exempted from toll. When the purposes of the Act should be completed, the tolls to cease, and the surplus-moneys to be applied to the repairs and lighting of the Bridge. See 1785.

The Corporation presented the Hon. William Pitt (afterward the great Chatham) and the Duke of Newcastle with the freedom of the city, in gold boxes.

The design of opening and building Park-street, with Great George-street and Charlotte-street, now began to be entertained. In 1596, Bullock's Park, alias Amery's Close, and the Grange, a part whereof was Tapley's Garden (the extent of which may be seen in Roque's plan of 1742), were leased from the 21st of December for one thousand years, at 1*d.* per annum, £45 to the representatives of Nathaniel Day, and 5*s.* per annum to the King, and now held by three several families (the Daubenys, the Deverells, and that of Woodward, bishop of Cloyne), together with two pieces of freehold land adjoining each other (at the foot of Park-street next to Frog-lane), originally bought of —— Worth, and of —— Hart, for one thousand years from Oct. 1, 1661. This year (1759), Sept. 29, part of the Boar's Head Inn yard, freehold, and another small piece next to it, were added, by purchase from Arthur Hart, executor of W. Hart, for the remainder of one thousand years. The progress which we have traced of this speculation, through all the changes of public credit and consequent mutations of individual interest, has left on our minds the impression that the view from College-Green would be fitly and justly terminated by a monument to the memory of the chief sufferer, inscribed with the venerated name of FRANCIS WARD.

1760   St. John's Bridge completed, just above that of the Water-Gate, on the Froom, opening a way, *within* the site of the gate, into Lewin's Mead.

A temporary bridge erected above the old Bridge on the Avon. Having been presented by Mr. Major (into whose hands the whole of Mr. Barrett's copper-plates and wood-cuts fell, by transfer from Mr. Lansdown, who bought them at a sale of Mr. Barrett's effects) with the identical block engraven for p. 80 of the "History of Bristol," we have thought proper to make the republication of it annexed. The outline-proportions, upon comparison with those of the new Bridge, we feel assured will be found correct.

Mr. Barrett says,—" No words can give the reader so just an idea of Bristol-Bridge as a view of the following draught of it, which was made in 1760, at the time it was about to be taken down; which being course, presents to the eye more truly the appearance of it.

" This Bridge, when naked and unincumbered with houses, (which were afterwards erected thereon by turning secondary gothic arches opposite the old ones, for a foundation for one end of the buildings to rest upon,) consisted of four neat, strong, semicircular arches, the passage over it being only nineteen feet wide, which must have had a parapet-wall at the sides before the houses were erected, to secure people from falling over into the river."

A. D.

1760   Lord Bottetourt rebuilt Stoke-House, Stapleton, the residence of the present Duchess Dowager of Beaufort.

Oct. 25, the King died suddenly, at Kensington, aged 77.
Succeeded by his grandson,

GEORGE III.

1761   Feb. 8, St. Werburgh's Church, the east end of which had
obstructed the entrance into Small-street, having been partly
taken down and rebuilt, was re-opened.   The tower underwent repair only at the top.   The Lord Chancellor presents
to the living.—Mr. Henry Smith possesses a drawing by
Halfpenny of the north side of this church, with the exterior
of its richly ornamented porch, as it now stood.

The fairs of March and September fixed by Act of Parliament.

Thomas Newton, thirty-third Bishop of Bristol—appointed
by the King without any intervention of a minister.

Nov. 13, commenced an affair of witchcraft that engrossed
the credulity and superstition of the city for the whole of the
ensuing twelve months.   The reader's taste in such "stuff"
of "waking dreams" may be gratified by *"A Narrative of
some extraordinary things that happened to Mr.* RICHARD
GILES's *Children* [Miss Molly and Dobby] *at the Lamb,*
[Inn] *without Lawford's Gate, Bristol; supposed to be the
effect of Witchcraft.   By the late Mr.* HENRY DURBIN,
*Chemist; who was an eye and ear-witness of the principal
facts herein related."*   Bristol printed, 1800.   From this
tract may be learnt that Miss Molly and Dobby (assisted by
fleshly confederates, of whom more anon) began their pranks
on the morning named, while in bed, by scratchings on the
windows and bedstead; and their hocus-pocus tricks,
adapted in extravagance to the growing appetite for the mar-
vellous, continued, as the Narrative relates, till the 27th of
November 1762; when the witchcraft was exploded by adoption of certain wise and delicate expedients that on the day
preceding had been recommended by "the Cunning-Woman
at Bedminster!"   This "cunning woman," the want of
whose veritable memoirs we know not how posterity can sur-
vive, had afterward the honour to be mother-in-law to a
knight-companion of the useful order of rags and lampblack,
who printed the maiden-volume of our fellow-native (born
in the house now occupied by Messrs. Goss and Fowler, in
Wine-street), the Poet Laureate.   But, that our inky brother
was not ambitious to share the Sybilline honours of his step-

1761 mother, was evidenced by the fact that when, within onr own knowledge, she flourished in the graces of supernaturality as well as *quant. suff.* of the grease of full-blown mortality (for she was "a ton of flesh"), her husband's son right worthily filled the office of singing-clerk in Castle-Green Meeting-house. To return to the Lamb,—

Poor Giles (who was not in the secret) had set up a fly-waggon for London, and, "as the Devil would have it," a rival common-carrier was said to be the suborner of invisible agency that at one time made his horses stand still on Kelson-Hill, and, at another, snap off their chain-traces, sending the fore-horses of the team scampering to their stable at Bath, whither the fragments of the traces arrived carefully tucked under the harness on their backs! So remorseless were the Genii of the Broomstick, that Richard could not withstand half the load of notoriety they conferred upon the maternal and filial members of his hopeful family: he sickened, and died on the intermediate 15th of May.—So far the "Narrative." Tradition, with her greater number of concurrent tongues, has informed us that the exorcism was effected in a widely different manner, and by a much wiser woman of the West!

Mrs. Haynes had the two girls to her house, still known as Wick-Court, and put them to sleep in one bed on a middle floor. Noises were heard in the night, as theretofore at the Lamb, and, on visiting the bed, Miss Molly was found wanting. Search being made, she was discovered hiding in an upper room, with newly made scratches on her innocent flesh. Nothing alarmed by these supernatural tokens, Mrs. Haynes directed the natural application of a birchen rod to Miss Molly's sensible posteriors; and Dobby was promised a spice of the same wholesome discipline, if she ventured any like experiment upon her hostess's credulity. The Spirit of Evil from that day departed from these precious lamb-kins, and was no more heard of.

The real plotters of this invasion of the public peace and news-loving propriety were Mrs. Nelmes and her daughter Mrs. Giles, the grandmother and mother of " Miss Molly and Dobby," for the purpose of depreciating the value of the house, of which Mrs. Nelmes became the purchaser. An elder sister of the two bewitched ones survived, to share with them the proceeds, on transfer of the premises to other hands.

[It may, from the apparent levity of our manner in treating matters so grave as the foregoing and that recorded under 1788, be imagined, by such as would profess themselves ten-

1761 derly alive for our salvation, and charitably prepared to kick us out of all Christian society accordingly, that we believe in neither Devil nor Hell. But, so far from it, we do believe that every man, woman, and child, who gives way to violent passion, is possessed of an Evil Spirit—that the house of scolding is a Hell upon Earth—that the drunkard puts a Devil into his mouth to steal away his brains—that the covetous man, who will not *let live*, while he himself either lives sumptuously or possesses the means so to do, the thief and murtherer, are infernals of precisely the same stamp and colour, and will alike eventually undergo either purgation or eternal extinction.—" Whence," it will perhaps be asked, " came your philosophy?" Briefly, we have in our time, now some few years since, endured personal insults and injuries that would have caused many a wight, under the same provocations, to blow out the little brains of his adversary, and cut his own more precious throat. At these, however, we have long, though it was but gradually, ceased to re-pine; since (besides the conviction that, but for the restraints so imposed upon our worldly progress, we might have died of repletion) we live to hold a pen for this humble tribute to the place of our birth—a nursery for many joys, domestic and social, beclouded as it has been by matters for regret, which have only tended to render those joys the dearer.]

Dec. 27, the Duke of York visited this city. He was received by the Corporation at Temple-Gate, where the freedom of the city was presented to him in a gold box—crossed the temporary bridge—was addressed by the Clergy and Merchants at Mr. Combes's house in Queen-Square—dined at the Merchants' Hall—supped with the Mayor (Isaac Elton)—breakfasted with Mr. Tyndall at the Fort, and, after viewing the glass-houses, returned to Bath. At this time the black bottle, flint-glass, and plate-glass manufacturers, occupied fifteen large houses.

1762 St. Nicholas Church commenced rebuilding. The following notice of the old altar-piece is copied from a MS. of Mr. George Symes Catcott's :

" It had greatly the advantage of the present altar-piece, by reason of its elevated situation; being erected over the ancient gateway, which was of height and breadth sufficient for admission of the tallest carriages; and therefore appeared in a very conspicuous point of view; the ascent being (if I remember right) by twenty-three steps of black and white marble, and, when viewed at a proper distance, had by far the most solemn appearance of any thing I ever

A. D.

1762 saw of the kind." "Although the present altar is embellished with the same sculpture and paintings, it loses much of its dignity, from its low situation, being placed almost on a level with the chancel.

"But, before I conclude, I hope it will not be thought unworthy of being committed to posterity, that, when the old gateway was taken down, two skeletons were found immured in stone coffins in the walls, one in the north, the other in the south end of the altar; and as this was the oldest church in Bristol, having been built nearly 900 years ago, they were probably reposited there when the gateway was first erected, and consequently coeval with the church itself."*

Sir Michael Foster resigned the recordership, and the Hon. Daines Barrington was chosen his successor.

Redcliff bells re-cast.

1763 The High Cross, which had been re-erected in the centre of College-Green, was now taken down and deposited in a corner of the Cathedral, where it remained till September 1764, when the Rev. Cutts Barton, upon being appointed Dean of Bristol, gave it to Henry Hoare, esq. of Stourhead. See its history, from the pen of Sir R. C. Hoare, bart., in The Bristol Memorialist, p. 123.†

* In November 1821, during a search in the crypt for the remains of Alderman John Whitson, where his monument had been originally erected, was found, under the centre arch of the north wall, in which it was partly inserted, with the lid standing higher than the floor, a coffin formed of Dundry stone, that had evidently received the remains of two persons; one of the bodies, excepting the skull, having been consumed to ashes, to make room for the other, of which the entire skeleton existed. The surface of the cover was carved with an ornamented cross, and a piece of metal had been sunk within the lines describing a cushion; but this was wanting. Mr. H. Smith made a drawing of the coffin, for his "Historical Collection of Sepulchral Monuments and Characters." On the right edge of the cover, presenting an obtuse angle, was an inscription, the letters filled with red paint, but much obliterated by time, of which we could make out only the following: " +MABEL. . . . . . . HAW.E . . . RICHARD: LE: DRAPE . . . . E IS . . . . . . 1311." By reference to the Mayors' Kalendar, it will appear that Roger le Draper was senechal in 1269, and mayor in 1287. The Mabel and Richard le Draper here buried were probably of the same family.

† The following Letter is copied from the original, in possession of Mr. Henry Wood, sculptor, as found among the papers of his grandfather's predecessor, Mr. Paty, in 1823:

"Sir,—The Dean of Bristol is so obliging as to write me word I may send for the Cross directly. I have therefore ordered my servant, Faugoin, to send out two waggons from Stourhead on Monday morning. I suppose they will be three days in and out; and if it is the Dean and Mr. Tyndall's opinion it should go all at once, as you think there is six loads of it from the point you marked in the print sent me, for the legs are not worth fetching, I beg of you to hire four more waggons to accompany mine, and to be so kind to see it safely and carefully packed and well bedded with hay or straw, and to let one of your men to come with it, to see it unloaded; and I make no doubt you will insist on *careful drivers*; and as I shall be at Stourhead the end of November or beginning of December, wish it may be convenient to you to come over, and let me see you and consult with you how to repair and put it up, and what base or support will be required to it; in all which I must request your assistance, which will much oblige, Sir, your very humble servant, "HENRY HOARE.

"London, Fleet-street, Oct. 2, 1764.

"To Mr. Paty."—.

N n

A. D.

1763   During the war now concluded, there was a depôt for French prisoners at Knowle, juxta Totterdown and Pile-Hill. A short time previous to the peace, one of the soldiers, on his return from guard, for a wager, with a single ball struck the weather-cock of St. Mary Redcliff tower. About nine years afterward the cock ceased to traverse, and on examination it proved that the gun-shot-wound had opened a passage for the rain, which corroded the spindle. The size of the cock is about that of what Bristol school-boys call a Durdham-Down† lion—the shagged emblem of patient endurance.

1764   Pithay-Gate demolished.

The Church of St. Philip and James this year underwent considerable repairs. See 1824.

Sept. 27, Mrs. Ruscombe, and Mary Sweet, her servant, found murthered in her house in College-Green; which must have been done between one and two o'clock in the afternoon. The Corporation offered a reward of £200, and Mr. Nugent, M.P. £500, for discovery of the perpetrator, but without effect.

Nov. 30, the foundation-stone of the Theatre in King-street laid.

The nett remittance of Customs-duties from Bristol, for this year, was £195,000—from Liverpool, £70,000. The number of vessels entered inward at Bristol was 2353.

1765   Bridewell-Bridge, heretofore of wood, rebuilt with stone.

In this the King's 6th year was passed an Act of Parliament, For widening the streets, lanes, passages and places, and taking down buildings on the banks of the Froom—to remove sheds, houses, &c. standing on the Butts, from Denmark-street to Tombs's Dock—take down St. Leonard's Church and the vicarage-house, and unite the parish with St. Nicholas—for enlarging the Shambles, Bull-lane, and Dolphin-street, extending from High-street to Narrow Wine-street—for removing St. Peter's Cross and Pump, standing in the way through St. Peter-street into Dolphin-lane, and selling the cross† and pump, and erecting another pump elsewhere —for regulating projecting signs and sheds, and altering water-

---

A letter to Mr. Paty from F. Faugoin, dated Dec. 5, 1764, advises that his master, Mr. Hoare, is now at Stourhead, and wishes to see him there as soon as he can conveniently spare time.

   * In a note to p. 29, we have said that *ham*, in pure Saxon, means eminent dwelling-place. We gather from the Rev. Edward Davies, in his " * Celtic Researches," royal 8vo. 1804 (pp. 1 to 80 of which were printed in Bristol), that the ancient Druidical and Irish symbol of the letter D was the expansive oak. " Its name was *Duir*, which may be a compound of *Du*, spreading over, and *air*, he arose." The oak-tree still abounds in the fields adjoining Durdham-Down,

            * Mr. Seyer spells this word Keltic.

† Now in the keeping of Sir R. C. Hoare, bart. at Stourhead.

A. D.

1765 spouts—to open the way through Lawford's Gate, by removing seven houses on the south side and three on the north side—to remove two houses at the corner of Quay-lane and Christmas-street, a house in Castle-street, eleven old houses and a brew-house on the south side of Baldwin-street, and a tenement on the south side of Back-street next to Baldwin-street—two houses in Silver-street, next to Lewin's Mead—a house on the west side and a flight of steps on the east side of Small-street Gate—premises on both sides of Narrow Wine-street, from Newgate to Chequer-lane, and three houses next to Dolphin-lane—three houses in Temple-street next to, and three houses in Tucker-street—part of gardens extending from College-Green to Limekiln-lane or Cow-lane, to increase the way twenty feet more in one place and thirty feet in another—to open and lay out a new street [Union-street] by taking down three houses in Wine-street, nine old tenements behind them in a place called the New Buildings, a yard and a court of three tenements behind St. James's Back, and five ruinous houses in Broadmead, opposite the Lamb Inn—to lay open and make a new street from the lower end of Corn-street through part of Marsh-street to the Quay, nearly opposite the Draw-Bridge, including fifty-four houses or tenements and cellars [see 1770]—to widen Hallier's [Haulier's] Lane, and make a new street [Nelson-street], extending thence to Broadmead, at least thirty feet wide, including two houses in Christmas-street and other premises, with part of the old Bowling-Green, thence to four old houses on St. James's Back fronting Broadmead—also to open a way to an intended new Square in St. James's, by taking down a house in Stoke's Croft [that part of it now called North-street] and a house in Milk-street.

1766 May 30, Friday, the new Theatre in King-street was opened with The Conscious Lovers and The Miller of Mansfield, for the benefit of the Bristol Infirmary. The prologue and epilogue were written by Garrick. The cost of the building was above £5000.

Castle-Gate was taken down and given to Mr. Reeve, of Brislington, who re-erected it there, at the entrance of his castellated stables, now (1824) one of the horticultural establishments of Mr. Miller, of St. Michael's Hill.

The houses at the head of the Quay began to be taken down, to widen Quay-lane.—St. Leonard's parish annexed to St. Nicholas.

St. John's Chapel, in Redcliff Church-Yard, which had been granted by Queen Elizabeth for a free grammar-school, taken down. In the wall under the west-window was found a stone coffin, with a figure carved on the lid, and under it, " Johannes Lamyngton," who was chaplain in 1393. The school was removed to the Chapel of the Virgin at the east end of the church, where is a statue of Elizabeth in wood.

A. D.

1766 John Dunning (afterward Lord Ashburton), Recorder of
Bristol.

1767 The statues of the two West-Saxon kings (said to have been
removed from the Castle to Lawford's Gate) given to Mr. Reeve,
who placed them in the two canopied niches facing eastward.
The two figures placed in the parallel niches on the inside
of this gate we do not believe to be portraits of Bishop Godfrey and Earl Robert, being disposed to consider them rather
as general personifications of venerable civil and religious
authority.   Robert, earl of Gloucester, was only 58 years old
when he died, and the statue holding a castle represents a
man of greater age.   There are other civic reliques about
the same building, particularly a well-executed head of
Henry VIII., when about eighteen or twenty years old, and
which proves his face to have been scarcely less handsome
than that of Judge Jefferys.

An Act of Parliament was obtained for raising money to
discharge debts contracted for rebuilding the parish-church
and tower of St. Nicholas, and to rebuild the spire and complete the said church, and for other purposes.   The computed
expenses of the whole, £7624 5s.

The Mud-Dock at the Grove completed, and the Quay-
wall continued round to the Market-house, St. Nicholas-
Back.   The cost was £10,000.

" On Thursday, 25 June, 1767, the last stone was set in
the centre-arch of Bristol Bridge, about six o'clock in the
evening; and the next day, between seven and eight o'clock
in the morning, I rode over on a few loose planks which
were placed there on purpose."—MS. by Mr. GEORGE
SYMES CATCOTT.   The " toll" was five guineas, given the
workmen to drink.   This particular we learnt from Mr.
Hague, the builder; and the writer feels pleasure in being
the first to give effect, in his own words, to the single-hearted
old chronicler's aspirations for posthumous fame.

July 1, Chatterton left Colston's School for the office of
Mr. Lambert, solicitor, below St. John's Steps.   It has not
before found a place in print, that Chatterton's favourite
book-shop was that of Mr. Goodall, in Tower-lane, afterward Joseph Lansdown's, nearly opposite to Cider-house
Passage.   Here (as Mr. Goodall informed the writer) our
youthful poet passed many hours in a day, buying such books
as came within his means, and sitting to read those which he
either did not wish to possess or could not afford to purchase.
His reveries were seldom distracted by the presence of other
customers.   He was particularly attached to one book, on

A. D.

1767 Saxon manners and customs, which remained in the shop after news arrived from London of his death, but was at last missed without the help of a purchaser.

1768 George Weare, on going out of office as mayor, was the first to ride over the new Bridge in a carriage.

Clifton Church enlarged by building a north aisle. After being closed for a year, it was re-opened Oct. 2.

St. Peter's Cross taken down.

The Painting of the Transfiguration put up in St. James's Church.

The Merchants' Dock finished. In January 1769, it received a 64-gun ship through the gates. See 1775.

Lawford's Gate taken down, and the entrance to the city widened.

In 1766 the Society of Merchant-Venturers, who are lords of the manor of Clifton, having received a proposition from James Waters, to erect a windmill near the ancient military station, agreed to advance him £200 for that purpose; the building to be at his own risk. The mill was thereupon raised, and served also as a dwelling for the miller and his family; but, one night previous to April in this year (when the Society appear to have issued an ejectment to recover possession of the land), the sails of the mill became loosened by a high wind, and the violent friction setting fire to the machinery, the whole interior was burnt to the ground.—So picturesque an object might be easily made contributory to purposes of moderate refreshment, within proper hours, for the numerous juvenile pedestrians who court the stimulant to wholesome appetite found in the breezes of the health-inspiring vicinity. We have tasted the Sally Lun's buns of Bath, and the Nag's Head cake of Bristol. Security from abuse of such an accommodation might be found in granting a lease of this mountain-refectory, upon condition that nothing were vended but *Clifton-Windmill* or *St. Vincent's* biscuits, milk, and Hotwell or Sion-spring water, and that the shop should be closed on Sundays in the afternoon.

1769 July 2, the remains of Mr. Powell the actor, manager of the Theatre, were met by the Dean and the Choir at the foot of College-Green, and conducted to the Cathedral.

The Bristol Fire-Insurance Office established by sugar-refiners, chiefly against their own risks. It was subsequently thrown open to the public, and the same establishment continues. Offices, Small-street Buildings, on the site of Deane, Whitehead & Co.'s banking-house, formerly the mansion of the Creswicke family. " Alderman Holworthy's house, opposite," where Charles II. and James II. lodged, in August 1643, was that now (1824) occupied by Messrs. Pinnell and Doddrell, grocers, the state-room or hall of which remains.

Oct. 1, Chatterton's description of the Friers passing the old Bridge appeared in Felix Farley's Bristol Journal—his first printed production.

St. Nicholas Church completed.

Note by Mr. CATCOTT, *upon* CHATTERTON's *Poem entitled* " *Happiness.*"—*Vide Southey and Cottle's ed. vol.* i. *p.* 131, *l.* 2.] " Alluding to my laying the top-stone of St. Nicholas Spire, in Bristol, and placing (in a cavity cut for that purpose) two pieces of hard metal, each five inches square; on one of which was very deeply engraved the following inscription:

' Summum hujusce Turris Sancti Nicholai Lapidem posuit, mensi Decembris ' 1769. GEORGIUS CATCOTT, Philo Architectos, Reverendi ALEXANDRI S. CATCOTT ' Filius.'

" The inscription on the other piece was as under:

' Barbara Pyramidum sileat miracula Memphis ' Pyramis hæc vera est Religionis opus.'

" The steeple is 205 feet high from the lower ground. The plates were fastened in with lead, the better to preserve them from the injuries of time."

Benjamin Donne published a Map of the Country eleven miles round Bristol.

The time for holding the two fairs changed, from Jan. 25 to March 1, and from July 25 to Sept. 1.

1770 The Bishop's Park, the site of College-street, &c. obtained by Samuel Worrall, on lease for 90 years, at £60 per ann.

An Act of Parliament was passed, to enable the Bishop of Bristol to grant a lease or leases of a close of ground called the Bishop's Park.

April. Chatterton left his native city for London.

Aug. 24, Chatterton died, being found to have taken poison, at his lodging, in the house of Mrs. Angel, a *saque* or mantua (not *sack*) maker, in Brook-street, Holborn. The only paper found in his pocket-book was a letter received two or three days previously from Mr. Catcott, to which he had written a long reply in his usual strain of good spirits and freedom, but certainly not in the best state of mind towards religious professors and their sentiments. Both letters are now in the possession of Mr. Richard Smith. The most recent collection of Chatterton's Works was published in 3 vols. 8vo. for the benefit of his sister (then living) in 1803, by Longman & Co., edited by Messrs. Southey and Cottle. In vol. iii. Mr. Cottle, who, when he began the task, was a *Rowleian,* has decided the question on the Chatterto-

77Onian side of the controversy. That some real documents
fell into our poet's hands is not to be disputed; and these
gave him themes and writing-character whereon, assisted
by Bailey's Dictionary, &c. he exercised his genius, with
the avowed determination of building a fortune. This he
was too wise to expect in his own proper person. Had he
been in possession of MSS. which he thought really valuable,
and had he been conscious, too, of poetical merit to the amount
of a hundredth part of that which has been awarded him
and his Rowley by the host of controversialists who have since
gratified his perturbed spirit, if it really revisited earth, in
its most ardent thirst after posthumous fame, that consciousness alone would have sufficed to keep him in love with life.

In considering the claims of Chatterton's memory to a
monumental tribute, it is, we presume, ridiculous to talk of
the looseness of his theological opinions. In the Monthly
Magazine for January 1820, under the head " Cornucopia,"
appears, upon Mr. Catcott's authority, Chatterton's Articles
of Belief.* Few boys of seventeen years think so intensely
upon the subject of religion, and fewer still afford such
admirable materials whereon to found the character of a
rational Christian. Any one qualified by talents and expe-
rience to advise with him, as a bosom-friend, might have
satisfied him that he had not lived long enough to attract
all the patronage he deserved in the estimation of his fellow-
citizens. He sunk under the pre-excitement of enthusiasm
unchecked by friendly restraint—the consciousness of genius
overwhelmed by its pride. The alloy of a little *vanity*
might have kept his spirits rationally buoyant for a stream of
affairs more propitious to his hopes. His mortal remains lie
in the burying-ground of Shoe-lane Work-house, London,
mingled, perhaps, with the most disregarded dust.

Mr. Catcott had lent Chatterton, while in Bristol, ten
guineas. Alluding to it, some time afterward, in a sportive
mood, he said he might as well give a receipt, and, taking a
scrap of paper, wrote the subjoined, which we copy from
the original, in Mr. Richard Smith's possession:

" Mr. Geo. Catcott

.to the Exors of T. Rowley   Dr
To pleasure rec^d on reading his Historic Works   5 „ 5
———————————— his Poetic Works   5 „ 5

1„10"

* Mr. Catcott's volume, alluded to in that communication, is now in the possession
f George Weare Braikenridge, esq. of Broomwell-House, Brislington Wick, the un-
'earied collector of all matters relating to the history and antiquities of Bristol.

A D.
1770   The following Poem was written by Chatterton, in the
presence of his juvenile and our venerable friend William
Smith (who is frequently named in the course of the controversy respecting his productions), some time previous to
his departure from home. At Mr. Smith's request, Chatterton gave him a transcript, retaining the original; and
Mr. Smith has repeatedly assured us of the identity of this
copy.

" SAY, O my soul! if not allow'd to be
Immortal, whence the misery we see,
Day after day, and hour after hour,
But to proclaim its never-ceasing power?
If *not* immortal,—then our thoughts of thee
Are but visions of *non*-futurity.
Why do we live, to feel of pain, on pain,
If, in the midst of hope, we hope in vain?
Perish the thought, in night's eternal shade!
To *live*—then *die*—man was not only made.
There's yet an awful something else remains,
Either to lessen or encrease our pains!
Whate'er it be, whate'er man's future fate,
Nature proclaims, there *is* another state
Of woe—or bliss! But who is he can tell?
None, but the good, and they that have done well.
Oh! may their happiness be ours, my friend!
The little we have here will shortly end;
When joy, and bliss, more lasting, will appear,
Or all our hopes translated into fear!
Oh, may our portion in that world above,
Eternal Fountain of eternal Love!
Be crown'd with peace, that bids the sinner *live*,
With praise to Him, who only can forgive—
Blot out the stains and errors of our youth;
Whose smile is mercy, and whose word is truth."

The sympathizing reader will not fail to remark the
kindred feeling as well as genius displayed in Lord Byron's
poem, written for Mr. Nathan's adaptation to a Hebrew
melody, commencing " When coldness wraps this suffering
clay;" and in another short poem, the publication of which a
friend prevailed upon him to suppress, as being too sombre
for his lordship's muse, beginning " They say that hope is

.770happiness;" on the rescue whereof from oblivion the noble
poet's death has conferred a melancholy degree of propriety.
A Charles Abraham Elton lives to award complete justice to
the memory of the Bristol blue-coat boy of Colston's School;
therefore more words in this quarter would be impertinent.

St. Leonard's Church, Corn-street, the tower and Blind
Gate upon which it stood, and the old house (the Goat
public-house) within the gate, taken down, preparatory to
opening a new street to the Quay, which was named after
Lord Clare, lately Mr. Nugent, M.P.

According to "*A Plan of St. Stephen's Church and its
Environs*," as surveyed this year,

In the view down Corn-street from the Post-Office, instead of
the Froom and St. Augustin's Back, was seen the termination of
St. Nicholas-street in the front of the Goat public-house, sharing
more than half the width of Corn-street with the *Blind-Gate*
(anciently Baldwin-Gate and St. Leonard's Gate), an arch on the
spectator's right hand supporting the east end of St. Leonard's
Church.* Half-way under the church, the gate led, on the left,
into Baldwin-street, and with a curve to the right, into *Fisher-lane*,
now, with parallel corners and widened, forming St. Stephen-street.
The ground at present occupied by Sir R. Vaughan & Co.'s ware-
houses, and the dwelling-house adjoining, was the *Fish-Market*,
with the *Conduit* or Key-Pipe at the end of it, towards the river,
as described by William of Worcester, under 1534, "a fair castellette, &c." (One of its ornaments, a head of Momus, is in the
possession of Mr. Miller, at his Nursery, King's Parade.) The
north-east wall of St. Leonard's Church, bounded by the present
St. Leonard's Lane, measured 30 feet, and the south-west wall
about 20 feet, reaching to that side of Messrs. Oliver and Stone's
tea-warehouse, a length of about 64 feet. Ten feet of the breadth
extended from the frontage of the same house into Clare-street. On
the north-west side of the Church, two flights of steps, one on each
side of a small dwelling-house (formerly the vicarage), descended
from St. Leonard's Lane into Fisher-lane; the farthermost flight
across the latter faced a passage behind the site of Messrs. Oliver
and Stone's two houses, called *Pile-end* (a name which we think
was derived from the means used to make good that bank of the
ancient course of the Froom in its way through Baldwin-street);
and here, on the left, commenced Marsh-street; while a passage
of 25 feet long led to the church-yard, with its south-east boundary of *St. Stephen's Lane*. The Argyle public-house, with its
passage leading to the church-yard, stood in Marsh-street, on the
ground now occupied by Mrs. Prosser's toy-warehouse. St. Stephen's Lane led round the church-yard, in the direction toward
the Quay, westward of St. Stephen's Avenue. There were two

* The form and elevation of this church are clearly defined, No. 15 in S. & N. Buck's
North-west Prospect of the City from Brandon-Hill, 1734.

A. D.

1770 other church-ways from the Quay, between St. Stephen's Lane and the Fish-Market, viz. *Canon-lane* and *the White Hart Passage*, so named from a public-house facing the base of the Church-tower, *Coopers' Arms Passage* led from an opposite public-house to the Quay, parallel with St. Stephen's Lane, and that, and two houses standing between the lane and passage, and five other houses in their rear, extending to Marsh-street, were taken down, to make the new opening of St. Stephen's Avenue. Midway between the Coopers' Arms Passage and Rosemary-lane (the east end of which remains, leading from Marsh-street into Clare-street), was Mr. *Alderman Dampier's Passage*, that led westward from a court to the Quay. See 1773. .

1771 The pavement before the Council-House altered, and the bronze pillars placed in front of the Exchange.—Clare-street, towards which the Chamber gave £2000, commenced building.—St. Stephen-street opened.—College-street begun.

Stage-coaches began to ply between Bristol and the Hotwells, at sixpenny fares.

1772 The new paving began all over the city.—Houses in Wine-street taken down, to open a way into Broadmead, named Union-street.—Redcliff-Gate removed.—To enlarge the church-yard and open the avenues of St. Stephen, the Corporation contributed £200, the Society of Merchants £200, and Mrs. Peloquin (widow of the Mayor in 1751) £200. By her will in 1779, that lady bequeathed for the same purpose £300 more, and in 1780, Dean Tucker gave £50.

April 5, the organ of St. Peter's Church opened.

Dec. 2 and 15, the Bristol Library-Society formed. See an account of this institution in The Bristol Memorialist, p. 201, with the signature "Bibliophile," by John Fry; to which we are enabled to add some particulars, not to be found elsewhere in print.

So early as 1603, the Corporation agreed that, provided Mr. Redwood would give them his Lodge, which adjoined the Town-wall, near the Marsh, for conversion into a Library, there should be a door made through the wall, to pass thence into the Marsh; and that such books as should be given to the City by the Archbishop of York or any other well-disposed person, for the furnishing a library, should be thankfully accepted. In 1615 (when, probably, Mr. Redwood. made or confirmed his grant by will, dated the 20th of March) the Corporation ordered that 40s. should be paid out of the Chamber, annually, to the keeper of the library. In 1634 they further ordered that the library should be enlarged, and Richard Vickris (sheriff in 1636 and mayor in 1646) gave a parcel of ground for that purpose. Perhaps this grant was

1772 first committed to writing at the date quoted by Mr. Barrett, April 12, 1636.

As stated in that gentleman's History (to which we think Mr. Fry had not access when he wrote the paper above referred to), in 1738-9 the Mayor, William Jeffreys, expended in building the library £184 6s. 7d. His successors, Stephen Clutterbuck and Henry Combe, added, the former, in 1739-40, £681 3s., and the latter, in 1740-1, £435 18s. 6d., making a total of £1301 8s. 1d.

The books, including those given by Archbishop Mathew and various other persons,* did not at this time amount to more than 500. Those of the Archbishop consist of the Fathers, Schoolmen, and a few of the Latin Classics (most of which bear his autograph), of course such only as had been printed previous to 1628; and he doubtless had in view the ability which " the Aldermen and Shopkeepers" might derive, for reading them, from the previous foundation of the Free Grammar-School; nor is it to be doubted that the projectors of the Society now formed took cognizance of the good prelate's liberal design, in their *deliberations for the future* conservation and government of the Library. " The Aldermen and Shopkeepers," at the time of the Archbishop's bequest, comprehended nearly the whole of the citizens.† Whatever may be thought of the mental restraints imposed upon the "free burgesses" by the constitution of the Bristol Library-Society, we have never heard of any obstruction to a gentlemanly application for access to the books, the property of the Corporation, even on the part of those of the citizens who are *not* free burgesses. Very many "free burgesses" are to be found among the holders of purchased shares, who are, besides, annual subscribers.

1773 July 1, the Bristol Library-Room was first opened.

---

* Among those other persons, was John Heylyn, esq. who, as we first learnt from a memorandum in the margin of a foolscap quarto page, written full of directions to bind the two volumes described below, shot himself in his bed, at seven o'clock in the morning of Sunday, Aug. 28, 1768, at his house in College-Green :—

" Theological Lectures at Westminster-Abbey, with an Interpretation of the Four Gospels. To which are added, some Select Discourses upon the principal points of Revealed Religion. By John Heylyn, D. D. Prebendary of Westminster, and Rector of St. Mary-le-Strand. Tonson and Draper, 1749." In a blank leaf at the commencement of vol. i. is written, " John Heylyn—given me by the Author, my honoured ffather, Bristol, May 20, 1749. New binding in October 1751 cost nine shill."

Mr. Heylyn's autograph appears in all the books of which he was the donor.—We regard the matter of this note as supplementary to the Memoir of Dr. Peter Heylyn, in Rees's Cyclopædia, and who died May 3, 1662.

† None but free burgesses, it was till long since understood, had a right to keep open shops, the last example of which is seen in that of Mr. Llewelin, High-street, next to St. Nicholas-street.

A.D.

1773 An Act of Parliament was obtained for making·commodious ways and passages within the parish of St. Stephen, and for enlarging the burying-ground.

1774 At the general election, the votes in Bristol were, for Henry Cruger, 3565—Edmund Burke, 2707—Matthew Brickdale, 2453—Lord Clare, 286. Burgesses who voted, 5384.

1775 March 17, the Rev. Mr. Newnham's death in Pen-Park Hole.

This year the way was made from Wine-street to Broadmead, called Union-street; and, May 1, St. James's Market was opened.

July. St. Michael's Church commenced re-building, excepting the tower.

Four houses on the bank of the Froom, at the foot of and facing College-Green, taken down.

The building of Park-street, in Bullock's Park, began. It was, we believe, at the completion of Park-street, that the conduit at the south-east corner of Unity-street was erected, for conveyance from the spring rising at the head of Park-street. Previously, on the site of Reeve's Hotel, College-Place, stood " the Water-House."

Blind Steps, leading from St. Nicholas Market to Back-street, taken down, enlarged and opened.

It was estimated at this time that £5970 per annum was expended for the poor of Bristol in the hospitals, &c. exclusive of £10,000 raised for the parochial poor; and that there were constantly 1032 persons of all ages, who lived wholly upon public charity.

1776 The trees growing across the middle of Queen-Square cut down. [We would earnestly recommend all whose taste for radical innovation extends to the cutting down of trees growing in a crowded city, to study the chemical doctrine of the transpiration of vegetables, in which most of their young friends can give them learned assistance.]

An Act of Parliament was obtained, " to remove the danger of fire amongst the ships in the port of Bristol, by preventing the landing certain commodities on the present quays, and for providing a convenient quay and proper places for landing and storing the same; and for regulating the said quay, and the lighters, boats, and other vessels carrying goods for hire within the said port of Bristol; and for other purposes therein mentioned." The object of this Act was to enlarge and occupy the Merchants' Floating-Dock, in Rownham Meads. From Sept. 29, all that part of the parish of Clifton that lay between the bound-stone of

A. D.

1776 the city on the east of a little brook, anciently called Wood-well-lake, but now a sluice under ground, at Limekiln-Dock, and the ferry called Rownham-Passage, and between the river Avon and the road which leads from the said bound-stone and the said ferry, were hereby separated from the judicial jurisdiction of Gloucestershire, and made part of Bristol, except with regard to taxes and votes at elections for knights of the shire.

Oct. 17, the limits of the New Docks marked out.

1777 Jan. 19, Sunday morning, between six and seven o'clock, a fire broke out in Bell-lane, which consumed several ware-houses, and burnt and damaged large quantities of wool belonging to Lewsly & Co. The incendiary proved to be James Aitken, who had set fire to the rope-house at the Royal Dock-Yard, Portsmouth, Dec. 17th previous, for which he was hung on the 10th of March. For other like deeds of " Jack the Painter," vide The Newgate Calendar.

June. St. Michael's new Church opened.

An Act was passed to enable His Majesty to license a Theatre in Bristol.

1778 The Gloucester, for 60 guns and 316 men, of 896 tons, and the Medea, for 32 guns, launched in this port.

This year the estates and rents of the Corporation of Bristol produced £14,000.

1779 Mrs. Mary Peloquin bequeathed £19,000 to the Corpora-tion, for various purposes, and her house in Prince's Street, for the perpetual residence of the rector of St. Stephen's.

The drawing of pitch and tar from pit-coal was now first discovered in Bristol.

An Act of Parliament was obtained for making and repair-ing several roads round the City of Bristol; reciting all the former Acts, inclusive of that of 31 Geo. II. 1751.

1780 Matthew Brickdale, esq. and Sir Henry Lippincott, bart. chosen representatives in Parliament.

1781 Sir H. Lippincott dying, Geo. Daubeny, esq. was chosen to succeed him.

1782 The old colonnade called the Tolzey, erected in 1616, taken down.—The house next to All-Saints' Church rebuilt, as an eastern wing of the Exchange.—The Conduit-house at the head of the Quay taken down, and the Fish-market there removed to Union-street.

John Purrier, merchant, of London, settled so much in the public funds as would make Mr. Colston's apprentice-fee from the School fifteen pounds. He also gave for the boys 100 silver and 100 brass badges.

A. D.

1783   The boys of Queen Elizabeth's Hospital (the City-School),
Orchard-street, and those of the Grammar-School, in late
St. Bartholomew's Hospital, Christmas-street, exchanged
places.   This change was afterward confirmed by Act of
Parliament, viz.

"An Act to enable the Corporation of the city of Bristol to exchange the building of the hospital called Queen Elizabeth's Hospital, for the building called the Bartholomews in the said City, and
for altering the times for holding the Bristol Fairs." The preamble
states that the Mayor, &c. are Governors of Queen Elizabeth's Hospital for the maintenance and education of poor children, in the
houses near College-Green, formerly the sole property of the Mayor,
&c. and by them given and converted to that purpose;—that they
are likewise Governors or Visitors of a free Grammar-School in the
Bartholomews.   "And whereas the apartments belonging to the
" said building called the Bartholomews are not large enough to
" receive and maintain *many* of the citizens' children, who have *a*
" *right* to be educated at the said Grammar-School, although the
" said apartments *are* sufficient to serve *all* the purposes for which
" the Hospital called Queen Elizabeth's Hospital was intended.
" And whereas it would be of great *reciprocal* convenience and ad-
" vantage, if the masters and scholars belonging to the said free
" Grammar-School at the Bartholomews aforesaid were removed to
" the said building called Queen Elizabeth's Hospital, and that the
" master and children belonging to the said Hospital were removed
" to the said building called the Bartholomews; but as it is appre-
" hended that such exchange, though it would *manifestly* be of *such*
" reciprocal benefit as aforesaid, cannot be made without the aid and
" authority of Parliament, may it therefore please your Majesty, &c."*

1784   The foundation of the present Infirmary laid.—The Hay-
market in Broadmead opened.—Hackney-coaches first
established.

Mail-coaches established by John Palmer, esq. The experiment was first tried between London and Bristol.—The

* His Majesty was not told that the master of the Free Grammar-School had married
the daughter of an alderman (Henry Dampier, sheriff in 1751 and mayor in 1755), who
very naturally preferred the light and air of College-Green to that of Christmas-street.
Mr. Alderman Dampier did well so to exercise his influence for his daughter's better
health and comfort; but whether the complaisance of his magisterial brethren ought to
have carried them so far, is another question. We are of opinion that his fellow-bur-
gesses without doors were the most to blame. To the fathers of "many of the citizens'
children" the exchange must have been a matter of indifference; for, from their disregard, up to the present time, of the original design of the Thornes in their favour, it is
fair to infer that the affectation of superiority to the advantages of a *free-school* (a syno-
nyme of *charity-school*) was the parent and nurse of that indifference.—The Thornes
would seem to have been anxious to repair the loss of Latin and its teachers in the persons of the priesthood expelled by the Reformation, and Archbishop Mathew to furnish
books for its exercise; but we cannot understand that the reading of those books was to
be altogether a matter of charity: they were to be kept in order, and their number
increased; and so, beyond all doubt, thought the citizens who did the good work of 1772.

A. D.

1784 necessary revolution in the economy of the General Post-Office, London, for discharge of all the posts at one hour, was effected by the individual example of Francis Freeling, esq. then a lad, sent for from the Bristol Post-Office for that purpose; the clerks having mutinied against the new plan, as impossible to be executed.

The House of Mercy on Colston's Parade, Redcliff Church-yard, for twelve poor widows, built and endowed by William Fry, distiller.

April 3, commenced an election for representatives in Parliament that lasted thirty-seven days. The votes were, for Matthew Brickdale, 3458—Henry Cruger, 3052—George Daubeny, 2982—Samuel Peach Peach, 373.

1785 April 5, the Mansion-House, Queen-Square, having been fitted up for the reception of the Mayor's family for the time being, the Banquetting-Room in Charlotte-street was opened.

In this year (the 26th of the King) an Act of Parliament was obtained to render more effectual the Act 33 Geo. II. for rebuilding, &c. the Bridge over the Avon—to take down the south side of Tucker-street, some of the houses on the west side of Temple-street, and some on the east side of St. Thomas-street, nearest to the Bridge, to open a new street (Bath-street) from the Bridge to Temple-street—for removing the statue of Neptune, the pipes, &c. and for taking down and re-building or selling the Cross in Temple-street.*

An Act of Parliament was also obtained for rebuilding Christ-Church, otherwise the Holy Trinity, and for widening the adjacent streets.

1786 May 8, William Isaac Roberts born. See his Poems and Letters. He died Dec. 26, 1806.

The Hay-market in Broadmead established.—Hackney-coaches began to stand in the streets, commencing with three at the Exchange.—Queen's Parade, Brandon-Hill, built.—Berkeley-Square commenced.— Old Christ-Church taken down : a statue of a Saxon earl, seated in a niche, was found walled in at the front. The foundation of the new Church was laid Nov. 4.—The wing of the City-Library erected.

1787 An Act of Parliament was obtained for dividing the parish of St. James, in the City and County of Bristol, and County

---

* It might have been rebuilt; for the ground in front of the Stars public-house, corner of Hawkins's Lane (from Sir John Hawkins), still presents sufficient room. Though we had not even dreamt of becoming an Antiquary, we could not forbear sympathizing in Mr. George Catcott's newspaper-lamentation at the time.

1787 of Gloucester, and for building a Church, and providing a cæmetery and parsonage-house within the new parish.

On the south-west side of Redcliff-Hill was built a school for girls.

The south side of Tucker-street taken down, to open the he of Bath-street.

1788 The east wing of the Infirmary completed.—Brunswick-Square built.

This year (the 28th of the King) were obtained the three following Acts of Parliament, viz.

" An Act for removing and preventing Encroachments, Obstructions, Annoyances, and other Nuisances, within the City of Bristol and the Liberties thereof, and for licensing and better regulating Hackney-Coaches, Chairs, Waggons, Carts, and other Carriages, &c. and Porters and other persons within and for certain distances round the city and liberties ; and for better regulating the Shipping and Trade, and the Rivers, Wharfs, Backs, and Quays, and the Markets within the said liberties; and for other purposes." By this Act the Corporation were empowered to make by-laws respecting the Draw-Bridge, to establish a market for raw hides and skins at the Back-Hall, regulate the fisheries on the rivers Severn, Avon, and Froom, &c. &c. The schedule contains Tables of Fees of the Quay-Warden and the Water-Bailiff.

" An Act for widening and rendering commodious Broad-street, and for enlarging the Council-House and Guild-Hall, &c." This Act provided for taking down the houses recently [1824] occupied by Mr. Davies, glover, and Mr. Sheppard, milliner, in Broad-street, and the house in Corn-street, formerly Foster's Coffee-house, latterly in part occupied by Mr. Tayler, brush-maker, and whatever was intersected therewith, including the City Printing-Office and the shop formerly occupied in succession by Mrs. Ward, Mrs. Bryan, Mr. F. Harris, and Mr. Page.

" An Act for regulating Buildings and Party-Walls within the City of Bristol and Liberties thereof." This Act provides that the external wall of all new buildings shall be carried up perpendicularly, and range in the general line of the street, &c.; and that when any external wall or part thereof, ranging with the street, shall be taken down, the wall to be rebuilt or repaired shall rise in a perpendicular line from the ancient story-post or foundation of such building. No new bow-windows or other projections to extend, in any street thirty feet wide or more, above ten inches, nor in a street less than thirty feet, above five inches. No cornice or covering, in the former case, to extend more than eighteen inches, nor in the latter more than thirteen inches, from the upright line of the building.

Bristol was destined to be this year once more the theatre of a farce like that of the Lamb Inn, West-street, in 1762. For any grave treatment of such details we are not, in this

1788case, disposed to do more than refer to a pamphlet, published in this same year, under the following title:

"A Narrative of the Extraordinary Case of GEO. LUKINS, of Yatton, Somersetshire, who was possessed of Evil Spirits for near eighteen years. Also an Account of his remarkable Deliverance, in the Vestry-Room of Temple-Church, in the City of Bristol. Extracted from the Manuscripts of several persons who attended. To which is prefixed, a Letter from the Rev. W. R. W. [dated Wrington, June 5.] The fourth edition; with the Rev. Mr. EASTERBROOK's Letter annexed, authenticating the particulars which occurred at Temple-Church." 8vo. pp. 24.

"The persons who attended," as the reader is informed in a note to p. 19, were "the Rev. Mr. Easterbrook, vicar of Temple; Messrs. J. Broadbent, J. Valton, B. Rhodes, J. Brettel, T. M'Geary, W. Hunt. With eight other serious persons." The press of the day teemed with other productions of believers as well as of unbelievers in *Mister Nicholas senior*'s potency. Among the latter, the most successful disputant was Mr. Norman, surgeon, of Yatton; and the ridicule that accumulated around the devoted heads of the confiding-ones, we believe, tended to shorten the otherwise really useful life of the Vicar of Temple, who was also Ordinary of Newgate; of the goodness of whose heart, whatever might be said of his share of that needful material of the head, common sense, derivable chiefly from close and excursive observation of human nature, there were scarcely two opinions.

Lukins was a psalm-singer, a ventriloquist, and an actor of Christmas plays or mummeries, and had practised upon the credulity of his immediate neighbourhood for eighteen years, when his fame reached to Bristol. He had exhibited in Temple-Church two or three times previous to the grand display of the "Narrative." Being employed as a common-carrier between Yatton and Bristol, he was known to many of our fellow-citizens. In the performance of his engagement to join the serious assemblage at the church, he once called at the shop of Messrs. Bath and Pinkney, the corner of Redcliff-street and St. Thomas-street, for the purpose of inviting those gentlemen to be witnesses of his premeditated calling of "spirits from the vasty deep;" but Mr. Bath (as Mr. Pinkney told the writer) affecting to doubt the conformity of infernal agency with human arrangements of an adverse tendency, contented himself with hastening George on his way towards Temple-street, lest the Devil should take it into his horned head to "play hell" among the

1788 hardwares and cutlery. Happening ourselves, about 1804 or 1805, to reside in the road of Lukins's journeyings to and fro, as he " toddled" along with an arm-basket and a stick, he was frequently the subject of observation, which he invariably acknowledged by a polite touch of his hat. He was then a fair-looking, cleanly dressed, little old man, of yet comely and not hard-favoured features, with a good-tempered simplicity rather than archness of expression, that sufficiently accounted for the readiness with which so many became the dupes of his innocuously diabolical vocation.

1789   St. James's parish divided into two parishes, St. James and St. Paul's.—The foundation-stone of St. Paul's Church laid, April 23, by Levi Ames, mayor.*

     Sept. 29, James Hill, Mayor; Henry Bengough and John Gordon, jun. Sheriffs.

     St. Thomas' Church taken down, for rebuilding, excepting the tower, which remains shorn of one of its pinnacles, and the wound clumsily covered with lead, not *quite* out of sight.

1790   New Christ-Church opened.

     John Harris, Mayor; James Morgan and Rowland Williams, Sheriffs.

1791   Nov. 8, John Dawes Worgan born; who died July 28, 1809. He was the author of " Select Poems," published with " some particulars of his Life and Character, by an early Friend and Associate; and a Preface by William Hayley, Esq." Crown 8vo. pp. 324.

     John Noble, Mayor; Samuel Span and Richard Blake, Sheriffs.

1792   Bath-street made passable.

     Sion-Spring, Clifton, 246 feet deep, opened by Mr. Morgan.

     Tresham's painting of Christ raising the Daughter of Jairus presented to Redcliff-Church, by Sir Clifton Wintringham, bart.

     With this the 33d year of Geo. III. terminated the printing of Acts of Parliament in 𝕭𝖑𝖆𝖈𝖐 𝕷𝖊𝖙𝖙𝖊𝖗 or 𝕺𝖑𝖉 𝕰𝖓𝖌𝖑𝖎𝖘𝖍 type. It should be known that none of previous date, except such as were so printed, can be given in evidence as law.

     James Morgan, Mayor; William Gibbons and Joseph Gregory Harris, Sheriffs. In this mayoralty commenced the observance of Good Friday, by closed shops, &c. The

---

* Mr. Barrett's History contains a list of the Mayors, &c. up to this time. It was our intention to reprint the whole, in the form of an Appendix; but the varieties of spelling, especially in the earlier names, adopted in about fifteen or sixteen different transcripts from the Mayors' Kalendar that we have seen, impose upon us the necessity for a separate and still more deliberate task than the present.

A. D.

1792 attempt of France to do without any religion was regarded as infectious, and needing every reasonable means of prevention. Papists found charity among us.

1793 The Penny Post-Office for Bristol and its suburbs established.

The body and eastern wing of the Infirmary opened.

The Asylum for the Blind, Lower Maudlin-lane, opened.

Dundry Church repaired.

Oct. 1. THE RIOT OF BRISTOL - BRIDGE. The writer having, in his then circle of acquaintance, stood alone in his estimate of the conduct of the magistrates in this affair, of which he was a close witness, being at the time a resident in Bridge-street,—having read all the contemporary publications,—and having hitherto met with no argument nor new matter to controvert his opinion,—he cannot resist the present opportunity of placing that opinion on record, for whatever judgment his readers may form beyond his sole motive; which is, by re-assertion of his belief that all shared alike in inflicting this imputed disgrace upon the municipal government, to neutralize all angry personal feelings in his surviving fellow-citizens.

The only limit of the Bridge-Act, as may be seen in that of 1785, was the accumulation of a balance of £2000 to vest at interest, for the purpose of lighting and keeping the bridge in repair. It should be premised that those alone who possessed horses and carriages were affected by the tolls, for foot-passengers had ever passed freely. David Lewis, a man with whose simplicity of character was blended an ardent public spirit, but which was rendered ineffectual by his almost total want of that part of education which teaches the best use of speech and letters (for the author, then an apprentice, was employed by him to write the latest of his several addresses as a candidate to represent the city in Parliament)—this man, though ordinarily penurious, being the renter of the tolls, gave up his profits from the 18th of September, by way of marking in the public mind the supposed letter of the law. Meantime, the Bridge-Commissioners, as theretofore, advertised the tolls to be let for another year, and, preparatory thereto, erected a new toll-gate at the south end of the Bridge; the citizens pusillanimously neglecting to call them to account for this apparent irregularity. The condition of the Bridge-fund was notorious, for the Trustees' statement of it was published annually in all the newspapers. Their last-published statement, dated Sept. 30, exhibited an estimate that the balance, when

1793 the debt of £2600 on the Bridge should be paid (towards which £1050 and upward of arrears remained to be received from the several parishes), would be only £1062; and the Trustees added that the interest of the sum allowed by the Act, £2000, would in their opinion be insufficient for the purposes of lighting and repairing the Bridge, and expressed their wish to continue the tolls for one year, to save the citizens the expense of another application to Parliament.

On Thursday Sept. 19, the toll-gates, and board with the rates of tolls payable, were pulled down and burnt. On Friday the 27th, the demolition of the new toll-gates and gutting of the toll-house and burning the books was undertaken by the very inconsiderable mob of scarcely twenty persons. During the whole of Saturday, Sunday, and Monday, immense crowds of people assembled, to witness the struggles between some of the magistrates in person, and riders and drivers, in enforcement and resistance of payment. The proclamation was first read on Saturday evening, about nine o'clock, and repeatedly afterward, but disregarded because it was not, from motives of humanity, promptly acted upon; the constant exclamation of individuals one to another being, "Oh! they don't dare to fire!" Not a petty constable's staff was to be seen—so that the writer himself mingled with the throng repeatedly, in perfect security. In the afternoon of Monday, the guards formed by the Hereford regiment of militia, under Lord Bateman, on the Bridge, were assaulted by boys and striplings, "aided, abetted, comforted and assisted" by the curious lookers-on who filled all the converging avenues. Thus goaded to resistance, the soldiers, under direction of the magistrates, fired, but mostly with elevated muzzles, or the slaughter would have been tremendous. The number of killed and wounded was altogether about thirty-six. The writer was at this instant, between seven and eight o'clock, in professional attendance at the Theatre, but so strongly was he possessed with the belief that only powder had been discharged, of which some of the flying-mob, whom he first met near the Back-Hall, repeatedly assured him, that he passed one man lying prostrate as if fallen in his flight through inebriety, at the foot of St. Nicholas' Church-steps, and, with unabated security, another man lying near the place of the watch-box in the church-yard-railing, from whom a stream issued down the pavement. A bonfire blazed on the Bridge, and the firing of musketry and roll of the drums had not ceased on the side of St. Thomas-street, when he continued onward, through two

A. D.

1793 lines of soldiers drawn from High-street to the north-west toll-house, and across the end of Bridge-street, without any interruption from them, either of word or act. The first unauthorized faces he saw were those of persons peeping out from the steps leading to Bridge-street Chapel. Before he reached the composing-room of Sarah Farley's Journal-Office, on the upper floor, which commanded a view of the Bridge, all was quiet. After eleven o'clock, he ventured out to view the scene of action, but a shower of rain had washed away every trace of blood.—He thought then, as he does still, that this disastrous event might have been prevented by a well-regulated exercise of every good citizen's public duty, in meetings to discuss the supposed abuse of their trust by the Bridge-Commissioners. The path of the Magistrates was plain: they were bound to preserve the King's peace by all the means in their power. The London riots of 1780, and the consequent lesson to pusillanimous magistrates, were freshly in remembrance. It was no less the duty of the inhabitants, for their own sakes, actively to support the magisterial authority, while on the other hand they sought to obtain legal redress from a disputed toll. The required deficiency of ways and means for lighting and keeping the Bridge in repair, to the amount of £1920 more than the balance in hand, was, after all, made up by private subscription among the quiet observers of the recorded mischiefs.—An eminent physician interested himself to obtain a meeting for enquiry into all the circumstances, and bring the matter before Parliament, but could not succeed in procuring a place wherein to hold such a meeting.

Henry Bengough, Mayor; Robert Castle and Joseph Edye, Sheriffs.

Dec. 21, the new Church of St. Thomas opened. Architect, James Allen.

794 June 29, St. Paul's Church was opened. The architect and builder was Daniel Hague, under the direction of the Rev. Dr. Small; who, though a Freemason, in his abandonment of all established orders of architecture, proved his practice of the mystic craft to be not quite orthodox.

Joseph Smith, Mayor; John Page and Charles Young, Sheriffs.

795 The Asylum for Orphan Girls established at Hooke's Mills, and the Chapel opened.—St. Peter's Church repaired.—The new Pump-Room of Sion-Spring opened.—The Ebenezer Chapel for Wesleyan Methodists, in Old King-street, opened;

A. D.

1795 the Room in Broadmead (built under the auspices of John Wesley himself) being abandoned through a dispute with the Trustees.

James Harvey, Mayor; David Evans and John Wilcox, Sheriffs.

Nov. 27, the Duke of York visited Bristol, making his public entry from Park-street to the Mansion-house, where he dined. After visiting the Theatre, His Royal Highness returned to Bath.

1796 A new Bridge, formerly Needless Bridge, erected across the Froom, from Broadmead to Duck and Haulier's Lanes, preparatory to the erection of Nelson-street.—The Quay, between St. Giles's and the Draw-Bridge, widened.—St. Mary Redcliff Church repaired, and the pinnacles on the south side rebuilt, under the direction of Mr. James Allen.

James Harvey, Mayor; John Foy Edgar and Azariah Pinney, Sheriffs.

1797 Besides the annual subscriptions to the funds of the Bristol Infirmary, £10,096 14s. 6d. was contributed, to extricate the Charity from its incumbrances. See 1805.

Thomas Daniel, Mayor; Edward Protheroe and John Span, Sheriffs.

1798 Robert Claxton, Mayor; Daniel Wait, jun. and William Fripp, Sheriffs.

1799 Vaccine inoculation introduced by Dr. Edward Jenner. Few prophets reap *honour* in their own country, and that, perhaps, is the reason why so many seek merely profit. Dr. Jenner on this occasion received honorary testimonies from the remotest parts of the world—from petty sovereigns of Indian tribes, and from the Autocrat of all the Russias. The cities of London and Edinburgh voted him their freedom in gold boxes; but the cities of Gloucester and Bristol reserved their sacrifice till after sun-set. Still nearer to his home, if there yet remains one spot upon the face of the globe deriving benefit from the discovery, as witnessed by the smooth skins of its damsels, and in which the preserver of so much beauty was held in utter disregard *as such*, that spot is Berkeley!— The amount of Dr. Jenner's expenses, incurred by correspondence, was more than £7000. This, however, was covered by the grant from Parliament of £10,000.

John Morgan, Mayor; Henry Bright (sugar-refiner) and Worthington Brice, Sheriffs.

1800 John Townsend, the surgeon, died, aged 70; leaving the population of Bristol very much indebted to him for helping so many of them first into the light.

A. D.

1800 William Gibbons, Mayor; Robert Castle and Samuel Birch, Sheriffs.

1801 The population of Bristol, excluding the suburbs, estimated at 63,645.

The Bristol Penitentiary, Upper Magdalen-lane, established.

Joseph Edye, Mayor; Samuel Span and Richard Vaughan, jun., Sheriffs.

1802 Robert Castle, Mayor; who died, and was succeeded by David Evans; J. F. Edgar and Sir Henry Protheroe, knt., Sheriffs.

1803 An Act of Parliament passed to convert the rivers Avon and Froom into a floating-harbour, by cutting a new course for the Avon, from the line of the city-boundary eastward, to the Red Clift, the seat of Dowager Lady Smyth, westward.

David Evans, Mayor; Samuel Henderson and John Haythorne, Sheriffs.

1804 May 1, the New Cut for the Avon commenced excavating in the mead near Wapping. We have already noticed, p. 6, in illustration of the earliest name of this city in the Welsh chronicles, the discovery of the waters having formerly flowed over a bed, of which the Avon is now but a very contracted channel.

St. James's Church repaired, with the addition of a south gallery.

Edward Protheroe, Mayor; Levi Ames, jun. and Philip Protheroe, Sheriffs.

1805 The amount of contributions for building the *west* wing of the Infirmary, and towards its support, independently of the annual subscriptions, was £10,602 12s. See the Table of Benefactions in the Committee-Room.

Daniel Wait, jun. Mayor; Wm. Inman and John Hilhouse Wilcox, Sheriffs.

1806 The Pitching and Paving Act passed. Quietness and economy require that this Act should be superseded by one for *steining* and paving.

Richard Vaughan, jun. Mayor; Henry Brooke and Edward Brice, jun., Sheriffs.

1807 Aug. 1, an Act of Parliament passed " for ascertaining and establishing the rates of wharfage, plankage, anchorage, and moorage, to be received at the lawful quays in the port of Bristol; for the regulation of crane-keepers in the said port; and for the better regulation of pilots and pilotage of vessels navigating the Bristol Channel."

Henry Bright, Mayor; who died, and was succeeded by

A. D,

1807 Samuel Birch; Sir Henry Protheroe and John Haythorne, Sheriffs.

October. The Prince of Wales and the Duke of Sussex dined at the Merchants' Hall. At eight o'clock the same evening their Royal Highnesses left Bristol for Berkeley Castle.

1808 The river Froom, owing to a heavy fall of rain, overflowed its banks, and inundated the north side of the city, without the line of its original walls, from Newfoundland-street to Broadmead.

John Haythorne, Mayor; Benjamin Bickley and Philip George, Sheriffs.

1809 May. The Floating-Harbour completed.

John Hilhouse Wilcox, Mayor; Edward Brice and Benjamin Bickley, Sheriffs.

1810 ·March 22, a Chapel for Calvinistic Independents opened near Countess or Counter-slip.

Aug. 6, 14, and 21, Joseph Lancaster delivered his three lectures, (the first two at the Tailors' Hall, and the third at the Assembly-Room,) which settled the foundation of his system of universal education in Bristol.—[In 1809, his friend Joseph Fox wrote "A Comparative View of the Plans of Education, as detailed in the publications of Dr. Bell and Mr. Lancaster." 8vo. pp. 80. In Jnne, this year, appeared "The British System of Education; being a complete Epitome of the Improvements and Inventions practised at the Royal Free-Schools, Borough-Road, Southwark. By Joseph Lancaster." 8vo. pp. 82. No one, than Joseph Lancaster, more sincerely rejoiced at the successful rivalry that hence ensued on the part of the Diocesan Schools throughout the empire; and which, within the two short years preceding the publication of this "Outline," has fostered the experiment of "The Hive," a twopenny weekly sheet in 8vo., until the number of similar appeals to the rational being of the people, embracing extracts from expensive works connected with nearly the whole circle of the sciences, amounts to upwards of sixty. This is indeed the triumph of the Press over stupid Tobacco-funking!—The History of Joseph Lancaster and his compeers remains to be written. Toward the materials, a sketch of his disputes with the Borough-Road Committee, bearing on its front the repulsive sentence, "Oppression and Persecution," instead of producing the justice due to truth and the benefit of a mirror to the writer for his better progress, fell still-born from the press. Particulars of the manner of his departure from this country, and his reception in America, will be found in the Monthly Repository for June 1819,

.

A. D.

1810(vol. xiv. p. 397), and in the Monthly Magazine for September following, p. 105. The newspapers have reported that, in April 1824, Joseph Lancaster and his family (a wife and daughter) sailed from Philadelphia for La Guira. Having searched that man's heart, and brought natural tears into his eyes by the questions we felt were due to our respect for his public character with reference to the reports of his faults and foibles, we declare that his final Judge alone may venture to pronounce against him without the utmost temerity. His greatest crime was his poverty—his greatest folly, in the estimation of Mammon's darling children, refusal of a sinecure of £365 per annum, because mistaken charity denied investigation of the charge of his having anonymously addressed a threatening letter to Joseph Fox. The debt of the petitioning-creditor under his bankruptcy, we believe, had been owing scarcely six months; and the act of bankruptcy was committed unconsciously, by accepting a seat in the carriage of a gentleman nearly related to one of the most popular members of the present Parliament. But how, it will be asked by the uninitiated, could Joseph Lancaster's claims upon the national gratitude be possibly repressed without *some* foundation? In the first place, he was too proud to prefer a claim except upon his own terms: he was no hypocrite, no sophister, in any sense of the words. In the next, the world abounds with very good people who, not being over-wise in tracing the sinuosities of human policy, will not suffer their native benevolence and candour to believe that any man, wearing the garb of goodness and notoriously in the performance of *some* good works, could become the inventor and propagator of false testimony against his neighbour. But Interest, the *alpha* and *omega* of not a few among us, can do wonders: ambition is sometimes too humble to reach Heaven: some among us would rather make sure of Earth, and take their chance for another and a better world!]

Sept. Mr. Sadler's ascent, with Mr. William Clayfield (the youngest son of Chatterton's liberal patron), in a balloon, from the Back-field, between Stoke's Croft and Wilder-street, which descended in the Bristol Channel on the coast of Somersetshire; but both of the voyagers were brought home, the following day, without injury.

Philip Protheroe, Mayor; William Inman and James Fowler, Sheriffs.

1811 September. The Commercial Rooms were opened, for the perusal of newspapers and other publications of trading

1811 reference; with suites of rooms for auctions, bankrupt-meetings, &c. Built by proprietary shares of £25 each. The subscriber who is not a proprietor pays the interest of a share (25s.) in addition to three guineas per annum; proprietors themselves subscribe three guineas per annum, for use of the rooms. Non-residents admitted free of charge for a month, upon having their names registered by a subscriber.—The architect of the building was C. A. Busby; the sculptor of the three statues over the pediment and of the group in bas-relief on the frieze within the portico, was J. G. Bubb.

The population of Bristol, including Clifton and Bedminster, estimated at 71,279. But this, as well as every other census in time of war, was very loosely taken; the disposition being scarcely less strong to evade such an enquiry, than to prevent a full assessment of taxes.

John Hilhouse Wilcox, Mayor; Edward Brice and Benjamin Bickley, Sheriffs.

1812 The Prince of Wales assumed the Regency.

The Rev. Samuel Seyer published " The Charters and Letters Patent granted by the Kings and Queens of England to the Town and City of Bristol. Newly translated, and accompanied by the original Latin." 4to. pp. 338.

July 21, Richard Hart Davis, esq. was returned as a representative in Parliament for Bristol, upon the retirement of Charles Bragge Bathurst, esq. The election lasted fourteen days, during which Mr. Davis polled 1907, and Mr. Henry Hunt 235 votes.

Michael Castle, Mayor; George and Abraham Hilhouse, Sheriffs.

Oct. 19, at the general election, after eight days' polling, Richard Hart Davis and Edward Protheroe, esquires, were returned. The votes were, for Mr. Davis, 2910; for Mr. Protheroe, 2435; for Sir Samuel Romilly, 1685; for Mr. Hunt, 455. The number of persons polled was 4500.

The Prudent Man's Friend Society instituted.

1813 The front of the Guildhall rebuilt. Mr. Henry Smith had previously made a drawing of the old front.

From Feb. 26 until March 11, a select committee of the House of Commons (Michael Angelo Taylor, esq. in the chair) was engaged in trying the merits of the late Bristol election. The petitioners were, Mr. Hunt and four of the electors. " An Authentic Report of the Evidence and Proceedings, &c." was published in 8vo. pp. 272, by an anonymous editor.—One of the effects of this enquiry was the

A. D.

1813 publication, in 1818, by " John Cranidge, *A. M.*," of " A Mirror for the Burgesses and Commonalty of the City of Bristol, in which is exhibited to their view *a part* of the great and many interesting Benefactions and Endowments of which the City hath to boast, and for which the Corporation are responsible, as the Stewards and Trustees thereof; correctly transcribed from authentic documents." 8vo. pp. 296. Mr. Cranidge (at the time of his publication, *M*aster of an *A*cademy at Upper Easton) was Mr. Hunt's especial secretary for the purposes of the scrutiny, and in that capacity " having had free access to the City-Books, by virtue of a warrant from the Speaker of the Commons House, in the months of January and February, 1813," offers his readers " many correct documents extracted therefrom" [meaning correct extracts from the civic documents], in the hope that his " extract" may " lead to a reduction of the parochial rates and public taxes." How far Mr. Cranidge's designed end will be ultimately obtained (to say nothing of the expectation of many of the " free and independent burgesses" that his labours would lead to something like a pauperizing allowance of we know not how many shillings per head per week) may be best ascertained by the perusal of the still more copious extracts from the same documents, as well as from the vestry-books of all the parishes, elucidated by personal examination of the most aged and intelligent of the free parishioners, made and taken by the Commissioners acting under Mr. Brougham's several Acts for enquiring into Charitable Trusts and Foundations. In the course of this enquiry, which is just [1824] terminated, the chairman (William Roberts, esq. A. M. and F. R. S., of Gray's Inn, barrister-at-law) declared his belief that more moneys had been vested in trust for benevolent purposes alone, in Bristol, than in the whole empire of France with its population of three millions. The Reports of the several Commissions now in operation throughout the united kingdom are in course of printing, by order of the House of Commons. Copies, as delivered to the Members, are accessible to the subscribers of the Commercial Rooms and the members of the Chamber of Commerce.*

* In the course of 1822 and 1823, such of the Reports of " the Commissioners for enquiring concerning Charities" as related to the Free Grammar-School, Queen Elizabeth's Hospital, and the Red Maids' School and other Charities under the Will of Alderman John Whitson, to be carried into effect by his Feoffees, were published in *The Bristol Observer*, and thence progressively reprinted in 12mo., with Introductions and Notes by a Barrister, who now fills an important judicial situation in a distant portion of the British Colonies. Part I. comprises 36 pages; Part II., 50 pages; and

A. D.

1813   The first report of the Adult Schools published.

Oct. 28, died John Eagles, collector of H. M. Customs. He was the author of a periodical paper in Felix Farley's Journal, under the title of The Crier. Proposals for re-printing the numbers in a collected form, by subscription, for the benefit of the Bristol Infirmary, were hereafter issued; but the names have been hitherto insufficient.

James, Fowler, Mayor; Benjamin Bickley and Philip George, Sheriffs.

1814   William John Struth, Mayor; William Fripp, jun. and James George, jun., Sheriffs. The Mayor and Richard Vaughan, esq. were knighted at presentation of an address to the Regent on peace with America.

1815   Sir W. J. Struth, knt. Mayor; Benjamin Bickley and Philip George, Sheriffs.

1816   Reynolds's Commemoration-Society formed.

June 20, an Act of Parliament was passed, for building a new Gaol in the City of Bristol, and for other purposes. It was herein provided that " the expenses of repairing, main-taining, and supporting the new gaol and other erections, of the salaries to the governor and other officers, and of main-taining and supporting the prisoners, should be defrayed by the Mayor, Aldermen, and Common-Council, out of the estates, funds, and revenues belonging to the Mayor, Bur-gesses, and Commonalty of the city." Towards the building of the gaol, it was enacted that £60,000 should be raised by a rate of not more than 2s. in the pound, on the annual value of all the lands, houses, &c. within the city and county of Bristol. The lands separated from the counties of Somerset and Gloucester by 43 Geo. III., and added to Bristol, were exempted. The land taken for the purposes of the Act lay in the parish of Bedminster, adjoining, on its north side, sun-dry messuages, &c. the property of the Dean and Chapter— anciently Trenelly, Trene, or Trine-Mill Mead.

July 27, the Duke of Wellington visited Bristol. He entered publicly through Park-street, dined at the Mansion-

Part III., 60 pages, including a " Memoir of Alderman Whitson, by G. S. Catcott." In addition to the monumental tribute therein described (which had been brought from the crypt to the vestibule of St. Nicholas Church, and is now restored to its original place), the Corporation have commenced the erection of a highly florid gothic ceno-taph, after a design by Mr. W. Edkins, carved in Painswick stone by Mr. Clark, enclosed with iron railing cast in a correspondent style. We wish, however, to see the railed northern gate of the vestibule exchanged for a window that may exclude the wea-ther and dust, and in place of its south window, a close porch and arcade cursing down to the pavement facing the river. There are at present only two entrances to the church, and those both together in St. Nicholas-street, where two carriages can neither pass each other nor turn round.

A. D.

1816 House, and was presented by the Corporation with the freedom of the city in a gold box. He departed the same evening.

John Haythorne, Mayor; Edward Daniel (barrister) and John Barrow, Sheriffs.

Oct. 16, *The Bristol Law-Library-Society* was formed. Each of the members (barristers and attorneys-at-law) deposited five guineas for his share in the foundation, which is maintained by an annual subscription of two guineas. The members now [1824] amount to seventy. The place of the books and meetings of the president and committee (of whom Mr. Wasbrough is honorary secretary) is the state or banquetting-room of Hugh Brown, one of the sheriffs in 1642 and mayor in 1650, over the grocery-warehouse of Mr. Fiske, in Corn-street.—The room is highly ornamented in the moulded style of that time. The carving of the fire-place is of superior execution. A group of three figures above the mantle represents Astrea holding a pair of scales. A youth is in the act of depressing the beam on one side, by blowing through a tube and filling the scale with bubbles; which an angel is about to counterbalance, by putting his finger into the other scale. This may be supposed to typify the sentiment, Man's breath is but as froth, when opposed to the divinity of Truth. In the distance, on one side, is a hall of justice or front of a castle; and on the other, a church, with a tower and a steeple like that of St. Nicholas or St. John.

1817 For an account of the appearance and progress of Cara-boo, princess of Javasu, alias Mary Baker, of Witheridge, Devonshire, see a royal 8vo. printed at the office of The Bristol Journal.

In the Edinburgh Medical and Surgical Journal, for July, p. 266—300, appears a communication from Dr. C. Chisholm, then senior physician to the Clifton Dispensary, " On the Statistical Pathology of Bristol, and of Clifton, Gloucester-shire;" and, by way of appendix, "A Geological Description of the City of Bristol and Parish of Clifton, communicated to Dr. Chisholm by G. Cumberland, Esq." In the latter, "Stock" must be read *Stoke*—" Potterdown," *Totterdown* —" Gotham," *Cotham*—and " Dandry," *Dundry*. [Sub-sequently, Dr. Richard Bright, M. D. communicated to the Geological Society a paper " On the Strata in the Neigh-bourhood of Bristol," which is published in their Tran-sactions, and was copied into The Bristol Observer of Sept. 23, 1819.]

A. D.

1817   Aug. 25, the Theatre in King-street was opened, under the new management of Mr. John Boles Watson, of the Gloucester and Cheltenham Theatres.

John Haythorne, Mayor; George and Abraham Hilhouse, Sheriffs.

Oct. 30, at eleven o'clock at night, the William and Mary Irish packet-vessel, from Bristol to Waterford, was wrecked on the Wolves rock, N. of the Flat Holmes. Of 56 persons, only 23 were saved.

Nov. 6 died, in child-bed, the Princess Charlotte, aged 22 years.

Dec. 17, Queen Charlotte, the Princess Elizabeth, and the Duke of Clarence, being visitors at Bath, were invited by the Corporation to visit Bristol. They were received at the Mansion-House, rode thence to Clifton; on their return visited Col. Hugh Baillie and his lady, at their house in Park-Row, now the property of Mr. Frederick Ricketts; and returned the same day to Bath.

1818   Jan. 20, Sir Robert Gifford, bart. solicitor-general, chosen Recorder of Bristol, on the retirement, through ill health, of Lord Chief-Justice Gibbs, who had filled that office more than twenty years.

March 3, the pile of buildings in Small-street, formerly the mansion of the Codrington family (see 1643), since occupied by Dean, Whitehead & Co., bankers, unaccountably consumed by fire. The chimney-jambs and mantle of the state-room now decorate the library of Broomwell-House, Brislington Wick.

May 7, a painted window by Egginton, of Birmingham, erected over the altar of Christ-Church.

June 16, an election commenced for representatives of Bristol in Parliament. The candidates were Mr. Richard Hart Davis, and (though they had personally declined any contest) nominally, through their several partizans, Mr. Edward Protheroe and Col. Hugh Duncan Baillie. The polling was closed on the 20th, with, for Mr. Davis, 3370 votes; Mr. Protheroe, 2259 votes; and Col. Baillie, 1684 votes. Mr. Davis and Mr. Protheroe were returned as members, the Sheriffs objecting to continue open the poll.

June 24, the chandeliers, scenery, &c. of the Theatre sold by auction, under a distress for rent.

The Mayor, John Haythorne, directed the monuments of St. Mark's Chapel to be cleansed of their white and yellow washing. A part of the imaginary improvements of this chapel, in 1721, consisted in the erection of a heavy though

1818handsomely carved altar-screen of Dutch oak, which being viewed, or rather, not to be viewed, under the light of a broad window, produced a sombre effect, likely to involve the mind in restless doubts as to the altar's pretensions to harmony with the rest of the building. In the search for a fitting space wherein to erect a monument to the memory of Alderman Bengough, the Vice-Chamberlain (now the Chamberlain), Mr. Thomas Garrard, being induced to mount a ladder for the purpose of ascertaining what had been concealed by the Dutch oak screen, discovered sufficient to convince him that some finely executed carving in Dundry stone had been rudely mutilated to admit it; upon removal of which, fragments of crocketted canopies were found at the foot of the original altar. The feeling of sound taste was hereby excited, and Mr. William Edkins, being employed to make a drawing of the ruin, succeeded in supplying all the parts necessary to form a perfect whole. Mr. Clark, an experienced carver in stone, was hence enabled to restore a beautiful gothic altar to its primitive freshness and magnificence. Similar restorations have since proceeded, particularly in the vestry-room, which was originally a chapel of the Poyntz family; for a description of which, as well as of the improvements within the chapel, the reader is referred to "William Wyrcestre Redivivus. Notices of Ancient Church-Architecture in the fifteenth century, particularly in Bristol. With Hints for practicable restorations." 4to. 1823. Dedicated to the Rev. Samuel Seyer, M.A. The author of this " right pleasaunt and pithy" mantle after the fashion of 1480, so cheeringly woven for the wardrobe of the venerable author of the " Memoirs," is the Rev. James Dallaway, M.D. vicar of Leatherhead, Surrey, earl marshal's secretary, Herald's College; who was baptized in the font of Saxon sculpture still preserved in St. Philip's Church; as was, Jan. 16, 1774, the present story-teller.

Mr. Barrett notices, in his p. 345, that "under the floor [of St. Mark's vestry] is a large vault, the entrance of which in 1730 fell in, and, upon examining the corpses there deposited, supposed to be those of the founders of the church, there was found a gold bodkin entangled in some hair." One of the bodies, as we learn from a note in Mr. H. Smith's illustrated copy of Barrett, was that of " a female, clothed in white satin (lying just under where the fire-place now is), having her robes fastened on the breast by a very handsome gold clasp, which was taken by and, as I am informed, is now in the possession of Mrs. Becher, in College-Green."

A D.

1818 These must have been the remains of Dame Margaret, the wife of Sir Robert Poyntz (see 1486), for whose obsequies, with his own, and those of Robert and Thomas Poyntz, sons to Sir Anthony Poyntz, knt., his son, he richly endowed the " Chapel of Jesus" and " the Church of the Gaunts," by will dated Oct. 19, 1520, a probate of which we have perused. This endowment, including " a certain messuage, lands and tenements, meadows, leasings, pastures, rents, &c. with woodlands, within the parish of Almondesbury, Stonehous, Tharseld, Huntingford, Hawkesbury and Leighterton, with their appurtenances, in the county of Gloucester," was one of the bonuses so freely bestowed by Henry the Eighth's supremacy upon his own matchless piety.—Mrs. Becher, (widow of Cranfield Becher, related to the mayor of 1721) for a close housewife, deserved the custody of such relics: she was born and lived in the same house, without having slept out of it more than one night, till she was removed by death about the year 1823. We hope, however, that both the bodkin and clasp will eventually find their way to the Corporation's intended museum of antiquities in the new Council-House.

Henry Francis Brooke, Mayor; Thomas Hassall and Nicholas Roch, Sheriffs.

This year the city of Bristol was first lighted with coal-gas, from a station with two gasometers erected on Temple-Back, near Tower Harratz. The Company was established by Act of Parliament. See 1824.

Oct. 27, arrived the Albion, Captain Buckham, the first merchant-vessel direct from the East-Indies, bound for the port of Bristol.

Nov. 17, died Her Majesty, Queen Charlotte, aged 75 years.

Nov. 20, Meerza Saafaz and Meerza Saulih, who three years previously had been sent on a mission to this country by the reigning Prince of Persia, Abbas Meerza, arrived in this city. On the 22d (Sunday) they visited the Cathedral, St. Mary Redcliff and other churches, and heard divine service at the Unitarian Chapel, Lewin's Mead. On the 23d they visited the Phœnix Glass-houses and other manufactories. Their costume was the Persian, but they spoke English fluently. The rites of domestic hospitality were administered to them chiefly by C. A. Elton, esq. at Belle Vue.

Dec. 20, the brother of the Emperor of Austria, the Archduke Maximilian, with a travelling suite of attendants, being in Bristol, attended divine service in the Roman Catholic

A. D.

Chapel in Trenchard-street. On the Monday the Archduke visited the principal manufactories.

1819 Jan. 18, a meeting of Col. Baillie's friends resolved to petition the House of Commons against what they considered the premature return by the Sheriffs of Mr. Protheroe, before fourteen days' polling had taken place. March 19, a committee of the House unanimously determined that the conduct of the Sheriffs was correct. The committee also resolved that the petition was neither frivolous nor vexatious, by a division of eight and seven. "An Authentic Report, &c. taken in short-hand by Mr. Gurney," was published from the Office of Felix Farley's Journal.

March 20, Mr. Protheroe announced his determination to decline the future representation of Bristol, in consequence of a misunderstanding with his committee for conducting the late election, upon the subject of his portion of the expenses. "A full Detail of the Facts, relative to the late Election of Edward Protheroe, esq., with a complete Justification of the Conduct of his Committee, by a Committee-man," was printed at The Bristol Observer-Office. This pamphlet produced one from Sir Henry Protheroe; but the dispute terminated in acquittal of the committee, by a letter from Mr. Wm. Fripp, jun., which appeared in The Bristol Observer of May 13.

March 29, the Theatre was re-opened under the management of Mr. William M'Cready. For materials towards a Memoir of this gentleman, see " Biographia Dramatica, &c." 8vo. 1812; vol. i. 478, and vol. ii. 329, art. 100; also what has and may hereafter be said of the brilliant career of his son, whose sur-name the London managers print, for distinction-sake, Macready; and who, in June 1824, did credit to his discrimination of female dignity and propriety in private life, as well as kindred genius, by his union with Miss C. M. Atkins, then unknown to the London boards.

June 14, an Act of Parliament passed " for repairing, widening, and improving the several roads round the city of Bristol, and for making certain new lines of road to communicate with the same."

Sept. 23, the two eldest sons of C. A. Elton, esq., Abraham and Charles, about thirteen and fourteen years old, while amusing themselves apart from the rest of the family, on a small island called Bernbeck, near the bathing-place at Weston-super-Mare, by the flowing of the tide on the causeway that separated the island from the shore, were drowned in their attempt to regain it. All search for the bodies

1819 proved unavailing.   The sympathetic exertions of Colonel
Rogers (a Somersetshire magistrate, and lieutenant-colonel of
the Mendip Legion), for ten hours in an open boat, brought
on a fever, of which he died on the 6th of October.   The
bodies of the two youths eventually floated to the shore of the
family-estate at Clevedon, where they were buried by their
grandfather, the Rev. Sir Abraham Elton, bart., without
permitting his son to share the renewed affliction of witnessing their injured remains.   Mr. Elton's grief found
vent and consolation, as his tone of mind recovered strength,
in "The Brothers, a Monody."

William Fripp, jun. Mayor; James George, jun. and
John Gardiner, Sheriffs.

Nov. 2, died Edward Bird, R.A., historical painter to
the Princess Charlotte. On the 9th, his remains were attended from his residence at King's Parade by upward of
300 friends and fellow-citizens, and deposited at the foot of
the steps from the Cathedral into the cloisters. Mr. Bird
having, on his appointment in 1813, presented Her Royal
Highness with his painting of *The Surrender of Calais*, the
royal widower, Prince Leopold, gave the widow of the artist
£100; and in February and March 1820, the Prince, with
the possessors of many other of his pictures, contributed to
their exhibition at the premises lately occupied by the Bristol
Fire-Office, in Corn-street.

Dec. 14, at night, a fire in High-street, at the entrance of
All-Saints' passage, destroyed, including one occupied by
Mr. Rees, bookseller, four houses, unveiled the ancient west-
window of All-Saints' Church, and the heat and smoke that
issued into the Church itself occasioned the discovery of a
walled-up recess, in which were found a black-letter bible
and other books that must have been secreted by the Catholic
priests during their alarm upon approach of the Reformation.
These, we hope, will at all times be found in possession of the
Church-Wardens.

1820   In January, the Floating-Harbour was so firmly frozen,
that skaiters had a free run over its whole surface. On the
16th, at eight in the morning, the thermometer stood at 8,—
24 degrees below the freezing-point. In another, on being
taken into the open air of Tyndall's Park, the quicksilver
sank into the bulb. The fluctuations of temperature within a
week, were from 8 to 46. Snow and rains brought on a gradual
thaw, and on the 24th the ice was no longer visible.

Jan. 23, died the Duke of Kent, aged 52 years.
Jan. 29, died the King, aged 82 years.

GEORGE THE FOURTH,

who had been eight years Prince Regent, and who completed 59 years of his age on the 12th of August following. Proclaimed in Bristol Feb. 3d.

Feb. 29, was laid the foundation-stone of a building at the south-west corner of Park-street, for the establishment of a Bristol Philosophical and Literary Institution. The ceremony was performed by the Mayor, assisted by the Sheriffs, some of the Aldermen, the Dean of Bristol (Dr. Henry Beeke, Oxford Professor of Modern History), Sir Thomas Lethbridge, bart. Sir John Cox Hippesley, bart. and a long train of resident friends to the undertaking. A metallic plate, with the following inscription, covering several medals, was deposited under an immense block of freestone, in the N.W. corner of the ground marked for the erection:

" The Foundation-Stone of this Building, for Literary and Philosophical Purposes, was laid on the 29th day of February, 1820, in the second month of the reign of George the Fourth, by the Right Worshipful William Fripp, junior, esquire, Mayor; in the presence of James George, junior, and John Gardiner, esquires, Sheriffs; the Aldermen and Common Council, and the other principal inhabitants of the City of Bristol. Charles Robert Cockerell, architect. George Jones and Thomas Willcox, builders."

The Building-Committee were,

The Very Rev. the Dean, Mr. Alderman Daniel, Mr. Alderman Fripp, the Rev. John Eden (rector of St. Nicholas), Messrs. R. B. Ward, John Sanders, S. Lunell, Henry Browne, John Cave, Joseph Reynolds, Richard Smith, W. H. Goldwyer, Richard Bright, J. S. Harford, M. Castle, M. H. Castle, W. B. Elwyn, A. G. Battersby, T. Jarman, J. L. M'Adam, Thos. Sanders, F. C. Husenbeth, Ralph Mountague, Robert Bruce, Dr. Stock, and Dr. Kentish.

In the afternoon, a party of 130 gentlemen dined at the Merchants' Hall. The Rooms were opened Nov. 25, 1822. —The published transactions of this and other like institutions, which it has roused into existence, will prove that the projectors of the building might have produced a more comprehensive plan with the certainty of success.

March 7. The circumstances preceding the election of representatives in Parliament for Bristol, that now commenced, proved enough to warrant the hope of a better mode of ordering such matters throughout the kingdom— that the age of wantonness in expenditure upon elections is fast passing away. On the 19th of February Mr. R. H. Davis had signified his determination to withdraw his pre-

1820 tensions as a candidate, on account of the usual invitation on the part of the Steadfast Society being withheld. On the 22d, Mr. Protheroe confirmed his former resolution to withdraw altogether. Mr. Philip John Miles had been invited by the Steadfast Society to permit his nomination, but declined. Mr. Henry Bright, second son of Richard Bright, esq., of Ham Green and Great George's street, having been named on the part of the Whig-interest, Col. Hugh Baillie, evidently foreseeing that an attempt to return two representatives of the same party-feeling would be unavailably expensive, preferred leaving the way clear for Mr. Bright. Some friends of Col. Baillie, however, professing no predilection for either Whiggism or Toryism, persisted in putting his brother, Mr. James Baillie, in nomination; and Mr. Davis having, by the universality of his attentions to the local interests of burgesses and non-burgesses of all parties, taken fast hold of the affections of burgesses who chose to act independently of the Steadfast Society, three days' polling thus operated: for Mr. Bright, 2997 votes; Mr. Davis, 2811; and Mr. James Baillie, 115. This experiment by Mr. Baillie's nominees being considered sufficient, the Sheriffs returned Mr. Davis and Mr. Bright as duly elected; and Mr. Davis having previously expressed his wish that, if elected, the ceremony of chairing should in this instance be dispensed with, on the 10th Mr. Bright alone appeared in a procession of splendour without example on similar occasions. This, it is to be hoped, will hereafter form the only feature of an election, for which our "free and independent" burgesses will even think of expending money not of their own independent and honest earning.

June 6, Queen Caroline arrived in London.

June 27 died, at Cambridge, Dr. Mansel, Lord Bishop of Bristol. The Rev. Dr. Kaye, (aged about 38 years,) Master of Corpus Christi College, and Regius Professor of Divinity in the University of Cambridge, was nominated his successor. "Dr. Kaye entered the church without patronage, and owed his advancement entirely to his literary attainments, biblical knowledge, and able discharge of the duties of his profession."

James Johnson, F.S.A., then the Deputy but afterward Governor of the Corporation of the Poor, published " An Address to the Inhabitants of Bristol on the subject of the Poor-Rates, with a view to their reduction and the ameliorating the present condition of our Poor." 8vo. pp. 80.— It was herein stated that the poor-rates, in 1815 and 1816,

1820 amounted to £15,500; in 1817, £20,500; and in 1818 and 1819, to £27,500. The rental of the city was estimated at £203,848—the highest rate 3s. in the pound. Illegitimate children were said to cost the city £1000 per annum.

Aug. 6, died the Duchess of York, aged 54 years, eldest daughter of the late King of Prussia by his first consort. She was united to the Duke Sept. 29, 1791, but never had any issue.

Aug. 25, the old Gaol of Newgate was evacuated, for the prison erected on the bank of the new river, facing the junction of the Avon and the Froom.

1820 Mrs. Jasper Leigh Goodwin, of Hoddesden, Herts, left by will, to the Bristol Infirmary, £500; to the Asylum for Indigent Blind, £200; to the Stranger's Friend Society, £200; and to the Asylum for Poor Orphan Girls, £200.

George Hilhouse, Mayor; Thomas Hassall and Robert Jenkins, Sheriffs.

The Chamberlain purchased, at a sale by Sir Paul Bagot of Gloucestershire, the stained glass which fills the great window over the altar of St. Mark's Chapel. The former window, now much decayed, represented the treachery of Judas, the scourging, the bearing of the cross, and the ascension. The figures were large and in good drawing.

Dec. 16, died Levi Ames, esq. senior alderman of Bristol, who was mayor in 1788-9. He bequeathed moneys sufficient for an expenditure, in every two years, of £72, to furnish the night-constable and nine watchmen of St. Maryport ward with a substantial great coat, hat, and pair of boots.

1821 Jan. 1, Mr. William Adye* sent to the Treasurer of the Maudlin-lane Institution for Diseases of the Eyes the donation of £100.

January. In excavating the ground of Messrs. Hurle and Co.'s premises, in High-street, without the south wall of what we consider to have been the House of the Kalendaries, was found the upper jaw of an alligator, about fifteen inches long and very perfect. It will be for inspection in the Corporation's intended museum of Bristol antiquities.

Jan. 29, Monday evening, Mr. and Mrs. Norris, a hapless pair who had recently begun, by a fish-shop in this city, to repair the waste of circumstances caused by the peculiar state of the times elsewhere, returning from a visit to an acquaintance who lodged on the south side of the outward lock of Cumberland Basin, then imperfectly lighted, and

* In our note to p. 230, we have erroneously Christianized this gentleman *George.*

1821the man being deaf, both walked short of the swing-bridge,
and fell into the lock. The newspaper-report of the accident
having reached a tradesman at Bath, who called on the
writer with information that Mr. Norris was an exemplary
Freemason, a train of benevolent feeling was excited for
their four infant-children. Mr. M'Cready having offered the
use of the Theatre, the balance of the receipts at a performance on the 15th of February, after deducting £24 for
the expenses, added £190 to the individual contributions,
which altogether amounted to about £500. This sum, under
the direction of a committee, being placed in trust, was
considered, with the assistance of an uncle in London, sufficient for their complete establishment in life. A poetical
address, written by Brother Charles Cummins, P. M. and
delivered by Miss Desmond (now Mrs. M'Cready, sen.) introduced three of the four orphans upon the stage with an
effect that every parent can more easily imagine than describe.
Mrs. Norris's remains were not found until the 8th of March,
giving time for the *duck*-like impatience of suspended conjecture, to blacken the poor woman's memory with the imputation that she had been the destroyer of her husband, and
absconded with life from her fatherless children! This
" dipping into the first dirty pool that presented a plausible
surface" was the alacrity of ever-uncharitable ignorance,
opposed to, perhaps, a too ready complaint on the part
of that super-grand-jury, the many-tongued public, against
the inferior lighting of what was not, certainly, a *common*
thoroughfare.

March 4, died the Princess Elizabeth, three months old,
daughter of the Duke of Clarence. The cause of her death
was announced to be *introsusception*.

April 2, at midnight, during a tremendous thunder-storm
from the N.W., the electric fluid struck the north end of
the tower of St. Mary Redcliff Church. Entering the upper
bell-loft window, and forcing a large aperture in the stone
framing, it so shattered the beam that supported one of the
bells as to render it useless, but without injuring the bells.
It then passed down the bell-wire of the clock, and escaped
on the south side of the tower, rolling up the lead from the
roof, and dislodging nearly 3 cwt. of the stone-work. Fragments of the wire bore the appearance of intense heat.—
At Stanton-Drew, thirteen sheep were killed. Several vessels were driven ashore in the Bristol Channel.

June. In piercing the wall at the eastern termination of
the south aisle of the Cathedral, for erection of a mural

A. D.

1821 monument to the Grossett family, discovery was made of the remains of an elegant gothic altar. The corresponding wall of the north aisle was then tried, and another altar, that of the second Maurice Berkeley, noticed under 1311, proved to have been unwittingly stabbed through its plastered coat, to attach the pyramidal tablet of Thomas Coster, esq., described in Barrett's History, p. 299.* Mr. O'Neill made drawings of both of these altars, which are in the possession of Mr. George Weare Braikenridge.†

July 19, the King's coronation. The manner of celebrating this event in Bristol is fully detailed in No. 208 and 209 of The Bristol Observer, as well as in the other newspapers of the time.

Steam-packets commenced their summer-voyagings between Bristol, Ireland, &c.

Aug. 7, Queen Caroline died, aged 53 years. Buried at Brunswick.

Sept. A letter from J. C. Harford, esq. to the editor of Felix Farley's Journal, relates an anecdote of Mr. Maddox, director in 1786 of the Opera, and keeper of a Vauxhall, at Moscow, who was nephew of "old Seward," of Fair-memory, in whose hands the sound of the trumpet produced its first impression upon the musical hearts of many a wight of the writer's standing. Wait, a Bristol professor, who died early, aspired after the neatly made little showman's silver tube, and possessed it (not like Gainsborough the painter, who coveted a lute he could not play, but) to accompany Bartleman in The Messiah, Incledon and Braham in Judas Macabæus, and a nameless orator of the same class in Martin Luther's hymn.

Sept. 11, the new church, built on Kingswood-Hill, Bitton, consecrated by the Bishop of Gloucester. Its name, the Church of the Holy Trinity.

Sept. 12, Mr. Henry Browne, banker, published a letter addressed to the Corporation and the Dock-Directors, containing a "Plan for cleansing the River Froom, without any inconvenience to the shipping."

* Mr. Coster was M. P. for Bristol in 1734, till his death in 1739. A scarce print of him is in possession of the Bristol Copper-Company, of which he was a partner, at their counting-house in Small-street.

† Mr. Braikenridge's collection of drawings illustrative of the antiquities and rural scenery in the neighbourhood of Bristol, amounted, in May 1824, to about six hundred; of which 435 were by Hugh O'Neill (whose death is recorded in the Bristol newspapers of the preceding 10th of April), and the remainder by Messrs. Holmes, Jackson, Johnson, and Cassin. The remains of O'Neill were interred in St. Stephen's Church-Yard, under the second window from the gothic porch—a spot which he himself would have chosen, had his frame of mind been less disordered by peculiar decay of body.

A. D.

Population of Bristol and the neighbouring Parishes, in 1821.

Parishes.	Houses inha- bited.	Number of Fami- lies.	Houses building and not inha- bited.	Other Houses uninha- bited.	Males.	Females	Total Males and Females	Increase since 1811	De- crease since 1811.
All Saints.........	30	30	1	17	76	97	173	23	—
St. Augustin........	1030	1735	3	58	2945	4376	7321	826	—
Castle-Precincts	236	342	—	10	703	823	1526	—	9
Christ-Church	137	209	7	17	530	499	1029	135	—
St. Ewen	21	21	—	—	35	64	99	—	4
St. James	1295	2426	7	97	3851	4953	8804	563	—
St. John	111	200	—	34	359	398	757	53	—
St. Leonard........	37	61	—	15	142	143	285	—	144
St. Maryport	44	55	—	22	123	179	302	86	—
St. Mary Redcliff....	961	1390	9	78	2696	3131	5827	1131	—
St. Michael	492	798	3	42	1521	1924	3445	342	—
St. Nicholas........	241	497	1	32	843	1049	1892	73	—
St. Paul	1076	1704	7	76	3099	4221	7320	1264	—
St. Peter	175	232	1	2	711	912	1623	77	—
St. Philip & Jacob...	593	910	3	46	1694	1979	3673	839	—
St. Stephen	234	484	—	41	921	1157	2078	407	—
Temple...........	823	1310	1	20	2590	2753	5343	653	—
St. Thomas	176	317	—	46	605	671	1276	18	—
St. Werburgh	22	22	—	19	58	58	116	—	28
Total......	7736	12,743	43	672	23,502	29,387	52,889		
Kingsdown (part of Westbury parish)	177	208	—	33	367	568	935	—	—
Bedminster	1412	1673	70	73	3830	4149	7979	3402	—
St. James & St. Paul Out-Parish	651	735	25	52	1322	2283	3605	1178	—
St. Philip & Jacob. Out-Parish	1875	2531	39	138	5512	6312	11824	1122	—
Clifton	1088	1905	42	77	3332	5479	8811	2077	—
Total........	5203	7052	176	373	14,363	18,791	33,154		

See Barrett's History, p. 99, for the number of houses in the eighteen parishes within the city, in 1712 and 1735.

Abraham Hilhouse, Mayor; Nicholas Roche and Thomas Camplin, Sheriffs.

Nov. 13, the centenary since the death of Edward Colston, whose munificent benevolence has been celebrated in our own time by three several societies, the Dolphin,* the Anchor, and the Grateful, dining together, and contributing, on removal of the cloth, to a charitable fund for distribution during the succeeding year. The Dolphin Society consists chiefly of Tories and Churchmen; the Anchor, Whigs and Dissenters; the Grateful (composed principally

* Named after his crest, which tradition says was assumed from the circumstance of a fish of that species having stopped a leak in one of his ships at sea.

A. D.

1821 of such as pride themselves in having been "Colston's Boys," yet among whom, though Chatterton was one, we have not heard that his memory has been toasted) profess to be exclusively neither. This year the collection for charity alone at the Dolphin, where 171 dined, amounted to £406 17s.— at the Anchor, £450 14s. 6d., out of which the charge for dinner and wine for 150 guests was defrayed; and at the Grateful, £190, exclusively for apprenticing poor boys and relieving women in child-bed.

Nov. 19, St. Nicholas Church re-opened after repairs, and the building of a new organ by William Smith, a native of this city. A MS. Anthem, the words from Ps. xcii., was sung, and a Sermon on the usefulness and excellency of introducing vocal and instrumental music in public worship, preached by the Rev. John Eden, incumbent of the rectory, which was afterward printed in 4to. with Notes.

Nov. 28, a meeting of subscribers to Mr. H. Browne's Plan was held in St. George's Chapel, Guildhall; and opinions of its feasibility by Messrs. Jessop, Plumley, W. Townsend, and W. Armstrong, surveyors, were published.

1822. March. A chronometer was completed on the front of the Exchange. Of course the writer hence " surceased the suit" upon petition of his juvenile acquaintance, the Christ-Church Quarter-Boys, to be restored, which had been preferred in The Bristol Mercury, some ten or eleven years previously.

May 15, an Act of Parliament passed " for the employment, maintenance, and regulation of the Poor of the city of Bristol; and for altering the mode of assessing the rates for relief of the poor, and certain rates authorized to be raised and levied within the said city by certain Acts for improving the Harbour there; and for paving, pitching, cleansing, and lighting the same city; and for the relief of the church-wardens and overseers from the collecting of such rates, and for amending the Act for paving, pitching, and lighting the said city."

June. A table, published in The Bristol Observer, of comparison between the prices of the following articles furnished to St. Peter's Hospital, shewed these averages:

	In 1769 to 1772. s. d.	1821:2. s. d.
Beef and mutton, per cwt.	20 8	29 0
Flour, per sack of 280 lb.	35 5	38 0
Malt, per bushel	3 6½	5 6
Cheese, per cwt.	28 9	29 0

1822 June 26 and July 3, the editor of The Bristol Observer
copied from the " London Museum" an account of the sale,
by Mr. Evans of Pall-mall, of the " Curious and valuable
Library, and richly sculptured Ivory Vases, of the late
W. Barnes, of Redland-Hall, Bristol." Mr. Barnes was
son of the Mayor of Bristol in 1776-7, and died Feb. 21,
1821. The " description of the books, with the bibliogra-
phical illustrations," was not the composition of the auc-
tioneer, but written by our fellow-citizen, John Fry, author
of the article in The Bristol Memorialist on the Bristol
Library. This catalogue was nearly the last of John Fry's
literary labours, for he died on the 28th of the present June.
A short memoir of him, from the pen of another acquaintance, was forwarded by us for The Monthly Magazine, in
which it appeared. Mr. Tyson obtained a plaster-cast of
his face. He was buried in St. Nicholas burial-ground,
juxta Crow-lane. His mother survives, in the house where
he died, near Bridewell-Gate.

July 13, the Prince and Princess of Denmark, and suite,
came to Bristol from Gloucester, by way of Blaize Castle,
the Cottages, and Clifton, where, at the Hotel (late Man-
geon's), they kept their court. On the Monday morning the
Prince took a seat at the Quarter-Session in the Guildhall;
and their Royal Highnesses afterward visited the Phœnix
Glass-Houses (where they made some purchases), and
Messrs. John Hare and Sons' floor-cloth manufactory. The
Prince, with his secretary, chamberlain, physician, &c. also
visited the mineralogical and geological museum of Mr.
Jas. Johnson, at Dowry Parade. In the afternoon, the royal
party departed for Bath, on their route for Longleat, Stone-
henge, Salisbury, and Dover, where the Royal Sovereign
yacht received them for conveyance home to Copenhagen.

Aug. 12 (Monday), a new Church and burial-ground for
the parish of Clifton were consecrated by the Lord Bishop of
Bristol. The form of the " Office, &c." was printed in an
8vo. pamphlet. The morning-service was performed by the
Rev. J. Hensman, and the Bishop preached from the text,
1 Cor. iii. 17. The choir of the Cathedral assisted.

The new Church commenced building in June 1819. It
is 70 feet long and 75 wide in the clear of the walls, and 39
feet high. The crypt or crowd is 7 feet 6 inches high, and
has graves formed under the whole of its floor, 8 feet deep.
The church is calculated to seat 1650 persons; 600 of the
seats, for both adults and children, being free. There
are three galleries, with two stone stair-cases, leading from

1822the entrance-lobbies, which are each 25 feet long by 12 feet wide. In these are placed most of the monumental tablets of the old Church, including that of Mrs. Green, the actress, daughter of Mr. Hippisley, author of "The Drunken Man" and proprietor of the Jacob's Well Theatre. The principal entrance to the Church is westward, under the tower, which is 110 feet high. The contractor for the building was Mr. William Stock; for whom Messrs. Foster and Sons operated as architects. An individual (Mr. Thomas Whippie) contributed £2000 towards the expense. The pulpit and reading-desk were erected by Mr. James, the resident manufacturer in British woods to the King. The organ-case was carved by Mr. Humberstone. The organ was built by Mr. William Smith, of Bristol. See Nov. 24.

Of the old Church, which originally consisted of its nave and tower, dedicated to St. Andrew, and was situated in the centre of the southern division of the present burying-ground, we find that William de Clifton gave it to the Abbey of St. Augustin, in the reign of Henry II. Roger, a subsequent Lord of Clifton, who was son and heir of Elias de Clifton, gave also to the Abbey " common or pasture in his manor of Clifton, and all the water-courses which were between the croft and the house which Adam his bailiff held, as far as the hill, and all the courses which were upon the Canon's Conduit at Wodewell [Jacob's Well] towards the hill, which they were at liberty to draw to their conduit [formerly " the water-house" in Limekiln-lane, now at the south-west corner of Unity-street] from his land at Clifton; and he gave them also liberty to have stone from his quarries at Clifton, to build any thing within the Abbey-gate, provided they did no injury to his arable land or wood."—FOSBROKE. The manor, in 1608, was vested in the Berkeley family, and sold by them to the Society of Merchant-Venturers of the city of Bristol; in whose possession it still remains.— The Vestry possesses no written documents of earlier date than 1723, when the north aisle was erected, to which the munificent Edward Colston contributed £50. The *south* aisle, and gallery extending along the whole of the thus increased western wall, were added in 1768. The only sculptured ornament within the church was the arms of Elizabeth. The rudely carved corbels supporting the moulded arch of the west-door, under the tower, were supposed to represent the heads of Philip and Mary. The living is a perpetual curacy; of which the incumbent is the Rev. James Taylor, a son-in-law of the late Right Hon. John Philpott Curran.

1822 James George, Mayor; Gabriel Goldney and John Cave, Sheriffs.

This year produced a considerable improvement of the point of egress from Park-street outward, in rebuilding the walls with iron palisading, and widening the road on both sides. This was accomplished by a subscription of private individuals, with the concurrence of the Corporation, at the instance of Mr. John Nash Sanders.

The Hotwell-House, erected in 1696, and its more modern appendages, having been taken down, throwing the road open for carriages under St. Vincent's rocks and up the acclivity to Clifton Down; a new house was erected, upon a plan of the Tuscan order by Henry Hawke Seward; which contains baths, with every accommodation, for invalids of the most delicate degrees of strength to embrace their salutary influence.

Nov. 24, the organ of the new Church at Clifton was opened on its completion, with an Anthem and Services composed purposely by a Bristol amateur-professor, whose trading-concern furnished the "paper—even a rag like this," of the present volume.

Dec. 11, the site of Newgate prison, part freehold and part leasehold, under St. John's vestry, paying a chief-rent of £3 10s., sold at auction by the Commissioners to the Corporation, for £655. The materials had previously obtained £500.

1823 Jan. 1, the ship Weare, of 450 tons, bound from Bristol to Jamaica, having sailed hence on the preceding morning, was wrecked at eight o'clock in the evening on the Irish coast, between Ballycotton and Youghall. Fifteen persons (including the master, pilot, two females, one infant, and three male passengers) perished. Thirteen escaped.

Feb. 13, the Bristol Chamber of Commerce began to be constituted. The president, vice-president, and directors, were named in April. The results (in June 1824) promise all the good of which calm enquiry and candid explanation between contending though not opposite interests are capable.

June. The Bristol Dock-Company declared a dividend of one per cent. to the holders of shares. See The Bristol Observer, No. 306.

July. The Reading-Room of the Bristol Institution in Park-street was opened. In the list of donations to the Institution now announced were,

By the Rev. W. D. Conybeare and Mr. De la Beche, "A Geological Map of the Course of the Avon, from Clifton to the River's

A. D.

1823 Mouth."—" Geological Maps of Mendip and the Country 24 miles round Bath."

By Mr. J. N. Sanders, " Copies of Colston's Settlements [4to. pp. 76] with MS. Legal Opinions."

By Mr. Benjamin Heywood Bright, " Authentic Copies, abstracted by special license from the Pontifical Archives, in the Vatican, relative to the Early Ecclesiastical History of Bristol."

Of the latter we expect that the Rev. Mr. Seyer will not fail to avail himself, in the approaching completion of his " Memoirs."

A Chapel of Ease for St. Augustin's parish erected, and a burying-ground laid out, on the north-west side of Great George-street, Park-street. (The ground was purchased by the Vicar of Augustin-the-Less, in 1819, for £1250, with the materials of seven unfinished houses, for £316 more.) The Chapel was consecrated on Sept. 23 by the Lord Bishop of Bristol, assisted by the Dean; Lord William Somerset, prebendary; the Rev. Samuel Seyer, bishop's chaplain; the Rev. Henry Green, chancellor; and officers of the Chapter, with the incumbent, the Rev. James Carter. The Church-Wardens, James Ford and R. Hunt, esquires, and Vestrymen of the parish, were accompanied by the Mayor, Mr. Sheriff Goldney, and Mr. Alderman Daniel. The sermon was by the Very Rev. the Dean, upon Ps. cxxii. 1. The Chapel was opened for divine service on Sunday, Oct. 5. The number of free sittings is 900.

The following inscription appears in brass on the east-wall of the south aisle of the crypt of St. Nicholas Church, and receives light through an aperture of the wall that closes the old south door, which, the crypt on the left-hand being boarded off, was used as a day-time thoroughfare into High-street by another porch at the corner of St. Nicholas-street:

" This crypt is traditionally an ancient Cemetery of the original Church of Saint Nicholas, which was founded in the reign of Canute the Great, about the year of Our Lord 1030. It appears to have been repaired and beautified during the reign of Edward III., in the year 1361 ; a head of his Queen, Philippa, being still perfect in the key-stone of the first groin in the south aisle. It was afterwards used by the fraternity of the Holy Ghost as a Chapel, in the year 1503, and was religiously preserved, when the ancient Church was taken down and rebuilt, in the year 1768. So long a period of time having injured some of the arches, the foundations were carefully examined and repaired, and the whole building was restored to its original strength and beauty, in the year of Our Lord 1823, under the immediate superintendance of Mr. JACOB WILLIAM ATTWOOD, one of the Church-Wardens; to record whose indefatigable zeal in the prosecution of so laudable a work, the Rev. John Eden, B.D.

1823 Vicar, and the other Members of the Vestry, have caused this Tablet to be erected."

[There is yet one trifling addition required to make St. Nicholas' crypt the full organ of its solemn truths,—an inscription upon the tomb under a mural arch opposite to its present south entrance, nearer the base of the tower. The executors of DAVID EVANS know that he was a sheriff of Bristol in 1795-6, mayor for the latter part of Robert Castle's year, 1802-3, and for the whole of 1803-4; and many of his fellow-citizens know also that he purchased with his own proper moneys the Room in Broadmead which was the first meeting-house of the Wesleyan Methodists, and, collecting among friends of all religious denominations a further sum, sufficient for an annual stipend to a minister, vested the whole in trust that natives of Wales might hear divine service in their own tongue. Who, we would ask, has not heard the vulgar imputation, the fruit of envy, that David Evans's prosperity in trade as a wholesale-grocer was the result of short weights unchecked by a single beam and scales of sufficient capacity throughout the whole principality? Those with whom this calumny originated knew well enough that the shop-keepers of South Wales for a short time so suffered, but we believe that neither by that cause nor effect were David Evans's hands ever polluted. The writer was present at a conversation, in the year 1805 or 6, between this his father's namesake and the late Thomas Holmes, of Tontine-warehouse memory, in which the redoubted grey-bearded plodders were comparing notes upon the fluctuation of markets and the prevailing disappointments to the most experienced speculators. With a mind most certainly free from all consciousness that in the thoughts of his auditors he was rebutting a charge with which his own good name had been assailed "behind his back," Mr. Evans related that his trade in South Wales, when greater than that of the other grocery-houses in Bristol collectively, at once most unaccountably declined. Buying his goods at the same marts, with no disadvantage that could arise from want of capital, and charging only a living profit, the mystery of this competition became more and more profound, until he bethought himself of prevailing with one of his lost customers in Carmarthenshire to let him order for his use a beam and scales equal to the weighing of a barrel of sugar in the gross. He did so. This was the first importation of that class and magnitude on the western shores of the Severn, and justice henceforward repaired the injury done to honour and mercantile confidence.

A. D.

1823 A weekly intercourse with the Alderman, as one of his agents in another concern, for more than five years, enables the writer to assert that, in David Evans, a clear head was united with exemplary singleness of heart. It has not rarely happened that people of fashionable life, in their manner towards those whom they considered mere tradesmen—and Bristol tradesmen, too!—forgot what was due to their own character for politeness. Often have we been amused in witnessing the mingled expressions of surprise and hauteur with which persons of the superior classes, as they doubtless thought themselves, received the manly and fitly worded though *Welshily* querulous expostulations of Mr. Alderman Evans, at their presuming to enter premises not their own, without the ceremony of first asking permission; and not less frequently have such persons tendered the warmest acknowledgements of his native urbanity, when, in return for their apology, our goodman bluff conferred personal attentions through every part of the Phœnix Glass-Manufactory, convincing his guests that churlishness could be equally a stranger to the counting-house as to the drawing-room.]

John Barrow, Mayor; John Savage and Charles Frederick Pinney, Sheriffs.

Oct. 1, was published No. 322, and the last, of the weekly newspaper called The Bristol Observer. It died, not for want of an ample portion of youthful vigour, but because its first nurses, having increased occupation of mind in other quarters, would not let it live for the risk, however remote, of growing ricketty or indolent in other keeping.* Bristol

* From the papers chiefly headed "Theatrical Observer," under Sept. 4 to 25, Oct. 2, Nov. 20, 1822, after which they bear the numbers vii.—xxxii. to May 28, 1823, thence Sept. 3, No. xxxiii. to xxxiv., may be gathered the chronicler's opinion of the Drama and Music in Bristol, for the time. In apology for what has been called the substitution of ribbons for birchen rods in the correction of players, we may remark that nothing is more easy than to find fault with this class of labourers for the public good: eighteen pence might at any time purchase a throne of condemnation, though not of justice. We have written the words *labourers* and *good*, and cannot conscientiously blot them out. No condition of life is more precarious—none, in the lower grades especially, more pregnant with industrious application; and we would not advocate the *abuses* of the Stage any more than of the Pulpit, in its uncharitableness of one religious sect towards another. The *uses* of both must ever go hand in hand. The animated parables of the former are scarcely less striking upon the moral sense, than the metaphorical types and symbols of the latter: the one is chiefly the medium of example, where the salutary pill is gilded with good humour; the other, the vehicle of precept, heretofore too often blended with the fulminations of hell-torments during eternity, in return for "a span" of sinning, and so "taking in vain the name" of an Almighty God of Love and Mercy! There are no such blasphemies uttered on the Stage. Priests were the first actors of the earliest plays, when Christianity is supposed to have laboured under fewer corruptions. Actors and actresses are entitled to no less protection of their credit in pursuit of honest livelihood than any other craftsmen or women. Security against the effects of inflated praise upon their interest is sure to be

A. D.

1823 now prints only four newspapers, viz. Felix Farley's Journal and The Mirror (formerly Bonner and Middleton's Journal), published on Saturdays, The Bristol Mercury on Mondays, and The Bristol Gazette on Wednesdays. That the Observer *Printing-Office* survives, the present volume is one of the many increasing symptoms.

1824   Jan. 10, died Thomas Edward Bowdich, the African traveller, who was born in 1793, in one of the houses now occupied by Mr. Wintle, linen-draper, in Clare-street. Such of his memoirs as have hitherto been published appear in The Literary Gazette for March 13 and 20. The Bristol Memorialist contains a list of his published works. The Governor of Cape-Coast-Castle, under whose auspices he engaged in the mission to Ashantee, was his uncle, a younger brother of his mother, whose family, named Smith, resided at the corner of Unity-street and College-Green. His widowed mother, with a brother, four sisters, and other relatives, still reside in Bristol. Mrs. T. E. Bowdich and her infant-children arrived home in June, to receive the tribute to her husband's merits of a liberal subscription, set on foot by Mr. Ackermann, of the Strand, and promoted in Bristol by Mr. John Mills, proprietor of The Bristol Gazette, who, among other donations, received one of £50 from a citizen, and £21 collected at a meeting of the Society of Inquirers. Previous to being superseded by Sir Charles Macarthy in the government, Mr. Smith received from the Ashantee sovereign, as a *present*, in token of respect and amity, his

found in the common sense of those auditors, the majority, no part of whose business it is to write for the press, and who will not be *puffed* into surrender of their discriminative faculties. The professionally grave ones need not be alarmed for the *levities* of the Stage; for we think we have discovered that one quality of the human mind, of which they can have had less opportunity for observation, is to forget that soonest which most excites risibility. To laugh heartily is not an act of the will that may be repeated at command: nothing rapturous can be of permanent effect. The tendency of "trifles light as air" is not, therefore, to leave a lasting impression. Wit ceases to surprise upon repetition, and soon becomes dulness; while brutal sensual stupidity is in equal danger of rejecting what is good, whether in a church, a chapel, or a playhouse. See Sept. 25, 1822, on the tendency of The Beggar's Opera, in particular.

In the number for Oct. 23, 1822, "The Ghost of Joseph Gayner," of equivocating memory, records some facts, under the head "Capital and Credit *versus* Commerce," that may yet be discussed with advantage. See also Nojoker's letter, of Nov. 20; and No. i. to iv. of "The Chamber of Trade, House of the Kalendaries, Parish of Christ-Church," on the licentiousness of the Press and its *legal* cultivation.

In No. 309, some memoranda relating to the history of Bristol are to be found, in our review of vol. iv. of Nichols's Illustrations of the Literary History of the Eighteenth Century.

Sept. 3, 1823, appeared an account of the discovery of the Great Stone House in Baldwin-street, the residence of Harding, who died in 1115. The key-stone there mentioned is transferred to the careful keeping of the host of Broomwell-House.

1824 own cousin, a young man now about 22 years old; who came with Mr. Smith to England, was baptized at St. Stephen's Church, Bristol, by the name of George King, on the 21st of August, 1823, and is now on a Continental tour with his patron, to whom his amenity of manners and aptitude for instruction render him a most interesting companion.

January. On the removal, this month, in St. Philip's Church, of a monumental tablet that had been affixed to the western pier of the two arches standing between the north or Kemys's aisle and the chancel, the pier was found to contain a stone stair-case that must have led to a rood-loft attached to its side eastward, under the arch. The materials with which the aperture was closed up comprised several painted and gilt fragments of capitals of pillars and cornices in the florid Norman style. These, with the massive lid of a stone coffin of the same period, which for years lay exposed without the church-walls, and a tablet of stone on which is carved a double mitre, are now carefully preserved in the chancel. The mailed figure under the east window of the north aisle is that of J. Kemys, who founded a chauntry, suppressed in 1547.

April 21, died, through a fall from his horse, Mr. Gresley Hellicar, solicitor, aged 25 years. He filled the office of Secretary to the infant-institution, the Chamber of Commerce; to which he was chosen from the ability shewn in a series of Essays (still in MS.) which he wrote, on the best means of improving the Commerce of Bristol, as competitor for a prize of 30 guineas, anonymously proposed by Mr. J. N. Sanders and another gentleman, who preferred that means of drawing forth what local knowledge might exist on the subject.

May 2, at St. James's Church, a new organ, planned by the organist, and erected by the Bristol "father Smith," in the old case, with the addition of a choir-organ, and raised upon a new gallery for the use of the children of the Sunday-Schools, was opened with MS. Services and an Anthem composed for the occasion. See The Bristol Mirror for May 8, and the Sermon and Musical Services, &c. published together, in folio.—In the evening of June 25, the germ of a Bristol Harmonic Institution was indicated by the full-score performance, in the same Church, of selections from Handel, Haydn, Beethoven, Pergolesi, and Martin Luther, and the new Anthem with orchestral accompaniments, by as many of the resident amateurs as the gallery could accommodate, to an auditory of 420 persons admitted by tickets at 5s. each,

A. D.

1824 in aid of the previous voluntary donations of the parishioners towards the architectural accessions named.

May 12 (Wednesday), at two o'clock, the Mayor, Aldermen, Sheriffs, and other officers of the Corporation; the Master, Wardens, and Society of Merchant-Venturers; the Governor, &c. of St. Peter's Hospital; the Clergy; the Church-Wardens of Christ-Church and St. Ewen; the boys of the City-School; Mr. Smirke, the architect; Mr. Phillips, contractor for the building, and Mr. W. Stock, carpenter, with others of the citizens, assembled in the Guildhall, and progressed under the arch of St. John's tower, through Quay-street, St. Stephen-street, and Corn-street, to the site of the old Council-House and St. Ewen's Church, as described in the Act of 1788. A large stone being sunk in the earth at the S.E. corner of the intended building, and another, measuring 3 feet 8 inches by 3 feet 6 inches, and weighing 25 cwt., suspended by tackling, a box was handed to the Mayor, containing a coronation-medal (given by the Chamberlain), other gold and silver coins of the present reign, and the current copper of the realm, which he called over, and then deposited the whole in a cell cut in the nether stone. He then covered the cell with an inscribed plate, and trimmed the mortar with a silver trowel. The suspended stone was then lowered, and his Worship (who is " a free and accepted mason") squared his work, striking it with a gavel or mallet. After the populace had cheered to the music of the city-waits and ringing of the " bonny Christ-Church bells,"—All-Saints' dome looking on in silent expectation of a happy greeting of its regenerated " rival,"— his Worship thus addressed the crowded auditory:

" Brother Magistrates, Gentlemen of the Corporation, Friends, and Fellow-Citizens,—Having the honour to fill the high office of chief magistrate of this city, it has fallen to my lot to lay the foundation-stone of this intended building. May God prosper the undertaking! and I sincerely hope and pray that, in raising the superstructure, he may be pleased to protect the artificers, labourers, and other persons employed in the work, from all danger and accidents; and when the edifice shall be completed, may it exist for ages, not only as a specimen of the architecture of the present day, but as a tribunal distinguished for justice and mercy!

" May the Magistrates, who may be called upon from time to time to preside therein, administer justice with the strictest impartiality, to the high and to the low, to the rich and to the poor; and may they, by their virtues and upright conduct, prove themselves to be the faithful guardians and protectors of their fellow-citizens!

" May the Corporation at all times encourage and support the increase of trade and commerce, and the general welfare of the city!

1824 May they ever maintain and uphold the dignity of the situation in which they are placed; and, while they conscientiously discharge the important duties reposed in them for the benefit of their fellow-citizens, may they defend with energy and firmness their lawful rights and privileges—rights and privileges which have for centuries past been held sacred by the Corporation, who have ever discharged their trusts with honour and fidelity to the public.

. " God, save the King, and prosper this ancient and loyal city!"

The procession returned down Broad-street to the Guild-hall. The Mayor, Aldermen, and Corporation, afterwards gave a splendid dinner to a number of their fellow-citizens, at the White Lion Inn, at which the Mayor presided. The Officers of the Corporation, &c. also dined at the Rummer Tavern. Mr. Alderman Daniel gave the boys of the City-School a dinner, not without plenty of plum-pudding, and each a shilling.

Inscription on the Plate.] " This Foundation-Stone was laid on Wednesday, the Twelfth day of May, in the year of Our Lord One Thousand Eight Hundred and Twenty-Four, and in the Fifth year of the reign of His Most Gracious Majesty King George the Fourth, by the Right Worshipful John Barrow, Esq. Mayor, assisted by the Worshipful the Aldermen, John Savage, Charles Pinney, esquires, Sheriffs, and the rest of the Common Council of the City and County of Bristol. The superstructure is dedicated to the administration of public justice, and to the maintenance of social order. Robert Smirke, architect."

On the inside-lid of the Box.] " The Committee for erecting the Building: John Barrow, esq. Mayor; John Noble, esq. Thomas Daniel, esq. Sir R. Vaughan, William Fripp, esq. James Fowler, esq. Aldermen; James George, esq. late Mayor; Thomas Garrard, Chamberlain."

May 27, the foundation-stone was laid of an avenue opened in Broadmead, westward of Alderman Evans's Welsh Chapel, thence crossing the Horse-Fair to the entrance, from its Alley, of St. James's Barton, to be distinguished as St. James's Upper and Lower Arcade.

Inscription.] " This stone, the first of an Arcade, for the better accommodation of foot-passengers, was laid on the twenty-seventh day of May, Anno Domini MDCCCXXIV. and in the fifth year of the reign of His Most Gracious Majesty, George the Fourth. MICHAEL WREYFORD, JOHN W. HALL, JAMES PATY, Proprietors. JAMES and THOMAS FOSTER, Architects."

May 28, the royal assent was given to " an Act for lighting and watching the parish of Clifton, in the county of Gloucester."

June 17, passed an Act of Parliament " for lighting with Oil-Gas the City of Bristol, and the Parish of Clifton in the County of Gloucester, and certain Parishes adjacent thereto."

1824 By this Act it is provided that the capital is not to exceed £30,000, in shares of £25 each.   The gas to supply a light cheaper than that obtained primitively from oil, and should the Bristol [coal] Gas-Company be unable to complete their contract, this company is to light the city upon the same terms. The station of the works is Limekiln-road, at the end of Canon's Marsh, next to the Glass-house.

June 19, the Bristol Institution opened their first exhibition of Pictures. The catalogue described 96 subjects by old masters, the property of gentlemen of Bristol and the neighbourhood, and casts from the statues found among the fallen parts of the Temple of Jupiter Panhellenius, in the island of Ægina, in 1811, with casts from the frieze of the Temple of Apollo Epicurius, near Phigalia in Arcadia, discovered in 1812.

The remains of the mansion called Mead-Place, Wraxall, noticed under 1491, are now occupied by Mr. Oldham, of Wine-street, Bristol, with improvements and restorations. The porch is in the style of A.D. 700. The arms of the *Vere* family, on one of the fire-places, bear the date 1624, and the *vane* is dated 1633.

July 3, the leaden figure of Neptune was removed from its second station, next to Dr. White's Alms-house, preparatory to being re-erected in Church-lane, Temple-street, opposite to the leaning S.W. corner of the Tower. The Alms-house itself is about being entirely rebuilt with a modern and simple gothic front, by Mr. Edward Brickden, an operative architect of the school of Smirke.—We have found nothing opposed to the belief that our Neptune was erected in commemoration of the defeat of the Spanish Armada. As " all the world knew that," so no one, perhaps, thought it necessary to write or print about it, till " all the world" had " died off."

ADDENDA

ET

CORRIGENDA.

" We almost pity the man who can find no enjoyment in the study of Antiquities. Next to the natural desire after the secrets of futurity, implanted in every breast, ranks, in our estimation, the more rational disposition to become acquainted with the genius and taste of the men of former days. In proportion to the supposed degree of obscurity in which their history is necessarily involved, from the circumstance of having preceded the Art of Printing, is the quickness of appetite, in every thorough-bred Antiquary, for developement of the mystery. Of all the Sects of Philosophy, certainly that of the Antiquaries presents the least individual jealousy—the least pretension to exclusive merits of discovery. Truth is the Antiquary's aim and end, and his ruling passion, excitement of a mere spark in the economy of facts to the effulgence of the noon-day Sun."—*Review of* FOSBROKE's *Encyclopedia of Antiquities.*

WE appreciate the following contribution by Dr. Shaw, F. A. S. the venerable Rector of Chelvey, the more highly, because, at the time it was made, he knew no more of our text etymological than was to be found in that part of our Prospectus which is transferred to p. xiii of the Introduction.

'At the time the Romans made such a progress in Britain as to establish a station at the place now called BRISTOL, the Caledonians and Welsh dialects of the Celtic, as well as the Armoric of Cornwall, were not so dissimilar in sound and orthography as they are now. The latter is now entirely extinct. That station the Romans called Venta Silurum, although Camden says it is *Caerwent* in Monmouthshire. Tacitus, in his Annals, calls the inhabitants of South Wales, *Silures.* The Romans have put the word Venta, I conceive *a venio,* " to come," before proper names of several places; as Venta Silurum, Venta Belgarum, &c.; intending to mean, perhaps, that they had reached so far, and, meeting with a check from the Aborigines, could then advance no farther. Bristolia, Bristowa, Bristulium, are subsequently known to be the Latin names of Bristol. The proper names of places, often among the Romans, always with the ancient Scotch and Irish, were generally *denominative,* i. e. descriptive of the natural situation of the place.

It is not only curious but useful, always pleasing and delightful to the Philological Antiquary, to trace the etymology of ancient names of countries, and towns and places. *Erin*, Ireland, is " the Western Island." Carlow, spelled Catherlogh, i. e. *Cathair*, " a city and logh or loch, a lake," i.e. a city on a lake or river, denominative of its actual situation. *Balintobair*, " the town by the well." *Baile na mona*, " the town by the Moss." *Uisge beatha*, i.e. Whisgy, from *Uisge*, " water," and *beatha*, " vitæ," i. e. aqua vitæ.

The last time I was in Arran, one of the Hebrides, my *natale solum*, Gershom Stuart, one of the clergy of the island, a man of good learning, and myself, in imagination travelled round the island, 24 miles long by 12 broad, and found the names of every farm and place denominative of its natural situation. Goatfield, or *Gaoidbhein*, is " the mountain of blasts and storms." The strait or frith between that island and Kintyre, the continent, is called *Caolas drandanach*, or " the whistling, murmuring strait or channel," because there is a constant breeze of wind in that passage from the surrounding hills. Kintyre, that promontory of Scotland reaching over from Tarbet to the Mull of Kintyre towards Ireland, is made up of *Ceann* and *Tir*, i. e. *Ceann*, " head," or " end," and *Tir*, " land," i. e. Land's end. *Mull*, or *maoll*, signifies " round end, a head without horns," a promontory; hence *Maoll Cheantirach*, " the Mull of Kintyre," the Epidium of Ptolemy; *Maoll Ghalilach*, " the Mull of Galloway."

What a Welshman may make of BRISTOL in his own language I at present know not, but will enquire of the first clergyman of that country I meet with.* *Bristolia, Bristowa, Bristulium*, in my dialect of the Celtic, without *fetching* an etymology so *far* as the merry, witty and facetious Dean (every body knows what Dean I mean), who made *Andromache* " the daughter of a Scotch gentleman named *Andrew Mackay*,"—*Bristulium* is immediately Celtic; for *Bras* (vide Shaw's Gaelic Dictionary, in the Bristol Library) signifies " quick, rapid," and *Tuile*, signifies " stream" or " flood;" *Brastuile*, " rapid stream." Bristol, therefore, means a place on a rapid stream. Or thus, perhaps more agreeably to the nature of the place: *Braois*, " a gap, gape, yawn, chasm, rent," and *Tuile*, " stream, flood." How descriptive of St. Vincent's rocks! *Braoistuil*, therefore, means, the place by the chasm or rent of the floods. *Tuile ruadh* is the Gaelic phrase for " the Deluge of Noah."

To prove how far this scheme of etymologyzing might be founded in truth, and what analogy there might be between the Eastern languages and the Celtic, I asked once an Officer, who had been twenty years in the service of the Company, to mention the names of some places in India with which he had been acquainted, and to inform me candidly whether the etymology of the names, as supposed allied to the Celtic language, given by me, were descriptive of the places he should name. *Sheanscrit*, in Gaelic, means " old writing," or " ancient language," from *Sean*, " old," and *sgriobhte*, " written." *Benares* I supposed to be a hilly country, where were many temples; and the gentleman granted that

---

* Vide our p. 7.

Benares was a hilly country, and that there were many temples in it. *Ber.*, or *bein*, signifies "a hill" or "mountain," and *Aros*, "a temple" or "house." Vide the Gaelic Dictionary. W. S.*

* Dr. William Shaw was born at Clachag, in the parish of Killmory, in the island of Arran, Buteshire, Feb. 3, 1749. He received the rudiments of learning at Ayr, and was well acquainted with and often rambled on the banks of the "bonny Doone," since become classic ground. He took his degree of A.M. at Glasgow, and in Divinity afterwards at Cambridge. In 1778 he published "A Grammatical Analysis of the Gaelic Language," 4to. In 1780, the "Gaelic and English and English and Gaelic Dictionary" referred to in our text, 2 vols. 4to. "An Enquiry into the Authenticity of the Poems ascribed to Ossian," 8vo. (pp. 80, and upward) procured for him the friendship of Dr. Samuel Johnson. "Suggestions for a Plan of National Education," 8vo. appeared in 1801. Next followed "A Scheme of a Fund for the Support of the Widows of the Clergy of the Church of England, by an Annual Rate to be paid from the Benefice of every Incumbent," 8vo. In 1809, "A Sermon preached before the Grateful Society at Bristol," 8vo. In 1810, "A Sermon preached at Bedminster, at the Visitation of the Archdeacon," 8vo. Subsequently "Latin Prosody made Easy," 8vo.—The Doctor is believed to be the author of a Criticism on the early Writings of Mrs. Hannah More, 8vo. which arose out of the Blagdon controversy in 1801. We understand he is now employed on a work of considerable labour, "On the Corruptions, Apostacy, and Imposture spiritual and temporal, of the Church of Rome; justifying the Necessity of the Reformation, vindicating the Gospel from the monstrous doctrines erroneously derived from it, with Reasons why equal privileges with other members of society should be denied the Papists, until they publicly renounce certain principles and doctrines maintained by them; and proving that the Religion of Rome is an Artificial Religion, the manufacture of Priests, and that the Popish Universities deliberately imposed on Mr. Pitt."—Hoping for pardon of our presumption in an attempt to review a book thus prematurely, we must add our critical belief that, next to the formation of a universal creed, excepting it be in the precise terms of Scripture as read in all languages, would be the difficulty of drawing up an Act of Renunciation which the foregoing sketch of Dr. Shaw's literary design would seem to propose. The Roman Catholics, like other Christian sects, where animal*ism* is suffered to embrace intellectual*ism*, now agree to differ among themselves; and no man possessed of but an ordinary share of manly pride, would be forward to confess his destitution of common sense and the advantages of education, by formally disavowing that which he never believed. Besides, Papists may, in their turn, with no less propriety, require, as the first step towards the fellowship enjoined by the common Father of us all, renunciation of certain uncharitable prejudices and misrepresentations against themselves, the recorded ravings of Protestantism in a fearful fever long subsided. Alas! for the degenerated breed of Popish bulls! we have seen that, so long since as 1226, his Holiness's demands upon the purses of his flock, even when a Protestant defection was not to be apprehended, could be peremptorily repelled. When the canon of the Scriptures has derived all the philological advantage of which the daily increasing accessions to the philosophy of language is capable, then will the distinctions of Papist and Protestant, Calvinist and Lutheran, Churchman and Dissenter, be of as much indifference in the scale of Christian love and estimation, as the names that distinguish the different children of the same domestic family. A finer piece of satire upon persecution for religious opinions, whether positive or negative, could rarely be imagined, than that produced by old Grimaldi, in 1780, when, to guard his house against the rage of the mob excited by Lord George Gordon's Protestant Association, he wrote upon his closed shutters, "No religion at all here!" * After all, if the Papal Clergy wish to retain their influence over their communicants, they will *not* advocate the question of political emancipation. The Sun of Toleration is very likely to make the Sectarian traveller throw off his strait-laced cloak, let its colour be the choosing of either Peter, Martin, or Jack.*—A word, by the by, for the hoarders of Irish title-deeds under ground, now long out of date, and withal valueless from any chance of a Catholic profession of religion conferring political power! Had the true policy of giving Ireland a better system of agriculture, in a full participation of manufacturing advantages, been preferred to instruction by the point of the bayonet, not a man of 'em

* See Dean Swift's "Tale of a Tub."

The running-title of p. 3 would have been more properly
THE CELTS AND THE BELGÆ. The reader who wishes to go
further into the History and Antiquities of the Britons is
recommended to commence with Brewer's "Introduction to
the Beauties of England and Wales," royal 8vo. 1818. The
ground on which Bristol stands was part of the district of
the Celts or Senones occupied by their sixth tribe, the *Hædui*.

In p. 5, the reader will prefix the letters B.C. to the year-
date 83 ; and instead of 74, after A.D. 45, say 47.

50   In p. 6, add to note upon the Avon, " The old Celtic
Amau, or Amon, ' a river,' in Irish, is pronounced *Avan;*
in Welsh, *Avon." Vide* DAVIES's *Celt. Res.* 404.

Our second note appended to the text under A. D. 50,
we think, notwithstanding an attentive consideration of
what Mr. Seyer has adduced to give Clifton a greater degree
of importance, sufficiently characterizes the military remains
on the summit of the hill. Granting that this station was
the original *Caer Odor*, how comes it not only that the ancient
British Chronicles, but the all-enquiring Latin historians, are
so very silent as to the migration of its inhabitants into *the
vale of the Baths?* If the station was really peopled to the
extent Mr. Seyer imagines, surely so eventful an accident
as a *chasm* or *rupture*, with reference to the safety of the
occupants, could not have passed without notice. That two
several parts of a town should be communicable by fording
a stream which must have been more of a torrent than now,
is alike improbable. Had he (instead of leaving Brennus
where he found him, in the cloudy region of fable) marked
the precise era of the foundation of *Brig-stowe*, we might
have been disposed, as we wished, to treat Part I. of the
" Memoirs" with more deference. Whatever might have
been the ancient importance of Clifton in a civil point of
view, we find, by the quotation under 1822, from an equally
industrious searcher of topographical records, that, about
A.D. 1170, it had dwindled into the demesne of an individual of no great note among his contemporaries.

700   Add to note of Christ-Church and the House of the Kalendaries,—In other cases the church and the parish are

would have wished to remember that he ever had a grandfather the owner of a potato-
garden. How much more patient and loyal would any Englishman have been, who felt
himself the dignified representative of a long line of hedgers and ditchers, on the very
estate which the founder of the family called all his own, and was snatched from him
without " value received?" Custom-houses should be as rare between Ireland and
England as between England and Scotland, and then the taxes might be equalized; for
Ireland would have wherewith to pay taxes and keep her poor at home.

N. B. We dedicate this note to Mr. Wilberforce, who has not yet advocated any scheme
to abolish the Slavery of Ignorant Poverty, under which no freedom can be worth having.

A. D.

700 more easily distinguishable. "A house situated in St. James's" may be readily received as meaning in the *parish* of St. James; but "a house in Christ-Church" needs the addition of parish, to prevent the confusion of place which has here so long prevailed. See 1318.

915 Add to this text,—The mingled waters of the Avon and the Froom westward of Bristol, at this time, were spread over the adjoining lands, so as to be called the commencement of the sea. The "Sea-banks" are situated just below "the mouth of the Froom," defending Canons' Marsh from the overflowings of the tide.

934 Of the legendary blending of matters of fact with fiction respecting Guy, earl of Warwick, see "An Historical Account of Redcliff Church, &c." (12mo. printed for the Sexton, 1815) p. 22—32, contributed by the present writer.

1003 This date, as connected with Bedminster Church, may be altogether dismissed. The Abbey of White Land, on the Tave, Carmarthenshire, Speed says, was formed by Rhys ap Tewdr, in 1086, for monks of the Cistercian order. The manor of Bedminster was sold by Robert, earl of Gloucester, to Harding (see 1069), and the church is therefore likely to have been erected by him, or rather by some of his family, after the date of Domesday-Book, for it never formed part of the revenues of the monastery. It is reckoned in "the deanery of Redclift and Bedminster, in the archdeaconry of Bath." Both Redcliff and St. Thomas Churches were originally chapels to Bedminster, and now, with Abbot's Leigh, form but one vicarage.

1016 May not "Bristow construxi" imply that Brictric rebuilt the walls of Bristol? St. Nicholas Church was built *on* the wall. His father, Algar, we have seen, built St. Leonard's also on the wall.

1086 There is a tradition that Stephen had a palace at Barton *Regis*. In Domesday-Book it is called only "Barton." A house, taken down by Mr. William Sheppard, now (1824) a resident there, was called the Royal Table. See 1153.

1147 Earl Robert's age was 57 or 58. Dr. Meyrick, in his work on Ancient Armour, i. 10, says it was Earl Robert who first improved the English horse by the importation of Arabians.

1176—1189 Isabella was also called Haweis. "One writer (Leland) says he had an intermediate wife, keeping the heiress of Gloucester but a year." See 1200.

1196 For £133 6s. 3d., say £133 6s. 8d.

1229 P. 58, for George & Co., read Stephen George & Sons.

u u

A. D.

1229 We think the bridge to the Quaker's Work-house, lately rebuilt, must have been the bridge meant by our informant.

1247 Gybb Tailleur—" from Gilbert le Taylor, or Gilbert the Tailor."—SEYER.

1267 In note, for 1747, say 1247.

1305 The second of this date should be 1306.

1313 P. 75, l. 5. Some remains of the foundation of this wall, of considerable thickness and stubborn construction, were discovered in May 1824, about twelve feet from the frontage of the houses on the eastern side of Dolphin-street, in digging to lay the main-pipes of the Oil-Gas Company; and previously, Mr. Strickland, silversmith, in digging for a common sewer, in a northerly direction towards the corner of Narrow Wine-street, came to a subterraneous aperture in part of the same wall, which the workmen failed to explore.

1320 P. 78, l. 3, read " north side" of Portwall-lane. Mr. Seyer, in his plate described c. xii. § 54, of Bristol between A.D. 1250 and 1350, assigns a situation for this Convent and Church in the S.E. part of the Rack-Close, near Tower Harratz; and on the spot above-mentioned he has placed Spycer's Hospital. See 1366 and 1393.—We only " speak by the card."

1341 Ralph Asche was the fourteenth abbot.

1347 " Appearinge" should be appeasinge.

1360 Leland says, vol. v. fo. 22, " A mason, being mastre of the bridge-house, buildyd a fundamentis, a chapel, propriis expensis."

376 THE CONDUITS.] We trace these ancient and ever-flowing veins of mother Earth, teeming with life-blood that has assisted in nourishing so many generations of our fellow-citizens, and extending their means of existence over half the globe in their ships, with a pleasure that language is too weak to express.

The Key-Pipe. The water brought to this point of delivery rises in a withy-bed north-eastward of the Orphan-Asylum, lying between the high land of Ashley-Court (described in our note to p. 219) and the mill-stream that flows from " the Boiling-Well," situated more remotely, on the same level, towards Stoke-House. In this withy-bed are two wells, which overflow into the leaden cistern of a conduit-house. Hence the water runs in pipes of lead along the north bank of the mill-stream, to Lower Ashley-House; there it turns under the bed of the brook, and crosses the fields south-westward, to a small house (mentioned in the Perambulation of 1373) at the entrance of a hamlet, erected on the bank of the river Froom within the last thirty years, called Botany Bay. From this conduit or second head, technically termed by plumbers a horse,

A. D.

1376 the pipe crosses under the turnpike-road leading from Ashley-Place &c. to Baptist-Mills, into Driver's Fields (so named from a former Keeper of the gaol of Newgate, who held a farm there), proceeding onward under Newfoundland-lane and street, Milk-street, passing close to the White Horse Inn, through the Horse-Fair, over Bridewell-Bridge (on which are two branches for supply of the prison and keeper's house), under Bridewell-lane, the north side of Nelson-street to the sugar-house, where it turns across to the pavement flanking St. John's Church, and so onward, through Quay-street, to the final cistern; whence the water is drawn by two cocks, from which, on account of its superior purity, the casks of nearly all the shipping of the port have been filled.

The water of *All-Saints' Pipe* (also noticed under 1400) rises in what was the garden of the Priory of St. James, which was supplied by a branch-pipe, the remains of which run under the paved court of a house at the head of Lower Maudlin-lane. The main-pipe crosses Upper Maudlin-lane (in the walls on the north side of which are two or three approaches to the spring-head, which forms a large subterraneous pool), through the courts of the Moravian Chapel, the site of the Black Friers, into Lewin's Mead; passing close to the court of the Unitarian Chapel, it turns over St. John's Bridge, up Christmas-street, under the arch of St. John's tower, up the Guildhall side of Broad-street, crossing the site of the old Council-House to the Stamp-Office; turns thence to the Norwich Union Insurance-Office (the front of which was the ancient place of delivery), and turns into a cistern with cocks and an overflow-pipe in All-Saints' lane, under the S.W. corner of the Church.

St. John's Pipe is supplied from a spring that rises on the Brandon-Hill side of Park-street, down which the water flows through a well-secured cavern of stone, to a pipe that ascends Frog-lane (after Queen Charlotte's cottage, affectedly named *Frog-more* and *street*), and turns along *Pipe*-lane, where a main cistern anciently supplied the Monastery of Carmelites, the Prior of which made a special grant* of a feather-pipe to the Vestry of St. John, which was renewed so lately as during the Protectorate. This continues along St. Augustin's Back, through Horse-street and Christmas-street, to its demi-"castellette," of Roman style in its decorations, within St. John's Gate, at the corner of Tower-lane.

St. Thomas' Pipe is a continuation of that of Redcliff.

1388 Henry, earl of Derby, and the confederate lords, having prevailed upon the King to abandon his favourites and their agents, Sir James Berneys or Berners and Richard Medeford or Metford, a clergyman, were sent to the Castle of Bristow; Sir Robert Tresylian, chief justice of England, was sent to Gloucester Castle. Sir James Berners was beheaded on Tower-Hill, London, May 12. Of Metford, see 1396.

* The original document (still in possession of St. John's Vestry) is a piece of parchment nearly the size of this leaf, to which is appended a silver tube of about half an inch bore, run upon a green silk cord, as a specimen of the pipe to be used.

A. D.

1466   The second monument of William Canynges (a recumbent figure), now in Redcliff Church, was originally erected in Westbury College.

1469   "Robert Ricard" this year lived at a house in Redcliff-street, latterly the York-House Tavern, and the house now occupied by Mr. Clements, plumber, the property of St. John's Church. See 1479.

1478   Thomas Norton was ancestor of the Norton of Leigh-Court, the host of Charles II. See 1549.

1483   Richard, of the house of " York," was Duke of Gloucester.

1486   Of Sir Robert Poyntz, see under 1818.

1487   "An Act" was passed "for the Mayor, Bailiffs, Sheriffs, and Commonalty of the town of Bristol, for paving the streets there."

1503   P. 127, the running-title should be HENRY THE SEVENTH.

1506   Oct. 16, complaints having been made that the brewers had taken back from their customers, the tapsters, "such ale as had been found fusty, dead, and unable to be drank, and, of craft and subtle, had used to put it among the ale at the next brewing, and so uttered the same unto the King's people within this town, whereby it was likely that some persons had heretofore taken infection and disease," it was ordered that such ale, instead of being taken home by the brewer, should be cast into the street before the door of the same customer, by the oversight of the Serjeant of the Ward where such default was found ; and upon proof of any contrary conduct, the brewer to forfeit 20s. and the tapster 3s. 4d. It was also ordered that " no brewers do put any hops among the ale that they shall brew hereafter, at any time of the year, but only in the months of June, July, and August," on pain of forfeiting, for every default, 10s. Half the penalties in all these cases to go to the Chamber, and half to the Sheriffs.

1514   " An Act for continuance of the Under-Sheriff of Bristol" was passed this year.

1518   In the mayoralty of John Williams, brewer, an Ale-conner was appointed, " who," it was ordered, "shall every shifting-day in the year boldly go into the houses of the common-brewers, before the shifting of every of their ale, and there shall taste the same ; and if he finds it good and wholesome for man's body, so to commend it ; and if he find it contrary and unlawful for the King's people, then he shall command the same brewer not to make any sale or utterance thereof to the subjects; and that every common-brewer shall obey him in the execution of his office, and make no resis-

A. D.

1518tance, let, or impediment against him, on pain of being fined 6s. 8d."—The time for shifting was ordered to be, in the winter, between Allhallows-tide and Candlemas, before five o'clock in the morning; and in the summer, between Candlemas and Allhallows-tide, before four in the morning.

1534 In Sir Robert Poyntz's will, his brother, Thomas Poyntz, *John Fitzjames*, with divers others, are mentioned as seized of the property with which he endowed the Chapel of Jesus, &c.

P. 136, l. 3, for 1764, say 1725.

It may be added to the note of Mr. Franklin's closet, that Mr. Joseph Manning, a pupil of Mr. King, has made fac-similes of the pictures in oil, for the Chamberlain, and water-colour drawings for Mr. G. W. Braikenridge.

1541 The exemption produced by Thomas White's deed of gift was not to " exempt the Severn-vessels from customs in the port," but to *free the city-gates from toll.*

1542 Reference to the " Statutes and Orders for the better Rule and Government of the Cathedral," we presume may be had in Sir Robert Atkyns's " Ancient and Present State of Gloucestershire," pp. 164—182; for Browne Willis, in his " Survey of the Cathedrals," vol. ii. p. 759, under that of Bristol, says, " The places of the inferior members being but small, they are seldom kept entirely filled, as provided for in the Statutes, which are, *mutatis mutandis*, the same with those of Gloucester and others of the new foundation, which may all be judged of by those of Rochester, printed in an octavo account of that church, ann. 1717."

1544 Oct. 24, Candlemas-fair, in St. Mary Redcliff parish, agreed to be discontinued, on condition of the Corporation paying £50 per annum toward the repairs of the Church.

1552 " 1551—1553. Those 2 years liv'd ill members in the p'ish, that sold away part of the Church-land and the house in Marsh-street."—*Conclusion of a MS. page, relating to the bargain with the Corporation; found among the loose papers of St. Ewen's Vestry.* This was probably written during the papistical ascendancy of Mary.

1556 Cardinal Pole visited Bristol, as appears by a charge of expenses in the vellum book of St. John's Church.

1559 August. See an anecdote of a citizen of Bristol, named John Tronton or Brunton, seized and subjected to torture by the Tribunal of the Holy Inquisition at Seville, in Bla-quiere's Historical Review of the Spanish Revolution. Had his royal mistress been a papist, this might not have happened.

A. D.

1569　Aug. 20, by a patent of " Robert Cooke, esq. *alias* Cla-
riencieux, principall and kinge of armes of the southe easte
and weste partes of this realme of England from the river of
Trent southewardes," the arms of the City of Bristol are declared to be "gules on a mount vert, issuant out of a castle
silver upon wave, a ship golde;" and the crest and supporters now granted, "upon the heaulme in a wreathe golde
and gules; issuant out of the cloudes two armes in saltour
charnew, in the one hand a serpent vert, in the other a pair
of balance gold; supported with two unicornes seant gold
mained, horned; and clayed sables mantled gules dowbled
silver." The motto, " *Virtute et industria.*"

1572　The Vestry-room of St. John's Church, now for the first
time so called, was previously the High Altar, which, being
erected on city-land, pays 1*s.* per annum to the Corporation.

1573　The Corporation ordered that if, after the feast of Pente-
cost, any fire appeared flaming out of any part of a house,
the owner should forfeit 6*s.* 8*d.* to the Chamber; and that,
after the feast of St. Bartholomew, no house should be
covered with thatch, upon pain of the same being pulled
down and taken away by command of the Mayor.

1581　Oct. 12, it was ordered that nobody should brew nor sell
any ale called crock-brewed, upon pain of forfeiting 20*s.*
The brewers to be licensed by the Mayor, &c. to brew good
ale for the citizens after the rate of 3*s.* 4*d.* per dozen, " until
the feast of the Annunciation of our Lady the Virgin Mary,
next coming," and not to alter it above that sum, on penalty
of £10.

1582　Read, the year ended March 24, 1583.

1583　The Corporation agreed that every member of the Common
Council should keep six buckets made of leather in his house,
to be in readiness against fire, or forfeit 20*s.* The Mayor
and Aldermen to appoint other substantial citizens to do the
same, under a penalty of 10*s.*

1588　Every inhabitant was ordered to pay 1½*d.* per yard for
pitching before his house; such pitching to be laid at the
direction of the Alderman of the ward or his deputy (a
Common Council-man).

1594　May 12, in a Court held at Greenwich, Bristol farthings
were ordered to be called in; and no one to make the like
without special license from the Mayor, &c.

1612　A quart of double-beer was ordered to be sold for a penny.

1622　Of the tavern at the Bridge-end, see also 1658. *Qu.* Was
the Richard Rogers of the riding-exhibition in October 1654
a degenerated son of this family?

A. D.

1624 It was ordered by the Corporation that the Mayor, on Michaelmas-day, do publish and declare openly, in the Guildhall, the names of persons who have received the loan of money of Mr. Thorne and Sir Thomas White, on pain of forfeiting £10. [In the progressive decrease of ready-money transactions and increase of sales for time, this ordinance was very likely to decrease the number of borrowers: few Bristol tradesmen would now wish to have it known that they stand in need of small loans. This, however, is very like the fabled pride of the cobbler's dog, who, not choosing to give the wall to a brewer's cart, was crushed to death. Had not the Nation *borrowed*, she might have been long since "keel upward." Knowledge, with honesty, is both riches and power.]

1625 For £1 6s. 0d. read £1 6s. 8d.

P. 174, of the bronze table. See a Hobson in 1608, and another in 1632. Hugh Hobson was rector of St. Stephen's from 1628 till 1641.

Brandon-Hill was parcel of the dissolved Monastery of Tewkesbury, and was sold by Queen Elizabeth to two private individuals. Queen Bess may hence be regarded as Bristol's guardian-genius of well-bleached smickets.

1629 There is a charge, in the Chamberlain's accounts, of £5 13s. 4d. paid to John Corsley, for gunpowder expended at Alderman Whitson's funeral.

The salary of the Common Raker was not augmented to £70, but, in addition to the £30 paid him by the Corporation, by only £10, to be levied on the citizens; the £30 to be supplied by the Corporation as heretofore. The Raker to provide sufficiency of carts, horses, and servants, and to cleanse more streets than he formerly did, and in a proper manner. To be paid, in respect of St. Nicholas, £6; St. Stephen, St. Werburgh, and Christ-Church, £4 each; All-Saints', £3 10s.; St. Leonard, £2; St. Ewen, £1 10s.; St. John, £3 10s.; St. Maryport, £2 10s.; St. Peter, £3 10s.; St. Thomas, for part of the Bridge, £1 10s.; St. James, £3; and St. Michael, £1 10s.—(The parishes of St. Mary Redcliff, St. Thomas, Temple, St. Augustin, St. Philip, &c. had now as little need of the scavenger as Clifton in 1824).

1631 An article in The Bristol Observer, for Feb. 11 and 18, 1819, occupying four of its columns, contains extracts from " Captain Thomas James's strange and dangerous Voyage, in his intended Discovery of the North-West Passage into the South Sea, in 1631 and 1632." This Narrative was originally published by order of Charles I. The undertaking

A. D.

1631 was by the Merchant-Adventurers of Bristol, whence Capt.
James sailed in the Henrietta Maria, a ship of 70 tons, with
22 men, victualled for eighteen months. Having, through
the ministerial offices of Mr. Palmer (probably Thos. Palmer,
vicar of St. Mary Redcliff from 1623 till 1636, and author
of a sermon entitled " Bristol's Military Garden," described
in The Bristol Memorialist, p. 131), invoked the protection
of " Him whose dominion is from sea to sea," the Henrietta
Maria left Kingroad on the 3d of May. On the 2d of October, after a devious course, and touching several other
points of land, she commenced wintering on Charlton Island
(so named by Capt. James in honour of his King), situated
in lat. 52 on the east shore of Labrador, and remained there
nearly ten months, leaving it on Monday July 2, 1632, for
return to England. The writer of the newspaper-article
remarks, in conclusion, that

Captain James " elucidated no inconsiderable part of Hudson's
Bay; having discovered all the south-east, south, and south-west
sides of that great expanse of water. With the application of astro-
nomical principles to the purposes of navigation, he seems to have
been well acquainted; and in the few tables preserved by him, and
which are affixed to his Voyage, the altitudes and azimuths of the
Sun, with the declination and variation of the needle, are carefully
noted down. Our great philosopher, Mr. Boyle, is also said to
have derived assistance in his experiments on heat and cold from
some observations in Capt. James's Narrative."

1634 In June, John Evelyn, esq. author of " Sylvia," was in
Bristol. See his Memoirs, vol. i. p. 275.

1636 Robert Skinner, the eleventh bishop of Bristol, was consecrated Jan. 15. After his translation to Oxford, in 1641,
he was the only bishop that continued to confer orders
throughout the Interregnum. William Prynne, in his "An-
tipathie of the English Lordly Prelacie both to Regall Mo-
narchy and Civill Unity, &c." published in the latter year,
says that Bishop Skinner " threatned to interdict a faire
kept in the parish of St. Iames in Bristoll, if they would not
set up a pair of decayed organs in that church." This quotation should form part of his epitaph in Worcester Cathedral.

1643 P. 187, of the Chapel on the Bridge. In 1649, Sir William Birch, of Westminster, granted to Walter Stevens and
Son the two stone arches on which the priests' tenements
formerly stood, which had been burnt, to be built upon.—
BARRETT, p. 187. Who was the James Birch to whom the
Mercers and Linen-Drapers' Company presented his picture,
in 1725?

P. 192, *note.* Dr. Ingelo's novel was printed in 1660.

A. D.

1643 The title, "Bentivolio and Urania, in Four Bookes." Pp. 314. Dedicated " to the Honourable William Brereton, Esq. eldest son of the Right Hon. William Lord Brereton, of Brereton in Cheshire." Its style is manly, rational, and unaffected though classical.

P. 7. Alderman Holworthy's house, in which Charles II. and James II. lodged, was that now chiefly occupied by Messrs. Pinnell and Doddrell.

1644 October. 80 cwt. 3 q. 13 lb. of biscuit, sent to the King at Cirencester, cost the city £80 17s. 3d.

1645 Feb. 1, Prince Charles lodging at the Great House, St. Augustin's Back, the Corporation presented him with a hogshead of Canary and three hogsheads of Gascoigne wine.

" Paid for a hhd. of Canary	14	0	0
——— 3 hhds. Gascoigne wine ..	16	10	0
——— Excise	5	0	0
——— Cooper	0	2	0
	£34	12	0

Between Dec. 17, 1642 and Feb. 20, 1643, Col. Essex was paid by the City, in cash, " for the present occasion of King and Kingdom," £3400; Fiennes, from March 2 to May 2, on the same pretence, £2000; Waller had, in April, £2000; and, from July 7, 1644, to April 30, 1645, the King and Prince Rupert had about £3400; all independent of the cost of fortifying the city, victualling the fort of Dungannon, paying the crew of the Lion frigate; " a gift of £5 in charity to the Bishop of Waterford, July 7, 1643;" at the same time " a butt of sack given to Lord Hopton, and sugar, £22"— " provisions sent to Clifton to Col. Washington, July 27, 1643, £9 4s. 6d."—In April 1644, the Queen, who lay at the Great House, St. Augustin's Back, was presented with £500, in three leather bags, collected among the inhabitants; the Corporation contributing £100.—In March 1644, 45 tuns of beer cost the Corporation £81.—Aug. 16, 1645, " Paid to Spurrier, for burying of the dead people about the line, £1 6s."—In Jan. 1642, ten barrels of gunpowder were spared to the City of Gloucester for £60. Dec. 30, 1643, Bristol lent to Somersetshire, on bond, £1000; and Nov. 23, 1644, £400 more. Jan. 16, 1644, the County of Gloucester was in like manner accommodated with £1000. In March 1643, plate was lent to Parliament, value, at 4s. 4d. per ounce, £600.

1649 Miles Jackson, &c. commenced as Mayor and Sheriffs in this year, not in 1650.

A. D.

1651   P. 213, for "MSS." read MS.—Note, P. J. Miles, esq. removed *from* "Nash-House" to his new mansion on the site of Leigh-Court.

1651   Richard Aldworth, M. P. revived the Bristol farthings, "holding forth unto the Councell of State the original of our square copper farthings; and, finding encouragement, he procured a round stamp, and engraved the city-arms on one side, with C. B., and round about in letters was written, 'A Bristol Farthing.' These were very beneficial to the poor, and for exchange of money amongst the people of the city; it being publicly made known that, if any man had too many upon his hands, the Chamberlain would exchange them for silver."

1652   "Upon the petition of the inhabitants of St. Nicholas' parish, for the erection of an Alms-house, it was ordered that the Surveyors of the City-Lands shall lay out a convenient quantity of ground for that purpose, under the Wall in the Marsh, near Back-street Gate; which shall be granted to them in perpetuity, on payment of 6s. 8d. to the Chamber per annum."

1654   Of the Apprentices. The reference onward should be to 1660.

The Castle was not destroyed "in a fortnight;" for so late as the 8th of March the magistrates ordered payment, till the work should be done, of 12d. per week, by those who did not assist in person.

Feb. 23, all importers of wood for fuel were ordered to wait upon the Mayor, and acquaint him with their price before landing, and not to land above the lower brass post on the Key.

June 6, it was ordered that no butter should be imported by merchants, to be exported, until first offered in the markets at 3d. per lb.

June 21, for the relief of the poor, 8d. was ordered to be paid out of every kilderkin of butter exported.

Sept. 4. "Forasmuch as Mr. James Read, of this citty, clerke, uppon Saterday ye 26th day of August last, did marry John Bradley and Sara Bannister according to ye old formes, as he hath confessed before us, It is therefore ordered that he finde sureties for his good behaviour and to appear at the next sessions, &c.   GEORGE HELLIER, Maior."

Sept. 23, the assize of bread, the general price of wheat being at 3s. the bushel. "The twopeny white loaf to be 22½ oz. weight. The twopeny wheaten loafe, to be 33 oz. ¾ and 1d. weight. The twopeny houshold loaf to be 45 oz. weight."

A. D.

1654 Oct. 4, an order was issued against badgers and regrators of corn. None to be brought until the market-bell had done ringing.

Oct. 25, Richard Rogers, blacksmith, and Ann Dabder, singlewoman of Tewkesbury, were apprehended, the woman in man's apparel, for having kept company together at the Seven Stars in Thomas-street, and at Thomas Beale's house on St. Michael's Hill, where the said Ann put on the man's apparel, and being both drunk the night before, when they abused the constables with very filthy language. They were ordered

" to be set upon a horse, back to back, and so to ride, the constable going before them, through High-street, Redcliff-street, St. Thomas-street, and Wine-street,—the said Rogers to be set down at Newgate and remain there till he found sureties for his good behaviour; Ann Dabder to be set down at Bridewell, to be whipped, and sent to the place of her dwelling, from tithing to tithing, with a pass. Alice, the wife of Thomas Beale, who aided the disguise, to be set in the stocks for being drunk, there to remain for three hours, she refusing to pay 5s. according to the statute in that behalf; and that she be committed to Newgate for trial at the general gaol-delivery, for being a common bawd and entertainer of lewd persons in her house, and prohibited from keeping any longer an alehouse within the city."

Nov. 3, Capt. William Davis claimed and received the benefit of an ordinance, to enable such soldiers as served the Commonwealth in the late wars in Scotland to exercise any trade within this city. [Many other instances of this sort of claim occur during the Protectorate.]

Nov. 11, Ann, wife of Thomas Ilsly, butcher, for swearing two oaths within the parish of Christ-Church, having forfeited 3s. 4d. each oath to the poor of the parish, and having refused to make payment or give security, was ordered to be openly set in the stocks for three hours. The husband having resisted the Sheriffs' officers in the execution of this order, he was committed to Newgate till he should find sureties for his appearance at the session.

Nov. 13, John Amory appointed lead-reeve, to dig for lead ore in the commons at the hill in the manor of Congresbury.

Dec. 19, an order against apprentices rioting in the streets.

" OLIVER P.

" You are, within seven daies after sight hereof, to draw all the forces out of the Castle within the Cittie of Bristol (except onely such as you shall thinke fitt to appoint for the guard of yᵗ house and family), untill the tenth day of May next ensuing, and

A D.

1654 to put them into the Great Fort above the said Cittie. And our former order for demolishing of the said fort and disbanding of the forces there, you are to suspend untill further order. Given at Whitehall the 27th December 1654.

    " To Coll. Scroope, Govr

       of the Cittie of Bristol."

1655   Jan. 3, the Common Council agreed to discharge and save harmless all the inhabitants of the Castle from all arrear of fee-farm rent, due for the Castle, houses and grounds there.

    Jan. 22, an order that John Camm and John Audland, " two strangers, who were before commanded to depart, and have again come to the city," be apprehended.

    Jan. 23, an order for the apprehension of John Camm, John Audland, George Fox, James Nailor, Francis Hogill, and Edward Burroe, as strangers who could give no account of their being here.

    Jan. 24, information was given that certain persons of the Franciscan order had arrived from Rome, and that the above-named persons, " under the notion of Quakers," were suspected to be Jesuits.

    " 10th Feb. 1655. Whereas I have been arrested and am now in prison at the suit of the Company of Taylors, for useing their trade; in consideration that the Taylors will consent to release me from prison, I doe hereby promise to depart out of ye Citty, by the tenth of May next, with my wife and children, and will not returne againe hither and offend in the like kinde.   JAMES CORBETT."

    " The 7th of Sept. 1655. I have now rec'd of Mr. Maior xlv*s.*, and therefore will be gone with my wife and children for Ireland, in the space of the fortnight next ensuing, if the wind serve, otherwise with the first faire winde.   JAMES CORBETT."

    April 3, it was ordered by the Corporation that two ladders, one long and the other short, should be provided by the church-wardens of every parish, for the better prevention of the dreadful consequences of fire.

    May 3, for the prevention of sickness, Mr. John Stone, merchant, was ordered to remove out of his cellar in Marse-street, over against Baldwin-lane, " all such trayne-oyle as there now remaineth, and that he place the same in some other convenient place, where it may not be noisome and offensive to the neighbourhood, &c."

    May 5, " for the prevention of sickness during this hot season of ye yeere, It is ordered that all inhabitants of this citty doe forbeare to throw any dust or filth before their doores, or in the streets or lands of this citty; and that they twice every day, during this hot weather, throw water before their doores in the said streets and lands."

A. D.

1655 May 9, Robert Rutter, a soldier, in Major-Gen. Skippon's and Col. Haynes's regiment, exhibited his certificates; and Richard Balcomb, shoemaker, and Thomas Reeve, also soldiers, claimed the exercise of trades.

"The disposall of the moneys to repaire the wayes, 1655: London, £30; Aust, £20; Horfield, £10; Batheway, Kainsam, £20; Pensford, £30; Bedminster, £10; Oxford, £20."

July 6. "An Account of the Collection made in the several parishes in the Citty of Bristoll, for the reliefe of the Protestants in the Dominions of the Duke of Savoy.

	£	s	d		£	s	d
St. Nicholas	64	07	07	St. Ewens	01	19	04
Redcliffe	05	10	03	St. Peter	07	16	00
Christchurch	14	13	03	St. Stephen	25	00	06
Little St. Augustine	09	00	06	St. James	14	09	07
St. Phillips	07	03	04	Temple	05	15	08
St. Leonards	17	10	00	St. Thomas	28	15	07
St. Maryport	06	03	08	St. Walborough	34	10	03
All Saints	08	16	04	St. Michaell	04	17	08
St. John's	13	13	04				

£270 02 10"

July 24, an order was received to demolish the Royal Fort, and remove the provisions of war to Chepstow Castle. (The demolition was not completed till after the ensuing 28th of February.)

Sept. 16, the Mayor, Mayor-Elect, and two of the Aldermen, being in St. Nicholas' Church, Margaret Thomas interrupted Mr. Farmer, the minister, whilst naming the text, and disturbed the congregation. She was committed to Newgate.

Sept. 23, John Smith, in the same presence, Mr. Farmer being in the prayer, appeared with his hat on, and disturbed the congregation. Also committed.

Sept. 27, John Doddridge, esq. sworn Recorder.

Temperance Hignell, for disturbing Mr. Brent and his congregation in Temple Church, ordered to find sureties for good behaviour.

Oct. 22, the innkeepers were restrained from taking more than 6d. for a night's hay for a horse, and for a bushel of oats only 2s.

Nov. 23, "Samuel Bearham made oath that a contract and intention of marriage betweene John Hardimer, of Christ-Church parish in Bristol, tayler, and Frances Donnoell, of the parish of St. Peter, hath beene published three market-days in three severall weekes within this citty."

Dec. 13, General Disbrowe wrote Mr. Mayor, to advise Mr. Sherman, Mr. Lock, and Mr. Knight, as he had re-

A. D.

1655 quested when last at Bristol, to withdraw themselves from the Corporation, as not in any measure qualified and spirited for government;" which, on the 18th of February following, they did, on the plea of age, weakness of body, and other infirmities.

1656 Arthur White, seaman, and the wife of John Olliver, having been found incontinent together, it was ordered, according to the ancient custom of this city, that the said parties should be set upon a horse, back to back, and so ride, the bellman going before them and publishing their offence, from the High Cross down High-street, and Tucker-street, so far as the dwelling-house of the said Olliver, and from thence return up High-street and go to Bridewell, there to be set down and discharged.

Feb. 20, the constables were ordered to assist Capt. Robert Doleman, commander of the Wexford frigate, in the impressment of two hundred able mariners, seamen, and watermen, above the age of fifteen and under sixty years.

June 4, the general assize of wheat being at 5s. the bushel, the twopenny white loaf was fixed to weigh 14oz. 3q. 1dr., the wheaten, 22oz., and the household, 29oz. 1q. 3dr.

July 2, Henry Chappell was committed for disturbing the congregation at St. Nicholas' Church, the last Lord's day, "both by putting on his hat in prayer-time, and after prayer was ended, crying out, ' Believe not in man!' and endeavouring to speak more if he had not been hindered, and, upon examination, giving the lie to Alderman Vickris."

Aug. 29, an order of the Mayor stated that

In pursuance of a statute of Jan. 25, 19 Henry VII., "the Masters, Wardens, and brethren of the fraternity and company of Innholders within this city, being an ancient fraternitie, time out of mind," obtained a confirmation, bearing date March 1, 3d of the late King James, under the hands and seals of the Lord Chancellor, Lord High Treasurer, and Lord Chief Justice of the King's Bench, of "certain ordinances and constitutions for the well ordering and governing of themselves. Amongst which ordinances a certain number of ancient Innes are declared to bee common Innes and hosterries within this cittie and liberties thereof, and that noe more or noe other than are therein particularized should bee made use of as Innes and hosterries. And whereas a certain messuage without Redcliffe Yate, within the liberties of this cittie, commonly called the Angell, was heeretofore used, employed, and allowed as a common Inne and hosterry, ass well by the Maior and Aldermen of the said Cittie as by the said Company, although not within the number allowed by the said ordinances and constitutions, and particularly soe confirmed in the yeare of our Lord God 1624; since which the said messuage haveing beene wholly taken downe

1656and demolished, and now againe newly erected and built, and made very large and commodious for entertainement of men and horses, and the present Master, Wardens, and Company of Inholders, together with Anne Pruett, widow, owner and occupier of the said messuage, makeing their application to us that the said messuage might be for ever allowed as one of the common Innes and hosterries within the cittie, soe as it might not be prejudiciall to the said ordinances and constitutions. We therefore, considering the said request, and their reasons enforceing the same, conceiveing it may tend to the common good of the people coming and travelling to and from this cittie, have thought fitt and doe declare our willingness thereunto," &c. &c.

Sept. 8, Capt. Morgan, of St. George's, apologized, by letter to the Mayor and Aldermen, for his tenants having built houses at Pill, and promised them no more should be erected without the Corporation's consent.—Aug. 19, 1658, the Water-Bailiff was sent to Crockerne Pill, to require Mr. Morgan and all his tenants to pull down the several houses built there contrary to the decrees of the Exchequer with which they had been served.

Nailor's entry into Bristol was Oct. 24, on horseback. Timothy Wedlock, of Devonshire, and two married women, Martha Symons and Hannah Stranger (whose husbands were in London), came before him, singing " Holy, holy, Lord God of Israel!" Two other women led his horse, with the reins in their hands. In this manner he rode to the High Cross, and the White Lion in Broad-street. That night he and his disciples, seven in number, were summoned before the magistrates; but such was their singing *Hosanna!* and *Holy, holy, holy!* with the concourse of people, that little was then said to them. But the next day, being Saturday, the magistrates examined first Nailor, who declared himself to be " the Son of God," adding, " and the Son of God is but one."

Monday, Oct. 27, Dorcas Erbury was examined, who said that James Naylor was the Holy One of Israel, and she would seal it with her blood. Being asked, " Why did you pull off his stockings and put your clothes under his feet?" she replied, " Because he is the Lord of Israel, and worthy of it." A copy of this examination was forwarded to the Parliament.

Part of the sentence (boring the tongue) was remitted. While in the pillory, one Robert Rich placed a paper over his head, on which was written, *"This is the King of the Jews."*

Dec. 8, an order was issued against private persons entertaining the horses of travellers to the prejudice of inn-

A. D.

1656 holders, who by the law and custom of England are responsible for all such horses. Another order against feeding horses in the streets, the owner to forfeit 6*d*. to the use of the poor. Inhabitants permitting a horse to stand to forfeit 1*s*. A constable or serjeant-at-mace bringing said horse to the next common inn, to receive 4*d*. from the owner, who was to pay the innholder 2*d*. for the standing of the horse.

Elizabeth Nut, of Chelvey, in the county of Somerset, being taken up as a vagrant, was ordered to be whipped from the High Cross to Redcliff-Gate, and so sent home.

1657 Feb. 6, Richard Jones, for disturbing Mr. Stubbs, minister, and hindering the beadle in execution of punishment on James Nailor, was committed till he found sureties for his good behaviour.

March 6, William Hobson, merchant, having been convicted upon the oath of two witnesses, for that he, within the space of six months past, had avowedly in words professed that the act of drunkenness might be committed without sin, it was ordered that, according to an Act of Parliament in that behalf, he should be committed to prison, there to remain for the space of six months without bail or mainprize, and until he should put in sufficient sureties to be upon good behaviour for the whole year.

May 9, John Johns, tailor, was committed to Newgate, for having, at the Wednesday's lecture-sermon in St. Philip's Church, disturbed the congregation, by reviling at the minister, Mr. Ralph Farmer, calling him " Jesuit, and deceiver of the people."

June 7, John Cottrell and Robert Jones, of Pensford, bakers, admitted to sell bread in the market, as two of the five bakers so privileged.

June 20, Katharine Hughes was convicted of going to Mr. Ralph Farmer* with a letter, and abusing him, saying that " the plagues of God would pursue him—that he was a murderer and oppressor of the prisoners—that he thirsted after blood, and such like words."

Mr. Knolls was disturbed, during his sermon in Allhallows Church, by one Nathaniel Milner.

July 17, a new inn, built by George Hele, tailor, adjoining that on which the George Inn in the Castle lately stood, allowed to be used as a common inn and hosterry.— Aug. 26, an order was obtained that no other inn should be opened within the precincts of the Castle.

* In 1660, Thomas Wall, by the Tolzey, published Ralph Farmer's Fast-Sermon, preached at St. Nicholas, April 6, dedicated to W. Pryn, Esq. M.P.

A. D.

1657 August. Complaint having been made that Edward Morgan, Thomas Wallis, Bartholomew Allen, and others, had digged wells in the vicinity of the head of the spring of All-Saints' Conduit, in Maudlin-lane, it was ordered that no more wells should be dug, and, upon injury to the spring-head appearing, that the wells already dug should be dammed up.

Sept. 20, John Bezar, a tailor, disturbed the congregation of St. Nicholas' Church, in view of the Mayor and Aldermen, and was committed to Newgate.

Dec. 6, John Johns disturbed the congregation at St. James's.

1658 April 29, Elizabeth Skreene, having confessed fornication, was ordered to be carted through the city, " in such sort as such lewd persons have formerly been used, time out of mind."

June 14, William Wilkes and John Barnes were committed for walking in the Marsh, about six o'clock on the preceding Sabbath-day, and not paying the fine.

October. A lecture having been set up without authority in St. Maryport Church, at seven in the morning of Sundays, the church-wardens were ordered not to suffer the bells to be rung nor the church-doors opened, nor any one to preach, without further order from the Mayor and Aldermen.

December. A weekly rate ordered for the liberty of the Castle, for the relief of its poor.

1659 Jan. 4, twenty city-watchmen were appointed; such as watched as a supply, and not on his own account, to be paid 4*d*. per night in the summer, and 6*d*. in the winter; all to be under the controul of Richard Hopkins, marshal.

March 27, Thomas Hiscocks and William Collins, two apprentices of John Johns, tailor, were taken up, about three o'clock in the afternoon, as they were going to Redland, where they said they were sent on an errand by their mistress; whereby they breaking the Sabbath, and forfeiting 10*s*. a piece, which they refused to pay, on the 12th of April they were committed till they should find sureties to answer it at the sessions; as was also Hugh Millerd, a journeyman-tailor, taken up by the constables of St. James's ward, for walking on the Lord's day in time of sermon, and refusing to pay the fine of 10*s*. John Whiting, a carpenter, having charged John Moats, one of the St. James's constables, as a persecutor in this particular, he too was committed, to answer for the offence.

The market in Broad-street ordered to be kept by country-

A. D.

1659 butchers only, and not by the city-butchers, who had shops elsewhere all the week long, on pain of forfeiting 6s. 8d. a day.

May 5, the Corporation received from the executrix of John Doddridge, esq., their late recorder, a legacy of £40, to be laid out in a piece of plate.

June 10, several matters of lewdness and incontinency having been proved against Richard Rogers and his servant, Katharine Chitty, " tending to the great dishonour of God and to the scandal of the magistracy and government of this city," it was ordered that the said Richard and Katharine be set upon a horse, back to back, his face being towards the tail, and so to ride through the city; and being set down, the said Katharine to be set in the House of Correction, there to be kept at work according to law.

July 18, Christopher Poole, tailor, with Sarah Harbert and Ann Long, ordered to be set on horseback (Christopher to ride in the midst, with his face towards the tail of the horse), and so to ride through the city and be set down at the House of Correction.

Oct. 1, the conduit-head by Breene's Mill having been found defective, whereby the current thence to the Key and Back Pipes was very much stopped, a survey was ordered.

Oct. 6, Thomas Johns committed to prison, charged with assailing the door of Mr. Knowles, minister in the Castle, with a chopping-knife, and abusive language before the Mayor and Aldermen. Being questioned as to what he would say to the accusation against him, he replied, " The Lord of Hosts will not answer thee."

Oct. 18, the Mayor and Aldermen directed search into all charters and books of records, writings and evidences, whatsoever, and a report to be made in writing.

It was ordered that the country-butchers leave the market in Broad-street on Saturdays by three in the afternoon.

1660   Feb. 4, the Apprentices appear to have kept guard in the Meal-market (now called the Guard-house), Wine-street. On the 10th they were ordered to deliver their arms at the Guildhall, and trustees and widows to make register of the apprentices and servants who went in arms.

May 14, an order issued against the erection of May-poles, being originally heathenish, and under the Gospel as scandalous.

1663   The first part of the note respecting Sir John Atkyns's residence is corrected in the second note at foot of p. 229.

1665   The John Yeamans now created a baronet was a barrister. " The Booke of the Mercers and Linen-Drapers Companie,"

A. D.

noticed under 1743, has this memorandum :—"1659. Paid to officers for seizures, for Counsel retaining fees to Mr. Jones, Mr. Ridott, and Mr. Yeamans, £3."

1667 Mr. Braikenridge possesses a drawing of " the great clumsy porter."

1671 Sir John Knight's house still stands, being the premises below Messrs. Johnson and Co.'s oil-warehouses, with four slender pillars in front. His son occupied what had been formerly the Templars' Hall, now Mr. Hayes' coach-manufactory.

1672 " An Act" was passed, " to enable the Dean and Chapter of the Cathedral Church of Bristol to exchange their vicarage of Berkeley, in the county of Gloucester, with George lord Berkeley, for his rectory of St. Michael's in Sutton Bennington, in the county of Nottingham."

1673 It was Roger, earl of Castlemain, whom James, on his ascending the throne, sent on an embassy to the Pope. We possess a folio, with eighteen finely executed plates, chiefly drawn and engraven in Rome, bearing this title :

" An Account of His Excellence Roger Earl of Castlemaine's Embassy from His Sacred Majesty James the IId. King of England, Scotland, France, and Ireland, &c. to His Holiness Innocent XI. Published formerly in the Italian tongue, by Mr. Michael Wright, Chief Steward of His Excellences House at Rome. And now made English, with several Amendments, and Additons. Licensed Roger L'Estrange. London, printed by Thomas Snowden for the Author. 1688."—Pp. of letter-press, 120, nearly three of which comprise complimentary verses, original and translated, by Nahum Tate. The frontispiece represents four whole-length cherubs bearing an oval medallion of the King through the air, and his Ambassador in the act of kissing the Pope's toe; while a female figure, perhaps designed for Religion, appearing to act as mistress of the ceremony, addresses His Holiness, pointing with one hand to his Lordship, and with the other to St. Peter's in the distance. A portrait of Queen Maria, daughter of the late Duchess of Modena, " R. White, sculp. Lond." and a vignette of an angel bearing a medallion of her Majesty, drawn by Gio Batta Lenardi, are prefixed to the Dedication. Six of the plates delineate the sides, back and front, of two of the Earl's state-coaches, and seven are devoted to the Hall of Monte-Cavallo and the chief ornaments of the banquetting-table.—This unseasonable publication must have spoken more of James's design to convert his subjects to the papal supremacy than met the eye. Our copy is labelled with " 1706" under the arms of " Gostlet Harington of Marshfeild in the Coun: of Glocester Gent."

1678 John King, probably the first spectacle-maker who resided in Bristol, was admitted to the freedom of the city, on payment of a fine of £3 and conditioning to follow no other trade.

A. D.

1683 . The writ of Quo Warranto and its adjuncts cost the Corporation ("paid towards perfecting the new grant by the King") £544 13s. 6d.

1685 The "John Wraxall" of the note was Master of the Mercers and Linen Drapers' Company in 1723. Nathaniel Wraxall was Sheriff the same year. See Biogr. Dict. of Living Authors, art. Sir Nath. W. Wraxall.

1686 The erection of the new market-house for corn, on Aldworth's Key, cost £582 1s. 9d.

1689 Jan. 7, Monday, the Mayor (William Jackson), Recorder, Aldermen, and "Commons of the principal citizens of the city of Bristol," waited upon the Prince of Orange, being introduced by His Grace the Duke of Ormond, their High Steward, and the Earl of Shrewsbury. The Recorder addressed His Highness with "thanks for his design of delivering the kingdom from Popery and arbitrary power." The speech was printed in "A Sixth Collection of Papers relating to the Present Juncture of Affairs in England. Licensed and entered according to Order. London printed, and are to be sold by Richard Janeway in Queen's Head Court, in Paternoster Row, 1689." There were twelve of such Collections printed in the course of 1688 and 1689; the first of which commenced with the Petition of the Seven Bishops to James, and the twelfth closed with the Coronation-Oaths of William and Mary in England and Scotland. Except that of London, the Bristol address was the only one of a Corporation so published.

"An Act" was passed "for erecting Courts of Conscience in the City of Bristol and Gloucester and the liberties thereof."

1694 This year Sir John Knight delivered a speech in the House of Commons, against the Bill for a General Naturalization, which (the Tories having dispersed copies of it throughout the nation) was ordered to be burnt by the hands of the common hangman. The speech (a copy of which is in the possession of Mr. S. C. Webb, printed on the broad side of a demy sheet) is curious for its eloquence, humour, and sarcastic irony. Sir John's appeal to the Bible is not what we should now consider in the best taste. Towards the close of his address, he says,

"Mr. Speaker, this nation is a religious, just, and jealous nation, who, in some of their fits and zeal, have not only quarrelled and fought for the same, but have murder'd and deposed kings, nobles, bishops, and priests, for the sake of their religion and liberties, which they pretend to prove from the Bible. We are the religious

A. D.

1694 Representatives of this religious people; let us therefore learn instruction in the case before us, from that good book, where we may be informed that St. Paul, from being born free of heathen Rome, escaped a whipping, and valued and pleaded that privilege."—Our orator then goes on to notice the policy of Joseph, a slave in Egypt, in taxing the Egyptians to lay up a store of corn, which in time of famine he made them purchase at a high rate; getting from them, " for that which was once their own, all their money, their cattle, their lands, and, last of all, their persons into slavery, tho' at the same time he did far otherwise by his own countrymen; for he placed them in the best of the land, the land of Goshen, and nourish'd them from the King's store," &c. " Sir, I perceive some gentlemen are uneasy: perhaps I have offended them, in supposing they are religious Representatives, or concluding that their religion is from the Bible. If that be it which displeaseth, I beg their pardon, and promise not to offend again on that score, and will conclude all with this motion: *That the Serjeant be commanded to open the doors, and let us first kick the Bill out of the House, and then foreigners out of the kingdom.*"

1699 " An Act for the better preserving the Navigation of the Rivers Avon and Froome, and for cleaning, paving, and enlightening the streets of the city of Bristol."

1700 It has been proved to us that the ground now known as Dame Pugsley's Field and Nine-Tree Hill was, in a deed dated Dec. 1723, transferring it to the family who still hold it, called " Steep-Hill" and " Conduit-Close," and this might have been ever the *written* law of our daisy-land before Dame Pugsley was born; but all the ink of all the lawyers this side dooms-day cannot gainsay the *common* law dictated by the little boys and girls of more than a century.—We have reason for conjecture that Mrs. Pugsley was somehow connected with a family named Cole.

1702 Sept. 1. " The sixty captains of ships were distinguished from the rest by knots of red ribbons in their hats. The Queen's twelve coaches were each drawn by six horses."— " The serjeants-at-mace, who before wore black gowns, now began to wear blue gowns, that they might be distinguished from their masters whom they walked with."—*Mr.* BRAIKENRIDGE, *sen.'s MS.*

1703 During the storm that commenced in the night of Nov. 26 (not 20), the water rose two feet at the end of Baldwin-street, next the Back. (See of Jessop's Survey, &c. 1793, forward.)

1705 Lime-trees planted in Queen-square.

1706 The " pent-house" against St. Nicholas' Church was also called " The Walk."

A. D.

1708 Richard Brent, "Tom Thumb," about whom Sir Edward
    Harington wrote, and whose portrait Benjamin Barker
    painted, was born at Wells, Dec. 28, this year. He died in
    July or August 1793.

1709 Much wheat was exported to Flanders for the army. The
    promised price per bushel to the colliers was 6s. 8d. Some
    of them notwithstanding remained, and for threatening
    words were seized and secured in the Council-House. The
    others, hearing of it, returned; and there was a bustle
    between them and the militia, in which two or three of the
    mob were wounded, and the Council-House windows broken,
    through which the prisoners escaped.

1711 In Hervey's Naval History of Great Britain, vol. iii.
    p. 320 (8vo. 1779), are some particulars relating to two
    privateers, named the Duke and the Duchess, commanded
    by Woods Rogers and Stephen Courtney, which had been
    fitted out by some merchants of Bristol, to cruize against
    the Spaniards, in 1708. In August, this year, they arrived
    in the Downs, after encompassing the world in three years
    and two months; having on board, as pilot, the famous
    Capt. Dampier, author of "Voyages, &c." In one of these
    ships also came home Alexander Selkirk, who had resided
    alone on the Island of Juan Fernandez nearly five years, and
    to whose history De Foe was indebted for his " Adventures of
    Robinson Crusoe." In 1712, John Rumsey, esq. presented
    to the Bristol Cathedral a pair of large silver candlesticks,
    of the plunder in this expedition, which cost him £114.

1714 Oct. 20. " In the windows of several of the houses [of
    the Dissenters] were the effigies of Doctor Sacheverell,
    designed by the inhabitants of them to be burnt."—Mr.
    BRAIKENRIDGE's MS.
        The Mayor, Anthony Swymmer, lived at the house now
    the property of James Harford's family, St. Augustin's Back,
    in which died the Countess of Westmorland, widow of Mr.
    Fane, who, previous to his succession in the peerage, was
    clerk to the Society of Merchant-Venturers.

1715 " St. James's Square," though perhaps at this time so
    intended, must here mean St. James's Barton. For the
    Square, see 1765.

1716 The intention respecting the figure of Neptune, it will
    be seen under 1824, was abandoned.

1717 " The Quay-wall was lengthened" 240 " feet, as far as
    the Gibb," and thence turned 200 feet to the Gibb-Slip,
    beyond which it was carried " 280 feet up the Avon, &c."
        Mr. Day died June 26.

A. D.

1729 The Mayor's sur-name was Stokes.

1734 According to "A List of the Freeholders and Freemen who voted, &c." in May, this year (and not in 1733, as arranged in p. 262), " printed by Felix Farley, and sold only by him, at Shakespear's Head, the upper end of Castle-Green," the number of *votes* for "John Scrope, esq." was 1866—for Sir Abraham Elton, bart. 2420, and for Thomas Coster, esq. 2071. The following are the numbers of *voters* in the several parishes, with such as were clergymen, and those who resided elsewhere; including the subjoined enumeration of voters who polled as freeholders.

Parish	Voters		Parish	Voters	
All-Saints' Parish	30—	6	St. Philip & Jacob.	421—41	
St. Augustine's	176—	15	St. Peter's	145—17	
Castle-Precincts	167—	28	St. Stephen's	243—27	
Christ-Church Parish	120—	16	Temple	285—53	
St. Ewen's	18—	5	St. Thomas	247—43	
St. James's	617—191		St. Werburge	37—16	
St. John's	120—	19	Bedminster	32	
St. Leonard's	43—	5	Clifton	25	
St. Mary-Port	74—	9	Clergymen	28—	5
St. Michael's	135—	25	Country-Voters	298—12	
St. Mary Redclift	350—	50			
St. Nicholas'	298—	47		3909	600

Of the freemen, 265 were weavers, 100 of whom resided in the parish of St. Philip & Jacob., 83 in Temple-parish, and 12 in the country; 1 doctor of medicine; 15 surgeons in the city, 1 at Clifton, and 1 each at Alveston, Abergavenny, Backwell, Keynsham, Gloucester, and Monmouth; 3 schoolmasters; 4 writing-masters; 2 musicians; 1 fiddle-maker; 1 printer (John Bonney); 1 engraver, and 1 freemason.

1737 The putting-up of the table of loan-money, &c. was an act of the whole Corporation, in Common Council assembled.

1739 For Snowgate, read Snowgale's Alms-house; which was re-erected in the time of opening All-Saints' street.

1745 The "two London privateers" were the Prince Frederick (Captain James Talbot) and the Duke. Their prizes were French, the Marquis d'Antin, mounting 24 guns, and El Lewis Herasma, 28 guns. They had been out four years, and, when captured, were last from Callao in Peru, where the treasure had been put on board them for greater safety, as war had not then been declared between France and England. Vide Hervey's Naval History, vol. iv. p. 277.

1750 The William Miller of the first Bristol Bank was not the merchant who resided in Queen-Square, but a wholesale grocer in Tailors' Court—" a hundred thousand pounder," as his representatives were enabled to testify.

1755 The Mayor's state-coach cost £354.

1761 *The Lamb Inn Witchcraft.*] The Rev. Mr. Symes, rector of St. Werburgh's, one Sunday, desiring the prayers of his congregation for two children grievously tormented, above half of them (church-goers, be it remembered—not infidel scoffers) instantly quitted their seats in disgust.

Innate veneration for the memory of Mrs. Haynes and her Temple of Rationality induced us to make enquiry as to the present condition of Wick-Court, which is depicted in a folding plate of Sir Robert Atkyns's History of Gloucestershire. This produced the following information from Mr. Richard Haynes, solicitor, the present representative of the family and owner of the mansion:

" Sir Robert Atkyns does not appear to have been quite correct in his account of the ancestry of this family, nor of the boundaries of the parish. In respect to the first, it is of no material note; but the second may misinform in cases of importance.

" In p. 200, he says, ' Thomas Haynes, son of Richard, married Joan, daughter of the Larager: his second wife was the daughter of Sir Anthony Pointz.' This passage, in my copy of the History, has been corrected, and I believe by the pen of my great grandfather, Richard Haynes, in the following manner: *His second wife was Mary, daughter of Mathew Pointz, of Alderley, brother of Sir Nicholas Pointz, of Acton, in this county.*—The next passage, ' Richard Haynes, son of Thomas by Mary Pointz, his second wife, married Margaret, daughter of Edward Trotman, of Cam: his second wife was Mary, daughter of William Capell, of Bromyard in Herefordshire;' has been corrected by the same hand, thus: *His second wife was Mary, daughter of Edward Capell, of How Caple, in Herefordshire.*

" Sir Robert, p. 655, places ' Breach Yate' in the parish of Siston. *The whole of Breach Yate lies in the parish of Wick and Abson.*

" He mentions that ' Rock Diamonds, Belumnites, and Astroites, Serpentines, &c. were frequent in this parish.' But, since his time, a considerable quantity of the species of fossils called *Geodes** has been discovered on this estate by the late Mr. Haynes; several of which have been shewn at the British Museum and to gentlemen of information on this subject. The collection is now in my possession, and, for magnitude and brilliancy of the specimens, their number and variety of colours, I understand that so splendid a cabinet of Geodes is nowhere else to be found.—The Roman coins and bricks mentioned by Sir Robert Atkyns, as having been found in a ground called Chestles, or Castles, in that parish, are also in my possession."

---

* " This word is evidently of Greek extraction: γῆ, *terra*, earth; and ῳδὴ, *cantus*, a song. Thos. Holyoke thus defines the Latin word, *Geodes*: ' A kind of stone having earth within its hollowness; and being laid to the ear, it maketh a noise.' "

A. D.

1762 A mezzotinto engraving, drawn by N. Hone and scraped by James M'Ardell, depicting a comely-looking personage in canonicals, named " The Rev. Emanuel Collins, A.M." is frequently to be seen in our print-shops. Mr. Collins was of Wadham College, Oxford, for which he had probationized at the Bristol Grammar-School, under the Rev. A. S. Catcott, and was vicar of Bedminster, where he kept a public-house, and performed the marriage-ceremony in it at a crown a couple—an abuse of the sacred ordinance which, we have been told, was chiefly instrumental in producing the Marriage-Act of 1752. He was the predecessor of Mr. Cocking, a former proprietor of Felix Farley's Bristol Journal, as master of a school for boys in Shannon-Court, and published " Miscellanies in Prose and Verse, &c." 153 pp. small 4to. " printed by E. Farley, in Small-street, 1762"—a work which shews that the man had more ability than good moral taste in the choice of subjects for his muse. Like the youth who, skilled in boxing beyond his fellows, is ever ready to bestow a knock-down blow, or, being an adept in riding or driving, prefers to all other pursuits, running both fortune and fame for more useful matters off their legs, Mr. Collins was nothing loth to employ his lively talent in lampooning his neighbours. A notable proof of ingenuity in blunting the means of punishment thus occurred. Having laid himself open to correction by the law, the offended party contented himself with proffering mercy upon the usual terms of a recantation of the calumny in one of the newspapers. To this Mr. Collins assented, with the proviso that he should be permitted to add or not, as he might determine at leisure, two lines only, by way of postcript. As the writer of the concession took care to have the libeller's signature to terms which were considered sufficiently degrading, so he regarded not what might be added. Accordingly, the repentant called at the printing-office too late for interposition between the following couplet from Hudibras and the hour of publication :

" He that's convinced against his will
Is of the same opinion still."

1764 The Corporation paid the Vestry of St. Nicholas' parish £216, in consideration of their opening the new way under the Tower, to the Back.

1766 Henry Jones, author of the tragedy of the Earl of Essex, &c. published his " Clifton : a Poem, in two cantos. Including Bristol and all its Environs." 4to., pp. 44. The inscription was to " the Right Hon. Norborne, Lord Botte-

A. D.

1766 tourt," the occupant of Stoke-House.—Jones would perhaps have written better, had not the spirit of his muse demanded the inspiration of a bottle of brandy per day. Flashes of wit so excited rarely extend their illumination beyond the surface of the nose. His hand-writing was so villanously hieroglyphical, that neither he himself nor any one else could decipher it, excepting one journeyman-printer; to whom, for that purpose, one of his MSS. was sent from London to Edinburgh. See vol. iii. of the " Life and Adventures of Timothy Ginnadrake [father of the late Misses Fleming, of Bath]," fcap. 8vo. 1771.

1768 Clifton Church was enlarged by building, not a north, but a south aisle and west gallery.

1775 The conjecture here advanced, respecting the spring-head of the conduit in Unity-street, is erroneous. That water comes from Jacob's Well; with which also the Bishop's Palace, &c. are supplied.

1793 J. Jessop, engineer, and W. White, surveyor, published " A Plan and Sections of Part of the Rivers Avon and Froom, viz. from Rownham Ferry to Temple Back, and from the Quay's Mouth to Traitor's Bridge." According to this, between Temple Back (the commencement of the new course of the Avon) and Rownham (where the locks of Cumberland Basin terminate the Floating-Harbour), there was a fall of twelve feet in the river's bed. At Temple Back, the land rises 25 feet above the bed, and at Rownham 37 feet; to which points rose the high tide of January 1792, overflowing the banks of each extremity. The ordinary low-water mark, all the way, was 6 feet, and the land-flood of that month rose to 12 feet above the bed. The following are elevations of the land above the bed of the river at intermediate stations.

At the level between Redcliff, St. Thomas, and Bath streets, about.. . . . . 33 feet.

Southern foot of the Bridge opposite the Savings' Bank .. 35

S. E. corner of St. Nicholas' Church, in High-street, nearly 40

At the crowd-door of St. Nicholas Church 37

Quay-wall, corner of the Back and the Grove, in view from St. Nicholas' Church, and to which the same high tide flowed 30

Summit of the Gib-slip, end of Prince's street, where also the high tide reached 32

Mouth of the River Froom. 34

(Here the zero of the *Quay-Gauge* stood 7½ feet above the bed of the Avon.)

Land of the timber-yards, on the south bank, juxta the Rope-walk 32

A. D.

1793 Brick-yard opposite to the Glass-House and Tombs's old
Dock... 35 feet.
Mouth of the Creek opposite to the Merchants' Floating-
Dock.. 33

At the Red Clift, the ground rises 36, 41½, and 39 feet
above the bed, in the course of a few yards. Here were
the trees imbedded, &c. noticed in p. 6, as felled by the
sudden rush of waters through the " chasm or rupture."

In the Rownham Meadows, the Clifton side of the river,
the land is.. 35

The bed of the Froom dips precipitately into the Avon
at 8 feet below zero of the Quay-gauge, beneath which the
low-water line ran about two feet. The level of the high
tide in January 1792 there flowed 24 feet on the gauge, or
32 feet above the bed, and five feet over the bed of the river
just above Traitor's Bridge; the fall thence to the Avon
being 27 feet. The surface of the water in the pond of the
Castle-Mill is little more than 3 feet above its bed; and the
fall from the Castle-Mill head, to the surface of Bridewell-
Mill pond, is five feet. The fall thence to the bed of the
stream is about 8½ feet; whence the low water ran less than
a foot to the Avon, over a gradual fall of eighteen feet.
Hence the level of the high tide of January 1792, which
was 24 feet on the Quay-guage, rose only two feet above the
surface of the Castle-Mill pond, or seven feet above its bed.

The land at the flood-hatches on the Narrow Weir, in
Castle-Mill pond, is 8 feet above the bed of the river; on
the Broad Weir, less than 7 feet. In Nelson-street, the
ground rises 20 feet higher than the bed of the Froom, an
elevation parallel with that of Traitor's Bridge; and these
are the highest stations on the whole line. The lowest,
over which the high tide of Jan. 1792 flowed a foot, is the
entrance of the little dock at the head of Canons' Marsh
rope-walk, where the land rises 24 feet above the gradually
inclining bed of the river. In the Plan, the bottom of the
cellar at the Hole-in-the-Wall public-house, Prince's street,
supposed to be one of the lowest, was shewn to be on a level
of 15 feet with the Quay-gauge, and 10 feet 7 inches from
the bed of the river.

The level of 16 feet on the Quay-guage, at which the
water in the Floating-Harbour is kept, gives the following
depths on the gauges of the respective docks for admission
of vessels.

In the Avon.

Tombs's Dock .... 12 feet,
Blanning's Dock 11

A. D.
1793

Osborne's (Tombs's old) Dock........... 11 feet.

Hilhouse's Dock....................... 15

Farr's Dock 11

Merchants' Dock 16

In the Froom.

Tombs's Little Dock.................. 9 feet.

The length of water in the Avon part of the Floating-Harbour is about 250 yards more than two miles. From Traitor's Bridge to the Quay's mouth, the Froom measures about 250 yards short of a mile and a half, or a mile and more than 3 furlongs.

1806   May 17, died John Brice Becket, long a respectable bookseller in Corn-street. He was a contributor to the philosophical journals of his time, and a valued correspondent of Dr. Priestley. He left a variety of valuable MSS., of which his acting-executor, Mr. John Mills, may be expected to make popular use.

1816   Mr. John Loudon M'Adam appointed General Surveyor of the Bristol Turnpike-Roads.

June 25, was passed " an Act for the more speedy recovery of small Debts, in the City and County of the City of Bristol, and the liberties thereof, and in the several parishes and places therein mentioned, in the Counties of Gloucester and Somerset."

1822   A younger brother of John Fry, named Richard, settled as a merchant at Cape-Coast-Castle, headed a detachment of 240 blacks in Sir Charles Macarthy's unfortunate expedition against the Ashantees, in 1824, and escaped with four body-wounds.

1824   May 2. Read *professors and* " amateurs, &c."

July 29, Mr. Graham, aëronaut, accompanied by Mr. Robert Saunders, solicitor, ascended with a silk balloon, at seventeen minutes after five o'clock, from the station of the Bristol Gas-Light Company, Avon-street, St. Philip's; and after a circuitous course, crossing and re-crossing the Avon, and becoming nearly stationary over the Severn at Aust, descended safely on Itchington-Common, Gloucestershire, about seven o'clock.

☞   The following are said by Mr. Hallam, in his " Middle Ages," to be fair multiples, when we would bring the general value of money in those reigns to our present standard: — Multiply any sum mentioned by a writer under Edward I. (1272—1307) by twenty-four. Henry VI. (1422—1461) by sixteen.

EXPENSES OF ROYAL AND NOBLE VISITS.

1585 The Earl of Pembroke's ungracious visit cost the city, including a present of sweetmeats, &c. £102 15s. 4d. He was received on his entrance from Wells by the burgesses in armour, and thirty-two chambers fired off in Redcliff Church-yard.

1587 The Earls of Leicester and Warwick came from Bath, and on Easter-day dined at Mr. Kitchin's mansion. Expense of this visit, including a present, £149 4s. 4d.

1612 Queen Anne, from Friday, June 4, till the following Tuesday, two o'clock. The bower built for Her Majesty cost £4 1s. 10d.; the water-sport, £41 9s. 10d.

1648 The Marquess of Worcester, Aug. 4, £138 6s.

1649 [Lord Lieutenant Cromwell's visit, in July, of more than a week, was without charge upon the city-fund!]

1654 Lord Whitelock, October, £20 14s. 8d. [See note to p. 192.]

1663 King Charles the Second, and his Queen, in September, £1390 10s. 9d. "Received of sundries towards ditto, £1380." £898 of this sum was borrowed of various individuals upon bonds. Their Majesties had been invited at Bath, Saturday, Sept. 5. A purse containing 130 pieces of gold at 22s. each, was presented to the Queen. The purse cost 7s. 6d.

1664 Sir Henry Vane, Nov. 4, £11 10s.

1665 The Duke of Ormond, at Sir Henry Creswicke's house in Small-street, £177 9s. 10d.

1676 The Duke of Ormond, July, in St. George's Chapel, £32 10s. 9d.

1677 Queen Catherine, July 11, £446 2s. 8d.

1681 The Marquess of Worcester, Sept. 8, at the Merchants' Hall, £186 10s. 8d.

1686 King James, Aug. 24, £573 0s. 1d.

1687 King James and his Queen, Monday, Sept. 12, £703 1s. 5d.

1702 Queen Anne, with Prince George, at Sir Thomas Day's great house in Redcliff-street, £466 4s. 7d.

1727 The Princess Amelia, May 9, £242 14s. 11½d.

1733 The Prince of Orange, Feb. 21, £297 1s. 3d.

1738 The Prince and Princess of Wales, Nov. 10 and 11, £954 19s. 11d.

1761 The Duke of York, Dec. 28, a dinner at the Merchants' Hall, £398 5s. 4d., and a ball at the Assembly Room, £104 6s.

A CATALOGUE

OF PORTRAITS IN THE CHAMBER OF BRISTOL.

[*The notes from Mr. Alderman* HAYTHORNE's *MS.*]

1531   No. 1.   Mr. Thomas White, mayor in 1529.   [See 1541.]
>   This picture was brought hither from Coventry.

1546   No. 2, 3.   Robert and Nicholas Thorne.
>   "1624. Paid the Dutch Painter for drawing [copying] the two Pictures of Mr. Thornes [in the Grammar-School] to hang up in the Council-House, £2 4s."

1555   No. 4.   Sir Thomas White, alderman and merchant-tailor of London, and founder of St. John's College, Oxford.   [See 1555 and 1566.]
>   "1625. Paid for Sir Thomas White's Picture that was sent from Coventry hither, instead of Mr. Thomas White's Picture [No. 1] that I sent for, he being a worthy benefactor to the City, £2 16s."
>   —*Ibid.*

1583   No. 5.   An Alderman (as conjectured from the dress), whose name was not preserved beyond the supposed all-sufficient notoriety of his day.   The picture bears only this inscription:
>   "Anno Domini 1583. Ætatis suæ 62."—Arms, a globe.

1591   No. 6.   Lord Treasurer Burleigh, who died in 1598.
>   "Paid unto Sergeaintt, painter at arms in London, for my Lord Treasurer's Picture, with his Arms, £3. For a new frame to set it in, and for carriage from London, 5s.; for 1 ell of taffeta for a curtain for the same, and making it, 6s.=pro memoria, £3 11s."

No. 7.   Robert Cecil, earl of Salisbury, who died in 1612.

1594   No. 8.   Alderman Robert Kitchin; aged, at his decease, 63 years.

1523   No. 9.   Thomas White, D.D.   [See A.D. 1610, where the quotation, as from this picture, is an error; also Barrett's History, p. 618.]
>   "1625. Paid unto John the Painter, for drawing of Dr. White's Picture, £2 10s."—His brother, a Bristol merchant, gave one of the bronze tables on the Exchange, 1631.

1625   No. 10.   King Charles the First. By Sir Anthony Vandyck.
>   "1633. Paid unto Flecher the Dutchman, for the new making the King's Picture, the Lord Treasurer, and Lord Cecill, and for the new trimming of the Pictures in the Council-House, £6."

No. 11.   The Earl of Pembroke.   [See 1621.]   Painted by Sir Anthony Vandyck.
>   "1627. Paid the Picture-Maker for drawing the Earl of Pembroke, £3 13s. 4d."

A. D.

1628   No. 12.   Richard Weston, lord treasurer, afterward earl of Portland.

1629   No. 13.   Alderman John Whitson.

> This picture was originally in the Alderman's house in St. Nicholas-street.

1630   No. 14.   Alderman George Harrington (brewer), mayor in 1617.

> Inscription: "Ætatis suæ 70. Anno Domini 1630."—A well-executed statue, reclining upon a cenotaph, which is kept concealed under an arcade of more modern construction in St. John's burial-ground, we have been told was erected to the memory of this gentleman. His deed of gift, dated March 24, 1637, gave £540, not "£240," as in Barrett, p. 620. His widow, Mrs. Thomasine Harrington, (not "Mr. Thomas H.") bequeathed £10 8s. annually, in bread, to the poor of St. Thomas, St. Michael, and St. Mary Redcliff parishes.

1660   No. 15.   King Charles the Second.   *Qu.* if by John Hoskins?

> "1675. Sept. 28, paid John Bevill, painter, for guilding the King's Picture at the Tolzey, £8."

1686   No. 16.   King James the Second.

> "1686. April 7, paid John Hoskins* for the King's Picture, £10 5s. Paid for gilding frame, 13s."

1691   No. 17, 18.   King William and Queen Mary.   *Qu.* if by the Chevalier Karel de Moor?

> "1691. Jan. 7, paid Mr. More for the King's and Queen's Picture, £13 5s."

No. 19.   Charles, earl of Dorset, lord chamberlain of the King's household.

1702   No. 20.   Edward Colston.

> "1702. Jan. 25, paid Alderman Yate, for Mr. Colston's Picture and other disbursements, as per note, £23 6s. 8d."

1703   No. 21.   Queen Anne.

> "1703. Sept. 29, paid Alderman Robert Yate, being so much paid for the Picture of Her Majesty, to be put up in the Council-House, £24 15s."

1716   No. 22.   King George the First.

> "1716. Paid to Nicholas Hicks, esq. [mercer and Mayor] for the King's Picture, £33."

1732   No. 23, 24.   King George the Second and Queen Caroline.

> "1732. May 26, paid expenses, carriage, &c. of their Majesties Pictures, from London, £1 13s. 6d. Paid Alderman Day's disbursements for ditto, £11 4s."—These, from there being no charge for painting, would appear to have been a present.

No. 25.   Sir Michael Foster.   Presented by Mr. Ludlow the town-clerk, in March 1822.

* *Qu.* if a son of the John Hoskins who died in 1664.

A. D.

1759   No. 25. Lord Clare. A present.

> Inscription: "Right Honourable Robert Nugent, esq. unani-
> mously re-elected Member of Parliament for Bristol, Dec. 26,
> 1759."

1782   No. 26. Lord Ashburton.

> " 1784. Sept. 8, paid Sir Joshua Reynolds for a portrait of Lord
> Ashburton, late Recorder of this city, by order of Common Coun-
> cil, 11 Dec. 1782, £105."

1792   No. 27. The Duke of Portland.

> " 1792. Oct. 20, paid Thomas Lawrence, esq. for a picture
> painted by him, and frame, of the Duke of Portland, £149."

1815   No. 29. George the Third.   Painted · in 1815, by
E. Bird, R.A.

No. 30. Sir Vicary Gibbs, lord chief justice.   Painted in
1815, by W. Owen, R.A.

DISCOVERIES ON DIGGING FOR THE FOUNDATION
OF THE NEW COUNCIL-HOUSE.

1824   About eight feet beneath the south-east part of what was formerly St. John's
Chapel, were found four graves of stones, rough-hewn, but closely fitted to the
human shape on the inside, with the heads west and feet eastward, two of them
lying close together. The covers were thin stones, also in several pieces. One
scull only gave evidence of their contents, and that crumbled to earth on being
handled. In other parts of the site of St. Ewen's Church were dug up fragments
of fluted bases, columns and capitals, in the Norman style, with some of their
painting and gilding, and pieces of the covers of stone coffins, one of them engraven with a cross. The mortar of the original foundation was more tenacious
than the stones it cemented. The excavators were liberally encouraged to seek
for and produce every article of value or interest to the antiquary, but they
found none except the following:

A shilling of Henry VIII. (No. 13 in Plate vii. of Ruding's " Annals of the
Coinage, &c.")—a sixpence of James I. 1603 (No. 4 in Pl. xvi.)—and a shilling
of Charles I. (No. 8 in Pl. xxii.), with six small brass, copper and mixed
metal coins, the devices and inscriptions nearly illegible. Some of them are
French or Norman, the letters like those used about the time of the Conquest.
One of them is a very small and thin local token, having on one side the device
of a pair of scales, surrounded by the words SAMVELL STAPLES; on the reverse,
in the centre, $_S{}^S{}_E$, and round it, OF THORNECOMBE, 68.

Under the church-pavement, behind what was Mr. Davies's shop, was found
the long hair only of a female; and about the middle of the remains of her coffin,
wrapped in yellow silk, an oval miniature, in oil-colours, on copper, of a gentleman aged about 50 years, dressed in the costume of the early part of the last
century, his flowing wig being of moderate di_____ us, neck-cloth rose-tied,
and coat a light brown, without collar.

Generally, the contents of the cemetery appear to have been rudely disturbed
on the demolition of the church, when those who laying claim to the ashes of relatives, had them re-interred in Christ-Church.

24 DE 61

TOPOGRAPHICAL INDEX.

Farringdon Castle, 1143
Feathers' Inn, Wine-street, 1654
Felonde or Failand, 1491
Ferry, Temple, 1651
Fisher-lane, 1770
Fish-Markets, 1615, 1717, 1782
Fishponds, Stapleton, 1746
Flat Holms, 918, 1373
Floating-Harbour, 1803, 1809
Fokeing alias Pucking-grove, 1373
Fortifications, 1642, 1645
Fort-lane, 1739
Foster's Alms-house, and Chapel of the
  Three Kings of Cologne, 1481, 1504,
  1702
———— Place, 1659 note
Fotheringay, 1429
Frampton-upon-Severn, p. 47 note
Franciscan or Grey Friery, 1226, 1274
French Protestant Chapel, 1721
Frome, Somerset, 1685
Froom River, 50. See Trench. 1803,
  1821, p. 362
———— Bridge, 1248, 1314
———— or the Water Gate, 930, 1520,
  1545, 1574, 1618, 1642, 1643, 1645,
  1694
Fry's House of Mercy, 1784
Fulham, 878
Gainsborough, 1013
Gaol, 1816. See Newgate
Garden, William of Worcester's, 1371,
  1480
Gas-Light Stations, 1818, 1824
Gate-House, College-Green, 1649
Gaunt's Hospital, 1170, 1220, 1229,
  1268, 1281, 1336, 1487, 1534, 1667.
  See St. Mark's Chapel
Geology, 1148 note, 1817
St. George's Chapel, Guildhall, 1353
———— Church, Kingswood, 1750
Gib Taylor's Ferry, 1217, 1577, 1611,
  1613, 1666, 1674, 1717, p. 338
Giles's Bridge, 930, 1314, 1754
———— Chapel, 1301, 1319, 1754
Glastonbury, 546, 718, 955, 1189, 1276,
  1304, 1539
Glastonbury Court, 1304
Glass-Houses, 1761
Gloucester, p. 5, 47, 461, 577, 955, 1042,
  1063, 1089, 1138, 1141, 1176, 1417,
  1532 note, p. 356
Golden Boy Lane, 1480
Grammar-School, the Thornes', 1528,
  1610, 1627, 1772, 1783
Gray's School for Girls, 1713
Great Britain, 946
Great Garden, 1643
Great George-street, 1759
Green Bank, 1709
Grey Friers, 1226, 1274

Grope-lane. See Haulier's lane
Grove, 1702
Guard-House, 1347, 1579, 1596
Guillows Inn, 1472
Guilders Inn, 1625. 1740
Guildhall, 1313, 1353, 1376, 1532, 1574,
  1569, 1685, 1788, 1813
Gunpowder Repository, 1722
Hales Croft, 1366, 1373
Halls of Crafts, 1449, 1743
Hambrook, 1084
Hanham, 1645, 1695, 1697, 1743
Hareclive, 1170
Harptree, 1084
Hawkins's Lane, 1785 note
Hauliers' Lane, 1665, 1796
Hay-Market, 1786
Henbury, Introduction, and p. 7
Henroost Slip, 1722
Hereford, 1016, 1130
Hermitage, Brandon Hill, 1351
———— St. Vincent's Rocks, 1480
High Cross, 1247, 1490, 1495, 1525,
  1574, 1633, 1697, 1733, 1763
—— street, 1348, 1472, 1490, 1608,
  1625, 1717, 1740, 1772 note, 1821
Holy Spirit, Chapel of the, 1207
Hooke's Mills, 1658
Horewood, p. 4, A.D. 1227
Horfield, 1222, 1227, 1643, 1646
Hors-strete, 1490
Horse-fairs, 1684
Hotwells, 1661, 1668, 1691, 1696, 1755
Huge Well, 1207
Hungroad, 1564, 1578, 1585, 1609
Huntingdon (Lady)'s Chapel, 1706
Huntingford Chase. See Horewood
Hutton, 1084
St. Jacobus of the Market, 1174
Jacob's Well, 1373
St. James's Priory and Chapel, now
  Church, 1129, 1130, 1147, 1174, 1241,
  1282, 1374, 1478, 1540, 1598, 1626,
  1657, 1679, 1698, 1721, 1768, 1804,
  1820, 1824, p. 344
———— Back, 1415, 1765
———— Barton, 1715, p. 358
———— Church Tower, 1374
———— Church-Yard, 1478
———— Fair, 1603, 1689, p. 344
———— Gift-House, 1537, 1604
———— Parish, 1603, 1787
———— Poor-House, Back, 1694
———— Poor-House, Barrs - street,
  1694, 1752
———— Square, 1765
———— Market, 1775
———— Arcades, 1824
James's Place and Parade, 1645
Jews' Chapel, St. Giles's Church,
  1319

Powlet (or Paulet) Manor, 1220
Prince's Street, 1779
Prior's Croft, 1373
——— Orchard, 1373, 1400
——— Hill Fort, 1643, 1645
——— Slip, 1671
Pucklechurch, 947, 1227
Pucking Grove, 1373
Pugsley's Well-Field, 1645, 1700, p. 357
Purbeck, 978
Quaker's Meeting-House, Rosemary-street, 1669
Quay. See Key
Quay-lane, 1765, 1766
Queen-street, Castle Precincts, 1480
Queen's Gate, 1659
Queen-street, St. Michael's, 1668
Queen-Square (see Marsh), 1698, 1702, 1710, 1726, 1735, 1751, 1776, p. 357
Queen's Parade, 1786
Radcleve, 1789
Ragland Castle, 1645, 1646
Raven's Well, 1366
Reading, 870
Redcliff and Church, 789, 1201, 1207, 1247, 1279, 1293, 1369, 1376, 1416, 1446, 1471, 1474, 1491, 1628, 1643, 1650 note, 1657, 1669, 1682, 1685, 1704, 1709, 1728, 1753, 1756, 1762, 1766, 1792, 1796, 1821, p. 337
——— Steeple, 1446
——— Back Ferry, 1717
——— Fair, 1529
——— Gate, 1247, 1446, 1520, 1545, 1645, 1730, 1772
——— Girls' School, 1787
——— Grammar-School, 1766
——— Hill, 1589, 1685
——— Hospital, 1671
——— Mead, 1685
——— Parade Ferry, 1717
——— Street, 867, 1281, 1320, 1490, 1550, 1665, p. 340
Redland, 1063, 1174, 1555 note, 1643
Red Lane, 1373
——— Lodge, 1598
——— Maids' Hospital, 1627, 1634, 1655
Ridley's Alms-house, 1740
Rivers, p. 6 note, p. 357
Roache's Lane, 1480
Roads, 380, 1542, 1569, 1593, 1613, p. 349, 364
Rochester, 884, 1000
Rose-lane, 1671
Rownham, 1610, 1661, 1685
Royal Fort, 1645, 1650, 1655, p. 347, 349
Rudeland. See Redland
Rud Hall, 789
Sanctuaries, 1486, 1495, 1503, 1534
Sandbrooke, 1185
Sandford, 1084
Sandwich, 1009

Satinors' Croft, 1373
Saxon Octarchy, 579 note
Scilly Island, 1278
Sea-Banks, p. 337
Sea-Mill Dock, 1712, 1750
Selwood Forest, 856, 878
Severn, 1430
Shambles, 1174, 1247, 1445, 1586, 1740, 1765
Shaftesbury, 1035
Sheppey I., 832
Sherborne, 836, 866, 1143
Ship-Yard, Quay, 1617
Ship Public-house, Steep-street, 1643 note
Shire Newton, 1644
Shoe-lane Work-house, 1770
Shooter's Close, 1129
Shuter's Ditch, 1373
Sieges, 1313, 1643, 1645
Sion Spring, 1792, 1795
Siston, 1154. Siston-House, 1613
Skadpull-street, 1301. See Marsh-street
Slimebridge, 1154
Small-street, 920, 1569, 1573, 1587, 1643, 1664, 1686, 1765, 1768, 1818, p. 345
Smiths' Hall, 1610
Snowgale's Alms-house, 1350, 1739, 1740
Sodbury, 1685
Southmead, 1173 note
Southwell-street, 1645
Spencer's Alms-house, 1493, 1604
Spicer's Hall, 1377
——— Hospital, 1393
Stallenge Cross, 1247, 1525
Stanlega, 1243
Stapleton, 1174
Steep Holme, 1373
——— street, 1252, 1481, 1550, 1643 note
St. Stephen's Avenue, 1772
——— Church, 1304, 1399, 1472, 1594, 1603, 1617, 1629, 1657, 1673, 1703
——— Lane, 1770
——— Street, 1087, 1770, 1771
——— Tower, 1439, 1469
Stevens's Alms-houses, 1679
Stews, 1544
Stoke's Croft, 1373
——— Alms-house and School, 1722
Stoke House, 1645, 1750, p. 362
Stone Bridge. See St. Giles's Bridge
Stourhead, 1763, 1765
Strange's Alms-house. See St John's Alms-house
Swan-lane, 1671
Swanwick, Hants, 877
Surgeons' Hall, 1740
Surveys, 1741, 1743
Sussex, 584, 642, 800
Tables. See Pillars
Tabernacle, 1753

Tailors' Hospital, Marsh-street, 1604
———— Alms-house, Merchant-street, 1701
———— Chapel, 1398, 1552
———— Hall, 1615, 1617
Taverns, 1552, 1743
Taunton Castle, 721
Templars, 1118, 1201, 1312
Temple Church and Tower, 1145, 1299, 1342, 1390, 1460, 1503, 1544, 1568, 1576, 1646, 1667, 1701, 1788
———— Cross, 1785
———— Fee, 1200, 1247, 1498
———— Gate, 1247, 1366, 1373, 1520, 1545, 1645, 1734
———— Mead, 1574
———— -street, 1411, 1490, 1610, 1765, 1785
———— Sanctuary, 1534
———— Gray's School, 1713
Terrill-street, 1173
Tewkesbury, 1107
Thanet, 864
Theatre (see Play-House), 1706, 1766, 1764, 1777, 1817, 1819, 1821 *note*
St. Thomas' Church, 1200, 1405, 1411, 1657, 1682, 1789, 1793
———————— Market, 1570
———————— Street, 1252, 1490, 1550, 1574, 1691, 1695, 1785
Thornbury, 1066, 1534, 1681
Three Tuns Tavern, Corn-street, 1743
Three Tuns Tavern, Wine-street, 1673
Tickenham Middle, 1491
Timsbury, 1084
Tintern, 610, 1331
Togbill, or Tughill, 1643
Tolzey, 1503, 1550, 1583, 1589, 1610, 1611, 1615, 1616, 1740, 1782
Totterdown, 1748
Tower Great, 1577, 1709
———— Harratz, 1247, 1373, 1645, 1671, 1722
———— Hill, 1279
———— lane, 1767
———— Slip, 1671
———— street, 1480
Traitor's Bridge. See Wade's Bridge
Trench, 1239, 1247
Trene or Trenelly Mills, 1247, 1373, 1607, 1671
Tretwr Castle, 1409
Tuckers' Hall, 1610
Tucker-street, 1340, 1490, 1704, 1714, 1757, 1765, 1785
Turnpikes, 1726, 1748
Twerton, 1084
Turtles, or Jonas Leazes, 1691
Tyndall's Park, 1336, 1658
Venta Belgarum, 120, p. 332
St. Vincent's Chapel and Rocks, p. 6, 305, 1480

Virgin Chapel, 1360, 1643, p. 338, 344
———— Redcliff Church, 1766
Virgin Tavern-lane, 1304, 1445
Union-street, 1765, 1772, 1775
Wædmor, 878
Wade's Bridge, 1685, 1781
Wallingford, 1142
Wapley, 1084
Wareham, 876, 1142
Ware Mead, 1373
———— Mill, 1220
Warwick, 905
Washington's Breach, 1643
Watchet, 918
Water Fort, 1645
Water-House, 1775
Walls of Bristol, 930, 1087, 1772
Weavers' Chapel, 1299, 1503
———————— Hall, 1503
Weedport, 928
Weir, 1490
Wells Cathedral, 1239
Welsh Chapel, 1795, 1823
Were, Somerset, 1061.   See Ware Mill
Wessex, 50, 519 till 934
St. Werburgh's Church, 1200, 1384, 1528 *note*, 1606, 1657, 1740, 1761
St. Werburgh, 1717, 1761
Westbury-upon-Trymme, p. 7, 824, 983, 1093, 1223, 1288, 1374, 1466, 1643
Westminster-Hall, 1099
Weston, 1084
Weston-super-Mare, 1084, 1819
Whitchurch, 1643
White's Alms-house, 1610, 1622, 1824
White Lodge, 1671
———— Tower, 1373
———— Lion Inn, 1610, 1622, 1685
Whitson Court, 1129, 1174
Wick, p. 4 *note*, 603
Wick Court, 1761, p. 360
Wight I., 684
Wilton, 871, 1143
Wimburn, 870
Winchester, 836, 934
Wine-street, 795, 1313, 1574, 1581, 1596, 1673, 1640, 1643, 1684, 1716, 1733 *note*, 1761
Winterbourne, 1553
Woodwill's Lake, 1373
———————— Lane, 1373
Worcester, 1093, 1139
Worship-street, 1247
Wotton Church, 1311, 1417
Wraxall, 1084, 1476, 1491
Wrington's Croft, 1373
Wynchcombe, 603, 795
Wyuch-strete. See Wine-street
Yatton, 1788.

Ingram Content Group UK Ltd.
Milton Keynes UK
UKHW032235150323
418612UK00009B/358